Tyndale New Testament Commentaries

Volume 3

Luke

For my beloved son Luke

Whether far or near, you are always with me in my heart.

Tyndale New Testament Commentaries

Volume 3

SERIES EDITOR: ECKHARD J. SCHNABEL
CONSULTING EDITOR: NICHOLAS PERRIN

Luke

AN INTRODUCTION AND COMMENTARY

Nicholas Perrin

Academic
An imprint of InterVarsity Press
Downers Grove, Illinois

InterVarsity Press
P.O. Box 1400 | Downers Grove, IL 60515-1426
ivpress.com | email@ivpress.com

Inter-Varsity Press, England
36 Causton Street | London SW1P 4ST, England
ivpbooks.com | ivp@ivpbooks.com

InterVarsity Press®, USA, is the book-publishing division of InterVarsity Christian Fellowship/USA® and a member movement of the International Fellowship of Evangelical Students. Website: intervarsity.org.

Inter-Varsity Press, England, originated within the Inter-Varsity Fellowship, now the Universities and Colleges Christian Fellowship, a student movement connecting Christian Unions in universities and colleges throughout Great Britain, and a member movement of the International Fellowship of Evangelical Students. That historic association is maintained, and all senior IVP staff and committee members subscribe to the UCCF Basis of Faith. Website: www.uccf.org.uk.

First published 2022

USA ISBN 978-1-5140-0535-4 (print)
USA ISBN 978-1-5140-0536-1 (digital)

UK ISBN 978-1-78359-922-6 (print)
UK ISBN 978-1-78359-923-3 (digital)

Typeset in Great Britain by Avocet Typeset, Bideford, Devon

Printed in the United States of America ∞

InterVarsity Press is committed to ecological stewardship and to the conservation of natural resources in all our operations. This book was printed using sustainably sourced paper.

Library of Congress Cataloging-in-Publication Data
A catalog record for this book is available from the Library of Congress.

British Library Cataloguing-in-Publication Data
A catalogue record for this book is available from the British Library.

30 29 28 27 26 25 24 23 22 | 12 11 10 9 8 7 6 5 4 3 2 1

CONTENTS

GENERAL PREFACE

The Tyndale Commentaries have been a flagship series for evangelical readers of the Bible for over sixty years. Both the original New Testament volumes (1956–1974) as well as the new commentaries (1983–2003) rightly established themselves as a point of first reference for those who wanted more than is usually offered in a one-volume Bible commentary, without requiring the technical skills in Greek and in Jewish and Graeco-Roman studies of the more detailed series, with the advantage of being shorter than the volumes of intermediate commentary series. The appearance of new popular commentary series demonstrates that there is a continuing demand for commentaries that appeal to Bible study leaders in churches and at universities. The publisher, editors and authors of the Tyndale Commentaries believe that the series continues to meet an important need in the Christian community, not the least in what we call today the Global South with its immense growth of churches and the corresponding need for a thorough understanding of the Bible by Christian believers.

In the light of new knowledge, new critical questions, new revisions of Bible translations and the need to provide specific guidance on the literary context and the genre of the individual passages as well as on theological emphases, it was time to publish new commentaries in the series. Three authors have revised their commentaries that appeared in the second series. The original aim remains. The new commentaries are neither too short nor unduly long. They are exegetical and thus root the interpretation of the text in its historical context. They do not aim to solve all critical questions, but they are written with an awareness of major scholarly debates which may be treated in the Introduction, in Additional Notes or in the commentary itself. While not specifically homiletic in aim, they want to help readers to understand the passage under consideration in such a way that they begin to see points of relevance and application, even though the commentary does not explicitly offer these. The authors base their exegesis on the Greek text, but they write for readers who do not know Greek; Hebrew and Greek terms that are discussed are transliterated. The English translation used for the first series was the Authorized (King James) Version, the volumes of the second series mostly used the Revised Standard Version; the volumes of the third series use either the New International Version (2011) or the New Revised Standard Version as primary versions, unless otherwise indicated by the author.

An immense debt of gratitude for the first and second series of the Tyndale Commentaries was owed to R. V. G. Tasker and L. Morris, who each wrote four of the commentaries themselves. The recruitment of new authors for the third series proved to be effortless, as colleagues responded enthusiastically to the opportunity to be involved in this project, a testimony to the larger number of New Testament scholars capable and willing to write commentaries, to the wider ethnic identity of contributors, and to the role that the Tyndale Commentaries have played in the church worldwide. It continues to be the hope of all those concerned with this series that God will graciously use the new commentaries to help readers understand as fully and clearly as possible the meaning of the New Testament.

Eckhard J. Schnabel, Series Editor
Nicholas Perrin, Consulting Editor

AUTHOR'S PREFACE

The Gospel of Luke holds out its central character Jesus Christ as
the fulfilment of the Scriptures and the human climax of redemptive history. In this respect, the third Gospel is eminently simple
in what it attempts to do: it tells the story of what this Jesus began
to do – Acts would pick up the story from there. In the Gospel's
opening pages, it quickly becomes apparent that Luke's tale does
not float about in the ether, as if the events he relates were somehow
strangely *above* history. No, it is a story about a God-man who
enters *into* history, only to collide with its most significant stakeholders. Think of how many aspects of Luke's Gospel can be
pinned down to a specific time and place. The Evangelist intended
it that way. As the first historian in the church, he insists that the
gospel contained within his Gospel was enmeshed in the messy
time–space continuum we know as human history.

   For the purposes of this commentary, I have attempted to take
this point seriously. After all, if Luke took human history seriously
then so too should his interpreter. *That* human history begins – as
far as our Gospel writer is concerned – with the story of Israel, as
contained in Israel's Scriptures. This has no uncertain hermeneutical significance. In the first instance, the weightiness of Israel's
prior story requires our attending to the redemptive-historical
storyline and avoiding the error of the second-century Gnostic
theologian Marcion, when he attempted to apply a scalpel to the
third Gospel in the hope of disassociating it from the Hebrew
Scriptures. At the end of the day, his was a vain endeavour. Wanting

to have Luke apart from its scriptural roots is like attempting to have the ocean without its salt. Of course, it is chemically possible to separate ocean water from its salt, but then at that point it would no longer be ocean water! The Hebrew Scriptures suffuse the thought-world of the New Testament authors across the board and Luke is no exception. Our exegesis should reflect as much. Though some of my readers may complain I am sometimes too quick to suppose intertextual correspondences between Luke's writing and the Scriptures, I would only remind these same readers of what the Evangelist himself wrote about Jesus: 'Then beginning with Moses and all the prophets, he interpreted to them the things about himself in *all* the scriptures' (24:27). It is impossible to do justice to this writing without circling back to the Scriptures at multiple points. The responsible identification of scriptural allusions in Luke's text necessarily depends on various criteria that allow for degrees of plausibility or implausibility, probability and improbability. Yet this is as much art as it is a science. In cases of an alleged echo of the Scriptures, New Testament commentators on the minimalist side will demand clear and convincing evidence before even mentioning the possibility of an allusion. By contrast, this commentary will set the evidentiary bar to a preponderance of evidence: where scriptural allusions are more probable than improbable, these deserve mention, even if there is a sliding scale of certainty in these matters.

If one distinctive of this commentary is its rather robust contemplation of the 'Old in the New', a second distinctive has to do with its compositional reading approach. In other words, I believe that the Early Church Fathers were on to something when they talked about the principle of Scripture interpreting Scripture. (The principle was in fact derived from a Judaism that preceded Luke.) The self-interpreting quality of the New Testament writings means that the Evangelist is not only in conversation with the Law and the Prophets, but also – as strange as it might sound – with himself. Like a Bach fugue, there is something intrinsically cyclical about Luke's narrative. In reading Luke, one gets the impression that he is ever circling back, but with each return – with each recapitulation – he expands the horizons of what has gone before. Scripture interprets Scripture even within the bounds of Luke.

The authors writing for this series are encouraged not to overdo it when it comes to engaging the secondary literature. For my part, I have chosen to restrict myself to a more or less fixed number of commentaries. These include Bock, Bovon, Edwards, Fitzmyer, Green, Johnson, Liefeld, Marshall and Nolland. I know or have personally met almost all of these scholars. As much as I have appreciated these commentators personally as individuals, this writing project has also allowed me to come away with a deeper appreciation for their distinctive voices. Though the commentary is based on the Greek text, my default translation throughout is the NRSV (1995). Translations from the Septuagint (LXX) are my own.

I owe a debt of thanks first to our editor Philip Duce of Inter-Varsity Press. His patience has been unfathomable. The same could be said for Eckhard Schnabel, the series editor. I am also grateful in the first instance for the privilege of not only contributing a volume but also serving as consulting editor for this series. Dr Schnabel's shrewd comments on my manuscript are much appreciated. Appreciation also extends to my colleagues at Trinity College and especially Trinity Evangelical Divinity School. What a privilege to have such a brain trust within a stone's throw of my office! At my previous institution, countless conversations with Wheaton College faculty and students (including my doctoral students, three of whom have dissertated on Luke) also have played an incalculable formative role. Last but certainly not least, Bryan Eklund gets a special call-out for his unending encouragement and occasional copy-editing, even on this manuscript. It is a sweet thing for a man to have such a close friend who shares his passion for the Scriptures.

The lion's share of thanks goes to my supportive family, especially my wife Camie who has patiently played the scholarly widow time and time again – and that without murmur or complaint. Conversations with my philosophically inclined son Nathaniel on various topics have likewise contributed to a project like this. Finally, I want to thank my artistically inclined son Luke. Like Luke the Evangelist, my own Luke has helped me to see the world as an unfolding masterpiece – a marred masterpiece but a masterpiece nonetheless. I dedicate this book to him.

Nicholas Perrin

ABBREVIATIONS

General

AB   Anchor Bible

ABD   *Anchor Bible Dictionary*, ed. D. N. Freedman (New
            York: Doubleday, 1972)

AnBib   Analecta Biblica

ANTC   Abingdon New Testament Commentaries

BDAG   *A Greek–English Lexicon of the New Testament and
            Other Early Christian Literature*, ed. W. Bauer,
            F. W. Danker, W. F. Arndt and F. W. Gingrich,
            3rd edn (Chicago: University of Chicago Press,
            2000)

BECNT   Baker Exegetical Commentary on the New
            Testament

BETL   Bibliotheca Ephemeridum Theologicarum
            Lovaniensium

BIS   Biblical Interpretation Series

BZNW   Beihefte zur Zeitschrift für die neutestamentliche
            Wissenschaft

CBQ   *Catholic Biblical Quarterly*

ConBOT   Coniectanea Biblica: Old Testament Series

COQG   Christian Origins and the Question of God

CTR   *Criswell Theological Review*

CurTM   *Currents in Theology and Mission*

DJG	*Dictionary of Jesus and the Gospels,* ed. J. B. Green, J. K. Brown and N. Perrin, 2nd edn (Downers Grove: InterVarsity Press, 2013)
EBC	The Expositor's Bible Commentary
EDNT	*Exegetical Dictionary of the New Testament,* ed. H. Balz and G. Schneider (Grand Rapids: Eerdmans, 1990–93)
EncJud	*Encyclopaedia Judaica,* ed. F. Skolnik and M. Berenbaum (Detroit: Macmillan Reference USA, 2007)
ET	English translation
EvQ	*Evangelical Quarterly*
FRLANT	Forschungen zur Religion und Literatur des Alten und Neuen Testaments
GCRW	Greek Culture in the Roman World
GNS	Good News Studies
ICC	International Critical Commentary
Int	*Interpretation*
JBL	*Journal of Biblical Literature*
JETS	*Journal of the Evangelical Theological Society*
JGRChJ	*Journal of Greco-Roman Christianity and Judaism*
JSHJ	*Journal for the Study of the Historical Jesus*
JSJSup	Journal for the Study of Judaism Supplement Series
JSNT	*Journal for the Study of the New Testament*
JSNTSup	Journal for the Study of the New Testament Supplement Series
LNTS	Library of New Testament Studies
LSJ	*A Greek–English Lexikon,* ed. H. G. Liddell, R. Scott, H. S. Jones and H. Stuart, 9th edn (Oxford: Oxford University Press, 1996)
LSTS	Library of Second Temple Studies
LXX	Septuagint (Greek) Text of the Old Testament
NICNT	New International Commentary on the New Testament
NIGTC	New International Greek Testament Commentary
NovT	*Novum Testamentum*
NovTSup	Supplements to Novum Testamentum
NTS	*New Testament Studies*

NTT	New Testament Theology
OBT	Overtures to Biblical Theology
PNTC	Pillar New Testament Commentaries
PRSt	*Perspectives in Religious Studies*
SBJT	*Southern Baptist Journal of Theology*
SBLDS	Society of Biblical Literature Dissertation Series
SBLRBS	Society of Biblical Literature Resources for Biblical Study
SBLSP	Society of Biblical Literature Seminar Papers
SBT	Studies in Biblical Theology
SCJ	Studies in Christianity and Judaism
Smyth	H. W. Smyth, *Greek Grammar*, rev. edn (Cambridge: Harvard University Press, 1956)
SNTSMS	Society for New Testament Studies Monograph Series
SP	Sacra Pagina
SVTP	Studia in Veteris Testamenti Pseudepigrapha
TBT	*The Bible Today*
TCGNT	B. M. Metzger, *A Textual Commentary on the Greek New Testament: A Companion Volume to the United Bible Societies' Greek New Testament*, 4th edn (Stuttgart: Deutsche Bibelgesellschaft, 1994)
TDNT	*Theological Dictionary of the New Testament*, ed. G. Kittel and G. Friedrich (Grand Rapids: Eerdmans, 1964–76)
Thayer	*Greek–English Lexicon of the New Testament*, ed. J. Thayer (New York: Harper & Brothers, 1889)
ThTo	*Theology Today*
TNTC	Tyndale New Testament Commentaries
TSAJ	Texte und Studien zum antiken Judentum
TynBul	*Tyndale Bulletin*
USQR	*Union Seminary Quarterly Review*
WBC	Word Biblical Commentary
WUNT	Wissenschaftliche Untersuchungen zum Neuen Testament

Ancient texts

Old Testament Pseudepigrapha

1 En.	1 Enoch (Ethiopic Apocalypse)
2 En.	2 Enoch (Slavonic Apocalypse)
2 Bar.	2 Baruch (Syriac Apocalypse)
4 Ezra	4 Ezra
Apoc. Ab.	Apocalypse of Abraham
As. Mos.	Assumption of Moses
Jub.	Jubilees
Pss Sol.	Psalms of Solomon
Sib. Or.	Sibylline Oracles
T. Ash.	Testament of Asher
T. Gad	Testament of Gad
T. Iss.	Testament of Issachar
T. Levi	Testament of Levi
T. Mos.	Testament of Moses
T. Sol.	Testament of Solomon

Dead Sea Scrolls

1QH	Hodayot (Thanksgiving Hymns)
1QM	War Scroll
1QS	Rule of the Community
3Q15	Copper Scroll
4Q175	Testimonia
4Q242	Prayer of Nabonidus
4Q500	Benediction
4Q521	Messianic Apocalypse
11Q13	Melchizedek
CD	Cairo Genizah copy of the Damascus Document

Josephus, Philo, Midrash, Talmud and related Jewish literature
Josephus

Ant.	Jewish Antiquities
J.W.	Jewish War

Philo

Abraham	On the Life of Abraham

Moses   *On the Life of Moses*

Targumic literature
Tg. Isa.   Targum Isaiah

Rabbinic literature
'Abot   Avot
b.   Babylonian Talmudic tractate
B. Bat.   Bava Batra
B. Meṣ   Bava Metzi'a
B. Qam.   Bava Qamma
Ber.   Berakhot
Exod. Rab.   Exodus Rabbah
Ḥag.   Hagigah
Ḥul.   Hullin
Kelim   Kelim
Kil.   Kil'ayim
m.   Mishnah Talmudic tractate
Mek.   Mekilta
Menaḥ.   Menahot
Mid.   Middot
Ned.   Nedarim
Pesiq. Rab.   Pesiqta Rabbati
Šabb.   Shabbat
Sanh.   Sanhedrin
Šeqal.   Sheqalim
t.   Tosefta tractate
Ta'an.   Ta'anit
Tamid   Tamid
Yebam.   Yevamot
Yoma   Yoma

Apostolic Fathers
Did.   Didache
Herm. Sim.   Shepherd of Hermas, Similitude(s)
Herm. Vis.   Shepherd of Hermas, Vision(s)

Other early Christian literature

Augustine, *Quaest. ev.*   Augustine, *Quaestionum evangelicarum libri II*
Eusebius, *Hist. eccl.*   Eusebius, *Ecclesiastical History*
Irenaeus, *Haer.*   Irenaeus, *Against Heresies*
Jerome, *Vir. ill.*   Jerome, *De viris illustribus*
Justin, *Dial.*   Justin, *Dialogue with Trypho*

Classical literature

Epictetus, *Diatr.*   Epictetus, *Diatribai*
Herodotus, *Hist.*   Herodotus, *Histories*
Seneca, *Polyb.*   Seneca, *Ad Polybium de consolatione*
Suetonius, *Cal.*   Suetonius, *Gaius Caligula*
Tacitus, *Ann.*   Tacitus, *Annales*

Bible versions

ASV	American Standard Version, public domain.
CEB	The Common English Bible. © Copyright 2011 by the Common English Bible. All rights reserved. Used by permission.
ESV	The ESV Bible (The Holy Bible, English Standard Version), copyright © 2001 by Crossway, a publishing ministry of Good News Publishers. Used by permission. All rights reserved.
GNT	The Good News Bible, The Bible in Today's English Version. New Testament © 1966, 1971, 1976 by the American Bible Society.
JB	The Jerusalem Bible, published and copyright © 1966, 1967 and 1968 by Darton, Longman & Todd Ltd and Doubleday, a division of Random House, Inc., and used by permission.
KJV	The Authorized Version of the Bible (The King James Bible), the rights in which are vested in the Crown, reproduced by permission of the Crown's Patentee, Cambridge University Press.
NAB	The *New American Bible with Revised New Testament and Revised Psalms* are copyright © 1991, 1986, 1970 Confraternity of Christian Doctrine, Washington,

SELECT BIBLIOGRAPHY

Commentaries on the Gospel of Luke

Bock, D. L. (2008), *Luke 1:1 – 9:50*, BECNT 3A (Grand Rapids: Baker Academic).

Bovon, F. (2002), *Luke 1: Chapters 1–9:50*, Hermeneia (Minneapolis: Fortress).

Edwards, J. R. (2015), *The Gospel according to Luke*, PNTC (Grand Rapids: Eerdmans).

Fitzmyer, J. A. (1981), *The Gospel according to Luke I – IX*, AB (New Haven: Yale University Press).

Gooding, D. (1987), *According to Luke: A New Exposition of the Third Gospel* (Leicester: Inter-Varsity Press; Grand Rapids: Eerdmans).

Green, J. B. (1997), *The Gospel of Luke*, NICNT (Grand Rapids: Eerdmans).

Johnson, L. T. (1991), *The Gospel of Luke*, SP 3 (Collegeville: Liturgical).

Liefeld, W. L. (1984), 'Luke', in EBC, Vol. 8: *Matthew, Mark, Luke* (Grand Rapids: Zondervan), pp. 797–1059.

Lieu, J. (1997), *The Gospel of Luke*, Epworth Commentaries (Peterborough: Epworth).

Marshall, I. H. (1978), *The Gospel of Luke: A Commentary on the Greek Text*, NIGTC 3 (Grand Rapids: Eerdmans).

Morris, L. (1988), *Luke: An Introduction and Commentary*, TNTC 3, repr. 2008 (Downers Grove: IVP Academic).

Nolland, J. (1989–93), *Luke*, WBC 35, 3 vols. (Dallas: Word).

Plummer, A. (1922), *Luke*, ICC, 5th edn (Edinburgh: T&T Clark).

Talbert, C. H. (1988), *Reading Luke: A Literary and Theological Commentary on the Third Gospel*, Reading the New Testament Series (orig. 1982; New York: Crossroad).

Tannehill, R. C. (1996), *Luke*, ANTC (Nashville: Abingdon).

Other works

Allison, D. C. (1985), *The End of Ages Has Come: An Early Interpretation of the Passion and Resurrection of Jesus* (Philadelphia: Fortress).

—— (1987), 'The Eye Is the Lamp of the Body (Matthew 6:22–23 = Luke 11:34–36)', *NTS* 33, pp. 62–66.

Anderson, K. L. (2006), *'But God Raised Him from the Dead': The Theology of Jesus' Resurrection in Luke–Acts*, Paternoster Biblical Monographs (Milton Keynes: Paternoster).

Ascough, R. S. (1996), 'Narrative Technique and Generic Designation: Crowd Scenes in Luke–Acts and in Chariton', *CBQ* 58, pp. 69–81.

Atkins, P. (1998), 'Luke's Ascension Location: A Note on Luke 24:50', *Expository Times* 109, pp. 205–206.

Bailey, K. B. (1992), *Finding the Lost: Cultural Keys to Luke 15* (Concordia: St. Louis).

Bauckham, R. (1990), *Jude and the Relatives of Jesus in the Early Church* (Edinburgh: T&T Clark).

—— (2006), *Jesus and the Eyewitnesses: The Gospels as Eyewitness Testimony* (Grand Rapids: Eerdmans).

Beale, G. K. (1999), *The Book of Revelation*, NIGTC (Grand Rapids: Eerdmans).

—— (2008), *We Become What We Worship: A Biblical Theology of Idolatry* (Downers Grove: IVP Academic).

—— (2011), *A New Testament Biblical Theology* (Grand Rapids: Baker).

Beasley-Murray, G. R. (1983), 'The Interpretation of Dan 7', *CBQ* 45, pp. 44–58.

—— (1986), *Jesus and the Kingdom of God* (Grand Rapids: Eerdmans).

Beavis, M. A. (1994), '"Expecting Nothing in Return": Luke's Picture of the Marginalized', *Int* 48, pp. 357–368.

Beckwith, R. T. (1985), *The Old Testament Canon of the New Testament Church: And Its Background in Early Judaism* (London: SPCK).

Ben-Sasson, H. H. (1972), 'Kiddush Ha-Shem and Hillul Ha-Shem', *EncJud* 10, pp. 978–986.

Bovon, F. (1992), 'The Role of the Scriptures in the Composition of the Gospel Accounts: The Temptations of Jesus (Lk 4:1–13 Par) and the Multiplication of the Loaves (Lk 9:10–17 Par)', in G. O'Collins, G. Marconi and M. J. O'Connell (eds.), *Luke and Acts* (New York: Paulist), pp. 26–31.

Brawley, R. L. (1999), 'Abrahamic Covenant Traditions and the Characterization of God in Luke–Acts', in J. Verheyden (ed.), *The Unity of Luke–Acts*, BETL 142 (Louvain: Louvain University Press), pp. 109–132.

Bridge, S. L. (2003), *'Where the Eagles Are Gathered': The Deliverance of the Elect in Lukan Eschatology*, JSNTSup 240 (Sheffield: Sheffield Academic Press).

Brown, R. E. (1977), *The Birth of the Messiah: A Commentary on the Infancy Narratives in Matthew and Luke* (Garden City: Doubleday).

—— (2008), *The Death of the Messiah: From Gethsemane to the Grave; A Commentary on the Passion Narratives in the Four Gospels*, 2 vols., AB (New Haven: Yale University Press).

—— (2010 [1961]), 'The *Pater Noster* as an Eschatological Prayer', in R. E. Brown, *New Testament Essays* (New York: Doubleday), pp. 270–320.

Brown, R. E., K. P. Donfried and J. Reumann (eds.) (1973), *Peter in the New Testament: A Collaborative Assessment by Protestant and Roman Catholic Scholars* (Minneapolis: Augsburg).

Callon, C. (2013), '*Adulescentes* and *Meretrices*: The Correlation between Squandered Patrimony and Prostitutes in the Parable of the Prodigal Son', *CBQ* 75, pp. 259–278.

Campbell, J. B. (2012), *Rivers and the Power of Ancient Rome*, Studies in the History of Greece and Rome (Chapel Hill: University of North Carolina Press).

Carson, D. A., *Scandalous: The Cross and Resurrection of Jesus* (Wheaton: Crossway, 2010).

Cave, C. H. (1968), 'Lazarus and the Lucan Deuteronomy', *NTS* 15, pp. 319–325.

Chapman, D. W. and E. J. Schnabel (2015), *The Trial and Crucifixion of Jesus*, WUNT 34 (Tübingen: Mohr Siebeck).

Cole, Z. J. (2017), 'P45 and the Problem of the "Seventy(-Two)": A Case for the Longer Reading in Luke 10.1 and 17', *NTS* 63, pp. 203–221.

Collins, R. F. (2016), 'Abraham in the Gospels', *TBT* 54, pp. 240–246.

Cook, L. S. (2011), *On the Question of the "Cessation of Prophecy" in Ancient Judaism*, TSAJ 145 (Tübingen: Mohr Siebeck).

Cosgrove, C. H. (1984), 'The Divine Δεῖ in Luke–Acts', *NovT* 26, pp. 168–190.

Cotter, W. J. (2000), 'Cornelius, the Roman Army, and Religion', in T. L. Donaldson (ed.), *Religious Rivalries and the Struggle for Success in Caesarea Maritima*, SCJ 8 (Waterloo: Wilfrid Laurier), pp. 279–301.

Crawford, R. G. (1978), 'A Parable of Atonement', *EvQ* 50, pp. 2–7.

Derrett, J. D. M. (1970), *Law in the New Testament* (London: Darton, Longman & Todd).

—— (1972), '"Eating Up the Houses of Widows": Jesus' Comment on Lawyers?', *NovT* 14, pp. 1–9.

—— (1987), 'No Stone Left upon Another: Leprosy and the Temple', *JSNT* 9, pp. 3–20.

Edwards, J. (1994), 'The Authority of Jesus in the Gospel of Mark', *JETS* 37, pp. 217–222.

Evans, C. A. (1991), 'In What Sense Blasphemy? Jesus before Caiaphas in Mark 14:61–64', *SBLSP* 30, pp. 215–234.

Fee, G. D. (1981), '"One Thing Is Needful": Luke 10:42', in E. J. Epp and G. D. Fee (eds.), *New Testament Textual Criticism: Its Significance for Exegesis; Essays in Honor of Bruce M. Metzger* (New York: Oxford University Press), pp. 61–75.

Fiensy, D. A. (2014), *Christian Origins and the Ancient Economy* (Cambridge: Clark).

Fletcher-Louis, C. H. T. (1997), *Luke–Acts: Angels, Christology and Soteriology*, WUNT 2/94 (Tübingen: Mohr Siebeck).

—— (2000), 'Jesus Inspects His Priestly War Party (Luke 14.25–35)', in S. Moyise (ed.), *The Old Testament in the New Testament* (Sheffield: Sheffield Academic Press), pp. 126–143.

—— (2001), 'The Revelation of the Sacral Son of Man: The Genre, History of Religions Context and the Meaning of the Transfiguration', in F. Avemarie and H. Lichtenberger (eds.), *Auferstehung – Resurrection: The Fourth Durham–Tübingen Research Symposium; Resurrection, Transfiguration and Exaltation in Old Testament, Ancient Judaism and Early Christianity (Tübingen, September 1999)*, WUNT 135 (Tübingen: Mohr Siebeck), pp. 247–298.

—— (2007), 'Jesus and the High Priestly Messiah: Part 2', *JSHJ* 5, pp. 57–79.

France, R. T. (2002), *The Gospel of Mark*, NIGTC (Grand Rapids: Eerdmans).

Giambrone, A. (2017), *Sacramental Charity, Creditor Christology, and the Economy of Salvation in Luke's Gospel*, WUNT 2/439 (Tübingen: Mohr Siebeck).

Gladd, B. L. (2008), *Revealing the* Mysterion: *The Use of Mystery in Daniel in Second Temple Judaism with Its Bearing on First Corinthians*, BZNW 160 (Berlin: De Gruyter).

Goodrich, J. K. (2012), 'Voluntary Debt Remission and the Parable of the Unjust Steward (Luke 16:1–13)', *JBL* 131, pp. 547–566.

Green, G. L. (2020), *Vox Petri: A Theology of Peter* (Eugene: Wipf and Stock).

Green, J. B. (1994), 'Good News to Whom? Jesus and the "Poor" in the Gospel of Luke', in M. Turner (ed.), *Jesus of Nazareth: Lord and Christ* (Grand Rapids: Eerdmans), pp. 59–74.

—— (1995), *The Theology of the Gospel of Luke*, NTT (Cambridge: Cambridge University Press).

Grindheim, S. (2013), *Introducing Biblical Theology* (London: T&T Clark).

Gronigen, G. van (1990), *Messianic Revelation in the Old Testament* (Grand Rapids: Baker).

Gundry, R. H. (1982), *Matthew: A Commentary on His Literary and Theological Art* (Grand Rapids: Baker).

Guy, L. (1997), 'The Interplay of the Present and Future in the
    Kingdom of God (Luke 19:11–44)', *TynBul* 48, pp. 119–137.

Hägerland, T. (2012), *Jesus and the Forgiveness of Sins: An Aspect of His
    Prophetic Mission*, SNTSMS 150 (Cambridge: Cambridge
    University Press).

Hartman, D. (2017), 'The "Children of Abraham" in Luke–Acts',
    Henoch 39, pp. 351–365.

Hartsock, C. (2008), *Sight and Blindness in Luke–Acts: The Use of
    Physical Features in Characterization*, BIS 94 (Leiden: Brill).

Hedrick, C. W. (1994), *Parables as Poetic Fictions: The Creative Voice of
    Jesus* (Peabody: Hendrickson).

Heil, J. P. (2000), *The Transfiguration of Jesus: Narrative Meaning and
    Function of Mark 9:2–8, Matt 17:1–8 and Luke 9:28–36*, AnBib 144
    (Rome: Pontificio Istituto Biblico, 2000).

Holgate, D. A. (1999), *Prodigality, Liberality and Meanness: The
    Prodigal Son in Graeco-Roman Perspective*, JSNT Sup 187 (Sheffield:
    Sheffield Academic Press).

Hom, M. and P. McClure (2018), 'A Short Note on Daniel 5 and
    the "Finger of God" Imagery in Luke 11:20', *NovT* 60,
    pp. 115–120.

Horbury, W. (1998), *Jewish Messianism and the Cult of Christ*
    (London: SCM Press).

Hultgren, A. (2000), *The Parables of Jesus* (Grand Rapids:
    Eerdmans).

Ilan, T. (1996), *Jewish Women in Greco-Roman Palestine* (Peabody:
    Hendrickson).

Jeremias, J. (1954), *Jesus' Promise to the Nations*, SBT 24 (London:
    SCM Press).

—— (1963), *Parables of Jesus*, ET (New York: Charles Scribner's
    Sons).

—— (1969), *Jerusalem in the Time of Jesus* (London: SCM Press).

Jipp, J. (2019), 'Abraham in the Synoptic Gospels and in the Acts
    of the Apostles', in S. A. Adams and Z. Domoney-Little (eds.),
    Abraham in Jewish and Early Christian Literature, LSTS 93
    (London: Bloomsbury T&T Clark), pp. 109–126.

Johnson, A. F. (1979), 'Assurance for Man: The Fallacy of
    Translating *Anaideia* by "Persistence" in Luke 11:5–8', *JETS* 22,
    pp. 123–131.

Johnson, L. T. (1977), *The Literary Function of Possessions in Luke–Acts*, SBLDS 39 (Missoula: Scholars Press).

Jonge, H. J. de (1977), 'Sonship, Wisdom, Infancy: Luke 2:41–51a', *NTS* 24, pp. 317–354.

Just, A. A., Jr. (1993), *The Ongoing Feast: Table Fellowship and Eschatology at Emmaus* (Collegeville: Liturgical).

Kelber, W. (1979), 'Redaction Criticism: On the Nature and Exposition of the Gospels', *PRSt* 6, pp. 4–16.

Kim, K. J. (1998), *Stewardship and Almsgiving in Luke's Theology*, JSNTSup 155 (Sheffield: Sheffield Academic Press).

Kingsbury, J. D. (1988), 'On Following Jesus: The "Eager" Scribe and the "Reluctant" Disciple (Matthew 8:18–22)', *NTS* 34, pp. 45–59.

Kloppenborg, J. S. (1989), 'The Dishonoured Master (Luke 16:1–8a)', *Biblica* 70, pp. 474–495.

Klutz, T. E. (1999), 'The Grammar of Exorcism in the Ancient Mediterranean World: Some Cosmological, Semantic, and Pragmatic Reflections on How Exorcistic Prowess Contributed to the Worship of Jesus', in C. C. Newman, J. R. Davila and G. S. Lewis (eds.), *Jewish Roots of Christological Monotheism: Papers from the St. Andrew's Conference on the Historical Origins of the Worship of Jesus*, JSJSup 63 (Leiden: Brill), pp. 156–165.

Knoppers, G. N. (2013), *Jews and Samaritans: The Origins and History of Their Early Relations* (New York: Oxford University Press).

Knowles, M. P. (2000), '"Wide Is the Gate and Spacious the Road That Leads to Destruction": Matthew 7.13 in Light of Archaeological Evidence', *JGRChJ* 1, pp. 176–213.

Kodell, J. (1969), 'Luke's Use of *Laos*, "People", Especially in the Jerusalem Narrative (Lk 19,28–24,53)', *CBQ* 31, pp. 327–343.

Koenig, J. (1985), *New Testament Hospitality: Partnership with Strangers as Promise and Mission*, OBT 17 (Philadelphia: Fortress).

König, J. (2012), *Saints and Symposiasts: The Literature of Food and the Symposium in Greco-Roman and Early Christian Culture*, GCRW (Cambridge: Cambridge University Press).

Kopas, J. (1986), 'Jesus and Women: Luke's Gospel', *ThTo* 43, pp. 192–202.

Kuhn, K. A. (2003), 'Beginning the Witness: The *autoptai kai hypēretia* of Luke's Infancy Narrative', *NTS* 49, pp. 237–255.

Laato, A. (1992), *Josiah and David* Redivivus: *The Historical Josiah and the Messianic Expectations of Exilic and Postexilic Times*, ConBOT 33 (Stockholm: Almqvist & Wiksell).

Landry, D. T. (1995), 'Narrative Logic in the Annunciation to Mary (Luke 1:26–38)', *JBL* 114, pp. 65–79.

Larkin, W. J. (1979), 'Old Testament Background of Luke 22:43–44', *NTS* 25, pp. 250–254.

Lehtipuu, O. (2007), *The Afterlife Imagery in Luke's Story of the Rich Man and Lazarus*, NovTSup 123 (Leiden: Brill).

Lewis, J. P. (1968), *A Study of the Interpretation of Noah and the Flood in Jewish and Christian Literature* (Leiden: Brill).

Liebenberg, J. (2001), *The Language of the Kingdom and Jesus: Parable, Aphorism, and Metaphor in the Sayings Material Common to the Synoptic Tradition and the Gospel of Thomas*, BZNW 102 (Berlin: De Gruyter).

Lull, D. J. (1986), 'The Servant-Benefactor as a Model of Greatness (Luke 22:24–30)', *NovT* 28, pp. 289–305.

McCown, C. C. (1938), 'The Geography of Luke's Central Section', *JBL* 57, pp. 51–66.

Maddox, R. (1982), *The Purpose of Luke–Acts*, FRLANT 126 (Edinburgh: T&T Clark).

Manson, T. W. (1951 [1931]), *The Teaching of Jesus: Studies of Its Form and Content* (Cambridge: Cambridge University Press).

Matera, F. J. (1993), 'Jesus' Journey to Jerusalem (Luke 9:51 – 19:46): A Conflict with Israel', *JSNT* 16, pp. 57–77.

Mattill, A. J. (1979), '"The Way of Tribulation"', *JBL* 98, pp. 531–546.

Mekkattukunnel, A. G. (2001), *The Priestly Blessing of the Risen Christ: An Exegetico-Theological Analysis of Luke 24:50–53* (New York: Peter Lang).

Miano, D. (2010), *Shadow on the Steps: Time Measurement in Ancient Israel*, SBLRBS 64 (Atlanta: Society of Biblical Literature).

Mihalios, S. (2011), *The Danielic Eschatological Hour in the Johannine Literature*, LNTS 436 (London/New York: T&T Clark).

Minear, P. S. (1974), 'A Note on Luke 17:7–10', *JBL* 93, pp. 82–87.

—— (1997), 'The Salt of the Earth', *Int* 51, pp. 31–41.

Moessner, D. P. (1988), 'Paul in Acts: Preacher of Eschatological
   Repentance to Israel', *NTS* 34, pp. 96–104.
Müller, C. G. (2003), '"Ungefähr 30": Anmerkungen zur
   Altersangabe Jesu im Lukasevangelium (Lk 3.23)', *NTS* 49,
   pp. 489–504.
Myers, C. (2008), *Binding the Strong Man: A Political Reading of Mark's
   Story of Jesus*, 20th Anniversary Edition (Maryknoll: Orbis).
Nelson, P. K. (1994), *Leadership and Discipleship: A Study of Luke
   22:24–30*, SBLDS 138 (Atlanta: Scholars Press).
Netzer, E. (2008 [2006]), *The Architecture of Herod, the Great Builder*
   (Grand Rapids: Baker).
Nygaard, Mathias (2012), *Prayer in the Gospels: A Theological Exegesis
   of the Ideal Pray-er*, BIS 114 (Leiden/Boston: Brill).
Olson, D. C. (2013), *A New Reading of the Animal Apocalypse of 1
   Enoch: 'All Nations Shall Be Blessed'*, SVTP 24 (Leiden: Brill).
Otten, J. (2017), 'I Alone Am Left: Elijah and the Remnant in
   Luke–Acts', PhD thesis, Wheaton College Graduate School.
Pao, D. W. (2002), *Acts and the Isaianic New Exodus* (Grand Rapids:
   Baker Academic).
Pao, D. W. and E. J. Schnabel (2007), 'Luke', in D. A. Carson and
   G. K. Beale (eds.), *Commentary on the New Testament Use of the Old
   Testament* (Grand Rapids: Baker), pp. 251–414.
Parrot, A. (1957), *Golgotha and the Church of the Holy Sepulchre*, tr.
   E. Hudson (London: SCM Press).
Perrin, N. (1998), 'Curse', in D. Reid (ed.), *The Dictionary of Biblical
   Images* (Downers Grove: InterVarsity Press), pp. 186–187.
—— (2010), *Jesus the Temple* (London: SPCK; Grand Rapids: Baker
   Academic).
—— (2011), 'Eternal Life', in D. Hays and J. S. Duvall (eds.),
   Baker Illustrated Bible Handbook (Grand Rapids: Baker), p. 660.
   Reprinted in *CSB Baker Illustrated Study Bible* (Nashville:
   Holman Bible, 2018).
—— (2013a), 'The Imperial Cult', in J. B. Green and L. M.
   McDonald (eds.), *The World of the New Testament: An Examination
   of the Context of Early Christianity* (Grand Rapids: Baker
   Academic), pp. 124–134.
—— (2013b), 'The Temple, a Davidic Messiah, and a Case of
   Mistaken Priestly Identity (Mark 2:26)', in D. M. Gurtner and

B. J. Gladd (eds.), *From Creation to New Creation: Biblical Theology and Exegesis; Essays in Honor of G. K. Beale* (Peabody: Hendrickson), pp. 163–177.

—— (2014), *Exodus Revealed: Israel's Journey from Slavery to the Promised Land* (New York: FaithWords).

—— (2016), 'Managing Jesus' Anger: Revisiting a Test-Critical Conundrum (Mark 1:41)', *CTR* 2, pp. 3–16.

—— (2018a), 'Jesus as Priest in the Gospels', *SBJT* 22, pp. 81–98.

—— (2018b), *Jesus the Priest* (London: SPCK; Grand Rapids: Baker Academic).

—— (2019), *The Kingdom of God: A Biblical Theology*, Biblical Theology for Life (Grand Rapids: Zondervan).

Phillips, T. (2003), 'Reading Recent Readings of Issues of Wealth and Poverty in Luke and Acts', *Currents in Biblical Research* 1, pp. 231–269.

Pitre, B. (2005), *Jesus, the Tribulation, and the End of the Exile: Restoration Eschatology and the Origin of the Atonement*, WUNT 2/204 (Tübingen: Mohr Siebeck).

Reicke, B. (1978), 'Jesus, Simeon, and Anna (Luke 2:21–40)', in J. I. Cook (ed.), *Saved by Hope: Essays in Honor of Richard C. Oudersluys* (Grand Rapids: Eerdmans), pp. 96–108.

Reid, B. E. (2012), 'An Overture to the Gospel of Luke', *CurTM* 39, pp. 428–434.

Rieske, S. (2019), 'A Tale of Two Families: "This Generation" and the Elect in the Book of Matthew', PhD thesis, Wheaton College.

Roth, S. J. (1997), *The Blind, the Lame, and the Poor: Character Types in Luke–Acts*, JSNTSup 144 (Sheffield: Sheffield Academic Press).

Rothe, U. (2019), *The Toga and Roman Identity* (London: Bloomsbury Academic).

Rowe, C. K. (2006), *Early Narrative Christology: The Lord in the Gospel of Luke*, BZNW 139 (New York: De Gruyter).

Savage, C. E. (2011), *Biblical Bethsaida: An Archaeological Study of the First Century* (Lanham: Lexington Books).

Schnabel, E. J. (2017), *Mark*, TNTC (London: Inter-Varsity Press).

—— (2018), *Jesus in Jerusalem: The Last Days* (Grand Rapids: Eerdmans).

Scott, B. B. (1989), *Hear Then the Parable: A Commentary on the Parables of Jesus* (Minneapolis: Fortress).

Sellew, P. (1992), 'Interior Monologue as a Narrative Device in the Parables of Luke', *JBL* 111, pp. 239–253.

Sherwin-White, A. N. (1963), *Roman Society and Roman Law in the New Testament*, Sarum Lectures (Oxford: Clarendon Press).

Shirock, R. (1992), 'Whose Exorcists Are They? The Referents of *hoi huioi hymōn* at Matthew 12.27/Luke 11.19', *JSNT* 46, pp. 41–51.

Siker, J. (1992), '"First to the Gentiles": A Literary Analysis of Luke 4:16–30', *JBL* 111, pp. 73–90.

Skinner, M. (2010), *The Trial Narratives: Conflict, Power and Identity in the New Testament* (Louisville: Westminster John Knox).

Smith, R. H. (1983), *Easter Gospels: The Resurrection of Jesus according to the Four Evangelists* (Minneapolis: Augsburg).

Snodgrass, K. R. (2008), *Stories with Intent: A Comprehensive Guide to the Parables of Jesus* (Grand Rapids: Eerdmans).

Strauss, M. L. (1995), *The Davidic Messiah in Luke–Acts: The Promise and Its Fulfillment in Lukan Christology*, JSNTSup 110 (Sheffield: Sheffield Academic Press).

Swarup, P. (2006), *The Self-understanding of the Dead Sea Scrolls Community: An Eternal Planting, a House of Holiness*, LSTS 59 (New York: T&T Clark).

Sweetland, D. M. (1990), *Our Journey with Jesus: Discipleship according to Luke–Acts*, GNS 23 (Collegeville: Liturgical).

Talbert, C. (1992), 'The Place of the Resurrection in the Theology of Luke', *Int* 46, pp. 19–30.

Tannehill, R. C. (1991), *The Narrative Unity of Luke–Acts*, Vol. 1: *The Gospel according to Luke*, ANTC (Minneapolis: Fortress).

Taylor, J. E. (2010), 'The Name "Iskarioth" (Iscariot)', *JBL* 129, pp. 367–383.

Thompson, M. M. (2000), *The Promise of the Father: Jesus and God in the New Testament* (Louisville: Westminster John Knox).

Torijano, P. (2002), *Solomon the Esoteric King: From King to Magus; Development of a Tradition*, JSJSup 73 (Leiden/Boston: Brill).

Troftgruben, T. M. (2018), 'Salvation "Today" in Luke's Gospel', *CurTM* 45, pp. 6–11.

Van Unnik, W. C. (1973), 'Once More St Luke's Prologue', *Neotestamentica* 7, pp. 7–26.

Waller, E. (1979–80), 'The Parable of the Leaven: A Sectarian Teaching and the Inclusion of Women', *USQR* 35, pp. 99–109.

Wiarda, T. (2000), *Peter in the Gospels: Pattern, Personality, and Relationship*, WUNT 127 (Tübingen: Mohr Siebeck).

Wilkinson, J. (1977), 'The Case of the Bent Woman in Luke 13:10–17', *EvQ* 49, pp. 195–205.

Wright, A. G. (1982), 'The Widow's Mites: Praise or Lament? A Matter of Context', *CBQ* 44, pp. 256–265.

Wright, N. T. (1996), *Jesus and the Victory of God*, COQG 2 (London: SPCK; Minneapolis: Fortress).

Zimmerli, W. F. (1979), *Ezekiel: A Commentary on the Book of the Prophet Ezekiel*, Hermeneia (Philadelphia: Fortress).

INTRODUCTION

1. The Gospel of Luke

For the greater part of two thousand years (at least since the time of the second-century writer Ireaneus [*Haer.* 3.11.8]), the Gospel of Matthew has been traditionally associated with the image of a man; Mark has been represented by a lion; and John, by an eagle. And the Gospel of Luke? This text has been classically signified by an ox. The choice of symbol for Luke is fitting for at least two reasons.

In the first instance, having eighty more verses than the second runner-up Matthew (and over 1,110 more words), Luke's Gospel is the longest book in the New Testament. As the ox of the New Testament canon, Luke muscularly carries the biggest load. Indeed, together the two complementary volumes (Luke–Acts) account for 28% of the New Testament materials, providing 16% more text than Paul. I suspect that many well-versed Bible readers would be surprised to discover this fact: among all the New Testament authors Luke is the most prolific.

Second, and perhaps more relevant to how this Gospel came to be associated with an ox in the first place, are the facts, first, that the ox is an animal of sacrifice and, second, that Luke's story begins and ends in cultic spaces. In the ancient world, the temple, typically perceived as the microcosm and centre of the universe, defined reality as a whole. Therefore, in the first-century world, when you set out to redefine the temple, you were setting out to redefine reality itself. Thus Luke's story is not just about the 'ox' and other bits of cultic business; it is about the cosmos and the scope of world history.

Of course, at the time of Luke's writing, the devotees of other religious spaces and religious-political systems, not least the synagogues and the temples dedicated to Caesar, had their own competing narratives. Fully aware of this dynamic, Luke consciously wrote his story of Jesus in dialogue with these alternative voices. According to the Gospel writer, shockingly so for those new to the Christians' message, everything revolved around not the law or Caesar but Jesus. Above all, the Evangelist knew that his hearers needed a clear account as to how and why Jesus came to be marked out as Messiah, Lord and Saviour of the world. Not only did his audience need to know that Jesus Christ had through his coming redefined all reality around himself; they also needed guidance on how to live in the light of the new in-breaking reality, the kingdom of God. Maybe, just maybe, the image of an ox gestures not only to a key Lukan interest, but also to the size of his argumentative yoke.

a. Early reception

Within a handful of generations after its composition, Luke's story began to provide raw resources for both Gnostic and proto-orthodox writers alike. Writing towards the last quarter of the second century, Irenaeus (*Haer.* 3.11.7) famously lamented the Gnostic Marcion and his 'mutilation' of Luke several decades earlier. Other 'Gnostic' writers, such as the composer of the (mid-to-late-second-century) *Gospel of Thomas*, made free use of Luke as well. Closer to the proto-orthodox vein, the *Epistle of the Apostles* (*c.* AD 140) seems to have drawn on texts familiar to us from Luke. The same goes for 2 Clement, another very early Christian text which has been ascribed a range of dates from the beginning of the second century to the middle.

As broadly as the Gospel of Luke circulated in the Mediterranean world, it seldom travelled alone. Right around the time of Irenaeus's writing, Tatian incorporated Luke (along with Matthew, Mark and John) into his fourfold Gospel harmony. Though the 'Western order' of the Gospels (Matthew, John, Luke, Mark) is preserved in Codex Bezae and some Old Latin codices, the vast majority and the earliest of the codices preserve the Gospels in the now-canonical order: Matthew, Mark, Luke and John. This order finds further support in the Early Church Fathers, not least Irenaeus, Origen, Eusebius and Athanasius.

b. Unity of Luke–Acts

Though our text was very quickly subsumed into a fourfold Gospel collection, Lukan scholarship of the past hundred years has repeatedly confirmed that the author of this Gospel also wrote its sequel, Acts. What is more, the Evangelist clearly intended his readers to recognize a fundamental unity between these two volumes. This is borne out not only by the two works' matching prologues (Luke 1:1–4; Acts 1:1–5) but also by a number of linguistic and structural markers shared between the larger stories. In one sense, Luke–Acts is two stories, the story of Jesus and the story of the apostolic church. Yet in another sense, the two stories are one story, held together by the thread of divine activity. So, then, Luke's Gospel is the first of two stories, yet also the beginning of one large still-unfolding story.

c. Genre

On the assumption that Luke knew and used at least one of the other now-canonical Gospels (whether Mark or Matthew or both), the writer must have construed his own project as a 'gospel' after the pattern of his precursor text(s). Whereas the genre of 'gospel' was a first-century literary innovation and that genre initially admitted only a very few members to its ranks, Luke knew that he was throwing his hat into a very small ring. The author must have written self-consciously within this newly established genre.

The closest Graeco-Roman equivalent to Luke's Gospel is the Hellenistic *bios*. Whereas this form of the ancient biography regularly takes an interest in its hero's youth, seeks to establish his merits, while exculpating him from slanderous accusations, Luke's Gospel does all these things and more. The scientific ring of Luke's prologue (1:1–4) confirms the seriousness of his biographical task. On a basic level, then, Luke's story aims to be understood as a biography like many other biographies of illustrious men.

Still the Hebraic cast of the narrative suggests that the issue of genre is not as clear-cut as might first be assumed. After all, if Luke's genealogy (Luke 3) reminds us of any ancient writing, it is texts like Genesis and 1 Chronicles. Perceiving the pervasive sense of fulfilment (not to mention the repetitive use of chiasms, repetitions and parallelisms), the well-versed first-century reader would have quickly recognized that Luke was setting up his literary shop in the world of the Scriptures. This is also the world of prophetic narrative, a world that often seeks to show the correlation between promise and fulfilment – an important theme in Luke.

And so Luke is something of a hybrid. With its vocabulary, concerns, structural elements and outlook, the Gospel presents itself as an extension of Old Testament Scripture, written into the present, as it were. At the same time, it fits right into a genre that would have been quickly recognized by Luke's first-century contemporaries. In order to take up a conversation on multiple cultural fronts, Luke appropriated a blended genre form, part *bios* and partially a pastiche of various scriptural forms, that resists simple literary categorization.

2. Origin of Luke

If as a rule we know frustratingly little about the historical circumstances surrounding the origins of the four canonical Gospels, Luke is no exception to this rule. Historical evidence demonstrates that Luke was circulating with some authority by the second half of the second century. But as to who wrote the third Gospel, where it was written, why it was written, when it was written and how it was written – these questions do not always fetch straightforward answers. That said, there is still much that we can say about the

Gospel's authorship, provenance, audience, purpose, date and sources.

a. Authorship

Over the past hundred years of critical scholarship, it has been generally – though perhaps erroneously – maintained that in the case of Matthew and John, the burden of proof falls on those wishing to maintain traditional authorship, while in the case of Mark and Luke, the burden of proof remains on those seeking to dispute traditional authorship. In relation to Luke, then, the greater part of modern New Testament scholarship would assert this: if one argues that Luke did *not* write the Gospel traditionally ascribed to him, then one must explain how a historical figure of such relative obscurity and unimportance came to be identified as its author. And precisely because *that* argument seems a rather difficult one to make, Lukan authorship should initially be presumed rather than doubted. External evidence (early tradition) and internal evidence only seems to support this presumption.

i. Early tradition

By the last quarter of the second century, Irenaeus (*Haer.* 3.1.1; 3.11.8; 3.13.3; 3.14.1) and the Muratorian Canon (§§2–8, 34–39) identify Luke's Gospel by name; the Anti-Marcionite prologue likewise associates Luke with the Gospel. Closer to the middle of the same century, Justin Martyr (*Dial.* 103.19) states that Luke was a travelling companion of Paul and also the author of one of the 'memoirs', a term which many take to be Justin's circumlocution for the Gospels. The earliest surviving manuscript containing Luke is contained in the remains of larger codex P75 (third century AD), most likely used for readings in church. There it sits alongside the Gospel of John, seemingly as part of a fourfold Gospel collection. Patristic evidence, together with early papyrological evidence, supports not only the traditional view of Lukan authorship but also that this Gospel was received as an authoritative text no later than the first half of the second century.

ii. Internal evidence

Lukan authorship is further supported by the 'internal evidence', meaning evidence from within Luke and the larger New Testament canon. In Luke's prologue, we discover that the author addresses his work to one 'Theophilus' (Luke 1:3). Though the addressee could be a fictive construct, most scholars are inclined to see this as either Luke's patron (financially underwriting the Evangelist's project) or his disciple – or both. At any rate, it is hard to imagine that Theophilus and his in-the-know acquaintances would have been silent as to the authorship of the text dedicated to the former. It stands to reason that Luke's first readers also knew the author's identity and that this would have been easily confirmed, directly or indirectly, by the dedicatee himself. And if that author *was* someone other than Luke, how is it that either the circles surrounding Theophilus or the broader scope of the text's readership would have allowed the pseudonymous ascription to deprive the real author of due credit?

As noted above, scholars regularly regard Luke and Acts as the work of a single hand. Therefore, any responsible investigation of the Gospel's authorship must also weigh the evidence for the authorship of Acts. Here we are helped by the so-called 'we' passages (Acts 16:10–17; 20:5–15; 21:1–18; 27:1 – 28:16), those sections where the otherwise anonymous narrator of Acts unobtrusively joins Paul as his on-again, off-again travelling companion. Since the list of Paul's named companions is fairly limited, and since Luke remains one of those companions (Col. 4:10–14; 2 Tim. 4:11; Phlm. 24), the case for Lukan authorship of the third Gospel is indirectly supported by a comparison of these texts from Paul and Acts. Furthermore, on considering the many similarities between Pauline theological concerns and those of Luke, not to mention their very similar formulation of the Lord's Supper, both at variance with the traditions of Matthew and Mark (cf. Luke 22:14–20; 1 Cor. 11:23–27), Luke and Paul's close acquaintanceship is eminently plausible. If Paul's friend Luke is indeed the author of Acts (as our best guess would indicate), then he is also almost certainly the composer of our Gospel. The witness of the church leaves us no other option.

iii. The historical Luke

Internal and external evidence conspire to paint a fairly coherent portrait of Luke the man, consisting of at least four strokes. First, Luke's Greek is very good, perhaps the best in the New Testament (though Hebrews would also be a contender). That would seem to indicate that he is well educated and that Greek was his mother tongue (cf. Acts 1:19). Second, our Evangelist knew his Scriptures, especially the Greek version of the Old Testament, the Septuagint or LXX. Third, Colossians 4:10–14 might indicate that Luke was a Gentile, though neither the grammar nor the logic of these verses strictly requires as much. Fourth, if Paul's Luke was indeed the author of the Gospel of Luke (as argued above), then the same Gospel writer was also a physician (Col. 4:14). This is borne out not only by the relative specificity of Luke's medical descriptions (compare, for example, the 'high fever' of Luke 4:38 with the nondescript 'fever' of Matt. 8:14//Mark 1:30) but also by the author's scientific genre as signalled in the prologue. The second-century Anti-Marcionite prologue affirms each of these points and adds, at no extra charge, that he also hailed from Syria, an assertion seconded by Eusebius (*Hist. eccl.* 3.4.6–8) and Jerome (*Vir. ill.* 3.7).

iv. Objections

Despite the strength of the arguments for Lukan authorship, a long line of scholarship has resisted such a conclusion. Setting aside outmoded arguments from earlier (nineteenth-century) scholarship, we can focus on four leading points, characteristic of the contemporary discussion. First, it is said that the author of this Gospel makes no claim to be an eyewitness; in fact, the historical distance he imagines (Luke 1:1–4) makes Lukan authorship a priori more unlikely than likely. Second, it is asserted that arguments for Lukan authorship which depend on Colossians 4:10–14, 2 Timothy 4:11 and Philemon 24 are intrinsically weak, since Colossians and 2 Timothy are widely (though not universally) considered to have been authored not by Paul but by a much later figure. Third, insofar as the argument for Lukan authorship relies on the judgment that the author of Acts and Paul were two peas in a theological pod, this argument is undermined by the fact that the theology of the Gospel and Acts is in some respects very un-Pauline. For example, whereas the Paul of the epistles focuses in on justification by faith and an atoning cross, the Paul of Acts emphasizes, quite differently, the resurrection. Fourth and finally, whereas the case for Lukan authorship relies on the historical integrity of the 'we' passages (as authentic recollections of the author of Acts), scholarly judgments that these same passages were inserted as fictive interpolations help to offset the case for Lukan authorship.

Though these arguments against Lukan authorship are by no means frivolous, they are open to rebuttal. First, to invalidate the Gospel's testimony on account of the author's failure to claim eyewitness status seems to miss the Evangelist's point, for he is not claiming to be an eyewitness to Jesus' life and ministry but rather to present a range of eyewitnesses and events, spanning from the time of Jesus' birth to Paul's imprisonment at Rome. Second, even if we were to discount the Pauline authorship of Colossians 4:10–14 and 2 Timothy 4:11 (granted for the purposes of argument but not conceded), this still leaves Philemon 24. (And if in response to this point it is countered that one Pauline witness is not sufficient, one might well ask in return, 'Well, why not?') Third, while there are obvious differences with Paul's theology as it is represented in, say, Romans, Galatians and the Corinthian correspondence, one might counter with the twin points (1) that Luke composed his narrative in order to make certain theological points appropriate to the occasion of his audience, and (2) that Paul wrote each of his epistles with somewhat different purposes in mind. One danger of conceptualizing theology as a series of abstract propositions is that it deludes us into thinking that the early church's kerygmatic message required uniform expression, no matter the author or the occasion. Fourth, if the 'we' passages of Acts are indeed a spurious insertion or fictive trope, then this begins to raise serious doubts about the historical faithfulness of Luke–Acts as a whole. This approach, though a path well travelled in much critical scholarship, seems to raise far more questions than it answers. A better path, even if it is a road less travelled, is to assume (1) that the author of the Gospel aspires to offer a credible history (per his own claims in Luke 1:1–4) and (2) that Luke implicates himself in the text precisely in order to vouch for his own account of the past.

b. Provenance, audience and purpose

Where did Luke write his Gospel? For whom and to what purpose? These are difficult questions but still questions deserving some comment, beginning with the matter of provenance. Some scholars suppose that Luke and his Gospel hailed from Syrian Antioch, a claim which is indirectly (though perhaps weakly) supported by the Western text (D) of Luke at Acts 11:28, which has Antioch as the point of departure in the first of its 'we' sections. Meanwhile, patristic traditions might incline us in the direction of Achaia (Greece). Still other traditions locate Luke's composition in Rome. The truth is we are unlikely to register anything more than a guess on this matter. And, frankly, given Luke's itinerant lifestyle, provenance hardly seems to matter.

As noted above, the stated audience is one 'Theophilus'. In our judgment, Theophilus was likely the Evangelist's benefactor who wished to be better schooled in the 'certainty' of what he believed. Of course, Luke is not simply writing his massive two-volume work for one man: he has a much broader audience in mind. If ever there were, among the four Gospels, a Gospel for all Christians, Luke has as strong a claim as any one of them. Luke wrote his Gospel not for one believer but for Christian believers everywhere.

And why did he write it, especially if he knew of other narratives already in existence (Luke 1:1)? Perhaps the Evangelist was motivated by the sense that Christian believers were in pressing need of further assurances. For example, persecuted by fellow synagogue members (Phil. 1:28; 1 Thess. 1:6–7), Paul's churches would have certainly appreciated a compelling narrative case that their allegiance to Jesus the Messiah was not in vain, despite the remonstrances of (fellow) Jews. At the same time, the strong-arm claims of Rome and the pull of emperor worship would have also challenged the early church's story of a suffering and crucified Messiah. Yet ultimately, if the Romans saw their epic founding story in Virgil's *Aeneid*, what Christians needed was something analogous, an epic spanning years and continents. Such a story would ideally lay the foundational narrative of the believing community, all the while showing that the *real* plot line was not bound up with the fortunes of Rome or the Jerusalem temple but in Jesus' life, death, resurrection and ascension, and the giving of the Spirit to a mission-oriented church. Though the reasons precipitating Luke's Gospel were likely manifold and complex (apologetics, for example, is strongly in the mix), the Gospel was likely written simply because the church needed its own story, precisely like the one found in Luke–Acts. Such a story, so Luke hoped, would underwrite the churches' own corporate self-understanding and mission.

c. Date
In dating the composition of the Gospel of Luke, contemporary scholars have posited four time periods as possibilities. The earliest (mid first century) and the latest (the first half of the second century) are very much minority positions. Much more common in the commentaries and handbooks are datings of either the 60s or even more commonly AD 75–85. We will restrict consideration to these two theorized time frames.

The case for a composition date of AD 75–85 depends primarily on two premises. The first, uncontroversially, is that Luke knew and used Mark. The second is that Mark should be dated in the early 70s. One of the leading reasons for dating Mark to the early 70s has to do with its account of the destruction of the temple (Mark 13). Because Mark's Jesus predicts the destruction of the temple with such accuracy, it can only be the case – so it is argued – that Mark put words into Jesus' mouth, creating a prophecy after the event (*vaticinium ex eventu*). Of course, the same argument applies to Luke with its prediction of the temple's destruction. If one assumes that it was not Jesus who predicted the future but the Evangelists who only made it look as if Jesus did so, then one must also surmise a dating after AD 70 for both Gospels, and a dating which allows lead time from the writing of Mark to the writing of Luke.

The case for a date in the 60s rides on three premises. First, those who adhere to this position generally hold that either Jesus in fact had extraordinary insight into the forthcoming temple destruction, or that Jesus is using generalized scriptural language to describe the temple's destruction given its disobedience (which may or may not entail miraculous predictive ability). Second, this position asks, if Acts breaks off so suddenly with Paul's Roman house arrest, would this not suggest the possibility that Luke wrapped up his two-volume work right around this time (mid 60s)? Third, given the trauma of the Neronic persecution in the later years of the 60s, how is it possible that a post-AD 70 Gospel could leave no hint of this terrible period in its pages? Surely, so it is reasoned, Luke completed his work before the Neronic persecution got underway. Though the matter cannot be definitely settled, the present author considers this last view the most persuasive: Luke was written in the 60s very close on the heels of Mark.

d. Sources

On the two-source hypothesis, Luke availed himself of Mark and the allegedly now-lost source Q (from the German *Quelle*, meaning 'source'), along with the special source L, in composing his Gospel. On the Farrer hypothesis, Luke used only Mark. On the Augustinian hypothesis, he used Matthew and Mark. The present commentary does not presume any particular solution to the so-called Synoptic problem. Agnostic on the issue of textual sources, we will generally avoid source-critical assumptions except for the assumption that Luke used Mark, which we will take for granted.

Though 'many have undertaken to set down an orderly account of the events that have been fulfilled among us' (1:1), Luke surely had non-textual sources at his disposal as well. Indeed, he claims to have consulted many 'eyewitnesses' (1:2). Included among these would have probably been the likes of Mary, the disciples, and certainly Paul who spent a good two years with Luke at Caesarea and laid claim to special revelations directly from the Lord. The thoroughness of Luke's method suggests that his approach was to leave no stone unturned and to present the facts as winsomely and effectively as possible.

3. Theological concerns

Luke tells the story of Jesus Christ with the goal of identifying him as the fulfilment of the Scriptures as well as the eschatological climax of redemption. This comes to surface not only through the Evangelist's recurring themes of fulfilment and divine necessity

(Greek: *dei*), but also through countless allusions to previous redemptive moments in Israel's history, not least the exodus and return from exile. For Luke, this core redemptive-historical fact about Jesus relates centrally to his distinctive salvation-bearing mission (its goals, values and strategies), which in turn serves as a template for the church as it undertakes (on the model of Jesus) its Spirit-directed and Spirit-empowered mission. This mission is characteristically marked by a hospitality that witnesses to Jesus' role as guest and host at meals, and by a concern for the poor, that is, the socially marginalized, including women, children and the Gentiles. Yet at bottom, all these threads conspire to set Jesus out as the author of salvation and the only hope for Israel and the world. The Gospel of Luke is the gospel of salvation.

4. Structure

In another writing, I have characterized Luke's structure as a seamless spiralling staircase, circling back repetitively while taking the reader higher and higher.[1] That said, some structure can be discerned. One of the most basic approaches stipulates four sections: the coming of Jesus (1:5 – 4:13); the Galilee ministry (4:14 – 9:50); the journey to Jerusalem (9:51 – 21:38); and the passion and resurrection (22:1 – 24:53). A more detailed version of this outline would add a prologue (1:1–4) and tease out a break between the infancy narrative (1:5 – 2:52) and Jesus' preparation for ministry (3:1 – 4:13). We would also submit the importance of distinguishing Jesus' journey *to* Jerusalem (9:51 – 19:27) from his ministry *in* Jerusalem (19:28 – 21:38). The passion (22:1 – 23:56) and resurrection narratives (24:1–53) also evince a clear break. A more detailed structure is now presented in the 'Analysis'.

---

1. Perrin, *Kingdom of God*, pp. 193–194. Werner Kelber ('Exposition', p. 14) similarly comments that Luke, like the other Gospels, is 'an intricately designed religious universe, with . . . retrospective and prospective devices, linear and concentric patterning, and a continuous line of thematic cross-referencing and narrative interlockings'.

ANALYSIS

1. **PROLOGUE (1:1–4)**

2. **INFANCY NARRATIVE (1:5 – 2:52)**
   A. Two birth announcements (1:5–38)
      i. Announcement of John's birth (1:5–25)
      ii. Announcement of Jesus' birth (1:26–38)
   B. Mary's visit to Elizabeth (1:39–56)
   C. Two births (1:57 – 2:20)
      i. Birth of John (1:57–80)
      ii. Birth of Jesus (2:1–20)
   D. Young Jesus at the temple (2:21–52)
      i. Presentation at the temple (2:21–40)
      ii. Sitting among the teachers (2:41–52)

3. **JESUS' PREPARATION FOR MINISTRY (3:1 – 4:13)**
   A. John the Baptizer (3:1–20)
      i. Inauguration of John's ministry (3:1–6)
      ii. John's message (3:7–20)
   B. Jesus' baptism (3:21–22)
   C. Jesus' credentials (3:23 – 4:13)

ii. Jesus mourns over Jerusalem (13:31–35)
J. Messianic banquet (14:1–24)
  i. Jesus heals a man of dropsy (14:1–6)
  ii. Honour at the feast (14:7–11)
  iii. The great feast (14:12–24)
K. The cost of discipleship (14:25–35)
L. Parables of lostness (15:1–32)
  i. Parable of the lost sheep (15:1–7)
  ii. Parable of the lost coin (15:8–10)
  iii. Parable of the prodigal son and his brother (15:11–32)
M. Parables of wealth (16:1–31)
  i. Parable of the shrewd manager (16:1–18)
  ii. Parable of Lazarus (16:19–31)
N. Sin and repentance (17:1–19)
  i. Faith and duty (17:1–10)
  ii. Jesus heals ten men of leprosy (17:11–19)
O. The coming of the kingdom (17:20–37)
P. Two parables about prayer (18:1–14)
  i. Parable of the persistent widow (18:1–8)
  ii. Parable of the two praying men (18:9–14)
Q. Upside-down kingdom (18:15–34)
  i. Jesus blesses the children (18:15–17)
  ii. The rich ruler (18:18–30)
  iii. The third passion prediction (18:31–34)
R. Approach to Jerusalem (18:35 – 19:27)
  i. Jesus heals the blind man from Jericho (18:35–43)
  ii. Zacchaeus (19:1–10)
  iii. Parable of the ten pounds (19:11–27)

6. MINISTRY IN JERUSALEM (19:28 – 21:38)
A. Entry into Jerusalem (19:28–48)
  i. Preparations for the entry (19:28–36)
  ii. Triumphal entry (19:37–44)
  iii. Temple action (19:45–48)
B. Conflict with Jerusalem authorities (20:1–26)
  i. Jesus' authority questioned (20:1–8)
  ii. Parable of the wicked tenants (20:9–19)
  iii. Taxes to Caesar (20:20–26)

COMMENTARY

1. PROLOGUE (1:1–4)

Context

In approaching any literary work, we will always find that genre matters. This should be obvious enough on considering the differing strategies readers adopt when they take in a newspaper article as opposed to, say, a science-fiction story. Consciously or unconsciously, we rely on certain textual signals as we discern a text's genre. This was as true in antiquity as it is today. As Luke beckons his readers into his story through the doorway of this prologue, he immediately offers us the calling card of a historian. Everything about Luke 1:1–4 seems to say in so many words, 'This is serious history.'

Modern Western readers tend to associate 'serious history' with a dispassionate and objective recounting of events. Good historians, we tell ourselves, at least *try* not to let on that they have a particular agenda. Nothing could be further from the case when it comes to ancient historiography. For the ancient historians, it was exactly their commitment to the facts *and* interpretation that qualified them to speak authoritatively. That is why Luke never claims to be objective, either here or at any other point in his two-volume set. He is unapologetically committed to the facts, true enough, but he is also – equally unapologetically – motivated by his theological interests. Like those before him who also had 'undertaken to set down an orderly account' (namely, Matthew and Mark), Luke wants to impress upon his readers the wonders of the earthly and Risen Lord Jesus Christ, as well as the necessity of placing faith in him.

Comment

1. Luke states that *many have undertaken to set down an orderly account* (*diēgēsis*), similar to the story he is about to tell. The word *diēgēsis* was a semi-technical term, referring to a 'well-ordered, polished product of the historian's work'.[1] This would certainly support the Evangelist's attempt to position his material as credible history. But in Luke's writing, the verbal cognate of the same noun is regularly used in connection with God's mighty acts.[2] This implies that the author seeks to provide not just a biography of Jesus but also a narrative of *God's works through Jesus*. These mighty works include certain salvific events which *have been fulfilled among us*. For Luke, then, the story which he is about to tell must be set in the broader context of God's purposes – past, present and future.

2. Eager to vouch for the accuracy of his own account, Luke next informs his readers that the materials he received were *handed on* (*paredosan*) by *eyewitnesses and servants of the word*. The verb here often refers to the transmission of official traditions (1 Cor. 11:23; 15:1–3; 1 Thess. 4:1–2), suggesting that the process of passing on 'Jesus stories' was a carefully executed, even solemn task. Meanwhile, governed by a single article, the nouns *eyewitnesses* and *servants* actually refer to two aspects of the same role. The mediators of this tradition are eyewitness-servants, who are likely the apostles themselves (cf. Acts 26:16).[3] The apostles *serve* God's people by

---

1. Van Unnik, 'Prologue', pp. 12–13.
2. Green, p. 38.
3. Though see Kuhn ('Beginning the Witness'), who wants to extend the term to select individuals from Luke 1 – 2.

collectively standing by their traditions as authoritative *eyewitnesses* of the events they relate. As such they are also the self-identified guarantors of the gospel truth which now stands to be perpetuated through established ecclesial structures.

3. Luke himself claims to have investigated everything (1) *from the very first,* (2) *carefully* and (3) in an *orderly* fashion. The phrase *from the very first* (*anōthen*) speaks of Luke's decision to begin with the birth narrative, as well as to the overall comprehensiveness of his biographical account.[4] Working within the framework of transmitted traditions yet building upon them, Luke claims to have done fresh investigative work according to the best historiographical practices of his day. He does so for the sake of one *Theophilus,* a figure who was either a fictitious construct representing every friend (*philos*) of God (*theos*) or, as maintained above, an actual person.

4. The point of all this is to assure the *truth* (*asphaleia*) or certainty of the proclaimed gospel – in regard to not only the isolated historical facts but also their apostolic interpretation. For Luke, salvific event and interpretation are inseparable; together both must stand up to scrutiny. History and faith together stand as the bedrock for the gospel story he is about to tell.

Theology

Luke calls his story an 'orderly account' or a 'narrative' (ESV) of events. Now, as Aristotle pointed out, the very concept of narrative – complete with a beginning, a middle and an end – assumes a logical sequence of events. The concept of sequence is important. Far too often, modern readers of the Gospels have treated the authorized stories of Jesus as a hodgepodge of random incidents and teachings with little discernible relationship to one another. The same readers may wonder whether there is any rhyme or reason to the ordering of the stories, aside from a rough chronological interest. But by identifying his story as a *diēgēsis* and therefore an orderly account, Luke is claiming that his plot has a

---

4. Some commentators (e.g. Fitzymer, p. 298), however, understand *from the very first* as from the start of Jesus' ministry in Luke 3:23.

linear progression. This means that the Evangelist's readers need to be sensitive to the narrative as a whole, even when examining the shortest of sayings or stories. Nothing is arbitrary: every word, sentence, paragraph, must be appreciated in relation to that which precedes and that which follows. Because Luke offers an organic narrative, the responsible interpreter must constantly look to the Gospel writer as his own best interpreter.

Moreover, because the Evangelist sees the events surrounding Jesus' life, death, resurrection and ascension as having been 'fulfilled among us', he also sees his own narrative as an authorized extension of the Old Testament narrative, the writings of the likes of 'Moses, the prophets, and the psalms' (24:44). If the second-century heretic Marcion reduced the four Gospels to a pared-down version of Luke's story simply because the third Gospel seemed to have the least to do with the God of Israel, it is only because he badly misunderstood that story in the first place. According to our Evangelist, the revelation of Jesus Christ is a progressive revelation, which fits snugly within the larger, overarching framework of the story of Israel.

2. INFANCY NARRATIVE (1:5 – 2:52)

A. Two birth announcements (1:5–38)

Context

The narrative action begins by focusing on Jesus' forerunner John, as well John's parents, Zechariah and Elizabeth. In all four Gospels, John the Baptizer plays an inestimably important role. Yet it is Luke, more than any other Gospel writer, who highlights John's significance. In 1:5–38, Luke puts the prenatal histories of John and Jesus side by side. He does so to anticipate their mutual association and to establish a contrast. As great as John was, Jesus was greater.

To put Gabriel's dual birth announcements in the same category as the many angelic appearances in Luke–Acts would be to miss the point. Gabriel stood at the top of the angelic hierarchy (cf. 1 En. 40:9). His appearance at the beginning of Luke's story strikes an auspicious note. Further, Luke's more well-versed readers would have been aware that when Gabriel first appears in Scripture, in the book of Daniel, he comes to reveal a flickering light of hope at the far end of the dark tunnel of exile (Dan. 8:16; 9:21). Now that flickering light, Luke begins to hint, is about to come into view.

The birth announcements of John and Jesus parallel each other in step-by-step fashion. Both conceptions announced by Gabriel are miraculous; both involve the Holy Spirit; finally, both are singled out as having redemptive significance.[1] Of course, there are contrasts as well. Two are salient. First, whereas the announcement of John's birth takes place in the temple in Jerusalem, news of the coming Messiah's birth is first broadcast in an insignificant and out-of-the-way location. Second, while the priest Zechariah disbelieves the angel's message and is rendered mute, the obedient response of a barely pubescent girl finally culminates in a declaration of God's praises (1:46–55). The movement from unbelieving priestly man to believing common girl, from officially sanctioned sacred space to newly established sacred spaces, augurs the overall thematic concerns of the Gospel itself.

Comment
i. Announcement of John's birth (1:5–25)

5. Luke sets the opening chapters of his Gospel in the time of Herod the Great (73–74 BC). *King Herod* was a ruthless and violent ruler, much feared and much despised. The very mention of his name in the lead-up to the births of John and Jesus would have reminded readers just what kind of world the Messiah and his kinsman forerunner were coming into.[2] The first characters introduced in Luke's story are John's parents. *Zechariah* belonged to the *priestly order of Abijah*, one of twenty-four priestly clans (1 Chr. 24:1–19) descendent from Aaron. His wife *Elizabeth* was also a *descendant of Aaron*. John's priestly pedigree, inherited from both sides of the family tree, anticipates his own unofficial priestly role which he will assume on entering the wilderness.

6–7. Luke now conveys three further pieces of biographical information regarding John's parents: they were morally upright, childless and advanced in years. Zechariah and Elizabeth's moral

---

1. On these and other similarities, see Nolland, p. 40.
2. On Herod, see Bond, *DJG*, pp. 38–82.

stature and childlessness invoke other scriptural characters: Abraham and Sarah (Gen. 18) as well as Elkanah and Hannah (1 Sam. 1). These linkages prepare us for the fact that God is once again about to intervene in the story of Israel, and that once again through a most unlikely biological process. The point is not simply to emphasize the extraordinary nature of John's birth but to demonstrate that the great forerunner, like Jesus after him, would be as integral to a renewal of the Abrahamic covenant as Abraham and Sarah were to its initiation, and as pivotal to the reinauguration of the Davidic covenant as Elkanah and Hannah were to that covenant's instigation. It was appropriate, too, that John and Jesus, who would each in their own way create something out of nothing, should be brought into existence virtually from nothing in biological terms.

8–10. On the week that his division is on duty, Zechariah is chosen by lot to burn the holy incense (cf. Exod. 30:34–38; m. Tamid 5:2).[3] Performed every morning and evening, this ritual would require – as Luke explains to his uninitiated readers – the priest to enter the Holy Place, while the worshippers remained at a safe distance. An important component of temple life, the incense-burning ritual symbolized the people's prayer going up before God. Little do the gathered worshippers know that their pleas for Israel's redemption – a recurring focus of Israel's corporate prayer as attested in the daily Jewish prayer of the Amidah – are about to be answered. The timing of this particular revelation could not have been any more appropriate.[4]

11. For now, the divine messenger is simply identified as an *angel of the Lord*. Because, as we shall learn from verse 13, the angel comes in direct response to Zechariah's prayer, it is only fitting that he appear *at the right side of the altar of incense* (a gold-enamelled fixture measuring some 3 ft high and 18 in. wide and deep), the central symbol of faithful prayer. The angelic encounter recalls Isaiah's

---

3. The set rotation involved each division serving two separate weeks per year; on this institution, see Fitzmyer, p. 322.

4. Divine visitations coinciding with this ritual were not unprecedented in Judaism; cf. Josephus, *Ant.* 13.282–283.

vision of the Lord at the temple, which also occurred when the smoke of incense filled the inner sanctuary (Isa. 6:4). Other similarities obtain between Isaiah and Zechariah's visions, not least the fact that both episodes culminate in the sending of a prophet to preach to Yahweh's remnant (cf. Isa. 6:8–13). It is almost as if the Baptizer were destined to close out what Isaiah, the preacher of exile, began. The angel's position next to the altar of incense, itself stationed directly in front of the temple veil, foreshadows the rending of the same veil at the end of the story (23:45). A veil at the beginning and at the end: seemingly like the Holy of Holies itself, Luke's Gospel, which contains the presence of God in the story of Jesus Christ, can be entered and exited only through the temple veil!⁵

12. On seeing the angel, Zechariah is understandably *terrified* (*etarachthē*). (The same verb *tarassō* characterizes the disciples' response to the Risen Lord; cf. 24:38.) Luke emphasizes the point by adding that *fear overwhelmed him*. In Luke (1:30; 2:10), as in other Scripture, fear is a common response to angelic appearances. But here the Evangelist seems to draw a line back to Daniel, who was likewise overcome by fear (Dan. 10:8–9), even as the same prophet was assured – again like Zechariah – that his prayers had been heard, and that no less at the hour of prayer (Dan. 9:21). The similarities are hardly accidental. Just as Daniel had longingly prayed for Israel's restoration from exile, Luke implies that the prophet's prayers were now being answered: restoration was on its way through the impending acts of God.

13. Employing elements characteristic of other scriptural visions, not least the command *Do not be afraid* (e.g. Gen. 21:17), Luke signals that this angelic sighting is a redemptive-historical milestone. And yet the vision carries a highly personal tone, as the angel addresses the aged priest by name, informing him that *your prayer has been heard*. In this respect, the name *Zechariah*, meaning

---

5. As early as the second century, we find Irenaeus (*Haer.* 3.11.8) comparing the Gospels to sacred space, when he identifies the four Gospels as pillars (*styloi*), that is, the posts that marked off the boundary of the tabernacle.

'God remembers', is not insignificant. As a result of Zechariah's prayers, the angel assures him, his *wife Elizabeth* will indeed give birth to a *son* who is to be named *John*, meaning 'God is gracious'. As the ensuing narrative makes clear, that graciousness extends not just to Zechariah and Elizabeth as childless individuals but to Israel as a whole (cf. Isa. 54:1).

14–15. As the angel describes John's destiny, he emphasizes the *joy and gladness* that this new life will bring to people, not least to Zechariah himself. The reason for this joy is stated in the last clause: *for [gar] he will be great in the sight of the Lord*, much as Jesus will be 'great' (v. 32). The angel continues by issuing a stipulation and a promise. The stipulation, forbidding John from partaking of any wine or perhaps beer, may be a version of the Nazirite vow (Num. 6:1–8) or simply an expansion of priestly protocol (Lev. 10:9). John's enforced abstention would at any rate become one of his defining traits (Luke 7:33), even as it more immediately puts him in company with Samson (Judg. 13) and Samuel (1 Sam. 1:11) – a deliverer and a prophet, respectively, who were also conceived through divine intervention. John's connection with Samuel is especially striking, given the latter's role in anointing David as king, for soon enough the Baptizer would anoint Jesus the new David (Luke 3:21–22). The promise that John will be filled with the Spirit *even before his birth* is later confirmed when John *in utero* leaps for joy at Jesus' presence (1:41). But John's Spirit-filling is only relative to a more robust filling that would later come on Jesus (cf. 1:35; 3:22; 4:18–21). In being *filled with the Holy Spirit*, John is marked out not simply for extraordinary spiritual experiences but for a specific prophetic purpose (cf. 1:41, 67; Acts 2:4; 4:8, 31; 9:17; 13:9).

16–17. The messenger now speaks of John's mission, namely, his task of bringing *the people of Israel* back to Yahweh. The Baptizer's vocation will not be without controversy, for although *many* will respond positively to God's overtures, not all will. Here and elsewhere in Luke (2:34; 5:15; 7:21; etc.), the term 'many' doubles as an elective term, as it does elsewhere in the Hebrew Scriptures.[6] That John will *go before him* (i.e. Jesus the Lord, v. 16)

---

6. See Marshall, p. 57.

in the manner of Elijah (Mal. 3:1) underscores the Baptizer's
Elijah-esque quality. Most basically of all, he will model himself
on Elijah by gathering a faithful remnant in the face of powerful
and wicked forces.

The allusion to Malachi 3 – 4 is not fortuitous. If Malachi 3
foresees the coming of a messenger 'before me [i.e. the Lord]',
Malachi 4 promises the sending of an Elijah who will turn the
'hearts of parents to their children' and vice versa (Mal. 4:5–6).
Functioning as the new Elijah, therefore, John is destined to go
before the Lord as his forerunner with the twin goals of securing
proper worship (Mal. 3:1–4) and forestalling the judgment of God
(Mal. 4:6b).[7] To accomplish this, in keeping with Malachi's stated
expectation, John will first *turn the hearts of parents to their children* and
the disobedient to wisdom. The implication is clear enough: on a
corporate level, renewed covenantal obedience would naturally
manifest itself through stable family relationships (even as the
predicted tribulation would entail the dissolution of family ties; cf.
Luke 21:16); on an individual level, the coming restoration would
result in the ungodly repenting of their sin. The goal of John's
ministry, then, is *to make ready a people prepared [kateskeusamenon] for
the Lord*, which is also to prepare (*kataskeuasei*) the way for the
Messiah (Luke 7:27).[8]

18. Zechariah's response to this astounding announcement is
anticlimactic, to say the least. Like Abra(ha)m (Gen. 15:8), he wishes
to have some palpable confirmation of the amazing promise (cf.
also Judg. 6:17–24). This is unsurprising, for just as Sarah and her
husband were getting on in years (*probebēkotes hēmerōn*, Gen. 18:11,
LXX), so too was Elizabeth *getting on in years* (*probebēkuia en tais
hēmerais autēs*). Perhaps Zechariah is looking for the same kind of
confirmation that was provided to Abram (Gen. 15).

---

7. See Perrin, *Kingdom of God*, p. 77.

8. The verb *kataskeuazō* is frequently applied to building and furnishing,
and in the Hebrew Bible to the building and furnishing of the temple
(BDAG, p. 418). That God's people should constitute a temple is a
common conceit in the NT writings (1 Cor. 3:10–17; 6:19; Eph. 2:19–21;
1 Pet. 2:4–8).

19–20. Regardless of Zechariah's intentions, the angel interprets the priest's response as an expression of unbelief and rebukes him accordingly. In the meantime, he identifies himself as *Gabriel* ('mighty man of God'), the one and the same angel who clarified Daniel's visions of oppression and comfort (Dan. 8:16; 9:21) and spoke of the advent of the Messiah at the close of the appointed seventy weeks. It was only appropriate now for the same Gabriel to return in order to announce that the appointed period of waiting had run its course. Offering his own credentials as one who stands *in the presence of God* (perhaps at God's right hand, even as he stands at the 'right hand' of the altar), he now speaks of his ambassadorial role, claiming to be the bearer of *good news (euangelisasthai)*.

A strategic word choice, the verb *euangelisasthai* would have struck two different chords. On the one hand, in the Jewish Scriptures, the proclamation of good news is associated with Yahweh's declaration that exile has run its course and that Yahweh himself now rules (Isa. 40:9; 52:7; 61:1). On the other hand, 'good news' also invokes Caesar's propagandistic communications, designed to remind the Roman subjects of the imperator's prowess and his divine right to rule. Gabriel's claim to preach good news hints that the Isaianic promise of 'good news' is now at long last coming to fruition, even as it suggests that Caesar's pretentious political claims will soon be shown up for what they are.

Zechariah's unbelief will not go without consequences. From this point forward, the aged priest will be rendered *mute* (and apparently deaf too; cf. 1:62–63) *until the day these things occur.* As it turns out, Zechariah's silence is not just a punishment but a sign: if Daniel could not speak until his mouth was opened by divine enablement (Dan. 10:15–16), the same would be the case for Zechariah, the new Daniel. The realities which Daniel foresaw were now set to transpire.

21. Given the repetition of the daily ritual of incense burning, one might fairly predict how long it should take for the priest to enter the Holy Place, light the incense and come back out again. This was not necessarily a trivial data point. Priests who entered the inner rooms of the temple were discouraged from dilly-dallying, lest their delay cause the people to wonder whether God had struck down the officiant in judgment (m. Yoma 5:1). As

Zechariah is delayed, the people begin to wonder and keep wondering (imperfect: *ethaumazon*).

22–24. True to Gabriel's words, when Zechariah does emerge he *could not speak to them*. Obviously, this would have been frustrating not only because his muteness would have prevented him from pronouncing the closing blessing (an honour which typically fell to the presiding priest), but also because he had quite a bit of news to share! Though Zechariah *remained* mute from this point forward, he finishes out his week, and then returns to his home in the Judean foothills (1:39). Eventually, Elizabeth is found to be pregnant in fulfilment of Gabriel's words and stays *in seclusion* for five months. Since three to five months is roughly the time period before a pregnant woman's stomach begins to show, perhaps she preferred to delay announcing the pregnancy until it was subject to public confirmation.

25. In Ancient Judaism, childlessness was typically regarded as a curse; the inability to bear children carried an inherent shame (Gen. 17:17; Judg. 13:2; 1 Sam. 1:2, 5, 11; Isa. 54:1). Freed from this shame, Elizabeth announces her pregnancy in the words of the once-childless Rachel (Gen. 30:23). Rachel was chosen by God to help perpetuate Israel's seed line, and now Elizabeth stands poised to serve the same purpose.

Although the present episode began by focusing on Zechariah, now he yields centre stage to Elizabeth. And for her part, having been granted the ability to bear children, Elizabeth participates in one of the blessings of Israel's covenantal obedience (Lev. 26:9). At the same time, through Elizabeth's body God has symbolically revealed that Israel's hour of redemption has come: the curse will be reversed and the nation will bear its shame no more. In this respect, Elizabeth embodies exiled yet soon-to-be-restored Israel.

ii. Announcement of Jesus' birth (1:26–38)

26–27. Careful to situate the announcement of Jesus' birth alongside the previous passage, Luke notes that some six months after Elizabeth's conception Mary receives from Gabriel news of her own baby. Gabriel's exalted position within the angelic hierarchy is juxtaposed with the lowliness of Mary's social station as a young girl. She is a virgin in a *town in Galilee called Nazareth*; she is also betrothed to Joseph, who is, not insignificantly, *of the house of David* – already anticipating that Jesus is the fulfilment of the Davidic promise in 2 Samuel 7. If Elizabeth's post-menopausal pregnancy is a miracle of one kind, the conception within Mary's womb is an even greater miracle.

28–29. Gabriel's words of *greetings*, blessing (*favoured one*) and assurance of divine presence (*The Lord is with you*) draw to mind Yahweh's comforting words to exiled Israel in Zephaniah 3:14–17; the Greek behind the last phrase (*ho kyrios meta sou*) is reminiscent of Judges 6:12 ('The Lord is with you'; LXX: *kyrios meta sou*), part of a larger passage (Judg. 6:11–18) where the angel of the Lord appoints Gideon to be Israel's delivering judge. Such language indicates that the divine deliverance wrought through Gideon and promised to Zephaniah is now again about to be realized. Hearing *his words*, Mary is *much perplexed* (*dietarchthē*) or 'deeply disturbed' (JB), wondering about the import of this greeting.[9] Mary knows her Scriptures (1:46–55) and she knows too that the angel's words signal God's intervention on Israel's behalf.

30. Gabriel's command not to fear is not only a pastoral response to Mary's perplexity but also a stock component of theophanic encounters. Nor is it insignificant, given earlier parallels between Gabriel's announcement and Zephaniah 3, that the imperative *Do not be afraid* also occurs in Zephaniah 3:16, further confirming Mary as a living metaphor of exiled Jerusalem. As if to drive home that she retains the status of 'favoured one' (*kecharitōmenē*), the angel offers that the young girl has *found favour* (*charin*) with God. Although this last phrase may give the impression that Mary has somehow merited divine attention, the expression simply denotes God's elective purposes.

31. The wording of this verse closely parallels the wording of the angelic announcement to Zechariah in verse 13, drawing attention to the close comparison between John and Jesus, as well as to God's close involvement in both births. Between Luke 1:13 and 1:31 there are of course differences as well. Among these is the

---

9. For other reasons as to why Mary might resist Gabriel's announcement, see Reid, 'Overture', pp. 428–429.

fact that in the case of John's birth announcement (1:13), it is the father who is given the child's name, whereas here it is the mother who *will name him Jesus* (cf. Matt. 1:18–25). Whereas Matthew's birth account tightens the connection between the name Jesus, which means 'God is salvation', and its significance for his future saving role (Matt. 1:21), Luke makes no comment along these lines.

32–33. The demonstrative pronoun 'this one' (*houtos*) or – more mundanely – *he* (NRSV) emphasizes Jesus' unusual qualities. First, like John (1:15), Jesus *will be great*, an assessment which will be shared by Jesus' contemporaries (7:16). Yet it is a greatness that can also in some sense be replicated through the disciples' humble service (9:46–48; 22:24–27). Second, he will also be called *Son of the Most High*. Since *the Most High* is normally a Gentile designation for Yahweh, its occurrence here in a conversation with a Jewish girl is puzzling, but can perhaps be explained as a nod to Luke's thematic interest in Gentiles. More to the point, since the divine epithet is especially characteristic of Daniel (occurring a staggering thirteen times), Gabriel seems to be reinforcing that that which he had conveyed to Daniel centuries earlier is now about to materialize. Climactically, Gabriel promises that Jesus *will reign over the house of Jacob for ever*, fulfilling the Davidic promise of an everlasting kingdom.

34. Although Gabriel's announcement did not specify as much, Mary somehow infers – correctly as it turns out – that her conception will occur entirely apart from Joseph's involvement.[10] Naturally, she is curious as to the biological process, since *I am a virgin*. Other complications would have quickly occurred to Mary, including daunting social and legal repercussions. For if, as we can only assume, she and Joseph were betrothed according to standard Ancient Jewish practice, her forthcoming marriage would have already been made legally binding through the betrothal deed and payment of the bridal price. This normally took place when the girl was roughly twelve. The last step of sexual consummation would occur about a year later.

---

10. For a persuasive handling of the source of Mary's insight, see Landry, 'Annunciation to Mary', pp. 65–79.

35. Gabriel speaks of the miraculous means of conception through two parallel promises. First, here at the beginning of the Gospel, the angel assures her that the *Holy Spirit will come upon you* (*pneuma hagion epeleusetai epi se*), just as, at the beginning of Acts, the angels assure the disciples that the Holy Spirit will come upon them (*epelthontos tou hagiou pneumatos ep'hymas*; Acts 1:8) for the sake of their witness. Second, Gabriel mentions an overshadowing by the power of God. On account of this event, the angel continues, Mary's baby *will be called Son of God*. The title is as appropriate to Jesus' divine conception as it is to his role as Davidic Messiah.[11] Just as Gabriel predicts, the epithet will be applied to Jesus by demonic beings (4:3, 9, 41), Caiaphas (22:70) and finally the apostle Paul (Acts 9:20).

36–37. The incredible nature of Gabriel's promise is made slightly more credible by what God has already done in the life of Elizabeth. The angel draws attention to this with the startling force of *And now* (*kai idou*) or 'And behold' (ESV). If God has the power to enable Mary's relative to become pregnant in her *old age*, is it really so incredible that he should do the same for this young virgin? The bottom line – in words reminiscent of the divine prediction of Isaac's miraculous birth in Genesis 18:14 – is this: *nothing will be impossible with God*. The promise made to Abraham concerning Isaac was an initial fulfilment of that which would come to fuller fruition in Mary's womb. The very story that closes out on Jesus' being raised from the dead begins with God bringing Jesus virtually out of nothing.

38. Gabriel has been emphasizing the fact of divine intervention through the interjection 'And now . . . !' (*idou*; 1:31, 36): Mary responds in kind by saying, *Here am I* [*idou*]*, the servant of the Lord*. In declaring herself a *servant of the Lord*, she acknowledges her elective status, as well as her place alongside the prophets (1 Kgs 14:18; 18:36; 2 Kgs 14:25; Isa. 20:3; cf. 1 Sam. 1:11), even as she soon will exercise a prophetic voice of her own (1:46–55). Mary's succinct response reflects her willingness to comply with God's purposes,

---

11. At the same time, by identifying Jesus as 'Son of God', Luke is 'moving toward a more ontological (and not only functional) understanding of Jesus' sonship' (Green, p. 91). Also see below on Luke 3:38.

no matter how potentially complicating those purposes might be: *let it be with me according to your word*. Once the mother of the Davidic saviour signifies her own submission to the plan, the angel's task is complete and he is free to depart.

Theology

Like Mark and John, Luke begins his story with Jesus *and* John. But unlike the other Gospel writers, Luke's elaboration of their respective ministries lays special emphasis on their shared relationship to the Holy Spirit. John's greatness as a prophet is ultimately chalked up to the Spirit's presence (1:15); Mary's pregnancy is possible only because of the overshadowing power of the Holy Spirit (1:35). For Luke, the Gospel story cannot even get off the ground apart from the Spirit. As the Spirit is key to the beginning of Jesus' story, he would be no less central to the beginning of the church's story (Acts 2).

That the Spirit is Luke's point of departure for both his Gospel and Acts is no mere coincidence. For just as the Spirit hovered over chaos in the first creation (Gen. 1:2), now the same Spirit comes again, Luke implies, this time to bring about *new* creation. This is not unlike what God would do when Jesus was raised from the dead, a moment which Paul tells us could not happen apart from the Spirit's close involvement (Rom. 1:4; Eph. 1:17–20). Whether in the creation of life or its recreation, the Spirit is the agent of *creatio ex nihilo*.

This would have been powerful consolation for Luke's original readers who in many cases saw themselves as having nothing, or close to nothing. If the first-century believers found themselves socially marginalized on account of their faith, and if (perhaps as a result) they were lacking in resources or position, this was no cause for despair. The Spirit has a long track record of comforting and empowering people in such circumstances. When God the Spirit moves, this passage would seem to say, he does so ordinarily through the most unlikely of individuals. This not only shames the strong and the powerful, such as Herod who haunts the Gospel from the very beginning (1:5), but shows that true power resides with God – and God alone. In a world twisted by abuses of power, the power of creation and *re*creation, the power of the Spirit, provides deep and abiding comfort.

B. Mary's visit to Elizabeth (1:39–56)

Context
Struggling for answers, Mary pays a visit to her relative Elizabeth.
The effect is a temporary convergence between the two conception
stories. (In 1:57 – 2:52, the stories of John and Jesus will again part
ways.) Elizabeth's reaction to Mary's arrival is remarkable. Not only
does the foetus John prove sensitive to the Messiah's presence, but
also his mother is inspired to offer an extraordinary blessing, theologically rich and chock-full of supernatural insight – all a clear
confirmation of Gabriel's promise. This prompts Mary to respond
with what traditionally has come to be known as the Magnificat, a
song focused on God's actions on behalf of Mary (vv. 46–50), on
behalf of the humble (vv. 51–53) and on behalf of Israel (vv. 54–55).
The seamless interchange between Mary's personal interests and
the interests of Israel renders the ensuing double-birth accounts
both a tale of two families and, more significantly, the story of
God's redemptive visitation.

Comment
39–40. Eager for some encouragement as she contemplates the
challenging months ahead, not least the burden of the social shame
she would incur as a result of a premarital pregnancy, Mary beats a
hasty path – almost certainly not alone – up through the Judean *hill
country* to her cousin. At length, she arrives and greets Elizabeth,
an appropriately deferential gesture for an adolescent girl approaching a much older relative.

41. But the normal hierarchy of honour is about to be reversed,
as Mary's greeting triggers a twofold response. First, deep within
Elizabeth's womb John leaps in reaction to the Messiah's presence,
signifying among other things that – in a head-on challenge to the
rampant Roman practice of child-exposure – the human unborn
are capable of humanity's highest calling of worship. Second,
Elizabeth herself is *filled with the Holy Spirit*. The same Spirit who has
created new life within Mary (1:35) is also now inspiring Elizabeth
to *interpret* the significance of that life through a providentially
arranged meeting. This sequence prepares for the Spirit's dual
function in Luke–Acts: recreating the cosmos through resur-

rection, and inspiring human agents to give witness to this new creation.

42. Elizabeth's *loud cry* of joy is not only consistent with a human response to divine action (Josh. 6:16; Pss 20:5; 98:4; Isa. 12:6; 58:1; etc.), but also points more specifically to the awaited messianic birth pangs (Isa. 26:15–21; cf. Isa. 66:5–11). Two blessings follow from Elizabeth's lips: one directed to Mary and the other to Jesus – no small comfort considering the trials ahead![12] This double macarism (blessing) anticipates the blessing which Jesus will impart to his disciples at the Gospel's close (24:50).[13] Ensconced between these two bookends are the blessings promised to heirs of the kingdom (6:20–23). Over the course of the narrative, then, Jesus the blessed one par excellence becomes the blesser par excellence.

43. Still under divine inspiration, Elizabeth expresses her astonishment that she is in fact welcoming *the mother of my Lord*. The statement is remarkable, since the older woman has not – as far as we know – been informed of Gabriel's announcement to Mary (1:26–38). Seemingly, Elizabeth's greeting is born out of supernatural insight. Whereas the Evangelist has already – drawing on various messianic epithets – revealed Jesus as the Son of the Most High, the heir of the Davidic kingdom and Son of God (1:32–33, 35), now the phrase *the mother of my Lord* hints at Jesus' divine status.

44–45. Feeling her baby bounding about within her, Elizabeth gathers that the inauguration of the messianic age, sometimes signified by leaping for *joy* (Isa. 35:6; Mal. 4:2), is now underway. Accordingly, she delivers a final blessing on Mary. More exactly, it is a blessing on anyone who believes *that there would be a fulfilment* of God's promises. God's blessings are not unconditionally and indiscriminately granted but are subject to a living faith anchored in the covenantal promises. Once again, Jesus' mother functions as a model for all those who take God at his word.

46. On receiving confirmation of the annunciation, Mary *magnifies* the Lord by ascribing to God a wide range of attributes

---

12. That Mary is *blessed . . . among women* is qualified by a more fundamental blessing falling on all those who obey God (11:27–28).
13. So Bovon, p. 59.

and functions. Like the song of Hannah (1 Sam. 2:1–10), Mary's rhythmic outburst celebrates a divinely facilitated birth; like so many psalms of praise (e.g. Pss 18; 145; etc.; cf. 1 Chr. 16:8–36; Rev. 11:17–18), it declares praise as well as its reasons. Though Mary's canto has been carefully stylized, this does not mean that its substance is either a community invention or a Lukan fiction.[14] The Magnificat's poetic form may easily be credited to Mary. Furthermore, although it is *generally* unlikely that the historical Mary was literate, this does not mean she would have been unfamiliar with Torah as it would have been read aloud in the regular services. It is quite possible, in other words, that the song's shape and many scriptural references (e.g. Deut. 10:21; 1 Sam. 2:1; Ps. 34:1–3) derive from the very voice (*ipsissima vox*) of Mary.

47. As Mary *rejoices in God my Saviour (ēgalliasen . . . epi tō theō tō sōtēri mou)*, her words recall Habakkuk who likewise rejoiced 'in God my saviour' (*agalliasomai . . . epi tō theō tō sōtēri mou*; Hab. 3:18, LXX). The parallel is likely intentional: just as the ancient prophet looked forward to Israel's eventual release from its pagan Chaldean overlords, so now Mary looks ahead to a final and lasting release from the latest resident pagans lording it over God's people – all to be accomplished through Jesus. Though the NRSV and many other versions have Mary rejoicing in the present, *ēgalliasen* is a perfective aorist. It is more on target, then, to say that Mary '*has* rejoiced'. That this and other verbs in the canto carry perfective force suggests that although the reign of the Messiah will unfold in the future, the very certainty of that reign permits Mary to speak of events as if they have already occurred in the past.

48–49. True to the form of the Hebrew psalm of praise, Mary now reveals the reasons for her acclamation: for starters, the God of Israel has had regard for her *lowliness* or humiliation (*tapeinōsis*). The humiliation is not simply hers but is shared by all of Israel – it is the humiliation of exile, painfully evidenced by the indignity of Gentile political control over the fortunes and sacred space of Israel. Because the messianic promise, which includes the promise of reversal of exile, is now about to be fulfilled even in her body,

---

14. Contra Brown, *Birth*, p. 347.

there is some sense in which Mary mediates the benefits of that
promise to Israel. Cognizant of this reality, and cognizant too of
the significance of the moment, she goes on to declare – with
intimations of the Abrahamic blessing (Gen. 12:3) – that successive
generations will declare her blessed. If Mary can say that *the Mighty
One has done great things for me*, it is because the divinely wrought *great
things* that Israel's exiles could only dream about will now soon
come to pass (Ps. 126:2–3).[15] God *has done great things* for Mary,
because God will soon use her in an extraordinary way to
accomplish his purposes.

50. Having earlier been instructed not to fear on receiving the
news of the messianic child (1:30), now Mary speaks of the *mercy*
awaiting those who exhibit a very different kind of holy *fear*.[16] This
implies, along with other texts (e.g. 10:37), that while God does not
unconditionally guarantee mercy to the nation of Israel, he does
guarantee mercy to those within Israel who fear God. This principle
is nothing new but has been operative *from generation to generation*.

51. The core of Mary's song catalogues a series of reversals that
foreshadow the many reversals to come in the narrative, not least
the scattering of those who are proud *in the thoughts of their hearts*. On
Luke's understanding, though such dark thoughts are not as
flagrant as public sins, they are no less pernicious (5:22; 6:45; 12:15–
21; 16:15; 24:25, 38). And when God repays such thoughts of the
heart with judgment, it is tantamount to a display of divine arm-
strength, as when Yahweh had *shown strength with his arm* to Egypt
(Exod. 3:19; 6:1; 13:9, 16; 32:11; Deut. 4:34; 5:15; 7:19). For Mary,
when inward thoughts are judged accordingly in real time (Luke
2:35; 5:22; 6:8; 11:17), this corroborates that a new and final exodus
is underway.

52–53. Although the precise outworkings of this envisioned
messianic revolution remain to be seen, the certainty of its socio-
political impact can hardly be doubted. Society's movers and

---

15. I am grateful to Bryan Eklund for pointing this out to me.
16. Luke is replete with divine encounters that inspire temporary fear (2:9–
    10; 5:10; 8:25; 9:34; etc.), but the point of these encounters is to lay the
    groundwork for the fear of the Lord.

shakers (the likes of Caesar, Herod, Pilate, Caiaphas and the priests) will be brought down *from their thrones*; those who are *lowly* (*tapeinous*) like Mary herself (v. 48) will be exalted (cf. Isa. 11:4; 49:13). Meanwhile, the hungry will be filled *with good things*, while the rich will be dismissed empty-handed. The former vision anticipates meal scenes in Luke where the hungry are filled (9:10–17; 22:14–23; 24:28–34; cf. 11:3); the latter, encounters where 'the haves', like the well-resourced ruler of 18:18–30, suddenly find themselves among 'the have-nots'.

54–55. God *has helped his servant Israel* in keeping with his merciful character and in remembrance of the Abrahamic promise (Gen. 12; 15; 17), which will be touched on two more times in this foundational stage of Jesus' story (Luke 1:73; 2:29).[17] The heart of that promise, it is to be recalled, pertained to land and seed. The promise of land is not unconnected with Luke's theme of Jubilee, centred on the restoration of land (4:16–19). The Abrahamic promise of a seed, through which the nations would be blessed (Gen. 12:1–3), presages the raising up of various children for Abraham (Luke 13:10–17; 16:19–31; 19:1–10; Acts 3:25; 7:2, 7–8; 13:26), along with the Gentile mission.[18] As Mary well knew, the promise of Messiah entailed the twofold promise of a newly constituted worshipping people *and* a newly constituted space.

56. Mary stays with Elizabeth for *about three months*, perhaps not coincidentally the same length of time that Jochebed hides her son Moses. She stays, that is, until the time of John's birth (since Elizabeth was now six months along). At the end of this time, Mary returns not to Joseph's house but to *her* house, assuring the reader that her virgin status remains intact.

---

17. As Jipp ('Abraham', pp. 113–114) rightly observes, given the obvious parallels between the miraculous births of Isaac and Jesus, Luke's concern is 'to portray to the reader that God's merciful kindness to Abraham has not been forgotten, and that . . . God is continuing the story and promises he had initiated with Abraham in Genesis'.

18. See Hartman, 'Children of Abraham'.

Theology

With the sentimentalization of the Christmas story in so much contemporary culture, it is easy to lose sight of the remarkable burden weighing on Mary following the angel's announcement – a burden matched by an equally remarkable obedience. If Mary's family adhered to the standard betrothal practices of the day, she would have been not much past twelve or thirteen years old at the time of Gabriel's announcement. One can hardly imagine the pressures on an adolescent girl tasked with giving birth to and eventually raising Israel's Messiah – this on top of the reputational damage that would tarnish her the rest of her years. How many among Mary's contemporaries would have believed her story? Some, like Elizabeth, yes; many others, not at all. Even before Jesus is born, those who are in on the messianic secret are called to share in the Messiah's pressures and shame.

Nor can one fail to observe the Magnificat's far-ranging vision – a vision of hope. Mary recognized that the promise of the ages was living inside her, that the fruit of her womb would cash out the promises made to Abraham of land and seed, and would close out the exodus initially set in motion under Moses. Yet with the image of the proud being deposed from their thrones, we also see glimpses of the Davidic covenant: one day those who walked in the footsteps of the false king Saul would yield their throne to Israel's rightful anointed, the seed destined to sit on the throne (2 Sam. 7). Within the tight confines of Mary's physical body, all the covenants – and in fact all of human history – were about to reach their climax.

The announcement of the Messiah's coming is not necessarily good news for all. Though many religious and political power brokers in Luke's day supposed that their positions would be consolidated either with the coming of the future kingdom or with the perpetuation of the current kingdom, such hopes are refuted by Mary's assertion that the existing power structures would be flipped. The announcement of Jesus' birth is an early warning that those on top would soon find themselves at the bottom; those at the bottom, on top. At the very least, the coming of the kingdom spells bad news for the social, economic, political and ideological systems that stand opposed to God. When the kingdom arrives, nothing in creation will be safe from its catalytic effects. For all his readers whose lives are embedded in present 'kingdom structures', Luke intends the Magnificat to elicit not just joy but heart-searching.

C. Two births (1:57 – 2:20)

Context

Having recounted the two stories leading up to the births of John (1:5–25) and Jesus (1:26–38), as well as the bridging of these two storylines in the meeting of Mary and Elizabeth (1:39–55), Luke now focuses on the boys' births. Structurally this section is analogous to 1:5–38. Each in turn, first comes the birth of John (1:57–80) and then the birth of Jesus (2:1–20). The chronological order of the two births, not to mention the order in which the births are related, parallels the temporal sequence of the two figures' respective roles in salvation history.

The present section foreshadows just how intertwined the destinies of John and Jesus are, and how their extraordinary ministries were anticipated by their equally extraordinary origins. The events following John's birth bring to a close Zechariah's muteness and inspire the once-disobedient priest to speak of the Baptizer's future (1:67–79). In this passage, traditionally identified as the Benedictus, he prophesies in a manner similar to Mary with her Magnificat (1:46–55). As breathtaking as events surrounding John's birth might be, Jesus' birth provokes a reaction of a higher order. John's role as the messianic forerunner is predicted on earth by the likes of Zechariah; Jesus' identity as Messiah is proclaimed in heaven by the angelic host (2:1–20). John may come first in time but Jesus comes first in significance.

Comment

i. Birth of John (1:57–80)

57–58. Roughly three months after Mary's arrival, *the time came* (*eplēsthē ho chronos*) or 'was fullfilled' (YLT) for Elizabeth to give birth – to *a son*, as Gabriel had promised (1:13). The sense of fulfilment conveyed by *the time came* pertains not simply to the baby reaching full term but also to a new day in salvation history.[19] Impressed that Elizabeth was able to give birth despite her years, her neighbours and kin celebrate along with her (with some parallels to two certain Lukan celebrations over lost items; cf. 15:6, 9). They rejoice because *the Lord had shown* [*emegalynen*, 'magnified'] *his great mercy* to Elizabeth, just as Mary had magnified (*megalynei*) the Lord on account of his mercy (1:46). Their joy is the very fulfilment of the angel's promise (1:14).

59–61. The extended family gathers *to circumcise* John *on the eighth day.* The irony should not be lost on the reader: while Elizabeth's friends and neighbours circumcise John to fulfil the demands of not just Torah (Lev. 12:3; m. Šabb. 18:3) but, more centrally, the Abrahamic covenant (Gen. 17:12), the same child would go on to play a crucial role in God's fulfilling of that same covenant (Luke 1:73). That the baby should be named on the day of his circumcision is unusual, since Jewish babies were typically named at birth (e.g. Gen. 4:1; 25:25–26). For whatever reason, however, perhaps under Greek influence, the newborn's family delays naming the baby until more than a week after birth.[20] Equally unusual is the fact that the relatives are determined to name him (conative imperfect: *ekaloun*) Zechariah, for a baby boy was usually named not *after his father* but after his grandfather. Whatever the motives of the friends and family, Elizabeth firmly rejects the idea (as the strongly worded Greek *ouchi alla*, 'no but rather . . . ', indicates) and insists that the infant be named John, in keeping with Gabriel's instructions (1:13). On hearing Elizabeth's proposal, puzzled family members object on the grounds that the name is unprecedented in the family history.

62–63. Wanting to get a second opinion, the gathered group now solicits Zechariah's input. That they should communicate with hand and head motions indicates that Zechariah is deaf as well as mute (1:20), as *kōphos* in 1:22 allows. At that point, Zechariah summons a *writing-tablet* to confirm his agreement with his wife. He writes: *His name is John*, meaning 'Yahweh is gracious' (Hebrew:

---

19. So too Fitzmyer, p. 373. This is likewise the case for 2:6 below.
20. Brown, *Birth*, p. 369.

Yôḥānān). The couple's shared determination to contravene baby-naming convention – not to mention their choosing the same name independently of each other – corroborates the reality of Gabriel's revelation. Inspired by awe, onlookers are duly *amazed (ethaumasan).*[21]

64. Once Zechariah has submitted to the divine purposes, his *mouth* is *opened and his tongue* is *freed.* After many months of speechlessness and still soaking in the significance of this new human life, the unlikely father finds that the only words appropriate to the situation are words of praise: 'Zechariah sings because he has now begun to believe.'[22] His singing is emblematic of an emerging corporate reality: whereas the dramatic shift from muteness to praise was predicted to mark Israel's return from exile (Isa. 35:5–6), the aged priest unwittingly presents himself as the embodiment of eschatological Israel, upon whom the promises have now come.

65–66. The uncanny chain of events makes a conspicuous impact. At a local level, the same *fear (phobos)* that had befallen Zechariah (1:12) now falls on *all their neighbours,* even as it would come upon the shepherds following Jesus' birth (2:9). But news of this event also extends to the surrounding *hill country of Judea,* where Mary had travelled earlier (1:39). While *all these things* are *talked about,* the populace lay up the extraordinary occurrence in their hearts (*ethento . . . en tē kardia;* cf. 2:19), all the while speculating on the infant's future calling.

But what narrative purpose might all this reportage have served? First of all, Luke is meeting his audience on their own terms, for in ancient biographies extraordinary birth accounts were typically brought in to help lay the groundwork for the recounting of an extraordinary life. In addition, the miraculous events straddling John's birth may also help explain the people's readiness to respond

---

21. At 1:21, the people wondered (*ethaumazon*) at Zechariah's delay in the temple. Now they register the same response in reaction to Zechariah and Elizabeth's joint decision to name the baby John. The verb *thaumazō* 'in both secular Greek and the LXX often refers to the reaction of people to the presence and action of a deity' (*EDNT,* p. 135).

22. Bovon, p. 69.

to his invitation some decades later (3:3–6). If historians are obliged to conform to genre expectations and explain causality where they can, Luke does not disappoint.

67–68. Just as his wife Elizabeth was inspired by the Spirit on Mary's visit, Zechariah *was filled with the Holy Spirit* as he pronounces prophetic revelation. Adhering, as Mary did in the Magnificat, to the genre of the Hebrew *berakah* (blessing), the aged priest infuses a familiar form of praise with new Christological meaning. The canto begins by declaring the blessedness of God, who is worthy of such blessing because *he has looked favourably* [*epeskepsato*] *on his people and redeemed them*. Forming an *inclusio* with the same verb in verse 78, the verb *episkeptomai* ('to inspect, go visit') has negative connotations when referring to divine judgment (e.g. Exod. 20:5; 34:7; Lev. 18:25) and positive connotations (e.g. Pss 65:9; 106:4; Jer. 27:22) when referring to divine redemption. Elements of both judgment and redemption are arguably in view here.

69–70. The working out of that redemption depends on God's raising up (*ēgeiren*) *a mighty saviour* (*keras sōtērias*, lit. 'horn of salvation'), that is, a mighty source of salvation *in the house* of David (cf. Deut. 33:17; Ps. 132:17). Jesus' origins from the house of David have already been well established (Luke 1:27, 32). Now his oblique identification as the Davidic saviour/horn indicates that Yahweh will 'visit' Israel in and through his person. Zechariah's use of *egeirō* ('to raise up') in connection with salvation is partially informed by its denotation of resurrection (Luke 7:14, 22; 8:54; 9:7, 22; 11:31; 20:37; 24:7, 34; Acts 15:13–18). But a more direct connection to Amos 9:11 ('On that day I will *raise up* / the booth of David that is fallen, / and repair its breaches, / and *raise up* its ruins, / and rebuild it as in the days of old'; emphasis added) seems to be in play as well, since the prophetic text speaks about the 'raising up' of a Davidide and comes to be applied to the resurrection (Acts 15:13–18). Though it is uncertain how much of this the character Zechariah (as opposed to Luke) understood in the moment, he is persuaded, as Mary was, that God is about to fulfil the terms of the promise made to David (2 Sam. 7).

71. The principal outcome of this imminent divine action is Israel's release from *all who hate us*, that is, *our enemies*. Such enemies no doubt include human political and religious autocrats, such as we will meet by name in Luke 3:1–2, as well as all those who will come to hate Jesus (19:14) and his followers (6:22, 27). But they also include the dark spiritual forces standing behind the hapless human pawns (11:14–23). For the Evangelist, salvation is unimaginable apart from the vanquishing of those powers and principalities that stand opposed to God.

72–73a. In his saving activity, Zechariah continues, God has shown *mercy . . . to our ancestors* (*tōn paterōn hēmōn*). Judging by a comparison with 1:55, it seems that the *ancestors* or 'fathers' in question are Abraham along with Isaac and Jacob (cf. Acts 3:13, 25), though the term may also include the believing lineage after Jacob. Impressed by God's power to secure Israel's redemption through his wife's unlikely womb (on the pattern of Sara), Zechariah follows Mary's lead (1:55) in interpreting the preternatural birth in view as a fulfilment of the Abrahamic promise. The fulfilment of the same covenantal promise is a show of *mercy* because in the Scriptures mercy is pre-eminently ascribed to Yahweh in his capacity as redeemer, whether leading his people out of Egypt (Exod. 33:19; 34:6) or out of exile (Deut. 30:3; Isa. 49:9–11).

73b–75. The goal of this divine redemption is not only the inheritance of land (as per the terms of the Abrahamic covenant) but also that God's people *might serve* (*latreuein*) Yahweh in priestly fashion (1) *without fear,* (2) *in holiness* and (3) in *righteousness* – conditions which will be provisionally met in the community after Pentecost (Acts 4:31–35).[23] By the same token, the phrase *all our days* signals that the experience of the apostolic church only presages a more perfected worship in the fullness of the eternal kingdom.

76–77. Now turning to his newly born son, Zechariah issues a prophecy regarding the boy's future calling, effectively answering the people's question in verse 66a ('What then will this child become?'). The core prediction about John complements the identity of Jesus: just as Jesus was to be 'Son of the Most High' (1:32), John will *be called the prophet of the Most High.* In this prophetic

---

23. 'The word for "serve" . . . connotes priestly service in worship (Exod 3:12), fulfilling the ancient ideal that Israel would be "a kingdom of priests" (Exod 19:6)' (Edwards, pp. 62–63).

role John will *go before the Lord to prepare* [*hetoimasai*] *his ways*, that is, Jesus' ways. This phrasing not only circles back to Gabriel's promise that John would appear as Malachi's eschatological Elijah (1:16–17; Mal. 4:5) who would also prepare the way (Mal. 3:1), but also looks ahead to the Baptizer's later identification as the Isaianic figure tasked with preparing (*hetoimasate*) the way in the desert (Luke 3:4–6; cf. Isa. 40:3). The linking of Malachi 3:1 and Isaiah 40:3 (through the key terms 'prepare', 'way' and 'Lord') is not unique to Luke (cf. Mark 1:2–3) and likely occurred in pre-Christian interpretation of the Scriptures. John is also tasked with bestowing a *knowledge of salvation* through the *forgiveness of their sins*. This prediction obviously looks ahead to John's ministry of baptism, which would be for the forgiveness of sins (Luke 3:3). Yet Luke's Zechariah stakes his claim carefully: John is the source not of salvation, but of the '*knowledge* of salvation'.

78–79a. This forgiveness of sins which Zechariah anticipates comes only on account of the *tender mercy* or 'bowels' (*splanchna*) *of our God.* In Hebrew thought, the intestines were regarded as the seat of deep feeling and affection. Accordingly, it is Yahweh's *splanchna* that compel him to rise up on behalf of his people. On account of the same mercy, the *dawn from on high will break upon us.* Trading on prophetic language which couples the eschatological dawn with the glorious presence of God (Isa. 60:1–2; Mal. 4:2), Zechariah's words look ahead to the Pentecostal granting of the Spirit (Acts 2), who is also the 'power *from on high*' (Luke 24:49, emphasis added).[24] Once so empowered by the Spirit, God's people will be positioned to *give light to those who sit in darkness and in the shadow of death*, who are, according to Isaiah (Isa. 9:2), one and the same as the Gentile nations yet to be incorporated into Yahweh's fold. If Zechariah is to be believed, the Spirit's first and foremost role is missional.

79b. A second consequence of this promised salvation is peace. For when the dawn of God appears, it will direct the feet of God's people *into the way of peace* (cf. Rom. 3:17). In Luke's narrative,

---

24. For Strauss (*Davidic Messiah*, pp. 103–108), the dawn is either salvation or the Messiah himself.

beneficiaries of such peace will include the woman who washed Jesus' feet with her tears (7:50), the haemorrhaging woman (8:48) and the disciples on welcoming the Risen Lord (24:36). In all these instances, peace is connected with salvation, forgiveness and wholeness. This is consistent with the Hebrew concept of shalom.

80. Luke rounds off his account of John's birth by summarizing his development from his youth up until his ministry. Here are two points of interest. First, Luke tells us that John *became strong in spirit*, presumably meaning effective under the power and suasion of the Holy Spirit. In this respect, John falls into the same distinctive category as Jesus who, like John, is not only conceived through the Spirit's activity but would also go on to be empowered by the same Spirit. Second, the Evangelist notes that John – unlike Jesus – remains *in the wilderness* until the commencement of his public ministry in the desert. John's seclusion from Israel's day-to-day life for a sizeable portion of his life confirms both the unique nature of his calling and the importance of personal preparation for that ministry. Moreover, his seclusion *in the wilderness* only reinforces the importance of the desert for John's calling (1:17, 76; 3:4). How and where the Baptizer spends his youth stands in contrast to young Jesus' activities and whereabouts (2:41–52).

ii. Birth of Jesus (2:1–20)

1. Humiliated by Roman taxation and an occupying military presence, Palestinian Jews at the time of Jesus' birth, along with many of Luke's own Jewish hearers, would have chafed at the mention of a fresh *decree* from Rome. In addition to bearing the economic burdens associated with a census (which were implemented for the purposes of taxation if not also military conscription), the Jews also had to reconcile themselves to the fact that their chief overlord *Emperor Augustus* was widely acclaimed as the principal mediator between humanity and the gods – Pontifex Maximus. His edict mandates that *all the world (pasan tēn oikoumenēn)* should be registered. Here, as in Acts 11:28, the term *oikoumenē* is used in the specific and more narrow sense of the Roman Empire.

2. Commentators here have long noted the historical difficulties posed by Luke's statement that this was the *first registration (apographē prōtē)* under the watch of Quirinius as *governor of Syria (hēgemoneuontos* *tēs Syrias*). Whereas Quirinius served as the Syrian governor in AD 6–9 and did in fact implement a notorious census towards the beginning of his administration, this is far too late a date to be linked with Jesus' birth which, judging by other bearings, must have occurred at least ten years earlier.[25] Perhaps the most promising solution to this problem is not to reject Luke's accuracy without further ado (since it is unlikely that an author of Luke's historiographical aspirations – as stated in Luke 1:1–4 – would commit such an obvious blunder), but to ask instead whether traditional translations have it wrong, especially in regard to the adjective *prōtos*. To wit, if we translate *hautē apographē prōtē hēgemoneuontos tēs Syrias* not as *This was the first registration and was taken while Quirinius was governor of Syria* (NRSV) but rather as 'This was the registration *prior* to when Quirinius was governor of Syria' (as is grammatically justified; see *LSJ*, p. 1535), then Luke is simply distinguishing this census from a more famous census which would occur some years later.[26]

3–5. Like so many others (Luke's *all* is meant as an informal generalization), Joseph must travel to his home town – an unusual though not unprecedented protocol. For Joseph as well as for Mary, who is both betrothed *and* pregnant, this meant going up to Bethlehem in Judea, situated some 70 miles south of Nazareth in the Galilee – a journey of roughly four days. On the basis of 1 Samuel 17:12 and other texts, Luke calls Bethlehem *the city of David* and explains that Joseph is required to go back to his home there because he is *from the house and family of David* (as already observed in 1:27; cf. also 1:32, 69). For the Evangelist, Joseph's return to Bethlehem cinches Jesus' genealogical connection to David, an important qualification for any would-be messiah (Mic. 5:1–2; cf. Matt. 2:5–6). Luke does not state outright that the couple's journey to Bethlehem serves to fulfil Scripture, as Matthew implies (Matt. 2:1–6). But to the extent that his readers would have understood

---

25. See Young, *DJG*, pp. 72–84.

26. This is precisely Luke's use of *prōtos* in Acts 1:1; see also John 1:15, 30; 15:18. The argument is supported by Nolland, pp. 99–102. For further discussion of this complex issue, see Marshall, pp. 97–104.

Joseph's return to his home town as a 'fulfilment' of Scripture, they might well have noticed that just as Roman political interests were the means by which God would achieve his purposes surrounding Jesus' birth, the same Roman self-interests would again be instrumental in advancing the divine plan when it came to Jesus' death (Luke 23:2).

6–7. During the couple's stay in Bethlehem, Mary's pregnancy comes to full term: 'the days are fulfilled' (*eplēsthēsan hai hēmerai*; cf. 1:57). Luke's description of their spare quarters confirms the humble character of Jesus' origins. The holy family settle down in a space normally reserved for livestock, because *there was no place for them in the inn* (*katalymati*). Although *katalyma* has been traditionally translated as *inn*, this is almost certainly incorrect. Only slightly more plausible is that the term refers to a public wayside shelter. But more likely still, Luke had in mind guest quarters of some kind near to a private home, much the same sense of *katalyma* in 22:11. That Jesus was born in a cave is amply attested by tradition (e.g. Justin, *Dial.* 78.4), and given first-century practice of keeping livestock in caves, not improbable. Jesus' placement *in a manger* (*en phatnē*) indicates that he was either laid in a feeding trough repurposed as a crib or kept in an animal stall repurposed as a nursery. Though the first of these two meanings of *phatnē* occurs more frequently, Luke's subsequent use of the same noun with the latter meaning (13:15) inclines us to imagine that Jesus was actually laid not in a manger but on the floor of a makeshift stall.

Certain details foreshadow what would later occur. Mary's wrapping of Jesus in *bands of cloth* anticipates the day of Jesus' death when his body would again be wrapped (23:53a), only then in a shroud. Meanwhile, Mary's laying (*aneklinen*) Jesus in a stall or cave points to the moment when his passive corpse is laid (*ethēken*) in the tomb (23:53b). Finally, Jesus is identified as Mary's *firstborn* (*prototokon*), presaging the Risen Jesus' status as firstborn (Rom. 8.29; Col. 1:15, 18; Heb. 1:6; Rev. 1:5) in early Christianity.[27] As firstborn, the Risen Christ would be declared to be the heir of renewed creation, and Luke hints at nothing less here.

---

27. Bovon, p. 85.

8–9. The narrative lens now swings to the nearby open countryside, where shepherds are *keeping watch over their flock by night.* There an angel of the Lord *stood before them* in the midst of the *glory* [*doxa*] *of the Lord,* much to the shepherds' trepidation (cf. 1:78–79).[28] If the *doxa* is in fact a fresh manifestation of the divine pillar of cloud that had occupied Solomon's temple (1 Kgs 8:10), then this is a theologically wrought moment. What could this mean except that the divine presence, which had long since departed with the exile (Ezek. 11:23), was now poised to redescend, not in a physical temple in Jerusalem but – of all places – in the Judean countryside. With the manifestation of God's glory to ordinary shepherds, who occupied the bottom of the socio-economic ladder, Mary's vision of reversal (1:52–53) is already beginning to materialize. In this new era, the glory of God would now occupy the most unexpected of places and reveal itself to the most unexpected of individuals.

10. True to the form of biblical theophanies, the angel commands the shepherds not to be afraid. He then goes on to proclaim (*euangelizomai*) the meaning of the event. The verb choice not only harks back to Isaiah's description of return from exile (Isa. 52:7; 61:1), but also takes off on a standard term associated with imperial propaganda. The former context suggests that the angelic announcement is part and parcel of Isaiah's vision of restoration (especially Isa. 9:1–7); the latter backdrop implies that Caesar's vain attempts at self-promotion have finally met their match in the birth of another Lord. Not surprisingly, then, the message promises to be a source of *great joy* [balancing the 'great fear' of the shepherds] *for all the people (laō)*, that is, the believing community.

11. The essential reason for this joy, as conveyed by the causal particle *hoti*, is the birth of the Saviour and Lord Christ. Appropriately, this 'Christ' (*Messiah*) is declared to be born *in the city of David*, heir of the royal promise that David would always have a descendant ruling on the throne (2 Sam. 7). That this Christ should also be deemed *Saviour (sōtēr)* and *Lord (kyrios)* aligns him in the first

---

28. Just as angels announce the entrance of the Messiah into the world, so too will angels announce his departure and imminent return (Acts 1:10–11).

instance with Yahweh himself, who is designated by both terms (Isa. 43:3, 11; 45:15, 21; 49:26; 60:16; 63:8; LXX). Yet insofar as these two terms were also applied to Caesar, Luke is implying that the exalted epithets normally accorded to Augustus must now be transferred to Jesus.[29]

12. Even though the term *sign* (*sēmeion*) occurs here for the first time in Luke's narrative, the angel's parting words to the shepherds mark the third and final angelic corroboration.[30] And yet here the sign, matched by the 'opposed sign' of 2:34, seems to perform a distinctive function similar to the Mosaic signs of the exodus which were performed both as an indictment and as a barometer of faith (e.g. Exod. 7:1–6). The sign is that the shepherds will find the baby *wrapped in bands of cloth and lying* in a stall (if not a manger). If early Christian interpretation is correct, then the fact that Israel's Messiah should be swaddled in an animal stall is not unrelated to Isaiah 1:3, a verse which laments Israel's failure to recognize its Lord.[31]

13–14. Quite *suddenly* an army (*plēthos stratias*) of angels now appears *praising God* and offering a blessing of peace *on earth* among 'people of favour' (*en anthrōpois eudokias*), that is, the elect (cf. 1QH IV, 32–33). If one of the recurring watchwords of the Roman imperium was 'peace and safety', the heavenly host now declares the establishment of a new peace settling in on the elect community. Here *peace* is to be understood not merely as the absence of conflict but as the eschatological state of blessing, health and wholeness. That an 'army' (NRSV *multitude*) of angels (cf. 1 Kgs 22:19; 2 Chr. 33:3, 5) should declare peace suggests that a holy war is underway against those who resist God's purposes; these can only vainly resist the divine fiat and are best served suing for peace (cf. 14:32).

---

29. See Perrin, 'Imperial Cult', pp. 124–134.
30. The first was Zechariah's muteness (1:20); the second, issued to Mary, Elizabeth's pregnancy (1:35–37).
31. 'The ox knows its owner, / and the donkey its master's crib; / but Israel does not know, / my people do not understand' (Isa. 1:3). So also Green, pp. 135–136.

15–16. By the time *the angels had left them*, the shepherds have enough information to begin looking for the child. In their excitement, they move quickly and eventually *found* [*aneuran*] *Mary and Joseph*, but only after some intense investigation – Luke's verb of finding connotes nothing less.[32] And with Mary and Joseph is the baby, *lying* just where the angel had promised. For the Evangelist's homiletic purposes, the shepherds' swift responsiveness and careful diligence provides a model of discipleship.

17–18. When the shepherds relate their experience in the fields, Mary and Joseph, together with the other witnesses of the shepherds' words, express their astonishment. But we must also imagine Jesus' parents having a sense of comfort that comes with confirmation. Meanwhile, making its rounds around the region, the shepherds' story would have surely functioned as a kind of independent witness to Jesus' Messiahship, even as it would confirm the veracity of Mary's story. In the midst of her shame, Mary finds much-needed corroboration for the almost unbelievable account of her pregnancy and birth – and that from the most unlikely of quarters.

19. Mary *treasured* (*syntērei*) the shepherds' words while 'pondering' (*symballousa*) them in her heart. The former verb (*synetēreō*) expresses the value which Mary attached to the shepherds' account; the participial form of *symballō* implies that she was connecting all kinds of dots in her own mind. Mary's awestruck processing of the shepherds' revelatory experience is a template for how Luke would have his hearers engage with his Gospel.

20. Unwilling to leave their sheep alone for too long, the *shepherds returned* to their fields. But as they go, they imitate the heavenly host by *glorifying and praising God*. Though the shepherds' response may seem like an incidental detail, in the Jewish thought-world the synchronization of heavenly and earthly worship was signal enough that the kingdom of God had arrived. Between their own experience of the divine self-revelation and the story related by Mary (*as it had been told them*), the shepherds are compelled to worship.

---

32. BDAG, p. 65.

Theology

For the better part of the modern era (for reasons that cannot be entered into here), biblical interpretation has largely ignored the political dimension of the Gospels. Today, while scholars will disagree as to what exactly Luke thought of Rome, there is little doubt *that* he must have done quite a bit of thinking about the Eternal City, if only because the Roman Empire was the dominant religious and political force of the day. Along with many first-century Jews, not to mention a handful of New Testament writers (1 Pet. 5:13; Rev. 17), Luke seems to have interpreted Rome as a kind of Babylon, perpetuating Israel's exile. After all, when Zechariah looks forward to Israel being 'rescued from the hands of our enemies' (1:74), or when the angels describe Jesus in terms typically reserved for Caesar (2:11), such data points suggest that Jesus' coming kingdom was destined to challenge Rome head-on: not because there was something exceptionally egregious about this particular empire but because, like other empires that had gone before and would come after, it was hell-bent on conforming God's people to its viewpoints and values.

Whereas the Roman Empire had touted itself as history's greatest kingdom, Luke announces the arrival of a new kingdom. The nature of this kingdom is indicated by John's future role as the Isaianic forerunner who would prepare the way in the desert (1:76). It was after all to be a return-from-exile kingdom, the adherents of which would inherit the salvation, peace and glory promised long ago by Isaiah. What is more, this kingdom would be ruled by a Davidic king (1:69; 2:4, 11), who would operate by an entirely different modus operandi. When this king prepared to pass through the womb, his parents would be forced to share borrowed space with livestock. And when this newborn king finally entered the world, he would be greeted not by the rich and powerful but rather by, paradoxically enough, a heavenly host *and* a set of poor shepherds who were living in an out-of-the-way field. In a surprising twist, yet in keeping with the scriptural promise, it turns out that the salvation, peace and glory that Isaiah had promised and Rome tried to manufacture were actually to be found in a child with the most humble and inconspicuous of beginnings. Insofar as Rome sought to define salvation, peace and glory according to the terms of its own narrative, Luke's presentation of Jesus' birth challenges and redirects that narrative altogether. In this respect, Jesus' kingdom *is* a political kingdom. But it is political in a way that no-one had ever expected.

D. Young Jesus at the temple (2:21–52)

Context

The two episodes recorded in 2:22–40 and 2:41–52 straddle Jesus' childhood, the former occurring just after his first week of life and the latter occurring when he was twelve. The two passages' mutual relation is further augmented by the repetition of closing editorial comments bearing on Jesus' growth in wisdom and physical stature (2:40, 52). Whatever Luke's motives for including this material, the two stories underscore the fact that the full-grown Jesus did not suddenly materialize out of thin air, as if by magic. Rather, he developed just as any human being would develop. Meanwhile, Jesus' movement from the north country (2:1–20) back to the temple in the south (2:22–38), matched by a repetition of the same geographical motion in verses 39–52, anticipates the larger-scale journey when Jesus would begin his ministry in the Galilee (4:14) only to set his face towards Jerusalem (9:51). At the same time, the present passage builds on earlier narrative. Providing complementary witness to a previous voice, Simeon's song about Jesus (2:28–32) parallels Zechariah's song about John (1:67–79), with earlier themes of salvation, peace and glory staying squarely in the foreground. Finally, while the story of the twelve-year-old Jesus does nothing to diminish Jesus' earthly parents, it now becomes clear that Jesus' title of 'Son of the Most High' (1:32) indicates a unique filial relationship, soon to be confirmed through the baptism (3:21–22).

Comment

i. *Presentation at the temple (2:21–40)*

21. Having recounted the remarkable occurrences surrounding John's circumcision (1:57–80), Luke narrates an even more remarkable chain of events at Jesus' circumcision. The scene is set as follows: *After eight days had passed, it was time to circumcise the child; and he was called Jesus.* The alert reader will not fail to note the parallelism between, on the one side, Zechariah and Elizabeth's naming of John in accordance with Gabriel's directive (1:13), and, on the other side, Joseph and Mary's naming of Jesus *also* in accordance with the archangel's words (1:31). God's oversight of the infants' respective namings reinforces the complementarity of their roles as well as their co-participation in the divine mission.

22–24. Following the day of circumcision, Scripture requires a thirty-three-day quarantining of the birth mother, on account of her uncleanness. Ideally this period would culminate with appropriate sacrifice (Lev. 12). Accordingly, once the period of *their purification* has run its course, Joseph and Mary proceed to the temple. The couple's offering of two birds (whether *turtle-doves* or *young pigeons*) instead of a sheep indicates their poverty. It is far from clear, however, whether their straitened circumstances had anything to do with their decision to consecrate Jesus rather than pay the ransom price for the firstborn (Exod. 13:2, 12, 15).[33] In waiving their right to redeem their firstborn son (cf. 2:7), the holy couple follow the example of Hannah (1 Sam. 1:11, 22, 28) in order to convey Jesus to God. They do so out of conviction of Jesus' future messianic significance.[34]

25–26. Simeon of Jerusalem is described in threefold fashion: he is *righteous and devout (diakaios kai eulabēs), looking forward to the consolation of Israel* and in communion with the Holy Spirit. First, as a *righteous* figure, Simeon finds himself in the company of *dikaioi* Elizabeth and Zechariah (1:6); as *devout*, he mirrors the demonstrably pious Anna (2:36–38). Such a character reference gives credibility to his impending pronouncement. Second, Simeon was renowned as one who awaited *the consolation of Israel*, the long-awaited return from exile (Isa. 40:1–2; 49:13; 57:18; 61:2). Whether Simeon's expectation was merely an inference on Luke's part or a publicly acknowledged fact (the latter seems more likely), Luke's descriptor

---

33. So, e.g., Green, pp. 141–142.

34. One might even go so far as to say with Reicke ('Jesus, Simeon, and Anna', p. 106) that through Jesus the 'sanctification of the firstborn son mentioned in Exodus 13.2 had taken place in a way that consummated the proper meaning of this Scripture'.

now serves to legitimize him as a qualified spokesperson for the righteous remnant.[35] Third, Simeon's distinguished character is related to the fact that the Holy Spirit *rested on him* (*ep' auton*), much as the Spirit would also be on (*ep' eme*) Jesus as Messiah (4:18). Simeon's Spirit-wrought conviction, that he would see the Messiah before going to the grave, is on the cusp of being confirmed. For Luke, whatever the distinction between the Spirit's activity in the era before Jesus' birth and in the days after Pentecost (Acts 2), that distinction is relative, not absolute.

27–28. In Luke–Acts, the phrase 'in the Spirit' tends to accompany significant redemptive moments (Luke 4:1; 10:21; Acts 19:21). For this reason, when Simeon enters the temple 'in the Spirit' (*en tō pneumati*), or perhaps led *by the Spirit*, or even 'by the power of the Spirit', the reader's expectations are high. The Spirit's guiding role is crucial not only in terms of timing (only by providential intervention could Simeon cross paths with Jesus' parents) but also in terms of inspiring prophetic speech. By the same token, the Spirit's role is necessary in alerting Simeon to the Christ child. Just as one righteous man in the temple foretells John's destiny (1:67–79), now another righteous man in the temple speaks of Jesus' future. Once again, Luke maintains the parallelism between John and Jesus in order to confirm their divinely ordained alliance *and* to bring out salient differences between the two.

29–30. Simeon's prayer begins in an unusual way, since it addresses God as *Master* (*despota*), a term which in the New Testament occurs only here and in Acts 4:24, where it is also used as part of a prayer. The word emphasizes, appropriately enough in this divinely orchestrated rendezvous scene, God in his sovereignty. Having seen the Messiah with his own eyes, Simeon realizes that he will soon close out his days *in peace*. On fulfilment of the Spirit's word (notably, tantamount to a divine promise), he now senses the time of his release. He realizes that in his arms is not just the human Messiah, but Israel's very *salvation* – more precisely, the means by which God will secure *salvation* for his people. The

---

35. This Simeon was possibly one and the same as the Sim(e)on who
  famously predicted Archelaus's dethronement (Josephus, *J.W.* 2.113).

angelic declaration of Jesus' coming and resultant peace (2:11, 14) is now being corroborated by human witness.

31–32. The salvation envisioned by Simeon is also *a light for revelation to the Gentiles* which God has *prepared in the presence of all peoples*. Here Luke's Simeon may have in mind Psalm 132:17 where God promises to *prepare* 'a *lamp* for my anointed one' in connection with a divine sprouting of the horn of David. If so, then this would be drawing from the same reservoir as Zechariah (see commentary on 1:69–70). The lamp is at any rate one and the same as the light dawning on the Gentiles (Isa. 9:2). Emphasizing the universal aspect of Jesus' mission, the convergence of biblical images, focusing on restoration and the Gentile mission, shares many of the same themes as Zechariah's song.

33. Although Mary and Joseph have already witnessed extraordinary events up to this point, they do not cease to be *amazed* at the thrust of the unfolding revelations surrounding their son.[36] Perhaps the bulk of their surprise revolves around the intimation that Gentiles will now – through *their* son – be included within God's plan. In Luke, wonder is in fact a recurring motif, a consistent human reaction to the revelation of God (1:63; 2:18; 4:22; 8:25; etc.). Mary and Joseph will soon be amazed again (2:48).

34–35. Having *blessed* the baby Jesus, Simeon now predictively blesses the child's parents, primarily Mary – her second blessing (cf. 1:42). According to Simeon's prophecy, Jesus will precipitate *the falling and the rising of many in Israel*, and that is because, given the phrase's allusions to Isaiah 8:14–15 and 28:16, Jesus is the scandalizing temple cornerstone (Luke 20:17–18). The text is slightly ambiguous: whether the 'fallers' and 'risers' constitute two different categories of many people or a sequence of experiences befalling the same group of *many* is uncertain. However, because Jesus is next described as a *sign that will be opposed* (the same confrontational sign who was wrapped in swaddling clothes, 2:12), I would maintain that the two categories break down as follows: on the one side are those who oppose the sign of Jesus, and on the

---

36. Their wondering here (perhaps unexpected) is no evidence for the story having been invented out of whole cloth; see Marshall, p. 115.

other side are those who finally rise after falling (Isa. 24:20; Prov. 24:16).[37] Examples of the latter category, such as the apostate Peter, the persecutor Saul or even the prodigal son, will for a time stumble over Jesus' identity, only to experience rising (*anastasin*), spiritually speaking in terms of their repentance and physically speaking in terms of their ultimate resurrection. Jesus' role as a sign means that he sheds light not just on God's purposes but also on the spiritual–moral character of those who observe him. As a result of his ministry, the *inner thoughts of many will be revealed*.[38]

Precisely on account of this fact, *a sword* will also pierce Mary's soul. While some commentators interpret this to refer to a mother's sorrows at her son's crucifixion, the expression more likely pertains to her own internal struggle regarding Jesus' messianic aims (2:48; 8:19–21; 11:27–28).[39] In the Scriptures, to allow the sword to pass through is to administer a judgment that sifts the righteous from the unrighteous (Exod. 32:27; Ezek. 14:17). Applied to Mary's soul, the phrase speaks not just of her internal doubts (as argued as early as Origen) but more fundamentally of her own halting allegiance to Jesus' messianic programme – liabilities perhaps not fully overcome until she joins the assembled church in Acts 1:14.

36–37. Like Simeon, an octogenarian by the name of Anna is of upstanding character and piety; unlike Simeon, she is explicitly designated as *a prophet*. Her remaining details (her genealogical descent, her short seven-year marriage, her devotion to ceaseless prayer and fasting) are marked by a certain verisimilitude, betraying the kind of accurate reportage Luke promises in his prologue. Her activities mirror those of a well-known Jewish heroine, Judith, who also gave herself to ceaseless prayer and fasting (Jdt. 8:1–8; 11:17; 16:21–25).

---

37. Similarly, Marshall, p. 122.

38. Examples of such revealed thoughts are found in Luke 3:7–9; 5:21–22; 7:40–47; 8:16–18; 9:18–20; 20:20–26; Acts 5:1–11; 8:9–25; 9:4; 12:19–24; 13:4–12.

39. Though the former approach is popular (held, e.g., by Nolland, p. 122), Bock (p. 249) rightly observes that its 'major problem is that Luke in his passion account does not explicitly mention Mary as present at the cross (23:49)'.

38. At 'that time' (*tē hōra*; NRSV *moment*, but *hōra* can refer to a longer period of time), Anna approaches the couple and echoes the benediction of Simeon. She *began to praise* God and to *speak about* him (*peri autou*). The antecedent of 'him' (*autou*) is ambiguous. Whether it refers to God (NASB, KJV), the immediate antecedent, or to the baby Jesus (NRSV, NIV), as per the larger sense of the passage, is unclear. The latter seems preferable. Interestingly, her message is not for all but only for those who, like Simeon, *were looking for the redemption of Jerusalem*. This perhaps sheds light on the division alluded to in Simeon's speech, that is, between those destined to fall and rise, on the one side, and those destined to oppose the sign of Jesus, on the other. In other words, Luke may be hinting that those who longed for Israel's restoration would be more likely to receive the Messiah.

39. The present verse forms an *inclusio* with the beginning of the passage, in two ways. First, standing opposite the remark in verse 22 that 'they brought him up to Jerusalem', the geographical note here frames this as a scene that has been self-consciously set in Jerusalem, establishing a parallel between the Jerusalem-based Jesus and the Jerusalem-based pre-Pentecost church (Acts 2:1–21). For both Jesus' ministry and that of the early church, the Jerusalem setting is apposite, since for the Ancient Jews salvation for the nations would issue from Zion (Isa. 2:1–4; Mic. 4:1–2). Second, we recall that the very reason Joseph and Mary had set out from Galilee in the first place was to satisfy the demands of the 'law of Moses' (v. 22) or the 'law of the Lord' (v. 23). Now we find that that mission, so to speak, has been accomplished. Again, Luke is keen to show that before and after Jesus' birth, the law had been scrupulously maintained – and indeed fulfilled.

40. The details of Jesus' early childhood were either largely unknown to Luke or irrelevant to his narrative purposes. The Evangelist did, however, have enough information to speak on a general level, so as to summarize this period of Jesus' life. Like any human boy, Jesus *grew and became strong*. Moreover, Jesus is described as being *filled with wisdom*, while the grace of God is *upon him*. Such biographical reminiscences, reaching back to childhood, are characteristic of the biographical genre (*bioi*) Luke employs.

ii. Sitting among the teachers (2:41–52)

41–42. Instituted in remembrance of the first Passover night and ensuing exodus, the Passover was the greatest of all Jewish celebrations. According to Jewish belief, the date of Passover (14 Nisan) was also the date of the Aqedah (Isaac's near sacrifice on Mount Moriah, i.e. the Temple Mount), even as it was the date on which the Messiah was expected to return to his temple. Luke's note that Mary and Joseph made the annual trek to Jerusalem is meant not so much to reveal their piety, since annual Passover attendance was a point of duty observed by countless Jews (Deut. 16:1–8), as to set the stage for the young Messiah's second entrance into the temple (the first occurring in Luke 2:22–40, the third in 19:45–48). That this episode should occur when Jesus was just twelve not only underscores his remarkable precociousness (an important element for Luke's readers accustomed to Graeco-Roman *bioi*), but also may give expression to Jesus' messianic status as the embodiment of Israel (twelve years corresponding to the twelve tribes).[40]

43–45. When the Passover week had run its course, Jesus *stayed behind* in Jerusalem, leaving his parents' caravan to head back north without him. Given the parallelism between the Spirit's descent on Jesus at his baptism (3:21–22) and the Spirit's descent on the disciples at Pentecost (Acts 2:1–4), the young Jesus' remaining in Jerusalem may be meant to parallel the disciples' remaining in Jerusalem (Luke 24:49). If so, then on the analogy with Pentecost, we have a right to wonder whether this episode is to be understood as somehow preparatory for the baptism. After a day of travel, Mary and Joseph eventually realize that the boy is not among trusted family and friends. Panicked by this realization, they head back to Jerusalem.

46–47. On their arrival in Jerusalem, Jesus' parents do not find their son right away but only *after three days* (give or take a day for

---

40. On the former point, see de Jonge, 'Sonship, Wisdom, Infancy', pp. 340–342. Graeco-Roman biographies often involved stories of their subjects at age twelve (Jonge, pp. 345–346) and apparently Luke is not willing to disappoint in this regard.

the trip back to Jerusalem). Mary and Joseph's three-day crisis, involving a Jesus gone missing, looks ahead to the distraught three-day period between the cross and resurrection, when Jesus also, so to speak, goes missing. When they do find the boy, he is in the 'midst of' (*en mesō*) the teachers, *listening* and *asking them questions* – a scene which sharply contrasts with the confrontational exchange which occurs the next time Jesus is in the midst (*eis ton meson*) of the teachers (5:17, 19). Apparently, the young Jesus is doing more than simply *listening* and *asking them questions*, for those who hear him marvel at his understanding and answers. Forebodingly, Jesus' theological and rhetorical agility presage his highly contentious debates which will occur during the final week of his life (20:1–44).

48–49. Mary and Joseph are likewise *astonished* at Jesus' abilities. But they are also perplexed by Jesus' seeming thoughtlessness and nonchalance over his absence. When Mary confronts her son, he responds not with an apology but with a counter-challenge comprising two questions. Jesus' first question (*Why were you searching for me?*) may, on the one hand, be Jesus' way of insisting on his personal prerogative to carry out God's will, which in this case demanded his remaining unencumbered in Jerusalem. On the other hand, he may be wondering why they had not first started their search for him at the temple, which, given the nature of his calling, is where they should expect to find him. If we translate the Greek of Jesus' second question (*ouk ēdeite hoti en tois tou patros mou dei einai me*) along the lines of the NRSV (*Did you not know that I must be in my Father's house?*), the second option appears more likely. But if we translate the question as 'Did you not know that I must be about my Father's *things*?', then it appears that Jesus is making a broader assertion about his vocation and its priority over his human filial obligations. In either case, Mary's emphasis on Jesus' obligation to *your father and I* is met by Jesus' insistence on his duty to his heavenly Father. It is a duty occasioned by divine necessity, marked by the impersonal verb *dei*, recurring in Luke.[41]

---

41. See also 4:43; 9:22; 12:12; 13:14, 33; 17:25; 19:5; 21:9; 22:37; 24:7, 44. See Cosgrove, 'Divine'; Green, pp. 28–37.

50. Apparently, Mary and Joseph – no less than modern-day commentators! – are mystified by Jesus' response. At least they are unable to grasp just what he means at the present moment. In due course, as the narrative develops, the meaning of Jesus' words will become clearer. If Jesus can call God his Father, then he truly is 'Son of the Most High' (1:32) and the messianic Son promised in Psalm 2 (cf. Luke 3:22).

51. Notwithstanding Jesus' shifting focus from his earthly father to the divine Father, he accompanies his parents back to Nazareth, thus bringing his family's geographical movements full circle (2:4). There, for the remainder of his upbringing, he continues to obey Mary and Joseph. Once again, Luke observes, Mary takes the event to heart (cf. 2:19); the editorial comment 'registers Mary's attempt to grapple with its significance', even as it 'serves with 2:52 as the conclusion of the Lukan birth narrative as a whole'.[42]

52. Luke closes out his account of Jesus' pre-ministry years with a concluding statement, parallel to a similar summary issued regarding John (1:80). Building on the earlier assertion of 2:40 (the two verses form an *inclusio*), Jesus is said to have *increased in wisdom and in years, and in divine and human favour* – as amply illustrated by the present passage marked off by verses 40 and 52. Here the emphasis falls squarely on Jesus as a developing human being. In Luke's Christology, Jesus' status as fully divine yet fully human does not preclude personal growth but rather demands it.

Theology
Sometimes Christian believers, to their detriment, tend to think of Jesus' humanity as being swallowed up by his divinity. But this is a grave error. Luke insists that Jesus *grew* physically, mentally, socially and spiritually (2:40, 52). How exactly this holds together with the fact that Jesus is also the divine Lord (2:11) is not always easy to explain. But, as the Evangelist hopes to show, the humanity of Jesus logically entailed a process of development – and vice versa. Jesus came to empathize with humanity precisely as he experienced humanity, namely, in and through the limitations imposed by

42. Green, p. 157.

human finitude and the natural process of maturation. Though the
Spirit was fully on Jesus, this fact did not eliminate his need for
personal development. And if Jesus' maturation as a human necessitated his *growing* in wisdom and stature, the same principle surely
applies to the Gospel's readers. This means, in the first instance,
that possession of the Spirit is no excuse for refusing educational
resources that promise to expand wisdom and understanding. In
the second instance, the incarnation also means that the Spirit's
presence does nothing to devalue the physical body, justify its
neglect or ignore its relevance to personal identity. Neither
fundamentalistic anti-intellectualism nor attempts to separate
human personhood from the biological body are compatible with
Jesus' full humanity.

3. JESUS' PREPARATION FOR MINISTRY (3:1 – 4:13)

A. John the Baptizer (3:1–20)

Context

Having devoted considerable space to John's and Jesus' birth and upbringing, Luke now lingers briefly on the ministry of the adult John. This brevity should not be taken as a measure of the Baptizer's relative importance, for 'among those born of women' (7:28) there is none greater than John. Here Luke manages to pack into the space of some twenty verses everything we need to know about John's message.

Through his words and chosen venue, the Baptizer squarely situates himself – in fulfilment of Zechariah's prediction in 1:76 – in the storyline of Isaiah 40, a passage which introduces a vision of Israel's return from exile through the desert. In the world of first-century Judaism, when messianic expectations were at a high simmer, activity such as this would have quickly got everyone's attention. And given the unusual circumstances around his birth, not to mention his priestly pedigree (1:5), all eyes are now on him.

Not surprisingly, many came to him, again just as had been promised (1:16). But what would have been surprising for these crowds was how John's message fell on their ears not as good news but rather as bad news. Though so many had come in the confidence that they were part of God's remnant and therefore poised to benefit from the impending eschatological turn, John disabuses them of all such presumption. True, Yahweh's remnant was about to be restored, but that remnant would need to be formed well within the boundaries of Israel – and, shockingly, outside Israel as well.

Comment

i. Inauguration of John's ministry (3:1–6)

1–2a. Like the inspired authors of Israel's histories, Luke drives a peg into the sand of history. Setting this scene on the stage of world history, the Evangelist links John's ministry, together with the ensuing narrative, to seven well-known figures holding office at the time. By listing the seven names serially, the Gospel writer is prioritizing these figures according to both their relative importance (from more powerful to less powerful) and their scope of jurisdiction (from broader to narrower). By grouping the names together, he implies a shared set of traits among them. Given just who is included in Luke's brief catalogue, his first-century Palestinian readers would have readily recognized this as something of a 'who's who' in the rogues' gallery of autocrats, large and small.

John's baptizing activity begins in the fifteenth year of Emperor Tiberius, that is, in AD 28 (if we do not count Tiberius's two-year co-regency with Octavian as part of those fifteen years). Following the lead of his predecessor, Tiberius (reign AD 14–37) perpetuated the idolatrous emperor cult initiated only decades earlier, a point which will be revisited (20:20–26). Though widely worshipped, the emperor was also loathed and feared by subject constituencies throughout the empire, not least the Jews in Rome whom Tiberius expelled in AD 19. While Pontius Pilate (AD 26–36) has gone down in creedal infamy as the prefect of Judea who handed Jesus over to be crucified, Luke's particular interest is to show his ruthlessness in the face of provocation (13:1) and pusillanimity in the face of political pressure (23:1–25). Not to be confused with his father Herod the Great, Herod Antipas (4 BC – AD 39) ruled as tetrarch of Perea and Galilee. In the Gospel, he bears double culpability: first and most immediately for his connection to John's wrongful imprisonment and execution (3:19–20; 9:7–9), then for his role in Jesus' death (13:31–32; 23:6–12). Herod's half-brother Philip (4 BC – AD 33) and Lysanias, tetrarchs of Ituraea and Abilene, respectively, do not figure directly in Luke's narrative; history tells us very little about the former and almost nothing about the latter. Annas (7 BC – AD 14) served as high priest before he was deposed on account of Roman political interests, although he retained the title *ad mortem* (cf. Acts 4:6); according to John, he is the first administrator formally to hear Jesus' case (John 18:12–24). One would be hard-pressed to think of a first-century Jewish leader who was more politically influential. By the outbreak of the First Jewish War in AD 66, Annas would have the distinction of having four sons (and one son-in-law) accede to the high priestly office. Finally, Caiaphas (AD 18–36), the high priest proper during the time of Jesus' ministry and Annas's son-in-law, proves to be instrumental in the final verdict of the Jewish Sanhedrin when they are convened to determine Jesus' fate. Interestingly, compared with the other Evangelists, Luke minimizes Caiaphas's role in the trial (22:54–71). Although the naming of these Jerusalem-based political heavyweights may seem incommensurate with the demographically and geographically broader scope of John's ministry, this is exactly Luke's point. The story which began in some out-of-the-way grazing fields and now makes its way to a remote corner along the Jordan will soon enough reach the ends of the earth (Acts 1:8), eventually making its way back into the halls of Roman power (Acts 9:15).[1]

2b. After the pattern of the divinely inspired Old Testament prophets (e.g. Jer. 1:1–3), *the word of God came to John son of Zechariah in the wilderness.* The Baptizer's prophetic reception of the word marks a redemptive-historical turning point, for the spirit of prophecy had not broken its silence since it was last heard through the voice

---

1. Edwards, p. 106.

of the fifth-century BC prophet Malachi.[2] The desert location is
vital, not only because it graphically recapitulates the wilderness
setting of Isaiah's vision of return from exile (v. 4; cf. Isa. 40), but
also because precisely this setting was the penultimate stop before
the tribes' entry into the land at the end of the exodus. In this light,
John's baptism ministry is cast as a new exodus and an Isaianic
return from exile.[3]

3. The Baptizer's activity in *all the region around the Jordan* mimics
Torah's description of Sodom (Gen. 13:10; 19:25). This hints not
only at Israel's spiritual condition but also at the possibility that
God is now about to make his face shine on the quintessentially
sinful – to give Sodom another chance, as it were. To that end,
John offers *a baptism of repentance for the forgiveness of sins (baptisma
metanoias eis aphesin hamartiōn)*. The construction *baptisma metanoias*
is a qualitative genitive, thus a 'repentance-baptism'. The *result* of
such baptism, the prepositional phrase *eis aphesin hamartiōn* informs
us, is the forgiveness of sins. John's baptism was no mere effort to
stimulate revival. Instead it marked an epochal shift which
intimated the imminent obsolescence of the current salvific
economy, including the Jerusalem temple (where sins were
typically forgiven); offered purification from uncleanness (Isa.
1:16; 4:4; Mic. 7:19; Zech. 13:1); and set forth a call to join a new
priestly (Lev. 8:6; Num. 19), return-from-exile movement (Ezek.
36:25–33), centred around John and focused on the imminent
arrival of the kingdom.[4]

4–6. The movement's return-from-exile self-identity follows
clearly from Luke's citation of Isaiah 40:3–5, a text focused on the

---

2. Pious Jews of the day would have seen his prophetic silence as an
   indictment of Israel. See Cook, *Cessation of Prophecy*, pp. 54–63.

3. For more on this in relation to Acts, see Pao, *New Exodus*.

4. In my view, John's baptism had an ordaining significance, if only
   because Zimmerli's comment on Ezekiel's sprinkled returnees from
   exile may be equally applied to John's followers: 'When reference is
   made here to "sprinkling with clean water" . . . we should see behind
   this image . . . the purpose of cultic purification' (*Ezekiel*, pp. 248–249).
   On this and other points, see Perrin, *Kingdom of God*, pp. 78–80.

forgiveness of Israel's sins in connection with its restoration to the land. John's 'forgiveness of sins' is therefore a national-level forgiveness, open to all who might come. His unique role in that restoration is to prepare the way 'for the Lord', who is none other than Jesus himself.

ii. John's message (3:7–20)

7. As the crowds come out to be baptized, John acidly identifies them as a *brood of vipers*, offspring of the serpent Satan. Such language makes clear that his call is not simply to reformation but to conversion. In the Baptizer's eyes, Israel as a whole had apostatized and those coming for baptism would need to follow through with repentance to have any hope of averting the looming judgment. In the context, such judgment would be understood less as a personal fate than as a public event in the course of Israel's history.

8. The key to such repentance lay in the command to *bear fruits*. Although this concept will continue to be unpacked in the course of the narrative (6:43–45; 8:5–15; 13:6–9; 20:9–18), for now the reader learns that fruit-bearing means choosing generosity over greed and eschewing acts of injustice (vv. 10–14).[5] Meanwhile, John warns, those who presume on their ethnic identity as 'sons of Abraham' will come to the startling realization that *God is able from these stones to raise up children to Abraham*. The assertion is polyvalent. Trading on a common Hebrew pun between 'sons' (*bānîm*) and 'stones' (*'ăbānîm*), John states that God will bring about a new humanity out of the earth's raw materials, as if in an act of new creation; such Abrahamic children (aka stones) will materialize in the course of Luke's narrative.[6] In style and content, John's preaching is

---

5. For the scriptural background, see Jer. 17:3b–8; 21:12–14; Ezek. 16:49 – 17:10; Hos. 10:12–13; Amos 8:1–6; Hab. 1:1–4; 3:17; Hag. 2:19.

6. See Luke 13:10–17; 16:19–31; 19:1–10; Acts 3:25; 7:2, 7–8; 13:26. Fitzmyer (p. 468), along with others, thinks that a targum of Isa. 51:1 is in the background. Bovon (p. 172) objects to this theory on the grounds that the Baptizer's 'sons' are Gentiles and that a stone is at any rate a different concept from the rock envisioned by Isaiah.

apocalyptic. His message promises a thoroughgoing transformation of the created order, involving a radical reconfiguration of the
boundary lines of God's covenant community.

9. The nearness of eschatological judgment is underscored by
the image of the axe *lying at the root of the trees*. Given Isaiah's application of arboreal imagery to the returning people of God (Isa.
55:12–13; 61:3), the well-versed among the crowds surmise that
Israel is liable to judgment for failure to bear fruit. This judgment
is symbolized by fire, a recurring image in the Gospel (9:54; 12:49;
16:24; 17:29). In Luke's theology, then, the most telling indicator of
salvation is fruitfulness, that is, those virtues and practices
consistent with personal righteousness and social justice.

10–14. On being asked *What then should we do?*, John focuses on
a specific set of ethical concerns.[7] Learning to be content, being
willing to share resources with others, and forgoing extortion and
price-gouging at the road tolls (the means by which most tax
collectors made their surplus wealth) all receive a mention. These
issues of stewardship and social responsibility will prove to be
thematic.[8] The queries directed at John come from various groups:
the crowds as a whole (v. 10), tax collectors (v. 12) and soldiers (v.
14). That the *tax-collectors came to be baptized* is highly surprising,
given their reputation as an accursed and godless lot. The last
grouping is even more remarkable, since any given crowd of *soldiers*
would likely include Gentiles.[9] The diversity among John's
enquirers confirms the great reversal signalled in the Magnificat
(1:46–55) and presages the universalistic thrust of the coming
salvation.

15–16. Steeped in the scriptural promises, John's hearers would
have noticed that he had all the marks of the long-awaited Messiah.
Speculations regarding his possible messianic status would have
been all but inevitable. Yet the Baptizer is quick to nip such musings
in the bud by drawing a contrast between himself and a 'coming

---

7. The question anticipates the Philippian jailor's 'What must I do to be
saved?' (Acts 16:30).

8. See also Johnson, *Possessions in Luke–Acts*; Kim, *Stewardship*.

9. So rightly Cotter, 'Cornelius'; contra Fitzmyer, p. 470.

one' (a circumlocution for the Messiah). It is a contrast in terms of both status and function. According to the Baptizer, the said coming one is *more powerful*, meaning either more powerful to save or more powerful to perform miracles, or both. In fact, this approaching figure is so great that even a prophet as great as John does not count himself worthy to be his slave (a role epitomized in the servant's task of removing the master's footwear). In terms of function, the Baptizer draws attention to the different kinds of baptisms introduced by himself and the approaching messianic future. For his part, John's baptism is only *with* or 'in' *water (hydati)*. By contrast, the one to come brings a baptism *with the Holy Spirit and fire (en pneumati hagiō kai pyri)*. While the history of interpretation has struggled to determine whether the fire-baptism is in fact a separate baptism from the Spirit-baptism, it makes sense, in the light of the Spirit's descent in flames of fire (Acts 2), to equate fire-baptism with Spirit-baptism.[10] The focus is on Jesus not as the eschatological punisher but as the mediator of the Spirit, who was expected to be poured out at the eschaton (Isa. 32:15–20; Joel 2:28–29; Zech. 12:10).

17. Continuing with the image of fruit, John says that the coming figure is poised to separate out the mixture of grain and chaff that now constitutes Israel. Those who respond favourably to him will be gathered into the divine *granary (apothēkēn*; cf. 1 Chr. 28:11, where the same noun is used in reference to the temple storehouses). Those who do not risk being subject to an *unquenchable fire*, that is, eternal judgment. When applied to the fuller narrative, this last assertion serves to frame Jesus' ministry as a winnowing process, suggesting that the varied responses to the Messiah are but manifestations of the responders' true identity, whether grain or chaff. Their identity in turn will determine their eschatological destiny, be that in the heavenly temple storehouse or in the eternal fire of judgment.

18. Luke's summation of John's preaching implies that his record of the Baptizer's speech has been selectively adapted to the Evangelist's theological purposes. It is through such exhortation,

---

10. Similarly, Bovon, p. 177.

the Evangelist writes, that John in fact preaches *good news* [*euēngelizeto*] *to the people*. In other words, John's call to repentance *is* the preaching of *good news*, because it signals that God's restoration of Israel has now been launched through John's proclamation. On this logic, the repentance John calls for is not a human-based attempt to secure God's favour but rather a response to the favour already shown through this long-anticipated declaration of forgiveness (Isa. 40:1—2).

19—20. Luke's account of John's preaching ministry is rudely interrupted by a figure fleetingly introduced in verse 1: *Herod the ruler*. As Josephus (*Ant.* 18.110, 136) likewise reports, Herod Antipas had set aside his first wife in favour of Herodias, the wife of his half-brother Philip (not the tetrarch mentioned in v. 1), an action which had drawn public criticism from the Baptizer. Soon enough Herod has John arrested and imprisoned at the fortress at Macherus, where he is eventually executed (*Ant.* 18.116—119; Mark 6:17—29). As one of the seven foreboding figures introduced in verses 1—2a, Herod's reappearance at the close of the passage forms an *inclusio*. It is almost as if John's preaching were hemmed in by Herod's menacing presence. Yet the very injustice alluded to here only confirms John's point. If Israel's top political ruler is apostate, then this bodes ill for the nation as a whole.

Theology
Down through the centuries, Christians have struggled to integrate personal and public ethics. For many Christians today, the relationship between personal piety and social justice is foggy at best. The result of this lack of integration, at least in the contemporary Western church, has been the splintering of ethics among various ecclesial camps and social-political groupings, with some churches (some political bases) emphasizing public justice at the expense of personal formation and others doing just the opposite.

For Luke, such a dichotomy is unthinkable, if only because it fails to do justice to his foundational biblical-theological commitments concerning the kingdom. When Isaiah looked forward to Israel's salvation (Isa. 40:3—5; cf. Luke 3:4—6), he anticipated what Ezekiel describes as a return from exile back into the land, along with the pouring out of the Spirit and cleansing water (Ezek.

36:24–38). The hallmark of this eschatological community was to be their covenantal obedience. Such obedience required a well-ordered life on the part of the individual and well-ordered relationships on the part of the community – righteous attitudes and behaviour before God and humanity. John's ethical appeal, therefore, is based not on any abstract moralism but rather on the redemptive-historical fact that God was now bringing about Israel's restoration, requiring the remnant to live according to the terms set out in texts such as Isaiah 40:1–5 and Ezekiel 36:24–38. The crucial pieces in achieving this new return-from-exile community would be the Messiah and the baptism of the Spirit. Neither right worship nor right human relationships are possible apart from dependence on the Messiah and immersion in the Spirit. The integration of horizontal and vertical ethics depends on being rightly related to Christ and the Spirit.

B. Jesus' baptism (3:21–22)

Context

All along Luke has been dropping hints that Jesus' role would be closely coordinated with the Spirit. Mary has been informed that the Spirit of God would overshadow her (1:35), while John has announced a 'coming one' whose distinguishing trait would be a baptism of the Spirit (3:16). There is an inner necessity in such promises, for according to the prophets, the presence of the Spirit is fundamental to the restoration of the sacred space. What is more, without the Spirit, God's people are effectively still in exile (Ezek. 11:22–25), and still without cleansing or the possibility of obedience. When it comes to the salvation of God's people, the Spirit is crucial.

In this brief passage the palpable manifestation of the Spirit finally occurs. In fulfilment of Isaiah (Isa. 32:15–18; 44:3–5), the Spirit now self-reveals in the presence of a repentant people who have submitted to John's baptism of repentance (Luke 3:1–20). But that Spirit would not come upon the people as a whole but rather only on Jesus. To this point, Jesus has come to us as the promised Davidic heir (1:32, 69) and the son of the Abrahamic promise (1:55, 73). Now, at his baptism, Jesus is confirmed as both.

Comment

21. Differently from Matthew and Mark, Luke has Jesus' baptism taking place alongside the baptism of all the people. This fact may help resolve the theological difficulty as to why Jesus would willingly undergo a baptism of *repentance*. For Luke, the answer seems to be that he is one among the people: Jesus must identify himself with sinful Israel. At the same time, Jesus' experience is unique, for as he prays heaven is *opened*. In Scripture, the opening of the heavens is associated with divine in-breaking into human reality (Gen. 7:11; Isa. 24:18; 64:1; T. Levi 18:6–8) and theophanic revelation (Ezek. 1:1). Through the baptism of Jesus, then, the self-revealing God is breaking into the world. That this opening of the heavens should occur in response to prayer is no accident, for elsewhere Jesus will affirm a correlation between prayer and divine 'opening' (11:9–10). In this respect, Jesus' baptism prayer prefigures his disciples' obligation to pray, 'Your kingdom come!' (11:1–2).

22. The descent of the Spirit *like a dove* does not necessarily mean the Spirit looked like a dove but that the manner of the Spirit's descent was visibly dove-like. While many explanations have been offered over the centuries for this comparison, the best explanation appeals to a certain Jewish interpretative tradition which held that at the cusp of creation the Spirit hovered over the primordial chaos as a dove (b. Ḥag. 15a). In this case, the Spirit's comparison to the dove signals that Jesus' baptism stands to usher in a new, better and final creation.

The voice from heaven identifies Jesus as the divine, beloved son. The filial epithet retrospectively clarifies earlier intimations of divine sonship (1:32–35, 41; 2:11, 49). Yet it also prospectively looks forward to, among other moments, the temptation (4:3, 9) and transfiguration (9:35) where Jesus' divine sonship is reconfirmed. The divine voice simultaneously draws on Psalm 2:7, where the royal-priestly David is installed on Zion, and Genesis 22, where the 'beloved son' (Gen. 22:2) Isaac is offered up to God.[11] If the former subtext serves to identify Jesus as the Davidic Messiah, the latter

---

11. Less direct though widely touted is an allusion to Isa. 42:1. See discussion in Perrin, *Jesus the Priest*, pp. 68–69.

passage implies that Jesus is destined to be offered as an atoning ransom, not unlike Isaac.

Theology

John had promised that God would imminently raise up new sons of Abraham from mere stones, and that in connection with the Spirit. Now the same hovering, dove-like Spirit who was instrumental in the first creation comes to rest uniquely on Jesus. As the baptism makes clear, new creation and all the eschatological promises regarding the pouring out of the Spirit are to be brokered through Jesus. Through his baptism and the words spoken over him, Jesus is also marked out as the fulfilment of the Abrahamic and Davidic promises: Jesus – and only Jesus – is heir to the land promised to Abraham and the final successor to the throne promised to David. His is the kingdom; his subsequent words and actions will define this kingdom, and whatever is true of the kingdom will also be true of the king.

Yet for all the Christological import of Jesus' baptism, there is no little missiological significance to this scene as well. As Luke will repeatedly remind his readers (Acts 4:23–31; 9:10–19; 13:1–13; 22:7–21), a prerequisite for effective ministry is divine empowerment through the Holy Spirit. If Jesus must be overshadowed by the Spirit before he inaugurates his ministry, how much more the church and the individual believers within it?

C. Jesus' credentials (3:23 – 4:13)

Context

It is one thing to be declared the Son of God (3:21–22); it is another thing to prove it. In this section, the Evangelist demonstrates Jesus' messianic calling by connecting two coordinated points: messianic pedigree (3:23–38) and messianic obedience (4:1–13). On both counts, in both passages, Jesus' link to Adam remains crucial. Once Luke's genealogy is properly understood, we begin to see Jesus and Adam as two pillars standing at either end of a carefully structured account of redemptive history. And once the temptation is understood, we see that where Adam had failed in the face of demonic suggestion (and where his seed, Israel, had also failed),

Jesus comes through with flying colours. In devoting an inordinate amount of space to Jesus' life before his ministry (at least compared with, say, Mark), Luke hopes to lay fulsome groundwork for Jesus' messianic identity.

Comment

i. Genealogy of Jesus (3:23–38)

23–38. Luke states that Jesus is *about thirty years old when he began . . .* (*archomenos*). Although modern translations typically supplement the elliptical force of the Greek syntax by adding a direct object to the present participle *archomenos* (*he began his work*, NRSV; 'he began his ministry', NIV, ESV), the sense of the sentence hardly requires it. The participle was in fact a technical term in Greek biographies, marking out the middle section of the text. That Jesus was roughly thirty at the time of his launch lands him in the same company as Joseph (Gen. 41:46), Ezekiel (Ezek. 1:1) and, perhaps most importantly, David (2 Sam. 5:4). Whatever the value of these considerations, given Jesus' anointing at the baptism, we should attach primary importance to the fact that thirty was the minimum age for entry into the priesthood (Num. 4:3, 23, 30, 35, 39, 43, 47; 1 Chr. 23:3).

The disconnect between Luke's genealogy and Matthew's (Matt. 1:1–17) has long been a source of puzzlement. Whereas Luke 3:31–34 matches Matthew 1:2–6 very closely, the list of names between Jesus' father Joseph and David (Luke 3:23–31), corresponding to the generational span of Matthew 1:6–16, lines up with the first Gospel at only two places: Zerubbabel and Shealtiel (Matt. 1:12, 13//Luke 3:27). This divergence has been explained in various ways. One solution has been to posit that Matthew's genealogy goes through Joseph, while Luke's goes through Mary. Another proposal is to suggest the possibility of multiple levirate marriages, whereby one Gospel writer records the name of the biological father and the other supplies the name of the adoptive father (following the death of the biological father). On top of these approaches, consideration should be given to a third option, namely, that Matthew's list represents a legal line of descent (marking out the rightful Davidic heir in each generation), but that Luke's genealogy is closer to a listing of the biological fathers and sons. The complexity of the issues evades our best attempts towards certainty.

Given this array of eminently plausible theories, and given Ancient Judaism's well-documented attentiveness to genealogical detail, we should be sceptical of facile assertions that this passage is essentially a homespun fiction. On the contrary, as Richard Bauckham asserts, the 'Lukan genealogy of Jesus is a more important historical document than has been generally appreciated'.[12] At the same time, the genealogy is a theologically rich, carefully structured document. Bauckham has also made the interesting proposal that Luke's genealogy, following the logic of the Apocalypse of Weeks, has been intentionally arranged in eleven 'weeks' or sevens, with each week culminating in a crucial event.[13]

Week 11	Jannai – Jesus (listed in reverse chronological order in vv. 23–24d)
Week 10	Maath – Joseph (vv. 24e–26a)
Week 9	Zerubbabel – Mattathias (vv. 26b–27c)
Week 8	Er – Salathiel/Shealtiel (vv. 27d–28e)
Week 7	Judah – Joshua/Jesus (vv. 29a–30b)
Week 6	Nathan – Joseph (vv. 30c–31d)
Week 5	Amminadab – David (vv. 31e–33a)
Week 4	Isaac – Admin (vv. 33b–34b)
Week 3	Eber – Abraham (vv. 34c–35d)
Week 2	Methuselah – Shelah (vv. 35e–37a)
Week 1	Adam – Enoch (vv. 37b–38c)

Structured within these eleven weeks, the sum total of names amounts to seventy-seven, which is the number of fullness (seven) to the nth degree (cf. Gen 4:24; Matt. 18:22). Occupying the seventy-seventh position from God, therefore, Jesus is a kind of 'fullness of fullness', even as the name of Jesus (= 'Joshua') also

---

12. Bauckham, *Relatives of Jesus*, p. 315.

13. The Apocalypse of Weeks is a pre-Christian Jewish document, embedded in 1 En. 91–105 (= 1 En. 93:1–10; 91:11–17), that orders history into ten weeks, each of seven generations.

falls at the forty-ninth place, the number of Jubilee (cf. commentary on Luke 4:18). Luke's structure implies that this genealogy not only spans the scope of redemptive history, but also fills in its individual 'chapters', with Jesus himself occupying history's climax. While it would certainly be impossible to 'prove' that this is what Luke had in mind when he laid out his genealogy, this theory is perhaps as strong as any in explaining the Evangelist's selection and numeration.

That this family tree reaches all the way back to God is unprecedented among ancient genealogies. Obviously, Luke draws a connection between Jesus being declared 'Son of God' at his baptism (3:22) and Adam's status as *son of God* (v. 38). A great number of commentators see the link as an attempt to show Jesus' solidarity with humanity. However, if this were Luke's objective, one is left to wonder why he was compelled to provide such an extensive list of names, and how this list actually serves to make Jesus more human. Against this interpretation, I propose that the Gospel writer is singling out Jesus and Adam *from* humanity (though of course both are human). Adam was the singular *son of God* inasmuch as he, at least for a time, served God in perfect obedience, faithfully reflecting God's image. As the one and only true image-bearer, Adam was the quintessential royal-priestly mediator between God and creation.[14] The strong link with Adam makes sense, too, because if Jesus was created apart from normal human reproductive processes (1:26–38), the same obtained for Adam (cf. 7:28). Made to stand at the climax of a circuitous history, Jesus is being presented as the one and only second Adam, at last completing what Adam failed to complete: full creation.

ii. Temptation (4:1–13)

1–2. Having been baptized by the Spirit (3:21–22), Jesus now *returned [hypestrepsen] from the Jordan, full of the Holy Spirit,* even as he is *led by the Spirit [ēgeto en tō pneumati] in the wilderness* much as Israel the son of God (Exod. 4:22–23) was divinely 'led . . . in the wilderness' (Deut. 8:2). Later, in Luke 4:14, he will return in the power of the

---

14. See Beale, *Biblical Theology*, pp. 614–648.

Spirit (*hypestrepsen . . . en tē dynamei tou pneumatos*). The repetition of
returned (*hypestrepsen*) and *Spirit*, encasing the present episode,
suggests that both Jesus' physical movements and his resistance to
the devil's overtures have more than a little to do with the
empowering Spirit.

At the close of a forty-day fast, Jesus, like Israel and Adam, is
tempted (*peirazomenos*) or tested by the devil. *Peirazō* embraces both
concepts. And in this story there are elements of both: Jesus is not
just tempted but confirmed in his identity as the messianic Son,
publicly conferred at the baptism.[15] If Jesus were simultaneously the
true Adam and the true Israel, the proof positive would be obedience.

Yet there are still other layers. Jesus' forty-day testing in the
wilderness also has affinities with the forty-day fast experienced by
both Moses (Deut. 9:9), as he received the law, and Elijah, en route
to Horeb (1 Kgs 19:8). Both of these figures show up at the transfiguration (9:30). And Jesus' ministry takes on qualities of both: like
Moses, Jesus will lead an exodus; like Elijah, he will call a remnant
to repentance. Such multilayered and intertwining typologies cast
no shade either on the historicity of the event or on Jesus' humanity.
In fact, Luke's remark that Jesus suffered hunger at the end of his
forty-day fast appears to be an intentional effort to refute those
who would diminish Jesus' humanness (Docetism) on the basis of
this story.

3–4. The wording of the devil's recommendation depends on a
prior knowledge of Jesus' sonship as revealed at the baptism. He
seeks not so much to question this identity but to lure Jesus into
plying his messianic powers inappropriately. By inciting him to
command this stone to become a loaf of bread (an action not unlike the
multiplication of the loaves and fishes, 9:10–17), the devil hopes to
coax Jesus into harnessing his title for self-serving ends, thereby
marring his entire messianic ministry.

Resisting the devil's overtures, Jesus responds by drawing
directly from the LXX text of Deuteronomy 8:3 ('*man will not live*

---

15. As Liefeld (p. 863) states it: 'In this temptation by the devil, the Lord
Jesus shows the validity of what God had just said of him, "With you I
am well pleased" (3:22).'

[*ouk . . . zēsetai ho anthrōpos*] by bread alone'). The rejoinder is intended not to inform the devil, who is already quite familiar with the Scriptures (Luke 4:10–11), but to model an appropriate response to temptation *and* to stake a Christological claim in the face of the devil's attempts to cast doubt. Challenging the diabolical assumption that life depends strictly and only on physical food, Jesus reasserts the force of Deuteronomy 8:3 which states that life ultimately finds its source in God's word. More than that, he gets special double duty out of Deuteronomy 8:3 by identifying himself as its unique fulfilment: in short, precisely as *the man* (*ho anthrōpos*) in the Adamic sense, Jesus alone will faithfully keep the word of God, and as a result 'will live' (*zēsetai*) via the resurrection.[16] Consistent with other New Testament writers (e.g. Rom. 5:12–21), Luke maintains that Jesus' perfect keeping of the law, decisively but not yet completely accomplished through the *peirasmos* of Luke 4:1–11, uniquely qualifies him as the second Adam.[17]

5–8. If the Spirit had led Jesus to the place of temptation (v. 1), now *the devil led him up* in order to show him *the kingdoms of the world* (*oikoumenēs*), a term already introduced at 2:1 in reference to the Roman Empire.[18] By introducing the same term here, the text implies that the discrete domains constituting the empire have been divinely granted to the devil and are therefore at his disposal (*for it has been given over to me, and I give it to anyone I please*). Astonishingly, in offering to transfer authority over these territories, the devil is essentially

---

16. This reading builds on the reasonable surmise that Luke's Jesus, like Paul (Gal. 3:11–12; cf. Hab. 2:4, LXX) and other Jews of his day, interpreted 'will live' (*zēsetai*) as shorthand for resurrection.

17. Contra Gooding (pp. 78–79), who writes that the 'Greek word for man which Luke uses (*anthrōpos*) is the one which means man in the sense of human being. Christ's reply, therefore, indicates that while he is indeed the Son of God, he is also human . . . a Son of Adam.'

18. Luke inverts the order of Matthew's second and third temptations. While Matthew is usually regarded as preserving the original order of the temptations as it was passed down in tradition, Luke's placement of the climactic temptation at the temple lines up with his temple-centric interest.

presenting Jesus with the immediate opportunity to become the new Caesar. Yet the offer is unacceptable. Although Jesus is confident that one day as Israel's Messiah he will indeed rule the world, the word of God spoken at his baptism has already intimated that his forthcoming role as the new self-surrendering Isaac will require him to lay down his life. His effectiveness as Messiah will directly depend on the nature of his kingly rule, and on that rule remaining different from that of the Gentile leaders (22:24–27).

Yet there is a hook in the devil's bait, namely, that Jesus *worship* (*proskynēsēs*) or bow at the knee before him. The term *proskynēsis* denotes a physical posture appropriate to demonstrations of religious devotion and social-political obeisance alike. In the first-century world, the gesture of public genuflection did not necessarily distinguish between honouring one's patrons and social superiors and honouring the gods. Contemplating the devil's offer, perhaps Luke's mid-first-century audiences drew an eery connection between this temptation and the Roman request that its subjects offer public homage to Caesar while receiving all the benefits for such religious-political conformity.[19] In any case, the devil tenders an offer which Jesus is compelled to turn down. He does so once again by appealing to Deuteronomy, and within that text a commandment insisting on Israel's undivided monotheistic allegiance (Deut. 6:13), a keystone of Jewish devotion. To capitulate to the devil's offer of authority and glory would be to betray Israel's foundational commitment to worship the one true God. The point for Luke's readers would be to recognize that wealth, power and status (authority), the central trappings of the kingdoms of the empire, are all in fact enticements to a self-compromising idolatry.

9–12. Leading Jesus into Jerusalem, now the devil perches him *on the pinnacle of the temple.* Repeating the protasis of the first temptation (*If you are the Son of God* . . . ; cf. v. 3), the devil seeks once again to induce Jesus to leverage his position improperly. If Jesus were to throw himself off the tower, so the devil reasons on the allegedly

---

19. In Luke's day, Rome's bid for allegiance came more in the form of cultural pressure than in the form of police state-style tactics employed towards the close of the first century.

scriptural grounds of Psalm 91:11–12, he could expect the angels to intervene before any bodily harm was done. The performance of such a stupendous sign would be especially tempting for Jesus as he anticipates hostile and eventually deadly sceptics. In response to this temptation, Jesus cites Deuteronomy 6:16, a verse prohibiting Israel's putting Yahweh to the test. A righteous person's refusal to put God to the test is a refusal 'to dictate to God how he must express his covenant loyalty and fulfill his promises'.[20]

13. His options exhausted, the devil departs from Jesus' presence, at least *until an opportune time* – no doubt the temptation scene at Gethsemane (22:39–46). That Jesus' ministry should be ensconced within two confrontations with the forces of darkness underscores not only the devil's grasp of the strategic nature of Jesus' mission, but also the relentless ferocity of the demonic opposition. Yet Jesus' faithfulness in the face of these temptations demonstrates that whereas Adam and Israel had failed, he had not. Jesus has proved himself as true Adam and true Israel – the quintessential human and the obedient one par excellence.

Theology
In his genealogy, Luke labours to show the symmetry between Jesus as the Son of God and Adam as the son of God. This prepares for the temptation scene, where Satan attempts to derail Jesus' ministry as 'Son of God' by either inciting him to some outstanding feat or seducing him with authority and glory. Yet Jesus refuses all the suggestions of a big splash. Instead, he responds as any believer might on our best days: by appealing to the higher authority of Scripture and resting on the empowerment of the Spirit. What does it mean to be 'Son of God'? If the genealogy demonstrates that Jesus is fully human while also emphasizing his unique relation to the directly created Adam, then the temptation shows that Jesus is simultaneously Messiah, Mosaic redeemer, a prophet like Elijah and true human being.

The last of these is often overlooked. We often make the mistake of tacitly believing that sanctification involves becoming more

---

20. Nolland, p. 181.

divine and less human. According to Luke, nothing could be further from the truth. Christ-followers are never more fully human than when they are struggling with intense temptations, remaining steadfast through humble reliance on the Word and Spirit.

4. MINISTRY IN GALILEE (4:14 – 9:50)

A. Inauguration of Jesus' ministry (4:14–44)

Context

Relating to the Galilean phase of Jesus' ministry, the larger section of Luke 4:14 – 9:50, to which 4:14–44 belongs, is marked by certain discernible patterns. First, the next five chapters are characterized by a sustained rhythm between deeds and words. The alternation between these two poles is almost certainly intentional. Perhaps Luke saw no other way to do justice to the programmatic citation of Isaiah in 4:18–19 than by showing how his inaugural sermon would work itself out in word and deed. Second, here Jesus begins to encounter very different reactions to his ministry or 'release' (an important word in this passage): some extremely negative, others extremely positive. These early controversies foreshadow later developments en route to Jerusalem and in Jerusalem itself. But it all begins in Galilee.

Having been baptized and tested, Jesus in 4:14–44 is now finally ready to undertake his ministry. He does so in his home town of

Nazareth. A sudden burst of ministry activity without explanation would risk leaving his observers mystified on too many fronts. So in his inaugural sermon, Jesus announces his agenda – and he does so, strikingly, with the words of Isaiah. Mary had perceived that the return from exile was nigh and that the climax of the covenants was underway (1:46–55); now Jesus confirms the same point.

Comment

i. Prefatory remarks to the Galilean ministry (4:14–15)

14–15. This couplet of transitional verses takes up a double duty in the narrative. Advancing beyond Jesus' last-mentioned whereabouts at the temple (v. 9), verses 14–15 note his transition to the *surrounding country* before eventually returning to Jerusalem (9:51). At the macro level, verses 14–15 introduce the entire Galilean ministry (4:14 – 9:50). Yet on a smaller scale, the two verses provide a bridge between the confirmation of Jesus' messianic identity (4:1–13) and his early implementation of his messianic ministry (4:16–30). The thread of continuity is the Spirit: whereas Jesus is *filled with the power of the Spirit* (v. 14) as an extension of the Spirit-indwelling before the temptation (v. 1), soon enough he himself will interpret that fullness in the terms of Isaiah's climactic prophecy (v. 18). Meanwhile, John's testimony about Jesus, the 'voice of one crying out in the wilderness' (3:4), now morphs into a collective report that is *spread through* the populated region of Galilee. Jesus' reputation is now preceding him, and that on account of the baptism and temptations, not to mention healings unreported by Luke (v. 23). All the while, verse 15 has a prospective force: when Jesus teaches *in their synagogues* and is *praised* (*doxazomenos*) or 'glorified' by everyone, this offers a fairly accurate preview of 4:14 – 9:50. The very glory which Jesus rejected in the second temptation (v. 6), then, is already circling back to him. Yet as 4:14 – 9:50 will also make clear soon enough, it is a glory deeply tinged with hostility.

ii. Kingdom preaching (4:16–30)

16. Returning to Nazareth (2:39–40), Jesus now makes his home town the geographical point of departure for his ministry. While one might ordinarily expect Jesus to utilize his home base to garner popular support, it is almost as if he launches from Nazareth precisely *because* of the resistance he expects to find there (vv. 23–24). Scepticism from his kith and kin here will soon prove to be a bellwether of his cool reception among the Jews in general.

Almost as if to reaffirm the intramural nature of Jesus' conflict with his fellow Jews, Luke confirms his Torah piety by noting that synagogue attendance was his Sabbath *custom* (cf. 1:9; 2:22, 39, 42). Having absented himself from Nazareth long enough to be considered both a 'home town boy done good' *and* a visitor, Jesus is granted the honour of offering the reading from the Prophets (which followed the reading of Torah but preceded the sermon proper) – a privilege appropriate to a distinguished visitor. Although in a typical synagogue service the ensuing sermon would often fall to a separate individual, Jesus retains the stage to elaborate briefly on the scriptural text.

17–19. Our knowledge of first-century synagogue practice is too scanty for us to be certain whether Jesus' passage would have been his choice or merely the assigned lectionary reading for the day. Either way, he reads from Isaiah 61:1–2 with a portion of Isaiah 58:6 tacked on for good measure. Also attracting the interest of the Qumran sectarians (e.g. 1QH XVIII, 14; 4Q521; 11Q13), Isaiah 61:1–2 seems to have been a major plank in the Ancient Jewish vision of eschatological restoration.[1] It is easy enough to see why, given the text's far-reaching promises. The passage envisions an anointed herald who declares the Jubilee (*the year of the Lord's favour*), involving (1) the proclamation of *good news to the poor,* (2) *release to the captives,* (3) *recovery of sight to the blind* and (4) the liberation of *the oppressed.*[2] Legislated in Torah, Jubilee was an institution that was supposed to have been implemented by the regnant high priest every forty-nine (or fifty) years (Lev. 25:8–17). It called for debt

---

1. Contra Edwards, p. 136; see Swarup, *Self-understanding,* pp. 23–24.
2. Jeremias (*Promise,* pp. 44–45) argues that Jesus' omission of Isa. 61:2b ('and the day of vengeance of our God') in his reading would have implied the Gentiles' immunity from divine judgment, and that this in turn was the provocation for Jesus' audience (vv. 22–30). Despite its pervasive influence, the argument is simply unsupportable.

remission, the emancipation of slaves and the restoration of property holdings to their erstwhile owners.[3] According to at least some Jewish eschatological hopes (11Q13), an eschatological high priest was expected to announce a kind of super Jubilee, exactly as envisioned in Isaiah 61, coinciding with the cashing out of Israel's eschatological promises. This would entail full return from exile, recouped land, a retrieval of Israel's political autonomy, restored worship and the Spirit's renewed presence. By declaring these events as having been fulfilled in the here and now, Jesus retrospectively interprets his baptism (3:21–22) as the anointing of the Jubilary high priest (Isa. 61:1) and prospectively signals a number of central themes awaiting development (the Spirit, good news to the poor, economic and spiritual release or forgiveness). With Luke's framing this text as a kind of inauguration speech unto itself, one could not imagine a more forceful demonstration of the organic unity between Jesus' vocation and the scriptural story of Israel.

20–21. Following his account of the reading from Isaiah, the Evangelist creates narrative tension by methodically describing Jesus' subsequent actions, namely, closing up the scroll, returning it to the attendant and sitting down. The actions mirror Jesus' movements in taking the synagogue floor: standing up, receiving the scroll and unrolling it (vv. 16–17). The effect is a chiasm, with the central term being the Isaianic phrase 'the Spirit of the Lord is on me'.[4] The thrust of these words is central to this episode, even as it is programmatic for the entire book.

As the audience intensely stares at him in wonder, Jesus declares the present-day fulfilment of the same scripture with the emphasis on *today*, a word which recurs in Luke consistently in connection with salvation (2:11; 5:26; 13:32; 19:5, 9; 23:43). Again, the Isaianic passage explains the linkage; here lies the root of all Luke's 'todays'. Through his reading and his declaration that *this scripture has been fulfilled in your hearing*, Jesus has effectively unleashed the benefits enumerated in Isaiah 61. The ensuing narrative will soon bear this out.

---

3. See Green and Perrin, *DJG*, pp. 450–452.
4. See Siker, 'First to the Gentiles', pp. 76–79.

22. The immediate response to Jesus' astounding assertion is mixed. On one level, the synagogue attendees support Jesus' claims by bearing witness (*emartyroun*) to him (NRSV *spoke well of him*); there is also a sense of astonishment (in keeping with earlier positive reactions to Jesus; cf. 2:18, 33) and wonder. Still, for the townspeople, other questions remain, not least Jesus' filial relationship to Joseph. Nazareth was a small village with a population numbering in the dozens. Here the highly unusual circumstances of Jesus' birth could hardly have been kept a secret. Even if Mary and Joseph had their supporters within the town, one can only imagine that there were a good number of sceptics as well. Now by drawing attention to Jesus as Joseph's son, the more vocal members of the synagogue are expressing their own sense of dissonance. To put the townspeople's unstated question bluntly: is it even possible that our local town bastard (*mamzer*) has become Israel's Messiah?

23-24. Sensing the resistance of his hearers, Jesus confronts them with two well-known aphorisms, connected here by the recurring catchword *patridi* (*home town*). With supernatural perception Jesus intuits that his childhood acquaintances will require an extraordinary amount of evidence before they accept his claims. Even though the people of Nazareth are aware of reports of healings performed in Capernaum (unrecounted in Luke's narrative), Jesus' abilities as a healer would apparently have to be scrutinized *de novo* by the folk of Nazareth prior to their giving any serious credence to his claims. However reasonable this approach may appear to many modern readers, for Luke their demand to *do here also* was nothing less than putting God to the test (cf. v. 12). Towards explaining the reasons for this unbelief, Jesus then goes on (in v. 24) to quote a second aphorism observing that *no prophet is accepted* [*dektos*] *in the prophet's home town*. Ironically, though Jesus offers the acceptable (*dekton*) year of the Lord's favour (v. 19), he remains the *prophet* who is not *accepted* (*dektos*) in the eyes of his own home town.

25-27. Now extending the point, Jesus appeals to two scriptural examples. In the first, Jesus capitalizes on the irony that although Elijah could have been sent to any one of countless widows among the Israelites during the three-and-a-half-year drought, he is sent only to a widow of non-Jewish pedigree (cf. 1 Kgs 17:8-24). A

similar irony marks the second example: although there must have
been countless Israelites with leprosy in Elisha's day, not one is
recorded as being healed by the prophet – only Naaman the
(Gentile) Syrian (cf. 2 Kgs 5:1–19). In the context of Luke–Acts,
such examples lay the initial groundwork for the church's universal
mission (Acts 10).

28–29. Whatever positive impressions Jesus had made at the
synagogue, these are now quickly forgotten in the wake of intense
anger. All too mindful of their oppression at the hands of this
empire of godless pagans, the townspeople are indignant at Jesus'
hint that the eschatological climax would enfold rather than exact
justice on the Gentiles. Not long after Jesus 'stood up' (*anestē*, v. 16)
to declare the day of Jubilee, the people *got up* (*anastantes*) with a
view to inflicting bodily harm. More exactly, in a makeshift act of
excommunication, the townspeople expel (*exebalon*) him from the
village limits (anticipating the vineyard workers' expulsion
[*ekbalontes auton exō*] of the son, 20:15), only to lead him up on a
nearby hill *so that they might hurl him off the cliff.* Such mob violence
was not without its reasons: the community is seeking to execute
Jesus for blasphemy, an offence which typically required death by
stoning, just as Stephen would be stoned at the close of his first
sermon (Acts 7:58).[5]

30. The Gospel tradition contains several stories in which Jesus
narrowly escapes stoning (John 5:18[?]; 8:59; 10:31), but none is more
inexplicable than this one. Luke informs us that Jesus *passed through
the midst of them and went on his way.* Even if the Evangelist's description
of the escape is tantalizingly spare, his readers would recognize
the similarity between this miracle and the devil's dare in the third
temptation (Luke 4:10–11). While Jesus had refused to put God to
the test on the devil's prompting, it remains the case that, when
necessity demands as much, God is able to intervene miraculously.

---

5. Stoning was accomplished either by throwing stones at the victim with
deadly impact or, more commonly in antiquity, by lofting the victim on
to the stones with equal results; cf. m. Sanh. 6:4.

iii. Kingdom activity (4:31–44)

31–32. At some later date, Jesus (re)enters Capernaum (cf. v. 23), a sizeable city on the north-west corner of the Sea of Galilee and home to Simon Peter (v. 38), among other future disciples.[6] Like the previous passage, this episode falls on the Sabbath and involves Jesus in a formal role in the synagogue service. Also like the previous episode, the present story offers a paradigmatic example of the activities described in verse 15. If at Nazareth the synagogue attendance was impressed by Jesus' gracious words, here they are moved *because he spoke with authority*. The authoritative quality of his presentation and content will soon (v. 36) be augmented by demonstrated authority over the spiritual world.

33. Jesus' teaching is suddenly disrupted by a man possessed by a *spirit of an unclean demon*, also translatable as an epexegetical genitive, thus: 'a spirit, that is, an unclean demon'. Language of uncleanness in connection with the demonic is unusual in the ancient literature overall, but standard in the Gospel tradition. Almost certainly it points back to the 'unclean spirit' of Zechariah 13:2, to be eradicated on the day of Israel's eschatological cleansing.[7] The Evangelists' specialized terminology, then, suggests that Jesus' exorcistic activity is to be understood as a facet of the redemptive-historical shift envisaged by Zechariah.

34. The Greek word *ea* may be translated either as an interjection, something like 'Ha!' (ESV), or as an imperative form of *eaō* with the meaning *Let us alone!* (NRSV). Perhaps the former makes slightly more sense, as it conveys the demon's combatively mocking stance. The following phrase (*ti hēmin kai soi*) is standard Greek idiom, here best captured by the NLT's 'Why are you interfering with us?' By identifying Jesus as a Nazarene, the demon seeks not only to control Jesus by identifying him and his origins, but also – through a wordplay – to expose his messianic credentials.[8] By identifying

---

6. On Capernaum, see Green, p. 222 n. 63.

7. See Perrin, *Jesus the Temple*, pp. 159–163.

8. The Hebrew root *nṣr* retained messianic connotations on the basis of 'the branch [*nṣr*] of David' in Isa. 11:1. See N. Piotrowskwi, *DJG*, pp. 624–625.

his exorcist as *the Holy One of God* (*ho hagios tou theou*), the demon confirms Jesus' sacerdotal right to declare the Jubilee release (vv. 17–21), for as *the Holy One*, Jesus is being designated as none other than the high priest (Num. 16:7; Ps. 106:16).[9] As the eschatological high priest, Jesus is also expected to wage a holy war against the kingdom of darkness – an expectation which clearly surfaces in the demon's question (*Have you come to destroy us?*). Ironically, while human observers struggle to grasp Jesus' identity and mission, the demon summarizes both with unsurpassable concision and clarity.

35. Swiftly rebuking (*epetimēsen*) the demon, Jesus reduces his adversary to silence. Like his source Mark, Luke embeds this episode within a larger theme of secrecy, commonly known as the 'messianic secret'. Jesus is more interested in controlling the timetable of his self-revelation than in accelerating a full disclosure of his identity, which could in turn lead to premature misunderstanding as well as (once the priesthood discovers there is another high priest in town) an untimely demise. With so many mistaken assumptions in place in the culture, Jesus will need the course of his ministry to show exactly what kind of Messiah he intends to be – a piece no less crucial than the fact of his Messiahship.

36–37. Like many accounts of Jesus' miracles, this scene closes out by registering the response of the gathered crowd. The people's speculation regarding the power of Jesus' *utterance* (*logos*) may at another level – allowing for a porous boundary between the spoken word of Jesus and the Word who is Jesus – be understood as Christological musing: 'Who is this Word [*logos*] that he commands . . . ?' (cf. John 1:1). No less significantly, Jesus' remarkable demonstration of *authority and power* (*exousia kai dynamei*), within a large struggle between clean and unclean forces, situates the exorcism within the narrative of Daniel 7. In that Danielic chapter, after all, the Son of Man will eventually prove his 'authority' (Dan. 7:14; cf. 7:6, 12, 26, 27, LXX) over the unclean, demonic beasts of the competing kingdoms. Jesus' exercise of authority (*exousia*) *over* the demonic world reinforces the significance of Jesus' earlier refusal

---

9. Perrin, 'Jesus as Priest', p. 83.

of *exousia* issuing *from* the demonic world (v. 6). Not surprisingly, Jesus' reputation continues to penetrate the region.

38. Having departed from the synagogue, Jesus *entered* the house of Simon (Peter), who is now mentioned for the first time in Luke.[10] He appears with the seemingly modest task of connecting Jesus with his mother-in-law who is stricken with *a high fever*. Her afflicted state is expressed with the verbal adjective *synechomenē*, which, though having the simple meaning of 'to suffer from', also denotes the sense of being hemmed in or held captive. Jesus' imminent healing of her fever is related as an outworking of his vocation to release the captives (v. 18). That this healing follows logically on the fact that *they asked him about her* implies faith on the part of the unnamed enquirers, who likely include Peter and other family members (though also cf. Mark 1:29).

39. Rebuking (*epetimēsen*) the fever just as he had rebuked the demon in the synagogue earlier in the day (v. 35), Jesus releases the woman from her affliction. More exactly, *it left her*, just as the demon had also exited the bodily space it had once occupied before Jesus' rebuke. While in Jewish antiquity not all illnesses are ascribed to demonic forces, some are – this one included.[11] The healed woman responds *immediately*. Rising up (*anastasa*), she begins to wait (imperfect: *diēkonei*) on them. If the afflicted mother-in-law is paradigmatic of those whom Jesus came to save, then the same woman now healed – having been raised up *to serve* – functions as a model of grateful discipleship.

40. The early evening influx of patients reflects that Jesus' healing of Peter's mother-in-law occurred on the Sabbath (the Sabbath like any Jewish day begins and ends at sundown). Once the Sabbath is over (or near enough over!), crowds begin to bring their loved ones for healing. The emphasis falls on Jesus' unflinching

---

10. Jesus' entrance implies a pre-existing relationship with Simon. Peter's appearance here anticipates the next passage (5:1–11) even as it secures early on his role as an eyewitness who both appears in and gives confirmation to Acts. See Green, *Vox Petri*, pp. 236–241.

11. Contra Liefeld (p. 873), who wonders aloud whether 'the fever is simply personified in effect'.

effectiveness as a healer: as for *all those who had any who were sick*, they do not leave disappointed.

41. As was the case with Peter's mother-in-law, many of these physically afflicted individuals are also severely spiritually afflicted, for *demons also came out of many*. Again, in these cases (which do not coincide with all the cases Jesus treats), an interconnection between demonic activity and disease is suggested. As the demons are exorcised, they mimic the wording of the baptismal voice. But Jesus is once again quick to silence them.

42. Marking the time of Jesus' departure, the transitional phrase *at daybreak* hints that his healing duties had occupied him the whole night, evidence of not only the numbers of the unwell in waiting but also the indefatigable dedication of the healer. Jesus now goes *into a deserted place* (cf. 5:16), perhaps to experience afresh the presence of the Spirit who had been closely associated with his last desert visit (v. 14). On discovering his whereabouts, the crowds follow in hot pursuit. On finding Jesus, they seek to detain him.

43–44. In response, Jesus insists on taking his leave, explaining that his proclamation of *the good news of the kingdom of God to the other cities* is necessary (*dei*). The verb *dei* is a favourite Lukan verb (e.g. 9:22; 13:33; 17:25; 19:5; 22:37; 24:7, 26, 44), denoting here and through the Gospel divine necessity. Just as the boy Jesus found it 'necessary' (*dei*) to be about his Father's business (2:49), so now the adult Jesus appeals to the same transcendent constraint. More exactly, he appeals to the necessity of proclamation (*euangelisasthai*) as well as to the fact of his sending (*apestalēn*), two key terms drawn from his programmatic Isaianic text (vv. 18–19). The proclamation centres around *the kingdom*, a term first signalled in 1:33 and now set into motion as a central concept in Luke's narrative. In the Greek sentence, the phrase *other cities* occupies the primary position, underscoring that Jesus' kingdom proclamation *must* have far-reaching scope, even reaching to *the synagogues of Judea*, which in Luke's parlance includes those situated in Galilee (cf. 23:5).

Theology

Sometimes modern-day Christians and their churches feel as if they are forced to choose between one of two roads: the path of proclamation or the path of social justice. Some churches pride themselves on 'preaching the Word'; others seek to engage with local communities through programmes, events or more personal involvement. All too rarely do we meet a church that truly excels at both. This is a false and unfortunate dichotomy.

This phenomenon may not be unrelated to two different kinds of criticism sometimes levelled against the church. It is no secret that people outside the church have sometimes regarded Christians – justly or unjustly – as busybodies who have nothing better to do than to make their orthodoxy a basis for telling others how they ought to think and act. Meanwhile, observers both inside and outside the church are rightly suspicious of Christian-style moralism bereft of convincing foundations. In this vein, the German philosopher Friedrich Nietzsche once complained – perhaps fairly – of the great British novelist George Eliot that inside her circles 'one must rehabilitate oneself after every little emancipation from theology by showing in a veritably awe-inspiring manner what a moral fanatic one is'. Some are fanatical about the finer points of their theology; others are fanatical about their moral stance on social-political issues.

When the townspeople of Nazareth converged in order to inflict violence on their Sabbath-day preacher, it was a misguided act of fanatical outrage which had foreclosed on the word of Jesus Christ and his ministry of release. Luke presents Jesus' acts of healing and exorcisms as the embodiment of his preaching; his preaching, as a commentary on his mighty acts. Together preaching, healing and exorcism *were* Jesus' ministry of release. In the person of Jesus, Christological word and Christological deed are mutually corroborating. And the necessary condition for the continuing integration of word and deed in the life of the church, Luke just might add, is the anointing of the Spirit described in Isaiah 61. The gospel is good news because the gospel – and only the gospel – brings freedom, and that freedom can be mediated only through a Spirit-endowed community.

B. Calling of the first disciples (5:1–11)

Context
From the baptism up until now, Jesus has been functioning as a 'solo act'. The reader has still not met his disciples, all of whom would become pillars in the movement, and some of whom would play a leading role in Acts. Just as Jesus' itinerant ministry is beginning to broaden out in geographic scope (4:43–44), the master now directs his attention to individual beneficiaries. The better part of Luke's remaining narrative is peppered with one-to-one encounters, each provoking an existential crisis. This is the first of such encounters. But what makes this meeting extraordinary is not only the stunning chain of events preceding Simon Peter's moment of decision, but also his significance in the early church. Luke wants to demonstrate the personal impact wrought by Jesus and, fittingly, there is no more paradigmatic example of this than in the life of the lead apostle Peter.

Comment
   1–2. Whatever the duration of the preaching tour reported in 4:44, Simon's presence in this episode leads us to believe that Jesus has now returned to Capernaum (cf. 4:31, 38). Apparently, Capernaum has now become a home base for Jesus, perhaps in place of unbelieving Nazareth (4:16–30). The episode is clearly one and the same as that recounted in Mark 1:16–20, but also clearly different – notwithstanding their striking similarities – from a story recounted in John 21:1–14.
   Setting the scene, Luke describes a crowd pressing in *to hear the word of God*. The presence of so many fervent listeners is an indicator of Jesus' mounting popularity; it may also serve as a point of reference for his later insistence that eager listening is insufficient (6:46–49; 8:13). There must also be faithful obedience, precisely as it is expressed in the response of Peter and the other disciples. Equating Jesus' preaching with *the word of God* (cf. 8:11, 21; 11:28), Luke characterizes it as both a word *about* God and a word *from* God contained in the person of Jesus. In order to secure some breathing space from the crowds, the teacher positions himself *beside the lake of Gennesaret* (cf. Mark 4:1–2; 2:13; 3:7–9), a body of water some 8 miles west to east

and 14 miles north to south. Eventually, Jesus decides it is not enough to stand beside the water; he must get *on to* the water, and spots two boats, either one of which might help accomplish just that. The craft's owners (whom on the basis of Mark 1:16–20 we surmise to be Simon, Andrew, James and John) had vacated them so as to wash the nets after a long night of luckless fishing.

3. The typical first-century Galilean fishing boat, roughly 26 feet (8 m) long by 6.5 feet (2 m) wide, would have been too big for Jesus to move himself. So on entering one of the two boats, the one which happened to belong to Simon, Jesus must enlist his friend's help in putting out from shore. Ostensibly this would be to achieve a better angle for communicating with the audience which was now lining up along the water's edge. Though it cannot be proved that Jesus knew whose boat was whose, Luke's detail that he had chosen *the one belonging to Simon* hints that the imminent call – sealing not only Simon Peter's salvation but also his role as a first among equals (*primus inter pares*) among the Twelve – is grounded in a larger elective purpose. Simon cannot be far away, since he complies with the request immediately; his prompt compliance is understandable, given Jesus' earlier healing of his mother-in-law (4:38–39). Now taking a seat on the boat (the typical posture of a teacher), Jesus continues to teach (*edidasken*).

4–5. Having concluded his teaching, Jesus repeats his request to Simon that the boat be put out, this time into the deep so that the fisherman and his hired help together might *let down* the nets *for a catch* of fish, more specifically, a species of tilapia today known as *musht* or St Peter's fish. Responding to Jesus, Simon addresses him as *Master* (*epistata*), a term of respect appropriate to rabbis, but a term too which will come to stand in sharp contrast to the fisherman's later form of address, 'Lord' (v. 8).[12] Simon hardly conceals his reluctance, naturally enough since he and his partners have just spent the night toiling with no results. Yet what tips the scales for Simon, despite these reservations, is the *person* doing the bidding: strictly on account of Jesus' *word* he agrees.

---

12. Marshall (p. 203) prefers to interpret *epistata* more specifically, stating the 'word is used only by disciples or near-disciples'.

6–7. Simon's obedience is quickly repaid with phenomenal success. The size of the catch, underscored by the near breaking of the nets and the virtual swamping of the two boats, would also be unprecedented for even the most experienced of fishermen.[13] Given that the other three Evangelists frame their boat scenes as symbolic narratives about the church, and given, too, Peter's remarkable sermon in Acts 2, the miracle is almost certainly meant to foreshadow his apostolic ministry.[14]

8–10a. The spectacular nature of the catch literally forces (now called) *Simon Peter* to *Jesus' knees*. The shift from Simon to *Simon Peter* is certainly intentional: it is Luke's way of signalling the fisherman's destiny, as the rock of the church (Matt. 16:16) is just now coming into view (cf. Luke 6:14; Acts 10:5, 18, 32; 11:13). Prostration is a typical response to theophany, and though it is unlikely that the astonished fisherman is inferring Jesus' full-blown divinity at this point, he has certainly become convinced of his divine origins in some sense. Now calling Jesus *Lord* (*kyrie*) (which may mean 'Sir' but in Luke's narrative carries far weightier connotations), Peter urges him to depart on account of his painful consciousness of sin.[15] Confronted by the holiness of Jesus, he recognizes that he is *a sinful man* (*anēr hamartōlos*) – not necessarily a profligate man (although the word can have that meaning in Luke [5:30; 19:7]), but a man who has in an instant discovered his unworthiness before the divine. Yet the astonishment is not Peter's alone. *All who were with him* share his reaction of amazement or a gripping fear (the sense of *thambos gar perieschen*), as do the

---

13. Hypothesizing the boats' weight capacity based on a size comparison to a typical first-century fishing boat, we might estimate the weight of the catch to have approached at least a ton of fish, roughly the equivalent of 500 or more mature *musht*.

14. According to Bovon (pp. 171–172), the presence of two boats 'may have something to do, in Luke's presentation, with the twofold character of the Christian church as Jewish and Gentile', even if 'Luke does not draw any explicit allegorical parallels'.

15. On the double meaning of 'Lord' at 5:12 and in Luke in general, see Rowe, *Narrative Christology*, pp. 89–91.

now-identified owners of the second boat, *James and John, sons of Zebedee.*

10b. In response to Simon's request, Jesus issues a command typical of theophanic encounters: *Do not be afraid* (cf. 1:13; 2:10), only then to make an assertion which is part prediction and part promise. By Jesus' reckoning, it is no longer sufficient for Simon to dedicate himself to catching fish: now is the moment to begin catching (*zōgrōn*) people. While the verb can be applied to contexts of fishing and hunting, its core meaning pertains to the notion of capturing alive or keeping alive (especially in the LXX; cf. Num. 31:15, 18; Josh. 2:13; 6:25). In this sense, to 'catch' is to enfold.

11. Although the episode has focused almost exclusively on Peter up to this point, now the lens widens to include the response of the other key players. Having beached the boats, the men now desert their trade in order to follow the 'master' who has just become their 'Lord'. Undoubtedly, Luke intends the movement from encounter to 'all-in' allegiance as a paradigm for all discipleship. For the Evangelist, here as elsewhere, the test of true repentance and discipleship is a willingness to hold loosely one's worldly goods.

Theology

Jesus had asked Simon two favours. The first was to put the boat out in the water so that Jesus might carry out his teaching more effectively. This was an entirely reasonable request. The second favour was to put out into the deep and put down the nets for a catch. This was *not* at all reasonable, at least not by Simon's reckoning. Regardless of the fact that his experience counselled him otherwise, our professional fisherman chooses to obey his carpenter master. He obeys strictly on the basis of Jesus' word. According to Luke, in other words, acts of faith take flight not in response to gut instinct or intuition or personal fancies, but in response to the word of God. Though Simon's faith was a begrudging faith, it was a sufficient faith to secure the miracle.

On recognizing God's activity through Jesus, Simon Peter is undone by his own sense of unworthiness and begs him to depart. Not budging an inch, Jesus instead calls the 'sinful man' to catch other sinful people like Simon Peter himself. It is this glorious task

that prompts the disciples to leave everything in order to follow
Jesus. And yet following Jesus is no guarantee of instant 'success'.
Simon himself does not begin to embrace this vocation until Pentecost in Acts 2. For Peter, between Luke 5 and Acts 2 stands a long
and winding road of discipleship. As far as Luke is concerned,
leaving all for Jesus' sake is no guarantee of evangelistic or
ministerial success. It is, however, the first step in a long journey of
day-in, day-out following.

C. Opposition from the Pharisees (5:12–32)

Context
With the calling of his first disciples (5:1–11), Jesus has taken on all
the appearances of a movement leader. This, combined with the
spectacular miracles performed in 4:31 – 5:11, now makes him a force
to be reckoned with, at least so far as the official religious leadership
is concerned – and a threatening force at that. In this string of three
passages (5:12–16, 17–26, 27–32), the conflict between Jesus and his
opponents comes to the forefront, beginning with the healing of a
man with leprosy (5:12–16). As impressive as the healing may be, the
leaders' determination to protect their own role as Israel's
gatekeepers, together with Jesus' seemingly blasphemous words
(5:21), causes them to turn a jaundiced eye on the next miracle (5:17–
26). Finally, with Jesus' consorting with the likes of tax collectors,
early silent opposition (5:21–22) gives way to open grumbling (5:30).

The root cause for the Jewish leaders' vexation is not unrelated
to the fact that all three of these passages deal with atonement. In
stipulating cases requiring atonement, the Hebrew Scriptures draw
no hard-and-fast distinction between moral lapse and ritual
uncleanness. Whether having incurred uncleanness due to a skin
ailment (as in the case of the man with leprosy) or being in need of
forgiveness of sin (as in the case of the paralysed man), or being
compromised in terms of both moral failings and ritual uncleanness
(as perhaps in the case of Levi), all such instances would have
required atoning measures (cf. Lev. 5 – 6). In this section, Jesus
shockingly presents himself as the sole agent of atonement. He
extends such atonement outside the standard protocols, personnel
and sacred space. To say that Jesus' actions had implications for the

entire Jewish cultus would be an understatement, and the Jewish leaders were among the first to realize this.

Comment
i. Jesus cleanses a man of leprosy (5:12–16)

12. Jesus' presence in a population centre within the region (*one of the cities*) helps explain the note in verse 15 regarding the broad circulation of the miracle's report. Suddenly (*idou*) appears a man whose body is racked *with leprosy*, more likely to be any one of a number of skin ailments rather than Hansen's disease.[16] On seeing Jesus, the man literally 'falls on his face' (*pesōn epi prosōpon*), a posture similar to that adopted by Peter in the previous passage (5:8). His prostration serves not only to express deep homage, but also, again, to mimic the characteristic human response to theophanic encounter. The same double function attaches to the man's address for Jesus, *Lord* (*kyrie*), which here conveys the simple sense of 'Sir', even as it betrays Luke's deeper Christological agenda.[17] While the man has no doubts regarding Jesus' power to render him clean through healing (thereby re-enfranchising him in the cultic life and broader society; cf. Lev. 13:45–46), he is uncertain as to whether Jesus in fact wishes to do so.

13. Very quickly any such uncertainties are dispelled, as Jesus extends his hand (*cheir*; just as accurately translated 'forearm') and effects an instantaneous healing. Jesus' touching the man with leprosy is remarkable not only because he does not ordinarily require physical contact in order to perform a healing (cf. 7:1–10), but also because the very act of touching an unclean individual normally rendered the toucher unclean. At a psychological level, Jesus may have recognized the man's need for physical touch. Yet on another level, Jesus' demonstrated ability to confer ritual cleanness by touch without himself incurring uncleanness marks him out as a kind of high priest, for only such could impart holiness/cleanness like a contagion.[18] Meanwhile, Jesus' extension

---

16. Fitzmyer, p. 517.
17. Rowe, *Narrative Christology*, pp. 89–92.
18. Fletcher-Louis, 'Messiah: Part 2', pp. 66–70.

of his arm in connection with leprosy brings to mind Moses' stretching out of his leprous arm (Exod. 4:6–8), one of several signs that Israel's redeemer enjoyed divine backing.

14. Jesus follows up the healing with a twofold instruction, first requiring the man who formerly had leprosy *to tell no one*, and, second, asking him to show himself to the priests *for a testimony to them (eis martyrion autois)* or perhaps a 'testimony *against* them'. Jesus' admonition of silence is part of a larger secrecy theme operative in all three Synoptic Gospels. Its historical origins in the life of Jesus can hardly be doubted and are easy enough to explain: on a very practical level, it would have been important for any would-be messiah to manage carefully the timing of the messianic 'roll-out'. The second instruction, namely, that the man with leprosy report to the priests, may be motivated by at least two concerns. First, though having already usurped the priestly role by declaring, 'Be made clean' (*katharistheti*) (cf. Lev. 13:6, 13, 17; etc.), Jesus still realizes the practical necessity of involving the priests in the man's reintegration into the cultus.[19] At the same time, when viewed against the backdrop of Moses' outstretched leprous arm, which was essentially a witness *against* Pharaoh, Luke's dative construction *to them (autois)* soon begins to look less like a simple indirect object and more like a dative of disadvantage: 'as a witness *against* them'.[20] Having experienced various levels of active and passive resistance from the Galilean religious leaders, Luke's Jesus intends the cleansed man to serve as 'Evidence A' that continued resistance would ensure the relinquishing of their priestly role to another.

15–16. The news of the healing sends a fresh shockwave through the region. *Now more than ever the word* concerning him goes out. In response, the crowds now come with a double agenda: to hear Jesus and to have their diseases healed. Meanwhile, Jesus meets the heightened attention by continuing (note the iterative imperfect *ēn hypochōrōn*) to retreat into the wilderness where he could pray.

---

19. Contra Nolland, p. 229.

20. In the former case, the man's showing himself amounts to an 'FYI'; in the latter case, it is closer to an indictment.

ii. Healing of a paralysed man (5:17–26)

17. Jesus' audience has now expanded to include religious authorities from every corner of Galilee and Judea, and within Judea, the greater Jerusalem area. They come to see this new teacher-healer for themselves and to investigate the basis for his meteoric rise (5:15). Meanwhile, in continuity with his inaugural activity (4:14, 36), Jesus retains *the power of the Lord* to heal. This is not necessarily to suggest that he had intermittent access to such power but rather to stress his continuity with the apostolic church, which also relies on the Spirit's power (Acts 1:8; 3:12; 4:7).

18–19. In the midst of his teaching, Jesus is interrupted by a small gathering of men lowering a paralysed man from the ceiling. Initially, the men had been trying to find (imperfect *ezētoun*) a way to bring the paralysed man to Jesus, but they could not even get near the door. Undeterred, they create an alternative route through the roof of the house.[21] In the end, they successfully lower – from at least 6 feet up – their companion both *into the middle* (*eis to meson*) of the gathered crowd and *in front of* or before (*enōpion*) Jesus. Luke's emphatic description of the healing space seems intentional, perhaps as if to symbolize the in-the-midst (*en mesō*) presence of the atoning high priest (cf. Lev. 16:16).

20. Strikingly the text yields no indication of the paralysed man's faith; rather, Jesus responds on perceiving the faith of his supporters. Such an insight need not have been preternatural, since the men's perseverance and ingenuity may themselves have been sufficient demonstration of their trust. If the paralysed man's unconventional entrance is unexpected, Jesus' response is all the more so: he declares that the man's sins have been forgiven.[22] The implications for communal, intercessory prayer hardly need elaborating.

---

21. Where Mark's version tells us that they 'dug through' the ceiling (2:4), as would be fitting for Palestinian mud roofs, Luke envisions the removal of clay tiles, perhaps as a way of accommodating his Roman hearers who would have been more familiar with tiled roofs.

22. Jesus' response is surprising but not incoherent; cf. b. Ned. 41a: 'Nobody gets up from their sick-bed until all their sins are forgiven' (my translation).

21–22. On hearing Jesus declare the man forgiven, the scribes and Pharisees are instantly riled. For them, his assertion constitutes a blasphemous usurpation of authority, since declarations of forgiveness could only appropriately be made by either Yahweh (Exod. 34:7; Ps. 103:12) or Yahweh's appointed agent.[23] On the face of it, the teachers' reaction is not entirely unreasonable, especially since Scripture clearly indicates that forgiveness is a strictly divine prerogative. But when Luke uses the verb *to question* (*dialogizein*), it usually conveys the sense of a perverse internal reasoning (12:17; 20:14); and given Jesus' stern rebuke in verse 22, we surmise that the religious leaders' mental processes are off the mark. Apparently, the furrowed brows should have known better. At this point, Jesus' insight into the hearts of his detractors exceeds the range of ordinary human perception; at this point, too, the promise of God scattering those who are proud 'in the thoughts of their hearts' (1:51) begins to be realized.

23. Having forced one sort of crisis among his hearers by the declaration of forgiveness, now Jesus adds a second layer of complexity by asking whether forgiving or healing is easier. On reflection, the query admits no straightforward answer. On the one hand, it may be easier to *say 'Your sins are forgiven'* than to *say 'Stand up and walk'* simply because the first claim by itself cannot be empirically disproved. On the other hand, it may be said that the act of healing is easier inasmuch as it does not necessitate the same priestly office required for forgiving. Jesus' question is rhetorical, designed not so much to solicit a specific answer as to force reflection on the monumental nature of his declaration.

24. Such a sign is immediately forthcoming in Jesus' threefold command to the paralysed man to rise, take up his stretcher and go home. The imperative *stand up* (*egeirē*) draws on resurrection language, which Luke arguably employs, here as well as in 6:8, to signal that Jesus is the source of resurrection hope. Such hope is provisionally intimated through this act of healing and, paradox-

---

23. Authorization for humans forgiving sin is not unprecedented: see 2 Sam. 12:13; Tg. Isa. 53:6; 4Q242, 3–4; 11Q13 II, 4–13; 2 En. 64:5; Josephus, *Ant.* 6.92.

ically, will come to take sharper form precisely through the very opposition which Jesus endures, even in this section of the Gospel. In complying with Jesus' directives, the erstwhile paralysed man becomes something of a walking public sign, the beneficiary of a miracle wrought *so that you may know that the Son of Man has authority on earth to forgive sins*. Of course, both in the original situation and in the house churches where Luke's Gospel was first read, this would have been heard as an astonishing claim!

In this the first use of *Son of Man* in Luke, the Evangelist is – despite the doubts of sceptical scholars – preserving historical reminiscence of Jesus' self-identification with the Danielic Son of Man. This supposition is supported by Luke's triangulation (even as he depends on Mark) of key terms and phrases from Daniel 7: 'Son of Man' (Dan. 7:13), 'authority' (*exousia* [Dan. 7:14, three times; cf. 7:6, 12, 26, 27, LXX]) and 'on the earth' (*epi tēs gēs* [Dan. 7:17, Theodotion], *en tē gē* [Dan. 7:23, Theodotion]). At the same time, Jesus' curious lead-in tag *so that you may know* flags up phrasing from the Exodus narrative (Exod. 8:22; 9:14, 29). Building on the Exodus imagery of Luke 5:12–16, the allusion establishes an analogy between Jesus' forthcoming miracle and the plagues of judgment against Pharaoh. Jesus' dependence on texts drawn from Daniel 7 and the Exodus plagues cycle suggests that his confrontation with the religious leaders finds its analogy in two familiar stories, both involving intense conflict between God's agent and the forces of evil. Luke's point is twofold: first, that the redemption which began in the exodus from Egypt was now about to come into its fullness in and through Jesus as a new Moses; and second, that Daniel's vision, which foresaw the capitulation of the pagan kingdoms to the kingdom of God, was now also about to be fulfilled through Jesus as the Son of Man.

25–26. Promptly complying with Jesus' command, the healed man exits the scene, glorifying God – no doubt hinting at Jesus' divinity. The crowd likewise glorifies God but remains bewildered by the *strange things* (*paradoxa*).[24]

---

24. Luke's characterization of the crowd may not be entirely positive; compare Wis. 5:2: 'When the unrighteous see them [i.e. the righteous

iii. Calling of Levi (5:27–32)

27–28. Following an indeterminate period (*after this*), Jesus spots a *tax-collector* (*telōnēs*) by the name of Levi and calls him to follow. Under contract with either the tetrarch or more local officials, Galilee-based tax collectors collected sales taxes, real-estate taxes and toll taxes imposed along travelling routes between cities. It was a role that lent itself all too well to extortionary practices. Given the high degree of contact between tax collectors and Gentiles in this profession, the stricter Jewish sects would have considered tax collectors inherently unclean, much like the man with leprosy of 5:12–16.[25] The Evangelist identifies this figure as Levi, though according to Mark 2:14 he was the 'son of Alphaeus' and according to Matthew 9:9 he is 'Matthew'. The discrepancy between Luke 5:27 and Matthew 9:9 has sometimes been said to reflect two different disciples, but this is unlikely. One explanation presents itself on the possibility that Matthew had followed Roman custom of retaining no fewer than three names (*praenomen, nomen* and *cognomen*).[26] An alternative explanation is that 'Matthew' served as a nickname, perhaps imposed by Jesus himself. Like the paralysed man before him (5:25) and the man with the withered hand after him (6:8), Levi is prompted to get up or rise (ESV) (*anastas*). The repetition of the verb speaks of a certain appropriateness in all three men rising, since all three experience transformations that together anticipate a much fuller rising (*anistēmi*) at the resurrection. And like the fisherman of 5:11, Levi is led to leave *everything* behind and 'follow him'. For Luke, following Jesus means leaving everything behind (cf. 14:33), not for the sake of duty or for the sake of sacrifice itself, but simply because Jesus says, *Follow me.*

(note 24 *cont.*) standing with great confidence] they will be shaken with dreadful fear, and they will be amazed at the marvel [*paradoxō*] of salvation' (translation my own).

25. DeSilva, *DJG*, p. 145.

26. Fitzmyer, p. 590, dubs this as 'theoretically possible'; Bock, p. 493, is more sanguine. As Eckhard Schnabel points out too, however, this theory is problematized by the fact that Levi and Matthew are Hebrew names, not Roman names.

29. Clearly out of a deep appreciation for Jesus' calling on his life, Levi makes *a great banquet (epoiēsen dochēn megalēn)*, much as Abraham had done – recounted with the very same Greek phrasing – on Isaac's weaning (Gen. 21:8, LXX).[27] If the connection is intentional, it would certainly be in keeping with Luke's interest in marking out Jesus as the new Isaac, the true sacrificial victim, now on the cusp of his ministry career. Invitees to this occasion quite naturally include members of Levi's network, whose reclining (*katekeimenoi*) posture conveys the formality of the event and therefore (with *a large crowd* in tow) its costliness.

30. The mixed company attending the banquet attracts the attention of the *Pharisees and their scribes*, presumably after the fact. Addressing their complaint (*egongyzon*) to a group of his disciples, they question the propriety of eating with tax collectors and sinners. The term for *complaining (gongyzō)* means 'to grumble', an activity characterizing the disobedient among the Sinai generation (Exod. 15:24; 16:7–8; Num. 14:2; etc.).[28] Given Luke's interest in presenting Jesus as the driver behind a new exodus, this may not be an insignificant point.

31–32. Responding on behalf of his followers, Jesus counters with a riddle that identifies Jesus with a physician and essentially divides the rest of humanity into two categories: the healthy *righteous* or the unwell *sinners*.[29] It is the latter whom Jesus calls *to repentance*. The riposte functions as a parable, forcing his hearers to identify themselves with one of the two groups, even as Luke forces his readers to do the same. Those who search their hearts and see themselves as unwell sinners will recognize that Jesus has come for them.

---

27. The phrase also occurs in 1 Esd. 3:1.
28. BDAG, p. 164.
29. Here the term 'sinner' (*hamartōlos*) generally denotes those who defiantly transgress God's law. But in Luke (e.g. at 18:9–14), it often designates 'someone . . . [who] had violated a group consensus as to how one should live a law-abiding life before God. So when Jesus is accosted for partaking of the company of sinners, it is because he and his disciples failed to adopt the particular way of life regarded as valid by . . . a particular sect such as the Pharisees' (Bird, *DJG*, p. 865).

Theology

By touching a man with leprosy, imparting forgiveness and healing to a paralysed man, and having table fellowship with tax collectors, Jesus was breaking all the rules – and is criticized accordingly. As we will learn from the rest of the story, he was in fact uniquely qualified to do all these things, simply on account of who he was, though Pharisees and scribes are not mentally prepared to accept this point. But the more fundamental reason that the religious leaders are quick to take offence is because they do not understand that they, no less than the tax collectors and sinners, are in dire need of an atoning physician.

The religious leaders of Jesus' day were not the only ones plagued by this tragic flaw. From experience, we know that sometimes members of a given social circle, network, race, tribe, demographic or political persuasion will gravitate towards an unbecoming us-versus-them polarity. In order to justify themselves, such group members will sometimes go so far as to denigrate these 'others' as especially sinful and therefore as unworthy of human embrace. Luke would remind his readers that whenever we consider ourselves morally superior to others, this not only dehumanizes those whom Jesus has called but also makes following the divine physician virtually impossible. Jesus came to call sinners. Yet it is a label that cannot finally be owned by those who are inwardly preoccupied with congratulating themselves on what they believe, what they do and what they stand for. Such, it seems, will tragically never hear Jesus' call or experience a life of following him.

D. Further controversies with the Pharisees (5:33 – 6:11)

Context

If there is a common thread connecting the three episodes contained in this section, it is controversy related to two basic Jewish observances: fasting and Sabbath-keeping. Yet as self-contained as this section appears, it also builds on what has gone before, for in 5:33–39 Jesus is simply offering a fuller explanation for his earlier dining (5:27–32). Meanwhile, he speaks into an ever mounting current of opposition. The silent murmurings of the

religious leaders (5:17–26), which had soon enough given way to
their interrogation of his disciples (5:30), now expresses itself in
direct confrontation with Jesus himself. As these controversies
unfold in the course of this section, matters only become more
intense. Indeed, by 6:11 the opposition is already entertaining
thoughts of inflicting physical violence on Jesus. For this reason, it
is not so surprising that Jesus, even at this early point of the story,
is already anticipating his death (5:35).

Comment
i. Questions about fasting (5:33–39)
33. Censure involving food-related matters now arises from
another quarter. If in the previous passage Jesus sought to defend
his followers by critiquing the holiness code of the Pharisees, now
certain unidentified critics are pointing out that the practices of the
Jesus sect are at variance with both the Pharisees *and* the followers
of the celebrated Baptizer. Since the Jesus community had enjoyed
close ties with the latter, any conspicuous differences between the
'Jesus group' and the 'John group' might be exploited by anyone
seeking to undermine the credibility of the former. In contrast to
John's followers, who *frequently fast*, Jesus' disciples are again (cf.
5:30) charged with profligate eating and drinking.[30]
34–35. In response to his critics, Jesus turns to a parable. His
rejoinder carries no criticism of the practices of either John or the
Pharisees; instead, it is a salvation-historical argument buoyed by
wedding imagery. In the ancient world, Jewish weddings were
extended festive events involving considerable consumption of
food and wine. To contemplate a fast during a first-century Jewish
wedding would be, in short, to imagine the unimaginable – as well
as the inappropriate. As Luke's readers would have understood
quickly enough, Jesus himself is the *bridegroom*; his disciples, the
wedding-guests. Beyond that, the metaphor is somewhat puzzling.
Equally mysterious would have been Jesus' reference to the time
when the bridegroom will be taken away from them. At least some of the

---

30. The combination of eating and drinking is distinctively Lukan; cf.
7:33–34; 22:30.

mystery is solved at a later point in the story, when it becomes clear in retrospect that Jesus here is anticipating his own death. Given the recurring scriptural comparison between human marriage and Yahweh's covenantal relationship with Israel, Luke's post-Easter readers would have readily found in this language hints of both Jesus' divinity and the announcement of a new covenant (Jer. 31:31–34). The exile, the time of Israel's mourning, was over (cf. Dan. 9:1–3); Yahweh was now poised to once again be husband to Israel (Isa. 54:5–6), and that through the person of Jesus. Again, this was to be an unusual wedding, for a time would come when the bridegroom would be taken away. And at that time fasting *would* be fitting. There is no reason to infer, on the basis of either these verses or the several references to fasting in Acts (13:2–3; 14:23), that Luke understands Christian fasting as continuing mournful reflection on the passion. Rather, for attendants of Jesus the bridegroom, fasting is appropriate preparation for a special imparting of the Spirit (Luke 24:49–53; Acts 1:1–11).

36–39. The festive imagery now finds some continuity in two analogies, both of which press home the dangers of imposing outmoded forms of spirituality on to the new salvific reality being ushered in by Jesus. Jesus is introducing *a new garment*, reminiscent of the radiant wedding garments promised to Israel's eschatological priesthood (Isa. 61:10); Jesus is also bringing *new wine*, like the wine of Isaiah 25:6, fitting for the messianic banquet at hand. To patch the Mosaic cultic system, symbolically torn (*eschisthē*) in the rending of the temple curtain (Luke 23:45), with bits and pieces ripped (*schisas*) from the new economy would not only be a mismatch but would violate the integrity of that which Jesus is establishing. To force the substance of Jesus' proclamation into the forms afforded under the law would be equally misguided. There is little choice but to receive what God is doing in the present day – to put on the new clothes and to drink the new wine.

ii. Questions about the Sabbath (6:1–11)

1–2. A certain Sabbath day finds Jesus and his disciples neither harvesting nor storing up grain from the fields, which would be a clear violation of the Sabbath (Exod. 34:21), but helping themselves to free-standing produce, as permitted by Deuteronomy 23:24–25.

Yet, on the Pharisees' reading of Scripture, any rights granted by
Deuteronomy 23:24–25 were rendered null and void by an
overriding concern to maintain the sanctity of the Sabbath.
According to the Pharisees, that is, the disciples' actions constituted
harvesting (m. Šabb. 7:2; Philo, *Moses* 2.4) and were therefore *not
lawful* – a serious charge.

3–4. Jesus defends his disciples by making a surprising appeal to
the precedent of David. More exactly, he points to the moment
when one Sabbath day the anointed king partakes of the sacred
bread of the Presence (1 Sam. 21:1–9), food ordinarily reserved for the
priests (Exod. 40:23; Lev. 24:5–9).[31] Hardly transparent in its
meaning, Jesus' argument has been variously interpreted. The
passage is often taken to mean that in the case of emergency situations, human exigency trumps cultic prescriptions. One problem
with this interpretation, however, is that there is no indication that
either David or his men (or, for that matter, Jesus and his men)
were in danger of malnourishment. Moreover, we agree with
Edwards when he writes that it would be 'inconceivable that Jesus
or any other rabbi would declare human supremacy over' the
Sabbath.[32] Another possibility is that Jesus as the Messiah had a
right to transcend the law, just as David had a right to do in a
smaller degree. But given countless indications of Jesus' interest in
keeping the law, this reading seems to render Jesus as a rather
capricious devotee of Torah. A third and better interpretation
begins with the premise that Jesus is invoking David not as a
representative human but as a high priest (Ps. 110). In this case,
Jesus is justifying his behaviour on the unstated grounds that he
and his disciples are priests in the same order as David – not a levit-
ical priest but a royal priest after the order of Melchizedek
(20:41–44).[33] This interpretation is confirmed in Jesus' description
of Davidic partaking (*labōn ephagen kai edōken* – and took and ate . . .

---

31. The Sabbath-day timing of David's visit to Ahimelech is presupposed
    in the Jewish tradition; see Bock, p. 524.

32. Edwards, p. 179.

33. Perrin, 'Mistaken Priestly Identity', pp. 169–176; *Jesus the Priest*,
    pp. 190–207.

and gave), which anticipates the phraseology of the Lord's Supper (*labōn arton . . . kai edōken* – 'took a loaf of bread . . . and gave', 22:19), where Jesus announces his own high priestly, messianic atoning role.

5. In an exegetical move that was already standard in the first century, Jesus then combines the figure of the eschatological David with the Danielic 'son of man' (Dan. 7), and then aligns himself with both figures. Given certain evidence that the *Son of Man*, like David, was also a priestly figure, and evidence, too, that priests had certain extraordinary authorities to perform work on the Sabbath, Jesus' point begins to come into view: quite apart from whether his disciples' actions should be considered unlawful Sabbath 'harvesting', both he and his disciples could rightfully glean on the Sabbath because he was establishing a new priesthood around himself as *lord of the sabbath*. This is no small claim: as 'Lord of the Sabbath', Jesus is the creator of time!

6–8. A second Sabbath controversy brews around a man with a withered hand. Whatever the exact nature of his disability, the condition was not just a physical problem, but entailed spiritual and social implications as well. Those with deformed limbs were forbidden full participation in temple life. The Pharisees, now joined by the scribes, are scrutinizing Jesus, even as they will do two more times in the narrative (14:1; 20:20). Though posing as willing members of Jesus' audience, they are less interested in the substance of his teaching than in finding grounds for legal charges. One such possible ground, so they thought, might surface if Jesus should choose to heal on the Sabbath, in contravention of Pharisaic practice (m. Šabb. 14:3–4; 22:6). Although aware of their inward thoughts (*dialogismois*, a term that consistently carries negative connotations in Luke; cf. 2:35; 5:22; 9:46–47; 24:38), Jesus nonetheless calls the man into the middle of the room. The first command in Jesus' instruction (*egeire kai stēthi*; 'Rise up and stand!') in the fuller narrative gestures towards resurrection, likely suggesting that the healing is meant as a picture of Israel's impending transformation from its withered spiritual state to resurrection.[34]

---

34. See pp. 102–103 above.

9. Moments before performing the miracle, Jesus turns to his opponents and asks whether it is better to *do good* and give life or to *do harm* and destroy life. Certainly, on any understanding of the Sabbath day (1 Macc. 2:39–41; m. Šabb. 16:1–7; m. Yoma 8:6–7; Mek. Exod. 31:13), the former option would have been the obvious choice. Thus the question is rhetorical, effectively serving a twofold purpose. On one level, Jesus is establishing the warrant for his own impending Sabbath healing, notwithstanding the inward objections of his opponents. On another level, Jesus is unmasking his adversaries' dark thoughts which stand in stark contrast to his own life-giving actions.

10. Having fixed his gaze on his opponents, perhaps after the fashion of Yahweh who fixes his gaze in judgment (Jer. 16:17; Amos 9:4), he orders the debilitated man to stretch out his hand. As the man heeds Jesus' instructions, his hand is immediately restored. The scene could hardly be more reminiscent, once again (cf. commentary on 5:13), of the moment when Yahweh instructs Moses to stretch out his hand as a sign for Pharaoh. Luke's point is clear enough: just as Moses had stretched out his hand before unbelieving Pharaoh in anticipation of much greater judgments, so too does this beneficiary of Jesus' healing powers.

11. The scribes and Pharisees respond to the miracle on both an emotive and a practical level. First, they are *filled with fury (eplēsthēsan anoias)*, a quality that denotes not only rage but also rash foolishness. Second, they now begin to confer with one another about *what they might do to Jesus*. The irony of Jesus' question to them has now come full circle. Having just been asked whether it is lawful to give or take life on the Sabbath, Jesus' enemies are now unwittingly framing their own answer by making plans to take Jesus' life.

Theology

In the aftermath of the French Revolution, in an effort both to eradicate earlier traces of a bygone rule and to show that a new day had dawned, the upstart regime implemented the so-called 'French Revolutionary Calendar'. The shift from the monarchy to the Republic was so profound, the revolutionaries believed, that an entirely new way of thinking about time was in order. As these three episodes together illustrate, an analogous transformation of the calendar was underway in the impending transition to Jesus' kingdom. In the first of these scenes (5:33–39), Jesus is not rescinding fasting in principle, for if that were the case it would be difficult to explain instances of fasting in the early church (e.g. Acts 13:2–3; 14:23). Rather, it seems, insofar as Second Temple Jews had long commemorated the destruction of the temple through fasting, such practices would no longer be necessary. This is because, as the Evangelist will make clear soon enough, Jesus is poised to establish a new and final temple (Luke 20:9–19). Meanwhile, whereas Judaism from the time of Moses observed the Sabbath on the *last* day of every week, early Christians chose, in the light of Jesus' resurrection, to move the day of rest to the *first* day of the week (Luke 24:1; cf. 1 Cor. 16:2; Rev. 1:10). For Jesus' followers, no less than for the French Jacobins, a new rule meant that the timing and particulars of earlier observances stood to be revised.

But what exactly did the coming of this new kingdom mean? Well, first, if we take the wedding imagery seriously, it meant worship in this new era was to be characterized by *celebration*. Second, just as new wine demanded new wineskins, Jesus anticipates his followers ever adopting new forms, new practices and new traditions, commensurate with this in-breaking reality. When it comes to their corporate practices, therefore, followers of Jesus must exhibit a Christ-honouring *flexibility*. Third, on the shared premise that Jesus was 'Lord of the Sabbath', Luke invites Christ-followers to enjoy – much as Jesus' hungry disciples enjoyed – a Sabbath marked by *restoration*. Fourth and finally, a proper Sabbath must have an outward-facing, life-giving aspect: the key word here is *mission*. Now that the kingdom has come, Luke would have us realize, days of fasting and Sabbath days must be celebrative, flexible, restorative and missional.

E. Calling of the Twelve (6:12–19)

Context

Jesus' baptism in the Jordan was an inaugural event (3:21–22); his temptation in the desert, an early milestone (4:1–13). Paralleling the sequence of events during and after Israel's exodus (Exod. 14 – 17),

Jesus' movement from watery initiation to wilderness testing symbolically points to him as the new Israel, embodied in the Messiah.

In this passage, by noting that Jesus was 'going out' (Luke 6:12) to the mountain, Luke takes the Exodus parallelism a step further: just as Moses had gone out of Egypt to a special mountain, so it was with Jesus. Under this new Moses, a new set of twelve tribes is now taking shape in twelve very ordinary men. As Luke's fuller story will demonstrate, these Twelve would witness revelatory events (e.g. 9:28–36) and acquire extraordinary authority (22:28–30). Eventually, these same apostles will be sent (Acts 1 – 2). If the apostolic ministry includes healing, exorcising and preaching, it is only because Jesus performs these same activities.

Comment

12. In order to pray, Jesus *went out* (*exelthein*) not to just any mountain but to *the mountain* (*to opos*). That Luke has a definite mountain in mind may indicate that, among the early Christians, this particular mountain was already famous for its significance as the birthplace of the apostolate. That Jesus *went out* after a series of escalating conflicts with the temple leaders, only to spend the night watching prayerfully, likely has something to do with the Exodus plot line. In the ancient story, Moses also 'went out' after protracted conflict with Pharaoh, summoning the twelve tribes by their divisions while God watched over them through the course of the night (Exod. 12:41–42).

13. After his night of prayer, Jesus calls a large gathering of *disciples* and selects *twelve* from among them. Whereas Mark (Luke's source) never indicates that the Twelve were drawn from a larger category of 'disciples' (cf. Mark 3:13–19), Luke distinguishes between *disciples* and *apostles*, two groups having different functions as well as two different levels of access to Jesus.[35] That Jesus chose *twelve* follows from the unique nature of his 'new exodus' mission. If the twelve tribes of Israel were brought into a formal alliance during a night of watching, then it was only appropriate that Jesus

---

35. See Sweetland, *Journey*, pp. 149–164.

also spend the night watching before reforming Israel around his own twelve 'tribal leaders'. These he names *apostles* (literally: 'sent ones'), which in Greek usage can refer to a military operation, but 'on occasion the term also designates a messenger or envoy (a herald, designated as *apostolos*, is sent to arrange a truce [Herodotus, *Hist.* 1.28])'.[36] In Luke's story, the sense of a military envoy fits well, for the Twelve will soon be enlisted in Jesus' strange holy war (Luke 12:31–33), even as they will follow their king who sues for peace (cf. 14:32; 19:37–42).

14–16. Luke's list of names was likely meant not only to document a historical reminiscence but also to authorize the Twelve. In this respect, Luke's catalogue of names, along with the other 'apostles lists' in the New Testament (cf. Matt. 10:2–4; Mark 3:16–19; Acts 1:13), would have functioned as part of a charter for the apostolic church. With *Simon, whom he named Peter* given top billing and the traitorous *Judas Iscariot* assigned to the bottom rung, Luke's list is not unlike those of Mark and Matthew. Given Peter's dramatic conversion in the previous chapter (5:1–11), not to mention his sizeable role in the future church (cf. 22:31–32), it is no surprise that Luke follows his predecessors in giving Peter pre-eminence.[37] The short interval between Jesus' invitation to 'catch people' (5:10) and his call to Peter and the rest of the Twelve here implies that their election to the apostolate was an extension and intensification of Jesus' earlier call to evangelize. For Luke, the role of the apostle was radically missional.

17. Whereas Matthew locates Jesus' Sermon on the Mount (Matt. 5 – 7) on a hill or mountain (Matt. 5:1), Luke's Sermon on the Plain (Luke 6:20–49) sets a very similar set of ethical teachings *on a level place*. The difference in topography across the two Gospels is problematic only if one needlessly assumes that Jesus issued this teaching only once and in one location. That said, there is nothing inherently unlikely in the surmise that Matthew and Luke are in

---

36. Schnabel, *DJG*, p. 34.

37. Luke's positive treatment of Peter sets the foundation for Acts. See Brown, Donfried and Reumann, *Peter*, pp. 118–119; Wiarda, *Peter*, p. 106.

fact recording the same event, since after all our Evangelist may be envisioning Matthew's mountain as a high plateau. In any case, Jesus is *with a great crowd of his disciples* together with a *great multitude of people*. Such phrases draw attention not only to Jesus' increasing popularity but also to the geographical diversity of his following, perhaps invoking the ethnically 'mixed crowd' (*epimiktos polys*) of the exodus which had followed Moses out of Egypt (Exod. 12:38).[38] They come from *all Judea* and *Jerusalem* to the south, as well as from the coast cities of *Tyre and Sidon* to the north. The presence of inhabitants from these two major coastal cities would not only further confirm the presence of Gentiles (cf. Mark 7:24–30) but also suggest that Jesus is – so to speak – conquering hearts from the boundaries of the land promised to Israel (Deut. 1:8). The responsiveness of crowds from these two cities here is likely related to Jesus' later remarks regarding their relatively superior receptivity, at least in comparison to Chorazin and Bethsaida (10:13–14).[39]

18. The Gospel writer explains not just *whence* the people came but *why* they came. Earlier, we learned that this proclamation was not merely conveyed verbally but was supported by acts of healing and exorcism (cf. 4:31–37, 38–41, 43). Later, in recounting the early church's practices of proclamation (Acts 2:14–41; 4:8–22, 33; 5:42; 6:4; 7:1–53; 9:20; 13:16–48; 16:10; 17:2–3, 10–13, 23; 18:4; 28:23–31), healing (Acts 3:1–10; 4:30; 5:12–16; 9:32–41; 14:8–10; 19:12a; 20:7–12; 28:5–9) and exorcism (Acts 8:7; 16:16–18; 19:12b–20), Luke will go on to imply that the mission of the church follows the pattern set by Jesus.[40] For Jesus as for the early church, proclamation, exorcism

---

38. Influenced by the literary technique of Graeco-Roman novels, Luke also uses the crowds as a gauge of Jesus' popularity; see Ascough, 'Crowd Scenes', pp. 76–77.

39. By including the city names of Tyre and Sidon, respectively derived from the Aramaic words 'rock' (*tur*) and 'to hunt' or 'to fish' (*tsud*), Luke may be attempting a wordplay. It is to be recalled that John the Baptizer promised that God would raise up new children for Abraham from stones (3:8), while Jesus has just challenged Peter to become a fisher of people (5:10).

40. On this point, see Perrin, *Kingdom of God*, pp. 153–168.

and healing constituted a trifecta of mutually interpretative kingdom signs.

19. The crowds realize that merely by touching Jesus, they could
tap into his healing *power*.[41] Though this scenario does not necessarily entail notions of magic (especially since the action of
touching Jesus' body remains a fundamentally *personal* interaction),
Luke wants to impress upon his readers that the magical powers
touted by the priests of paganism (scattered across the Roman
Empire) could not compare with the effectiveness of Jesus' power.

Theology
The prophets had made clear that the regathering of the tribes
would coincide with return from exile (e.g. Ezek. 34 – 37). In this
light, Jesus' decision to call – of all possible numbers – *twelve* men
to himself symbolically yet powerfully indicated that Israel's restoration was imminent. Yet it also clarified the pattern for God's
saving dealings in at least two ways. First, it was not Jesus' disciples
who called and chose Jesus, but Jesus who had called and chosen
them. Though in the process of salvation human choice remains
very real and vital, it is ultimately God who saves through Jesus'
initiative. Second, we note that the Twelve are 'named apostles',
that is, designated as 'sent ones'. This implies that whatever
occupational, societal, tribal or familial identities these twelve men
owned, these were to be secondary to their new God-given identity
as those who had been chosen and sent out. The inference for
Luke's diverse readership is clear: whenever believers prioritize the
interests of their affinity group over the gospel mission, it means
that they have failed to grasp that like the Twelve they too are 'sent
ones' above all.

---

41. More so than the other Evangelists, Luke tends to speak of Jesus'
     power as if it were a self-contained entity (Luke 8:46; Acts 19:12).

F. The path of discipleship (6:20–49)

Context

Looking back to Luke 4:1 – 5:11, we discern an alternating sequence moving from opposition (4:1–13), to inaugurated calling (4:16–19), to more opposition (4:22–30), to another calling (5:1–11). Now we discover the continuation of the same pattern: further opposition (5:12 – 6:11) once again gives way to calling (6:12–16), an apostolic calling. The terms of this apostolic vocation are spelled out in a text now familiar to us as Luke's Sermon on the Plain (6:20–49). Of course, Luke intends the Sermon on the Plain (much as Matthew intended his Sermon on the Mount) to be an ethical road map not just for the twelve apostles but for all those who would follow Jesus. Resisting the urge to regard 6:20–49 as an utterly self-contained unit, we should appreciate its placement within a broader pattern described here. That Luke inserts Jesus' summative ethical blueprint in the midst of stories of persecution is worth pondering. The sermon itself divides neatly into four subsections: blessings and woes (6:20–26); love for enemies (6:27–36); on judging (6:37–42); and two ways (6:43–49).

Comment

i. Blessings and woes (6:20–26)

20. Raising his eyes in the direction of his disciples, Jesus declares a series of blessings or 'beatitudes', beginning with what has now become the most famous of the Beatitudes: *Blessed* (*makarioi*) or 'happy' (CEB) *are you who are poor*. Luke's omission of 'in Spirit' (as found in Matthew) unmistakably designates these *poor* (*ptōchoi*) simply as the impoverished. Since in its prior attested usage the Greek term has no other referent than the economically destitute, we should be cautious before spiritualizing the term, as if *only* an inner attitude were in view. Jesus' down-and-out addressees are *blessed* (*makarios*) or happy because they possess *the kingdom of God* – here and now! For first-century ears as well as our own, Luke's point is not far short of shocking: if the *present* advent of the kingdom in the person of Jesus creates a new reality of blessedness, it is a reality that is first and foremost (though not exclusively) on offer to the poor.

At the same time, given striking verbal similarities between the Beatitudes and Jesus' inaugural sermon on Isaiah 61 which, we recall, was the scriptural basis for Jesus' mission to the poor (Luke 4:18–19), the blessed poor must also be Isaiah's poor, the returnees from exile (Isa. 41:17; 58:7; 61:1). Thus, the *poor* Jesus has in view are not only recipients of the kingdom but also the fulfilment of the return-from-exile movement Isaiah had envisioned so many centuries beforehand. What does all this mean? Just this, I think: that Jesus is inviting all the socially and/or economically marginalized among his hearers to take advantage of their socio-economic poverty (unencumbered by the trappings of position, power and possessions) by joining Jesus' return-from-exile movement. For Luke, as for other New Testament writers (e.g. Jas 1:9), the poor more than make up in spiritual advantage what they lack in terms of material or social advantage.

21. Those who are *hungry* and those who *weep* will be blessed; the proof of this, Jesus continues, will be in their future experience of fullness and laughter. The promise that the *hungry* will be filled is integral to Mary's vision of the messianic reign (1:53), as well as to the Lukan feeding miracle (9:10–17) and also to the messianic feast (14:15–24; 22:16). Under Jesus' kingdom rule, in other words, the poor are now already being filled, a proleptic sign of the eschatological fullness to come. Likewise, when we meet the many mourners in Luke's Gospel (e.g. the widow of Nain, 7:11–17; the sinful woman, 7:36–50; Jairus and his mourners, 8:40–56), these will be understood as those who will one day laugh out loud. The repetition of *now* (*nyn*) in both of the beatitudes only sharpens the contrast: if this age is *now* fraught with sin, now mired in death, disease, deprivation and loss, the coming age will be no less extreme in its reversal of such things.

22–23. Jesus next insists that, not 'if' but *when* his followers are hated, socially excluded, insulted or slandered on account of their commitment to *the Son of Man*, the appropriate response will not be despondency, self-loathing, anger or retaliation, but rather joy. Kingdom people are to rejoice in the face of social marginalization, Jesus says, because they have joined company with the rejected prophets of yesteryear, a fellowship that both Jesus (20:9–18) and his disciples (21:10–19) will soon share.

24–26. Corresponding to each of the four blessings specified in verses 21–23 are four woes or sorrows. The rich are warned of impending *woe* because, inoculated against the comfort of God, they have already received their comfort (*paraklēsin*). Meanwhile, those who are currently full will experience hunger at the eschaton, presumably because they will be excluded from the messianic table. Similarly, those who laugh now will one day find themselves in a perpetual state of deep grief. Finally, Jesus concludes, those who are widely praised will one day be revealed as companions of the false prophets, who, while claiming to speak for God, self-servingly told people exactly what they wanted to hear. Certainly, Luke finds no shame in the church's possession of a good reputation (Acts 2:47), but he also makes it clear that the gospel will always be unwelcome news to the ideologies and values of even the most allegedly 'gospel-friendly' of human cultures. To choose to follow Jesus is to join the ranks of the prophets; it is also, inevitably, a choice to be hated along with Jesus.

ii. Love for enemies (6:27–36)

27. Jesus' words are not meant for all, but only for *you that listen* (*hymin . . . tois akousin*), those who obey, for Hebrew thought did not distinguish faithful listening from faithful doing (cf. Deut. 6:4). Accordingly, to listen to Jesus was to obey the covenant; by the same token, failure to obey him constituted a breach of Israel's solemn obligation. At the heart of this new covenantal responsibility was a commitment to love even one's enemies. Jesus' point is not that love for enemies takes priority over love for one's own friends and kin, but that the former category of people should not receive any less of our goodwill. The phrase *love your enemies* is parallel to – and therefore partially explained by – *do good to those who hate you*. The love which Jesus requires, then, cannot be reduced to inward sentiments or attitudes. It must be expressed through practical action.

28. Inviting kingdom citizens to do good to their enemies, Jesus also demands that they make it their business to *bless those who curse* them. Although the verb *eulogeite* may convey little more than the communication of goodwill, the context suggests that the power to impart such blessing lies only with those who have received the blessings announced in the Beatitudes. Thus, by responding to their enemies with blessing, Jesus' followers demonstrate their own blessedness, their present participation in the kingdom. Another vocation entailed in kingdom life is interceding for one's verbal abusers. Such prayer likewise presupposes not only the disciples' forgiveness of their enemies but also their reception of divine forgiveness (cf. 11:4). To summarize, Jesus' followers are called to respond to human hostility in two different ways: on a horizontal level, by answering with words of blessings; on a vertical level, by answering with words of prayer. Because blessing and prayer are distinctively *priestly* activities, Jesus is teaching that members of his kingdom belong not only to the company of prophets (6:23), but also to a new priesthood. It is exactly at the crosshairs of such opposition, Luke's beatitudes also hint, that the prophetic voice becomes most clear and the priestly service attains its truest form.

29. Unlike other religious teachers within Judaism (we think, for example, of the author of the Qumran text 1QM, who looked forward to a holy war between God's elect and God's enemies), Jesus insists that his movement be characterized by the practice of non-violence. Jesus brings home the radical nature of this vocation by requiring his disciples both to forgo retaliation and to embrace enthusiastic cooperation with their enemies, despite any negative impact this might have on their person or personal resources. In due course, Jesus will model his own teaching by patiently enduring the cruel blows of his Roman captors (22:63–65) and surrendering himself to a process which will eventually deprive him of his clothes (23:11). For this reason, extreme as Jesus' demands may appear, they cannot be written off as either rhetorical exaggeration or a hopeless ideal. Jesus practised what he preached and expected his disciples to follow suit.

30. Driving the point home, Jesus now envisions two scenarios: one in which personal boundaries are respected; the other, in which such boundaries are transgressed. Despite the difference in intention in the two scenarios, the end result is the same. To the one who asks, whether with or without force, Jesus says, 'Give!' – no questions asked. What is more, he continues, once one's possessions have been surrendered, the better part of wisdom is to surrender all hope of reimbursement. Undoubtedly, such demands would be virtually impossible apart from a prior decision of faith to entrust oneself and one's affairs to divine providence.

31–34. Having described what love is, Jesus now explains exactly what love *is not*. He does so by ruling out any alternative approach that restricts love to *those who love you*, or limits benefaction to one's benefactors, or lends only to one's creditors. Jesus rhetorically asks, 'In such situations how could such a response be a *credit* (NRSV, NIV, NASB) or "benefit" (ESV) to you?' Perhaps both of these translations can be improved upon. After all, the operative word here is *charis*, a word typically translated as 'gift' or 'grace'. While either of these renderings might initially seem awkward, I suspect the point is this: if *sinners* (those outside the covenant community) reflect no divine *charis* in their lives when they live according to a quid pro quo or the Roman principle of 'I give to you that you might give', then the distinguishing mark of God's 'grace' is the ability to love individuals who have no means to reciprocate.

35. Against such self-serving strategies, Jesus reiterates the necessity of loving one's enemies, doing good to them and lending without any expectation of repayment.[42] The motivation for this extravagant self-giving is twofold. First, for those who give according to this prescription, Luke's Jesus holds out the prospect of great reward (*misthos . . . polys*), a turn of phrase reminiscent of God's promise to Abraham that his reward would be great (Gen. 15:1, LXX: *misthos . . . polys*). If the allusion is intentional (certainly a possibility worth considering), then this would imply that the disciples' obedience to this ethic of radical love will one day be crowned by the right to participate in the Abrahamic inheritance.[43] In this case, then, Jesus' call to radical love is not a reversal of Old Testament ethics (as has often been claimed) but rather the culmination of the way of life inaugurated under Abraham. Second, in faithfully carrying out this love command, Jesus' followers should

---

42. Some manuscripts retain the phrase 'hoping for nothing again' (so the KJV). As best as we can tell, the phrase is a later scribal addition.

43. This would not be extraordinary. On the importance of Abraham in Luke, see Brawley, 'Abrahamic Covenant Traditions'; Collins, 'Abraham'.

expect to become *children of the Most High*, standing to inherit the land of promise from Yahweh even while mirroring God's unconditional kindness. Here, as with other instances of this title in Luke (1:32, 35, 76; 8:28), one may find undertones of Daniel, where 'the Most High' is a circumlocution for God.[44] This, together with the mention of the Danielic Son of Man in connection with persecution (v. 22), has the effect of embedding the substance of Jesus' teaching in the fabric of Daniel's story. The climax of that story is of course the victorious coronation of the Son of Man, not to mention the defeat of his enemies, including those who have set themselves to opposing some of Luke's believing readers.

36. Rounding out this string of commands, Jesus summarizes his teaching by introducing the concept of mercy. *Be merciful* (*ginesthe oiktirmones*), he says, if only because this is what it means to imitate the merciful Father. Whereas first-century Graeco-Roman culture openly looked down on the unfortunate, Jesus enjoins a visceral reaction to the hardships of others – the term *oiktirmos* and its cognates denote nothing less (*TDNT* 5, p. 159). Modelled repeatedly by Jesus in Luke's narrative (19:41–44; 23:28), such affective depth is recommended as the principal disposition guiding Christians in their ethical decision-making. According to Luke, to retain a merciful outlook in the face of human need is to give full expression to one's identity as one (re)created in the image of God.

iii. On judging (6:37–42)

37–38a. Turning to a new topic, Jesus issues a string of four second person plural commands (after all, these are *community* requirements), two negative and two positive: (1) *Do not judge*, (2) *do not condemn*, (3) *forgive* and (4) *give*. The most interpretatively difficult are the first two imperatives, regarding judging (*mē krinete*) and condemning (*mē katadikazete*). Clearly Jesus is *not* ruling out ethical judgments of any kind, for otherwise this would make a nonsense of verses 43–45 where he enjoins the making of moral distinctions. Moreover, unless the first two commands are utterly redundant, we must somehow distinguish judging from condemning. It seems

---

44. See Dan. 4:34; 7:18, 22, 25, 27; also Gen. 14:18–20.

that condemning has to do with the mental (as opposed to formal and legal) act of assigning irreversible guilt, thereby forestalling the possibility of reconciliation and/or restoration. Meanwhile, judging has to do with the uncharitable postures which lead us to ascribe base motives on the basis of limited evidence. A refusal to judge in this sense involves not a mindless unwillingness to differentiate right from wrong, but an attitudinal commitment to believe the best about another, notwithstanding possible evidence to the contrary; it is, in Paul's turn of phrase, to 'believe all things' and 'hope all things' (1 Cor. 13:7). The entailment of this generosity of spirit is a willingness to forgive and to give freely. The result of such generosity (or lack thereof), Jesus promises, is repayment in kind: those who are judged will be judged, those who are condemned will be condemned, and so on. While commentators differ as to whether this promised recompense is of divine or human origin, the language of the fourth petition of the Lord's Prayer ('And forgive us our sins, for we ourselves forgive everyone indebted to us', 11:4) prompts us to focus on the latter without entirely ruling out the former.

38b. In order to illustrate his point, Jesus invokes the familiar world of the marketplace where grain and countless other dry goods were traded by volume. While shrewd (if not dishonest) vendors would find ways to reduce the amount of product actually contained in the measured unit, either by skimping or by somehow puffing out the contents, Jesus calls his followers to do the opposite in their giving, that is, by compressing as much as possible and by filling up the container beyond the brim. Of course, the point is metaphorical, as if to say that whatever our capacity to give, we must give in keeping with our utmost ability – and then some (*running over*). In time, Jesus further promises, such largesse will be measured right back into our laps.

39. Although verses 39–42 appear to present three discrete sayings (vv. 39, 40, 41–42), all three demand to be interpreted in relationship one to another. Forging an *inclusio* with the 'hypocrite' of verse 42, the metaphorically blind person is admonished not to lead another blind person (much less a sighted person!), lest the entire party end up in *a pit* (*bothynon*). Though the term typically refers to a cistern or catchment, its connotations of disaster cannot be ignored (LXX Isa.

24:17–18; 47:11; Jer. 48:43). On one level, the saying is a stern warning against those who, overestimating their own spiritual progress, presumptuously take on the role of teacher – not unlike the 'blind guides' of Matthew 23:24–26. On another level, the saying is also an exhortation, directed to those who aspire to spiritual leadership. Teachers of God's Word must be ruthlessly honest in self-examination, lest they play the self-deceived hypocrite of verse 42, blinded by an eyeful of log!

40. An added reason for watchfulness in this regard has to do with a certain universal leadership principle, namely, that the life of the *teacher* will inevitably reproduce itself in the lives of those who follow the teacher – for better or for worse. Therefore, again, would-be disciples must be very choosy when it comes to deciding whom to follow, even as would-be leaders are obliged to exercise regular self-evaluation.

41–42. Through two closing rhetorical questions, Jesus asks his hearers to contemplate an absurd scenario involving a contrast between, on the one hand, a minute *speck* in the eye of one's neighbour and, on the other hand, an immense *log in your own eye*. The first rhetorical question gets at the fallen human tendency to focus on the faults of another, while ignoring one's own obvious faults; the second question deals with the related urge to redress another's moral failings without acknowledging one's own. To be clear, Jesus does not rule out the attempt to point out another person's sin. Instead, the point is to underscore the ever-present danger of hypocrisy motiving such transactions. Luke 6:41–42 is no bar to moral confrontation. Rather, Jesus' saying serves to remind his disciples of the enormity of their own sin (which on Jesus' comparison dwarfs the sins of others) even as it underscores the crucial role of honest introspection prior to acts of correction.

iv. Two ways (6:43–49)

43–44a. Verses 43–45 present a self-contained unit establishing an analogy between trees and people. The simple point of the analogy is to illustrate the organic connection between patterns of human behaviour and spiritual identity. Just as the type of any given plant can be safely inferred from its fruit, so too a person's

identity as a *good tree* or a *bad tree* can be inferred by the demonstration of fruit, good or bad.[45] The image of fruit is grounded in
the story of Israel, a people called time and again to bear fruit by
maintaining covenant faithfulness.[46] While Luke's Jewish readers
would have agreed with the basic premise of the metaphor (namely,
that Israel had the covenantal obligation to bear fruit), the
comparison implicitly raises the logically prior question – without
settling it one way or another – as to whether the nation had the
capacity to discharge its fruit-bearing responsibilities. The comparison, then, undermines any assumptive correlation between
socio-ethnic identity and covenant privilege (i.e. status as a *good
tree*), even as it emphasizes that the best evidence for one's elective
status is the demonstration of covenant faithfulness.

44b. Though it may seem that Jesus' concrete examples of *figs*
and *grapes* (along with thistles and brambles) are simply intended to
drive the same point home, this would be to overlook the allusion
to – among other resonances – Hosea 9:10:

> Like grapes in the wilderness,
>   I found Israel.
> Like the first fruit on the fig tree,
>   in its first season
>   I saw your ancestors.
> But they came to Baal-peor,
>   and consecrated themselves to a thing of shame,
>   and became detestable like the thing they loved.

Though Yahweh had elected Israel even while it was still in the
desert to bear – metaphorically speaking – figs and grapes, God's
people had turned to idols and therewith failed to produce their
appointed fruit. The parable hints that though God is still looking

---

45. In Isaiah, trees represent the returnees from exile (Isa. 55:12–13) as well
    as those destined to experience the eschatological fullness of the
    kingdom (Isa. 61:3).
46. Jer. 17:3b–8; 21:12–14; Ezek. 16:49 – 17:10; Hos. 10:12–13; Amos 8:1–6;
    Hab. 1:1–4; 3:17; Hag. 2:19.

for such fruit from Israel, one cannot expect as much if the plant itself has strangely morphed into another species of plant altogether.

45. Building on the logic of the previous verses, Jesus now invites his hearers to discern fruit on the level of the *good person* (NRSV) or the 'good man' (*agathos anthrōpos*), perhaps hinting that, ultimately, Jesus alone fulfils this criterion as the unique good man (cf. 18:19). If so, then the saying is less ecclesial than Christological. In any case, in this metaphor, the heart serves as a storeroom for treasures – some good, others evil. The moral quality of that heart/storeroom, Jesus continues, will be manifest not just through the fruit (or lack thereof), but also through the words of the mouth, which express the *abundance of the heart*. In the Graeco-Roman world, where persons were generally valued by their ethnicity, pedigree, social status, rhetorical eloquence and learning, Jesus' focus on the moral quality of human speech would have been innovative.

46. Even more startlingly, Jesus' rhetorical question *assumes* that his hearers call him *Lord, Lord*, but do not in fact do what he says. The sharply worded question, in other words, shockingly assumes *some* level of hypocrisy on the part of his hearers. To this extent, it is a call for self-examination, forcing Jesus' followers to ask themselves not *whether* they have failed to do what their Lord says, but *how* they have failed. The term *Lord* would have been as fitting for Jesus' first hearers (where the term takes on the meaning of 'Sir' or 'master') as it would have been for Luke's first readers and even us today (where 'Lord' carries the meaning of divinity).

47–49. As if to put some teeth on his warning, Jesus closes out his Sermon the Plain, appropriately enough, by emphasizing the critical importance of not just hearing Jesus' words but *also* obeying them. Here the contrast is between a man who *dug deeply* and built his house *on rock* and another builder who was content to build his house *on the ground without a foundation*. The former house is able to withstand the torrents of *the river*; the latter gives way to the same river, yielding a great *ruin*. Here one cannot fail to pick up the hints of the destruction of the temple in Jerusalem.[47] After all, 'the house'

---

47. Though scholars are divided as to whether Luke was written before or after that destruction (see Introduction above), an allusion to its

in Luke's Gospel is classically the house of God (2:49; 6:4; 13:35; etc.); the rock seems to stand for the rock of Zion (Isa. 28:16); the 'river' may well represent the empire founded on – and therefore symbolized by – the Tiber River.[48] In this case, Jesus assumes that his own community will become like a temple which, firmly founded on his words, will have the wherewithal to withstand even the torrential forces of Roman military might.

Theology

So far in Luke's story we have seen Jesus and his disciples getting resistance from all quarters. But if Jesus really were the Messiah, Luke's readers would naturally ask, why should he and his followers meet so much opposition? In response, Luke's Sermon on the Plain seems to say that such opposition was no unanticipated oddity but was actually *intended* to mark out the kingdom of God, at least in the present time. Eventually, however, there would come a day when God's kingdom would arrive in fullness and all this would be made right and whole. The reality of present-day kingdom suffering also partially explains Luke's recurring Exodus imagery. Just as the nation of Israel was given birth through the harsh trials leading up to the exodus, so too, Luke's Gospel promises, before God's people could inherit the future kingdom, they would have to face their own trials and their own pharaohs – and they would have to do so Jesus' way.

Jesus' way was of course exactly the opposite of how most of us would prefer to handle life. While most people do what they can to amass wealth, Jesus declares that it is not the wealthy but the poor who are blessed, for with poverty comes trust. While people of this world would sooner laugh than mourn, Jesus says that there is an inscrutable value – a kingdom value – in mourning, for with mourning comes a willingness to feel and even embrace the pain of living in a far-from-perfect world.

---

destruction would be appropriate in a Gospel where the fall of the temple has been all but assured (21:5–24). On this interpretation, see Wright, *Victory of God*, p. 334.

48. See Campbell, *Rivers*.

Likewise, those who are well regarded in the culture's eyes will one day find themselves in the dubious company of the false prophets: those who are reviled on account of Jesus, by contrast, will inherit blessing. In every way, Jesus' kingdom is an upside-down kingdom. No wonder the message of Jesus and his followers has been so roundly rejected: it threatens the very foundation of the world's operating system.

G. Jesus' prophetic ministry (7:1–17)

Context

The narrative's next five scenes (7:1–10, 11–17, 18–35, 36–50; 8:1–3), sandwiched by the Sermon on the Plain (6:20–49) on the front end and two parables (8:4–15, 16–18) on the back end, are action-packed. The first two of these five passages (7:1–10, 11–17) constitute the present section under consideration. The pair of episodes illustrate not only Jesus' ministry of release but also his prophetic aspect. We recall that, in the aftermath of his inaugural sermon at Nazareth, Jesus adduced Elijah and Elisha as examples of two prophets who, like himself, were not well received in their home towns (4:24–27). Elijah, Jesus reminded his hearers, was sent to a widow; her son, the scriptural story reminds us, would be restored to life by the prophet (1 Kgs 17:17–24). For his part, Elisha healed a Gentile military commander (2 Kgs 5:10–14), but also raised a young man from the dead (2 Kgs 4:32–37). Given these scriptural backdrops, the healing of the centurion's servant (Luke 7:1–10) and the raising of the widow's son from the dead (7:11–17) conspire to depict Jesus' prophetic ministry in the vein of Elijah and Elisha. That Jesus should refer to Elijah and Elisha in Luke 4 only to enact variations of their miracles here gives his earlier declarations a quasi-predictive force, further confirming his prophetic status.

Comment

i. A centurion's faith (7:1–10)

1. As with Matthew's Sermon on the Mount (cf. Matt. 5:1; 7:28), though *all* the *sayings* of Luke's Sermon on the Plain are initially addressed to his disciples (6:20), his discourse now comes to a close *in the hearing of the people.*[49] From here Jesus once again enters Capernaum, where, it will be remembered, he had been violently opposed for insinuating the Gentiles' inclusion in the kingdom (4:24–27). Now, as Luke's story is about to make clear, certain Gentiles are already responding in extraordinary ways to Jesus.

2. The first of these 'certain Gentiles' is a Roman centurion (the commander of a hundred men); his *slave* (*pais*), greatly esteemed by his master, is on the cusp of dying from an unspecified illness. First-century Roman centurions were normally persons of high social rank. In fact, given Capernaum's modest size, not to mention the generosity of the centurion's public benefaction (v. 5), this man would have been among the most socially powerful figures in the region. That he is eventually able to engage Jesus (v. 6) suggests that the latter's mission to the poor (4:18) did not preclude his responsiveness to the powerful outside this social category. Though the centurion's presence in the garrison town of Capernaum would not have been surprising for first-century readers familiar with the Galilee, his appearance on the heels of Jesus' momentous announcements in 6:20–49 may have been. Though Jews were known to serve in the Roman army, Luke's readers would have likely surmised that this figure was a *Gentile centurion* and therefore an unlikely beneficiary of Jesus' healing powers.[50]

3. Although the centurion had never personally witnessed the miracles that Jesus had performed during his earlier stint in Capernaum, reports about the extraordinary healer had obviously got around, even as far as the headquarters of the local Roman encampment. Alerted to Jesus' return, he asked a contingent of Jewish elders to intercede on his behalf in the hope of recruiting the famed healer's powers (cf. vv. 7–8). In this connection, two points deserve mention. First, though a Roman centurion in

---

49. Moses' Song (Deut. 32), which closes out the terms of the Sinaitic covenant, seems to be in play: 'Moses came and recited *all the words* of this song *in the hearing of the people*' (Deut. 32:44, emphasis added). This would imply a correlation between Jesus' sermon on an unspecified plain and Moses' issuance of a covenant on the plains of Moab.

50. The centurion's Gentile identity is supported by vv. 5 and 9.

distress would have been ordinarily scorned by pious Jews (if only on account of what he symbolized), here the elders carry out their delegation enthusiastically and with a deep sense of gratitude for his benefaction. Second, while the centurion never intends for Jesus to come to his house (vv. 7–9), the elders nevertheless pitch their request on the assumption that Jesus' personal presence would be necessary for a successful healing.

4–5. Although Jesus' earlier encounters with the Jewish leadership of Capernaum had been adversarial (5:17 – 6:11), now at least some of these same leaders are enlisting his help. Their heartfelt devotion to the man who *loves our people* and has *built our synagogue for us* is reflected not only in their sheer willingness to mediate on the centurion's behalf but also in the fact that they *appealed . . . earnestly* (*parekaloun . . . spoudaiōs*), with the imperfect verb conveying a sense of repetition – in other words, 'they *kept appealing* to Jesus earnestly'.

6–7a. As Jesus follows the elders back to the centurion's house, it appears (though this is not explicitly stated) that someone had run ahead of the entourage, now attracting a crowd of curious onlookers (v. 9), to update the Roman officer. Yet even while this is taking place, a second delegation of *friends* (*philoi*) sent by the centurion meets Jesus and company en route. Mortified that Jesus is actually coming to his house (contrary to the initial intentions of the centurion who likely understood the real or perceived risks of defilement attached to such a visit), the commander has this time sent ahead a personally worded statement in order to ensure clear communication. Two remarks are apposite. First, the centurion addresses Jesus as *Lord* (*kyrie*). While in this context this word probably means nothing more than 'Sir' or something of the sort, Luke seems to suggest a double meaning: Jesus is being recognized both as an honourable man *and* as someone close to if not fully identical with divinity.[51] Second, while the elders had earlier appealed to the centurion's worthiness (v. 4) as grounds for their plea, ironically the commander emphasizes his deep sense of unworthiness (anticipating the so-called 'prodigal son', 15:19, 21). The inner sense of moral inadequacy that prompted the centurion

---

51. Rowe, *Narrative Christology*, pp. 114–117.

to send the first delegation turns out to be the same motivation for sending the subsequent contingent.[52]

7b–8. Remarkably, the officer envisages a healing performed merely on Jesus' *word*. Drawing an analogy between himself and Jesus as *a man set under authority*, the centurion reasons that if his own role in the military (as one under authority) authorizes him to give orders to lower-ranking soldiers, then Jesus (as one also under authority) should be able to manipulate creation in the same way. The analogy is filled out with three concrete examples, involving hypothetical subordinates being instructed to *Go*, *Come* and *Do this*. While Luke's centurion may appear to be belabouring the point, the threefold illustration strikingly anticipates three of Jesus' own commands issued elsewhere in the Gospel.[53]

9. Jesus' response to the centurion's words is one of pleasant shock: he is *amazed* at the soldier's faith, for the centurion clearly expected Jesus to heal without the kind of intermediary techniques typically associated with ancient healings. Jesus' point is not that such faith was unprecedented but that it was unprecedented *in Israel*. That a Roman centurion – of all people – should emerge as the leading example of faith not only underscores the theme of reversal in Luke's Gospel but also contributes to the more specific theme of Gentile-inclusive mission. Just as Elisha had his Naaman (Luke 4:27; cf. 2 Kgs 5:10–14), Jesus had his centurion.

10. Without either a physical gesture or even a word, Jesus now leaves off, allowing the second delegation to return to the centurion's house, where they and the centurion would find the servant restored to full health. As far as we know, the centurion's second and carefully worded communication to Jesus is the single precipitating cause of the healing. This may imply the inherent power of Christ-centred faith, whereby the very expression of faith proves sufficient for securing the ends such faith desires.

---

52. Edwards' (p. 211) assumption that the 'centurion grounded his first appeal in his worthiness' is unwarranted. There is nothing in the centurion's instructions to his first embassy to contradict his claim *I did not presume to come to you* (v. 7).

53. E.g. 'Go' (5:14), 'Come' (9:23), 'Do this' (22:19).

ii. The raising of the widow's son (7:11–17)

11. The phrase *soon afterwards* aligns the action of verses 11–17 with the previous passage. The crowd that had attached itself to Jesus by the end of the Sermon on the Plain has now expanded – partially due to the miracle of 7:1–10 – into *a large crowd*. Along with the disciples, the throng accompanies Jesus to a town some 25 miles (40 km) to the south-west of Capernaum called *Nain*.

12. As Jesus and his followers approach the town, another *large crowd*, perhaps of comparable size, is coming towards them heading out of town. Their attention is focused on a dead young man, the only son of a widow, stretched out on a funeral bier. The details of the surviving 'family' have at least a twofold relevance. First, Luke's readers would have understood that the death of an adult only son would have exposed the surviving single mother to grave uncertainty at best and dire economic consequences at worse. The man's death is thus a tragedy on several levels. Second, as mentioned above, in the light of Jesus' earlier mention of the widow of Zarephath (4:25–26), the story will invite a comparison with Elijah's raising of the widow's son (1 Kgs 17), retrospectively sharpening up an otherwise vague comparison between the Roman centurion (Luke 7:1–10) and Naaman (2 Kgs 5). On this emerging pattern, Jesus is beginning to be singled out as a prophet like Elijah. While the significance of an Elijah–Jesus interchange is disputed, I have become persuaded that Jesus imitates the prophet precisely as the human anchor of God's continuing remnant.[54]

13. In a culture where hearty expressions of grief were expected at funerals, Jesus' request – which comes not as a word of consolation but as an implicit promise that he will raise the young man – that the widow stop weeping verges on the socially unacceptable. On one level, Luke's audience would have understood Jesus' command here alongside other apostolic enjoinments not to grieve for the dead as the world grieves (1 Thess. 4:13). On another level, this instruction draws attention to itself as the first of three dominical injunctions not to weep (cf. 8:52; 23:28), all of which may possibly relate to Jeremiah's instruction not to weep over the dead

---

54. See Otten, 'Elijah and the Remnant'.

but to weep instead over those destined for exile (Jer. 22:10; cf. 31:16–17). This possibility is supported by Luke's observation of Jesus' *compassion*. While Jesus' emotional response to the widow's plight is meant as a model response, we should not lose sight of the fact that *compassion* is also the leading divine motivation for Yahweh's enacting Israel's return from exile.[55] In this case, the story acquires two levels. On the most basic level, the episode shows that Jesus the prophet has the power to restore dead sons to their mothers. On another level, the passage shows that Jesus is the catalyst for return from exile as he brings the corporate 'son' (Israel) back from the dead.

14–15. As if Jesus' words to the widow were not arresting enough, now he proceeds to approach and then touch *the bier*, an action which would normally result in his instantly becoming ritually unclean. Caught off guard by this increasingly odd turn of events, the pall-bearers stop dead in their tracks, unsure of either what to do with Jesus or how to proceed at this point. Yet the tension of the moment does not last long, for Jesus addresses the corpse: *Young man, I say to you, rise* [*egertheti*].[56] Immediately, the dead man comes to life before a now-stunned crowd of onlookers, only then to begin speaking (perhaps as Luke's proof that this was not the kind of thing that could be explained away by rigor mortis or something of the sort). Finally, Jesus *gave him to his mother* (*kai edōken auton tē mētri autou*), much as Elijah 'gave him to his mother' (*kai edōken auton tē mētri autou*), that is, gave the widow of Zarephath her son (1 Kgs 17:23, LXX).

16–17. Seized by *fear* (*phobos*), the onlookers glorify God, while making two assertions. First, the people are convinced that in Jesus *a great prophet has risen among us*, one in the order of Elijah. Second, they declare that *God has looked favourably on*, or, better, 'visited' (ESV, NASB), *his people*. While the people's summation may appear to be a verdict of comfort, the verb also carries connotations of judgment (e.g. Zech. 10:3), visitation (*episkeptomai*) being associated with the convergence of divine initiative and divine power – coming as

---

55. See Perrin, 'Jesus' Anger'.
56. The verb used here (*egeirō*) is typical of resurrection language.

good news for some but bad news for others.[57] Given the spectacular nature of this miracle, it is no surprise that word gets out, penetrating the breadth of Judea and the surrounding countryside.

Theology

In the Hebrew Scriptures, prophets are known to make true predictions, challenge and encourage God's people, respond to the leading of the Spirit, perform miracles and embody the word of God. Having declared the Spirit's anointing (4:18), Jesus discharges his prophetic vocation first through the Sermon on the Plain and then in this pair of passages centring around the miraculous restoration of life. Because Jesus' prophetic role is epitomized by the giving of new life, Luke's readers can take comfort in the truth that, though circumstances and humanly derived probabilities may shout otherwise, there is no person, no life, no relationship, no family, no community, no institution and no cause that is beyond the hope of restoration. Even when others have given up hope (as the centurion's friends had), even when others weep inconsolably (as the widow's son's mourners did), the prophet Jesus still has the power to retrieve from death. First and foremost, prophets are to be messengers not of doom but of renewed life. The principle applies no less to Jesus' followers than to Jesus himself.

H. Wisdom's children (7:18 – 8:3)

Context

The three scenes (7:18–35, 36–50; 8:1–3) which this section comprises speak not just about the person of Jesus but also of his impact. Perhaps the most significant of these three scenes is 7:18–35, where he clarifies the nature of his messianic ministry on the heels of having 'just . . . cured many people of diseases, plagues, and evil spirits', while also claiming to have raised the dead and preached good news to the poor (7:21–22). The catalogue of activities is retrospective. The curing of diseases, plagues and spirits has already taken place throughout the course of 4:31 – 6:11,

---

57. Bock, p. 654.

the raising of the dead in 7:1–17 and the 'gospelizing' of the poor in 6:20–49. In this light, 7:18–35 is Jesus' attempt to explain his activities Christologically. Yet as Jesus describes his ministry, he draws on a confluence of texts from Isaiah (Isa. 29:18; 35:5–6; 42:18; and 61:1), implying that these demonstrations of power are evidence that the prophet's vision of the restored kingdom is now coming into view. Jesus' hearers are not all equally prepared to concede the point: Jesus and his paradoxical outworking of the kingdom will leave some puzzled (Luke 7:18–24a), others scandalized (vv. 23, 29–35, 39, 44) and still others transformed (7:36 – 8:3). Those who belong to this last category are Wisdom's children, living proof that Jesus really is the Messiah he implicitly claims to be.

Comment
i. John the Baptizer and children in the marketplace (7:18–35)

18–20. John's disciples relate *all these things* (i.e. the miraculous events of vv. 1–17) to their imprisoned mentor (3:20; cf. *Ant.* 18.119). Once updated, John now sends two disciples (the minimum number of witnesses for a legally binding testimony, Deut. 17:6; 19:15) in order to investigate Jesus' putative messianic status.[58] Languishing in his fortress cell, John wonders whether Jesus really is *the one who is to come* (as the Baptizer had initially been led to believe according to 3:16) or whether he and the rest of the faithful should redirect their hopes elsewhere.[59]

21. The question is well timed, for according to Luke's report *Jesus had just then cured many people of diseases.* The Evangelist's summary invokes Isaiah's Suffering Servant who likewise had 'cured' or 'healed' (Isa. 53:5) 'many' (Isa. 53:11–12) of their 'diseases'

---

58. Fitzmyer, p. 665.
59. As Bock (p. 665) points out, the 'coming one' is also used in a messianic sense in 13:35 and 19:38; see also Marshall, p. 290. The use of the second person pronoun ('you') plus the verb 'to be', as found in John's question *'Are you* the coming one?' (*sy ei ho erchomenos*), recurs in the Gospel's major Christological confessions (3:22; 4:41; 22:67; 23:3, 39).

(Isa. 53:4). And so, even if Jesus is not responding to evil in a way that John might have expected from a Messiah, Luke's echoes of the Suffering Servant confirm that God's purposes will indeed be achieved through Jesus as the fulfilment of Isaiah 53.

22. Jesus instructs John's emissaries to report back on what they *have seen and heard*, not in their own terms but with language carefully drawn from Isaiah 26:19; 29:18–19; 35:5–6; and 61:1. At first blush, the sequence of actions appears strangely anticlimactic: the list climaxes not with the *dead* being *raised* to life but with the preaching of good news to the poor – as if this preaching were the most impressive and climactic point![60] For if both miraculous healing (the centurion's servant) and raising from the dead (the widow's son) had precedent in Elijah's ministry (1 Kgs 17:17–22), it is above all Jesus' vocation to preach to the poor that uniquely marks him out as the fulfilment of Isaiah 61:1, just as he had announced in his inaugural sermon (Luke 4:18–19).

23. Following his summation of his own ministry, Jesus declares a macarism (blessing) on individuals who might otherwise 'take offence' (*skandalisthē*) at his Messiahship. In its root sense, the verb *skandalizō* means 'to make stumble'; in metaphoric usage, it means 'to cause to disbelieve, to cause to sin, to give offense'.[61] Paradoxically, for some, Jesus will be the fulfilment of the messianic high priest (Isa. 61:1); for others, he will be the hazardous temple stone described in Isaiah (Isa. 8:14–15), a source of stumbling.

24–25. Once John's messengers make their way back to their master, Jesus debriefs the crowd on what must have been a highly charged moment. By questioning Jesus' messianic status, John has potentially raised questions about *himself*, not least in the eyes of Luke's readers. As if to allay any such doubts in regard to his forerunner, Jesus now pays tribute to John by posing a pair of rhetorical questions aimed at revealing his forerunner's role and identity. Similarly worded, the two questions presume that the

60. The Qumran text 4Q175 ascribes a very similar catalogue of actions, precisely in the same order, to the coming Messiah.
61. Stählin, *TDNT* 7, pp. 339–358.

crowds had gone out into the desert for the purpose of observing John. Now by focusing on what the crowds *did see* and *did not see*, Jesus hopes to clarify just what made John so different from the other influencers of the day.

What did you go out into the wilderness to look at? The first possible answer in Jesus' multiple-choice quiz is this: *a reed shaken by the wind.* A familiar sight in Palestine, especially along the Jordan River where John ministered, the wind-tossed reed is a fitting metaphor for individuals who are easily morally compromised due to external pressures or internal desires.[62] That John was *not* such a person would have been clear from the very fact that he was at the moment locked up in Herod's prison, all because he had spoken out against the tetrarch's adulterous marriage. At the same time, the blown reed *was* an appropriate image of Herod Antipas, whose impetuousness was known to leave a wake of human wreckage (Mark 6:14–29). That Jesus alludes to Herod is confirmed by evidence from contemporary coins, showing Herod on the obverse (heads) and a reed on the reverse (tails). Unlike the morally flexible Herod, John is no vacillating reed.

What did the crowds go out to see? A second theoretical possibility is this: a man *dressed in soft robes.* Certainly no-one would associate John's coarse camel-hair cloak with *soft robes.* More than that, the kinds of people who did wear such luxurious clothing lived in palaces and villas. Why does Jesus offer two possible responses to his own rhetorical question, only then to reject them both? To underscore that, like the righteous prophets of old, John was paying the standard price for having opposed the reigning evil king of Israel. Jesus draws attention to the fact that John had all the characteristic traits of a prophet.

26–27. Given historical evidence that the rank and file of first-century Israel had perceived John to be *a prophet* (Josephus, *Ant.* 18.116–119), quite apart from any supporting testimony from Jesus, it is unlikely that Jesus is introducing any startling new information here. He is simply confirming what the crowds have already come to know and believe about John. Yet Jesus also insists that

---

62. Contra Bock, p. 671, who understands 'reed' literally.

John is some*thing* greater (neuter: *perissoteron*) *than a prophet.* Just what this means is illuminated by a subsequent citation of Malachi 3:1 and Exodus 23:20 (two verses that overlap considerably in verbiage). In Malachi, the forerunning messenger seems to be identified with Elijah (Mal. 4:5). So, then, John is the long-awaited Elijah redivivus – not just another prophet like Elijah but something greater, something *more than a prophet* (cf. 1:17).[63] Jesus' declaration of John as the 'new and improved' Elijah, as it were, confirms the Baptizer's divinely assigned role as preparer of the way of the new exodus (3:4–6).

28. More than that, *among those born of women no one is greater than John.* Even with momentary reflection, one can hardly miss the extraordinary nature of the claim. Of *all* those born of women (including such bright lights as Abraham, Moses, David, Elijah, etc.), *none* is greater than the Baptizer! Though a conventional circumlocution for humanity (Job 11:2, LXX; 14:1; 15:14; 25:4; 1QS XI, 11; 1QH XIII, 14; XVI, 23–24; XVIII, 12–13), the phrase *born of women,* unless a redundancy, may hint that there is in fact one who is *greater* than John, namely, the one *not* born of woman, that is, Adam. Given Luke's interest in correlating Jesus and Adam (cf. Luke 3:38), the Evangelist may have retained these words, at least in part, to implicate Jesus as the new Adam and therefore also as the one living figure greater than John. As if the shock of this statement were not overwhelming enough, Jesus then goes on to inflict mental whiplash on his audience by declaring John's inferior status when compared with any and all members of the kingdom – down to its very least. Clearly, the kingdom reality now being introduced by Jesus would prove far superior to anything that God's people had heretofore known.

29–30. In an uncharacteristic move, Luke now inserts an editorial aside on the divergent reactions to Jesus' provocative statement. In response to Jesus' words, *all the people who heard this,* including 'even' (*kai*) the tax collectors, 'justified' (*edikaiōsan*) God: they *acknowledged the justice of God*'s activity. Meanwhile, the religious

---

63. On the expectation of an eschatological Elijah, see Sir. 48:10; 2 Esd. 6:25–28; Exod. Rab. 32:9.

authorities, the Pharisees and the *lawyers* (those who rigorously trained under a rabbi), rejected the thrust of Jesus' words and therewith the very *purpose* (*boulē*) of God.[64] The split reaction among Jesus' hearers, Luke informs us, is not unrelated to these same hearers' earlier divided response to John's baptism. As it would turn out, those who had submitted to the baptism were now finding themselves on the right side of redemptive history; those who had not submitted to John's baptism were tragically setting aside God's purposes. Apparently, the great divine sorting process, which John had promised in Luke 3, had already begun taking place even through his administration of baptism.

31–32. The Evangelist's editorializing segues into a comparison between *the people of this generation* and small *children* in a *market-place*. On one level, *this generation* refers quite obviously to Jesus' contemporaries – more specifically, those who finally reject his words. On another level, the phrase invokes texts like Deuteronomy 32:5 (cf. Gen. 7:1; Pss 78:8; 95:10), where 'a perverse and crooked generation' refers to the disobedient among Israel destined to incur continuing exile. In the apocalyptic literature of Second Temple Judaism, the term 'generation' typically retains this negative evaluative force (see the Apocalypse of Weeks: 1 En. 91:11–17; 93:1–10). Jesus intends nothing less here.

Although children in Luke are generally characterized in positive terms, in this instance the case is otherwise. The children in the imaginary scene are irritated because their musical efforts have not garnered the reaction they had hoped for. When they had played joyful music, the other children's response was not sufficiently joyful; when they had played mournful music, the response was not mournful enough. The imagery has a universal resonance: morally developing adolescents often struggle to see beyond themselves even as they are quick to impose their unrealistic expectations on others. Whereas the two protests issued by the parabolic children in the marketplace correspond to two different kinds of responses to John and Jesus' respective dining habits, Jesus is essentially

---

64. The concept of the purpose (*boulē*) of God is important in Luke's writings (cf. Luke 23:51; Acts 2:23; 4:28; 5:38; 13:36; 20:27; 27:12, 42).

challenging his detractors with spiritual childishness.[65] On a more general level, he suggests that those who resist the way of God will continue to cling to rigid and wrong-headed expectations.

33. Insofar as dancing is connected with feasting, the one who refuses to dance along with the Pharisees' merry tunes must be John. In the historical context behind Luke's Gospel, John's diet and abstinence from alcohol had drawn no little attention from his contemporaries (Mark 1:6); in the world of the narrative, Luke has already alerted the reader to the reason for John's teetotalism (Luke 1:15). Apparently, John's dietary commitments had prompted a number of his contemporaries (presumably among those who had rejected his baptism) to suppose that demonic forces were at work in the Baptizer – a very serious charge.

34. Whereas the Pharisees and scribes had played a flute for the ascetical John, for the dining Jesus they had sung a mournful dirge. In the terms of the parable, by refusing to fast (5:33–39) Jesus had also refused to mourn. But Jesus objects to his critics' darned-if-you-do-darned-if-you-don't inconsistency, for when *the Son of Man has come eating and drinking*, they level accusations of gluttony, drunkenness and ill-advised consorting. With the words *eating and drinking*, Jesus means not simply the ingestion of food and alcohol, but the kind of overindulgence the first-century world associated with bawdy Graeco-Roman symposia (feasts). That Jesus in his day participated in feasts sharing some traits of the symposium is virtually beyond question; that Luke has already recorded Jesus as doing so alongside *tax-collectors and sinners* is also patently clear (5:27–31). Now by designating himself (along perhaps with his followers) as the *Son of Man*, Jesus sets all these allegations within the context of the cosmic battle taking shape in Daniel 7.

35. Jesus has drawn attention to the fact that he and John have been forced into a catch-22. Any effort to meet their critics'

---

65. Some interpreters (e.g. Fitzmyer, p. 680) understand Jesus and John to be the children, playing the flute and singing the dirge, respectively. But for all its merits this interpretation finally stumbles, since it would awkwardly align these two righteous figures with the wicked generation.

expectations, like meeting the standards of silly children in the marketplace, would prove to be futile. Yet rather than leave the disagreement at an impasse, Jesus appeals to the 'children of Wisdom'. To be a child of Wisdom is quite simply to follow the path of wisdom, one and the same as the path of God; it is to partake of her feasts (Prov. 9:1–6). In other words, the children of Wisdom are those who eat at the table of Jesus, who is also the Son of Man. The vindication of the ministries of John and Jesus will emerge not through disputes over proper Halakha (Jewish ordinances), but through the transformed lives of those who now embody the wisdom or Torah of God. Just as the likes of the tax collectors and sinners had justified God (v. 29), so too will they justify wisdom itself, that is, Jesus. Jesus and his followers are both justifiers and justified.

ii. Jesus anointed by a sinful woman (7:36–50)

36. The Evangelist sets the stage for this poignant scene by introducing *one of the Pharisees*, who plays host to Jesus. That Jesus *took his place at the table* (*kateklithē*) in a reclining position, as suggested by the verb, points to a formal gathering. In picturing this scene, we imagine Jesus propped up on his elbows, lying down along with the other guests around the eating area, with his feet pointing to one edge of the room.

37. Without warning (*idou*) a woman appears; she is simply identified as *a sinner* (*hamartōlos*), that is, a prostitute by trade. Having been alerted to Jesus' presence at the Pharisee's house, she has brought with her *an alabaster jar of ointment*, myrrh to be exact. Myrrh was the primary ingredient in the oil mixture used to ordain the high priest (Exod. 30:23); a similar ointment would later be applied to Jesus' crucified body (Luke 23:56). Thus, although this anointing scene probably reflects a historical event different from the anointing at Bethany (Matt. 26:6–13//Mark 14:3–9//John 12:1–8), Luke understands this anointing (as the Gospel tradition understands the anointing at Bethany) as a consecratory act. More than that, if the Evangelist intends to link this woman to Psalm 45's 'daughter', who bows to her myrrh-anointed messianic king, then this implies not only Jesus' messianic status but perhaps also the sinful woman's newly acquired status of royal daughter (cf. Ps. 45:6–15).

38. Four main verbs (three of which are durative imperfects, suggesting continuous action) draw attention to four principal actions. The surprise intruder (1) dampens Jesus' feet with tears, (2) wipes them with her hair, (3) kisses his feet and (4) anoints them. Strikingly, all her actions are concentrated on Jesus' feet, stretched out towards the outer edge of the room. The woman's position on the fringe of the gathering gives spatial expression to Luke's theme of reversal, where the social outsiders become – by Jesus' reckoning – the new moral exemplars. In the first-century world, the feet were considered the most shameful parts of the body. Very practically, they would also quickly become filthy from dirt and dust (not to mention other even less desirable materials!), as one travelled from point A to point B. As Jesus will soon point out (vv. 44–46), while the host had failed to carry out his socially expected duties, the marginalized woman in effect steps up in his place, discharging the hosting duties that should have been performed by Simon. She does so with exceeding extravagance.

39. *The Pharisee who had invited* Jesus begins thinking to himself, thereby undertaking one of many interior monologues in Luke.[66] Though we suspect that a Pharisee in such a situation would have ordinarily banished the woman from his house without further ado, if only to protect his guests from ritual impurity, the host's decision to observe and interpret the unfolding event as evidence against Jesus (*If this man were a prophet, he would have known who and what kind of woman this is who is touching him*) is itself significant. From this, we sense that Simon's motives for inviting Jesus in the first place were not so much a show of friendship as an attempt to put the upstart religious figure in his place. The Pharisee who had invited or called (*kalesas*) Jesus to dinner in this scene is but an example of the implacable children from the last scene, calling out (*prosphōnousin*) to the likes of John and Jesus (7:32).

40–43. Responding to the Pharisee's inward thoughts, and thereby proving that he is in fact a prophet, Jesus rehearses a fictive story involving two debtors with different levels of indebtedness: *one owed five hundred denarii, and the other fifty* (v. 41). In

---

66. See Sellew, 'Interior Monologue'. Cf. 12:16–20; 15:11–32; 16:3–4.

the time of Jesus, the silver-based denarius was the standard pay for a day's wage. This means that the debtors owed the creditor roughly 500 and 50 days' worth of wages. Yet both of these debts are cancelled. Jesus then closes out his imaginary scenario by directing a follow-up question (*Now which of them will love him more?*) to his host, now identified as Simon. In response, Simon offers the logical answer: *I suppose the one for whom he cancelled the greater debt* (v. 43).

44–46. At this point Jesus turns *towards the woman* while continuing to address Simon. He draws the Pharisee's attention to her as a model, so as to contrast his host's social failures (indicative of a deeper moral failure) with the woman's praiseworthy efforts. According to first-century hospitality customs, Jesus would have had the right to expect water for his feet, a kiss on his cheek or hand, and oil for his head. As it turns out, all these expectations were frustrated, only to be strangely and unexpectedly met through the woman's emotional outpouring.

47. As far as the present company was concerned, Jesus' next words would have been as shocking as they were puzzling. *Therefore,* he says, *her sins, which were many, have been forgiven; hence she has shown great love.* Notably, Jesus does not whitewash or otherwise minimize the woman's sin. Indeed, he acknowledges the multitude of her sins, while at the same time *also* acknowledging that those same sins were forgiven, precisely on account of her actions. Here it would be overreading the text to understand this as a salvation-by-works theology, as if the woman's actions had somehow contributed to her justification. Rather, the point seems to be that her great love is evidence of her deep experience of forgiveness. Her love in turn is evidenced not just by her affective state but by the price she was willing to pay for the sake of this demonstration of love: the financial cost associated with purchasing the myrrh, as well as the huge social risk.[67] Such extravagant generosity and unflappable

---

67. To put this in perspective, it is to be recalled that she is essentially a streetwalker, and therefore a walking contagion of ritual impurity. Her barging into a gathering of socially powerful figures, whose overriding goal was to maintain cultic purity, is a very bold move.

courage testify to a profound love that can proceed only from an equally profound forgiveness.

48. Although Jesus already declares the woman's sins to have been forgiven, now he turns to address her directly with the same announcement: *Your sins are forgiven* (*apheōntai*). The *perfect* form of the verb assures us that the forgiveness is an act that has already taken place in the past with continuing validity into the future. As such, the forgiveness Jesus imparts is a *permanent* forgiveness. The verb's *passive* voice invites us to interpret this as a divine passive. The forgiveness, in other words, is of *divine origin*.

49. Not surprisingly, the guests observing this interaction now begin talking among themselves, speculating about Jesus' identity. Jesus had just 'cleared' a conspicuously sinful woman. In Ancient Judaism, only God (Exod. 34:6; Ps. 103:12) could forgive – more exactly, only God and his properly anointed spokesperson or priest.[68] What were these eyewitnesses to make of these events? The scene is reminiscent of Jesus' healing of the paralysed man, where very similar questions are asked (Luke 5:21). Of course, once again Luke provides no closure to this question but invites his readers to consider the matter themselves.

50. To this point, Jesus has mentioned the woman's love and state of forgiveness. Now he explains that it is in fact her *faith* that has *saved* (*sesōken*) her. This hardly contradicts his earlier statement. In early Christian thought, faith was expected to express itself through love (Gal. 5:6). Therefore, it is not simply the woman's perception of Jesus' willingness to forgive that caused her to love, but rather her appropriation of that forgiveness through faith, a faith acted out in extravagant acts of love. As beneficiary of the salvation offered by Jesus, the woman was now free to *go in peace*. Having heard of her forgiveness as a statement of fact (v. 48), now she receives a *direct* word of forgiveness from Jesus himself. Only then can she *go in peace*.

---

68. See discussion in Hägerland, *Forgiveness of Sins*, pp. 1–12.

iii. Jesus' supporters (8:1–3)

1. *Soon afterwards* Jesus proceeds systematically *through cities and villages*, proclaiming and preaching good news (*kēryssōn kai euangelizomenos*) as he goes, in keeping with his earlier stated mission (4:43). For Jesus, to preach *is* to bring the good news – and vice versa. The Twelve are also with him. Having been called (6:13), Jesus' closest associates now re-emerge to the foreground, travelling alongside their master in a more visible way.

2–3. Jesus is also accompanied by 'certain women' (*gynaikes tines*), three of whom are mentioned by name, probably on account of the spectacular nature of their deliverance. First, there is *Mary* from Migdal, a city 3 miles outside Tiberias. Her claim to fame consists in having had *seven demons*, which Jesus had apparently exorcised. The specification of *seven demons* not only underscores the severity of Mary's earlier state but may also hint, since seven is a number of fullness, at the thoroughness of the demonic control. Next there is *Joanna*, who was married to *Chuza, Herod's steward* (*epitropou Hērōdou*). In the Roman world, such a person would have been a top-level functionary, a steward being a highly honoured position with considerable responsibility. The Herod in view is undoubtedly Herod Antipas who himself had mixed feelings about Jesus, at best. That Jesus should win sympathizers from members of households occupying such high-level positions shows that these same households were being divided over him; some were already living out his demands for absolute allegiance (14:26). Indeed, that Joanna should leave her husband at home to manage Herod's household while she wandered the countryside with Jesus must have been seen as extraordinary, even scandalous. Both Mary Magdalene and Joanna will show up later at the empty tomb (24:10). Of *Susanna* we know nothing, though she was most likely known to Luke and his audience. These three women and many others ministered (*diēkonoun*) to Jesus and the Twelve from out of their worldly goods.[69]

---

69. In antiquity, it was not unusual for women to financially support rabbis (Josephus, *Ant.* 17.33–35). The KJV has the women 'ministering unto *him* of their substance' (emphasis added), but this translation is based on a suspect text-critical reading. See Metzger, *TCGNT*, pp. 120–121.

That two of the three women named here are unmarried is significant.[70] When we consider the widow of Nain (7:11–17), together with the sinful woman of the previous passage (who likewise would have also been unattached), we realize that Luke 8:1–3 is truly a summary of Jesus' modus operandi. Even as Jesus' community continued to expand by including socially marginalized women within its ranks, a new family was beginning to take shape. As Luke makes clear to a first-century culture that was often swift to denigrate women's contributions, the Jesus movement depended not only on the financial benefaction of such women but also on their itinerant co-partnership. No wonder the commentator Alfred Plummer once remarked, 'the Third Gospel is in an especial sense the Gospel for *women*'.[71]

Theology

The present section reveals contrasting responses to Jesus' ministry. In answer to the wavering John, Jesus exhorts faith and reaffirms the blessing of not falling away. Meanwhile, he likens the unbelieving religious leaders to spoiled children. Then there is the sinful woman who is saved by her faith, a faith that Jesus' Pharisaical host patently fails to demonstrate. Luke also weighs in by pointing out that the responsive children of Wisdom are proved right and by recording for posterity the presence of women who faithfully minister to Jesus out of their own resources. Both belief and unbelief come in different shapes and sizes.

Yet Luke also wants to show that there are certain attitudes and postures appropriate to faith. Those who encounter Jesus, the Gospel writer would have us know, will either follow the Pharisees' lead in requiring him to perform on their terms, or follow suit with the humility and generosity modelled by the sinful woman and Jesus' female financial backers. This saving faith is no mere mental assent. Faith has certain behavioural attributes. Faith has 'a look'.

Ironically, some of the best models of this faith are the notoriously sinful. Even as the Magnificat and the Sermon on the

---

70. Had they been married, their husbands would have been mentioned.
71. Plummer, p. xlii (emphasis original).

Plain have already promised, the lowly likes of prostitutes and tax collectors – and not the religious leaders – are proving to be the children of Wisdom. The most unlikely of people are coming to faith, and Jesus remains faith's focal point. God's saving work cuts across all social barriers and conventional hierarchies.

I. Discipleship explained (8:4–21)

Context

The Jesus movement is now gaining an increasing number of prospective adherents and curious observers – just the kind of reaction one might expect the Messiah to provoke. But now, at the very cusp of his popularity, Jesus offers a parable that anticipates the mixed reaction he will soon receive from the public. This passage, part of a larger section focusing on the word of God (vv. 4–21), neatly divides into two parts: the parable itself (vv. 4–8) and its interpretation (vv. 9–15). This is followed by further warnings regarding the necessity of hearing (vv. 16–18), followed in turn by a case study of certain individuals – the kind who might be expected to hear well but in fact do not (vv. 19–21).

Comment

i. Parable of the sower (8:4–15)

4. As a result of Jesus' itineration, *a great crowd* has converged; the crowd includes people from various cities who are travelling great distances to experience the phenomenon for themselves. Like Luke, Matthew and Mark also situate the parable of the sower (sometimes called the parable of the soils) immediately after a report on the size of Jesus' following (Matt. 13:2//Mark 4:1//Luke 8:4). In this light, it seems that the Synoptic tradition as a whole has understood the parable either as Jesus' tactical response to his increasing popularity (separating the serious enquirers from the less serious through verbal puzzles) or as his interpretation of it (hinting that the presently massive following is not all that it seems) – or both.

5a. The parable begins simply enough with a narration of a nondescript *sower* who *went out to sow his seed*. The agricultural imagery would have struck a chord with the agrarian audience, as most of them would have been very familiar with such a scene. At first blush, Jesus' parable lays hold of what is entirely familiar and then makes it strange through an *apparently* pointless story. However, those who may have sensed that there was more to this story than first met the ear would have pressed for further explanation.

5b–8a. Corresponding to four different types of soil, the four lots of scattered seeds produce four kinds of results. The first type lands beside *the path* or 'way' (*para tēn hodon*) (the NRSV's reading of *on the path* is unlikely), only to be *trampled on*, and eaten by *birds*. While the interpretation attached to this seed comes soon enough (v. 12), already Luke's readers have some sense of its meaning: if John and Jesus' following was a movement of the 'way' (1:79; 3:4; 7:27), then this seed *beside* 'the way' will come to represent those who have opted out of the proffered return from exile 'on the way' (Isa. 40:3). These hearers will be fated to be trampled on, just like the judged city of Jerusalem (Luke 21:24). A second category of seed falls *on the rock*. This is not soil peppered with stones as some translations suggest but a thin layer of soil overlaying a large, natural sheet of rock. Although the initial plant would have every appearance of health, eventually due to lack of moisture it would dry up. Like the second seed, the next category of seed also has the appearance of a promising start. But as it lands *among thorns*, the seeds-turned-germinating plants are doomed to be choked out. Finally, still other seed *fell into good soil*. Far more promising, these plants grow and eventually produce a *hundredfold* crop.[72] As to whether this is in fact a miraculous harvest, scholars have in the past been divided. The best evidence suggests that this would have been an excellent return in the first-century world but not beyond the realm of human possibility.[73] In any case, the emphasis is on the astounding degree of fruitfulness. The parable of the sower is a study of contrasts, more specifically, a contrast between three non-fruit-bearing soils, on the one side, and one fruit-bearing soil, on

---

72. Luke shortens the more expansive 'thirty and sixty and a hundredfold' of Mark 4:8, tightening the allusion to Isaac's blessed harvest of a hundredfold (Gen. 26:12). See Perrin, *Jesus the Priest*, p. 104.

73. Hedrick, *Parables*, pp. 172–173.

the other – a contrast that becomes clear only with the passage of time.

8b. The parable proper closes with a solemn warning which Jesus shouts out (*ephōnei*), as if for emphasis. It is an exhortation directed not to all, but only to those with *ears to hear* – reminiscent of a similar call made by the exilic prophet Ezekiel (Ezek. 3:27). The exhortation presumes in the first place that not everyone will in fact have such ears, and so the thrust of the parable will inevitably be lost on some, especially those who have become spiritually deaf (and blind) through the worship of senseless idols (Isa. 44:9–20).[74] As for those who can hear, however, it now behoves them to attend closely. In this instance, hearing means far more than sensory perception: it means actual obedience. Indeed, in enjoining obedience to his mysterious parable, Jesus may also be ascribing his words a significance rivalling the fundamental article of Jewish faith, the Shema ('Hear, O Israel . . . '; Deut. 6:4). The ability to hear and obey indicates one's own position within the good soil. Failure to hear, however, is in effect to prove oneself as unproductive seed and the bearer of an idolatrous heart.

9–10. As one might expect, the disciples are perplexed by the unusual story and turn to its teller to enquire into its meaning. In response, Jesus promises that to them belong the *secrets of the kingdom of God*, even as for others the parable remains a mystifying riddle. Following Mark 4:12, Luke's Jesus explains the secretive nature of his story as a fulfilment of Isaiah 6:9: *so that* (*hina*), or in order that, *looking they may not perceive, / and listening they may not understand*. The *hina* (purpose) clause has been a source of much stumbling among commentators, not surprisingly. But, one asks, is it really the case that Jesus preached the parables *in order* to harden his hearers? While various approaches to this difficult question have been offered, I suggest that though the *so that* (*hina*) clause of verse 10b does not necessarily explain Jesus' entire motivation for giving the parable, it does at least unpack one of his motivations, namely, to seal the judgment of the *others* (v. 10) who do not come for an explanation. Just as Isaiah was mandated to preach repentance to

---

74. Beale, *What We Worship*, pp. 165–166.

an ostensibly spiritually resistant Israel, so it is with Jesus, as witnessed by the fact that he could garner little response with the short-sighted individuals who couldn't be bothered to push further. But Jesus' preaching ministry is not just analogous to Isaiah's preaching but the fulfilment of it. As Luke makes clear, the long-awaited return from exile first predicted by the prophet was now being realized in Jesus, and only those who proactively responded to Jesus' teaching held promise for participating in it.

For Luke's purposes, too, the parable of the sower speaks of what must have been a standard objection to Jesus' Messiahship, to wit, the failure of the Jesus movement to win Israel over en masse. The reason why Jesus' proclamation has not produced a more far-ranging response within Israel, the parable seems to suggest, is because (1) much of God's elect nation has remained hardened (cf. Rom 9:30 – 10:21), and (2) God is in fact leveraging this hardness to establish a newly defined remnant involving unlikely converts both within and outside Israel. The *secrets of the kingdom* are precisely those kingdom purposes that are even now being realized through fruitful *and* unfruitful responses to the preached word. In the first-century setting, this by itself would have been not far short of stupefying. The simultaneous acceptance *and* rejection of the messianic kingdom would have thwarted all Jewish expectations of a clean break between 'this age' and the glorious 'age to come'.

11. Towards revealing the meaning of the parable, Jesus first identifies the *seed* as *the word of God*. This identification of the word as seed conjures up a similar metaphor from the prophets (Isa. 55:10–13) as well as other Jewish literature (4 Ezra 8:38–41; 9:29–37). In these cases, it is Yahweh who sows his seed as the word; in these cases, too, the seed-as-word retains its own inexorable generative power. Paradoxically, the seed, precisely as the 'seed of Abraham', is also the remnant Israel.[75] This dual reference is hardly problematic but gives fitting expression to the expected day of restoration envisaged when the word of Yahweh would coalesce with the righteous remnant in a new and powerful way. The imagery of seed is

---

75. Ezra 9:2; Isa. 1:9; 6:13; 43:5; 44:3; 45:26; 53:10; 54:3; 60:21; 61:9; 65:23; 66:22; Jer. 24:6; 31:27; 32:41; 46:27; Hos. 2:23; Amos 9:15; Zech. 8:12.

also appropriate for Luke's purposes since throughout the Gospel Yahweh's overriding concern is for fruit (Luke 3:9; 6:43–45; 13:6–9; 20:9–18), the fruit of covenantal obedience. In Jesus' messianic kingdom, such fruitfulness *cannot* occur apart from the successful sowing of the word. And since Jesus is now the bearer of the word, he no less than God is the sower of the seed.

12. The seed beside *the path*, Jesus explains, refers to those who have lost the implanted word to marauding satanic forces, symbolized in verse 5 by the birds. Having been deprived of the life-giving word, such individuals cannot believe, much less be saved. From this, we learn that the proper reception of Jesus' word is no exercise in mere cognition, but involves a battle with dark spiritual forces. People's failure to accept the words of Jesus stems not from a lack of information but from the hardened condition of their hearts; at the same time, behind this moral failure stands the deception of the satanic kingdom. Proclamation, Luke means to say, is at its heart a spiritual battle.

13. The seeds falling on the rocky soil are interpreted as the flash-in-the-pan conversions to Jesus. True, such persons at one time may have received the word with joy, but this is no assurance that the word will actually carry through its prescribed purpose. In the *time of testing* (*en kairō peirasmou*), they stumble, failing to live out – as we shall see – the thrust of the sixth petition of the Lord's Prayer: 'Lead us not into temptation [*peirasmon*]' (ESV). On one level, this 'hour' is the period of the promised tribulation (Dan. 7:22; 11:35); on another level, it refers to any moment when Jesus' followers are tempted to cave in to social or political pressure.

14. Quickly recognized as impediments to agricultural fruitfulness, thorns are broadly associated with cursing (Gen. 3:18; Num. 33:55; Isa. 5:6; Jer. 4:3–4), in this case the curses of worldly cares, riches and pleasures of life. At the same time, especially in Isaiah, thorns symbolize external threats to Israel's spiritual life (Isa. 9:18; 10:17; 27:2–4). Given that Jesus himself is being supported through the resources of some notable women (8:1–3), his warning against wealth cannot be understood as a blanket condemnation. Rather, the focus is on wealth's power to sway the human heart, distracting it with trivial pleasures and weighing it down with *cares* (*merimnōn*), a morally negative term (cf. 12:25).

15. In describing the fruitful soil, Luke makes two important changes to his source. First, he emphasizes that fruitfulness is directly tied to *an honest and good heart*. This builds a bridge back to 6:45, where the good person speaks out of the abundance of his or her 'good heart'. Second, Luke's good soil produces with *patient endurance (en hypomonē)*. This anticipates Jesus' insistence on the necessity of the same patient endurance during the tribulation (21:19). The brunt of the test of fruitfulness awaits future tribulation, a tribulation which Jesus and his disciples will soon undergo.

ii. Parable of the lamp (8:16–18)

16. Following an extended parable (8:4–15) about hearing the word, this mini parable of sorts offers a variation of the same theme by exploring the rewards and dangers attached to, respectively, obeying and disobeying. Here Jesus draws a comparison between effective hearing and an oil-fuelled house *lamp (lychnon)*, commonly employed for night-time illumination. He asks his readers to imagine lighting a lamp, only then to put it – in a bizarre move – *under a jar* or *bed*, thereby nullifying its function. Because the envisioned lamp provides lighting not for those in the house but rather for *those who enter*, the metaphor seems to emphasize that the primary benefits yielded by faithful hearing are the saving benefits which stand to be embraced by the not-yet enfolded.[76] By the same analogy, the comparison also warns that faithless hearing of the word has the effect of concealing or otherwise obstructing the light of salvation. In short, the disciples' choice to obey or disobey is not without its own missional implications.

17. As Jesus acknowledges, there is a good deal that is *hidden* and *secret*, not least the realities anticipated in the parable of the sower (8:10). Nevertheless, Jesus also promises, all things will eventually come to light, for *nothing is hidden that will not be disclosed*. On the eschatological day, all human beings will be shown up for the kinds

---

76. As Nolland (p. 391) puts it: 'His intention is that those who still need to find their way in may see the word of God streaming out from those already inside.'

of hearers they are, even as the truth of the preceding parable of the sower runs its course in human reality. In the final analysis, then, Jesus' followers must put the light of obedience on the lampstand, as it were, because God is in the business of bringing all things to light, not least the messianic light that is already beginning to burn within Jesus' community. The truth will out!

18. On the basis of verses 16–17, Jesus exhorts his followers not just to listen but to *pay attention to how you listen*. For Jesus, in other words, the life of discipleship requires not just an attentiveness to the word of God, but an uninterrupted attentiveness to the quality of one's attentiveness. The result of such faithful listening is superabundant reward: the just deserts of *not* listening are losing the little one has. In practical terms, though responsiveness to God's word may be a sign of God's initial grace, this is no guarantee against such grace being withdrawn as a result of spiritual neglect.

iii. Jesus' true family (8:19–21)

19. Having occupied a prominent role in the Gospel's opening chapters, only to disappear from sight for five chapters, Mary now reappears, this time along with Jesus' brothers. They are daunted by the very practical results of Jesus' burgeoning popularity, namely, the people compressed around him. Unable to get to Jesus *because of the crowd (dia ton ochlon)*, they face the same predicament as those who had been earlier carrying the paralysed man (where the same Greek phrase is used; cf. 5:19).

20. When Jesus is informed that his immediate family members are hoping to see him, the implication is that he is being summoned. That Jesus' family should expect him to be at their beck and call reflects a posture noticeably different from that of the four men carrying the paralysed man (in 5:17–26) who, as we recall, having likewise been hindered by the crowd, nevertheless pressed forward into Jesus' presence. Nor is it incidental that Mary and her sons are described as *standing outside (hestēkasin exō)*, for generally speaking in Luke, to be *outside (exō)* is to be outside God's salvific purposes (13:25, 28; 14:35; 22:62). On these considerations, it appears Mary comes to us as an instantiation of one who has received the word (Luke 1 – 2) but who also, notwithstanding the warning of the previous passage (8:16–18), has failed to improve consistently on it.

21. For this reason, perhaps shockingly, Mary's status as the mother of Jesus, as well as the status of Jesus' biological brothers, now becomes qualified. By Jesus' reckoning, true family relations are constituted not biologically but spiritually. Only those who *hear the word of God and do it*, as the parable of the house on the rock has demanded (6:46–49), can claim rights as Jesus' mother and brothers. In Luke's editorial handling, the moral weaknesses of Jesus' family not only temper any potential tendency among his readers to glamorize members of the holy family (outside of Jesus) but also serve to establish the circle of obedience as the fundamental community in the emerging kingdom of God.

Theology

The central thread running through these scenes is the theme of hearing. Consider Jesus' story involving four categories of seeds and four soils. The first measure of seed falls beside the path, representing those who fail to hear ultimately because they have fallen victim to demonic forces. The second grouping of seed/soil symbolizes those who take in the word but finally cave in to persecution. Meanwhile, the third seed/soil marks out those who fail to hear due to life's distractions – whether born of prosperity or trouble. In contrast to all these, the seed that falls on good soil stands for those who truly hear the word of God and as a result bear fruit. On the parable's logic, then, the fundamental question is not whether or not one has 'converted' to Jesus (which would have been true for the second, third and fourth seeds), but whether or not one bears fruit of obedience. For Luke (not to mention the NT as a whole), the most accurate barometer of one's standing in the kingdom is the quality of one's life. And, from the human vantage point, the crucial predictor as to whether Jesus' hearers will bear such fruit is the quality of their listening to him. The word of God is no respecter of persons. Even Jesus' own mother and brothers could not guarantee their position inside Jesus' family, especially if they failed to listen.

But the parable of the sower is not just about human listening, for it is also about God and what God is doing in Jesus. It announces an already-but-not-yet kingdom, one that is taking shape in the present and destined to emerge fully in the future. While Jesus' first-century hearers were expecting a clean and definitive break between the present age and the kingdom to come, this parable portrays the kingdom of God as a sphere of reality that exists concurrently alongside cheap and idolatrous kingdom imitations, that is, spheres of human reality that fail to engage his word. As Jesus saw it, the advent of the kingdom did not mean the eradication of things such as persecution, temptations and apostasy. Rather, strangely and paradoxically, the kingdom is due to emerge through such things. The path to the kingdom is laid with the stepping stones of trial and opposition.

J. Messianic signs (8:22-56)

Context
In the previous chapter, in an attempt to allay perplexities surrounding his own putative Messiahship, Jesus alluded to the activities he had performed up to that point in the story, including healing diseases, exorcising demons, raising the dead and preaching the good news (7:21-22). Such activities were not only characteristic of Jesus but also just the kinds of things one would expect of the Messiah. And because several of these same messianic functions also crop up in the last two of the three episodes making up 8:22-56, one could not be much amiss in suspecting Luke's interest in reinforcing the messianic signs. Meanwhile, the first of these three scenes (8:22-25), the so-called 'stilling of the storm', naturally builds on the parable of the sower (8:4-15) and provides a lens through which to view the subsequent two scenes. Whereas the parable has urged appropriate responsiveness to the sown seed of God, Jesus' calming of the storm serves to plant a seed of its own kind, putting him in a category reserved for God. As these events make clear, Jesus' Messiahship is not merely extraordinary: it is tinged with divinity.

Comment
i. Calming of the storm (8:22–25)

22. The seemingly innocent segue *one day* (*en mia tōn hēmerōn*), plausibly to be translated 'on the first day', may be carrying more freight than first meets the eye, especially since Luke uses the same phrase to introduce Jesus' healing of the paralysed man (5:17). Given that similar language also marks the first Easter morning ('but on the first day of the week', *tē de mia tōn sabbatōn*; 24:1), Jesus' imminent stilling of the storm, together with the healing of the paralysed man (where questions of Jesus' divine prerogative are in play), may be pointing forward to the new creation of resurrection. It is not implausible that Luke intends both miracles, themselves concerned with authority, as harbingers of the divine authority more fully to be revealed at the resurrection. Getting into the boat along with his disciples, Jesus directs his band to go *to the other side of the lake*, that is, the eastern side of the lake, which is also Gentile territory.

23. As the boat sails, a sudden gust of wind descends on the lake. When cool air from the Golan Heights collides with warm air over the low-lying Sea of Galilee, waves have been known to crest up to 3 feet high. In this case, it would be only minutes before the boat became entirely swamped. Among the three Evangelists reporting this event (cf. Matt. 8:23–27//Mark 4:35–41), Luke alone editorializes that the men on board *were in danger*. And yet Jesus appears to be sleeping through it all!

24. While Matthew's disciples try to rouse Jesus with the title 'Lord' (Matt. 8:25) and Mark's disciples call him 'Teacher' (Mark 4:38), Luke's terrified sailors address him as *Master* (*epistata*, vocative) – twice in fact, as a realistic expression of their franticness. Their panic is understandable, as they believe they *are perishing*. Though some argue that by designating Jesus as *Master* the disciples are betraying an inadequate Christology, this does not square either with other applications of the same epithet in Luke where there is no hint of critique (5:5; 9:33, 49; 17:13) or with Judaism's designation of God as 'Master' (e.g. Sir. 23:1). Most likely Luke is simply hoping to get double duty out of the term: Jesus is at once the disciples' human master *and* the lord of the universe! The same incarnational theology underwrites Jesus' remarkable ability to sleep through the furious squall. As the fully faithful man, the sleeping Jesus exhibits complete trust in the providential care of his heavenly Father; as God incarnate, Jesus is roused on the model of Yahweh who likewise is awakened by the faithful in order to quell the forces of chaos (Pss 7:6; 44:23; 59:5; Isa. 51:9). The stilling of the elements at Jesus' rebuke (cf. 4:35, 39) equally corroborates his divine identity, since God alone controls the weather (Job 28:25–27; Ps. 135:7; Jer. 10:13). The point is not just that Jesus is God but that Jesus is a God who saves the wayward (see parallels with Ps. 107:23–30).

25. Having commanded the disciples to join him in visiting Gentile territory (v. 22), Jesus may now be faulting them for their failure to believe that such a directive was tantamount to a guarantee for safe passage. In response to Jesus' stinging question, the disciples are *afraid and amazed*, and now question among themselves his identity – an issue which will not be resolved until 9:20.

ii. Healing of a demoniac (8:26–39)

26. If the phrase *of the Gerasenes* was in fact original to Luke (some manuscripts have 'of the Gergesenes' while others read 'of the Gadarenes'), then *the country of the Gerasenes* represents an expansive district that included the steep slopes that still loom today over the north-eastern shore of the Sea of Galilee. Positioned *opposite Galilee* on the lake, the eastern territory was populated mostly by Gentiles. This fact alone would have given pious Jews ample cause to avoid the area. For Jesus' band, the area's undesirability would only have been exacerbated by its providing garrison for a nearby detachment of the Romans' Tenth Legion, space for a number of tombs (which in the rabbis' estimation were the 'mother of uncleanness') and a herding ground for a large number of ritually unclean boar. In coming here, Jesus could not have visited a less congenial place. Clearly, he came with some kind of purpose.

27. No sooner does Jesus step ashore than a certain *man of the city* (perhaps paralleling the sinful 'woman in the city' of 7:37) appears on the scene. He was a highly conspicuous figure, going about *for a long time* naked and unhoused, and lingering among the tombs. Though such activity is (and was) not uncharacteristic of the mentally ill, Luke assures his readers that this man *had demons*. The demoniac's naked and homeless state gives expression to the demons' ravaging effects, including deprivation and uprootedness. In mentioning that the unnamed demoniac *met* (*hypēntēsen*) Jesus, Luke chooses a verb (*hyantaō*) that normally has connotations of aggressive confrontation, suggesting that the demon-possessed man was about to engage Jesus in a spiritual conflict.

28–29. Now approaching Jesus, the demoniac *fell down* before him. The man's prostrate posture not only prepares for his forthcoming pleas for mercy, but also, within Luke's broader eschatological perspective, anticipates the universal obeisance which all beings, visible and invisible, would one day give to the victorious Risen Christ (Phil. 2:10–12). By addressing Jesus as the *Son of the Most High God* (cf. 1:32, 35, 76), the beleaguered Gentile – undoubtedly prompted by the demons' preternatural insight shared with Satan (4:3, 9) – acknowledges Jesus as the Son of the God of *Israel* (cf. 4:31–37).[77] The impetus for the whole encounter is that *Jesus had commanded the unclean spirit to come out of the man*, presumably even as the demoniac was en route to meeting Jesus. The comparison between Jesus' authoritative command here and his earlier rebuke of the natural elements (8:24) is hardly incidental. Because the ancients regularly ascribed meteorological disruption to demonic forces (1 En. 69:22; Jub. 2:2; T. Sol. 16), Luke must have seen Jesus' earlier stilling of the storm (8:22–25) as foreshadowing the present passage. Juxtaposing the two uncanny events while highlighting their shared threads, the Gospel writer implies that Jesus' authority over the demonic is of a piece with his sovereignty over fallen creation.

30. In compelling the demon to give his name, Jesus complies with exorcistic practices of the day, where successful exorcism often depended on knowing the name of the invading spirit.[78] The

---

77. Josephus (*Ant.* 16.162–164) notes that this term was the Gentiles' epithet of choice for the God of Israel. At the same time, the divine epithet may conjure Dan. 7, where the cosmic battle between the unclean forces of the pagan kingdoms and the royal-priestly Son of Man comes to a head (Dan. 7:18, 22, 25, 27).

78. At the same time, in failing to perform rituals or prayers prior to his exorcism, Jesus is decidedly *unlike* any contemporary exorcist. See Klutz, 'Exorcism', pp. 159–160, 164–165.

demoniac's terse response (*Legion*) underscores not only the abundance of demons (as Luke points out), but also their association with the nearby occupying Roman soldiers. Elsewhere, I have argued that in the original historical context the convergence of unclean spirits in this area may have had something to do with the nearby Roman soldiers engaging in (idolatrous) worship of their military standards.[79] Given the imminent demise of 'a large herd of swine' (vv. 32–33), and given, too, the fact that the wild boar was the official mascot of the local legion, Luke's readers may well have read between the lines to learn that the powerful forces of pagan Rome would one day succumb to Jesus' power.[80]

31–33. Once Jesus secures their collective name, the demons know they are outmatched. Accordingly, they beg Jesus not to send them *into the abyss* (*eis tēn abysson*), that is, the holding place for evil spirits pending the day of judgment.[81] More than that, they ask permission to enter a large herd of swine feeding *on the hillside* – more simply 'on the hill', perhaps another surreptitious nod towards Rome, the famed 'city on the hill'. While in a seemingly surprising show of leniency Jesus grants their request, justification may lie in the scriptural image emerging from the now-demon-possessed pigs descending *down the steep bank into the lake*.[82] Just as Pharaoh's forces were doomed to drown in the Red Sea, so too, Luke seems to say, the Roman Empire (symbolized by the swine on the hill) would one day succumb to a judgment no less decisive.

34. Exactly how much the pig herders saw of all this is anyone's guess. Certainly, the sight of an entire herd of swine plunging to its watery death would have been remarkable enough – even

---

79. Perrin, *Jesus the Temple*, pp. 163–170.

80. The Romans were impressed by wild boars' brute strength. The animal became the chief symbol of the First Legion (*Italica*) and Twentieth Legion (*Victrix*), the latter of which was stationed not far from the scene of this exorcism.

81. On the abyss, see Jeremias, *TDNT* 1, pp. 9–10.

82. On the other hand, because 'abyss' can also refer to the sea (e.g. Gen. 1:2; 7:11), there is some sense in which Jesus refuses the demons' request; see Bovon, p. 437 n. 59.

terrifying. Understandably, *they ran off (ephygon)* or 'fled' (ESV); as they go, they proclaim *(appēngeilan)* the amazing turn of events *in the city and in the country*. Notably, the same two verbs *(phygō* and *apangellō)* also occur in Isaiah 48:20 ('Go out from Babylon, *flee* from Chaldea, / declare this with a shout of joy, *proclaim* it, / send it forth to the end of the earth; / say, "The LORD has redeemed his servant Jacob!"'; emphasis added), perhaps suggesting that the demoniac's redemption from 'Legion' symbolizes apostate Israel's return from exile. By this analogy, the state of the demoniac (naked, unclean and without a house) would also represent those who reject Jesus and choose instead to continue in exile: naked, unclean and without a properly functioning temple.[83] On the flip side, the metaphor also promises eschatological redemption from exile, a redemption now taking place through Jesus.

35. Eventually, a crowd of fascinated spectators comes out to see what has happened.[84] After examining the remains of the drowned swine, they come to Jesus who, along with his disciples, had obviously lingered long enough to allow the alarmed swineherds to return (with an intrigued contingent in tow). Even more startling than the herd's collective plunge was the presence of the once-notorious demoniac, now *clothed and in his right mind*. More than that, he is *sitting at the feet of Jesus (para tous podas)*, thus again bearing some resemblance to the sinful woman who stood weeping next to Jesus' feet *(para tous podas, 7:38)*. At this sight, so we might imagine, *they were afraid*.

36. Not unexpectedly, the original eyewitnesses repeat their story: *those who had seen it told them* – an action described with the same verb of proclamation *(apangellō)*. The content of that proclamation is simple enough: the man who had once been demon-possessed had been *healed (esōthē)* or 'saved'. Though Luke also uses *sōsō* in connection with salvation stemming from the preaching of the gospel, the Evangelist seems to understand this dramatic exorcism as a kind of salvation.

---

83. This interpretation is supported by 11:14–26; see commentary below.

84. Though the Greek does not specify a subject, the NRSV rightly supplies the word *people*.

37. By this time, members of a crowd have gathered from the surrounding countryside; on hearing the eyewitnesses' most recent report, they are *seized with great fear.* As if the sight of the transformed man were not unnerving enough, even more awe-inspiring was the realization that the power to bring about such transformation was concentrated in this person Jesus. Like Peter before them (5:8), the locals are psychologically overwhelmed by Jesus' display of power and ask him to leave. Much to their relief, he obliges by getting into the boat and prepares to head back to the western shore.

38–39. Yet even while Jesus and the disciples board, the transformed man pleads with Jesus *that he might be with him (einai syn autō).* Perhaps because 'being with Jesus' was a privilege restricted to the Twelve (8:1; cf. Acts 1:21–22; Mark 2:14), Jesus declines. Yet as he dismisses the erstwhile demoniac, he gives him a charge: *Return to your home, and declare how much God has done for you.* Here two remarks are in order. First, strikingly, in enjoining the restored man to *declare* God's works on his behalf, Jesus uses the same verb *(diēgeomai)* the Evangelist himself will use in describing the apostles' post-mission debrief (9:10), when they report back on what God has done through them. It is also the same lexical root with which Luke introduces his Gospel as narrative (1:1). In so many words, then, the liberated man is encouraged to present his own 'gospel story', revolving around his own experience of Jesus' power – all on the model of the apostolic proclamation and even of Luke's very own Gospel account. Second, though the man is told to declare what God has done, he instead proclaims *how much Jesus had done for him.* The implication could not be any clearer: from Luke's point of view, to declare God's great works on humanity's behalf is to declare what Jesus has done – and vice versa.

iii. Restored women (8:40–56)

40. On Jesus' return *(en de tō hypostrephein)* to the west side of the lake, the crowds welcome him, for they had been eagerly *waiting for him (prosdokōntes).* The latter verb has already been used in connection with messianic expectation (3:15; 7:19–20) and may be hinting at the same here. If some report of Jesus' stunning exorcism (8:26–39) had already preceded him, then this news, together with popular expectations regarding the Messiah's power over the demonic (1 En. 55:4; T. Mos. 10:1), would have convinced the crowds of Jesus' messianic candidacy.

41–42. Though the two female characters in this scene remain anonymous, the suppliant synagogue ruler is identified as Jairus, meaning 'Yahweh shines'. Casting aside all the dignity of office, he falls at *Jesus' feet* (not unlike earlier characters; cf. 7:38; 8:35), repetitively begging (iterative imperfect *parekalei*) the much touted healer to come to his aid. Like the centurion (7:1–10), Jairus intercedes on behalf of a loved one who lies gravely ill back at home – and to this extent he evidences faith. Yet unlike the Gentile officer, ironically, the Jewish ruler does not have sufficient faith to believe that Jesus can heal from a distance.

As if the prospect of losing one's young daughter were not grim enough, the threatened tragedy is compounded by the fact that she is the synagogue ruler's 'only-born' (*monogenēs*) and is about twelve years old, the age at which young Jewish girls are typically *about to be* married through betrothal, and therefore on the cusp of perpetuating the biological family line. Despite the high-stakes situation, Jesus is impeded by the crowds who in their curiosity are continually pressing (*synepnigon*) upon him – much to the ruler's vexation.[85]

43. Yet matters are about to change from bad to worse, for Jesus is now delayed by a certain woman who *had been suffering from haemorrhages for twelve years*. Due to this condition, which we might suppose to be chronic menorrhagia (prolonged menstrual bleeding), the woman *had spent all she had on physicians*, and *no one could cure her*.[86] Quite apart from its debilitating physical effects, a contin-

---

85. Having used the same verb (*sympnigō*) in connection with the thorn-choked plants in the parable of the sower (8:14), Luke may intend a parallel between Jairus's anxiousness and the word-choking worries of life.

86. The original wording of Luke 8:43 is uncertain. The NRSV here (along with the ESV and many other translations) retains mention of her medical costs; other translations (e.g. NIV, NLT and NET) omit it. The manuscript evidence is ambivalent, but in my view the evidence favours the phrase's inclusion.

uous menstrual flow would have rendered her a permanent *niddâ* (menstruating woman) (Lev. 15:19–23), not only consigning her to a ritually unclean state but also isolating her from others. Such a woman would have required nothing less than a financial, physical, social and spiritual restoration.

Noting the Evangelist's careful interweaving of these two stories, the alert reader senses that both females are made to symbolize something much larger than themselves. Unless the exact match between the twelve-year duration of this woman's illness and the age of Jairus's daughter is sheer coincidence (as commentators disinclined to recognize metaphorical layering are inclined to believe), it seems that both women – one standing in for errant virgin Israel (Jer. 31:4, 21), the other for exiled unclean Israel (Ezek. 22:26) – are being marshalled to represent Israel poised to be restored by Jesus. If the fertility of both women is under threat (albeit for different reasons), Luke seems to say, Jesus comes to renew the people of God in their Adamic mandate to 'be fruitful and multiply' (Gen. 1:28).

44. As in 7:36–50, a distraught woman approaches Jesus from *behind* (*opisthen*), this time not to offer precious ointments but to extract Jesus' healing power by covertly grasping *the fringe of his clothes* (*tou kraspedou tou himatiou autou*).[87] The woman is not disappointed, for on seizing the garment she experiences immediate relief, proving that just as Jesus had power over enthralling unclean spirits and unclean surroundings (8:26–39), the same power could also be brought to bear on the woman's ailing and unclean body. Together, both extraordinary acts of purification point, on the one side, to Jesus as the eschatological priest who declares the unclean clean, and, on the other side, to the people of God who are now – with the advent of Jesus – in the process of being cultically repurified. The retrieval of such purity of course is not an end in itself but the necessary prelude to the vocation of worship.

---

87. The fringe would have also included four tassels designed to remind pious Jews 'of "all the commandments of the Lord" so that they would do them (cf. Num 15:37–39). But the woman is violating a purity commandment by touching this fringe' (Tannehill, p. 149).

45. Jesus' question (*Who touched me?*) may be either a genuine enquiry born out of real ignorance or a rhetorical question posed in order to 'smoke out' the woman from the crowd. *When all denied it*, Peter remonstrates with the master, pointing out that the crowds are both surrounding (*synechousin*) and pressing in (*apothilbousin*).[88] The first of these two participles denotes intense compression, with possible connotations of oppression; the second may be justifiably translated as 'squeezing'. Together, the two words not only explain Jesus' difficulty in moving forward but also metaphorically allude to a crowd's power to choke out faith through peer pressure.[89]

46–47. Despite Peter's exasperation, Jesus remains adamant, convinced *that power had gone out from* him. Though the Evangelist does not say as much, at this point one can only imagine Jesus now turning both head and body around with a searching gaze – and that was enough to solve the mystery. Though some translations (e.g. ESV, KJV) imply that the woman behind him had been attempting to conceal herself for a time (albeit unsuccessfully), she may have actually been rejecting that option outright: 'knowing that she was not about to hide' (*idousa de hē gynē hoti ouk elathen*). And so we are graphically reminded, 'nothing is hidden that will not be disclosed, nor is anything secret that will not become known and come to light' (8:17). Against the backdrop of 8:17, then, Luke's Jesus calls out the woman not to embarrass her, but to put the light of her faith on a lampstand.

In Ancient Judaism, if a *niddâ* or any unclean person were to make physical contact with another, the unclean state would transfer like a contagion. That meant that if the woman's condition and actions were to come to light, she might ordinarily expect a stern reaction from those she had touched. Of course, part of Luke's point is that in this respect, too, there is something decidedly *unordinary* about Jesus. Though conflicted and trembling (*tremousa*) with swirling emotions of guilt and fear, the woman entrusts

88. The KJV's inclusion of 'and sayest thou' before repeating Jesus' query depends on manuscripts which likely reflect a copyist's decision to conform Luke's version to Mark 5:31.

89. Similarly Green, p. 348.

herself to her healer by prostrating herself, getting right to an explanation for her socially unacceptable actions: *she declared in the presence of all the people why she had touched him, and how she had been immediately healed.* As in the immediately preceding passage (8:34, 36), this verb of reporting (*apangellō*) retains a kerygmatic, proclamatory aspect. The woman's testimony declaration speaks not only of her personal transformation but also of her motivations for seeking Jesus.

48. Perhaps to everyone's surprise, Jesus does not chide the prostrate woman but profoundly affirms her by addressing her as *daughter.* As the newest member of Jesus' family, she does the will of God (8:19–21). And if she has done the will of God precisely by touching Jesus' garment and confessing no less, then she need not fear recrimination. Though Jesus has intimated that it was his 'power' that healed the woman, this is qualified by *your faith* that *has made you well (sesōken se)* – 'has saved you'. Divine power and human faith combine in the saving transaction. Finally, Jesus instructs the now-healed woman to *go in peace.* That is, she is to go forth not just in a state of emotional peace, but with the assurance of health, wholeness, blessedness and right-standing before God.

49–50. Even while Jesus is *still speaking,* a messenger from Jairus's house announces that the ruler's daughter has passed. For the moment, as far as the synagogue ruler is concerned, Jesus' drawn-out interaction with the former *niddâ* proves to be a tragic distraction at best, an act of gross negligence at worst. Yet Jesus remains unruffled. On hearing the news, he turns to Jairus with a negative command (*Do not fear*), a positive command (*Only believe*) and a promise (*and she will be saved*). That Jesus uses the same verb of saving (*sōsō*) for both his healing of the bleeding woman and his imminent restoration of Jairus's daughter frames the 'saving' of the first miracle as a kind of down payment for the second. The theological dividends of this story – as a storied metaphor of Christ's redemption from restored purity to future resurrection – are not hard to come by.

51. Finally arriving at Jairus's house, Jesus restricts entrance to Peter, James, John and the girl's parents. The decision to allow the parents to accompany him is patently sensible. But by inviting these three disciples, apart from the Twelve, Jesus establishes an inner circle within the apostolate – the same three will have the sole privilege of accompanying Jesus at the transfiguration (9:28–36).[90]

52–53. As the six adults prepare to enter, Jesus admonishes the *weeping and wailing* bystanders: *Do not weep; for she is not dead but sleeping.* Though astute members of the crowd might have recognized that Jesus was using sleep as a metaphor for death (Dan. 12:2), the parable falls on spiritually deaf ears: they all (*pantes*, v. 52) laugh at Jesus. Relating this episode on the far side of 6:21b ('Blessed are you who weep now, for you will laugh') and 6:25b ('Woe to you who are laughing now, for you will mourn and weep'), the Gospel writer is undoubtedly leveraging the combination of mourning and laughter to fill out the meaning of the earlier stated paradox. It is not mourning per se but rather mourning with the ears of faith that seals one's participation in the kingdom. While some mourning quickly devolves into laughter *at* Jesus, other mourners, not least those who witness life from death, will have their weeping turn to joy.

54. That Jesus should take the girl by her hand is striking, especially since Luke's readers are aware that Jesus' healings do not require physical proximity, much less physical touch (cf. 7:1–10). Yet by coupling this gesture with the command *Child, get up!* (*hē pais egeire*), Jesus not only expresses practical care for the girl but also draws on a scripturally rooted analogy between her and himself, on the one hand, and Yahweh and exiled Israel on the other: 'Rise up . . . O captive daughter Zion! . . . The LORD has bared his holy arm' (Isa. 52:2, 10). On another level, the phrase *hē pais* is meant to round out a complementarity of gender. The centurion's male *pais* (7:7), who also lay gravely ill at home, has now found its female counterpart in the *pais* of the resuscitated girl. Jesus' saving powers are for both male and female.[91]

---

90. Mark identifies these three as being present at Gethsemane (Mark 14:33), but Luke's account does not specify individual names (Luke 22:39–46).

91. Gender pairing has been regularly noted in Luke's Gospel; see e.g. Kopas, 'Jesus and Women', p. 192.

55. On Jesus' command, the spirit of the girl returns and the girl herself – in literal compliance with that command – gets up. Next Jesus orders that she be given something to eat, in part because she may have gone without food for some time, in part, too, in order to prove that the restored girl is no ghost but a flesh-and-blood reality. Another interpretative level may also be in view, with the mention that her *spirit returned (epestrepsen to pneuma)*. If the return of the spirit to the girl is a figure of the eschatological return of the Spirit to Israel, which Ezekiel associates not just with return from exile but also with resurrection (Ezek. 37), then the food which Jesus commands for the recovering child stands for the food promised to restored Israel (Ezek. 36:29–30). Luke's story, then, speaks of Jesus' deep compassion for an individual, but nods to God's compassion for Israel as a whole.

56. Now Jesus instructs the *astounded* parents *to tell no one*. Exactly why Jesus enjoins silence in this case (but not in the case of the resuscitation of the dead man at Nain) is unclear. In any event, like Mark the Evangelist, Luke is also concerned to take up the theme of secrecy. Jesus is keen to keep word of such astounding events within a tightly controlled circle, at least until the resurrection should make all things clear.

Theology

As Luke's story has already made clear, there is no predicting who will – and who will not – respond to the word of God. And for that very reason, Jesus invites his disciples to join him on a trip to the east side of the lake – into Gentile country. They go into this spiritually uncultivated territory to sow the word, so to speak, even if that 'word' turns out to be almost entirely without verbal content. The decision to cross the Sea of Galilee sets in motion a train of extraordinary events. Consider this: had Jesus never led his disciples across the lake in the first place, the miraculous events recorded in this passage might never have transpired. Once again, mission sets the stage for God's performance of mighty deeds through Jesus.

In this section, we again find Jesus raising the dead, healing the diseased and exorcising the demon-possessed. Yet before performing any of these activities he calms the unruly waters, just as Yahweh did in Genesis 1 when he asserted his kingdom over and against the realm of chaos. As the first in a series, the stilling of the storm illuminates the events that follow. Whereas exorcism, healing and raising the dead confirm that Jesus the Messiah has come to establish his kingdom, the prior stilling of the storm asserts Jesus' divine identity. As the disciples obediently accompany Jesus on increasingly risky missions like these, they come into closer contact with his identity as Messiah *and* Lord. Knowing Jesus as Messiah and Lord is no theoretical acquaintance. Such knowing, Luke reminds his readers, occurs pre-eminently in the rough and tumble of divinely prompted mission.

K. Ministry of the Twelve (9:1–17)

Context

We recall that Jesus summoned his disciples in 5:1 – 6:19, only then in the Sermon on the Plain (6:20–49) to sketch out the terms of that vocation. Now in 9:1–9, as an early indication of the kinds of tasks the church would be about in Acts, he commissions the Twelve. They are to bring along no earthly supplies but only their experience of Jesus who has now shared his authority with them. If the success of this initial mission was not evidence enough of this granted authority, the point is further driven home by the feeding of the five thousand (9:10–17). The movement from mission to feeding suggests not only that the disciples bear – to their surprise –a responsibility in hosting the crowd but also that this show of hospitality is somehow integral to their role as the Twelve. This in turn helps explain the frequency of meals in Luke–Acts (Luke 5:27–39; 14:1–24; 22:14–38; 24:13–35; Acts 1:4; 10:1 – 11:18; 27:33–38). The feedings which Jesus performed as Messiah are meant to be replicated, metaphorically and literally, in the ministry of the Twelve.

Comment

i. Commissioning of the Twelve (9:1–9)

1–2. Though the Twelve have gone virtually unmentioned after their appointment (6:12–15), now they re-emerge to receive Jesus' delegated *power and authority* over the demonic realm and over

disease. Their charge? To exercise the same prowess Jesus demonstrates in subduing the unruly realms of spiritual darkness and
physical disease (6:17–19). Insofar as 6:20 – 8:56 narrates Jesus'
modelling of kingdom power, the Twelve must now function as an
extension of Jesus. The concepts of *power* and *authority* are related
but distinct. Whereas the former typically carries the sense of
ability or capacity, the latter pertains to office or station. In granting
the Twelve both power and authority, then, Jesus conveys both
special abilities and special rights; as such, they are empowered to
heal and to proclaim the kingdom in the face of dark forces.[92]
Again, the distinction between the content of the kingdom proclamation and its authentication, the 'what' and the 'how' of the
kingdom message, recedes to the point of almost disappearing.

3. Jesus' list of prohibited items includes precisely those things
that one would expect to take on a journey.[93] In part, Jesus seems
to impose such restrictions in order to foster God-directed dependence rather than self-reliance. In part, too, by undertaking a journey
without such provisions, the Twelve would be imitating the twelve
tribes of the exodus who were prevented from storing up food
(Exod. 16) or packing clothes (Deut. 8:4; 29:5). For the Twelve, the
modality of their exodus-like existence becomes part of their
message.

4. The Twelve are also discouraged from moving from house to
house. Perhaps the logic here revolves around the Twelve needing
to build a solid relational base, which would seem to require longer-
term (rather than shorter-term) enjoyment of the supporting
family's hospitality.

---

92. The mission of the Twelve prepares for a much more significant
    mission set to unfold in Acts 2. Nolland (p. 426) comments: 'As the
    rejection in Nazareth is a kind of dress rehearsal for the passion of
    Jesus, so this mission is something of a dress rehearsal for the post-
    Pentecost role of the Twelve.'
93. It is sometimes claimed (see e.g. Johnson, p. 148) that the Twelve's
    modus operandi is meant to resemble that of Cynic philosophers (cf.
    Epictetus, *Diatr.* 3.22.50); if this were the case, Luke could have
    certainly done much more to strengthen the parallel.

5–6. Jesus is aware that while some villages will welcome his emissaries, other places will not. In the latter such cases, Jesus instructs the Twelve that when they are *leaving that town* they are to *shake the dust off* their *feet as a testimony against them.* Because dust is associated with the curse (Gen. 3:14), the disciples' act of shaking dust off the bottom of their soles would be to place that town under a curse, sealing the community's separation from the divine covenant. Having received their brief, they depart and follow Jesus' orders to a tee, preaching good news to the people and healing their sick.

7a. *Herod the ruler* (or the tetrarch) has already been mentioned in Luke's 'who's who' of power brokers (3:1). Now the high-ranking figure is reintroduced as one who is bewildered by these activities. Bewildered – and threatened. In proclaiming the kingdom of God, the Twelve, exactly as the symbolic representatives of the twelve tribes of Israel, were powerfully signifying Jesus' subversive intentions of reconstituting Israel around himself. This could also mean that Jesus had designs on replacing the current political structure in Galilee, which included Herod as its head.

7b–9. The Twelve's deeds were not only creating a stir in their own right but also provoking speculation regarding Jesus' origins. Depending on whom one talked to, Jesus was either (1) a John the Baptizer redivivus, (2) a manifestation of Elijah the prophet or (3) the re-emergence of a long-dead prophet other than Elijah.[94] As Herod considers these options, he seems to rule out the possibility that Jesus is a second version of John. After all, as Herod says, *John I beheaded.* As for options (2) and (3) – the tetrarch doesn't even bother to ruminate. In contrast to the rank and file's tendency to link Jesus to some deceased holy figure, Herod's puzzlement drips with disdain: his words might be rendered, 'Who is this fellow' (*houtos*: this one) *about whom I hear such things?* Still his interest is piqued, for he keeps trying (imperfect: *ezētei*) to see Jesus.

---

94. As Tannehill (p. 153) points out, *one of the ancient prophets* 'could suggest that Jesus is the prophet like Moses, which will be affirmed in Acts (3:22; 7:37; cf. Deut 18:15)'.

ii. Feeding of the five thousand (9:10–17)

10. Once their mission is complete, the apostles report back on *all they had done*, prompting Jesus to initiate a private retreat. The Greek word *hypechōrēsen*, translated here as *withdrew* (NRSV), has connotations of a fugitive status or flight from political persecution – not surprisingly since Herod is almost certainly trying 'to see' Jesus (9:9) with ill intent.[95] Their destination is *a city called Bethsaida*. Luke's phrasing suggests that the small fishing town on the northern tip of the lake would be unfamiliar to many of his readers.[96]

11. Despite the unexpected arrival of the crowds, Jesus exercises hospitality by welcoming the people in all their neediness. For the benefit of some, he heals; for the benefit of all, he then speaks about the kingdom. Yet even before the issue of food arises, Jesus' actions reflect those of the consummate host.

12. For the moment, however, the Twelve appear to surpass Jesus in their seeming sensitivity to the crowds' needs. For as the day ebbs, the disciples have already formulated – strikingly apart from Jesus – a plan for the crowd and now inform their master regarding his prescribed role in it. *Send the crowd away*, they instruct Jesus, in order that they might disperse to the surrounding towns and countryside in the hope of finding food and lodging (*katalysōsin*).[97] After all, the Twelve continue, *we are here in a deserted place*. Ironically, while the disciples should have perhaps recognized the combination of crowds and desert as an important clue that Jesus was preparing to re-enact the miraculous desert feeding of the exodus (which in turn might have implied their shared responsibility in feeding the people), the Twelve see their wilderness location as grounds for dismissing the crowds altogether.

13–14a. To the disciples' surprise, Jesus responds with a counter-imperative of his own: *You give them something to eat* (*dote autois hymeis phagein*). The laconic Greek sentence, which lacks an immediate

---

95. BDAG, p. 1043.
96. On Bethsaida, see Riesner, *DJG*, p. 51; also Savage, *Bethsaida*.
97. The verb *katalyō* implies taking advantage of another's hospitality; see BDAG, pp. 521–522.

direct object for 'give' (i.e. 'you give them to eat'), looks ahead to the Last Supper, when Jesus 'gave it [i.e. broken bread] to them' (*edōken autois*, 22:19), for their eating (*phagein*) (22:15). Just as, as we shall see, the meal of Luke 22 is both a 'new exodus' meal and a 'new covenant' meal, the feeding miracle here takes on both redemptive-historical and sacramental significance. In the former aspect, the feeding miracle signals the arrival of the kingdom and marks out Jesus as its appointed presider; as a prelude to the Eucharist, it designates the apostles as delegated hosts, as it were, laying the foundation for the continuing performance of the Lord's Supper in the church. Meanwhile, faced with such scant resources (*five loaves and two fish*) and such a massive crowd (*about five thousand men*), the apostles remain perplexed as to how they might hope to discharge Jesus' command. They contemplate aloud the possibility of buying food for the crowds but do so only to underscore the sheer absurdity of the idea. Whereas Luke's Jesus has already insisted that his followers give (*dote*) without reserve (6:38), the Twelve's tepid response to Jesus' 'Give!' (*dote*) here betrays spiritual shiftlessness. As this passage makes clear, if Jesus bids his followers to give freely, unconditionally and lavishly, their principal constraint is not lack of resources but lack of faith.

14b–15. Jesus' immediate followers started out in this passage as 'apostles' (v. 10) and the 'twelve' (v. 12), but now – for all we know – they have been demoted to *his disciples*. They receive orders to have the crowds *sit down in groups of about fifty each*. Though the majority of English translations join the NRSV in rendering *kataklinō* as 'sit down', the YLT's 'cause them to *recline* in companies' (emphasis added) gets at an important nuance. Whereas everyday Jewish meals were taken sitting down, festive meals, including the Passover, were enjoyed in a reclining position. Passover of course was the segue to the exodus. This is not unrelated to Jesus dividing the five *thousand* into roughly a *hundred* groups numbering *fifty* – all in imitation of Moses who parcelled the exodus generation into 'thousands, hundreds, fifties, and tens' (Exod. 18:21).

16. Luke now describes Jesus' actions with three main verbs (*blessed . . . broke . . . and gave*), precisely the same verbs predicated of Jesus at the Last Supper (22:19); the string of clauses is preceded by two participles: *taking* and *looked up*. That which Jesus 'takes' is none other than the previously mentioned bread and fish, again drawing to mind the Mosaic wilderness feeding.[98] Jesus' heavenward gaze seems to show that had the disciples themselves previously looked to heaven, they might have been better positioned to fulfil his request. But perhaps Luke's point is actually that neither heavenly mindedness by itself nor human resourcefulness by itself is sufficient to meet the needs of Christian ministry. Rather, the potential of our meagre resources is fully realized only when Jesus takes them and offers them up – through blessing, breaking and redistribution – to God the Father.

17. The crowds not only *ate* but *were filled*. Their satiety makes impossible the reading commonly handed down in the nineteenth-century liberal interpretation that the real miracle here was not that Jesus multiplied loaves and fish (which is said to be too incredible), but that everyone shared. This kind of abundance was also characteristic of the messianic banquet, as Second Temple Jews understood it (Isa. 25:6; Ezek. 34:17–30). Luke also tells us that the Twelve collected the leftovers in *twelve baskets* (*kophinoi*), containers roughly 2 gallons (4 litres) in size used for transporting daily provisions. If Jesus' disciples had managed to fill twelve such *kophinoi*, totalling 24 gallons (48 litres) altogether, such a volume would far outstrip the volume of the original five loaves and two fish. Given Israel's hope of a restored remnant, the vision of the scrap-gathering Twelve perhaps pictures the restoration of the twelve scattered tribes, which themselves are fragments of once-unified Israel. Through the feeding of the masses, Jesus reveals himself as the messianic king who cares for Israel *and* also his own imminent role in the eschatological restoration of the tribes – all sure-fire evidence that the kingdom had come in Jesus.

Theology
Though the Twelve's first mission was a spectacular success by any human measure, the afterglow of their achievement is quickly

---

98. Second Temple Jewish interpreters sometimes interpreted the quails from the sea (Num. 11:31) as a kind of flying fish; see Bovon, 'Scriptures', p. 29.

dampened by their failure to grasp that the same God who miraculously supplied their needs on their missionary journeys could equally provide for the crowds. To be sure, in fairness to the disciples, one could hardly imagine, especially in that desert setting, a greater disparity between supply and demand. Such a vast need and yet so scant the supplies! Both the Twelve's mission and the subsequent feeding miracle illustrate that wherever resources are scarce, God's miraculous provision becomes all the more conspicuous. In both passages, Jesus bids the Twelve as he does in order to show that the kingdom normally advances not through abundance and strength but through scarcity and weakness. Once turned over to Jesus, our meagre resources become God's opportunity.

L. Messianic revelation (9:18–50)

Context
This section is an important hinge in the Gospel's structure. Peter's confession of Jesus as Messiah builds not only on the preceding feeding miracle (9:10–17), where the apostles have surmised their master's royal role (i.e. by effectively feeding the people as kings should do), but also on Jesus' baptism (3:21–22), where he is marked out as a Davidic son – and therefore as the Messiah. Next, the transfiguration recapitulates the divine voice first heard at the baptism, declaring Jesus' sonship. And yet these scenes are intermixed with two predictions concerning Jesus' death, which at last shed light on his earlier mysterious remarks about the bridegroom being taken away (5:35). Immediately following this section, at 9:51, Jesus will turn his face towards to Jerusalem in order to die. Straddling these twin emphases of messianic glory and messianic suffering, 9:18–50 epitomizes Jesus' full messianic self-disclosure.

Comment
i. Peter's confession (9:18–27)
18–19. By this point in the story Jesus has already prayed alone twice: right before his baptism (3:21–22) and immediately before calling the Twelve (6:12–15). On discovering Jesus again praying

alone, we suspect that we are on the verge of another major turning point (see also 22:39–46). As it turns out, each of these prayer scenes anticipates a crisis in terms of either Christological identity (Who is Jesus and how will he discharge his vocation?) or apostolic identity (Who are the Twelve and how will they discharge their vocation?). Consistent with this pattern, the present passage marks a major stride in resolving the question 'Who is this Jesus?', even as it spells out the unexpectedly arresting terms of both Jesus' calling and the calling of those who would follow him. But first Jesus quizzes his disciples: *Who do the crowds say that I am?* Without committing themselves, they respond by mentioning three different possible identities, identical to those contemplated by Herod (9:7–9).[99]

20. The lead position of the second person pronoun *you* (*hymeis*) in the Greek of Jesus' query is emphatic: 'But *you*, who do *you* say I am?' Characteristically speaking on behalf of the Twelve, Peter tersely responds, *The Messiah of God*. Whereas only angels and demons have assigned Jesus a messianic role up to this point (2:11; 4:41), here for the first time – likely in answer to Jesus' prayers (v. 18) – a human voice confesses the astonishing truth. In Peter's mouth the term *christos* would not necessarily entail notions of either transcendence or divinity. Instead, the disciple is affirming that Jesus is the long-awaited fulfilment of the Davidic promise (2 Sam. 7), the one who would be tasked with restoring Israel's sacred space, regathering the twelve tribes, driving out the Gentiles and restoring the Davidic throne. Given Herod's recent queries (9:7–9), Peter's public confession is a bold and even dangerous move, effectively linking his fate to the fate of his master.

21. Notwithstanding the formal accuracy of Peter's response, he is met by a 'stern order' (*epitimēsas*) – the same response which Jesus had earlier issued to an unclean spirit (4:35), a fever (4:39) and the unruly waters (8:24). And so rather than congratulating his lead disciple at this moment, Jesus rebukes him. He does so seemingly because Peter and the rest of the Twelve still harbour grave and ultimately satanic misunderstandings regarding the nature of Jesus'

---

99. See commentary above for 9:7–9.

Messiahship. For this very reason, until Jesus' messianic vocation should be clarified through his death and resurrection, it is imperative that the Twelve keep this astounding disclosure to themselves.

22. Self-identifying not only as the Messiah but now also as the Danielic Son of Man, Jesus foretells his suffering, his rejection by – ironically enough – the temple elite, his death and finally his being raised *on the third day*. All these events are a matter not just of imminent certainty but of divine necessity: it is necessary (*dei*). Given the parallels between Jesus' predicted sufferings and vindication, on the one side, and the suffering and vindication of the Son of Man of Daniel 7, on the other, Jesus' resurrection must correspond to the Son of Man's enthronement as the Messiah (Dan. 7:13–14).[100] How will the unclean pagan nations threatening God's people finally be routed? According to Jesus' mysterious logic (still incomprehensible to the Twelve), this will occur through the resurrection of the Son of Man.

23. On the assumption that 'all' in the phrase *he said to them all* refers to an audience now perhaps larger than the Twelve, Jesus' stipulations are intended as a challenge for his immediate followers as well as generalized instructions for those who would later receive the apostolic message.[101] Jesus' requirements for discipleship are threefold, involving (1) self-denial, (2) daily cross-bearing and (3) following. The condition of self-denial pertains especially though not exclusively to the realm of material possessions. This may be inferred from the fact that the Twelve had just come off a leanly supported missionary journey (9:3), even while Luke's most prominent examples of self-denial have revolved around financial sacrifice (7:37; 8:3). Second, that true disciples must also *take up their cross daily* indicates that the decision to follow Jesus is no glorious

---

100. On the messianic interpretation of the Son of Man, see Beasley-Murray, 'Interpretation'.

101. The more public nature of Jesus' teaching is supported elsewhere. For example, when the angelic figures speak to the women at the tomb, they presume that the women were privy to Jesus' teaching at just this point (24:6–8).

one-off: on the contrary, it entails a day-in, day-out recommitment to carrying the same kind of ignominious burden that Jesus himself would be forced to carry. Third and finally, those who would come after Jesus must *follow me*. On one level, Jesus is referring to the convention of rabbinical discipleship *simpliciter*. On another level, however, with Jesus' journey to Jerusalem (9:51) on the horizon, Luke's readers are made to sense that they too must, so to speak, make their own ominous journey to Jerusalem on the pattern of Jesus.

24. Jesus' severe conditions for discipleship do not remain as naked fiats but are now supported by explanatory remarks introduced by *for* (*gar*). Here again Jesus depends on a paradoxical line of reasoning, where it is only those who *want to save their life* (*tēn psychēn autou*) who *will lose it*, while *those who lose their life for my sake will save it*. The term *life* (*psychē*), the equivalent of the Hebrew *nephesh*, is virtually untranslatable, referring to the sum total of the human person without our modern-day sharp distinctions between physical, mental, spiritual and volitional aspects.[102] It denotes all that one is and all that one stands for (attachments, desires, commitments, goals, values and behaviours) as these come to expression in the course of life. Thus to *lose* or 'destroy' one's *psychē* is to undergo a complete reorientation that is virtually tantamount to the annihilation of the self, giving way to a renewed self. All this, Jesus says, is *for my sake*. Thus Jesus offers himself as not just the primary motivation for this paradoxical exchange but also its goal. He is the human blueprint for the eschatologically saved life.

25. Mindful of the high stakes of his challenge, Jesus seeks to elicit further reflection by posing a rhetorical question. Drawing on conventional accounting language (*profit* [*ōpheleitai*] . . . *gain* [*kerdēsas*] . . . *forfeit* [*zēmiōtheis*]), Jesus asks his hearers to create a mental balance sheet, comparing the prospective assets of *the whole world* against the liability of losing oneself. Since Jesus has already turned down 'all the kingdoms of the world' (4:5) for the sake of his appointed mission, and since too the 'nations of the *world* [*kosmou*]' are themselves on an errant course (12:30), it is to be surmised that

---

102. Schweitzer, *TDNT* 9, pp. 608–660 (especially p. 620).

there is no real comparison between these ephemeral realities and the human *psyche*. Yet the notional framework for this cost–benefit analysis involves not a Platonic-style pitting of eternal/spiritual things against temporal/material things. Rather, with his gesture to the Danielic Son of Man (9:22), Jesus calls his hearers to decision with reference to the fact that he will finally judge the unclean rulers of the world, just as Daniel 7 promises.

26–27. Jesus also contemplates the eschatological assizes where humanity will essentially be divided into two categories: those who have been *ashamed of me and my words* and those who have not. If the present verse has any continuity with verse 25, the choice to identify with or distance oneself from Jesus is closely tied to another dilemma: whether to gain the world while losing oneself or to save oneself by losing oneself. On this logic, Luke's reader gathers that worldliness most fully emerges not so much through the more conspicuous sins as, more quietly, through the individual's failure to identify publicly with Jesus. If picking up one's cross entails embracing social shame for the gospel's sake, the corollary of the same principles means guarding against the temptation to cave in to social pressure. Although Jesus' promise regarding *some standing here* has often been taken as evidence that he and/or the early church expected the parousia within the lifetime of the Twelve, it is more probable that the seeing of the kingdom which Jesus has in mind actually occurs in the very next scene (9:28–36).

ii. Transfiguration (9:28–36)

28. The phrase *after these sayings* links the present passage with Jesus' promise (9:27) that some of his immediate hearers would see the kingdom of God prior to death. Closely tied to the previous passage, the ensuing transfiguration scene proves to be a fulfilment of that promise. Whereas Mark (and Matthew) has six days separating Peter's confession and the mountaintop experience, Luke prefers to think of the same period as being *about eight days.*[103]

---

103. Even if Luke had said 'exactly eight days', this would not necessarily
     have contradicted his Markan source. Ancient counting practices

Perhaps this approximation is meant to establish a parallel with the earlier eight-day window spanning Jesus' birth (2:1–20) and naming (2:21). After all, on the day of Jesus' birth, as well as on the day of Peter's confession, Jesus is identified as Messiah (2:11; 9:20), then on the eighth day after both of these events, Jesus' identity receives further specification (2:21; 9:35). In any case, Jesus takes *Peter and John and James* – the same group of disciples (listed in the same order) selected to observe the resuscitation of Jairus's daughter – up to the mountain to pray.

29. In the midst of his prayer, the appearance of Jesus' face becomes 'other' (*heteron*), even as *his clothes became dazzling white*. While it may not necessarily be incorrect to explain this event with reference to the glory of Moses' face (Exod. 34:29–35), a more apt comparison is found in the high priest's clothing, more exactly his breastplate, studded as it was by precious stones that had a light-emitting appearance (Exod. 28:15–30).[104] This is supported by Peter's plea. Given his proposal to build 'dwellings' (*skēnas*; Luke 9:33), which invokes a feast of Tabernacles setting behind the whole event, and given too evidence that the high priest normally acceded to office during the feast of Tabernacles (Josephus, *Ant.* 15.50–52), we tentatively conclude that Luke's transfiguration scene is modelled on the high priest's enthronement.[105]

30. *Suddenly* (*kai idou*) two individuals appear to speak with Jesus; they are identifiable as *Moses and Elijah*. Exactly how Peter recognizes these two figures is unclear. In any event, their presence – as opposed, say, to the presence of David and Abraham – is intriguing.

---

sometimes included and sometimes excluded the first and last items; cf. Miano, *Time Measurement*, pp. 49–62.

104. For Second Temple rumination on this property of the high priest's embedded stones, see references in Fletcher-Louis, 'Sacral Son of Man', pp. 294–295.

105. Horbury (*Jewish Messianism*, pp. 111, 134) teases out striking parallels between the priestly ordination of Aristobolus III (during the feast of Tabernacles) and the transfiguration; cited in Fletcher-Louis, 'Sacral Son of Man', p. 296. On the feast of Tabernacles background to the transfiguration, see Bock, p. 871; Fitzmyer, p. 108; Green p. 383.

One traditional interpretation holds that Moses represents the law and Elijah, the prophets. But this is forced: Moses was himself a prophet (cf. 9:8) and there is no reason why Elijah should be singled out as the chief representative of the prophetic guild. More to the point, it seems, are the mysterious circumstances surrounding their deaths as well as the highly conflictual nature of their ministries while alive. According to Scripture, Elijah was translated directly to heaven; Moses was buried by God (though according to some traditions he, like Elijah, was also translated into heaven). In their role as divine spokespersons, both experienced hostility and rejection. Given these considerations, along with the subject of their conversation (v. 31), their fellowship with Jesus, precisely as the Son of Man who is destined for suffering and exaltation (v. 22), can be explained as a function of not only their rejection but also their unusual transition to post-mortem reality. But between Jesus and his precursors important differences remain:

> In contrast to Moses and Elijah Jesus will attain heavenly glory, not by
> forgoing death or after dying a natural death, but by being raised by
> God after being put to death by his own people as an innocent and
> righteous prophetic figure.[106]

31. If the glory now enveloping Moses and Elijah was the same glory that would accrue to the Son of Man (Dan. 7:14), then the whole scene powerfully reminds Luke's readers that this same glory also awaits God's faithful agents on the other side of suffering. The substance of the three figures' conversation is Jesus' *departure* (*exodos*) or exodus, which he was about to *accomplish* or fulfil (*plēroun*) in Jerusalem. The term *departure* is intentionally ambivalent, referring simultaneously to Jesus' impending death and to the theological significance of that death, entailing as it would a new exodus for the people of God. This new exodus would occur not in Egypt or indeed in any pagan territory but, ironically, in Judaism's holy city, suggesting that the present temple space was not the terminus for such exodus but a point of departure.

---

106. Heil, *Transfiguration*, p. 99.

32. Luke mentions the sleepiness of the disciples to show, among other things, that they presently overcome the same temptations that will later overcome them at Gethsemane (22:45–46). In the future garden scene, the disciples will spectacularly fail: for now, despite being *weighed down with sleep*, they remain watchful (cf. 21:34–36) and as a result of their perseverance behold *his glory*. Like the Twelve, Luke's larger narrative seems to say, followers of Jesus will experience varying degrees of success in overcoming spiritual lethargy and, consequently, varying levels of insight into God's glory.

33. Just as the two patriarchs begin to distance themselves following their conversation with Jesus, Peter brusquely breaks the disciples' awed silence by proposing to build *three dwellings*, most likely Sukkoth booths, one for each of the three spiritual heavyweights. Wowed by the extraordinary experience (*it is good for us to be here*), Peter is perhaps hoping that by extending their celebration of the feast of Tabernacles, he might detain this gathering of venerable personages for just a while longer. *Not knowing what he said*, the disciple has intruded on the solemn convocation, while patently failing to understand the thrust of the patriarchs' speech. For whereas by the first century the annual Sukkoth ritual of building booths was designed to symbolize the eschatological exodus, when God would finally bring about a full release from the 'Egypt' of the present evil age, Peter's proposal that the three figures submit themselves to the same ritual revealed his inability to grasp the eschatological significance of the moment: rendering the long-standing feast of Tabernacles ceremony redundant, Jesus was now tasked with implementing the final exodus.

34. As Peter is still speaking, almost as if to answer the disciple's prattling, a cloud appears and quickly *overshadowed them*. The cloud in view is none other than the very cloud of glory that had once 'overshadowed' (*epeskiazen*) the Mosaic sanctuary (Exod. 40:35).[107]

---

107. See also the angel's words to Mary ('The Holy Spirit will come upon you, and the power of the Most High will *overshadow* [*episkiasei*] you') in Luke 1:35.

Since this pillar of cloud was also understood to prefigure the great eschatological light at the final feast of Tabernacles (Zech. 14:6–7), its appearance here corrects Peter's misapprehension by reinforcing the fact that the eschatological day of the Lord, predicted in Zechariah 14, is in fact now taking place.[108] For the disciples, it is a forceful reminder indeed: for *they were terrified as they entered the cloud.* The disciples' reaction corresponds to the response of the exodus generation as they encountered God in the cloud on Sinai (Exod. 20:18). In this respect, the transfiguration combines imagery of the future pillar of cloud with the self-revelation of Yahweh at Sinai.

35–36. In the aftermath of Sinai, Israel was instructed to receive and heed the law, encapsulated in the Shema ('Hear, O Israel . . .', Deut. 6:4). But now the disciples receive a different sort of 'Shema': *This is my Son, my Chosen; listen to him!* As the Son of God, Jesus not only supplants the law by giving the law its fullest expression (cf. Heb. 1:1–4), but also overrides the Sinai generation's preference for Moses' mediation, reverting to the unshielded glory of God (Exod. 20:18). Within Luke's narrative, this heavenly announcement is not the first of its kind, for a very similar pronouncement occurs at Jesus' baptism (3:22). While the baptism clarified Jesus' identity as divine Son, the transfiguration extends the idea by insisting that this same Son is now also the supreme focal point of divine self-revelation. For Luke, this Christological claim does not stand opposed to monotheistic Judaism but is in continuity with it. Indeed, after the voice speaks, Jesus is found *alone (monos)*, signifying not only that the two patriarchs had disappeared but also, on a theological level, that Israel's monotheistic faith had been reconfigured around the person of Jesus.

iii. Exorcism of an afflicted boy (9:37–45)

37. On one level this passage relates Jesus' increasing popularity as well as the limitations of the disciples' powers when confronting

---

108. As Grindheim (*Biblical Theology*, p. 117) reminds us, the feast of Tabernacles' 'light ceremonies reminded the Jews of the pillar of fire that had led them in the wilderness (Exod. 13.21). They also pointed forward to the light of the new creation (Zech. 14.7).'

the tenacity of the dark forces. But in order to make full sense of this puzzling scene, we must also recognize that the Evangelist is leveraging the event as a recapitulation of the apostasy of the wilderness generation (Exod. 32). The evidence for this interpretation emerges soon enough. While Jesus is on the mountain, a *great crowd* remains attentive to his return. In the time of the exodus, it was also a 'great crowd' that followed Moses through the desert and – restlessly and faithlessly – awaited his return down the mountain (Exod. 12:38). For Jesus as for Moses, the mediator of revelation comes back down from his mountaintop experience only to find God's people in the valleys of spiritual darkness.

38–41. Within the crowd stands a man who is desperate to find a solution for his *only* son (cf. 7:12; 8:42) – the last of three only children in Luke. The direness of the situation is heightened by the emotional charge of the man's appeal, the grim effects of the boy's condition and the disciples' inability to remediate the problem. The last point is curious because Jesus had earlier granted the disciples authority to drive out all '*all* demons' (9:1, emphasis added). Later on, the seventy-two sent out by Jesus seem to have mastery over the demonic forces (10:17). But here matters are at a standstill.

But why? Was this an unusually intransigent demon that could withstand all merely human efforts? Or perhaps someone was to blame – maybe the disciples or even the boy's father? Fortunately, Jesus himself sheds light on the issue by identifying those around him as part of a *faithless and perverse generation* (v. 41). Jesus' castigation of the onlookers echoes Moses' charges against the Sinai generation, a people who had given themselves over to false gods and sacrificed to demons (Deut. 32:5, 19–20). The fundamental problem, it seems, is not just the severity of this particular demonic possession but also the fact that Jesus' generation still remained – like Moses' 'faithless and perverse generation' – in exile. It was a spiritual exile born of idolatry. The key to overcoming such idolatry – the key for healing the demon-possessed boy – was in bringing the matter to Jesus: *Bring your son here* (v. 41).

42–43a. As the boy is brought to Jesus, the demonic forces within become agitated and violent. No surprise: in the Gospels Jesus' very presence regularly provokes the demons. Jesus responds with a threefold action: rebuking the demon, healing the boy and returning the young man to his father. Understandably, those gathered respond in astonished worship of God's majesty. Here, then, is a story of an extreme exorcism. Yet it is also an enacted parable of Jesus' actions on behalf of Israel, indicating that though Israel has nearly been destroyed by the forces of darkness, Jesus has responded by encountering the demonic, healing Israel of its sin and returning the nation to Yahweh. This in turn would result in grateful worship.

43b–45. In this the second passion prediction, Jesus once again foretells that the Son of Man is to be *betrayed into human hands*. A reprise of such shocking news was not to be treated lightly, and so Jesus asks his disciples to *Let these words sink into your ears*. Earlier, following his parable of the sower, Luke's Jesus had invited those with ears to hear (8:8). Presumably, then, those without ears could not hear and despite their best human efforts the disciples cannot hear well. Again, their inability to penetrate the mysterious fate of the Son of Man is not unconnected to the idolatry of the heart which forecloses on the possibility of fruitfulness. That the disciples fail to understand *and* fail to enquire suggests that their present status is for now in grave question.

iv. The greatest in the kingdom (9:46–50)

46. Luke's particle *de*, a Greek word which typically goes untranslated, gestures towards a contrast with what has gone before. It is a stark contrast, as the disparity between Jesus' predicted sufferings (9:43b–45) and the disciples' vainglorious squabbling could not be more pronounced. An *argument* (*dialogismos*) has arisen among the disciples, apparently in Jesus' absence – a telling detail in itself. Equally telling is this: wherever Luke uses *dialogismos* (2:35; 5:22; 6:8; 24:38), a word which carries connotations of doubt as well as legal wrangling, it is decidedly negative.[109] Whereas the NRSV (as well as ASV, CEB, ESV, etc.) translates *eisēlthen de dialogismos* as *an argument arose*, the YLT's 'And there entered a reasoning among them' more effectively conveys the spatial element introduced by the

---

109. See Schrenk, *TDNT* 2, p. 97.

chosen verb. On Luke's wording, the *dialogismos* becomes a personal or impersonal force in its own right, entering into the community of disciples.

47–48. Characteristically, Jesus is fully *aware* of their dark *inner thoughts* (*dialogismos tēs kardias autōn*).[110] By way of response, he brings to his side a *paidion*, a term generally applied to children seven years old or younger, as part of an object lesson. In Ancient Graeco-Roman society, 'a child was seen as an unfinished or imperfect adult', and thus as inherently flawed and valued only insofar as the child held potential for contributing to the adult world.[111] To be sure, while first-century Jews laid a higher intrinsic value on children than did their pagan counterparts, the Hellenistic spirit would have certainly had a corrosive influence on the first-century Jewish concept. And it is precisely this spirit which Jesus takes head-on, when he lays down a string of logical conditions: if anyone welcomes *this child in my name*, then that person also welcomes Jesus himself; and those who welcome Jesus (who by implication is God's emissary) welcome God. Therefore, according to the syllogism, the one who receives a child, including but not limited to the *paidion* next to Jesus, receives God. Luke does not mean to suggest that God is uniquely present in children, but rather that God finds no better expression in fallen humanity than in a mere child who, unlike the disciples, has neither pretensions nor aspirations of social power. This is not to sentimentalize children but to idealize the humility and unselfconsciousness characteristic of children in general.

49. John, one of the select three witnesses to Jesus' transfigur-ation, begins to process Jesus' teaching with a specific question related to the phrase 'in my name'. If children are to be received in Jesus' *name* simply because they are children, John begins to wonder, then what about adults who cast out demons in Jesus'

---

110. The weight of the manuscript evidence is divided evenly between *eidōs*, 'knowing' (e.g. ESV, NASB, NIV), and *idōn*, 'seeing' (e.g. ASV). In the end, the NRSV's *aware* arrives at something of a compromise between the two competing manuscript options.

111. Reeder, *DJG*, p. 111.

name? Thus John's words (*Master, we saw someone casting out demons in your name, and we tried to stop him, because he does not follow with us*) is perhaps more of a question than a statement. The question for John is, 'When we see some outside our circle engaging in exorcistic activity in the name of Jesus, should we stop them?'[112]

50. For Jesus, the short answer to this question is 'No'. After all, *whoever is not against you is for you.* Though there is a sense in which those who are not with Jesus are against him (Matt. 12:30), it is also true, Luke seems to remind his readers, that there is no reason to make enemies of individuals who, though not part of the 'in-group', are to all intents and purposes allies.

Theology
By all appearances, Second Temple Jews did not expect a Messiah who was also divine. An exalted figure? Perhaps. But on a par with the God of Israel? No. This historical fact makes Luke's unfolding report of Jesus' messianic identity all the more striking. If Elijah was a great prophet and Moses a great lawgiver, even regarded in some circles as of quasi-divine status, Jesus comes to us as one who surpasses both Elijah and Moses, in terms of both personage and role. More than a prophet and lawgiver, Jesus is, once again, both Messiah *and* God.

Yet, strangely enough, Jesus' transcendent status in no way exempts him from his appointed calling of suffering and co-identification with the weak. On the contrary, suffering and weakness are the modes through which his divinity and Messiahship would be most clearly revealed. This truth lies at the heart of the gospel mystery. This truth is also *the* scandal of the gospel, virtually impossible to comprehend.

---

112. Elsewhere (Perrin, *Jesus the Priest*, pp. 122–128), I argue that John's question is based on the unstated assumption that the Twelve retained a quasi-priestly role, which included the responsibility of performing exorcisms. For Jesus' closest disciples, the very fact that Jesus-sympathizers outside their own circle were performing exorcisms *in his name* potentially undermined their exclusive standing as eschatological priests in the making.

On a formal level, to be sure, Peter accurately identifies Jesus as the *Christos*. In other words, he is right in regard to the 'Who?' question. But on a substantive level, when it comes to discerning *how* this Messiah and his followers would operate, he and his peers could not be any further off the mark. This is demonstrable from the fact that even just after Jesus' sobering prediction of suffering, the disciples are still bickering among themselves about who would be the greatest. Luke is well aware that his readers are not so very different from Peter. Knowledge of the Messiah's identity is merely the precondition to knowing what is at stake in following him — and choosing to follow him despite the cost.

5. JOURNEY TO JERUSALEM (9:51 – 19:27)

A. Jesus' kingdom mission (9:51 – 10:24)

Context

The bulk of the narrative up to this point has been preparing for the climactic announcement of Jesus' Messiahship (9:18–27), followed by the transfiguration (9:28–36). Now, having built on these revelations with some remarks on the cost of discipleship (9:37–50), Luke's Jesus turns his face towards Jerusalem (9:51), marking the beginning of the story's longest section and anticipating the grim fate awaiting him. The present section (9:51 – 10:24) also bears a few striking parallels to Jesus' final approach to Jerusalem (18:31 – 19:27). The Samaritan rejection of Jesus (9:51–62) anticipates the Jewish leaders' rejection of Jesus (18:31–34), even as the seventy-two's commission to enter the cities (10:1–12) foreshadows the parable in which the parabolic lord bestows an inheritance of cities on his servants (19:11–27). Retrospectively, the sending out of the seventy-two is a more extensive version of the missionary campaign executed in 9:1–6. Its successful completion marks the demise of Satan, who himself sought Jesus' defeat chapters earlier (4:1–13).

Comment

i. The cost of following Jesus (9:51–62)

51. The Father's extraordinary endorsement of Jesus at the transfiguration seems to have been the necessary prelude to his fateful journey. Jesus must now *set his face to go to Jerusalem*. In the biblical literature, 'setting one's face' invariably denotes judgment against those to whom the face is directed (Lev. 17:10; 20:3, 5; Jer. 21:10; Ezek. 4:3, 7; 6:2; etc.). The same overtones cannot be excluded here. Yet with the expression Luke also intends to link Jesus with the Servant figure of Isaiah, who in his confrontation with Israel declares, 'therefore I have set my face like flint, / and I know that I shall not be put to shame' (Isa. 50:7). Even if Jesus' unbending commitment to the will of the Father brings him a temporary shame, this same Jesus – so the analogy implies – will be vindicated, even as he provides atonement for the people of God.

52–53. Now moving from Galilee in the north to Jerusalem in the south (roughly a three-day journey), Jesus sends messengers ahead to a Samaritan village situated along the way to arrange for lodging. As it happens, they are turned away, simply *because his face was set towards Jerusalem*. Though first-century protocol required showing hospitality to travelling visitors, this would not have been entirely unexpected, since there seems to have been a pattern of Samaritans failing to welcome Jews en route to Jerusalem (Josephus, *Ant.* 20.118; *J.W.* 2.232). While elsewhere in Luke Samaritans are depicted in a positive light (10:33–37; 17:11–19), here the villagers' affront is ultimately directed not to the messengers but to Jesus himself. They are the negative example of Jesus' maxim 'Whoever welcomes me welcomes the one who sent me' (v. 48).

54–56. Angered by the village's breach of hospitality, James and John offer to re-enact Elijah's judgment of fire, which had been issued against the Samaritan detachments sent by Ahaziah (2 Kgs 1:9–12). The suggestion is remarkable on two counts. First, correctly or incorrectly, James and John obviously thought that they had Elijah-esque abilities to call down fire from heaven at a moment's notice. (Perhaps they inferred their possession of such abilities following their earlier fellowship with Elijah at the transfiguration; cf. 9:28–36.) Second, the brothers' proposal reveals their dramatic failure to love their enemies (6:27–31). It is at any rate a suggestion which Jesus flatly rejects. Whereas up to this point in the narrative Jesus' reproofs have been largely reserved for demons (4:35, 39, 41; 8:24), his rebuking (*epetimēsen*) the disciples here may be tracing their vindictive impulses to a demonic origin. By Jesus' reckoning, the best response to this unanticipated rejection is simply to move on to another village.

57–58. Jesus and his disciples are now well *along the road*, more exactly, 'in the way' (*en tē hodō*), thereby fulfilling the Isaianic return-from-exile charter (Luke 1:76; 3:4). As they travel, an unidentified individual approaches in a bid to join the movement: *I will follow you wherever you go.* Despite the seemingly unconditional nature of this proposal, Jesus obliquely turns it down by contrasting the lot of the Son of Man with that of foxes and birds. Here it is commonly argued that Jesus turns away the aspiring disciple because he does not fully grasp the rigours of the disciples' itinerant lifestyle.[1] This interpretation seems implausible, not least because it squares so poorly with the fact that Jesus does in fact have *some* place to lay his head (5:29) and indeed is generously though probably not lavishly funded (8:3), even while his followers are instructed to take residence in houses as they can (9:4).[2] More likely, Jesus perceives in the would-be disciple a thirst for messianic revolution and eventually military occupation, only then to discourage this zealotry by (1) alluding metaphorically to birds of the air and the foxes (or jackals) as a carefully coded way of referring to the well-situatedness of Herod and the Gentiles, respectively, and (2) pointing out that the suffering Son of Man

---

1. A slightly less common alternative is that *the Son of Man* here represents humanity in general, so Jesus is simply making a philosophical point about humanity. However, as Marshall (p. 410) aptly points out, Jesus' 'saying is not true of man in general', since many people do in fact have a place to lay their heads.

2. Similarly Kingsbury, 'Following Jesus', p. 50.

would not dislodge those rulers any time soon but rather at the indeterminate eschaton.[3]

59–60. Whereas the first interlocutor in this string of three exchanges seeks to follow Jesus on his own political terms, the next two conversations centre around the well-intentioned but ill-advised prioritization of one's family over the kingdom – all underscored through the repetition of *first* (*proton*) (vv. 59, 61). In verse 59, Jesus' potential recruit unintentionally rebuffs the master by begging leave to bury his father. Whether or not said father was actually deceased (or soon expected to be) is unclear. If the father was dead, most of Luke's readers would have perceived this as an entirely reasonable request: in the ancient world, burial rites were extremely important and few obligations were more solemn than the obligation to ensure a proper burial for one's own parents (cf. Gen. 50:5; Tob. 4:3; 6:15). Even so, Jesus contests these cultural norms by insisting, in metaphorical terms, that *the dead bury their own dead*. If Jesus' counter appears callous, this is almost certainly part of the point. When Jesus issues his call to *Follow me*, and to *go and proclaim the kingdom of God*, this vocation must override all pre-existing roles. Accordingly, those who have been so called must be willing to demit even their most fundamental responsibilities. Some tasks, even perhaps the task of attending to the funeral arrangements of one's own father, are better left to the spiritually dead (cf. 15:24, 32) – all for the kingdom's sake.

61–62. The third and final exchange involves a request that, again at first blush, does not seem to be out of the ordinary. But, once again, it is exactly the seeming ordinariness of the appeal, together with its rejection, that underscores the extraordinary demands of the kingdom. Here the man makes lofty promises of obeisance (*I will follow you, Lord*), only immediately to compromise that profession by attempting to establish a relationship with Jesus on his own terms: *let me first say farewell to those at my home*. In rejecting the man's bid, Jesus summons the image of a plough in order to compare the man's ill-conceived request to Elisha's equally

---

3. On this interpretation, see Manson, *Teaching of Jesus*, pp. 72–73; Perrin, *Jesus the Priest*, pp. 208–218.

misguided response to Elijah's calling ('Let me kiss my father and my mother, and then I will follow you' [1 Kgs 19:20]). Thus Jesus imposes on his disciples the same terms and conditions which Elijah imposed on Elisha. For Jesus and Elijah alike, nothing less is required – metaphorically speaking – than an outright burning of one's ploughs (1 Kgs 19:21), foreclosing on the possibility of retreat or reverting to one's previous way of life. Those who put their hand to the plough but look back longingly on kith and kin are not useful (*euthetos*), or suitable, or *fit for the kingdom of God*. Following Jesus requires utter self-surrender.

ii. The mission of the seventy-two (10:1–16)

1. The transitional phrase *after this* refers to both Jesus' rejection at Samaria (9:52–53) and his interaction with the three less-than-qualified disciples (9:57–62).[4] Accordingly, when Jesus sends out the seventy-two, roughly on the model of the mission of the Twelve, he does so in the aftermath of fierce opposition and half-hearted allegiance occurring during the Jewish–Samaritan mission. If (as I argue below) the mission is in some sense a mission to Gentile populations living in these towns, then this second sending may logically follow on the palpable spiritual resistance coming out of Israel and Samaria (cf. Rom. 11:11–24). Three further points deserve comment. First, the emissaries are *appointed* (*anadeizen*), a formal term potentially invoking the context of diplomatic service – appropriate for the kingdom of God. Second, in sending out these missionaries *to every town and place where he himself intended to go*, Jesus clearly anticipates a circuitous path to Jerusalem, including towns not directly on the route.[5] As important as Jesus' business in Jerusalem may have been, the preliminary mission of preaching the kingdom was not to be cut

---

4. So also Matera, 'Journey', p. 67.

5. Nor is Jesus necessarily determined to move as quickly as possible. McCown ('Geography', p. 58) may be correct when he writes that Jesus 'made a most leisurely progression from city to city, something after the manner of an itinerant Evangelist, stopping often for days at a time'.

short. Third, the distribution and overall number of these missionaries is not without significance. Their pairing (*ana dyo*)
complies with the legal requirement that there be two or three
witnesses for legally binding testimony (Deut. 17:6; 19:15), even as
it sets the template for the apostles (Acts 3:1; 8:14; 13:2; etc.).
Meanwhile, that the messengers number seventy-two (not, I think,
seventy as per the translation of the NRSV and others) can be
explained by an intended correlation with the seventy-two nations
of the earth catalogued in Genesis 10 (LXX).[6] If the first mission
involving the Twelve was oriented to Israel, the second mission of
the seventy-two contains hints of being geared to the Gentiles:
first for the Jew, then for the Gentile.

2. Yet there is an order of business more pressing than preaching
the kingdom: struck by the contrast between the immensity of the
harvest and the paucity of the labourers, Jesus invites his appointed
messengers to *ask the Lord of the harvest to send out labourers into his
harvest.*[7] While agricultural imagery is used elsewhere in the New
Testament in relation to Christian ministry (e.g. 1 Cor. 3:6–9), the
term *harvest* carries an eschatological charge (e.g. Isa. 27:2–12; Joel
3:13–16). In this way, Jesus' command implies that the preaching
mission of the seventy-two is an early instalment of an extended
eschatological process, culminating in the great assizes. Moreover,
it is *the Lord*'s harvest, a point not unrelated to Jesus' identification
as 'Lord' in verse 1.

---

6. So also, e.g., Marshall, pp. 414–415. The issue, however, is a difficult
   one. The weight of the manuscript evidence at Luke 10:1 is evenly
   divided between 'seventy' and 'seventy-two'. The former reading is
   adopted by NRSV, ASV, KJV; the latter, by the CEB, GNT, ESV, NASB, NIV,
   NJB, NLT. Cole ('Longer Reading', p. 213) accurately opines that the
   'two major text-critical criteria are at a gridlock: the external evidence
   is evenly split, and intrinsic probability – with respect to the author's
   use of numerical symbolism – is frustratingly inconclusive'. Even so,
   the scales seem to tip ever so slightly in favour of 'seventy-two'.
7. 'The NIV [and also NRSV] translation "ask" is too anemic for Greek
   deisthai (v. 2), which means "to implore, entreat, pray"' (Edwards,
   pp. 305–306).

3. Yet prayer by itself is not enough: the seventy-two must also *go*. Jesus' accompanying warning (*I am sending you out like lambs into the midst of wolves*) probably alludes to Isaiah's vision of the eschaton, where wolves and lambs will peacefully coexist (Isa. 11:6; 65:25). In this respect, Jesus' metaphorical double comparison not only emphasizes the severity of forthcoming opposition, but also intimates that the eschatological peace predicted by Isaiah was even now being realized through the seventy-two's mission.

4. Whereas on their missionary journey the Twelve are forbidden from bringing along a staff, a knapsack (*pēran*), bread, money or a spare tunic (9:3), the seventy-two are prohibited from carrying a purse, a knapsack (*pēran*) or sandals. The directive on sandals probably does not mean that the missionaries are to go barefoot, but rather that they are to avoid carrying a second pair of sandals. The overall emphasis is on under-packing rather than overpacking, carrying less cash rather than more – all the while learning dependence on God's providence. Their task is also urgent, preventing even the possibility of greeting another on the road (cf. 2 Kgs 4:29).

5–6. Jesus' instructions for the Twelve regarding their lodging (9:4–5) are now expanded. The first of these additions is a directive to bless the host's dwelling: *Peace to this house!* The same peace that the angels had promised to the elect at Jesus' birth (2:14), which is also the same peace which Jesus imparted to the sinful woman (7:50) and the bleeding woman (8:48), now extends to those who will host these missionaries. Yet there are no guarantees that this peace will finally be received. For if *anyone is there who shares in peace* (*ean ekei ē huios eirēnēs*), or perhaps more woodenly, 'if anyone there is a son of peace', that peace will naturally *rest on that person*. If not, that peace will 'boomerang back' (*anakampsei*). The saving shalom soon to flow from these seventy-two has its own motion, but the peace itself cannot be disrupted.

7. Like the Twelve (9:4), the seventy-two are told to *remain* [*menete*] *in the same house* without moving about. In Luke, the verb *menō* signifies more than just having a roof over one's head; instead it includes the fuller experience of hospitality (Luke 19:5; 24:29; Acts 9:43; 16:15; 18:3; etc.). As part and parcel of the Son of Man's 'eating and drinking' ministry (7:33), the seventy-two are not to back down from the celebratory eating practices which Jesus' adversaries had found so scandalous. In this context, then, food and drink are not simply the wages (*misthos*) which *the labourer deserves* but also a polemical sign of the messianic feast.

8. At first blush, the command *eat what is set before you* (*esthiete ta paratithemena hymin*) may appear as little more than a challenge to the finicky eaters among the seventy-two. But it is more likely that Jesus is actually anticipating what Peter (Acts 11:7–10) as well as Paul and Silas (Acts 16:34) would have to do in sharing meals with Gentiles: set aside well-entrenched scruples of retaining ritual purity during table fellowship. More than that, when Luke pens this verse, he likely also has in mind – as comparisons of the Greek demonstrate – Paul's instructions to the sensitive consciences at Corinth to 'eat whatever is set before you' (*pan to paratithemenon hymin esthiete*; 1 Cor. 10:27). If so, then Luke may be attempting to recall the Pauline injunction to accept and gratefully enjoy a host's meat that had been sacrificed to idols, and then to root the same principle in the mission of the seventy-two. For Paul and Luke alike, because mutual hospitality is an important component in the formation of this emerging kingdom community, Jewish followers of Jesus must willingly set aside their kosher scruples precisely by recognizing that the coming of the kingdom has made all things clean. To this extent, the seventy-two's willingness to 'eat whatever is set before' them functions as an eschatological sign.

9. Yet there are two further signs, once again matching the remit of the Twelve (9:2): curing the sick and proclaiming *The kingdom of God has come near to you*. The verb *ēngiken* is in the perfect aspect, implying that the kingdom has already drawn near without necessarily also implying that it has fully arrived.[8] In no case can the verb be pressed to suggest that the kingdom has fully arrived or, conversely, that it has not yet arrived in any sense. Again, healing and the inauguration of the kingdom go together hand in hand, because healing means the reverse of the disease of exile (Deut. 28:21–22, 58–63) and the restoration of the created state.

10–12. Having laid out a course of action for situations where the missionaries are well received, now Jesus imagines the

---

8. See Perrin, *Kingdom of God*, p. 210.

alternative: *whenever you enter a town and they do not welcome you* (v. 10). In such case, the missionaries are to go into the streets for a very public announcement involving – in dramatic fashion – shaking dust from the soles of their feet, as well as the affirmation of the coming kingdom. By removing even the dust of such towns from their soles, the seventy-two are acting out an utter and absolute separation from the targets of God's imminent judgment. And because dust is associated with God's creational curse (Gen. 3:14), shaking out dust over a particular geography would undoubtedly signal that the same space has been – even through this dramatic gesture – consigned to the curse's unmitigated force. Such a town, Jesus goes on to warn (v. 12), is destined to fare worse than the archetypal city of judgment, Sodom (Gen. 19).

13–15. Almost as if to pre-empt the impression that the towns in the seventy-two's path would be shown up as especially sinful, Jesus retrospectively issues three sets of woes against three towns to the north: Chorazin, Bethsaida and Capernaum.[9] All three (mostly Jewish) towns were crowded around the north side of the Galilee, where Jesus had carried out the bulk of his ministry (4:14 – 9:17); all three had been witness to his *deeds of power*. Coupling Chorazin with Bethsaida, Jesus morally ranks both towns below Israel's evil rivals Tyre and Sidon. As for Capernaum, the impending judgment is even more severe, not unlike the fall of Babylon (and in Second Temple interpretation, Satan) described in Isaiah 14:13–15. In a rhyming sing-song Greek, Jesus asks:

will you be exalted to heaven?
  No, you will be brought down to Hades.

Mē heōs ouranou hypōthēsē?
heōs tou hadou katabēsē.

_____

9. Located roughly 2 miles north of Capernaum, the precise location of Chorazin is uncertain. Little is known about the ancient town except for its grain production (Menaḥ. 85a). In the NT, it is mentioned only here and in the Matthean parallel to this passage (Matt. 11:21).

16. Rabbinic Judaism was familiar with a principle whereby the 'sent one' (*šaliah*) carried a kind of legally binding power of attorney on behalf of the sender. Jesus' phrasing, which has the seventy-two being sent by Jesus, who in turn is sent by *the one who sent me*, appears to be a classical formulation of said arrangement. That which Jesus declares on behalf of his sender is to be treated as if the sender had declared it; that which is pronounced by the seventy-two on Jesus' behalf is for all intents and purposes as binding as Jesus' own words. Therefore, *whoever rejects you rejects me*. With such authorization, the seventy-two were not only empowered to speak and act freely, but also granted insight into why their important message might in some instances be rejected.

iii. The seventy-two return (10:17–24)

17. Forgoing details about the seventy-two's mission, Luke jumps to a summary of their impressions after the fact. Returning to Jesus, the missionaries exult in their ability to subdue *even the demons*. The reflection deserves at least two comments. First, though Jesus had authorized the Twelve to exorcise demons (9:1), no such responsibility had been assigned to the seventy-two. This suggests that the missionaries' exorcistic duties were either generally assumed all along or, more likely, logically entailed in their remit to heal and proclaim (10:9). Second, the seventy-two's pleasant surprise at their spiritual powers is itself surprising, since both Jesus' immediate disciples (9:40) and those outside the inner circle (9:49) had already had publicly observable success in driving out demons. In any case, the seventy-two's abilities had somehow exceeded their expectations and the result is *joy*.

18. In response, Jesus relates the contents of an ecstatic vision, coinciding with the seventy-two's missionary journey and symbolically representing its effects.[10] The aorist participle behind *fall* (*pesonta*) does not indicate a thoroughgoing plummet; indeed, the devil's later activities (22:3, 31) militate against such an inter-

---

10. While Jesus' statement may only be a poetic summary of the missionaries' activities, the imperfect *I watched* (*etheōroun*), or 'I was beholding' (YLT), implies a protracted experience on Jesus' part.

pretation.[11] At the same time, the comparison with lightning suggests a meteoric fall, swift and decisive (cf. T. Sol. 20:6–17).[12] Through such efforts as those undertaken by the seventy-two, Satan will slowly meet his end.

19. Towards explaining the missionaries' exorcistic prowess, Jesus remarks that their received *authority* includes, first of all, an ability *to tread on snakes and scorpions*. Since this is precisely the same ability promised to the messianic 'seed of the woman' after the fall (Gen. 3:15), Jesus' words not only speak of the seventy-two's power over the demonic but also hint at their incorporation into the messianic seed.[13] Second, this authority is comprehensive: superior to *all the power of the enemy*. Considering that the devil possesses authority over all the kingdoms of the earth (4:5–6), this is considerable power indeed. Third, the missionaries are promised immunity from retributive injury: *nothing will hurt you* (*hymas ou mē adikēsē*). But given Jesus' subsequent predictions (21:12–16), not to mention the disciples' subsequent experiences of bodily harm (Acts 5:40; 7:54–60; 14:19; etc.), the promise cannot be understood as an absolute guarantee against physical injury. When read in its context, the promise in fact suggests that the only true and lasting harm is spiritual in nature. Such an injury Satan cannot inflict.

20. Though the seventy-two may be tempted to rejoice in the fact *that the spirits submit to you*, Jesus urges them instead to *rejoice that your names are written in heaven* (cf. 6:23). Here Luke's image of the heavenly roll book may be most directly rooted in Daniel 12:1, but the concept is also found elsewhere (Exod. 32:32–33; Pss 69:28; 138:16, LXX; Mal. 3:16–17; cf. Phil. 4:3; Heb. 12:23; Rev. 3:5). On Jesus' exhortation, the one who has received extraordinary spiritual

---

11. The earlier-used 'the devil' (*ho diabolos*) now gives way to 'the Satan' (*ho Satanas*) for the rest of Luke's narrative. On this title, see 1 Chr. 21:1; Job 1:6–12; 2:1–7; Zech. 3:1–2.

12. Again, an allusion to Isa. 14:13–15 seems to be in play, essentially painting Babylon and Capernaum with the same brush.

13. Whereas Gen. 3:15 had already accrued messianic significance by the time of Luke's composition (cf. Gal. 3:16), power over demons was itself a messianic sign.

power must forgo revelling in such abilities thereby making such power an end in itself.

21. Like his emissaries, Jesus speaks with joy; *unlike* them, however, he rejoices *in* or by means of *the Holy Spirit*, returning thanks (*exomologoumai*) to the *Father, Lord of heaven and earth*. Typically meaning 'give consent to' or 'confess' (as in the only other two Lukan usages, Luke 22:6; Acts 19:18), *exomologoumai*'s occurrence here is slightly unusual, as the giving of praise and/or thanks is more typically expressed by other verbs. Perhaps the word choice hints that Jesus not only praises God for electing *infants* (*nēpiois*) but also cheerfully submits to and confesses the divine purposes (cf. 1 Cor. 1:18–29). Of course, the term 'infant' denotes not literal infants but, metaphorically, those who are helpless and utterly dependent (cf. Luke 9:48). Given Paul's earlier elaboration of the 'wise' in 1 Corinthians 1 – 2 with, arguably, reference to the book of Daniel, one suspects that *the wise and the intelligent* here refers on one level to the religious leaders who reject Jesus, and on another level to their spiritual forebears, specifically, Daniel's misguided 'wise men' (*sophoi*).[14] Like the pagan court astrologers who could not discern either Nebuchadnezzar's dream or its kingdom significance, the learned recipients of the seventy-two's message cannot – apart from the elective purposes of God – penetrate the meaning of secret divine revelation. Like, too, the seed sown on the first three soils in Jesus' parable of the sower, they are not privy to the Danielic mystery of the kingdom (8:10). In this way, Luke 10:21 subtly taps into the Danielic narrative on several levels, hinting not least that the same Spirit (Dan. 4:8, 9, 18; 5:11) who granted Daniel insight into God's immutable purpose now empowers Jesus to unveil the paradoxical salvation of the coming kingdom. To take this approach a step further: when Jesus says *I thank you* [*exomologoumai*], *Father* for revealing these 'hidden things' (*tauta*), he is imitating Daniel who also gives thanks (*exomologoumai*) for revealing these hidden things (*tauta*) contained in Nebuchadnezzar's kingdom dream (Dan. 2:23, LXX). In the light of Jesus' summary,

---

14. On the Danielic background of 'the wise' in 1 Corinthians, see Gladd, *Revealing*.

the preaching of the seventy-two, together with the earlier preaching of the Twelve, has served to actualize the parable of the sower. From a human point of view, one can no better explain why some seed grows and other seed does not than one can explain why Daniel was made to interpret the writing on the wall while others could not.

22. Jesus' transaction with the Father, whereby *all things have been handed over* (*panta moi paredothē*), strangely parallels the delegation of authority to Satan.[15] The term *all things* (*panta*) is ambiguous. If it refers to the created universe, then Jesus is now essentially claiming rights over that which Satan had earlier claimed for himself (4:6). However, because the preceding context seems to require that *panta* signifies *knowledge* of all things, which is tantamount to a knowledge of the Father's identity (*tis estin ho patēr*), it is more likely that Jesus is claiming to be – precisely as the unique mediator of divine knowledge – the repository of all wisdom. It is a knowledge that is already being revealed, even if partially, through Jesus' now-explicit familial language. Just as Satan mediates his entrusted earthly glory to those under his thrall, the Son mediates knowledge of the Father on the basis of his sheer pleasure.

23–24. The same revelatory activity is in view when Jesus now turns *privately* to *the disciples* and declares their eyes blessed.[16] Assuming that *the disciples* refers to the Twelve and not the seventy-two, Luke's reader is struck by the fact that it is only the former (and not the latter, notwithstanding their dedication and abilities) who are made privy to the person of the Father. The disciples and their eyes are *blessed* not only in the sense that they are fortunate enough to belong to the elect, but also – as in the Beatitudes (6:20–22) – in the sense that they are proleptic partakers of eschatological blessedness. In this respect, they are made to see that which *many prophets and kings desired to see* but could not.

---

15. 'And the devil said to him, "To you I will give their glory *and all this authority* [*tēn exousian tautēn hapasan*]; for it *has been given over to me* [*emoi paradedotai*], and I give it to anyone I please"' (4:6, emphasis added).

16. The passage has a close parallel in Matt. 11:25–27.

Theology

In Jesus' day, as in Luke's day, different people registered different responses to the Galilean's messianic claim. Refusing to welcome Jesus, the Samaritans reject outright his announcement of the kingdom. Elsewhere on the spectrum, ardent enthusiasts express their willingness to follow, only to be turned back on the grounds of their half-hearted faith. Still others seem to have responded well, at least so the text seems to imply. By the same token, others would be met with severe judgment, again by implication. If Jesus truly is the Messiah, one may ask, wouldn't he have garnered a more positive response? Why is 'the Messiah' receiving mixed reviews?

The reasons, the present passage seems to suggest, are complex but not beyond detailing. In the first place, as 10:21–24 makes clear, appropriate response to the preaching of the kingdom is first and foremost *animated by divine election*. That is to say, just as in Daniel's day Yahweh had for inscrutable reasons granted insight to some but not to others, the same principle applies here: human insight into the divine mysteries depends on God's willingness to reveal. Second, as the varied responses to Jesus in this passage well illustrate, the kingdom's advance is at least partly *dependent on human receptivity*. How this element of human responsiveness squares with divine sovereignty does not seem to be of immediate concern to the Evangelist. The bottom line is that any true receptivity to the kingdom involves a concurrence of divine initiative *and* human willingness. Third and finally, the kingdom's advance is *impacted by invisible realities, good and evil*. The raising up of labourers depends on earnest prayer, even as the disciples' report (10:17–20) underscores not just the devil's personal interest in countering the kingdom but also the importance of exorcism in securing it. God's purposes, the human heart and the vicissitudes of spiritual opposition all have a role in explaining receptivity to the kingdom announcement – or the lack thereof.

B. Life of service and listening (10:25–42)

Context

Jesus' recent encounter with an inhospitable Samaritan village in 9:51–56 makes it all the more ironic that, in this section, he should now tell a parable about a heroically merciful and eminently hospitable Samaritan. The parable's cast of characters also includes priests and Levites, who, while occupying a relatively minor role in Luke's Gospel, belong to the recalcitrant temple establishment. The parable powerfully illustrates the teachings of the Sermon on the Plain, especially the requirements of showing mercy (6:36) and demonstrating generous love, even to one's enemies (6:27). Following the parable, Luke goes on to draw back the curtain on at least two of the women who made up Jesus' behind-the-scenes supporting cast (8:1–3). The interactions between Mary, Martha and Jesus in 10:38–42 serve both to exemplify the ideal alluded to in the preceding parable and to qualify it.

Comment
i. The parable of the good Samaritan (10:25–37)

25–26. The NRSV's *just then* effectively conveys the suddenness of *kai idou* (cf. 5:12, 18; 7:12, 37; 8:41; etc.), as if the *lawyer* were interrupting Jesus' speech (10:17–24). The tight temporal connection between this passage and Jesus' remarks on the spiritually obtuse 'wise' and 'intelligent' (v. 21) raises the question as to whether this same lawyer is one of those misguided 'wise'. Certainly, that the scribe 'tests' (*ekpeirazōn*) Jesus is an ominous sign, since in Luke the only other tester is Satan himself (4:12).[17] By the same token, Luke's initial characterization may not be wholly dark, for the very fact that the lawyer *stood up* (*anastas*) to put Jesus to the test may be an oblique ray of hope, suggesting his willingness to relinquish his judgmental 'sitting' position so characteristic of his scribal colleagues (5:17; 7:32). His question, bearing on the quest for *eternal life* (cf. 18:18), was a standard one in the day and as such would not have caught Jesus off guard. Given Luke's description of the lawyer as *ekpeirazōn*, one may be forgiven for wondering whether the query was less an honest question than an attempt to force Jesus to 'go public' on an issue which had divided the rabbis of the day, thereby – so it might have been hoped – alienating those who were presently undecided about Jesus.

---

17. The verb *ekpeirazō*, an intensive form of *peirazō* (to test, to tempt), connotes entrapment, even the entrapping of God (cf. e.g. 1 Cor. 10:9).

The question itself should not be misinterpreted (as it so often has been) as asking, 'How can I spend eternity in a disembodied reality?', but rather 'How can I stake my claim in the new creation come the final resurrection?'[18] In a brilliant counter-manoeuvre designed to force his interlocutor to show his cards first (as it were), Jesus enquires after not only the contents of Scripture (*What is written in the law?*) but also its proper interpretation (*What do you read there?*).

27. The foiled scribe now has little recourse but to respond according to the party line. With only slight changes to the wording, Luke's scribe quotes Deuteronomy 6:5 (LXX), adding *and with all your mind*. Alongside this, the 'greatest commandment' (Matt. 22:37//Mark 12:30), the scribe attaches Leviticus 19:18: *and your neighbour as yourself.* Building on Leviticus 19:18's broad currency in the church of his day (Rom. 13:9; Gal. 5:14; Jas 2:8), Luke introduces an innovation by fusing the two commandments 'into a single unified command so that "love of neighbor" has the same force as "love for God"'.[19] By the canons of first-century Christian belief, Luke's scribe could not be any more correct.

28. Nevertheless, though the lawyer answers *orthōs*, that is, 'correctly' or in an orthodox manner, orthodoxy by itself is not enough. Picking up on the scribe's own language of 'doing' and 'life', Jesus closes out the thought: '*Do* this and you will *live*.' On the face of it, his challenge appears theologically problematic. For if up to this point Jesus had insisted on unbending commitment to himself (9:23–26, 58–62), the absence of any trace of Christology or soteriology would be jarring. Yet the problem is mitigated if, in the fuller context, Luke's Jesus means to say that those who truly love God and neighbour will do so only by availing themselves of the mediatorial Son, as spelled out in verse 22. Put differently, if 'whoever welcomes me welcomes the one who sent me' (9:48), then one who truly loves God and neighbour on God's terms will also love Jesus as well, and inherit eternal life.

29. Luke has also already informed us that, paradoxically, while sinners have 'justified' (*edikaiōsan*) God (7:29), the 'Pharisees and the

---

18. Perrin, 'Eternal Life'.
19. Johnson, p. 174.

lawyers rejected God's purpose' both by bringing charges against the Son of Man (7:30, 31, 34) and by failing to justify God. Now, still on a personal mission to uncover new evidence against Jesus, this lawyer is *wanting to justify* [*dikaiōsai*] *himself*, essentially compromising himself (16:16; 18:14). His hoped-for vindication turns on a seemingly innocent follow-up question: *And who is my neighbour?* Of course, the well-schooled lawyer knows that if the question of eternal life might fetch a variety of answers in the Judaism of the day, so too would the query 'Who is my neighbour?' Hoping to deflect the Scripture's claim on his life, the lawyer raises the question not in order to understand but in order to parlay interpretative uncertainty into a warrant for inaction.

30. At this point, Jesus offers not a concise proposition but a story, involving a certain *man* (*anthrōpos tis*; cf. 14:16; 15:11; 16:1, 19; 19:12; 20:9) who was *going down from Jerusalem to Jericho*. An 18-mile (29 km) stretch leading from the elevations of Jerusalem (2,500 ft or 762 m above sea level) *down* to the lowlands of Jericho (800 ft or 244 m below sea level), the road would have been familiar to Jesus' hearers. Judging by archaeological evidence of first-century Roman sentry points along the way, it also appears to have been a notoriously unsafe road, in part due to its surrounding landscape providing bandits with countless cavernous hideouts. But if Jesus' mention of *Jerusalem to Jericho* is an attempt to enhance the story's verisimilitude, it may also be drawing a parallel to David's flight along this very road, as he escaped the – ultimately ill-fated – revolt of Absalom (2 Sam. 15:13 – 16:14). The link with 2 Samuel gains strength on recalling that the unfolding conflict between Jesus (and his followers) and the temple elite (and their supporters) already has a certain Davidic character: just as the rightfully anointed David suffered injury and exile at the hands of certain usurpers along with their priestly supporters, Jesus would endure a similar fate a fortiori. Indeed, the parable's *robbers* (*lēstais*), who leave their victim stripped, beaten and half-dead, do not seem to be unconnected to the 'den of robbers' (*spēlaion lēstōn*) who oversee the cult (19:46) and ultimately have some role in Jesus' stripping (23:11) and crucifixion. In this case, the hapless man represents not just the random innocent victim but also a suffering David figure, re-embodied in history by Jesus and his persecuted followers. In this case, too, the parable's call to be a neighbour to the victim includes a more specific call to be a neighbour to Jesus, even as he is manifest amid his suffering community.

31-33. A priest, a Levite and a Samaritan now make their entrance. For Jesus' Jewish hearers, the first two figures would have represented the height of religious respectability; the Samaritan, by contrast, belonged to an ethnically and religiously contemptible race, a virtually invisible society in Jewish eyes.[20] The story's biting irony is that while those who retain prominent religious positions *passed by on the other side*, the Samaritan is *moved with pity*. Here the parable seems to be operating on two planes of meaning. On a basic level, the point is that love for one's neighbour must be actualized through concrete acts of mercy, unconstrained by cultural barriers thrown up by social, ethnic or religious identity. On another level, because all this takes place 'on the road' (*en tē hodō*), and 'road' (*hodos*) in Luke is the stretch of road separating the Holy City from the land of exile, the religious leaders' turning a cold shoulder 'on the road' may be sealing their destiny of continuing exile. This is confirmed by the fact that they are *going down* the road, meaning that they are moving from Jerusalem to Jericho, the opposite direction from which Jesus will initiate his dramatized return-from-exile march from Jericho to Jerusalem (18:35 – 19:44).

34-35. In caring for the victim, the Samaritan is conscientious, generous and thorough. More than just bandaging the man's wounds, he applies *oil and wine*, commonly applied as salves in the ancient world.[21] More than simply bringing the recovering man to

---

20. Jewish hostility towards Samaritans (i.e. Shechemites) went back centuries before the time of Jesus (Neh. 4:1–2), as exemplified in Sir. 50:25–26: 'Two nations my soul detests, / and the third is not even a people: / Those who live in Seir, and the Philistines, / and the foolish people that live in Shechem.' For historical background, see Knoppers, *Jews and Samaritans*.

21. Augustine (*Quaest. ev.* 19) sees the oil and wine as referring to the comfort of hope and the exhortation to work, respectively. In my view, if the Evangelist intended an allegory at all, a stronger case could be

an inn, he goes on to attend to the man himself, before hiring the innkeeper to take care of him for the price of two denarii.[22] *Whatever more you spend*, he promises the innkeeper, 'I myself will repay.' In some sense, if Jesus is identifiable with the victim, he is also identifiable with the extravagantly saving good Samaritan.[23] In this case, the *innkeeper* (*pandochei*), which may also be translated as 'host' in a generic sense, represents all those whom Jesus entrusts with resources, in order that they might generously host on his behalf, that is, until he returns and pays them back.

36. The lavish, above-and-beyond quality of the man's care serves to reframe the lawyer's question entirely. Loving one's neighbour, Luke's Jesus means to say, is not a matter of asking, 'What is the minimum requirement in order to fulfil the basic duties demanded by Leviticus 19:18?' Rather, it is a matter of asking, 'How can I reflect the extravagant love of God in my own dealings with others, including my enemies?' Likewise, Jesus' concluding question is designed not so much to get information (since the question's answer is obvious) but to invert the lawyer's original question and to issue a personal challenge.

37. The lawyer's continued engagement in the conversation, together with his response to Jesus' parting question, leaves hope that he is not beyond the pale. By verbalizing the correct answer himself, an answer once again centred around 'doing mercy' (*poēsas to heleos*), the lawyer is faced with an existential decision. Will he *go and do likewise* as Jesus bids – or not? Luke's readers, of course, are also faced with same decision.

(note 21 *cont.*) made for the oil and wine representing the Spirit and Jesus' blood, respectively.

22. A denarius was a day's working wage. Jeremias (*Jerusalem*, p. 122) calculates that two denarii would have purchased room and board for twenty-four days.

23. Early rumours identifying Jesus as a Samaritan (cf. John 8:48) may be in the background here. The inference might have followed from Jesus' ministry beyond the ethnic boundaries of Israel, as Samaritans denied the Jewish claim that Jews alone were children of Abraham.

ii. Martha and Mary (10:38–42)

38–39. The present story, unique to Luke, connects with the previous passage through the pairing of the remark that the band *went on their way* (*poreuesthai*) with Jesus' command that the lawyer '*Go* [*poreuou*] and do likewise' (v. 37, emphasis added). Entering an unidentified village, Jesus and the disciples are received by two sisters identified by name: Martha and Mary.[24] The former *welcomed him into her home*, thereby qualifying herself as a recipient of Jesus' peace (10:5–6). Meanwhile, her (presumably younger) sister Mary is sitting *at the Lord's feet* (*pros tous podas*; cf. 7:38; 8:35, 41), listening intently and without interruption (as suggested by the durative imperfect: *ēkouen*).[25] Like any male disciple sitting at a rabbi's feet (Acts 22:3) (a female sitting at the feet of a rabbi would have been radical though not completely unprecedented in the Judaism of the day), she listens to 'his word' (*ton logon autou*; KJV), the same mesmerizing word spoken at Nazareth (4:32, 36), identical with the word of God (5:1).

40. The adversative particle *de*, translated as *But* in the NRSV, underscores a contrast between Martha's attitude and Mary's attentiveness.[26] The source of Martha's distraction is 'much service' (*pollēn diakonian*), putting her – despite the noblest of intentions – in the category of the seed 'choked by the cares . . . of life' (8:14). Though Martha addresses Jesus as *Lord* (*kyrie*), her tone is at once self-pitying and strident, if not impertinent; her approach is both confrontational (*Lord, do you not care . . . ?*) and directive (*Tell her then to help me*). Yet Luke invites us to have a balanced portrait of Martha. On the one hand, her expectations are not unrealistic: normally the older sister *would* expect the younger sister to help shoulder the burden of the necessary preparations. On the other hand, there are already sufficient hints in her interaction with Jesus that the fundamental problem lies not so much with Mary but with Martha.

---

24. John (11:1), however, identifies the village as Bethany, several miles east of Jerusalem.

25. Martha's welcoming of Jesus suggests her leadership over the home and therefore her seniority.

26. Using a verb that expresses anxious preoccupation, Luke writes that Martha was *distracted* (*periespato*).

41–42. Jesus' repetition of the name (*Martha, Martha*) strikes a calming, pastoral note. Even so, he does not leave his beloved complainant unchallenged. According to the Lord, Martha errs by being *worried and distracted by many things*. And these *many things* stand in contrast to the *one thing* (*henos*) that is needful.[27] In some sense, that *one thing* is obviously the *better part* (*agathēn merida*) chosen by Mary, that is, listening to Jesus. Yet the disjunction between the feminine noun *merida* (lot, portion) and the masculine or neuter gender of *henos* (one) leaves open the possibility that the *one thing* is actually one (masculine singular) *person*, that is, *ho theos*, the one God. In this vein, Jesus hints that Martha's distractions are not just unnecessary but ultimately idolatrous. As for Mary, her lot – strikingly the same term used for a real-estate inheritance – will *not be taken away from her*. By listening at the feet of Jesus, then, she acquires an eternal plot of land akin to that which had been sought after by the lawyer (10:25).

Theology

Like many a good song, Luke 10:25–42 begins and ends on the same note, in this case, the theme of hospitality. But Luke never intends his readers to practise hospitality merely for the sake of hospitality. On the contrary, for the Evangelist, the only proper motivation for service is Christological.

If my reading of the parable of the good Samaritan (10:25–37) is on target, then Jesus is both innocent victim and saving hero, both recovering guest at the inn and the silent sponsor supporting the innkeeper. As humanity's saviour, Jesus generously cares for those who have been stripped and bloodied by life's road bandits, including the bandit of sin. As the victim-turned-guest, Jesus identifies with the needy in their plight. Perhaps this dual identification corresponds to a life of discipleship, which inevitably calls Christ-followers to seasons of generous giving as well as to seasons of humble receiving. The Risen Christ is in both trans-

---

27. With its insertion of the phrase 'and yet few are needed', the JB has followed the text of certain weighty manuscripts. However, the phrase is likely spurious; contra Fee, 'One Thing'.

actions, because paradoxically Jesus is the definitive 'guest-host'.

To be sure, Jesus' followers likewise are called to be both guests and hosts, but there is an asymmetry in this dual vocation. On the heels of the parable, Martha administers care through her active service, while Mary receives care by listening to Jesus. Both emphases are important but priority is given to listening to and receiving from Jesus. Well-intentioned activism that is not rooted in listening to Jesus has fallen short of the worshipful life God requires. For Luke, simply being in Christ is more important than doing for Christ.

C. Praying for the coming of the kingdom (11:1–26)

Context
As much as the seventy-two's announcement of the kingdom (10:1–16) unsettled the demonic realm (vv. 17–18), it also provoked human opposition (vv. 13–15). This sets the stage for what follows. When the disciples approach Jesus for guidance in prayer (11:1–13), they do so because they have already begun to experience demonically inspired tribulation. The master himself likewise encounters the same kind of persecution, not least when his opponents accuse him – ironically so – of being in league with Beelzebul (11:14–26). In the midst of such conflict, Jesus asks his disciples to discern the contours of the true battle lines. On the one side is the kingdom; on the other side, the kingdom of Beelzebul. As Jesus' followers pray what has come to be known as the 'Lord's Prayer', Jesus himself will play the strong man against the adversary and the adversary's kingdom.

Comment
i. Teachings on prayer (11:1–13)
1. In the first of several treatments of prayer, the Evangelist sets out what his first-century readers might have already recognized as *the* prescribed prayer of the church. Attentive modern readers of Luke and Matthew will notice differences between their two respective versions of the prayer, in wording as well as in context. In Luke (differently from Matthew), one of the disciples asks Jesus

to teach them to pray, just as the Baptizer had instructed his disciples to pray. There is no reason either to doubt the historical authenticity of this request or to resist the surmise that Jesus' disciples were prompted by the same kinds of concerns which had led John's disciples to request a prayer appropriate to their circumstances.[28] In my view, because John had been in prison for some time (3:20), and because too the Baptizer seems to have interpreted that imprisonment as a part of the much anticipated tribulation leading up to the Messiah's coming (7:18–19), John's disciples were most likely seeking for something like a 'tribulation prayer'. That the Lord's Prayer was originally intended in the same vein helps make sense of the Lukan context. Perceiving signs of tribulation (Luke 10), not least in their battle with the demonic, the disciples request a new prayer for leveraging divine aid in the face of dark resistance. Jesus' carefully formulated response delivers on the disciples' immediate request even as it has provided a rubric that has served the church down through the ages.

2. Whereas the Hebrew Scriptures attest to many different epithets for Israel's God, the most central being 'Yahweh' (cf. Exod. 3:13–14), Jesus' disciples are to begin their prescribed prayer with an address that is striking in its simplicity: *Father.*[29] It is a familial term appropriate to the new family coalescing around Jesus. To be sure, though *Father* may in part speak of the unprecedented intimacy of the individual's encounter with the divine, its significance bears no less on the dawning of a new era now being initiated by Jesus.[30] This is because in naming God as 'Father', community members were asserting not only their solidarity with Jesus the Son (cf. 3:22; 4:3, 9, 41; 9:35), but also their incorporative status as fellow members of Yahweh's firstborn *son* (Exod. 4:22–23), Israel.[31] Just as Yahweh's son

---

28. So Marshall, p. 456.

29. The KJV's inclusion of 'which art in heaven' almost certainly reflects a late scribal interpolation, which in turn came from an urge to conform Luke to Matthew (6:9).

30. On the dangers of overreading this text as a source of Jesus' inner experience of God, see Thompson, *Promise*, p. 31.

31. Perrin, *Kingdom of God*, pp. 224–225.

(Israel) was called to engage in worship in the face of powerful countervailing political forces (Exod. 4:22–23), the same vocation now fell to Jesus' disciples as they modelled their sonship after the example of Jesus *the* Son. The address of 'Father' was entirely appropriate for a movement called to undertake a new exodus.

Pursuant to this 'new exodus' identity two imperatives follow: *hallowed be your name* and *your kingdom come*. The former of these pleas is again best understood against its scriptural context. In accordance with the promise that God would 'hallow his name' by restoring his people to a re-sanctified land (Ezek. 36:22–25), the so-called first petition asks the heavenly Father to lay the spiritual groundwork for the fulfilment of the restorational promises. The request for hallowing is closely related to the second petition, which asks for the coming of the kingdom as part and parcel of return from exile, envisioned in Micah 4:1–8 (especially v. 8). By Jesus' day, the hallowing of God's name further touched on the notion of an atoning death through martyrdom.[32] In Luke's theology, then, the coming of the kingdom and Israel's restoration are but two sides of the same coin.[33] Introduced at the beginning of Jesus' prescribed prayer, the coming of the kingdom, one and the same as return from exile, stands at the very top of the agenda.

3. Interpretation of the third petition for *daily bread* is flummoxed by the uncertain meaning of *epiousion*, the operative Greek participle behind *daily*. There are at least three interpretative possibilities. First, the Greek word may represent a convergence of *epi* ('for') and *ousia* ('being'), potentially generating the translation 'necessary for existence'. A second possibility, the so-called 'quotidian interpretation', sees the participle as an elliptical rendering of *epi tēn ousian hēmeran* ('for today'). This is the basis for the oft-used translation, dating as far back as the fourth-century Latin Vulgate, 'daily bread'

---

32. Ben-Sasson, *EncJud* 10, pp. 978–986.

33. Commenting on the second petition, Brown ('Eschatological Prayer', p. 299) rightly remarks: 'The Christians are not primarily asking that God's dominion come into their own hearts ... but that God's universal reign be established – that destiny toward which the whole of time is directed.'

(*panem nostrum cotidianum*; cf. KJV, NASB, NRSV, etc.). The third and in my view best option is to take *epiousion* as a participle for *epeimi* ('to come upon' or 'to follow'), a favourite Lukan verb for expressing future time (Acts 7:26; 16:11; 20:15; 21:18; 23:11), yielding the meaning 'future bread' or 'tomorrow's bread'. This interpretation would certainly line up with Luke's narrative interest in the messianic banquet (14:7–14), where the chief menu item would be bread. On this reading, the third petition encourages the disciples to pray for the bread of the messianic banquet, which is to pray metonymically (i.e. as a part for the whole) for the eschaton itself. At the same time, praying for the community's eschatological bread arguably includes the series of day-to-day provisions leading up to the messianic banquet, the culminating feast capping off an indeterminate set of forward-looking celebratory meals in this age.[34] Along these lines, I suggest that verse 3 is a prayer not only for the eschatological meal but also for daily, corporate sustenance leading up to that moment.[35] Because Luke's Jesus has ministered to the crowds by issuing bread together with teaching (9:11), which is a form of spiritual bread (Isa. 55:2; Amos 8:11), standard patristic interpretation of this verse is likely correct in maintaining that the petition for daily bread includes in its purview both physical and spiritual nourishment through the Word.

4. Whereas Matthew records 'debts' and 'debtors', Luke has *sins* and *everyone indebted to us*. The difference between 'debts' and 'sins' should not be overemphasized, since Hebrew thought regarded sin as a kind of debt. Apparently, Jesus would have his community be a place of forgiveness, more exactly, a space where forgiveness is freely and regularly granted, just as it is freely and regularly received. The request for divine forgiveness blends nicely with the so-called sixth petition: the plea to be spared *trial* (*peirasmon*). While some commentators see more 'temptation' than 'eschatological trial' in the Greek word *peirasmos*, I think both concepts are in view but primarily the latter. After all, an eschatological tribulation would

---

34. See Dennis, *DJG*, p. 93.

35. I say 'corporate sustenance' simply because the prayer reflects community needs more so than private needs: 'Give *us our* daily bread.'

not be unconnected to Jesus as the instigator of a new exodus. For it seems that just as Israel the son of God had to go through the trials (*peirasmoi*; cf. Deut. 4:34; 7:19; 29:2, LXX) of the plagues as a prelude to their exodus experience, so too Jesus' followers would have to endure their own trials en route to their own exodus-like experience.[36] Whichever of these two options the interpreter takes, a sharp notional distinction between 'temptation' and 'trial' is hardly sustainable.

5–8. After conveying the content of his prayer, Jesus now emphasizes the *why* of persevering prayer by inviting his disciples to imagine a hypothetical scenario in which they imagine themselves as hosts receiving an unexpected guest *at midnight*. Without food and thus unable to fulfil the basic obligations of hospitality (a serious faux pas in antiquity), *you* the host go to the house of another friend hoping to borrow *three loaves of bread*.[37] Because the friend's family has long since retired for the night (a typical Palestinian home would have everyone sleeping together on one floor mat in the main room), he is initially hesitant to respond. When the friend is reluctant, he risks putting himself in a bad light, for ancient hospitality customs demanded that a village pool its resources in meeting the needs of travelling strangers. Ultimately, however, because of the friend's commitment to maintaining his own honour or *anaideia* ('state of shamelessness') in a tight-knit village where gossip and the sound of late-night requests for bread carry, he accedes to the demand despite the nuisance. A standard alternative interpretation ascribes *anaideia* not to the friend in the house but to the breadless host, and translates the Greek word as 'persistence'. But this is problematic, not least because it presumes an unusual meaning for *anaideia*.[38] If we go down

---

36. This exodus will be signalled again when, on the eve of his crucifixion, Jesus performs the definitive Passover meal at the so-called Last Supper (22:14–23). Jesus' death and resurrection are the means by which the passage from 'Egypt' occurs.

37. The three loaves may be connected to Jesus' subsequent parable involving three measures of flour in Luke 13:21, the same amount used for Abraham's three visitors in Gen. 18:1–8.

38. For references, see Nygaard, *Prayer*, p. 142.

this route at all, then a slightly better option sees Jesus exhorting not persistent prayer but shameless (i.e. bold) prayer. But again, in my view, it makes most sense that the focus of the parable is on neither human persistence nor human boldness but on God's overriding commitment to his own honour (*anaideia*) – and that in turn becomes the basis for persevering prayer.[39]

9–10. Extending the point, Jesus issues a threefold exhortation which logically follows from the illustration of verses 5–8: *ask*, *search* and *knock*. In response to each of these actions, Luke's Jesus grants unqualified assurance of divine aid. Nor is such confidence to be restricted to a few extraordinarily righteous or deserving individuals; rather, the emphasis is on the universality of the promise: *everyone* who asks receives. Searching and knocking are not so much alternatives to asking as alternative ways to think about asking, for in Luke's theology of prayer, divine intervention consistently depends not on any vague hoping or wishful thinking but on the concrete act of asking. In order to attain the fullness of divine blessing, nothing less than persevering petition will do.

11–13. In closing out his exhortation, Jesus again draws an analogy with his hearers' personal experience. If a child were to ask for either a *fish* or an *egg*, no-one in his or her right mind would meet such an appeal by supplying a *snake* or a *scorpion*. In the parallel in Matthew 7:9–10, the hypothetical parent offers a stone in response to a request for bread and a serpent in response to a request for a fish. The ominous reptilian images, replete with demonic overtones, suggest that though human beings are essentially *evil* (a point which is taken for granted), they are rarely so evil as to intend harm to their children. This comparison in turn serves as the premise for Jesus' a fortiori argument: if evil human beings generally manage to do right by their own children, how much more might the disciples depend on the beneficence of their heavenly Father, who willingly grants *the Holy Spirit to those who ask him*. The initial granting of that gift occurs of course in Acts 1:14 – 2:4. That Luke expected his readers to continue asking for the Spirit – as the highest aspiration of all their prayers – well

---

39. So, e.g., Green, p. 448; Johnson, 'Assurance'; Nolland, p. 626.

beyond Pentecost follows from the placement of verse 13 within a general exhortation.

ii. The cosmic war with Beelzebul (11:14–26)

14. Luke's record of this exorcism, not as spectacular as the one at Gerasa (8:26–39), cues up the following discourse (11:17–26) even as it graphically drives home Jesus' agenda.[40] The offending demon is *mute* (*kōphon*) and has inflicted its muteness on its victim, who, once freed of the menacing spirit, is able to speak freely – all to the crowd's amazement. In delivering the man, Jesus is making good on his promise to release God's people from their bondage (4:18–19). Yet the exorcism also takes on the quality of an enacted parable drawing on familiar scriptural concepts. According to Isaiah, God's exiled people have become mute, much like the voiceless idols they have worshipped (Isa. 46:7; cf. Pss 115:6–8; 135:16–18; Jer. 10:5; Hab. 2:18; 1 Cor. 12:2). Since Luke's Jesus has already explained his exorcisms and healings with reference to Isaiah (Luke 7:21–22), one may interpret this astonishing transformation as a dramatization of Jesus' mission to reverse Israel's spiritual muteness by curing the nation of its idolatry and restoring it from exile (Isa. 35:5–6).[41]

15–16. The amazement of the crowds (v. 14) triggers two kinds of reactions corresponding to two groups of observers. The first group (*some*), on comparing notes, concludes that Jesus *casts out demons by Beelzebul, the ruler of the demons.* Synonymous with Satan, 'Beelzebul' can mean 'Lord of dung' (a mocking play on the Ekronite god Beelzebub, 'Lord of the flies') but also 'Lord of the house', a meaning not unrelated to Jesus' 'house' language to follow (v. 17). *Others*, making up a second group, are less curious about the origins of Jesus' authority but hope to test the upstart exorcist by asking for a confirming sign. Such aspirations do not put these *others* in good company. In Luke's story, Satan has already put Jesus to the test by seeking signs (4:1–13); similarly, in the Hebrew Bible,

---

40. Jesus' enduring and far-ranging reputation as an exorcist is corroborated in rabbinic tradition (b. Sanh. 43a).

41. See commentary above at Luke 8:26–39.

the sign-seeking Sinai generation puts Yahweh to the test (Exod. 17:1–7; Num. 14.20–23) and this an offence to God.

17. Once again responding to his interlocutors' unspoken thoughts, Jesus maintains that an internally divided kingdom cannot endure but will eventually turn into *desert*. In such a case, too, *house falls on house*. The transformation from kingdom to desert is strange but explicable as a nod towards Israel's exile, metaphorically described as a desert-like experience (Isa. 35:1; 41:18; 43:19). Meanwhile, the phrase *house falls on house* is ambiguous since it may envision either a house collapsing on itself or a house being crushed by another house. If the temple 'house' and its priestly overseers are in view, then the ambiguity perhaps serves to give a double meaning After all, by Luke's reckoning, the temple in Jerusalem will collapse under the weight of its own malfeasance (Luke 6:48; 21:6), even as the same temple will suffer the impact from the house that is the kingdom of God (20:18; cf. Dan 2:44–45).

18. Jesus further explains that if Satan *is divided against himself*, it would be impossible for his kingdom to remain standing. In other words, so the logic goes, if Satan did share his dark powers with Jesus only to see his own demonic minions driven out as a result, this would be incredibly short-sighted on Satan's part. As Jesus engages in a rhetorical duel with his sceptics, his *reductio ad absurdum* argument scores high points.

19–20. These two verses are interpretatively complex on several levels. First, translators disagree on the best equivalent for the Greek phrase *hoi huioi hymōn* ('your sons') in verse 19a. NRSV reads: *Now if I cast out the demons by Beelzebul, by whom do your exorcists* [*hoi huioi hymōn*] *cast them out?* But the NRSV's *your exorcists* (*hoi huioi hymōn*) may be equally translated as 'your followers' (CEB, NIV, GNT), or 'your people' (NEB), or even 'your experts' (JB). Still one more approach would be to take 'sons' at face value, that is, as biological descendants, and by extension, fellow ethnic Jews (ESV, KJV, NASB, RSV). Without putting too fine a point on it, then, we are left with two possibilities for *hoi huioi hymōn*: (1) those who belong to the Pharisees' movement or (2) compatriot Jews. The first option is made difficult by verse 20, which would imply by this reading that Jesus' opponents are helping to usher in the kingdom.[42] This seems counter-intuitive on a number of levels. But if we go with option (2) and suppose that 'your sons' refers not just to compatriot Jews *simpliciter*, but more specifically to Jesus' (Jewish) disciples as they cast out demons (9:1–2; 10:17), this would better square with (1) Luke's insistence that the kingdom advances by the Spirit (Luke 3:22; 4:1, 14, 18; 10:21; 12:12; Acts 1:2, 5, 8; 2:18; 4:31; etc.), and (2) his narrative pattern, whereby the Pharisees are depicted as being opposed to the Spirit (Luke 12:8–12; Acts 7:51; 28:26–28).[43] In this case, it seems that Jesus is challenging his opposition as if to say, 'If you want to accuse me of being allied with Satan, very well. But then you will also have to charge not just the Twelve with the same crime, but also the seventy-two disciples – the sons of Israel who are doing the faithful work of an exorcist!' Aware of the countless individuals who had benefited from the seventy-two's highly effective exorcistic ministry tour (10:17), the Pharisees quickly realize the political liability in pressing this attack any further and, hence, back down.

Now going on the offensive, Jesus next invites his critics to consider the alternative: *But if it is by the finger of God that I cast out the demons, then the kingdom of God has come to you [ephthasen eph' hymas]* (v. 20). But what exactly does Jesus mean when he says that the kingdom of God has *come to you*? Here it should be noted that the Greek verb *ephthasen* connotes an explosive and unexpected coming – maybe even a violent coming associated with judgment.[44] Connotations of judgment are reinforced by the *finger of God*, which, according to numerous commentators, is a re-extension of the

---

42. Despite this difficulty, Nolland (p. 639) and Green (p. 456) take this approach.

43. To date, the definitive case for this view has been set forth by Shirock, 'Whose Exorcists'.

44. While the perfective aspect of *ephthasen* intimates that the kingdom has arrived in a completed sense, there obviously remains a strong sense in which the kingdom has not yet come. For discussion on Luke 11:20 and its Matthean parallel (Matt. 12:28), see Beasley-Murray, *Kingdom of God*, pp. 75–80; Fitzer, *TDNT* 9, p. 92.

same 'finger of God' once pointed at Pharaoh's demonically inspired magicians (Exod. 8:19; cf. Jub. 48:9, 12).[45] At the same time, we should not rule out an allusion to the ominous finger of God that, according to Daniel, scrawls out words of judgment (Dan. 5:5).[46] By implicitly comparing his exorcisms to Moses' plagues, Jesus casts himself and his opponents in the roles of Moses and Pharaoh's magicians, respectively; by comparing his exorcisms to the mysterious writing on the wall, a Daniel-esque Jesus predicts the doom of those who oppose him. For Jesus, his exorcisms were evidence enough that the kingdom of God was indeed at hand – and with the full coming of the kingdom in the future, imminent judgment.

21–22. Shifting gears, Jesus likens Satan to a *strong man, fully armed*, who seeks to guard *his castle* (*tēn heautou aulēn*). The term *aulē* typically does not mean 'castle' but 'courtyard', and it acquires precisely this latter meaning in reference to the high priest's enclosure (22:55, the noun's only other occurrence in Luke). Given Luke's careful word choices, this verbal link may hint to some connection between Satan's *aulē* and the *aulē* of the high priest. If so, then this would suggest not that the Jewish priesthood was essentially satanic, much less that Judaism was inherently evil, but simply that the evil one had insinuated himself among the securely ensconced temple leaders. Yet perhaps an equally good case can be made that the fully armed strong man stands for the Roman military, taking the reader back to Jesus' earlier exorcism of a *legion* of demons (8:26–39), with its decidedly anti-imperial implications.[47] Yet, again, perhaps *both* Jerusalem and Rome are in view. In any instance, the satanic strong man's possessions will soon be taken away and redistributed as plunder – this will occur thanks to *one stronger*, Jesus himself. Those whom he liberates will be his prized booty.

---

45. Matt. 12:28 has 'Spirit of God' instead of 'finger of God'. On the Exodus backdrop of the Lukan rendering, see Bock, p. 1079; Green, p. 457; Marshall, p. 475.

46. As argued persuasively by Hom and McClure, 'Daniel 5'.

47. So, among others, Myers, *Strong Man*, pp. 190–193.

23. While some within the crowd had no qualms about publicly criticizing Jesus, others remained silently sceptical. For the sake of the latter, Jesus wants to make clear that hedging one's bets is no safer an option: *Whoever is not with me is against me, and whoever does not gather with me scatters.* As this pronouncement formally contradicts Jesus' earlier statement ('whoever is not against you is for you') in 9:50, the tension between the two sayings clearly puts us in the realm of paradox. In some cases, 9:50 seems to be saying, those who are not against Jesus are actually for him; in other situations, 11:23 now affirms, those who fail to support him are actually against him. Moreover, those who are against Jesus are, wittingly or unwittingly, participants in a process of scattering. More exactly, they are scattering the twelve tribes of Israel by perpetuating the very exile that Jesus intends to reverse.

24–26. Jesus now describes a situation in which an exorcised demon departs from an individual, wanders for a time in the desert (the traditional haunt of the demonic) and then returns to its original location, a well-swept and ordered house, rendering *the last state of that person . . . worse than the first.* Apparently, it is in the very nature of the demons to seek out a resting place. Apparently, too, an isolated demon can join forces with other demons in the hope of reinvading the human individual. That the demon should invite seven demons – the number of fullness – suggests a thoroughgoing possession. Jesus' words stand as a warning against the dangers of a superficial moralism. For both the individual and Israel as a whole, it is not enough to drive out the unclean spirits: one must also fill the house with a sustaining power that will prevent future demonic infestations from occurring. Such power, the power of the Spirit, will appear in 'the house' in Acts 2.

Theology

Having preached the kingdom on at least several occasions (4:43; 8:1), and having tasked others to do the same (9:2; 10:9), Jesus now reveals that the crucial factor in securing the kingdom is not preaching but prayer. As members of the same family, Jesus' followers are to call on God as 'Father'. And as co-conspirators in the same familial mission, their first prayer is that God would re-establish his rule and holy presence in the land, with the result that God's people might rightly honour God as king and worship God as God. This is the all-important prayer to which all subsequent prayers are secondary. When it comes to following Jesus, everything must centre around the coming of the kingdom.

But ultimately it is not even prayer that establishes the kingdom of God but Jesus himself. And when Jesus does so, this will mean nothing less than the overthrow of the strong man holding humanity in bondage. Temporary repentances, including personal moralistic endeavours or vain attempts at societal improvement, may discourage demonic forces for a time. But in the end, such measures will only backfire. The only means by which the kingdom may come is through the exertions of Jesus. And the first order of business, as far as Jesus' followers are concerned, is prayer.

D. Pronouncement of blessings and curses (11:27–54)

Context
If the four passages composing the current section were brushstrokes on a painting, they would alternate between tones of bright felicity and dark judgment. Jesus begins by pronouncing blessing on those who do his will (11:27–28), moves to condemning the present disobedient generation (11:29–32), continues with inviting his hearers into the light (11:33–36) and concludes with an extended litany of woes directed against the Pharisees and the scribes (11:37–54). So much of this is but a further elaboration of what has gone before. When Jesus had very suddenly calmed the storm (8:22–25), much as Yahweh had suddenly calmed the storm in the case of Jonah, this in retrospect now appears to be an anticipation of the fuller sign of Jonah to come (11:29). When Jesus was brought into the world with a great display of light (2:9) and shortly thereafter identified as a light for the world (2:32), this now turns out to be only a prelude to a subsequent moment in which divine light would also be imparted to his followers. Like a rose coming into bloom, initial insights into Jesus' person continue to unfold.

Here Jesus is calling for a radical obedience, an obedience which has nothing to do with any supposed advantage associated with certain social roles. In fact, those conventionally renowned for their piety are now being unmasked. Nor is it enough simply to declare blessing on those associated with Jesus or to take safe harbour in one's Jewish ethnicity. Instead, everything depends on one's relationship to Jesus and following him on his terms.

Comment
i. True blessing (11:27–28)

27. According to Second Temple Jewish expectation, one of the Messiah's appointed tasks was to rid Israel of unclean spirits.[48] This is why, even while Jesus is speaking authoritatively about the demonic realm (vv. 24–26), a certain *woman in the crowd*, inferring that he is in fact the awaited Messiah, pronounces a blessing on the womb that bore him and the breasts that once nurtured him.[49] Of course, the woman seeks to bless not the parts of Mary's anatomy but Mary herself! The blessing is not inappropriate. After all, Elizabeth has – seemingly with the Evangelist's approval – already declared a blessing on Mary before Jesus' birth (1:42).[50]

28. At the same Jesus pushes back, not so much to correct the woman's assertion as to qualify it. Though Mary is uniquely blessed on account of her unique role, how much more blessed, according to Jesus, are *those who hear the word of God and obey it!* True blessedness, in other words, consists not in genealogical connection but in covenantal obedience (cf. 6:46–49).

---

48. Zech. 13:1–2; 1 En. 55:4; T. Mos. 10:1. See also Perrin, *Kingdom of God*, pp. 158–160.

49. Though Marshall (p. 482) notes a similar saying about the mother of the Messiah in Pesiq. Rab. 149a, he is unpersuaded that 11:27 amounts to 'an implicit confession of Jesus as Messiah'. I demur: the woman's observation of Jesus' prowess as an exorcist, together with her blessing, conspires to make this an all but certain messianic confession.

50. Whereas Luke presents exemplars of faith as Wisdom's children (7:35), it is *perhaps* no accident that this anonymous woman *raised her voice* to declare truth to the crowd, just as Lady Wisdom 'raises her voice' to speak true words before the people (Prov. 8:1, 4). In this respect, the nameless woman is Wisdom.

ii. The sign of Jonah (11:29–32)

29. The blessing woman (vv. 27–28) who nurtured hopes of Jesus' messianic destiny was not an anomaly: the masses were also beginning to share this conviction. This partly explains the fact that *the crowds were increasing*. But whereas other messianic movements before and after the time of Jesus were historically driven by demagoguery, this Messiah was no rabble-rouser. Instead, he lumps the crowds together as members of *this generation (genea hautē)*, that is, an *evil generation (genea ponēra)*. Whereas some commentators understand *this generation* strictly in the temporal sense, that is, as referring simply to Jesus' contemporaries, this fails to account for the scriptural background of the idea, not least Deuteronomy 32:5 and Genesis 6:9 (cf. Luke 7:31; 9:41). The former text refers to the 'perverse and crooked generation' of the exile, prophesied by Moses; the latter, the warped generation of Noah's day, doomed to the flood. As has been persuasively argued elsewhere, the Evangelists' phrase 'this generation' retains not just a temporal sense but also a moral sense.[51] By applying the term to his audience, Jesus is essentially saying that the cosmic conflict between the two great oppositional seed lines, the seed of the woman versus the seed of the serpent (Gen. 3:15), has continued down into the present day. Indeed, that even some of his own followers belong to the wicked seed line is demonstrated by their perverse demand for a sign (v. 29), despite ample miracles and exorcisms testifying to the kingdom. In the face of such scepticism, Jesus insists that *no sign will be given . . . except the sign of Jonah*.

30. The meaning of the 'sign of Jonah' is now spelled out through a comparison between the famed reluctant prophet and the Son of Man. Just as Jonah, having been swallowed and regurgitated by a whale, was a sign to the Ninevites, so too would the crucified and risen Son of Man become a sign *to this generation*.[52] Yet there is more at play here than a typological analogy between Jonah's emergence from a whale and Jesus' impending resurrection,

---

51. See Rieske, 'Two Families'.

52. The parallel in Matt. 12:40 makes explicit the connection between the sign of Jonah and resurrection.

for in the case of both figures the miraculous life-from-death event is closely coupled with the authoritative proclamation. Thus we agree with Fitzmyer that the sign of Jonah is 'the person of Jonah and his *preaching*'.[53] In the aftermath of Easter, that repentance should be preached (whether by Jesus or his followers) and that Jesus should be raised from the dead – together these would be sign enough.

31. Switching to a different scriptural story, Jesus now assures his audience that the *queen of the South* (the queen of Sheba) would be raised up (*egerthēsetai*) for eschatological vindication, because she had travelled *from the ends of the earth* (*ek tōn peratōn tēs gēs*) in order to hear Solomon's wisdom (1 Kgs 10:1–13).[54] More than that, Jesus continues by saying, almost certainly to his hearers' amazement, that she, though a Gentile, would stand in judgment over the Jewish crowds who constitute *this generation*. Though the logical relationship between the story of this royal tête-à-tête and the 'sign of Jonah' may seem obscure, Jesus' invocation of the former actually makes sense in the context of verses 14–28, since in the Ancient Jewish mind Solomon's reputation as a sage par excellence would not have been separable from his exorcistic abilities.[55] Motivated by second-hand reports of Solomon's connection with the divine and travelling a great distance to *listen to* (*akousai*) his wisdom, the queen of Sheba serves as a model of faithful hearing. By contrast, Jesus' contemporaries remain eerily unmoved by their own first-hand experience of Jesus' feats of exorcism (vv. 14–16) and wisdom (vv. 17–26). Such callousness seems to be at least partially connected with a certain complacency born out of ethnic pride. For Jesus promises a day when the Gentile queen of the South, together with the equally Gentile Ninevites, will serve as

---

53. Fitzmyer (p. 933), emphasis original; contra, e.g., Edwards (p. 350), who suggests that the sign of Jonah is simply 'the preaching of Jonah'.

54. Not insignificantly, the resurrected Jesus will later call his apostles to take the gospel *to* the 'ends of the earth' (*eschatou tēs gēs*, Acts 1:8; cf. Acts 13:47).

55. Solomon's control over the demonic would have been inferred from his capacity as a sage. See Torijano, *Solomon*, pp. 110–128.

proof that God is more impressed by responsive obedience than by race or family lineage – the very same point he just sought to drive home in verse 28. But for Jesus' contemporaries, the stakes are even greater than they were in Solomon's day, since *something greater* [neuter: *pleion*] *than Solomon is here!*

32. Circling back to the story of the Gentile Ninevites, Jesus explains how they too will rise up and judge *this generation*, because they had repented at the 'preaching' (*kerygma*) of Jonah while Jesus' present company had not. Once again, his immediate hearers are more liable to judgment not only because they have failed to repent but also because they have an advantage that the Gentile respondents of the earlier era had lacked, for *something greater* [*pleion*] *than Jonah is here!* Exactly why Luke has 'some*thing* greater than Solomon' and 'some*thing* greater than Jonah' rather than the more expected masculine singular 'some*one* greater than . . .' requires some explanation. What is the *something greater*? On the one side, when we coordinate Solomon and Jesus as outstanding examples of a sage, and then, on the other side, link Jonah and the apostles together as fellow proclaimers of the 'resurrection', we begin to see that Jesus' focus is not so much on himself as on another person. That which is *greater* (Greek neuter singular: *pleion*) than both Solomon and Jonah, so it would seem, is the Spirit (Greek neuter *pneuma*) who on the pattern of Solomon is already operative through Jesus' display of wisdom (4:14) and exorcistic capacities (4:31–37; 11:20), and who also on the pattern of Jonah would soon bestow on the apostles extraordinary powers of preaching (Acts 2:14–41; 4:8–22; etc.). In this reading, Luke's point is more pneumatological than Christological: the advent of the Holy Spirit, working in and through both Jesus and the disciples, means the arrival of qualitatively superior revelation. All the while, it is no accident that the most outstanding respondents to Solomon and Jonah were not those within Israel but Gentiles on the outside. This presages the ensuing narrative of Acts, where we witness the more direct presence of the Spirit and the Spirit's relatively greater impact among the Gentiles.

iii. Light of the body (11:33–36)

33. Having previously drawn a contrast between the blessed obedient ones (v. 28), on the one hand, and the wicked generation (vv. 29–32), on the other, Jesus now presents his hearers with an existential choice between two diametrically opposed destinies: a body filled with light and a body filled with darkness (vv. 34–36). But first Jesus asks us to consider the absurdity of someone lighting a *lamp* only to put it into a *cellar (kryptēn)*, as well as the reasonableness of putting a lamp *on the lampstand so that those who enter may see the light.* Here, as in the parallel Matthew 5:14–16, Jesus' interest is not in physical lamps but in the human person as a living source of divine illumination. Since in Luke the *krypt-* word group typically refers to that which has yet to be revealed eschatologically (8:17; 12:2), we infer that the lamp on the lampstand and the entrance of *those who enter (eisporeuomenoi)* together refer to the long-awaited illumination of the eschatological temple (1 En. 14:8–23; 71:2–47; Sib. Or. 3:787; 5:420), along with the ingathering of the tribes at that temple (Isa. 60:1–3, 19–20; Zech. 14:6–7; Tob. 13:10–11). Now that Jesus has come, the light of salvation is no longer meant to be hidden away but rather is to be exposed to as many as possible.

34. In antiquity, the eyes were variously regarded not just as windows on an illuminated external world but also as portals through which light would emanate from the inside.[56] For this reason, though these verses have often been interpreted as a rumination on how spiritual light might most effectively enter the body, Jesus' point is likely just the opposite. In other words, *if your eye is healthy (haplous)*, then the external observer will regard *your whole body* as *full of light.* Conversely, if the human eye is *not healthy (ponēros)*, morally speaking, then the body will be seen as being *full of darkness.* Though the NRSV's translation of *healthy (haplous)* and *not healthy (ponēros)* makes sense, it masks the unevenness of the contrast. The term *haplous* means not just 'whole' but also 'showing integrity' or even 'being generous'. Meanwhile, the juxtaposed term *ponēros* generally refers to sexual immorality but also on a wide level covenantal unfaithfulness. At the risk of overreading

---

56. Allison, 'Lamp of the Body'.

the former Greek term by assuming that the totality of its semantic range is operative here, it is possible that the word choice of *ponēros* is meant to prepare for Jesus' subsequent teachings against greed (12:13–21) and adultery (16:18). If so, then Luke's point is not only that human spiritual vision is impaired by lust and greed, but also that a vision of life sustained by singleness of heart and generosity promises to release the spiritual light within to a watching world without.

35. The upshot of this teaching is that Jesus' followers must *therefore* [*oun*] *consider* or take pains (*skopei*) to ensure that the inner light is not darkness. This implies on the part of Luke's readers the obligation of undertaking a regular and continuing spiritual self-audit. To be clear, it does not seem to be the case that this internal light has anything to do with natural faculties within the human person. Instead, the light Jesus has in mind must be more or less equivalent to salvation itself.[57]

36. Jesus closes out the point by holding forth the ideal: *If then your whole body is full of light, with no part of it in darkness, it will be as full of light as when a lamp gives you light with its rays.* Now reading verse 33 from the perspective of the present verse, it becomes clear that Jesus' instructions bear on the mission of his followers, namely, to bear the light within by ensuring the health of their spiritual eyesight.

iv. Woes against the scribes and Pharisees (11:37–54)

37. In the midst of Jesus' exhortations (vv. 29–36), indeed *while he was speaking,* a certain Pharisee invites him for a formal meal (*aristēsē*). Such an invitation would likely never have been issued had the Pharisee grasped the extent of Jesus' disapproval. Such obliviousness perhaps helps explain the severity of Jesus' indictment (vv. 39–52), undoubtedly intended to jar his interlocutor to his senses. This is not Jesus' first tableside confrontation with a Pharisee. Earlier Jesus had rebuked one Pharisaical host for his spiritual smugness (7:36–50). Now at the present supper with the present Pharisee, his reproach will verge on utter condemnation.

---

57. See Hartsock, *Sight and Blindness.*

38. According to Luke, the Pharisees had made a point of scrubbing their dishes prior to meals, and this ritual was neither practised nor endorsed by Jesus.[58] In the moment, the host is *amazed* (*ethaumasen*) by Jesus' failure to *wash*.[59] Just how the Evangelist knows so much about the host's internal reaction we do not know. On the one hand, such amazement may have been expressed through body language or perhaps through comments now lost to history. On the other hand, given Jesus' track record for penetrating the inner thoughts of others (6:8; 9:47; 19:11; 24:38), we do not rule out this being yet another instance of his supernatural abilities as a mind reader.

39–40. Though Jesus never claims that the Pharisaical ritual is *inherently* objectionable, he does insist that the sectarians, in the very act of focusing on such matters, had become distracted from weightier concerns, not least the besetting evils of *greed and wickedness* (*harpagēs kai ponērias*). Jesus' concern with the former vice ties in with Luke's larger themes of generosity and stewardship; his emphasis on *wickedness* is of a piece with other teachings revolving around repentance from sexual impurity (5:30; 7:48). Through this complaint, Jesus' host, along with the Pharisees as a whole, becomes the *negative* embodiment of Jesus' kingdom ethics. Indeed, the dinner host and his sectarian confrères merit the morally charged epithet *fools* (*aphrones*) (cf. Pss 14:1; 53:1), for in their divorcing of external realities from internal realities they had missed the more obvious point that the creator of the *outside* of the dish had also formed the *inside* of the human person, that is, the heart.[60] On Jesus' analysis, the Pharisees' inordinate interest in purity concerns had eclipsed the more foundational moral entailments of God's status as creator.

---

58. The pre-meal washing practice mentioned here finds modest but sufficiently credible historical attestation in the rabbinic literature (b. Ḥul. 105a).

59. Judging by Luke's choice of the verb *thaumazō* ('to be amazed'), it seems that this reaction was roughly on a par with that of those who witnessed his miracles and exorcisms (8:25; 9:43; 11:14)!

60. Literally 'your insides' (*to esōthen*); cf. Bock, p. 1113 n. 13.

41. Towards remediating the vices of greed and wickedness, Jesus recommends that his hearers *give for alms those things that are within*. On the face of it, this is an odd expression. But assuming that *those things that are within* (*ta enonta*) are the scope of one's personal values, desires and moral disposition, we might understand Jesus to be calling for essentially giving one's very being as a kind of alms.[61] Here there are elements of both continuity and discontinuity with Jesus' contemporary Judaism. In step with traditional Jewish teaching, which considered almsgiving to be an important pillar of piety (Tob. 12:8–9; Sir. 7:10), Jesus attaches paramount significance to 'doing mercy'. But by insisting that the substance of such giving includes first and foremost *those things that are within*, Jesus also breaks from the way in which most Jews thought about almsgiving, namely, as an external action. 'Do this', Jesus says, 'and *see, everything will be clean for you*.' And so, much to his audience's surprise, Jesus radically transposes ritual purification into ethical terms.

42. Building on this exhortation, Jesus now unleashes a more far-reaching indictment against two categories of persons. Earlier in Luke's story, Jesus had declared four blessings (6:20b–23) together with four woes (6:24–26). Now in verses 42–52, Jesus issues six more woes, the first three of which are directed against the Pharisees; the second three, against the scribes. Within this first set of three, Jesus approves of the Pharisees' practice of tithing herbs (*these you ought to have practised*), while also chiding the sectarians for neglecting issues of *justice and the love of God*. Somehow the Pharisees' priorities had become misaligned. So far as Jesus was concerned, their practical inability to assign the norms of Torah their proper weight resulted in an imbalanced and ultimately warped moral framework.

43. The second woe is directed not to any of the Pharisees' ritual practices but to their craving for human approbation, expressed in such tokens as *the seat of honour in the synagogues* and respectful

---

61. Alternatively, if we take *ta enonta* to be an accusative of respect, the rendering would be something like 'give alms with respect to what is inside'.

greetings *in the market-places*. By exposing the sectarians' quest for the sought-after chairs, Jesus is in his own way fulfilling Mary's prediction that he would bring 'down the powerful from their thrones' (1:52). Similarly, by conjoining the Pharisees' fixation with these same seats with their unhealthy interest in being greeted in the marketplace, Luke's Jesus is inviting us to align them with the 'children sitting in the market-place and calling to one another' (7:32). In the same passage (7:31–35), Jesus had implied that his detractors' failure to accept John and the Son of Man was somehow connected with their self-serving 'groupthink'. Likewise, the fact that the Pharisees *love* (*agapatè*) these symbols of social power helps explain their neglect of the 'love of God' (v. 42). Craven obsession with human approval is a serious hindrance to our experience of the love of God.

44. Jesus' third woe bears not so much on any behaviours or attitudes on the Pharisees' part as on their toxic effect on the unsuspecting who come into contact with them. In Ancient Judaism, the corpse – and by extension the grave – was considered a 'Father of all uncleanness'.[62] By comparing the Pharisees to *unmarked graves*, Jesus is charging them with ritually defiling unwitting passers-by who, while walking about (*peripatountes*), have been injured by their baneful influence. The irony is biting: whereas the sectarians had prided themselves on retaining cultic purity, Jesus now designates them as the chief source of impurity. Yet the image carries out a double duty, for in Scripture it is the wicked who will one day be trampled underfoot (Isa. 28:18; Mic. 7:10; Zech. 10:5). And so the comparison also speaks of the Pharisees' impending judgment, now already being unleashed in the present time.

45. Earlier in Luke's narrative an unidentified lawyer emerged from the crowd, calling out to Jesus as 'Teacher' (10:25). Now the pattern is repeated, as a scribal interlocutor once again addresses Jesus by the same title, but in this instance not to pose a question (cf. 10:25) but instead to point out that the denunciation of the Pharisees (vv. 39–44) is more far-reaching than Jesus himself may

---

62. b. Kelim 1:1.

have realized. After all, as the lawyer complains, countless scribes would have also self-identified as Pharisees: therefore, *you insult* [*hybrizeis*] *us too*. While the NRSV's translation of *insult* may lead us to think of merely verbal abuse, the verb (*hybrizō*) carries a broader sense of ill-treatment within a social context, underscoring the dishonouring effects of Jesus' words.[63]

46. Much to the scribe's surprise, Jesus now unleashes a threefold litany of woes against *you lawyers*, lodging a different accusation with each successive woe. In the first of these, Jesus condemns the scribal elite for loading (*phortizete*) people with *burdens hard to bear*. Of course, the loads (*phortia*) in view are metaphorical, almost certainly referring to particular scribal prescriptions which the religious authorities had added to Torah legislation. In the literature, the cognate *phort-* root behind both the verb and the noun is commonly associated with pack animals, perhaps suggesting that these legalistic requirements had a dehumanizing effect. To compound the problem, Jesus continues, the same authoritarian scribes are callous, not even willing to *lift a finger to ease them*. No doubt Luke's recording of this first woe would have been at least partially motivated by a pastoral interest. Within this newly emerging messianic community, the Evangelist wants his readers to know, leaders must not only avoid burdening people unnecessarily but also strive to come compassionately alongside those who struggle under the mantle of the kingdom.

47–48. The second woe criticizes the scribes for building *the tombs of the prophets whom your ancestors killed*. Since the last of the prophets had perished centuries earlier (cf. v. 51), such 'building' likely involved layers of architectural or decorative improvements on the original monuments. At first blush, the criticism seems counter-intuitive, as one might expect that such improvements to a prophet's grave would honour the deceased. But Jesus offers a different interpretation, for *so*, in the very constructing of such tombs, *you are witnesses and approve of the deeds of your ancestors*.[64] When

---

63. BDAG, p. 1022.

64. The virtually untranslatable particle *ara* (NRSV *so*) is regularly used in the apodosis of conditional sentences; see BDAG, p. 104. In this

we compare the *deeds* [*erga*] *of your ancestors* (v. 48) with Stephen's description of the Mosaic-era golden calf, the 'works' (*erga*) of those ancestors' hands (Acts 7:41), this raises the possibility that such pious adornments are actually artifices of idolatry. If so, then we may also rightfully wonder whether in the same sentence Jesus' designation of the scribes as *witnesses* lays the veiled claim that they are – like exiled Israel of Isaiah 40 – 66 – 'witnesses' to their own idolatry (Isa. 43:10, 12; 44:8). Though there is a perverse division of labour between the scribes and their ancestors (*for they killed them, and you build their tombs*), their essential motive and mission is the same.

49. In response to the intergenerational resistance, the *Wisdom of God* promised to send *prophets and apostles* who would be met with stiff and even deadly resistance. The brief narrative of Wisdom's ill-fated delegation parallels the forthcoming plot line of the parable of the wicked tenants (20:9–19), where a vineyard-owner (representing God) sends a series of envoys (representing the prophets and Jesus) who are harshly treated. Amid the obvious similarities stands an important contrast: whereas in Luke 20:9–19 the sender is God, in Luke 11:49 the sender is the *Wisdom of God*. The epithet recalls the familiar figure of personified Wisdom who stands at the city gates (Prov. 8:1–3), calls out to humanity (vv. 4–11), identifies herself as the embodiment of creational wisdom (vv. 12–31), holds out the prospect of life or death (vv. 32–36), even while sending out servants (*ně'ārôt*) as part of her proclamation (9:3). Given that Jesus has already identified himself as Wisdom, and his followers as Wisdom's children (Luke 7:35), Luke's attentive reader now retrospectively gathers that the Twelve's earlier apostolic mission (9:1–6) was in fact the climactic component of a re-enacted narrative of Proverbs 8:1 – 9:3. All this serves to frame the scribes' resistance to Jesus as a variation of the same resistance facing Wisdom (Prov. 9:7–8, 12–18). Strikingly, the waves of envoys set in motion by Wisdom/Jesus are a direct response (*Therefore: dia touto*) to the disobedience shared by the ancestors and Jesus' opponents.

---

respect, perhaps a preferred rendering would be 'you build the tombs of the prophets . . . so *then* you are witnesses . . .'

This perhaps anticipates Paul's threefold indictment of disobedient Israel in Acts 13:46; 18:6; and 28:26–27, whereby the apostle's repeated call to eschatological repentance not only underscores divine patience but also – in the case of Israel's continued unrepentance – increases the severity of corporate guilt.[65]

50. The introductory Greek conjunction *hina* may be translated either as 'in order that' or *so that* (NRSV). If we take the NRSV as resultative, this would mean that the brutal rejection of the apostles and prophets was divinely leveraged to establish the guilt of *this generation*. Alternatively, the *hina* may imply a stronger cause-and-effect relationship between the persecution of Jesus' disciples and *this generation*'s condemnation. Given certain conceptual and verbal parallels with Luke 8:10 as the climax of the parable of the sower, where (as I have argued above) Jesus very purposively gives parables 'so that [*hina*] looking they may not perceive', a telic force ('in order that') here seems more probable. This is not to say that the *generation* has been set up for failure against its own best intentions; rather, such fierce opposition to Wisdom's entreaties is palpable evidence of a profound spiritual resistance within, finally providing warrant for divine judgment against the temple (21:5–38). In larger perspective, then, the failure of Jesus' peers to recognize Wisdom's overtures in and through Jesus (cf. 19:44) gives both climactic and summative expression to the disobedience of God's people down through the ages.

51. To underscore the scope of this national disobedience, Jesus declares that all the spilt blood of the prophets, *from the blood of Abel to the blood of Zechariah, who perished between the altar and the sanctuary*, will certainly *be charged against this generation*.[66] The statement may mean, on the one hand, that the guilt of the present generation is comparable to Israel's incurred guilt from Abel to Zechariah. Abel is the first biblical figure to die at the hands of the wicked (Gen.

---

65. For more on the reiteration of Paul's call to repentance, see Moessner, 'Paul in Acts'.

66. The Greek verb *ekzētēthēsetai* (*ekzēteō*) behind the NRSV's *charged*, occurring here and in the previous verse (v. 50), has the sense of recompense or retribution (BDAG, p. 240).

4:10). Alternatively (or additionally), the assertion may envision the sin of the previous centuries devolving on to *this generation*. As for *Zechariah*, this could refer to any one (or more) of various historical figures of the same name, but among these the martyred Zechariah of 2 Chronicles 24:20–22 seems most likely.[67] The location of Zechariah's murder is striking, reminding us that the prophet's death was not only wicked but also profane.

52. A final woe is lodged against the scribes on account of their having *taken away the key of knowledge*. Though Jesus never makes explicit exactly what access might be granted through such a key, the subsequent language of *entering* virtually forces the conclusion that he is speaking of the kingdom. In this, the last and more serious of the three accusations, the lawyers are doubly condemned, for, by actively removing the key from sight, they have not only forfeited their own entry but also prevented others from entering.

53–54. That Jesus *went outside* perhaps augurs the parable of the wicked tenants, where the beloved son will also be put outside (20:13–15). In any case, Jesus' diatribe marks a watershed moment, when the *scribes and the Pharisees* join forces, as they *began to be very hostile (deinōs enechein)* and avail themselves of every opportunity to cross-examine him.[68] Such cross-examination proceeds not from intellectual curiosity but from a compelling desire to adduce evidence which might ultimately be used against Jesus. The language of *lying in wait (enedreuontes)* and 'catching' *(thēreusai)* is reminiscent of those scriptural passages which describe the machinations of the wicked against the righteous, most notably Psalms 10:9 and 59:3. Both are (arguably) Davidic psalms – appropriately so. As the conflict between Jesus (the Son of David) and his politically powerful detractors escalates, this serves only to advance the

---

67. So too, e.g., Bock, pp. 1123–1124; Nolland, pp. 668–669. Gundry (*Matthew*, p. 471) and Beckwith (*Canon*, pp. 217–221) argue that the saying (preserved also in Matt. 23:35) intends a conflation of the Zechariah of 2 Chr. 24:20–22 and the author of the eponymous biblical book by the same name.

68. Jesus' opponents now bring an emotional intensity: BDAG (p. 173) translates the adverb as 'fearfully, terribly'.

outworking of the fuller Davidic narrative in a new key. If David suffered en route to becoming Israel's great king, the same must surely be the case – so Luke's language hints – for Jesus.

Theology
Social psychologists and marketing experts will sometimes speak of a 'halo effect', that is, a phenomenon whereby positive impressions in one area have a spillover effect on other areas. The woman who calls Jesus' mother blessed does so because she assumes a certain virtue by association. The same thinking seems to have characterized the Pharisees and scribes who, on account of their scrupulous religiosity, saw themselves as deserving of the best seats at a public meal. And yet the same thinking, again, seems to have belonged to Jesus' immediate hearers who assumed – incorrectly, as it turns out – that they would one day stand in judgment on the queen of the South and Jonah's Ninevites. Membership within an ostensibly devout family, people group, geography or religious in-group can conjure a sense of self-confidence.

And yet, Luke warns his readers here, such confidence is invariably *false* confidence. Such false confidence tends to be rooted in a complacent refusal to look beyond the surface of things. Though the Evangelist makes no case for a morbid self-absorption in the life of the disciples, there does indeed seem to be a place for healthy introspection – all with the goal of confession and repentance. As Luke sees it, whereas social advantages can be deceptive, Jesus calls his followers to cultivate a rigorous self-honesty that can be fully realized only as the divine light fills the whole body.

E. Warnings and encouragements (12:1–12)

Context
In his recent diatribe against the Pharisees and scribes (11:37–54), Jesus was not content simply to expose the religious leaders' sin, for he also had something to say about their baneful influence. The latter point now receives further elaboration in this passage. And yet the bulk of these twelve verses bears on Jesus' instruction regarding appropriate response to persecution. Such persecution will be a natural consequence, he implies, of faithful kingdom

proclamation. By any showing, it appears that Jesus is anticipating a broadening effort to preach the good news: the missionary charge which had originally been restricted to the Twelve (9:1–6), and then granted to the seventy-two (10:1–12), would even be expanded to include members within the crowd.

Comment

1. Jesus' conflict with the religious leaders' (11:37–54) has done nothing to hinder his rising popularity. In 11:29 'the crowds were increasing'; now these same crowds have *gathered in thousands*, having *trampled on one another* in the process. Such trampling (*katapatein*) also describes the infertile seed beside the path (8:5), perhaps hinting that the crowds, like the hapless seed, represent spiritually tone-deaf hearers of the word. Such would perhaps, too, share the grim fate of the trampled Pharisees (11:44). Despite the arrival of the crowds, Luke remarks that Jesus *began to speak first [prōton] to his disciples*. The function of *prōton* is ambiguous, as *first* could refer either to the priority of his audience or the significance of the content: 'he began to speak to his disciples of what was of first importance'. This second option is less preferred among commentators – and for good reason: as important as it may be to avoid hypocrisy, it strains credulity that Jesus considered this principle 'first' in relation to, say, the Great Commandment (Matt. 25:35–40; Mark 12:28–34).

Jesus' speaking to the disciples *first* draws attention to the fact that Luke 12:1–12 is the first of four linked speeches in this chapter; it is followed by a speech to the crowds (vv. 13–21); another speech to the disciples (vv. 22–53); and then a final speech to the crowds (vv. 54–59). The alternating rhythm between the disciples and the crowds is not unconnected with the specification *thousands*, which reinforces an analogy between Jesus, his disciples and the *thousands*, on the one hand, and Moses, Moses' judges and the 'thousands' of the exodus (Exod. 18:21), on the other. The priority of the disciples in Luke's four speeches corroborates an inescapable hierarchy: for both Moses' appointed judges and Jesus' disciples, it made sense that they – and not those under their charge – be instructed *first*.

On a basic level, Jesus' warning against the *yeast of the Pharisees* seeks, while drawing on a familiar symbol of contamination, to criticize the members of this religious group for caving in to social pressures. At the same time, given the analogy with the Sinai masses hinted at not least by the *thousands*, together with Jesus' warning against leaven, which was ordinarily supposed to be removed in preparation for the paschal feast in memory of the exodus (Lev. 23:5–8), one may discern another layer of meaning beyond the more obvious. To wit, Jesus' warning against the Pharisees' *hypocrisy* amounts to a reissuing of a long-standing Passover stipulation, appropriate to the higher ethical standard of his 'new exodus' movement. In order to be part of this movement, Jesus admonishes, his disciples must eradicate any hint of the Pharisees' divided loyalties (11:37–54), which, if left unchecked, will spread throughout the community like leaven.

2. The basis for Jesus' warning is eschatological. Because there is nothing *covered up that will not be uncovered* and *nothing secret that will not become known*, all such hypocritical posturing will soon enough be shown up for what it is. In an earlier chapter, Jesus had promised that 'nothing is hidden that will not be disclosed, nor is anything secret that will not become known and come to light' (8:17), and this was soon fulfilled in a Christ-honouring confession (8:47). But now basically the same saying seems to cut in two directions: not only will those who confess Jesus be revealed in due course (8:17, 47), but so too will those whose faith is disingenuous – as will also become clear (cf. Acts 5:1–11; 8:9–25; 9:13–16). Though human motives are, much like leaven, hidden from human observation, the consequences of such motives, again like the effects of leaven, will soon enough be seen for what they are. In ushering in the kingdom, Jesus accelerates eschatological disclosure, bringing it forward into present time.

3. The same principle equally applies to the sphere of spoken words. While some commentators restrict *whatever you have said* and *what you have whispered* to ill-advised words (making v. 3 a mere repetition of v. 2), verse 3 makes better sense as a general remark, promising just deserts for every utterance spoken in private – whether appropriate or inappropriate.[69] Secret words spoken out of

---

69. The parallel in Matt. 10:27 refers to utterances spoken by Jesus in private. Thus, Matthew clearly sees the saying as referring – at least – to divine revelation.

a personal moral darkness will one day be outed; quiet confessions spoken *behind closed doors*, that is, in the innermost rooms of one's house (*en tois tameois*), will likewise be rendered public. Every thought and word will be laid bare before the living God.

4–5. The transitional phrase *I tell you* develops the line of thought begun in verses 1–3, suggesting that those otherwise unidentified people who *kill the body* do so in response to the disciples' future 'housetop proclamation' (v. 3). If and when the disciples meet up with these violent persecutors, Jesus continues, they must not be afraid, for once such murderers have done their worst to the body, they will have exhausted their options. Inviting his disciples to consider the broader eschatological horizon, Jesus redirects their fears from their human malefactors to the one who *has authority to cast into hell* (*geennan*), that is, Gehenna. The underlying Greek *geenna* is a transliteration of the Hebrew *gê-hinnōm* (Josh. 15:8; 18:16), a ravine on the south-west side of Jerusalem associated with child sacrifice (2 Chr. 28:3; 33:6; cf. 2 Kgs 16:3), temporal judgment (Jer. 7:30–33; 19:1–13; 32:34–35) and eschatological judgment (Apoc. Ab. 15:6; 2 Bar. 59:10; 85:13; 4 Ezra 7:36; Sib. Or. 1:103–104; 2:292–306; 4:186; m. 'Abot 5:19).[70]

As to the identity of the one bearing this authority, commentators have advocated for one of three options. One line of interpretation suggests that the one who casts into Gehenna is Satan. Though not impossible, this reading would problematically entail Jesus recommending his followers to fear Satan, which seems theologically out of accord with other Scripture (cf. 1 John 4:4). A somewhat better option and far more popular view maintains that God is the intended referent.[71] But this approach, too, is not without its problems, for authority is not typically something God 'has' (as if authority were not intrinsic to God's very self) but something which God *gives*. In my judgment, the best option is to regard Jesus himself as the authorized judge, precisely in his capacity as the coming Son of Man. The key text is once again Daniel 7, which envisions the Son of Man consigning his enemies to the flames

---

70. See Bocher, 'γέεννα', *EDNT* 1, pp. 239–240.

71. Bock, p. 1136; Marshall, p. 513; Tannehill, p. 202.

(Dan. 7:11), while also being accorded all authority (v. 14). Corroborating this interpretation is Jesus' repetition of the command: *Yes, I tell you, fear him* (*touton*), or 'fear *this one*'. Elsewhere in Luke the demonstrative pronoun 'this one' (*touton*) often stands in for Jesus (19:14; 20:12, 13; 22:2; 23:14; 23:18).

At first blush, two objections may be lodged against this reading. First, this interpretation appears to stumble on the initial imperative (*fear him who, after he has killed, has authority to cast into hell*), at least insofar as it is difficult to imagine Jesus as a killer! However, the NRSV's translation *after he has killed* takes unnecessary liberties in inserting the pronoun *he*; indeed, the Greek *meta to apokteinai* hardly requires our supplying any subject for the Greek infinitive 'to kill' (*apokteinai*). (The NIV's rendering is preferable: 'fear him who, after your body has been killed, has authority to throw you into hell'.) Second, it might also be objected that in the Gospels, and indeed in the larger New Testament record, Jesus is presented not so much as the focus of our fears but rather as the supreme object of our love. True as this may be, it should be remarked that the fear which Jesus enjoins here is qualified by the phrase *my friends* (*tois philois mou*; v. 4), implying a pre-established covenant of love between the Son of Man and those who are instructed to fear him.[72] Thus a healthy fear of the judging Son of Man – thereby avoiding the hypocrisy of fearing human beings – is set within the framework of a loving relationship. In summary, though the disciples' future housetop proclamation may very well cost them their lives, such sacrifice is warranted in the light of the resurrection hope, which promises not only to restore the martyr's body for a post-mortem kingdom but also to vest the Son of Man with authority for final judgment. Of course, the disciples would hardly have understood all this in the historical moment. Rather, Jesus' admonition is based on a forthcoming reality that he himself would 'show' (NIV) through his resurrection (future *hypodeixō*; cf. use of *hypodeixō* in Acts 9:16).

6–7. The *assarion*, also known as the 'as' (its common English translation) or the 'penny' (as it is also translated), was a small

---

72. The immediate referent is of course the disciples; cf. Stählin, *TDNT* 9, p. 163.

Roman copper coin which was worth one-sixteenth of a denarius or about 6% of a daily wage. Jesus equates the value of *two pennies* with *five sparrows*. Sparrows that had been trapped for human consumption were not hard to come by in the marketplace; in the human economy the life of a sparrow was worth precious little. And yet, Jesus maintains, *not one of them is forgotten in God's sight*. The contrast between the sparrows' low market value and their significance in God's sight underlines the depth and breadth of God's loving attentiveness to the creaturely order. But ultimately, of course, the real concern here is not with birds but with God's providential care for his disciples in the midst of persecution.[73] Applying a *qal wahomer* argument (from the lesser to the greater), Jesus wants to drive home the point that if a perished sparrow does not go unmourned by God, then how much more significant are the lives of his disciples, for *you are of more value than many sparrows*.

Jesus asserts not just the inestimable value of human life (higher by the way than an animal's life) but also God's intimate acquaintance with human individual existence: *even the hairs of your head are all counted (ērithmēntai)*. Jesus' focus on human follicles is striking for at least three reasons. In the first place, the image draws attention to the fact that divine knowledge of the human person attains a depth that far exceeds the personal knowledge of even the most intimate of human relationships. Second, the Greek verb *ērithmēntai* ('counted') is a perfect passive, indicating that such divine knowledge is not achieved by a process of investigation (as if God would need time to count what may be upwards of 100,000 hair follicles) but is a perfected knowledge, serving to emphasize God's immediate and comprehensive knowledge of the human person. Third, given the fact that human hair has no physiological function and yet is still on God's 'radar screen', one infers that God's intimate knowledge of the human person goes well beyond issues of mere functionality or physical well-being. The image tacitly argues that God's knowledge and love tenderly extend to the

---

73. It is no coincidence that in the Scriptures persecuted individuals are sometimes compared to sparrows on account of their slight size and helplessness (Pss 11:1; 102:7; 124:7; Lam. 3:52).

whole scope of one's personal existence, touching on even the most incidental details such as the number of hairs on our heads. For all these reasons, Jesus' followers should be free from anxiety, even when their lives are being threatened due to their proclamation. To seal the point, Jesus closes with a reiteration of the initial command first intoned in verse 4: *do not be afraid*.[74]

8. The phrase *and I tell you (legō de hymin)* recapitulates the same phrase in verse 4, introducing a new paragraph comprising verses 8–12 (matching the earlier paragraph marked out, vv. 4–7). The concern of the present paragraph lies in public confession: *everyone who acknowledges me before others, the Son of Man also will acknowledge before the angels of God.* In earliest Christian thought, one of the key evidences of saving faith was one's willingness to declare Jesus publicly (Rom. 10:9; 1 Cor. 12:3; 1 Tim. 6:12; 1 John 4:2). To acknowledge or confess Christ in the present age was to set the stage for one's own acknowledgment in the divine courts.

While the Matthean (Matt. 10:32–33) and Markan (Mark 8:38) parallels also witness to an eschatological confession before the Son of Man, Luke alone includes angels in the prospective scene. This functions to strengthen the tie back to the vision of Daniel 7, where the Son of Man judges the blaspheming beasts (Dan. 7:11), only then to acknowledge his faithful followers when 'the greatness of the kingdoms under the whole heaven / shall be given to the people of the holy ones of the Most High' (Dan. 7:27). If the Danielic 'holy ones' are one and the same as *the angels of God* (Luke 12:8), then the latter likely includes not just celestial beings but also glorified saints who in the post-mortem state have attained a quasi-angelic status.[75]

9–10. In this case, verses 9–10, which in the first place envisage some who will be *denied before the angels of God*, signal a great separation involving the Son of Man presiding before the gathered heavenly community. For Luke's readers who are familiar with the rest of his story, however, this presents a potential problem. After

---

74. 'The verb "fear" (*phobeomai*) is used five times in verses 4–7, and will return in v. 32' (Tannehill, p. 202).

75. See Fletcher-Louis, *Luke–Acts*, pp. 70–72.

all, Peter will go on to deny Jesus in due course (22:57), even as he will later charge his audience with denying Jesus (Acts 3:13–14). Almost as if in an attempt to resolve the tension between verse 9's cut-and-dried warning and Peter's forthcoming denial in 22:54–62, Jesus continues by saying that *everyone who speaks a word against the Son of Man will be forgiven*. Still, how might one resolve the seeming contradiction between verse 9 (condemning those who deny the Son of Man) and verse 10a (promising forgiveness for those who speak a word against him)? It is a notoriously difficult interpretative issue, but perhaps the aspect of the verbs gives us some help. When Jesus speaks of the one who *denies* (*arnēsamenos*) him, he employs an aorist participle, suggesting that the denial in view is in fact the culmination of a systematic series of renunciations. By contrast, the present tense of *speaks* (*erei*) in verse 9 suggests a renunciation that is less than definitive. Verse 10a, then, significantly qualifies verse 9 by promising that those who have denied Jesus on a given occasion in real time will always have, like Peter, the opportunity for repentance, forgiveness and restoration. Still, even more qualification follows from verse 10b, which assures that *whoever blasphemes against the Holy Spirit will not be forgiven*. Towards understanding *this* saying, we are aided by the wider context, namely, the repeated blasphemy directed against the Spirit-empowered mission in Acts (Acts 13:45 *blasphēmountes*; 18:6a *blasphēmountōn*), leaving Paul in both instances to declare that he would be turning to the Gentiles (Acts 13:46–48; 18:6b) in accordance with the promises of Isaiah.[76] This suggests, at least in Luke–Acts, that the blasphemy against the Holy Spirit looks ahead to the apostolic mission and signals that hardened resistance to the church's proclamation would be the leading indicator that such resisters have disqualified themselves from the Isaianic return from exile (prophesied in Isa. 6:8–10). As a result, they risk standing condemned. If rejection of the pre-Easter Son of Man admitted the possibility of forgiveness even for the Jewish religious leadership, then the same leadership's

---

76. The same pattern arguably applies in 28:25–28, where drawing on Isaiah 6, Paul responds to the verbal rejection of the Jews with a reaffirmation of his mission to the Gentiles.

post-Pentecost rejection of the Spirit's activity extinguishes, as it were, all but the slimmest of hopes of a second chance. In the era of the church's proclamation, the stakes are raised considerably for one and all.

11–12. All the while, the key to the apostolic mission will be dependence on the same Spirit: *for the Holy Spirit will teach you at that very hour what you ought to say.* The phrase *that very hour (autē tē hōra)* not only refers to the moment of the disciples' assured appearance before *the synagogues, the rulers, and the authorities*; it also signifies the Danielic hour (*hōra*) (Dan. 8:17, 19; 9:21; 11:35, 40, 45; 12:1, 13), the hour of tribulation. At such a time – not if but *when* those encounters do occur (cf. 21:12–19) – the disciples can count on the Holy Spirit to aid them in their moment of need (cf. John 14:25–27). Jesus' words would of course be fulfilled, as the narrative of Acts clearly demonstrates (e.g. Acts 4:8, 31).

Theology
One of the most important influences on modern post-Enlightenment thought has been the seventeenth-century thinker John Locke. One of Locke's primary contributions to Western thought and culture has been his emphasis on religion as a matter of purely inner belief, that is, a set of convictions which must be distinguished from public matters such as politics, public policy or economics. Thanks in part to Locke, along with other like-minded thinkers and certain cultural forces, modern Western Christendom has assumed that Christian belief must properly remain a *privatized* belief. This is why today's followers of Jesus are often 'put in their place' with sentiments such as 'If it's true for you, so be it. But don't force your faith or your morality on others!' This way of conceiving of the Christian faith persists both in Western culture and in Christianized societies which have felt the impress of Western influence. Tragically, too many Christians in these same cultures are all too glad to capitulate to this way of thinking.

But if we take Luke's record seriously then confession of Jesus as the messianic Son of Man is not something we safely whisper to ourselves in the privacy of our rooms. No, Jesus' lordship must be publicly (though also wisely) confessed – no matter the risk, no matter the public shame, no matter the persecution. Wishing to avoid displeasing their unbelieving peers, all too many Christians practise a thoroughly private faith and do so earnestly believing that Jesus would have it no other way. Yet, as this passage makes perfectly clear, such thinking is a trap. However self-identified followers of Jesus justify their silence, Jesus' words are clear: it is only a public confession of the Son of Man that gives one any shred of confidence to stand before him when he comes.

F. Teachings on stewardship (12:13–34)

Context

The two complementary episodes contained in Luke 12:13–34 circle back to Jesus' earlier indictment of the Pharisees' greed and wickedness (11:39) as well as to his charge to avoid their baneful influence (12:1). From another vantage point, the section is an extended commentary on the thorny soil of Luke 8:7 and 14, receiving seed 'choked by the cares and riches and pleasures of life, and [whose] fruit does not mature' (8:14). Yet the section also looks *forward* to Jesus' warning not to be 'weighed down with ... the worries of this life' (21:34). Both greed and worry are spiritual maladies that must be remedied through an expanded time horizon. For Luke, the key to the proper management of resources and people hangs critically on eschatological expectation.

Comment
i. Parable of the rich fool (12:13–21)

13. No sooner does Jesus speak of the dark persecution and glorious recompense awaiting the faithful (12:1–12) than *someone in the crowd* interrupts hoping to leverage Jesus' status as a high-profile figure for a personal agenda. Notwithstanding Jesus' vision of eschatological inheritance (v. 8), the man in the crowd is ironically more immediately concerned with his temporal *inheritance*. His request that Jesus intervene would not have been highly unusual: religious authorities were likely summoned to settle disputes of this kind.

14. On the face of it, Jesus declines the man's request, but does so with intimations of an analogous dispute involving Moses' uninvited attempt to mediate between two fighting Hebrews

(Exod. 2:13–14). Jesus asks, *Who set me [tis me katestēsen] to be a judge or arbitrator over you?* Meanwhile, according to Exodus 2:14 (LXX), one of the two street fighters asks, '*Who set you [tis se katestēsen] to be a ruler and judge over us?*' (my translation). Of course, in the Exodus account the fighting Hebrew's question is rhetorical and assumes the answer 'No-one', meaning that the uninvited Moses had no right to stick his nose into the Hebrews' quarrel, at least not until Yahweh had authorized Moses to be judge (Exod. 18) and king of Israel. By slightly tweaking the very same question, Jesus invites an exploratory comparison between himself and Moses. Yet the query also raises a probing Christological question: who indeed has set Jesus to be judge and arbitrator over the two brothers or, for that matter, the rest of humanity? The answer to this question – should this enquirer piece it together – has already been baked into Jesus' statement contained in 12:8: 'everyone who acknowledges me before others, the Son of Man also will acknowledge before the angels of God'. Just as Jesus will, after the pattern of Moses, finally acquire the right to judge, so too will the Danielic Son of Man be given authority to judge.[77] Thus, while on the surface Jesus appears to be putting off the man in the crowd, he is in fact throwing down the gauntlet for further engagement. 'First answer my question correctly,' Jesus seems to say, 'and then you will find that both your life and the things that you seek in life will take on an entirely new framing.'

15. Turning *to them*, the crowds, Jesus makes an example out of the man's request by issuing a double warning: *Take care! (horate)* and *Be on your guard (phylassesthe).* The twin imperatives, including the verb 'to guard', seem to be an emphatic variant of the earlier admonition of guarding (*prosechete*) against the leaven of the Pharisees (12:1). And what are Jesus' disciples to guard against in this instance but *all kinds of greed.* If Jesus deemed the Pharisees' lust for mutual approval as a particular expression of greed, now he makes a more generalized statement regarding greed in all its various manifestations, not least

---

77. Hence Edwards (p. 370) ultimately gets it backwards when he remarks that the point of the Exod. 2:14 allusion is 'that Jesus was *not* willing to play the role of Moses in his fraternal dispute' (emphasis original).

the perverse desire for an *abundance of possessions*. Be alert, Jesus insists, because one's life is not derived from such things.[78]

16–17. Expanding on the thrust of verse 15, Jesus tells a parable about a *rich man* (*plousios*) and his land. Already with this adjective the unfolding story carries an ominous tone, for Jesus has already touched on the woes awaiting the wealthy (*plousious*, 6:24). The man has a seemingly wonderful problem: his crops are yielding a greater harvest than he is able to store. For Luke's readers, because agricultural productivity was seen as a direct blessing from God, the man would have ordinarily been regarded as divinely favoured. But as he contemplates his growing wealth he mistakenly turns inward, asking himself, *What should I do?*

18–19. The rich man considers a vision characterized by expansion (*I will pull down my barns and build larger ones*), accumulation (*and there I will store all my grain and my goods*) and hedonism (*And I will say to my soul, Soul, you have ample goods laid up for many years; relax, eat, drink, be merry*). As we discover in verse 21, the fundamental problem with this approach consists in the rich man's putting a higher priority on his own pleasures and interests than on the interests of God.[79] To be sure, the parable does not strictly target the rich, as if the non-wealthy were naturally immune from the selfish impulse which Jesus describes (they are not). But the parable does seem to imply that those who require inordinate storage for their possessions, stockpile their material goods and make a luxurious lifestyle an end in itself are precisely those at gravest moral risk. In the first-century Roman world, where conspicuous acquisition and conspicuous consumption were the rule among the wealthy, Jesus' challenge would have been prophetic.

---

78. The phrase *ek tōn hyarchontōn* (*of possessions*) may be either a genitive of material (Smyth §1323) or a genitive of source (Smyth §§1410–1411). In the first sense, personal possessions are not among the key components for life; in the second sense, possessions have no power to give life. I suspect that Luke would hold both senses to be equally valid.

79. Green (pp. 490–491) speculates that the decision to store rather than sell the grain promised a negative economic impact on the peasant-based economy.

20. Making an unexpected entrance, God interrupts the rich man's reverie with a reproachful epithet, *fool* (*aphrōn*), typically connoting both senselessness and rashness. The rich man is a *fool* not because he fails to foresee the timing of his own death but because he has not taken to heart the fleeting nature of either his possessions or even his very existence. In the larger scheme of things, since he cannot say with certainty *whose* [*things*] *will they be*, his investments of time, energy and attention have proved to be badly misguided. God's notice that the man will not make it through the *night* reminds us of the divine indictment of Belshazzar who responded unwisely to the mysterious writing on the wall and as a result forfeited his life 'that very night' (Dan. 5:30).[80]

21. Concluding his parable, Jesus induces a universal principle: *So it is with those who store up treasures for themselves but are not rich towards God.* Though one might infer from the parable proper (vv. 16–20) that the problem consists in the man's actions, as if storing up treasures for oneself were intrinsically evil, verse 21 shows otherwise. Notably, it is not the storing up of goods that is chiefly problematic, but such actions combined with a tight-fisted posture towards God. Reviewing the parable, we discover that such churlishness surfaces not so much in any explicit failure of benevolence but rather in the self-focused ruminations of verses 18–19, which preclude any trace of God-oriented concern. Though the post-mortem fate of the rich man goes unremarked, the implicit comparison between the rich man and Belshazzar, aligning the parable's central figure with one of the pagan arch-villains of Daniel's day, does not bode well. When pushed further, the point goes on to suggest that those who think and act like the rich man risk putting themselves in the company of a notorious pagan ruler who opposed the people of God; they can therefore expect to be judged accordingly. In Jesus' estimation, the fools who in their hearts fail to be rich towards God meet with the

---

80. On another level, Jesus may also be alluding to Herod the Great who prior to his own sudden death stored grain and other valuable goods in the temple storehouses. For potential veiled references to other political figures, see Fiensy, *Ancient Economy*, pp. 70–71.

same fate as the fools who 'say in their hearts, "There is no God"'
(Ps. 14:1).

ii. On worry (12:22–34)

22. Having offered a glimpse of the judgment awaiting those
who have been stingy towards God yet generous towards self
(12:13–21), Jesus now very practically applies – as *therefore* (*dia touto*)
makes clear – the preceding parable together with the whole of
verses 1–21. Directing his disciples to account for providence and
future judgment, Jesus exhorts them to avoid worrying both *about
your life* and *about your body*. By *life* (*psychē*) Jesus specifically has in
mind *what you will eat*; with *body* the focus is on *what you will wear*. The
teaching builds on the two earlier accounts of mission (9:1–6; 10:1–
12), where God's provision was demonstrated. Now Jesus elaborates
on the attitude appropriate to this modus operandi by urging his
followers to reject dark impulses towards anxiety.

23. Anxiety derives from a misunderstanding of the purpose of
human life, for *life is more than*, or greater than, *food, and the body more
than clothing*. That is, when people pursue food or clothing for its
own sake rather than as a means to a higher end, they tragically
underestimate the glorious end (*telos*) of all human existence. That
higher purpose can be grasped only in an eschatological horizon.
The disciples are called to set their eyes on a prize (finally spelled
out in vv. 33–34) far higher than that which could be obtained
through the consumption of food or the acquisition of clothing.

24. In calling his disciples to *consider the ravens* or crows, Jesus
makes an object lesson out of an unclean species (Lev. 11:15; Deut.
14:14). At least some Jewish communities regarded these scavenging
birds as a symbol for exploitative Gentiles (the sacrilegious Syrians,
to be exact) who preyed on the helpless flock of Israel (1 En. 89:1 –
90:19).[81] Notwithstanding the ravens' low station, in terms of both
purity and moral association, *God feeds them* – and that apart from
activities of food production or building of storage spaces. The
point virtually speaks for itself: if God cares for loathsome birds,
how much more will God bestow *at least* the same level of care on

---

81. Olson, *Animal Apocalypse*, pp. 136–139.

his children, quite apart from their toiling. Given the metaphorical usage of ravens, Jesus may be gesturing beyond the natural world to the segment of humanity behind the allegorical symbol, that is, oppressive Gentiles. On this reading, then, Jesus is also saying, 'If God provides for even the godless Gentile, then he will assuredly also care for his own' (cf. Matt. 5:45). While in the original historical moment Jesus is likely renewing a call (cf. Luke 5:10–11) that his immediate followers rely on God as they pursue their itinerant ministry, for Luke's readers Jesus' words come as a reminder that believers' sustenance depends not finally on their own efforts or diligence but on a God who provides.

25–26. Jesus exposes the pointlessness of human anxiety by framing two rhetorical questions. The first is rendered interpretatively difficult by the ambiguity of two key Greek words: *hēlikia* (which can mean 'height' or 'life span') and *pēchys* (which typically means 'cubit' but could be extended to mean hour). Though some interpreters and translations (NIV, ESV) prefer the sense of NRSV, that is, *add a single hour to your span of life*, the more typical meaning of *pēchys*, together with Jesus' penchant for mind-bending images (e.g. 6:24; 18:25), inclines us to prefer the thrust of the KJV: 'add to his stature one cubit' (cf. BDAG, p. 812). Nurturing anxious thoughts about circumstances beyond one's control is as ridiculous as trying to make oneself taller merely by wishing it so. A person's height is rarely if ever relevant to his or her chances of flourishing: in this respect, it is a 'small thing'. Yet even *so small a thing as that* is well beyond human control. The point is this: with so many things beyond our own powers, it is folly to *worry about the rest*.

27. Following his reflection on ravens (vv. 24–26), Jesus now takes up a similar a fortiori argument by calling his disciples to *consider the lilies (ta krina)*. A wide range of different flowers may be in view.[82] Once again, Jesus contrasts the hectic quality of human

---

82. 'In this connection the principal opinions include the autumn crocus, Turk's cap lily, anemone, or gladiolus, but the data do not permit certainty. Perhaps Jesus had no definite flower in mind, but was thinking of all the wonderful blooms that adorn the fields of Galilee' (BDAG, p. 451).

self-care with the seeming effortlessness with which nature preserves itself under divine providence. Luke wishes to show not so much that toiling and spinning are inherently misguided activities, but that believers need not preoccupy themselves with either the production or – by extension – the acquisition of clothing. Called to transcend a world of incessant striving, Jesus' followers are to be distinguished by their inward reliance on divine provision. This provision comes about through a mysterious means, perhaps not unlike the organic process by which lilies grow.

Nor should Jesus' followers expect this provision to be a shabby minimum: if the adornment of the fields surpasses even the sartorial grandeur of Solomon, then how much more will God do for his children? As Jesus ascends from Solomon to lilies to the disciples, he implies increasing gradations of stylishness. But how do we explain Jesus' promise that the disciples will be clothed two levels, as it were, above the wealthiest king in Israel's history? For all we know, the comparison retains additional eschatological thrust. After all, Jesus has already declared that 'something greater than Solomon is here' (11:31). So by promising that his disciples will be garbed more splendidly than the lilies, which in turn are more splendidly arrayed than the great king in his day, Jesus not only affirms God's provision of decent clothing in the present age but also hints that the believers' earthly wardrobe is but a fleeting transition to far more glorious raiment, that is, once their union with 'something greater' is consummated.

28. Whereas grass and people are somehow comparable in their adornment, their life expectancy is very different. People live for years: grass by contrast is *alive today and tomorrow is thrown into the oven* (*klibanon*) or furnace. On one level, the logic is simple: if God should take pains to beautify grass, fleeting as it is, then how much more will the same God attend to believers' clothing – and fashion no less – since humans live much longer than grass?[83] Once again,

---

83. Here it does not go unnoticed that, contrary to the Platonic tendency of many Bible interpreters down through the centuries, Jesus affirms the value of aesthetics.

Jesus' followers can count on their heavenly Father to provide their clothing needs.

The comparison between grass and humanity appeals not only to the natural order but also to a set of scriptural images associated with return from exile as described in Isaiah 40. In this chapter, a key chapter for the Evangelist (cf. e.g. Luke 3:4–6), the prophet compares unredeemed 'flesh' to the fading grass and the flowers of the fields, both of which are then contrasted with the enduring word of God (Isa. 40:6–8). This word, so Isaiah's reader also soon discovers, would one day be embodied in those who had been redeemed from exile (Isa. 55:9–13). On this logic, if Luke depends on the emerging arbour of Isaiah 55 to underwrite his parable of the sower (8:8, 15; cf. Isa. 55:9–13) with its representation of Jesus' faithful hearers, then the Evangelist also appropriates the grass and flowers of Isaiah 40:6–8 to make a point about well-clothed unbelievers (perhaps like Herod; cf. Luke 7:25) who will – despite their finery – wither in exile. Indeed, in Luke's hands the veiled symbols go on to hint that this same unredeemed grass-like humanity risks very soon being thrown into the furnace, more exactly, the furnace of Gehenna, as Jesus has just warned (12:5).

Closing out his exhortation, Jesus chides his hearers as those *of little faith* (*oligopistoi*). The term (occurring only here in Luke but multiple times in Matthew; cf. Matt. 6:30; 8:26; 14:31; 16:8; 17:20) makes clear that Jesus gives no excuse for anxious thoughts. The root cause of all such apprehension is unbelief.

29. The resumptive *kai* beginning the Greek sentence (translated as *and* in the NRSV) draws out the practical implications of the meditation contained in verses 24–28. In the light of the durative aspect of the two present-tense imperatives, it seems that Jesus has in mind neither the natural urge for food and drink nor the isolated worrisome thought but rather granting such thoughts and urges free reign: *do not keep striving for what you are to eat and what you are to drink, and do not keep worrying* (*meteōrizesthe*). The Greek behind *striving* (*zēteō*) implies a sense of focused determination; the later verb (*meteōrizō*), which occurs only once in the New Testament, connotes the metaphorical sense of a storm-tossed boat being thrown up in the air, an image appropriate to the feeling of suspense. Yet more centrally the latter verb conveys the sense of arrogantly 'making oneself high', in a sense, attempting to increase one's own height (v. 25).[84] Thus Luke's Jesus connects worry with arrogance (as does e.g. 1 Pet. 5:6–7). In the final analysis, all our anxious preoccupations belie an arrogant conviction that we can and should control that which is strictly under God's oversight.

30–31. Verses 30–31 draw an implicit contrast between *the nations of the world* (a circumlocution for Gentiles) and the disciples at their best. One of the palpable differences between unbelievers and those who are Jesus' own is that while the former make *these things* the primary objectives of their lives, the latter by contrast *strive for his kingdom*. This is not to suggest that God regards *these things* as inconsequential: on the contrary, *your Father knows that you need them*. For Jesus, the core issue revolves around how one orients oneself in response to life's most basic and pressing needs. On the one hand, those who mentally and emotionally devote themselves to the pursuit of food, drink, clothing and other material provisions will be aligning themselves with pagan idolaters – with no guarantees that their quest will be successful. On the other hand, those who in faith prioritize the kingdom's interests will obtain that which they seek and, strangely and mysteriously, find all 'these things' *given to you as well*. Though on any worldly reckoning such advice seems foolish, Jesus nevertheless invites his disciples to embrace a new and paradoxical logic, one which calls into question human inward fretting over life's basic necessities.

32. Jesus' exhortation to seek the kingdom raises the question as to how, especially in matters of salvation, human willing relates to divine election. Though Jesus does not necessarily resolve this question, he does affirm *the Father's good pleasure to give you the kingdom*. Paradoxically, then, the kingdom is something to be sought by humans, even as it is something to be given by God. At any rate, believers need *not be afraid* but have every reason to be confident that God's eschatological purposes for them will be fulfilled. Just as provisions of food and clothing are not finally dependent on human hustle and bustle, so it is with salvation. In all these realms, divine agency and human action conspire.

---

84. As rightly stressed by Edwards, p. 375.

Such assurances are directed to the disciples as members of a *flock*. Luke applies the same pastoral image to the believers elsewhere (Acts 20:28), as do other early Christian writers (John 10:14–30; 1 Pet. 5:3). The roots of this comparison are scriptural. In the Scriptures, the scattered tribes of Israel are compared to scattered sheep (Jer. 23:1–4; Ezek. 34:6); the regathering of the same sheep into one flock signals that return from exile is underway (Isa. 40:11) precisely in and through Jesus' band of disciples. And though the flock be *little*, one senses that in God's plan this diminutive community will – like the seed of a mustard tree (13:18–21) – soon grow well beyond its initial proportions.

33. The NRSV's insertion of a comma between *sell your possessions* and *give alms* is unfortunate, as it muddies their logical relationship. The NIV's rendering ('Sell your possessions and give to the poor') better retains the sense of the Greek, which suggests that by selling their possessions the disciples will have the resources for almsgiving. That Jesus' double command should be fulfilled in Acts (2:44–45; 4:32–37) should caution us against both over-interpretation and under-interpretation. On the one hand, because Jesus' command is specifically fulfilled in the early church community *as an apostolic community*, we cannot assume that his exhortation applies equally to individual believers of all times and places. Indeed, texts like Luke 8:3 militate against this kind of blanket interpretation. On the other hand, by noting that the apostolic community *had* in fact taken Jesus' command literally, Luke seems to be encouraging his readers around the Roman Empire to contextualize the principles of communal sharing in their own setting.

The command to self-divest and 'reinvest' in more lasting repositories of wealth is appropriate to the eschatological hour at hand. According to Jesus, the accursed present age is threatened not only by thieves (Hos. 7:1; Zech. 5:3–4), such as the Romans, who would soon enough pillage the temple (Luke 21:5–38; cf. Joel 2:9), but also by the destroying moth, which may be taken as a symbol of God in his capacity as judge of Israel (cf. Hos. 5:12). The imminent redemptive-historical shift presaged by Jesus' preaching required a new level of generosity that would ensure future participation in an eschatological reality.

34. In inviting his disciples to redirect their material resources to an 'unfailing treasure in heaven' (v. 33), Jesus' *ultimate* interest is not in offering investment advice on material possessions (although material eschatological reward is partially in view; cf. 18:29−30), but in the *heart*. Where one's treasure *is* (*estin*) the heart *will be* (*estai*). On this principle, the fibre and direction of one's willing, desires and emotions will inevitably depend on one's prior personal investments. Shaped over the course of one's life by daily and seemingly mundane decisions, the heart will determine the depth of one's eschatological felicity. All manner of personal investments (how one spends one's time, treasures and talents) will have a direct effect on one's eschatological future.

Theology

Whereas to pray for the coming of the kingdom (11:1) without also seeking the kingdom (12:31) would be hypocritical, to seek the kingdom while also pursuing worldly wealth would be self-delusional. A pernicious and prevalent vice so far as the Evangelist is concerned, greed is poised to overtake both the anonymous man in the crowd (12:13−21) and the 'little flock' who fret over their provision (vv. 22−34). Whatever its form, avarice is among the chief obstacles to the fulfilment of God's kingdom purposes.

Whenever the lust for possessions takes root in the human heart, Luke seems to say, this is ultimately symptomatic of spiritual short-sightedness. The eschatological 'long view' challenges such narrow thinking. It reveals in the first place that any attempt to manage one's resources and oversight responsibilities without reference to one's heavenly treasure will ultimately result in mismanagement before God. For Luke, faithful stewardship is a function of faithful eschatology.

G. Readiness for the master (12:35−48)

Context

Luke 12:35−48 develops at least two concepts from earlier narrative. First, the parable's wedding-feast backdrop (12:36) takes the reader back to a moment when Jesus had intimated himself as the messianic bridegroom (5:34−35). Second, the subsequent shift to the metaphor of a forcible break-in (12:39–40) recalls the parable of the strong man (11:14–23). This section also bears comparison with 17:7–10, which makes a point that, though seemingly very different from the message of 12:35–48, is actually complementary to it. Continuing the thrust of the previous section (12:13–34), this passage draws out further implications from the fact that the eschatological horizon was now closing in on human history.

Comment

35–36. The 'parable' (v. 41) related in verses 35–48 marks a new point of departure but one not unrelated to the theme of anxiety developed in the preceding passage (vv. 22–34). If worry is the vain attempt to grapple mentally with the uncertainties of life, then dissipated living, the primary concern of this passage, typically results from the equally fruitless attempt to escape such anxieties. For those destined to leadership in Jesus' kingdom, the latter failing can have especially serious consequences at the judgment (vv. 45–48). By exhorting his followers to faithfulness, Jesus trades on images from a domestic scene: *Be dressed for action, have your lamps lit* and *be like those who are waiting for their master to return*. The first of these commands (*estōsan hymōn hai osphues periezōsmenai*) might be more literally if not archaically translated as 'Let your loins be girded' (YLT). In antiquity, tunics were worn down to the ankles and secured at the waist by a belt. While performing activities requiring free leg movement, such as manual labour or fighting, it would be necessary to bundle the low-hanging hem of the tunic underneath one's belt. In the light of this background, the injunction 'Let your loins be girded' asks that the disciples be ready for service requiring exertion. Highlighting the importance of sustained mental focus (cf. 21:34), Jesus next requires that his disciples keep their metaphorical lamps burning so that they can stay awake through the course of the night (v. 37). Both imperatives take on greater definition in Jesus' third exhortation: that his disciples play the role of servants who await their master's late-night return from *the wedding banquet*. In sum, because the master will knock on the door (cf. Rev. 3:20) unexpectedly, they must be ever alert (with lamps burning) and ready for action (with loins girded up). When this string of images is coordinated with the first-century expectation of the

Messiah's return to the temple in the middle of the night, all three activities (girding up the loins, keeping lamps lit and serving) now take on the cast of distinctively priestly duties.[85] That Jesus should specify the detaining event as '*the* wedding banquet' (*tōn gamōn*; cf. 5:34–35) implies that the celebration in view marks nothing less than the consummation of the covenant between God and God's people, soon to be signified in Luke's narrative through the Last Supper (22:16–23).

37–38. Together, these two verses constitute a chiastic (ABCB'A') structure. On the outer edges of the chiasm (A, A'), the servants are described as *blessed* (*makarioi*) or happy (vv. 37a, 38b). The next layer (B, B') focuses on the indeterminate timing of the master's coming: *when he comes* (v. 37a); *If he comes during the middle of the night, or near dawn* (v. 38a). Finally, at the structural centre (C) lies the main point, to wit, the master's surprising actions on behalf of his servants: *truly I tell you, he will fasten his belt and have them sit down to eat, and he will come and serve them* (v. 37b). Whereas servants are generally expected to serve their master, in Jesus' imagined scenario it is the master who girds up his own loins (*perizōsetai*), makes his servants recline (*anaklinei autous*) and serves them (*diakonēsei autois*). In being so served (by their *kyrios*, no less!) in response to their own faithfulness, the servants will naturally be surprised and delighted (*makarioi*). All this points to the breathtaking and upside-down nature of the coming kingdom, which will also witness the servants of the Lord (*kyrios*) entering into the blessed (*makarioi*) state on the arrival of the Son of Man (v. 40).

Within the limits of the story, the master's actions point both backwards and forwards. In feeding the five thousand, Jesus has already made the crowds recline for their meal (9:15); later, in Luke 13 (close to the immediate context), Jesus will envision the patriarchs reclining at the eschatological banquet table (13:29). Finally, bridging the gap between these temporal and future realities is the Last Supper where Jesus has the apostles recline (22:14), even as he

---

85. The standard term for priestly ministry is 'serve'. For priests girding up their loins in preparation for sacrifice, see Jdt. 4:14; for keeping the temple lamps trimmed, see Exod. 27:20–21; Lev. 24:2.

will invert the hierarchical distinction between those who recline and those who serve (22:27).[86] Within this broader context, then, the parable promises that Jesus will one day return, not to be served but to serve his kingdom subjects at the climactic messianic banquet. For that reason, Luke's readers must watch for the Son of Man as one who will gird up his loins and wait on tables. They must do so, not knowing whether that coming should occur during the second or third watch of the night, midnight and pre-dawn, respectively.

39–40. Commentators have sometimes regarded verse 39 as a non sequitur that has been awkwardly inserted within the tradition, but this is an unwarranted judgment. In fact, once properly interpreted, the verse falls into place as a logical development of what has gone before. I have argued above that Luke's house on the rock is in fact the Jerusalem temple (6:48–49), and that though this house/temple is also presently under the sway of Satan the strong man, it nevertheless remains vulnerable to imminent intrusion (11:14–26). If verse 39 has the same violated house in view, then the *owner of the house* (*oikodespotēs*) must refer to the high priest.[87] Meanwhile, given the parallelism with verse 40, the thief can only be Jesus the coming Son of Man (similarly in Rev. 16:15). Connecting the dots this way, we surmise a cautionary tale. If the high priest had known *what hour* was at hand, namely, the hour of divine judgment, he would have ensured that he and those within his administration were spiritually prepared. In the same way, Jesus warns, as the disciples prepare to assume priestly oversight of their own household 'temple', they too *must be ready*.

41. Peter has grasped the parable's twofold point. First, Jesus will come into his temple as Israel's rightful Messiah and will do so unexpectedly, at any time; second, Jesus' faithful followers must

---

86. The post-Pentecostal church will take this inversion seriously as the church's leaders wait on tables (Acts 6:2).

87. Identifying the owner of the house (*oikodespotēs*) with God does not make sense, for two reasons. First, the owner is unknowing; second, the Greek noun pertains more to management responsibilities than to ownership.

discharge their priestly responsibilities as they operate a makeshift temple-like community. But then just who exactly, Peter wants to know, are these 'priests'-in-waiting? Is Jesus enjoining these responsibilities and promising blessedness *for us or for everyone* in the community?

42–43. Responding to Peter's question, Jesus poses a query of his own. His intent is not to solicit information but rather to identify responsibilities and character traits for anyone who aspires to the role of *manager* within God's house, only then, ultimately, to attain the blessedness described in verses 37–38, 43. What is the manager's task? Quite simply, it is to give the household servants *their allowance of food at the proper time*. While one may be tempted to interpret this strictly as a metaphor for spiritual teaching, Luke's subsequent accounts of food allotments under the apostles' authority (Acts 6:1) suggest that the *allowance of food* here intends both spiritual *and* literal feedings. If Jesus' disciples must ask God for their daily bread (11:3) and that bread refers to both physical and spiritual nourishment, then it would make sense for leaders within the church to distribute allowances of food that meet both physical and spiritual needs.[88] All the while, the qualities of faithfulness (*pistos*), involving the conscientious discharge of one's studies, and prudence (*phronimos*), the ability to perform one's tasks with understanding, are paramount. Such a slave will be *blessed* when the master *arrives*.

44. So far in the story, the substantive plural participle of *hypoarchō* ('possessions, property') has been used in connection with those redeemed from the strong man (11:21), as well as with personal property (12:15, 33). On the latter use, Jesus not only warns his disciples about the dangers of wealth, but also calls them to divest themselves of it for the kingdom's sake. Now Jesus promises that the coming *kyrios* – seemingly in exchange for such earthly sacrifices – *will put that one in charge of all his possessions* (*hyparchousin*) at the parousia. Given Luke's development of 'possessions', not to mention other forthcoming assurances (18:29–30), the promised reward would seem to include not only eternal property holdings

---

88. See commentary on Luke 11:3.

but also even leaderships roles within the eternal kingdom (cf. 1 Thess. 2:19–20).

45. Whereas verses 41–44 have envisioned a model set of behaviours followed by a blessed outcome, verses 45–48 consider several scenarios with less favourable results. In each of these, the stumbling point is not so much the master's delay itself but rather the conclusions which the faithless and unwise servant draws from it. The trouble begins, as it does in other places in Luke (12:16–20; 15:11–32; 16:1–8; 18:2–5), with self-talk: 'if that slave says in his heart . . . ' (NASB). Sensing no accountability, the servant *begins to beat the other slaves . . . and to eat and drink and get drunk.* Though eating and drinking have already become marks of Jesus' community (5:30; 7:34; 10:7), here (as in 12:19) Jesus warns against an untethered conviviality which also involves the unfaithful servant beating those under his charge, both *men and women.* By including this teaching, the Evangelist seemingly speaks of cases not only of ecclesiastical abuse (whether physical, financial, spiritual, emotional or sexual) but also of self-indulgent neglect among church leaders. Spiritual leadership that is not firmly oriented on the eschatological horizon alternately lends itself to forms of active and passive aggression.

46. For *that slave* the master *will come on a day when he does not expect him and at an hour that he does not know.* This is not to say that obedient servants should be able to predict the Son of Man's coming (the NT tradition clearly indicates otherwise). Rather, the point is that as far as the faithless servant is concerned, the master's coming will seem especially sudden and unexpected. And when the master does come, he will subject the faithless servant to dismemberment, a punishment which the ancient world reserved for the most egregious of criminals. That Christian leaders should stand in danger of eternal judgment on account of their malfeasance would have been a sobering corrective for any leaders in Luke's audience who might otherwise see their spiritual office as a guarantee of eternal felicity.

47–48. The punishment to be dealt out to such malefactors will be a function of their awareness of Jesus' demands: those who should have known better will *receive a severe beating*; those without such awareness will *receive a light beating.* Thus, while ignorance is never presented as a 'free pass' from judgment, the extent of the eschatological punishment will be scaled against the individual's knowledge. On Jesus' vision, whatever personal resources one may have to hand (be it time, treasures, talents and wisdom, or something else), these must be regarded as a sacred trust. The arresting truth is just this: the greater one's resources, the greater one's responsibility before God.

Theology

By Luke's estimation, right standing before God requires membership within the returning master's household. That said, membership within the household of faith is hardly a sufficient condition for salvation. Jesus requires his servants to be *ready*, to live and to act without the prospect of shame at the Lord's coming. Belonging to the people of God, in other words, is not just a matter of affinity and allegiance; it is also a matter of attitude. Believers must live expectantly, ready for divine interruption at any moment. And when leaders fail to exhibit this sense of expectancy, they are at grave risk of abusing those under their charge. Here is a sobering thought: those who neglect or otherwise abuse those under their charge will – notwithstanding their reputation or office – be assigned the same fate as unbelievers.

H. Interpreting the times (12:49 – 13:21)

Context

Jesus' exhortations on stewardship in the previous section (12:35–48) would be little more than wishful moralizing apart from some evidence of the kingdom's immanence. And though he had intimated that 'the kingdom of God has come to you' (11:20), it was undeniable that the kingdom had not arrived in the way that most first-century Jews had come to expect. Indeed, there was so much about Jesus, his style and his message that seemed to contradict his kingdom claim. What exactly did Jesus mean when he said, 'The kingdom of God has come to you'?

In many respects, the whole 'Journey to Jerusalem' section (9:51 – 19:27) serves to answer that very question. But it is especially now in the present section (12:49 – 13:21) that Jesus makes the following observation: since in the kingdom things are not always as they appear, superficial impressions are bound to be misleading. Therefore, when it comes to receiving the kingdom, one has to penetrate the mystery of Jesus' identity, as if in a moment of divinely fostered insight. Just as it fell to the reader of Daniel to discern the prophesied eschatological 'hour' (*kairos*) or 'time' (Dan. 12:1), so too it now fell to Jesus' hearers to interpret the present hour (*kairos*) (Luke 12:56) – the realization of what Daniel had been pointing to.

In order to understand this hour, one must first grasp not only the nature of Jesus' mission but also the crossroads at which Israel had found itself. As for God's people, the nation had very little going in its favour. It was bound to face the judge (12:57–59); its citizens were no less guilty than those who had perished prematurely (13:1–5). Israel was comparable to a barren fig tree (13:6–9) and, like the stooping woman encountered in 13:10–17, bent over under demonic oppression. Meanwhile, despite earlier angelic promises of his bringing 'peace on earth' (2:14), Jesus himself now insists he will be the cause of deep conflict (12:49–53). At the same time, paradoxically again, if Luke's readers penetrate the meaning of Jesus' healing of the bent-over woman (13:10–17) and the mustard seed parable (13:18–21), they will also see Jesus as the singular source of healing, hope and community. And should the crowds interpret these matters rightly, they would be well positioned not only for the present hour but also, as the ensuing section of 13:22 – 14:24 makes clear, for the future.

Comment

i. Coming division (12:49–53)

49. In the present paragraph (vv. 49–53) Jesus specifies three components of his mission: casting 'fire to the earth' (v. 49), undergoing a 'baptism' (v. 50) and sowing 'division' (vv. 51–53). The first of these appointed tasks puts Jesus once again in company with Elijah, who twice in his prophetic career brought down fire from heaven: once in a spectacular competition with the priests of Baal (1 Kgs 18:38) and then again in a twofold strike against Ahaziah's dispatched troops (2 Kgs 1:9–15). In both events, fire is the vehicle of judgment. And so, as if to expand on verses 45–48,

Jesus reasserts himself as a prophet like Elijah. This means, perhaps among other things, that he is tasked with bringing judgment on an apostate Israel. While the fire is not yet kindled, it will – so it seems – eventually descend in the person of the Holy Spirit (Acts 2:3) and this in fulfilment of John's words (Luke 3:16).[89] For Luke, therefore, Pentecost is a moment not only of empowerment for the people of God but also of decisive judgment against the pagan nations.

50. The Greek connective *de* (left untranslated in the NRSV) implies a logical connection between Jesus' anticipated baptism and the coming kindling. That the baptism stands to be *completed* (*telesthē*) or 'accomplished' (ESV, KJV) implies a degree of purposiveness, suggesting even that this metaphorical baptism is a climactic moment – anticipated through his literal baptism of 3:21–22 – within a much larger divine plan. On account of a variety of factors within Luke, not to mention supporting theological tradition outside the Gospel (Rom. 6:3–4), the baptism in view here must be understood as Jesus' death (cf. Mark 10:38). Not surprisingly, Jesus reports being under *stress* (*synechomai*) or 'distressed' (NASB) or 'pressed' (YLT) until that moment should come. Luke's choice of verb is striking, since Jesus has already experienced the press (*synechō*) of the crowds (8:45) and will do so again (19:43), even as his mockers detain (*synechontes*) him (22:63) after his arrest. The constraint which Jesus experiences, at seasons of popularity and ignominy alike, not only lies at the very heart of the Hebrew concept of curse, but also becomes a piece in a great exchange in Luke's atonement theology: Jesus willingly underwent constraint in order that those he came to rescue might be liberated (4:18).[90]

51–53. Jesus poses a rhetorical question only to give a surprising answer. To this point in the story, the reader has been conditioned to think of Jesus as a bearer of peace (1:79; 2:14; 7:50; 8:48; 10:5–6). But now Jesus adamantly denies such a mission, claiming instead

---

89. See also Luke 17:29. Interpreters often feel forced to decide whether the fire refers to judgment or to the Spirit (see e.g. Johnson, p. 209), but this is a false disjunction.

90. See Perrin, 'Curse'.

to bring *division* precipitated by himself. The nature of this division is such that it will penetrate into the most fundamental of social units: the *household*, where oppositional lines are soon to be drawn right down the middle of the family – all in fulfilment of Micah 7:6, part of a larger passage (Mic. 7:1–7) lamenting the apostasy of Israel.[91] It is hardly incidental that the prophetic language belongs to a broader register of scriptural texts interpreted as predictive of a great tribulation. Because such tribulation was also understood to precede messianic redemption, Jesus presents himself as the instigator of the very tribulation which will also become concentrated on his person through his 'baptism'. Jesus' logic thus follows a sequential timeline: from Pentecost (v. 49) to the cross (v. 50), and from the cross to the controversial preaching ministry of Jesus (vv. 51–53).

ii. The future crisis (12:54–59)

54–55. Confronting the crowds with their shallowness (cf. 12:13–21), Jesus issues a stern twofold warning in the form of two rhetorical 'why questions': the first highlights their inability to interpret the times (vv. 54–56); the second, their failure to judge rightly (vv. 57–59). Laying the groundwork for the first of these two queries, Jesus notes the crowd's ability to interpret weather patterns: *When you see a cloud rising in the west, you immediately say, 'It is going to rain'; and so it happens. And when you see the south wind blowing, you say, 'There will be scorching heat [kausōn]'; and it happens.* The two cause-and-effect sequences are not only accurate enough but also frequent enough to have been a matter of common knowledge. When moisture gathers in cloud formations over the Mediterranean Sea, this tends to produce rain showers. Likewise, southerly wind from the sun-scorched desert is typically accompanied by hot, dry air. More than a lesson drawn from nature, Jesus' allusion to shifting weather conditions seems to have a scriptural lining, for when Israel's drought drew to a close, Elijah looked west and recognized 'a little *cloud . . . rising* out of the sea' as the harbinger of the fact that

---

91. Strikingly, Jesus' mission appears to be the opposite of John's mission which is to turn the hearts of fathers to their children (1:17).

God was about to lift the curse from the land (1 Kgs 18:44, emphasis added). By the same token, a withering, *scorching heat* (*kausōn*) is regularly associated with divine judgment (LXX Jer. 18:17; Ezek. 17:10; Hos. 13:15; Jon. 4:8). Thus, despite the appearance that these are randomly selected weather conditions, Jesus is actually reflecting on his mission as a catalyst for both blessing (i.e. the reversal of curse) and judgment. For those who could interpret the eschatological hour and respond accordingly, there would be redemption. For those who did not see what was happening, there would be scorching judgement.

56. The crowds earn the epithet *hypocrites* on account of their failure to transfer their weather-predicting skills to what God is doing in and through Jesus. They *know how to interpret the appearance of earth and sky*, but they are unable to assess the significance (*dokimazein*) of this 'present hour' (*kairon touton*), the appointed eschatological *kairos* (Dan. 7:25; 12:7) and 'the time [*kairos*] of your visitation from God' (Luke 19:44).[92] Had members of the crowd penetrated beyond the surface of things and gained insight into the meaning of Jesus' ministry, their response would have been entirely different.

57. One good question deserves another, one which builds upon the first. If the appropriate first step is correctly interpreting the times (v. 56), the second step involves drawing practical implications from that interpretation, requiring the ability to *judge for yourselves what is right* (*to dikaion*). The neuter substantive *dikaion* denotes not some abstract ethical principle but a proper response within the context of a legal or covenantal relationship. Judging *for yourselves* also has its own extrinsic motivation, since those who do judge for themselves are more likely to avoid their just deserts, meted out by unappeasable figures who have been entrusted with executive and judicial duties (vv. 58–59).

58. Whereas a number of commentators understand the four roles (*accuser, magistrate, judge* and *officer*) as nothing more than civic actors, it makes sense to extend the language metaphorically,

---

92. Likewise, it is 'the crucial time when the hearers must respond to Jesus' call or let a great opportunity slip away' (Talbert, p. 215).

pointing to specific suprahuman individuals. In Second Temple Judaism, the *accuser* (*antidikos*) is an equivalent term for Satan (Job 1:6–8; Zech. 3:1–7). Similarly, the term commonly translated as *magistrate* (*archonta*) might just as well be glossed as 'ruler' (YLT), one who is at any rate probably to be linked with Beelzebul 'the ruler [*archonti*] of the demons' (Luke 11:15). On this logic, the *judge* (*kritēn*) would be God and the *officer* (*praktōr*) or bailiff would likely be an angelic figure tasked with guarding the doomed. In this case, too, the *prison* is akin to superterrestrial prisons mentioned elsewhere in the literature (1 Pet. 3:19; Rev. 18:2; 20:7; 1 En. 21:10), which are holding places for condemned beings. Jesus urges his hearers not so much to *settle the case* (*apēllaxthai*) with the demonic chieftain (as the NRSV among other translations would have it) as to be 'delivered' from him (rightly, KJV). They are to do so while they are *on the way* (*en tē hodō*), a phrase which in Luke refers to return from exile (1:76; 3:4; 7:27; 8:12; etc.), dramatized by Jesus' journey to Jerusalem.[93] In short, to join Jesus' return-from-exile movement even while he proceeds to his fate is to extricate oneself from all-but-certain punishment.

59. Extending the parable one more step, Jesus declares that once the guilty are condemned they will not be able to get out until they have paid *the very last penny* (*lepton*), a coin of almost negligible value. The coin denomination is significant, not least because Luke's reader will later meet a widow who will self-sacrificially give to God her very last two pennies (*lepta*; 21:1–4). In this broader context, then, Luke's point seems to be that securing deliverance from judgment in this life has *something* to do with one's selfless giving of one's own resources, as modelled by the widow. Conversely, the failure to 'pay it forward' in this life will result in a

---

93. Johnson (p. 209) is correct when he writes: 'In Matt 5:25–26, the exhortation to make things up with an adversary before going to trial is a teaching to the disciples on fraternal relations. But in Luke, it is parabolic for this moment in the narrative of the Prophet's progression to Jerusalem. They are ones "on the road" (12:58) who must make their decision now, before it is too late.'

sort of a fine and consequent thoroughgoing forfeiture at the eschatological judgment.

iii. Parable of the fig tree (13:1–9)

1–3. Though a case could be made for separating Jesus' warnings (13:1–5) from the parable of the barren fig tree (vv. 6–9), the two passages are more usefully considered together, especially since both sections (as I will argue below) gesture to the impending disaster of the Jewish Revolt (AD 66–70). According to Luke, *there were some present who told him about the Galileans whose blood Pilate had mingled with their sacrifices.* Given the lexical weight of *pareimi* ('there were some present') and the Evangelist's other uses of this verb (Acts 10:21, 33; 12:20; 17:6; 24:19), these individuals seem to have recently arrived, perhaps with the intention of reporting the massacre.[94] Coming on the heels of Jesus' dire warning to the crowds (Luke 12:54–59), the messengers' announcement *at that very time* (*en autō tō kairō*, 13:1) is issued in response to it. By identifying these tragic events with God's judgment, the messengers of the news are perhaps seeking Jesus' assurance that they themselves will be shielded from his promised judgment. Meanwhile, Luke's strategically placed Greek *en autō tō kairō* also frames the two calamities described in verses 1 and 4 as two aspects of the same Danielic hour (*kairos*) just announced in 12:56.[95] As such, the mishaps are no random occurrences but rather integral components of long-expected tribulation leading up to the messianic revelation – palpable signs that the redemptive-historical shift is already underway.

---

94. BDAG, p. 624. Though the incident alluded to in Luke 13:1 is not historically attested outside the Gospel, such brutality is certainly consistent with Pilate's reputation (Josephus, *Ant.* 18.85–89; *J.W.* 2.169–177). A similar incident occurred in 4 BC when Archelaus had about three thousand Passover pilgrims slaughtered next to their sacrifices; *J.W.* 2.10–13, 30.

95. While 'the phrase "in that time" does not have eschatological overtones outside the prophetic books, . . . in the prophetic literature, "in that time" is primarily used with an eschatological sense' (Mihalios, *Eschatological Hour*, p. 17).

Judging by verse 2, it seems that Jesus had detected a hint of moral self-congratulation in the messengers' tone and responds accordingly by posing a rhetorical question aimed at exposing their self-righteousness and undermining their false sense of security. To their surprise, he assures the crowds that apart from repentance they too *will all perish as* (*homoiōs*) the Galileans did (v. 3). The choice of the adverb *homoiōs* ('likewise, equally, in the same way' [Thayer]), over the alternative option of the weaker *hōs* ('as'), serves to emphasize similarity in the manner of death. Whether Jesus is warning his hearers of an impending premature and violent death or, more specifically, a premature and violent death in the midst of a cultic act, is not entirely clear. But given the following parable's allusion to the temple's destruction, the latter is more probable. In which case, Luke's Jesus is prophesying that some in the crowd – if they continue in their present waywardness – may one day find themselves mortally wounded in Israel's sacred space, even as Jerusalem falls.

4–5. Having discouraged unwarranted inferences from the massacre of the Galileans, Jesus now extends the same principle to tragic accidents which might – in the parlance of the insurance industry – be characterized as 'acts of God'. The focus turns to *those eighteen who were killed when the tower of Siloam fell on them* (v. 4).[96] Once again Jesus criticizes any attempt to correlate such tragic events with moral culpability. Once again, as well, his primary interest is to discourage the crowd's finger-wagging by insisting that in God's eyes they are no less deserving of the same fate. This 'death by architectural structure' here anticipates the sack of the temple, when not one stone will be left on another (19:44; 21:6).

6–9. This parable, like the parable of the wicked tenants (20:9–19), is a story of – at least from the owner's point of view – a failed harvest. Given the scriptural backdrop (Isa. 34:4; Jer. 29:17; Hos.

---

96. No mention of this event survives outside of Luke 13:4. The tower seems to have been the same one mentioned by Josephus 'above the fountain of Siloam' (*J.W.* 5.145); cf. John 9:7. Perhaps not coincidentally, eighteen is also the number of years marking Israel's bondage to alien powers (Judg. 3:14; 10:8).

2:12; 9:10; Joel 1:7; Mic. 7:1), the fig tree is likely a symbol for God's people; the planter, God. Meanwhile, Jesus himself plays the role of gardener – not surprising since Luke has already underscored his Adamic quality (3:38). The expected fruit is covenantal right-eousness, marked out by both personal and corporate justice.[97] The man's concern is not only with the tree's failure to produce fruit but also with the resulting waste of *the soil* (*tēn gēn*), that is, the land. The noun carries some redemptive-historical cargo. Because the land was essentially on loan to Israel as a platform for fulfilling God's purposes, Israel's continued disobedience was proving to be a poor use of the sacred space. Cutting down the tree, then, is equivalent to a kind of exile.

That Israel's probationary period should be set at *three years* relates, in the first instance, to the fact that three years is a typical period of judgment (cf. 4:25). On a more literal level, one suspects that the onset of the triennial period coincides with the Baptizer's demand for fruit (3:8–9) near the beginning of Jesus' ministry. In this connection, it is not too speculative to suggest that God the planter has requested Jesus the gardener to tear down the fig tree, and that this prerogative would soon be dramatized in the temple cleansing (19:45–48) – at the tail end of Jesus' three-year ministry. Beyond the three-year mark, Jesus' efforts of digging and manuring are not his earthly efforts but the convicting and enriching activity of the Spirit through the church. Should Israel remain unfruitful during the course of the additional year (which is perhaps an indeterminate or extended period of time rather than a literal year), then the planter's initial plan to cut down the tree will be implemented. In the meantime, the gardener asks that the planter *let it alone* (*aphes autēn*) or, to translate the Greek otherwise, 'forgive it'. In this light, the request of the crucified Jesus that his persecutors be forgiven (23:34) actualizes the same intra-Trinitarian script Jesus intimates here, preparing for the apostolic ministry recorded in Acts.

---

97. See commentary above on Luke 3:8 along with scriptural references.

iv. Healing of the disabled woman (13:10–17)

10–11. Jesus' Sabbath day teaching at the synagogue takes us back to his inaugural Sabbath sermon (4:16–30) when, following his proclamation of release, he met a variation of the same resistance he now meets here (13:14). But in focusing on Jesus' power to reverse the handiwork of Satan (13:16), the present passage is also reminiscent of his encounter with a demon-possessed man (4:31–37), again in a synagogue on a Sabbath day. That the woman has been suffering for *eighteen years* links not only with the eighteen victims at Siloam (13:4), but also, more distantly, with the eighteen years marking off two regimes in the oppressive era of the judges (Judg. 3:14; 10:8).[98] Thus the specified time span not only speaks of the chronic nature of the woman's condition but also hints at her status, within the narrative, as a metaphor for oppressed Israel.

The woman's postural issues are severe. So *bent over* is the woman that she is *unable to stand up straight* (*mē dynamenē anakypsai*), at least not fully (*eis to panteles*).[99] In Greek usage, *anakyptō* means to stand erect physically or to be lifted up emotionally or spiritually (BDAG). On a related note, Jews regarded standing as an especially appropriate posture for praise (Neh. 9:5; Pss 134:1–2; 135:1–2). Looking to the future, Luke's Jesus will promise a coming day when the elect would 'stand up [*anakypsate*] and raise your heads, because your redemption is drawing near' (21:28). But for now a posture of praise is impossible, that is, so long as this enfeebling dark spirit is at work.

12. Summoning the hunched woman, Jesus addresses her simply as *Woman* (*gynai*). In using this term of address, Jesus sets up the scene as a companion piece to the healing of the paralysed man (5:17–26) who, prior to his healing, is called 'man' (*anthrōpe*; 5:20) – consistent with Luke's habit of establishing gender complement-

---

98. See note at commentary on 13:4. Nolland (p. 724) thinks that eighteen years is a circumlocution for 'a long time' but this is speculative.

99. Marshall (pp. 557–558), along with some other commentators, prefers to translate *eis to panteles* as 'at all', in which case she is completely unable to stand straight. Wilkinson ('Bent Woman') suggests that the illness is Bechterew's disease, an arthritic condition rendering the spine inflexible.

arity between two analogous pericopae, reinforcing a new creation motif: 'male and female he created them'. Jesus' declaration that the woman has been *set free (apolelysai)* from her weakness involves the perfect aspect, indicating a perfected act (or an imminent perfect act, given the subsequent laying on of hands in v. 13). The combination of the two concepts (liberation and weakness) in Jesus' announcement perhaps calls to mind Isaiah's Suffering Servant who redeems Israel from its infirmities (Isa. 53:4; cf. Matt. 8:17).

13. Luke emphasizes not only the immediacy of the woman's healing but also the worshipful character of her response: *she stood up straight and began praising God.* The healing itself comes about through a laying on of *his hands (tas cheiras)*, consistent with Jesus' earlier healings (4:40; 5:13) and anticipating the later apostolic practice (Acts 5:12; 19:11; 28:8). Jesus' gesture not only embeds this healing within the exodus underway (assuming an analogy between Jesus' hand and the redeeming hand(s) of Moses and Yahweh), but also sets the stage for the apostles' use of the same action not just for healing but to signal their perpetuation of the same movement (Acts 6:6; 8:14–19; 13:3).[100]

14–15. Whereas the synagogue leader in Corinth responds positively to Paul's proclamation of the gospel (Acts 18:8), this *leader of the synagogue* does not. He is happy enough for people to come in order to be healed – only not on the Sabbath.[101] On one level, this might not seem an unreasonable request, but Jesus will have none of it. The synagogue leader's complaint only prompts Jesus to address a much larger crowd of opposing religious stakeholders (v. 17) who are hovering nearby. He applies to them the same term he

---

100. On this point, see Perrin, *Exodus Revealed*, pp. 114–116. On *cheir* (arm, hand) in the exodus, see among other texts Exod. 8:5–6, 16–17; 9:3; Deut. 4:34; 5:15; 7:19; Pss 77:20; 136:11–12; Isa. 23:11; Zeph. 1:4.

101. In the rabbinic writings, exemptions to Torah's Sabbath legislation (Exod. 20:8–11; Deut. 5:12–15) are made when it comes to caring for animals, and the same principle becomes the basis for Jesus' a fortiori argument in 13:15. Meanwhile, the stricter Qumran community seems to have resisted providing any form of help to animals on the Sabbath; cf. CD XI, 13–14.

applied to those who failed to interpret the eschatological hour
(12:56): *hypocrites*. They are *hypocrites* in the sense that they are willing
enough to perform Sabbath work when it comes to caring for their
own oxen or donkeys, but they are unwilling to tolerate those who
extend Sabbath-day care to human beings.

16. Though the NRSV inserts an indefinite article (*a*) before
daughter of Abraham, in the Greek the phrase is closer to '*this* [*tautēn*]
daughter of Abraham'. The demonstrative adjective ('this')
occupies first position, as if Jesus were proudly announcing her as
a new family member within the newly reconstituted family of
Abraham – and, prospectively, a sibling to Zacchaeus the 'son of
Abraham' (19:9). Luke's Jesus also inserts the interjective *idou*
('behold') before the phrase *eighteen long years*, yielding the possible
translation: 'whom Satan has bound for – hey, look! – eighteen
years'. If, as I have suggested, eighteen years is specified so as to
draw out a comparison with the duration of Israel's oppression
under alien powers, and if, too, Jesus is presenting the miracle as
a dramatic representation of Israel's deliverance from Satan's
thrall, then the miracle is both discharging *and* enacting his earlier
inaugural promise of effecting Israel's corporate release (4:18–19;
11:22). In this light, Jesus' point is not so much 'that any time is
appropriate to come to God for healing and restoration' (Bock,
p. 2012), but rather that there is a certain appropriateness or even
necessity (*dei*) that this miracle of release, quintessentially
characteristic of the Jubilee (4:18–19), occur on the Sabbath. After
all, Jubilee was not just to be announced on the Sabbath; it marked
the culminating Sabbath year within a set of seven Sabbath years
(Lev. 25) – a 'super Sabbath', as it were.

17. Within the Ancient Near Eastern shame–honour culture,
there were few misfortunes greater than public shaming. By
dictating the permissible time frame in which the people could and
could not be healed, the leader of the synagogue had sought to
circumscribe Jesus' unimpeachable authority to heal within his
own authority as a religious leader, and this amounted to an attempt
to shame the unruly Sabbath-violating healer by putting him 'back
in his place'. But on Jesus' rejoinder, it is the outmanoeuvred synagogue leader and his cohort of antipathizers who are put to shame.
The same power which enables Jesus to put his debating partners

to shame, ahead of the great day of eschatological shaming (Ps. 119:78; Isa. 26:11; 44:11; 45:16, 24; Jer. 23:40; Dan. 12:2), will also be at work in the early church (cf. Luke 21:15). All the while, the *crowd was rejoicing*. If the eschaton was to be characterized by sharp contrasts of joy and shame, then the eschaton was now.

v. Two seed parables (13:18–21)

18. The inclusion of *oun* (*therefore*) logically connects the two parables of this section with the prior miraculous healing (13:10–17).[102] The connection seems to be this: if Jesus really was the Messiah, then the stiff opposition he had just faced from the religious leaders (13:14–17), despite his healing, remains puzzling. The solution to this puzzle promises to be contained in the pair of parables. While many had expected a glorious kingdom that would command assent from Israel's leadership, the kingdom promised by Jesus was obviously turning out to be very different. This kingdom was to be characterized by surprisingly inconspicuous beginnings and even marginalization, only to transition towards a glorious destiny. And so Jesus probes his audience's imagination with a double question.[103]

19. The parable of the mustard seed begins with a 'man' (despite the well-meaning NRSV *someone*), who, as the analogue of the 'woman' of verse 21, takes a mustard seed and sows it in the *garden* (*kēpon*). A garden of course is the quintessential creational setting, as well as an eschatological symbol (Isa. 61:11; Ezek. 36:35).[104] And, despite the claims of some commentators, the planting of the mustard seed in a garden is neither particularly subversive of any

---

102. This follows the pattern suggested by Liebenberg (*Language*, p. 306), who argues that the entire travel narrative may be subdivided into three sections (9:51 − 13:21; 13:22 − 17:10; 17:11 − 19:28), with each section including a healing miracle followed by a kingdom discourse.

103. The double question is reminiscent of 7:31, where Jesus also reflects on resistance to the kingdom.

104. In John's Gospel, the garden is also where Jesus (like the mustard seed) is buried and risen (18:1, 26; 19:41), and this is perhaps no coincidence as far as Luke is concerned.

cultic purity laws in particular nor generally controversial.[105] The parable's crucial element is the dramatic difference in size between the mustard seed, which is around one-sixteenth of an inch (between 1 and 2 mm) in diameter, and a fully developed mustard bush, which can attain heights of well over 10 feet (3 m). Eventually, the mustard seed-turned-tree provides a haven for 'the birds of heaven', which appear to represent the Gentiles, at least judging by various relevant texts (Ps. 104:12; Ezek. 31:6; Dan. 4:12; 1 En. 90:30, 33, 37) and by how some of these texts were interpreted in the day.[106] A no less relevant subtext is Ezekiel 17:23, where the exilic remnant is pictured as being planted 'on the mountain height' (i.e. Zion). This kingdom envisaged by Jesus is therefore not only a highly inclusive community (composed of all the returnees from exile, including the Gentiles) but also a worshipping community. Seemingly insignificant at first, it looms large as it approaches the eschatological future.

20–21. Like the first parable in this two-parable set, the parable of yeast emphasizes the hidden growth of the kingdom. The focus is not on yeast as a corrupting agent but on its astounding capacity to penetrate.[107] While many commentators see *three measures (sata tria)* or three seahs (equivalent to 9 gallons or 34 litres of dry measure) as having no especial significance, one cannot help but notice the correspondence with Sarah's three-seah batch of cakes that she prepared for three visitors on a journey (Gen. 18:6).[108] And if Luke intended a connection, it would not be fortuitous. Whereas the mustard tree of the previous parable promises to provide a home for the Gentiles on the basis of Psalm 104:12; Ezekiel 31:6;

---

105. Whereas planting mustard seeds near grain crops is proscribed by (the later) m. Kil. 3:2, the text never hints that the bush is inherently unclean; contra Scott, *Parable*, pp. 382–387.

106. The connection between the birds and the nations is disputed by Fitzmyer, p. 1017.

107. Leaven had both negative *and* positive connotations in Jewish antiquity. See the helpful comments of Snodgrass, *Intent* (p. 233).

108. The connection with Genesis is doubted by a number of commentators, but see Waller, 'Parable'.

and Daniel 4:12, the parabolic batch's invocation of Sarah's leavened bread (Gen. 18:6) speaks of another kind of hospitality – directed, like Sarah's, to God's very self, embodied in human form.

Theology

Luke 12:49 – 13:21 touches on a number of paradoxes pertaining to the kingdom. The first of these is a paradox of visibility versus imperceptibility, that is, divine disclosure versus divine hiddenness. The coming of Jesus was itself a clear indication that God was poised to intervene dramatically in the affairs of humanity. And yet that intervention is not always immediately visible to the naked eye. That is why, on the one hand, Jesus challenges his hearers to interpret the *kairos* (12:56), while, on the other hand, the kingdom quietly does its work well beneath the surface, like a buried mustard seed or leaven mixed into dough (13:18–21), quite apart from human reception. In this respect, Jesus reasserts the kingdom as a mystery which many though 'looking . . . may not perceive' (8:10). Access to this mystery is finally granted on the basis of divine election, as was the case for Daniel.

Closely related to the modality of the kingdom's revelation is the issue of time. As it turns out, in the kingdom time is both durative (provoking a gradual response like the growth of a mustard seed or the slow spread of leaven in a batch of dough) and punctiliar (demanding an immediate decision in the here and now). Jesus warns his hearers that they should '*on the way* make an effort to settle the case' (12:58), before it is too late. Before anyone knows it, he warns again with the same urgency, the three-year probationary period will have expired and then the fig tree will be cut down (13:6–9). The kingdom demands immediate response with not a moment to waste. And yet, by the same token, the kingdom growth will continue into the indeterminate future, until its function as the hosting platform for the nations is fulfilled, until the dough of the kingdom is finally ready to be enjoyed as bread.

Finally, the kingdom triggers both rejoicing and humiliation (13:17), depending on one's response to it. There will be those who, like the bent-over woman, will respond to Jesus' call (13:12), receive his healing and stand up straight before God in worship. Yet at the very same time, Israel's rulers are being brought down, much as Mary had foreseen (1:52). So too will be those who, so busy judging the less fortunate (13:1–5), are unable to recognize their own guilt before God. In this respect, Luke presents Jesus as the most divisive figure the world will ever know: 'Do you think that I have come to bring peace to the earth? No, I tell you, but rather division!' (12:51). If people resist Jesus, this is no cause for doubt but is in keeping with the inherently controversial nature of the kingdom.

I. Eschatological warnings (13:22–35)

Context
Having laid emphasis on the nearness of the kingdom (12:49 – 13:21), Luke now revisits the kingdom's paradoxical nature with special emphasis on the great reversal to come. At the judgment, those who thought themselves likely candidates for the kingdom will prove to be disqualified, while those normally considered the last will be first (13:30). For this very reason, Jesus exhorts his hearers not only to struggle their way into the master's house (13:25) but also to allow themselves to be gathered in by Jesus, all the while rejecting the temptation of trusting in Jerusalem or its centrepiece, the Herodian temple (13:34–35). In order to stem any false hopes, Jesus makes clear that entrance into the master's house is not a matter of physical proximity to himself. Indeed, while those from the far reaches of the earth would sit down at the great banquet table, many of the locals who might otherwise pride themselves on their familiarity with Jesus would be excluded (13:24–30). This arresting announcement lays the groundwork for further teachings on the messianic banquet (14:1–24) as well as on Jesus' identity as the true tower-builder (14:28–30).

Comment
i. The narrow gate (13:22–30)
22. According to Luke 9:6, the Twelve had executed their short-term mission (9:1–6) among the villages (*kata kōmas*). Now Jesus undertakes a similar journey (perhaps among some of the same villages) while this time including larger population centres, the 'towns' (*poleis*). Though he had decisively set his face towards

Jerusalem (9:51), his journey proves to be neither the quickest nor the most direct: side excursions were apparently justified for the purpose of *teaching as he made his way to Jerusalem*. Whatever the purpose of this preaching campaign, it would set a precedent for the early church's missionary movement among the towns and villages of the Mediterranean world (Acts 8:25, 40; 14:6; 16:4; 26:11).

23. No doubt Jesus commended his own teaching as the source of Israel's salvation. Otherwise, it would be hard to explain *someone* in the crowd asking, *Lord, will only a few be saved?* [109] Whether the impetus for this question was the stringency of Jesus' ethical demands or his stern warnings to those who might have ordinarily expected to be *saved*, one can only guess. In any case, the anonymous enquirer likely expects that the question will be answered in the affirmative.

24. Yet Jesus fails to answer, at least directly. As if averse to speculating on the fate of third parties, he confronts his entire audience by insisting that they *strive [agōnizesthe] to enter through the narrow door*. The main verb is an imperative form of *agōnizomai*, a term with connotations of athleticism, sometimes meaning 'to contend for a prize esp. in the public games', and more broadly 'to struggle' (as the NEB has it here) or 'to exert oneself' (LSJ, p. 18). Quite clearly, 'easy believism' has no place in Luke's theology.

The focal point of such exertions is hoped-for entrance through *the narrow door (thyra)*, which *many . . . will try to enter and will not be able.* That Jesus should direct his hearers to a *narrow (stenēs)* door associates this entrance with tribulation (cf. Luke 21:23; Acts 8:1; 11:19; 14:22; 20:23).[110] And that Jesus should direct his hearers to '*the* narrow door' suggests the availability of one or more wider doors. If we are to be guided by the parallel to Luke 13:24 at Matthew 7:13,

---

109. The question was a standard one in Judaism, as in m. Sanh. 10:1; for further references, see Marshall, p. 564.

110. In this connection, Acts 14:22b ('It is through many *persecutions* [*thlipseōn*] that we must enter the kingdom of God') is particularly instructive, since *thlipsis* denotes both constraint and persecution. See Mattill, 'Tribulation', esp. p. 532.

which contrasts the narrow, life-giving gate (*pylē*) with the wide gate of destruction, then Jesus' warning locates itself squarely in the genre of the 'two ways' tradition (Deut. 30:19; Ps. 1; Jer. 21:8; Sir. 21:11–14; 2 Esd. 7:6–14; T. Ash. 1:3, 5; 1QS III, 20–21), offering a way of life leading to the kingdom and, implicitly here, a way of death.[111] Since Luke's Jesus has already – through veiled terms – identified his movement with reconstituted sacred space, this narrow door may also be pitting itself against the massive golden double doors of the inner gate leading to the sanctuary in Herod's temple (Josephus, *J.W.* 5.211).[112] Strikingly, it is not that the *many* are unconcerned to enter through the narrower gate, but rather that their best efforts to enter will prove in vain. The contrast, then, is not between the religious and the irreligious but between two different subcategories of the former.

25. The reappearance of *the owner of the house* (*oikodespotēs*), recognizable from 12:39, invites comparisons with the parable of 12:35–40. The similarities and differences are instructive. As for the key points of comparison, both parables involve a crucial entrance door and a celebratory meal. The principal contrast is twofold: whereas in 12:35–40 the servants open the door for the master of the house, in 13:25 it is the master who plays gatekeeper to the members of Jesus' audience. Moreover, here the house owner *has got up* (*egerthē*), which, not insignificantly, may be equally translated 'has been raised'. The coded implication is that once Jesus is resurrected as rightful owner of the house (cf. Heb. 3:3), he will *shut the door*, leaving some if not all of Jesus' immediate hearers standing *outside* (*exō*), not unlike Jesus' mother and brothers who were standing outside (8:20) – all in contrast to those who do the will of God (8:21). At that time, too, Jesus promises, these same excluded will *knock at the door, saying, 'Lord, open to us'*. In response, Jesus continues, the risen owner will declare, *I do not know where you come from*, presenting an interesting difference from the Matthean parallel (7:23): 'I never knew *you*'

---

111. Judaism regularly thought of the kingdom as having a gated entrance. See Rev. 22:14; 4 Ezra 7:1–16; Pesiq. Rab. 179b; Herm. Sim. 9.12.5.

112. See Knowles, 'Archaeological Evidence', pp. 200–201.

(emphasis added).[113] Whereas Matthew 7:23 focuses on the necessity of Jesus' personal knowledge of the elect, Luke emphasizes the importance of Jesus recognizing their origins, including presumably their animating agency (demonic or otherwise) and motivations.

26–27. At this moment, these same rejected persons will object that they had eaten and drunk with the lord of the house, just as, for example, certain Pharisees had dined with Jesus (7:36–50; 11:37–54).[114] They did so even while Jesus *taught in our streets* (*plateiais*). These of course are the same *streets* (*plateiai*) in which the seventy-two were instructed to pronounce curses on the uncongenial (10:10). Unfazed by such protests, however, the owner of the house simply repeats himself (*I do not know where you come from*) but this time also appends a dismissal: *go away from me, all you evildoers!* Notably, the imperative (*go away, apostēte*) is a form of *aphistēmi*, a verb which has already been used in connection with Satan's departure from Jesus after the temptation (4:13), and with those 'seed' who, planted on shallow soil, fall away (8:13).

28. The adverb *ekei* ('there, in that place') in the first position, left untranslated by the NRSV, emphasizes the close time–space connection between the dismissal of the hapless aspirants and their *weeping and gnashing of teeth*.[115] Such distress has to do with the disappointing fact that *you* will *see Abraham and Isaac and Jacob and all the prophets in the kingdom of God, and you yourselves thrown out*. The contrast is stark. On the one side, the three great patriarchs along with the prophets will be included in the kingdom of God. On the other side, the very members of Jesus' audience will be banished outside (*exō*).

---

113. Certain important manuscripts of Matthew have *hymas* ('you') instead of *pothen este* ('where you are from'). The decision is difficult, but the evidence finally supports the former.

114. Writing for a church-based audience, Luke's parable may be intended to warn believers against putting false confidence in their participation in the Lord's Supper.

115. The phrase, occurring only here in Luke, is much preferred by Matthew, where it occurs six times (Matt. 8:12; 13:42, 50; 22:13; 24:51; 25:30).

29. The anticipated pilgrimage of the Gentiles to Zion is an important component of Jewish eschatology.[116] By envisioning individuals coming from all four directions by name, Jesus not only clarifies that he knows where they are from (in contrast to vv. 25 and 27) but is also obliquely setting the parable within this end-time scenario. With the four directions named one by one, the global end-time gathering is shown to be comprehensive in scope. And what will such pilgrims do but *eat in the kingdom of God*, much as Jesus and his disciples have been eating (5:27–32; 7:36–50; 9:10–17; 11:37–52). The meal in view is the messianic feast (Isa. 25:6–8).

30. If Jesus' hearers are surprised that those at the door have been turned away, they should not be. Paradoxically, some *are last who will be first, and some are first who will be last.* In other words, those who might be considered most likely to inherit the kingdom will be barred, while those typically deemed least likely, including Gentiles such as the queen of the 'South' (11:31), will sit alongside the luminaries of Judaism.

ii. Jesus mourns over Jerusalem (13:31–35)

31. Though the Evangelist's portrait of the Pharisees is largely negative, it is not uniformly so. In this case, certain sympathizing *Pharisees came* to him with an urgent warning. The NRSV's *Get away from here (exelthē kai poreuou enteuthen)* might alternatively be translated 'Get up and go!' Jesus must leave, because word was out that Herod Antipas, tetrarch of Galilee and Perea, had had enough of Jesus' messianic posturing – his miracles, exorcisms and teachings – and was seeking to do with him what he had already done with John (3:19–20; 9:9). Jesus' safest course was to cut short his trip to Jerusalem (v. 22) and exit safely out of Herod's jurisdiction.

32. Unmoved by the well-intentioned advice, Jesus instructs the Pharisees to inform *that fox* that he has no intention of changing course. In antiquity, scavenging foxes were symbols of cunning and opportunism; in Jeremiah, they represent Judea's corrupt

---

116. See Isa. 2:3; 60:5–14; 66:18–20; Jer. 3:17; Mic. 7:12, 17; Hag. 2:7; Zech. 8:21–23; 14:16.

leaders.[117] Earlier in the story, when Jesus sent emissaries back to a puzzled John the Baptizer, he focused on his messianic activities (7:22–23). Here he does much the same, but this time with the stated intention of completing those activities uninterrupted *today and tomorrow*. Moreover, on the third day *I finish my work* (*teleioumai*), or perhaps more accurately if not more vaguely, 'I will complete', or 'I will attain my end' (JB), or even 'I shall be perfected' (KJV).[118] The third day on which Jesus 'completes' may be the day of Jesus' death (cf. John 19:28–30; Wis. 4:13–14) or more likely the resurrection day, the day on which Jesus will not just complete his work but bring all things to their fulfilment in himself (Luke 24:44; cf. Eph. 1:9–10, 15–20; Col. 1:15–20).

33. In remarking on his obligation to continue his journey to Jerusalem, Jesus employs the language of divine purpose (*dei*, 'it is necessary').[119] The verse not only constitutes Jesus' first clear (albeit still implicit) self-identification as a prophet; it also serves to group his death with the demise of other righteous prophets before him. As a rule, according to Jesus (uniquely so in the Jewish literature), prophetic martyrdoms *must* occur within Jerusalem. Whether that curious 'rule' was governed by some principle of irony, or a larger redemptive-historical logic, or something else altogether, is unclear.[120] It is possible that because Isaac's near death on Mount Moriah (Gen. 22) was thought to have occurred in a space that later became the temple space within Jerusalem, and because this self-offering was an obedience to death, subsequent martyrdoms taking place in the Holy City (2 Kgs 21:16; 24:4; Jer. 26:20–23; 38:4–6; 2 Chr. 24:20–22) are to be understood as recapitulations of the Aqedah.

---

117. Ancient Hebrew did not distinguish between jackals and foxes; see Song 2:15; Jer. 10:22; 14:6; 49:33; 51:37; Ezek. 13:4.
118. Tannehill (*Narrative Unity*, p. 154) maintains that Jesus is speaking about the completion of his journey to Jerusalem, but this fails to do justice to the deep scriptural resonances of the phrase *third day*.
119. On *dei*, see commentary on 2:48–49.
120. Green (p. 537) seeks to solve the puzzle of this saying by claiming that Jerusalem 'stands as a cipher for Israel as a whole', but there is no evidence to this effect.

34. Pivoting with an apostrophe (a rhetorical gesture in which a speaker addresses a third party, present or absent, animate or inanimate), Jesus picks up a new stream of thought. While the Pharisees warn Jesus out of a concern for his safety (v. 31), he is more concerned about the sacred city's welfare, especially given its recalcitrance, borne out by the city's refusal to accept Jesus himself. Accordingly, he takes up a lament for Jerusalem and its inhabitants, not unlike the one which he will invite on the way to his death (23:28–32). Here he touches on not just the city's long history of violence against God's messengers, but also Jesus' own strong desire *to gather your children together* (*episynaxai ta tekna sou*). The language of assembly is not incidental. Whereas Jesus had already been successfully gathering (*episynaxtheisōn*) the multitudes (12:1), and this gathering is likely related to the divine purpose of gathering the tribes from exile (Pss 106:47; 147:2; Isa. 27:12), the culmination of this redemptive-historical project and the core of Jesus' longing involves Jerusalem. This background may also explain the image of a *hen*, or more accurately and more generically a bird (*ornis*), taking its brood under its wings: it is precisely in Moses' ominous prediction of exile that he insists that Yahweh, like a vulture, has spread its wings over disobedient Israel while in the desert (Deut. 32:11).

35. In the Greek, Jesus prefaces his concluding statement with the same interjective *idou* ('behold') that introduced his message for Herod a few verses earlier (v. 32): *See [idou], your house is left [aphietai] to you.* The repeated use of the term suggests a structural comparison between verse 32 and verse 35. If Jesus offered his exorcisms and healings as a sign of the kingdom to Herod, then the divine abandonment of the house (implied by the divine passive *aphietai* and reminiscent of Jer. 12:1–7) likewise presents itself as a kind of kingdom sign. Such abandonment seems to be already underway in the invisible realm (11:14–26), only soon to be more fully realized in the temple action (19:45–48) and in the destruction of the temple (21:5–36). Exactly how the solemn declaration of verse 35a relates to the prediction in verse 35b (*And I tell you, you will not see me until the time comes when you say, 'Blessed is the one who comes in the name of the Lord'*) is not patently clear. Given that the crowds will indeed chant these words, drawn from Psalm 118:26, during Jesus' triumphal entry (Luke 19:38a), one surmises that verse 35b relates to verse 35a in two respects. On one level, if Jesus' prophetic prediction regarding the people's words (the *you* of v. 35 referring back to the 'children' of Jerusalem in v. 34) proves true, which it will in Luke 19:38a, this will serve to confirm Jesus' status as prophet and therefore the truthfulness of his statement regarding the divine abandonment of the temple. On another level, God's rejection of the temple will be sealed by the temple leadership's glaring failure to receive Jesus in the midst of those chanted strains of Psalm 118 (19:38–40) – a rejection which in turn will be followed by Jesus' second and final lament over the city (19:41–44). The 'open door that Jesus mentioned in the previous parable is closing to this generation'.[121]

Theology
In this passage, Jesus predicts that many who had witnessed his day-to-day ministry would one day presume to receive a 'free pass' to the kingdom, simply by virtue of having somehow been tied in with Jesus. Such presumptions, Jesus warns, will prove badly mistaken. At the same time, Jesus predicts that Jerusalem's overall resistance to his ministry – of a piece with the city's historic resistance to the prophets – will likewise be met with punishment. This much will become clear on the destruction of the temple. If familiarity breeds contempt, the principle certainly applies to Jesus' own generation. But in this case, too, such easy familiarity also gives way to self-deception.

On the one hand, Luke includes these teachings of Jesus in his story in order to explain why so many in Israel had failed to respond appropriately to the Messiah in their midst. On the other hand, the unmistakeable pastoral point for Luke's readers is this: if such self-deception could overtake so many in Israel, there is no inherent reason why Jesus' own disciples could not fall into the same trap. For the Evangelist, discipleship paradoxically involves both an active striving to enter the kingdom and a passive willingness to be gathered up by the messianic hen. If Jesus' disciples do not find this

---

121. Bock, p. 1243.

holy blend of striving and surrender in their own lives, they perhaps ought to ask themselves whether they are not in fact trusting in some vague and misleading familiarity – either with Jesus or with the trappings of his church. The self-deceived, both in and outside the church, who harbour such vain dependencies will suffer the consequences.

J. Messianic banquet (14:1–24)

Context

Luke 14:1–24 is structured in three parts. The first part (vv. 1–6) thematizes the issue of Sabbath healing; the second (vv. 7–14), humility and honour; the third (vv. 15–20), the messianic banquet. Luke 14:1–6 builds on three previous episodes: an earlier meal scene at a Pharisee's house involving an uninvited visitor (7:36–50); another meal scene at another Pharisee's house focusing on particulars of the law (11:37–54); and a controversial Sabbath-day healing (13:10–17). Next, Jesus' teaching on honour (vv. 7–14) gives concrete expression to the kingdom principle of reversal, which maintains, as we discovered in the very last scene, that the first will be last and the last will be first (13:30). Finally, Jesus' elaboration of the feast in the kingdom of God (14:15) likewise picks up on the previous passage with its mention of the kingdom feast (13:29). Jesus' treatment of the messianic feast is the logical culmination of verses 1–6 and verses 7–14, for it is above all at the great eschatological banquet that God's people will receive Sabbath-day life and be seated around the table according to a strangely reversed hierarchy.

Comment

i. Jesus heals a man of dropsy (14:1–6)

1. If the meal of 11:37–54 leaves off with the Pharisees looking for a chance to 'catch him in something he might say' (v. 54), this meal potentially gives them that sought-after opportunity. In two previous scenes, as mentioned above, Jesus takes a meal in a Pharisee's house (7:36–50; 11:37–54), but this third and final such meal is set at *the house of a leader of the Pharisees*. The rising political importance of Jesus' religious dining partners is no indication that he is gaining favour with the establishment: on the contrary, Luke's

remark that *they were watching him closely* alerts the reader that things
have reached a point where now the Pharisees' top brass are hosting
Jesus on the Sabbath, but only with the specific intention of
catching him out on one or more Sabbath code violations.

2. *Just then* (*idou*) an oedematous (*hydrōpikos*) man appears with
the unstated mission of receiving healing. Though oedema or
dropsy (the swelling of the soft tissue, usually around the hands
and ankles) may not be noticeable in all cases, the present case must
have immediately been conspicuous and therefore severe.[122] The
man stands not behind Jesus, as did the uninvited sinful woman
(7:38), but *in front of* him (*emprosthen autou*). What might this pos-
itional shift mean but that the very same boldness encouraged in
11:5–13 is now playing itself out with increasing effect.

3. Though most translations omit translating the participial
phrase *kai apokritheis* (by contrast, the KJV has 'answering'), the
sense is one of Jesus responding. Of course, he is answering not any
given spoken word but rather the hidden thoughts of *the lawyers and
the Pharisees* (cf. 5:22; 9:47); he does so by taking the offensive in a
kind of cross-examination. Calling for a clear 'Yes' or 'No' vote in
regard to Sabbath healing, Jesus gives an all-but-final opportunity
for those in the room to make a right judgment and break from the
official party line. It is an opportunity they collectively decline.

4. The icy silence of the scribes and Pharisees indicates that they
are not interested in defending their own position, much less
engaging Jesus in debate. Outwardly, they remain non-committal,
even if they have already committed themselves inwardly.
Meanwhile, as for the patient before him, Jesus *took him and healed
him, and sent him away* (*auton kai apelusen*). Judging by the comparison
with 8:38, where Jesus 'sent away' (*apelusen de auton*) the healed
demoniac so that he would share what God had done, this sending
away may be as much a commission as a dismissal.

5–6. Once the formerly oedematous man has left the scene,
Jesus follows up on his question (v. 3) by issuing another question,

---

122. Dropsy refers to a set of symptoms traceable to an assortment of
    ailments, including heart failure, kidney malfunction and malnutrition
    (lack of protein).

one with a patently obvious answer that also resolves the first question. Given a scenario where one's son or even one's ox falls into a well on the Sabbath, Jesus asks, who would not *immediately* pull him out?[123] If the analogy between the man's condition and finding one's family member or animals at the bottom of well holds water, the argument is difficult to resist.[124] As the Evangelist notes, Jesus' interlocutors are not up to the challenge of countering Jesus. Though it is they who have drawn Jesus into rhetorical battle by setting up this Sabbath-day exchange over a meal, it is they who – much to their shame – must for now admit defeat by quiet default.

ii. Honour at the feast (14:7–11)

7. When it came to formal meals, the first-century Hellenistic world attached considerable significance to the guests' seating arrangement, which was as a rule sequenced hierarchically, according to social importance. Those who sat closest to the host held 'the place of honour' (v. 8), while those at the far end of the table held 'the lowest place' (v. 9). When Jesus notices *how the guests chose the places of honour*, he sets out to discourage such one-upmanship through *a parable*. Though, as we shall see, the parable applies to the situation at hand, it does so only indirectly.

8–10. Precisely because Luke classifies the speech of verses 8–11 as parable, the reader should resist the temptation of interpreting Jesus' words as moralizing remarks on the importance of humility, much less as an isolated tip on etiquette. Notably, the repast imagined by the parable is not just any meal but a *wedding banquet*

---

123. Some fairly weighty manuscripts have 'donkey' (*onos*) in place of 'son' (*huios*). Likely mistranscribed through faulty hearing, the more difficult reading of 'son' is to be preferred. The pairing of 'son' and 'ox' likely has to do with the historical Jesus' Aramaic wording which would have included a wordplay: *běra* (son) and *bě'ira* (ox).

124. Members of the Qumran community would have objected to Jesus' premise, since the community rules proscribed pulling an animal out of a pit on a Sabbath (CD XI, 13–17). Rabbinic legislation (Šabb. 128b), preserving the legacy of Pharisaic thought, allowed for animals to be helped in such circumstances.

(*gamos*).[125] Earlier parables have already allegorically represented Jesus as a bridegroom (5:34–35), as well as a 'lord' (*kyrios*) who has gone away to a wedding feast (12:35–40). In both these instances, the wedding imagery serves to paint a picture of the eschatological scenario – that is, the messianic banquet promised in Isaiah 25:6.

Construed with this logic, the inviting host (a certain *someone*, *tinos*) refers not first and foremost to a merely human figure, but to God or, more likely, Jesus the bridegroom/host. Those who have been *invited* (*kekl ēmenos*) have been called by Jesus, whose stated mission is to call (*kaleō*) (5:32).[126] The parable's guests stand for the elect (just as in 13:28–29); the assignment of seats, the final judgment. There is a complicating twist: though the parable's host will have the final say in assigning the lowest place as well as the place of honour, it is presumed that the invited guests have some freedom in choosing their seating (*kataklinō*). As such, the parable retains an already-but-not-yet quality, as the banquet in view seems to have eternal aspects, pertaining to realities on the far side of the general resurrection, as well as temporal aspects, pertaining to earthly realities. This wedding banquet will seemingly be initiated in this age and undergo shifts as it transitions into the age to come.

As we make sense of this paradox, the verb *kataklinō* appears significant, if only because it is used in connection with both the feeding of the five thousand (9:14, 15), which clearly looks ahead to the Last Supper (22:14–20), and the Emmaus road meal (24:30), which clearly looks back to the same meal. On the observation that all three of these meals also retain a paradoxical already-but-not-yet quality, one might propose an interpretation of the passage on two levels. In the original setting, Jesus seems to have presented his parable not only to subvert the rigid social hierarchies reinforced by the highly influential institution of the symposium (a meal coupled with considerable drinking along with philosophical

---

125. The relevance of this point is either missed or denied by commentators; see e.g. Bock, p. 1263; Fitzmyer, p. 1046; Johnson, p. 227.

126. As Marshall (p. 581) notes, *kaleō* 'is a key word which binds the whole of this section together: 14:8, 9, 10, 12, 13, 16, 17, 24'.

discussion or sensuality), but also to discourage the jockeying for social power that was characteristic of such events.[127] On a second level, taking aim at his own post-Easter readers, Luke includes this parable partially in order to raise the same kinds of concerns first raised by Paul (1 Cor. 11:17–34), when he decries the Corinthians' practice of perpetuating social distinctions in their celebration of the Eucharist. Luke's point is that a humble posture in both sacramental and more broadly ecclesial gatherings is fitting both on account of the possibility that on the day of judgment *someone more distinguished than you* (including the likes of the patriarchs mentioned in 13:28!) might – to your shame – bump you from your place, and on account of the possibility that Jesus himself might – to your honour – call you *Friend* and ask you to *move up higher.*

11. The principle (*For all who exalt themselves will be humbled, and those who humble themselves will be exalted*) which summarizes the parable (and is repeated at 18:14) is neither novel nor inconsistent with the Hebrew Scriptures (2 Chr. 7:14; Prov. 18:12; Mic. 6:8). Yet given that this principle is uniquely and decisively actualized through Jesus' coming (1:52–53; 6:20–26), not to mention quintessentially epitomized through the cross, resurrection and ascension, it follows that we are dealing here not simply with a platitude of Jewish wisdom but rather with a promise regarding the eschatological event now already beginning to unfold.

iii. The great feast (14:12–24)

12. Having instructed his fellow guests on how to be good guests (vv. 7–11), Jesus now challenges his host on the kinds of guests one ought to invite to *a luncheon* (*ariston*) or *a dinner* (*deipnon*). The *ariston* was a midday meal, lighter than the *deipnon* – its closest modern-day analogy would perhaps be the business lunch. The *deipnon*, typically held just before sunset or slightly later, was more formal and often involved multiple courses and even entertainment. For all such events, Jesus urges, *do not invite your friends or your brothers*

---

127. On the symposium, see König, *Saints and Symposiasts*, pp. 3–29. On Jesus' meals as a strategy of subversion, see Perrin, *Jesus the Temple*, pp. 170–179.

or your relatives or rich neighbours, lest they should return the favour
with the unfortunate result that this 'might become to you a
recompense' (*genētai antapodoma soi*). Observing how the well-to-do
throw luncheons or dinners only for those in their own tight-knit
social networks, only in turn to be later invited by the same
erstwhile guests, Jesus is criticizing a well-established social convention based on the principle of quid pro quo. Such transactions,
Jesus points out, are an unprofitable zero-sum exchange.

13. In order to break the cultural institution of reciprocity, it
would be necessary for those with means to make a sharp turn
(note the strong adversative *alla, but*) by inviting not their wealthy
contacts and kin but *the poor, the crippled, the lame, and the blind* –
almost certainly to the astonishment and resentment of the former.
The *poor* (*ptōchoi*) in this instance are both the cash poor and by
extension the socially poor.[128] Meanwhile, those who are *crippled*,
lame and *blind* do not so much take their place alongside *the poor*;
rather, they are subcategories of a broader demographic classifiable
as *the poor.*[129] In an economy driven by manual labour, where such
disabilities would directly impact employability, *the crippled, lame* and
blind were ordinarily reduced to begging. Such individuals were not
only among the most marginalized in first-century Roman society
but also precisely those whom Jesus came to redeem (7:22). Because
the kingdom was especially oriented towards the poor (4:18), Jesus
now urges his host to invite those same poor to his next *banquet*
(*dochēn*).

---

128. This precise meaning of 'poor' in Luke has been disputed in modern
     scholarship; see Phillips, 'Wealthy and Poverty'. In the Greek literature
     before Luke, the word *ptōchos* consistently denotes poverty in an
     economic sense, i.e. being reduced to beggary; see Hauck, *TDNT* 6,
     pp. 886–887. At the same time, the weight that Green ('Good News')
     and Beavis ('Marginalized') place on the term's social aspect (i.e.
     poverty as social marginalization) cannot be far off the mark.
129. In his study of these categories, Roth, on the one hand, seems to
     criticize treating *the poor* as an all-embracing term (*Character Types*, p. 17),
     but, on the other hand, cannot help but subsume those with disabilities
     under the same heading.

14. According to Jesus, the one who obeys this teaching will be blessed (*makarios*), for such under-resourced individuals *cannot repay you*. According to Jesus' kingdom economics, it seems, God is 'on the hook' for reimbursing the elect for that which they have paid out in this life – even through the currency of banquets – to the poor. This further implies, on Luke's theology, that human fiscal and social capital, potentially shareable through events such as banquets, is essentially on loan from God. Put differently, in bestowing such social and material benefits on the poor, kingdom participants are essentially lending to God, who will then repay at the resurrection.[130]

15. Picking up on Jesus' makarism (*makarios*, 'blessed'), an anonymous guest (*tis tōn synanakeimenōn*) interrupts him, declaring the blessedness of *anyone who will eat bread in the kingdom of God*. The unprompted benediction is not unlike that spoken by the woman in the crowd in 11:27 ('Blessed is the womb that bore you and the breasts that nursed you!'). If in that scene, Jesus' response (11:28) suggested that the interjection was both formally correct *and* at a deeper level a distortion of his own Beatitudes (6:20–22), here a similar dynamic seems to obtain. On the surface, there is nothing technically inaccurate about the man's statement. Yet Jesus' fuller response (vv. 16–24) will indicate that this joyful interruption belied a misplaced confidence. A crucial yet subtle element is at play: by invoking the common hope of the eschatological banquet in the context of a Pharisaic meal, the fellow guest inevitably aligns the current gathering on the trajectory leading up to the great banquet. But Jesus is about to challenge any presumed continuity between this breaking of bread and the kingdom meal.

16–17. Without designating it as such, the Evangelist now introduces a kingdom parable, pertaining to a certain *someone* (*anthrōpos tis*; cf. 10:30; 15:11; 16:1, 19; 19:12; 20:9) who *gave a great dinner (epoiei deipnon mega)*.[131] It is an abundant meal, to which *many* (*pollous*) are *invited (ekalesen)*, not unlike the banquet which Yahweh

130. See the far-ranging study of Giambrone, *Creditor Christology*.
131. The parallel in Matt. 22:2 has 'wedding banquet' (*gamous*). If (as is likely) Luke is responsible for this change, he might have hoped to

would 'make for all peoples' (Isa. 25:6). The parable's 'certain
someone' may refer to an ideal human figure (as I believe it does)
but it also refers – more basically – to Jesus. Within the Lukan
context, 'many' describes the crowds who follow Jesus (5:15; 14:25).
More immediately the word ties back to the 'many' who, though
standing at the door of the kingdom (13:24), will be bitterly
disappointed. Consistent with these usages, the invited *many*
symbolize the human funnel of Jesus' audiences who receive the
call of God through his invitation to repentance and fellowship. At
the same time, the word of invitation, *Come!*, resonates with
Yahweh's invitation to exiled Israel to participate in a divinely set
feast (Isa. 55:1). This may not be unrelated to the fact that the one
through whom the invitation comes is a *slave* (*doulē*) or a 'servant',
reminiscent here of the Isaianic Servant of Isaiah 53, who justifies
'many' (*pollois*, LXX 53:11).

Not only does the servant instruct his hearers to come, he also
explains *why* they should come: *for everything is ready now*. The not
unreasonable assumption that the adjective *hetoimos* (*ready*) modifies
an unstated *panta* (*everything*) follows both from context and from
the parallel in Matthew 22:4 ('everything is ready', *panta hetoima*). By
the same token, the presence of the phrase *at the time* (*tē hōra*) or 'at
the hour' in the same verse makes it possible that it is not only the
meal that is ready but also the hour, that is, in the sense of being
fulfilled (cf. John 7:6).

18–20. In an unfortunate and unexpected twist, the invitees *all
alike began to make excuses*. Bringing social shame on the host, the
excuses are many and manifold, betraying their hollowness if not
their intentional coordination. Edwards is certainly correct (p. 421)
when he comments that when all three excuses 'are combined –
property, occupation, and family – they comprise the essential
commitments of life', the same idolatrous commitments represented in 9:57–62. At the same time, intimations of Deuteronomy
20:5–7 and 24:5 (where men are exempt from war if they have
recently built a house, planted a vineyard or married) may also be

---

strengthen the comparison between the eschatological banquet
(*deipnon*) and the present meal scene.

discernible. A strong case cannot be made either way, but given my interpretation of the parable of the warring king in nearby Luke 14:31–33 (where I argue that the attacking king is Jesus; see below), a glance at the legal code of Deuteronomy 20:5–7 and 24:5 is probable, hinting ahead of time that a refusal to come to the master's banquet is tantamount to a refusal to enlist in the divine king's holy war.[132]

21. Returning to the master (*kyrios*), the servant reports back on *this* (*tauta*). Enraged, the master urges his servant to seek out a new set of guests by stipulating a new target geography for the invitations as well as a different 'clientele'. First, the envoy is told to hurry into the *streets and lanes of the town* (*tas plataeias kai rhymas tēs poleōs*). The allegory is thinly veiled. Jesus and his disciples have already ministered in the streets (*plataeiai*) (10:10; 13:26); soon the early church will extend its reach into the streets (Acts 5:15) and the lanes (Acts 9:11; 12:10). The principal locus of all this activity in both Luke (Luke 4:31, 43; 5:12; 7:11; 8:1; etc.) and Acts (Acts 4:27; 5:16; 7:58; 8:5, 8–9, 40; etc.) is the *polis*. Second, the servant is sent to summon precisely the same four audiences mentioned in 14:13 (though curiously the order of the 'lame and the blind' is inverted in 14:21). Of course, the same people have also been the focus of Jesus' ministry (7:22). In a stroke, therefore, the parable defines the ministry of Jesus and of the apostolic church as the preliminary stage of a great banquet. The call to repent in view of the kingdom's arrival, issued by both Jesus and his followers, is essentially a call to the messianic supper. The sent servant (*doulē*) is simultaneously Jesus and the apostles, both (arguably) manifestations of the Suffering Servant.

22. The servant had already anticipated the master's request to pursue more guests yet still there is *topos* (*room*), a not uncommon circumlocution for the sacred space (Exod. 15:17; Deut. 12:5, 11; 2 Sam. 7:10; 1 Kgs 8:29; 11:36; 14:21; 2 Kgs 21:4, 7; etc.). Given the master's interest in filling 'my house' (v. 23), and given that the

---

132. *Pace* Pao and Schnabel ('Luke', p. 340), who reject any echoes of Deuteronomy 'since the features of war and king are absent from the parable'.

'house of the Lord' is also a stand-in term for the temple, the phrase *there is still room* must be another way of saying, 'There is still room in the sacred space marked out by the expanded people of God.'

23. Determined that his *house may be filled*, the master repeats the command of verse 21 (*Go out, exelthe*) but this time suggests a more distant destination.[133] Now the servant is not to go into the 'streets and lanes of the town' but the *roads and lanes*. Wherein lies the difference between these two sets of destinations? Whereas the 'street' (*plataeia*) refers to the narrow roadways within the isolated population centre of the city (*tēs poleōs*), likely *the* city, that is, Jerusalem, the term 'road' (*hodos*) pertains to the sprawling pathways that connect cities. And though the NRSV offers the same translation ('lane') for *rhymē* (v. 21) and *phragmos* (v. 23), their nuances differ: the former primarily refers to an alley, the latter to a countryside hedge (BDAG, pp. 737, 865). The second 'going out' (*exelthe*) alluded to in this parable, then, is the going out to the ends of the earth later fulfilled in Acts. The distinction between the two sendings speaks not so much of the mission to the Jews and the mission to the Gentiles, as of the mission in and around Jerusalem and the mission to the populace (Jew and Gentile) in the diaspora, thereby roughly reflecting the two parts of Acts.

24. The text is unclear as to whether the present verse is being spoken by the master within the parable or by Jesus himself. The connective *for* (*gar*) would seem to point to an unbroken continuity with verse 23 and therefore point to the former; meanwhile, the phrase *I tell you* (*hymin*) would point to Jesus, since if the master were addressing the servant, one would expect a singular pronoun. The ambivalence is not only intentional but also in keeping with the two-storey meaning inherent in the parable. On one level, the master of the house is the ideal follower of Jesus who must make up his or her mind to close the door on the first line of invitees in order to make room for the poor. On another and more fundamental level, Jesus is offering a road map for his own ministry, as well as for the ministry of the apostolic church. How the parable's

---

133. Notably, the Spirit fills 'the entire house' when the nations are assembled for Pentecost (Acts 2:2).

hearers might plot themselves and Jesus himself within this parable remains the existential decision demanding resolution.

Theology

Whereas the Pharisees had presumed that their invitation to the messianic feast (14:15) was secure, Jesus undermines such misguided confidence by urging a different set of practices as more reliable indicators of future inheritance. These include not least the celebration of Sabbath-day healings (14:1–6), gravitation towards the lower end of the table (14:7–11) and reaching out to the marginalized of society (14:12–24). Given the rigid divisions between the social classes of the first-century world, it is difficult to overstate the disruptive nature of such teaching. Nevertheless, it is a message which Luke expects to be taken seriously.

In any given society, it is not uncommon to find that socio-economic well-being is loosely or tightly tied to one or more demographic factors (geography, profession, gender, ethnicity, race, family lineage, religious background, etc.). Where such correlations exist, as they did in Jesus' and Luke's world, it is inevitable that any concerted effort on the part of the well-to-do to include the poor must also involve the crossing of various boundaries. Without downplaying such challenges, Jesus envisions an eschatologically minded community where the socially and/or economically powerful ask the less well-to-do to join them for a meal. Such meals are not an end in themselves but the platform for continuing relationship. In other words, the socially powerful must find everyday ways to harness their social resources so as to include and empower the marginalized.

Within the community of Jesus' followers, one very ordinary but highly strategic platform for such inclusion and empowerment is the community meal. Jesus essentially asks: since the poor and disenfranchised believers will be treated as special guests of honour at the messianic banquet, why not create that culture now through your hosting practices? It falls to the church not only to be a window into the inverted hierarchy of the future kingdom but also to be a prophetic challenge to present-day cultures where the socio-economically powerful all too often perpetuate social inequalities by refusing to share their material and social capital.

K. The cost of discipleship (14:25–35)

Context

From Jesus' parable of the great banquet (14:15–24), Luke's readers have gathered that the kingdom of God is a highly inclusive space. True as this may be, the present passage now seems to indicate just the opposite. This is the nature of the great paradox. On the one hand, one and all are invited to the messianic table. On the other hand, before the crowds fully commit themselves to following Jesus, he invites them to count the cost. Such an invitation comes in the form of three parables: one relating to an unfinished tower; the second, relating to a war; the third, having to do with salt. So far as these parables are concerned, as was the case in the parable of the sower, not everyone would have ears to hear (14:35; cf. 8:8).

Comment

25. The *large* or many (*polloi*) *crowds* that journey with Jesus are inevitably linked with the 'many' (*pollous*) invited to the great banquet (v. 16). That Jesus *turned* (*strapheis*) to speak to the same crowds is reason to believe that he had been at the front end of the human parade, walking ahead of the masses as they followed along. Before the crowds continued any further, they would need to hear his stark terms of discipleship. While it is true that Jesus has graciously invited one and all to his feast (vv. 15–24), it is equally true that participation in this event is not without its own conditions.

26–27. Verses 26 and 27 end with the same apodosis (the 'then' clause in an 'if . . . then' statement): *cannot be my disciple*. As such, the two verses together spell out, in negative terms, two necessary conditions for following Jesus. The first condition (v. 26) bears on one's closest family relations; the second (v. 27), on one's willingness to *carry the cross*. In the world of the Ancient Near East, family ties were the most foundational of all bonds. And so Jesus could not have issued a more iconoclastic demand: that his followers *hate father and mother, wife and children, brothers and sisters*. Indeed, he continues, his would-be follower must hate *even life itself* (*tēn psychēn heautou*), or 'even their own life' (NIV).

Such words are not without difficulty. How is it possible, it may be asked, that Jesus reaffirms Torah's command to love others (Luke 10:27–28) while also enjoining hatred towards one's kin as a condition for discipleship? Towards resolving this tension, some maintain that Jesus' speech is hyperbolic. On this reading, Jesus is not intending to be taken literally but rather is enjoining a love so profound that even the strongest of one's earthly attachments amounts to hatred by comparison. Against this 'flattening out' approach, it may be proposed that Jesus is in fact commanding a hatred of sorts. But such a hatred is not a burning disdain but an act of the will – an intentional disowning of one's kith and kin in order that one might find one's proper place in a newly reconstituted family (2:49; 8:21; 9:59–60; 11:2, 27–28; 12:52–55; 21:16). Following Jesus means giving him absolute primacy in all areas of life.

Luke's Jesus has already twice predicted his death (9:21–22, 43–45) and that prediction will be fulfilled through Roman crucifixion. As we shall see, for Jesus as for many victims of crucifixion, carrying the cross will be part of the punishment (23:26–31). For this reason, it is Jesus himself, as the cross-carrying crucified one, who gives shape and definition to what he means when he demands that his followers *carry the cross and follow me*, as Simon of Cyrene quite literally would do (23:26). In this light, to carry the cross is to share in Jesus' physical and emotional suffering, his social shame and his agenda of subjugating one's entire being – goals, aspirations and livelihood – to the demands of the kingdom. Thus Jesus' requirement that his followers carry the cross fills out what he means by hating *even life itself* (v. 26).

28–30. The remainder of the section consists of several brief parables setting out two hypothetical scenarios: the first of these concerns a venture in tower-building (vv. 28–30); the second, a king preparing to go to war (vv. 31–32). While the majority of interpreters understand the two parables as a 'what if . . . ?' thought experiment in which aspiring disciples are invited to fancy themselves as tower-builders or warring kings, this commentary regards this approach as roughly correct so far as it goes but insufficient.[134] In my

---

134. See fuller discussion in Perrin, *Jesus the Priest*, pp. 120–122.

judgment, the parables are not *primarily* about Jesus' hearers considering the cost of discipleship but about Jesus himself counting the cost of undertaking his ministry. The Christological thrust of the parables does not cancel out the necessity of human cost-counting but rather provides its basis.

The first line of evidence for this reading is simply this: wherever else a parable is introduced with the phrase 'Who among you' (*tis ex hymōn*), the lens is consistently focused on God or Jesus.[135] In this connection, so much interpretation of the parable of the tower-builder gets off on the wrong foot by failing to wrestle with the question as to why Jesus would mentally summon the extraordinary task of building a *tower*? Israel's most familiar 'tower' in that day was of course that of the temple; the most famous tower-builders were Herod and his successors, who made a decades-long project out of refurbishing the temple.[136] Often suspending the project for years at a time due to lack of funds and inaccurate projections, the Herodian rulers likely incurred the ridicule of the populace, not unlike the parabolic tower-builder who is also met with *ridicule* (*empaizen*; v. 29).[137] With this background in mind, one cannot avoid the conclusion that Jesus, having recently denigrated Herod as 'that

---

135. Luke 11:5; 15:4; 17:7; as pointed out by Fletcher-Louis ('Priestly War Party', pp. 127–128), among others.

136. A close co-identification between tower and temple, inspired by Isa. 5, is readily found in the primary Jewish (e.g. 4Q500; Sib. Or. 5:414–433) and Christian literature (Matt. 21:33; Mark 12:1; Herm. Sim. 8.2; 9.3–31; Herm. Vis. 3.2.4–3.7.6). The temple–tower connection might have been further supported by the actual architecture of the Herodian temple, which retained the tower of the fortress of Antonia on the north-west corner.

137. Herod the Great (73–4 BC) initiated the temple project in 20 BC. While the initial phase of the project proceeded quickly, the construction of the courts and outer buildings under successive 'Herods' took the better part of eighty years, finally being completed during the procuratorship of Albinus (AD 62–64); cf. John 2:20. For details, see Fletcher-Louis, 'Priestly War Party', pp. 134–135. See also Netzer, *Architecture*, pp. 137–178.

fox' (13:32), is now beginning to poke fun at Herod's never-ending tower project.

At the same time, it bears mentioning that in the Gospel tradition Jesus is presented not just as the true king of the Jews, and therefore as the photographic negative of each 'King Herod' (Matt. 2:1–2 [Herod the Great]; Mark 6:14 [Herod Antipas]; Acts 12:1 [Herod Agrippa]), but also as a kind of messianic tower-builder.[138] After all, more than once Jesus lays implicit claim to the role of messianic temple-builder (Luke 6:46–49; 19:45–47; 20:9–18; cf. John 2:19). This role is not unrelated to the otherwise inexplicable observation that both the tower-builder and the warring king 'first sat down' (*prōton kathisas* [tower-builder] . . . *kathisas prōton* [king]) (vv. 28, 31) before undertaking their contemplated task. Perhaps not coincidentally, Jesus himself twice sits down in anticipation of two separate ministries in the Luke–Acts narrative: first, at the inauguration of his earthly ministry (*ekathisen* [Luke 4:20]) and then at the inauguration of his session in the ascended state (*kathisai* [Acts 2:34]). If Jesus the king declares his holy war in Luke 4, he initiates the building out of his temple in Acts 2.

In addition, the two parables highlight the similarities and differences between Jesus and his Herodian counterparts – with rich theological implications. For its part, the Herodian dynasty laid the foundation for the temple, struggled to bring the project to completion and – for all we know – opened themselves up to ridicule behind closed doors. Yet Jesus also laid the foundation of a temple, appeared to have failed and was mocked accordingly (18:32; 22:63; 23:11). If both the Herodian line and Jesus laid the foundations for their respective temples, and if both were mocked for failing to complete their projects, Jesus' mockers (18:32; 22:63; 23:11) will finally be silenced by the resurrection.

31. Jesus is not just a builder; he is also a king going to war. Recall that earlier Jesus had gathered 'thousands' to himself (12:1). But now by issuing these demands of discipleship he anticipates

---

138. As Wright (*Victory of God*, p. 205) crisply puts it, 'the Temple-builder was the true king, and vice versa'.

that his force will be greatly reduced. For this reason he says, *what king, going out to wage war against another king, will not sit down first and consider whether he is able with ten thousand to oppose the one who comes against him with twenty thousand?* The phrasing invokes Gideon, who at God's instruction pared down his army by twenty-two thousand to ten thousand by dismissing the timid (Judg. 7:3). And if one legitimate answer to Jesus' question (*what king . . . ?*) is Gideon, then the problem with an army of ten thousand was that such a force was not too small but rather too large (cf. Judg. 7:4–23)! In the vein of Gideon's against-all-odds victory, then, Jesus seeks to assure his followers that the imminent dwindling of his following will be an early sign not of defeat but of victory. Knowing that his hard teachings will cause him to lose support in numbers, the priestly warrior-king has already counted the cost ahead of time.

32. Despite the assurance of ultimate victory, this same king cannot – in the short run anyway – oppose the numerical strength of the opposing king, perhaps representing the whole operative system under Herod. Accordingly, *he sends a delegation and asks for the terms of peace.* Such terms are presented in so many words in Luke 19, when having sent his disciples as envoys ahead to Jerusalem, Jesus himself draws near to shouts of '*Peace* in heaven and glory in the highest heaven!' (19:38b), and laments, 'If you, even you, had only recognized on this day the things that make for *peace*! But now they are hidden from your eyes' (19:42; emphasis added). One day, however, the parable also predicts, the tables will be turned and it will be the very same people who rejected the earthly Jesus who will play the part of the parable's outmatched king.

33. In view of the cost that Jesus has counted, and in view of the costs required of would-be disciples, it is imperative to *give up all your possessions.* Apart from that divestiture, Jesus, warns, *none of you can become my disciple.* Jesus' disciples must relinquish that which holds them back.

34–35a. While these verses have been variously interpreted, I have argued elsewhere that the salt in question here is the 'salt of the covenant' (cf. Num. 18:8–19; 2 Chr. 13:5), which must pass through the fire, symbolizing the eternal covenant perpetuated by the community of priests operating under Jesus' new hierocracy

and anticipating persecution to come.[139] Salt must be *good* in the face
of such opposition because the disciples are called to 'do good' to
their enemies (6:27, 33, 35).

Through the flames of such opposition Jesus' would-be 'priests'
would either solidify their place in the eternal covenant or be
'thrown away'. The salt is thrown away because it is *fit neither for the
soil* [*gēn*] *nor for the manure heap* [*koprian*] (v. 35a) – a difficult phrase to
make sense of. In my judgment the two terms refer back to the
'soil' (*gē*) and 'manure' (*kopria*) of 13:7–8, materials which, as we
recall, were metaphorically brought to bear on the struggling fig
tree of the temple. This implies that those who reject the covenant
of salt have not only opted out of Jesus' mission to renew the
temple but also sealed their own excommunication from the Jesus
community. In sum, whatever renunciations Jesus requires, in
terms of either social status (taking up one's cross) or possessions
(giving up one's possessions), perseverance is paramount.

35b. Repeating the same summons issued on the heels of the
parable of the sower (8:8b), Jesus invites only those with *ears to hear*
to *listen*. And just as in 8:8b (see commentary above), to *listen* is to
listen in the sense of obeying. Though all of Jesus' teachings are
meant to be obeyed, Jesus knows full well that this especially hard
instruction will be unpalatable to many. It would be only those
with *ears to hear*, one and the same as the 'good soil' of Luke 8,
unencumbered by the snares of idolatrous commitments, who
would respond positively. Such a response is wise because there is
certainty not in human calculation but in Jesus' having sat down
and counted the cost ahead of time.

Theology
Building on the previous passages, Luke 4:25–35 embraces one of
the paradoxes – if not *the* paradox – of the kingdom of God: its
gracious yet conditional nature. On the one side, the kingdom is a
banquet to which both the high and the low of society have been

---

139. Likewise Minear ('Salt', p. 36), who maintains that 'the metaphor has
    an ominous overtone . . . those designated as salt are engaged in a task
    that leads inevitably to violent rejection'.

invited. On the other side, Jesus insists that his followers hate their closest personal relationships and pick up their own cross of shame. No ifs, ands or buts: discipleship on any other terms is no discipleship at all. Herein lies the tension: Jesus' kingdom is characterized by open-invitation banqueting *and* stringent cross-carrying. The invitation is free, but it comes with a mission attached.

In this passage, this mission is represented by the metaphors of building and war. Though King Herod's administration and the politically self-interested high priesthood will get the better of Jesus in the short run, in the long run all the earthly powers will yield the stage to a new war and a new temple-building project instigated by the Risen Lord. In short, Luke reminds his readers that the church must be engaged in both a holy war and a holy building project. (His text is not the only one to do so; Ephesians also develops both concepts, Eph 2:19–22; 6:10–20.) The metaphors of holy war and temple-building create an important tension in the church's conception of its task. So long as the church is faithful to its mission, that mission will be inherently constructive *and* conflictual. Yet in all its endeavours, the church must remain focused on the true tower and the true battle: when the church gets caught up in the wrong building projects or fighting the wrong battles, it has already drifted from its mission.

L. Parables of lostness (15:1–32)

Context

Engaging an audience steeped in Jewish eschatological expectation, Luke has devoted attention (14:1–24) to redefining the much-anticipated messianic meal – not as a distantly future and abstract hope but as a reality that was already taking shape around Jesus in the form of 'mini messianic meals'. When Luke recounts Jesus hosting such meals over the course of his ministry, the Evangelist consistently drops hints of their social diversity. More so than the other Gospel writers, Luke is determined to illustrate and justify Jesus' inclusive – not to mention controversial – dining practices.

Entering Luke 15, we find that the lingering controversy over Jesus' dining partners is now once again resurfacing among the religious leaders (15:2). Against this backdrop, the three parables of

Luke 15 together form a triadic response to such misguided misgivings. Towards driving his point home within these parables, Jesus brings together themes of exile (lostness), recovery ('found-ness'), repentance and joy. As Luke presents it, Jesus' meals with disreputable 'sinners', as controversial as they may have been, were not just an ad hoc celebration of return from exile and repentance but also a matter of divine obligation.

Comment
i. Parable of the lost sheep (15:1–7)

1–2. Not for the first time (5:27–39; 7:29, 34; cf. 3:12), the *Pharisees and the scribes* are vexed because *all the tax-collectors and sinners were coming near to listen to him*.[140] Clearly, Jesus' continuing fellowship with such unsavoury individuals remains a preoccupation for his opponents. As the one who *welcomes sinners and eats with them,* Jesus has remained unswerving in his dining practices – to their dismay. Nevertheless, unlike the religious leaders, Jesus' improbable adherents are positioning themselves to hear (*akouein*) Jesus with a view to obeying. At least, this use of *akouein*, along with Luke's earlier uses of the same verb (8:8; 11:31), hints at such obedience. In fact, in retrospect, the tax collectors and sinners in view here are the fulfilment of Jesus' recently expressed wish that those with ears hear (14:35b). Nor is it insignificant that the verb of motion (*engizontes*) predicated of these hearers is also applied to the priests' approach for cultic service (Exod. 19:22; 34:30; Lev. 10:3); in the more immediate narrative of the so-called 'prodigal son', it applies to the wayward son who draws near home (15:25).[141] Luke's purpose in deploying this verb may well be an attempt to affirm that repentance is the necessary and sufficient condition for service in the newly emerging priesthood.

---

140. For more on 'tax-collectors' and 'sinners', see commentary at 5:27–28 and 5:31–32.

141. The double occurrence of 'come near' (15:1, 25) forms an *inclusio*, confirming that the prodigal son and the sinners are mutually interpretative.

3-4. The present parable sets out to underscore the importance of every last sheep, *especially* those who have wandered from the fold (cf. Ps. 119:3; Isa. 53:6).[142] That a first-century shepherd would generally be willing to risk ninety-nine sheep for the sake of recovering one lost one is not empirically certain, but to do so was probably a low-risk venture, especially if other herders were present to lend a watchful eye.[143] Nor is the number itself insignificant, since one hundred is not just a number of fullness but also the size of Gideon's force as he prepared to attack (Judg. 7:19).[144] The risk of having permanently lost even one of these hundred sheep demanded swift response, even if this posed a slight risk to the larger group. That the flock was *in the wilderness* reminds the reader of Moses' herding in the desert both actual sheep (Exod. 3:1-4) and the sheep of God's people (Ps. 78:52) ultimately under Yahweh's shepherding guidance. More fundamentally, the lost sheep in the desert may be doing double duty as a metaphor for Israel scattered by exile (Ezek. 34:11-16). Because the eschatological David tasked with restoring Israel was thought to be one and the same as the Messiah, it was natural that the image of a shepherd was closely tied to the Messiah (4 Ezra 2:34; Pss Sol. 17:40). On a redemptive-historical level, then, the parable speaks of Jesus' role as the new Moses and the new Davidic shepherd entrusted with gathering every last member of the elect. On a more basic and pastoral level, the parable speaks of the necessity of God's shepherd untiringly pursuing *the one that is lost until he finds it.*

5-6. If the average sheep weighs between 100 and 200 pounds, hoisting even a small lost sheep on the shoulders is no small feat. Yet in antiquity, this was a typical means for transporting individual sheep.[145] That the imaginary shepherd in this parable *lays it on his shoulders* might possibly carry atoning significance, insofar as

---

142. In the Matthean parallel (Matt. 18:12-14), the sheep strays (*planēthē*; v. 12); in Luke, the sheep is lost (*apolesas*).

143. Bailey, *Finding the Lost*, p. 72.

144. Allusions to Gideon can be found in the immediately preceding pericopae; see commentary on 14:31-32.

145. The historical evidence for this is substantial; see Fitzmyer, p. 107.

the officiating high priest was to bear the names of the tribes on his shoulders (Exod. 28:9–12).[146] The sheep-owner *rejoices* and calls for *friends and neighbours* to rejoice along with him. The same joy distinguishes the messianic age (6:23; 10:20) and this also provides the explanation for Jesus' celebratory meals with the socially untouchable. The shepherd and his guests rejoice because what was *lost* has been *found*. So it is with Jesus and his friends and neighbours, that is, the followers in his movement.

7. Jesus interprets his parable by identifying the single lost sheep as a *sinner* (*harmatalos*); the ninety-nine sheep left behind, as *righteous people who need no repentance*. When the former *repents*, the event garners more *joy* than the sheer existence of a much larger population not needing repentance. The joy is finally God's joy, but also the Messiah's. Whether the ninety-nine sheep merely perceive themselves as not needing repentance or actually do not need repentance in the sight of God is a debated issue.[147] It seems that the ninety-nine are in fact the righteous who have already repented and are in good standing with their shepherd.

ii. Parable of the lost coin (15:8–10)

8. Whereas the parable of the lost sheep (15:4–7) featured 'a certain man' (*tis anthrōpos*; 15:4), this parable, the so-called parable of the lost coin, tells of 'a certain woman' (*tis gynē*). Again, Luke's characteristic pairing of gender across two related passages not only serves to relate the teaching to men *and* women, but also hints at the Adamic image of God, in which male and female are combined. The woman has lost a silver coin (*drachmēn*), roughly equivalent to a denarius or a day's wage. That this lost currency constituted a tenth of her holdings, consisting of *ten silver coins*, is apparently relevant to Luke's point. In the first place, her initial possession of *ten* coins anticipates the parable of the *ten* pounds

---

146. Bailey (*Finding the Lost*, pp. 91–92) also detects atonement theology riding on the shepherd's shoulders.

147. Marshall (p. 602) follows the lead of the NRSV by supplying the sense of *mallon* ('more'): *more joy* accrues to the repentance of an individual and less joy to those who are in the covenant.

(19:11–27), in which a nobleman distributes his ten coins.[148] In the second place, the 10% ratio in this parable is somehow loosely related to the previous parable's interest in the one sheep that made up 1% of its flock. Though the percentages differ, the underlying idea is the same: people who lose property, whether a sheep or a coin, search carefully for it, nor does the consolation of their remaining possessions dissuade them from doing so. For this reason, the woman makes up her mind to *light a lamp, sweep the house, and search carefully until she finds it*.[149] This needs to be read against the backdrop of the fuller story: Jesus of course is the kerygmatic lighter of the lamp (8:16–18) and the exorcistic sweeper of the house (11:25).

9–10. Like the owner of the lost sheep, when the woman finally finds that which she had lost, she invites her *friends and neighbours* with the simple agenda: *Rejoice with me*.[150] And with the same transition (*just so*), Jesus fills out the terms of the analogy. If in the first parable the 'one sinner who repents' occasioned 'joy in heaven', here the one sinner who repents prompts *joy in the presence of the angels of God*.

iii. Parable of the prodigal son and his brother (15:11–32)

11. The primary concern of this parable is not the misadventure and return of a younger son, as is often supposed, but rather his father, introduced as a certain *man* (*anthrōpos tis*; cf. 10:30; 14:16; 16:1, 19; 19:12; 20:9). Traditionally, the father is understood to represent God and this makes sense, not least in the light of Jesus' invitation to call on God as 'Father' (11:2). At the same time, one cannot deny the figure of the father a Christological aspect. If, as has been

---

148. Whether Luke intends his reader to infer a conceptual parallel between the two parables on the basis of this similarity is an intriguing question but one which will be left unexplored here.

149. First-century Palestinian floors were typically laid with pavers that allowed coins to drop through the crevices. Moreover, because windows tended to be very small, lighting lamps was a practical necessity before looking around.

150. The Greek *philē* denotes that these are female friends.

argued above, the man in the parable of the lost sheep and the woman in the parable of the lost coin combine to point to the image of God (male and female), then we might expect this third parable to build notionally on the *imago Dei*. The expectation is confirmed by the fact that the *man* of 15:11 has two sons who, like the two sons of Adam, Cain and Abel, have a strained fraternity!

12. More than a show of heinous greed, the younger son's request (*Father, give me the share of the property that will belong to me*) is an outright affront to the father. In antiquity, to ask for one's inheritance ahead of time would have been akin to saying, 'Drop dead!' In the same way, the father's decision to grant the request and divide his property (which according to the stipulations of Deut. 21:17 would have left the younger son with no more than a third of the estate) was essentially a decision to endure social humiliation. If one were forced to speculate on the roots of such reckless rebellion within the Gospel text, one might conceivably go back no further than the Lord's Prayer (11:1–4). Though impossible to prove, for all we know a comparison is intended between the younger son's request ('Father, give me the share of the property that will belong to me', *Pater, dos moi to epiballon meros tēs ousias*) and the bread petition: 'Father . . . give us [*Pater . . . didou hemin*] us each day our daily bread' (11:2–3). By way of comparison, both the Lord's Prayer and the younger son's request for an allotment to be granted earlier rather than later. By way of contrast, whereas Jesus asks his disciples to request bread for 'us', the community, the son asks only for himself. For the young man, the root issue is one of greed.

13. With the inheritance now in hand, the younger son once again does the unthinkable, this time by cashing out the inheritance. It is 'unthinkable' morally, since a family's legacy was normally preserved through real estate.[151] It is also unthinkable legally, for Jewish law frowned on any such divestitures as long as the father was still alive (B. Bat. 8:7). In a very short time (*a few days later*), the wayward son *gathered all he had*, or more exactly 'gathered everything' (*synagagōn panta*), yielding the disturbing impression that

---

151. Forsaking life on the farm was considered morally suspect; see e.g. in T. Iss. 6:2.

in collecting his inheritance the young man had made a comprehensive sweep. The verb choice 'to gather' (*synagagō*) is not
incidental, recalling, first, Jesus' warning that 'whoever does not
gather [*synagagōn*] with me scatters' (11:23), and, second, the rich
fool's determination to gather up (*synaxō*) the surplus crops (12:17–
18). As we shall see, in this parable, as in Luke 11 and 12, a
misconceived gathering ultimately results in a tragic scattering. For
soon enough, having *travelled to a distant country* (*apedēmēsen eis chōran
makran*), a circumlocution for Gentile territory, the son squanders
his inheritance *in dissolute living* (*asōtōs*).[152] Whereas most interpreters
do not see any intimations of exile in the comparison between the
lost son's trajectory and Israel's redemptive history, this commentator, convinced by Luke's interest in the theme of restoration,
concurs with the view that the son's trip to a Gentile country
emblematizes, at least on a second level of meaning, Israel's
squandered inheritance of the land.[153]

14. Far more so than modern economies, the ancient economy
was especially vulnerable to the impact of famine, and even more
so a *severe famine* or 'a mighty famine' (KJV). The famine is not so
much an unforeseeable disruptor as an aggravating circumstance
besetting the son's great spend down: after all, the prodigal runs
out of money at some point *before* the famine hits. Needless to say,
once the spendthrift young man had exhausted his financial
resources, finding work in the midst of an agricultural and economic crisis would have been difficult.

15. Unable to secure an income where he was residing, he *went*
(*poreutheis*) on a journey of indeterminate distance as a vagabond.
The verbal link with the earlier parable of the lost sheep deserves
comment: whereas the shepherd 'goes after' (*poreuetai*) the missing
animal (15:4), here the father stays at home and it is the errant son
who travels (*poreutheis*). This may serve a certain homiletical point:
when it comes to pastoring the straying believer, perhaps Luke

---

152. Holgate (*Prodigality*, p. 144) demonstrates that to live in dissolution
      (*asōtōs*) is by definition to engage in sexual immorality; see also Callon,
      'Squandered Patrimony'. Contra Johnson, p. 236.

153. As argued most notably by Wright, *Victory of God*, pp. 126–131.

means to say, the better part of wisdom is in knowing when to travel after the lost sheep and when to allow the prodigal to travel unfollowed. Eventually, the young man *hired himself out (ekollēthē)* to *one of the citizens of the country*. Yet this too is part of the downward spiral, for the verb *kallaō* suggests that his new Gentile association – far from being a casual employment relationship – is a form of personal solidarity (cf. Acts 5:13; 8:29; 9:26; 10:28; 17:34).[154] His task, prohibited by Jewish purity requirements (m. B. Qam. 7:7), was to feed the swine.

16. The Greek which the NRSV translates as *he would gladly have filled himself* has alternatively been translated as 'he longed to fill his stomach' (NIV) and 'he was desirous to fill his belly' (YLT).[155] And that which he longed to fill himself with was the carob pods, regularly used for animal fodder. That *no one gave him anything* implies that he had been robbed of all autonomy, even lacking authority to help himself from the pigs' food apart from – presumably – being severely punished. Now beginning to starve, the young man has been reduced to a level lower than the lowest of unclean animals.

17. Comparing his own sorry lot (whether he was literally *dying of hunger* is impossible to say) with that of his father's *hired hands* (*misthoi*), the prodigal comes to grips with the depths to which he has sunk. A *misthos* was a day labourer, drawing pay that was at or slightly above sustenance-level income. If his father's hired hands had *bread enough and to spare (perisseuontai artōn)*, this would have likely put the father on the more generous end of wage-payers. At the same time, the comment puts the *misthoi* in company with Jesus' five thousand guests who, following the desert meal, had bread scraps to spare (*to perisseusan*; 9:17). On this analogy, the father's estate has a striking resemblance to the kingdom of God.

---

154. For the relevant definition, BDAG (p. 441) has 'join oneself to, join, cling to, associate with'. The parallel between the prodigal son joining himself to Gentiles and the Roman-sponsored tax collectors, who we recall are the very reason for Jesus' parables (15:1–2), does not go unnoticed.

155. The verb *epethymei* is either a durative imperfect (he kept wanting to . . .) or an iterative imperfect (he repeatedly wanted to . . .).

18–19. Necessity now leads the prodigal to conjure a bold plan to *get up* (*anastas*), return home to his father and offer a speech – all with a view to being taken back into the home whence he came. That he must first *get up* is indicative of the fact that he has, in some metaphorical sense, fallen. At the same time, the verb *anistēmi* can mean 'to resurrect', terminology – perhaps not coincidentally – also applied to Israel's return from exile (Ezek. 37). The young man's premeditated speech consists of three components. First, recognizing that all offences against other people are ultimately offences against God, he intends to acknowledge the vertical (*against heaven*) and horizontal (*before you*) dimensions of his sin. Second, he plans to declare himself unworthy of his filial status. Third and finally, he will ask to be put in the same category as the well-supplied day workers.

20. True to his intention (v. 18), the young man rises and *went to his father.* Privy to the son's inner thoughts (vv. 17–19), the reader expects that the best possible outcome is one in which the father begrudgingly grants the son's request. The adversative *de* (*but*), however, is initial indication that the father's graciousness will far exceed all expectations. Then follow four significant responsive actions on the father's part. First, the father sees the son *while he was still far off,* as if on the horizon of the landscape. Whereas the father's glimpse of his son may have simply been a matter of his happening to look up in the right direction at the right time, we are instead invited to imagine the father spending his days anxiously scanning the horizon in the hope of catching sight of his lost son. Second, given the gravity of the son's offences, Luke's first-century reader would have ordinarily expected the father to have been furious (precisely the response of the older son; cf. v. 28).[156] Instead, in keeping with the counter-intuitive nature of the kingdom, he is *filled with compassion* (*esplagchnisthē*). Within the story, the father's compassion is owing to his feeling – more than anything else – the weighty effects of his son's destructive choices. Simultaneously, in the broader canonical context, it does not go unobserved that the

---

156. The father would have been within his rights to invoke Deut. 21:18–21 and call for his son to be stoned.

scriptural tradition 'consistently correlates Israel's return from exile with Yahweh's compassion (Isa. 14:1–3; 30:18; 54:10; 60:10; Jer. 42:12; Ezek. 39:25; cf. Deut. 30:3)', especially as this is 'rooted in Yahweh's first revelation of empathy at the first Exodus (Ps. 78:38)'.[157] Third, casting dignity aside, the father runs to his son and puts his arms around him, more specifically, by pulling his neck and head towards himself. By now, Jesus' point to his critics could not be any clearer: whatever cold shoulders the Pharisees and scribes were inclined to give to the sinners and tax collectors, Jesus' heavenly Father by contrast excitedly embraces such individuals, much as a father embraces a long-lost son. Fourth and finally, the father affectionately *kissed* the son. The entire range of actions (*his father saw him and was filled with compassion; he ran and put his arms around him and kissed him*) drives home the father's profound, even undignified, love for his rebellious child.[158]

21–22. Almost oblivious to these signs of affection, the son rehearses his premeditated script (vv. 18b–19). Yet before he can come to the part in his speech where he asks to be made into one of the day labourers, the father interrupts by issuing several sets of instructions to the servants. The first instructions aim to clothe the son with the best robe, a new ring and new shoes for his feet. Since servants were tasked with putting shoes on their masters, these instructions imply that the servants would indeed resume their role of being the son's servants too, showing that the son has been fully reinstated into the family.

23. The second set of instructions involves a celebration following the slaughtering of *the fattened calf*. As '*the* fattened calf', it

157. Perrin, 'Jesus' Anger', p. 8.
158. Luke's text runs very close to Gen. 33:4: 'But Esau ran to meet him, and embraced him, and fell on his neck and kissed him.' The similarities raise the intriguing possibility of a parallel between the man's younger son and Isaac's younger son Jacob. Not unlike Jacob, the prodigal had in some sense robbed his older brother of his inheritance and fled far away for a long period of time. And once again like Jacob, the young man anticipates a reunion marked by recrimination only to be pleasantly surprised by a gracious welcome.

is the one and only animal on hand worthy of such a celebration. The calf is not simply 'killed'; the father's words may equally be interpreted as 'sacrifice [*thysate*] it' (cf. Luke 22:7; Acts 14:13, 18; etc.). Portending Jesus' impending death, this celebratory meal within the parable takes its place alongside the Last Supper (22:7–38).[159]

24a. The father closes out his directive with a rationale for all the fuss: *this son of mine [houtos ho huios mou] was dead and is alive again; he was lost and is found.* The Greek subject has some resemblance to God's words over Jesus at his baptism ('You are my Son', *sy ei ho huios mou*, 3:22) and even more so at his transfiguration ('This is my Son', *houtos estin ho huios mou*, 9:35). What do we make of the parallels between the father's words over his lost son and God the Father's words over Jesus? It is difficult to say with certainty, but it may bespeak a soteriological principle, namely, that insofar as the parable's homecoming prodigal represents all repentant prodigals everywhere, such individuals have come to share in Jesus' identity as divine Son, precisely as confirmed by the baptism and transfiguration.

More immediately, the son's status as 'lost and found' puts him in the same category as the lost-and-found sheep of the first parable of this parabolic triad as well as the lost-and-found coin of the second. The double correlation fills out and extends the earlier stories. For Luke's Jesus, lostness is not merely a deviation from the course or a temporary misplacement, it is death itself. Likewise, to be found is to be made alive again, akin therefore to resurrection.

24b–27. As per the father's instructions, a celebration gets underway. All the while, however, the older brother has been *in the field* of his father (interestingly, not entirely different from the younger son who had also been 'in the field', v. 15). Eventually, he approaches the house and, to his surprise, hears the sound of *music and dancing.* As if half fearing that these festivities have been occasioned by the return of his younger brother, he remains at a distance. Unwilling to dignify such a celebration with his own presence, he summons and queries one of the servants. The servant in turn explains that *because he has got* the prodigal *back safe and sound (hygiainonta)*, the father has chosen to celebrate. The word

---

159. See Crawford, 'Parable'.

choice helps to clarify Jesus' earlier dictum 'Those who are well [*hoi hygiainontes*] have no need of a physician, but those who are sick' (5:31). The implication is that the repentant son does not have need of a physician, now that he is repentant.

28. When the older brother *became angry and refused to go in*, he bears a vague resemblance to the snubbed master of the banquet who was angered (same word: *orgistheis*) by the three refused invitations to his banquet (14:21). If the Evangelist intended to depict two parabolic banquets across two chapters, both marked by responses of anger (in the first instance the anger of the host and in the second instance the anger of the invitee), this would seem to have far-reaching implications. Together, the two banquets would seem to indicate that the human refusal to participate in the kingdom banquet, already underway in Jesus' dining practices, can take the form of either indifference (in the case of 14:16–20) or resentment (as here, in 15:28), even as the divine rejoinder to such responses includes both anger (in the case of 14:21) and fatherly imploring: *His father came out and began to plead with him.* The father goes out (*exelthōn*) in order to persuade the older son to come in (*eiselthein*) – an ironic reality, since the younger son had earlier gone out (v. 13) only later to come back in. The father's pleading before the older son may anticipate the relatively unheeded pleading (*parakalei*) of Peter before the diasporic audiences at Pentecost (Acts 2:40).

29–30. As the older brother puts his anger into words, he draws a contrast between his own faithfulness and the unfaithfulness of the younger son: *For all these years I have been working like a slave for you, and I have never disobeyed your command.* Very differently, his younger brother *devoured your property with prostitutes.* The shared hinge between the two comparisons is the dedication of an animal for celebratory purposes. Resentful that the father has *killed the fatted calf* for the prodigal, the older brother imagines a more modest and yet-unrealized scenario in which he is given a *young goat* in order to *celebrate with my friends.*[160] The invitees include only the older

---

160. Hultgren (*Parables*, p. 81) reckons that the price of a goat was roughly a tenth of the price of a calf. Still, as Nolland (p. 787) remarks, 'It is not a goat as such that he wants . . . but recognition.'

brother's friends: strangely and strikingly lacking from this imagined party is the father's presence.

31–32. The address *son* (*teknon*) is a term of affection. And whereas most translations agree with the NRSV in rendering *teknon* this way, the translation 'my child' makes clearer the possible connection with the tragically resistant *tekna* (children) of Jerusalem whom Jesus had longed to draw together under his wing (13:34). The father's rejoinder to his son consists of two points. First, he points out the fact of his continuing presence (*you are always with me*) and that everything at his disposal has also been at his son's disposal. Second, celebration (cf. 12:19 and 16:19) and rejoicing were not simply a good idea but a matter of necessity (*edei*). And because in Luke language of necessity is almost always language of divine necessity, it follows, according to the argument of the parable, that Jesus' festive table practices are likewise a matter of divine necessity. Rejoicing and celebration are essential and non-negotiable elements of the kingdom age that Jesus is introducing.

As to what happens next, however, that is something Jesus leaves to his hearers' imagination. Does the older son come round to see the father's point and join in the festivities? Or does he continue to sequester himself in pouting isolation? It is almost as if Jesus in his turn and Luke in his turn were inviting all hearers of this parable to complete the story with their own choices, their own lives.

Theology

It is no overstatement to say that the scribes and Pharisees are virtually obsessed – in a critical sort of way – with Jesus' practice of eating with sinners and tax collectors. In order to understand this preoccupation, it is important to note that Jesus' dining habits were inherently destabilizing, posing a threat to the religious leaders' social power. After all, if members of Israel's well-entrenched in-group could preserve their power base only as long as they refused to associate with the excluded out-group (sinners and tax collectors), then what would Jesus' undiscriminating choice of dining partners mean but the dissolution of such social boundaries? In these parables, both Jesus and God have been compared to a shepherd eagerly searching for his lost sheep and a woman searching for a lost coin. From this it follows that the same passion that Jesus has for the lost ought to characterize his followers. In the kingdom, then, the leading resources are to be devoted not to those who are safely well ensconced but to those who are at risk and at the margins.

M. Parables of wealth (16:1–31)

Context

In order to drive home the dangers of greed, the Gospel now introduces a fictional shrewd manager (16:1–13) who, like the prodigal son of 15:11–32, squanders his entrusted wealth – or at least is reported as having done so. The manager is gainfully attached to a certain rich man, just as the central character of another passage in this section, Lazarus, is likewise associated – not so gainfully – with a rich man (16:19–31). Whereas the prodigal son gives himself over to the greed of profligacy (and the shrewd manager is charged with the same moral failing), Lazarus's wealthy acquaintance suffered from the no less culpable greed of stinginess. In between the stories of the shrewd manager and Lazarus are teachings about the heart and divorce (16:14–18). The topical shift is not as abrupt as one might think: where divorce follows from adultery, greed of another kind is not far removed.

Comment
i. Parable of the shrewd manager (16:1–18)

1–2. With the characteristic introduction 'there was a *certain man* [*anthrōpos tis*]', Jesus returns us to the now-familiar territory of parable.[161] This is not the first time the reader has encountered a *rich man* (cf. 12:16; 14:12), a *manager* (*oikonomos*; cf. 12:42) or the *squandering* of property (cf. 15:13). The so-called parable of the shrewd manager seems to combine a handful of Lukan interests: wealth, waste and stewardship. In larger, Roman-style households,

---

161. The same Greek phrase also introduces parables at 10:30; 14:16; 15:11; 19:12; and 20:9. Its nearby occurrence at 15:11 perhaps draws more immediate comparison.

it would not be uncommon for a wealthy householder to have an *oikonomos*, a hired person or, more commonly, a slave who would take charge of the day-to-day administration of the estate.[162] In this story, the manager is charged with squandering (*diaskorpizōn*). Though the accusation is never verified, apparently for the owner of the property the complaint itself is enough reason to give notice to his employee: having *summoned him*, the master requests a final *account of your management*. The window of time required for this accounting, between notice of termination and the actual event of termination, allows the manager to devise a plan.

3. In the midst of his personal crisis, the manager entertains an internal monologue – the third such instance of self-talk in Luke, once again giving us a glimpse into the character's motivations.[163] Here there are similarities with the earlier soliloquies, not least in the words *What will I do ...?* (*ti poiēsō*), which matches the deliberative question confronting the greedy man who ruminates over insufficient storage space (12:17). As the manager considers losing his current livelihood, neither of his two imagined alternatives are viable, for he is *not strong enough to dig* and is too *ashamed to beg*. Given evidence that the manager has been administrating an estate of considerable scale (see below on vv. 6–7), it is striking that he should visualize himself occupying two roles at the very bottom of the socio-economic register. Once his reputation had been tarnished by the allegations of waste, so the manager reasons, he would be forced to endure the most extreme of financial *and* social demotions.

4. As the manager mulls the problem over, the solution comes to him in a stroke.[164] He quietly formulates a plan that, once executed in verses 5–7, promises to land him as a guest or an employee in the homes of others. Even now the meaning of the parable becomes apparent. Since according to Luke the extending

---

162. Though one might ordinarily assume that the *oikonomos* is a slave, his contemplation of begging suggests that he is not a slave facing punishment but an employee facing termination.

163. Cf. 7:39; 12:16–20; 15:11–32; see Sellew, 'Interior Monologue'.

164. *I have decided* may alternatively be rendered 'I've got it!' (Morris, p. 270).

and receiving of hospitality is a hallmark of discipleship and
eschatological salvation (10:3–12; 18:29; 19:5–10), we take it that
Jesus' point (only to be confirmed in v. 9) is to connect the strategic
deployment of resources in this life with the enjoyment of future
hospitality in the life to come.

5–7. Summoning two of his master's debtors in separate conversations, the manager renegotiates each debt by setting new and
extremely favourable terms for the debtor in both cases. On the
manager's authority, the first debtor is allowed to cancel half of the
originally owed amount of a *hundred jugs of olive oil*. The NRSV's 'jug'
or ESV's 'measure' (Greek *bathos*) was a volume which varied
between 5 and 10 gallons. Assuming, as many commentators do, a
standard *bathos* of 8.75 gallons (33 to 34 litres), this would mean that
the debtor was being forgiven the equivalent of seventy-five
harvested olive trees or the cash equivalent of eighteen months'
worth of wages.[165] In the case of the second debtor, the manager
reduces the *hundred containers of wheat* owed his master to eighty
containers or cors (Greek *koros*), roughly the output of eighty acres
of grain field, yielding a total debt reduction equivalent to about
two years' wages.

Whereas commentators widely agree that these newly established terms are generous, they disagree on the intent of these
reductions. On one standard interpretation, the manager is
essentially embezzling from his master in the hope of ingratiating
himself with his master's debtors. Thus he is ostensibly a 'dishonest
manager' (v. 8) but nevertheless shrewd because his master would
virtually be forced to accept the new arrangements rather than
suffer the public humiliation of going back on the word of his
entrusted manager.[166] Another line of argument holds that the
steward is not skimming from what is due to his master but rather
relinquishing his own rightful commission, likewise in the hope of
eventually obtaining a quid pro quo.[167] A third approach maintains
that the original loan arrangements were usurious, and that by

---

165. Bock, pp. 1330–1331.
166. So, e.g., Tannehill, pp. 245–249.
167. Fitzmyer, pp. 1097–1101.

reducing the owed amounts, the manager is ensuring that the debtors pay back an amount equal to no more than the original principle, in accordance with Jewish law (Exod. 22:25; Lev. 25:35–37; Deut. 23:19–20).[168] On this interpretation, the manager had acted shrewdly (v. 8) because he left his master little choice in the public eye but to accede to what Torah had prescribed. According to the second and third interpretations, the manager is 'dishonest' only insofar as he has been *accused* of wasting property (v. 1) – not on account of anything he actually *does*. Against both the second and third options, however, the text gives no evidence of either a built-in commission or usurious interest rates.[169] Yet if we go with the first option, this leaves us with a virtually unfathomable situation in which a master praises a manager for 'shrewdly' or 'wisely' defrauding him of funds![170]

In the final analysis, we should not assume that the manager had acted underhandedly, for Luke's readers would have likely recognized this debt reduction as an ethically legitimate transaction. More specifically, we are best off regarding this as an instance of *remissio mercedis* (rent remission), a business practice involving massive rent discounts which were 'not only a sensible course of action to secure consistent and long-term profitability, but also a prudent strategy for obtaining debt repayment'.[171] In this case, the manager is simultaneously serving his master's best interests and serving his own best interests by 'paying it ahead', as it were.

8a. The NRSV along with other translations may be overstepping the bounds of the Greek when it renders *kai epēnese ho kyrios* as *and his master commended . . .* , since the original text simply reads 'the Lord commended . . . ' This deserves notice because while *ho kyrios* almost certainly refers to the master of the parable, the ambiguous

---

168. Derrett, *Law*, pp. 56–63.

169. As has been demonstrated by Kloppenborg, 'Dishonoured Master'.

170. In v. 8 the master congratulates the manager for acting 'shrewdly' (*phronimōs*; NRSV); given that the related adjective *phronimos* is elsewhere paired with 'faithful' (12:42), the adverb in v. 8 is better translated as 'wisely' (so KJV).

171. Goodrich, 'Debt Remission', p. 555.

noun is almost certainly meant to connect the landowner of the parable with *the* Lord, that is, Jesus himself. On the latter reference, the praise in view is eschatological praise. Either way, the basis for such commendation, whether coming from the manager or from Jesus at the eschaton, is a wise course of action (*phronimōs*) – in stark contrast to the malfeasant and self-serving behaviour which had initially been attributed to the manager.

8b–9. With the first word of verse 8b *hoti* (NRSV *for*), Jesus now gives some explanation as to why he gives this parable. To wit, *the children of this age are more shrewd in dealing with their own generation than are the children of light*. With these words, Jesus chidingly encourages his disciples to learn from the example of the wise manager. This involves, in the first instance, using *dishonest wealth* (*mamōna tēs adikias*) in order to *make friends for yourselves*. While some commentators infer that *dishonest wealth* refers to funds that the manager has immorally secured, we take this as a genitive of quality, in which case Jesus may simply be referring to the fallen nature of wealth in general. The paradox which he hopes to impress on his hearers is this: while some may understand wealth as inherently corrupt and therefore as irrelevant to 'spiritual concerns' or the things of God, Jesus is in fact advocating the wise use of money in order to advance the divine purposes and even one's own personal eschatological lot. Positioned on the heels of the parable of the prodigal son, which among other things warns against squandering resources, this parable invites – as if to balance out the parable of the prodigal (15:11–32) – a kind of holy squandering. When disposed of wisely, such largesse will prove to be a wise investment in the lives of others, eventually yielding return on investment both for the master of the kingdom and for oneself.

10. According to Jesus, faithfulness is a consistent virtue. It is never contingent on the scope of the stakes or the level of entrusted responsibility: *Whoever is faithful in a very little is faithful also in much.* Likewise, those who are *dishonest* (*adikos*) in the small things will be equally dishonest in the large things. The statement serves as a warning to those who might be tempted now and again to make small moral compromises on the rationale that such compromises are supposedly minor. More positively, Jesus' words are an encouragement for believers to attend closely to 'the little things' entrusted to them. Small choices for good or for ill in the present are the best predictors of character and moral decision-making in the future.

11. The contrast between *dishonest wealth* (*adikō mamōna*) and *true riches* (*to alēthinon*) is further evidence that the 'dishonest wealth' (*mamōna tēs adikias*) of verse 9 is not any illicitly acquired wealth but simply financial resources – the holy grail of an unjust and fallen world. The conditional sentence implies a close correlation between one's handling of such resources and the obtaining of a more lasting – and hence more *true* – wealth. At its core, the contrast contained in the 'if ... then' statement is a contrast between temporal and eschatological. As such, verse 11 now clearly decodes the manager's quest to be welcomed in the 'homes' of others (v. 4) as a metaphor for the believer's concern to be welcomed in a lasting home on the far side of death. Even so, it is possible, even likely, that the divine conferring of 'true wealth' may also entail the granting of spiritual responsibility within the parameters of the church's mission.

12. Because there is never any possibility of the parabolic manager transitioning from the stewardship of his master's property to the possession of his own, we should not work too hard in pressing the logic of verse 12 into the storyline of verses 1–8. Rather, verse 12 is merely a continuation of verse 11. Unfaithfulness with one's entrusted financial resources will not only preclude opportunities for managing true wealth but also jeopardize any possibility of eternal ownership.

13. Jesus states a general principle (*no slave can serve two masters*), only then to apply it more specifically: *you cannot serve God and wealth*. The existential dilemma, which is presented in a very different context in Matthew (6:24), underscores the grave danger – indeed the impossibility – of twin allegiances. Falling on the heels of verses 11–12, the aphorism implies that faithful stewardship begins by taking on the mind of a steward but culminates with a heart filled with a love for God undiluted by the love of money. A proper disposition towards God and wealth involves the whole person.

14. Even though Jesus had directed the parable of verses 1–13 to his disciples (v. 1), the Pharisees within earshot disrupt his teaching with ridicule (*exemyktērizon*).[172] They do so, Luke informs us, because they are *lovers of money* (*philargyroi*). In other words, the Pharisees deride Jesus' teaching on stewardship precisely because they are unsettled by the relevance of that teaching to their own lives. In the face of Jesus' moral challenge, the Pharisees – consciously or unconsciously – seek to deflect its force through mockery.

15. Jesus now exposes his critics' motives by tracing their ridicule back to participation in a kind of mutual admiration society: *you are those who justify yourselves in the sight of others; but God knows your hearts*. In modern society, we are all too familiar with self-appointed moral gatekeepers who gleefully denigrate a non-conforming viewpoint only to consolidate their own collective sense of self-righteous moral superiority. If the transition from verse 14 to verse 15 is to make any sense at all, Jesus can only be citing his opponents as an example of just this social phenomenon.[173] Preoccupied with obtaining a 'horizontal righteousness', the religious leaders stand in stark contrast to those who justify God through repentance (7:29). Of course, all such posturing is ultimately for naught, for *God knows your hearts*, even as Jesus knows their hearts in the very moment. Moreover, from God's point of view, such an orientation is an *abomination* (*bdelygma*), that is, a profaning sacrilege that invalidates the Pharisees' participation in true worship.

16. In first-century Judaism, it was widely held that the coming of the kingdom would entail the cessation of the Mosaic law; the same point also seems to have been taken for granted by Jesus. Yet, according to Jesus, the key transition figure – from *the law and the prophets* to the preaching of the kingdom – was John. From John's ministry onwards, the kingdom was being faithfully proclaimed and *everyone tries to enter it by force*. While the scope of *everyone* has

---

172. The verb *ekmyktirizō* is often used in reference to the wicked's persecution of the righteous (LXX Pss 22:8; 35:16). In Luke, the same verb describes those who mock Jesus on the cross (23:35), hinting that the moral challenges which Jesus sets forth in the parable of the shrewd manager contribute to his arrest and execution.
173. In the Greek, the emphatic pronoun *hymeis* (*you*) takes first position, adding emphasis: '*You* are the ones who justify yourselves!'

been variously interpreted, I argue that it refers not to everyone in an absolute sense but specifically to those who oppose Jesus, including those who had just mocked him (v. 14). The attempt of Jesus' opponents to secure an inheritance in the kingdom while failing to submit to him on his terms is tantamount to an ultimately futile breaking and entering (cf. John 10:1–10).

17. While for Jesus the transition from the age of the law to the era of the kingdom implied a phasing out of the Law and the Prophets on some level, the redemptive-historical shift did not imply a wholesale vacating of the law's moral force. Indeed, it is *easier for heaven and earth to pass away, than for one stroke of a letter* (*keraia*) – the miniscule horn just visible on certain letters in the Aramaic scripts – to fall away. In short, Jesus insists, the central thrust of the law will remain effective *in toto*, notwithstanding the kingdom's arrival. So long lasting is the law, indeed, it is more durable than *heaven and earth*. Given that *heaven and earth* is sometimes used as a circumlocution for the temple, Jesus' reference to the passing away of heaven and earth is not so much an invitation to contemplate a theoretical but highly improbable possibility; rather, he is likely alluding to the imminent destruction of the temple (21:5–36). One day, so Jesus hints, the Law and the Prophets together with the current Mosaic temple (*heaven and earth*) would indeed pass away, while the law down to its smallest detail would endure, finding its fulfilment within the community of believers.

18. Luke's insertion of Jesus' teaching on divorce and remarriage at first glance seems an unanticipated shift in thought. But when the saying is understood in conjunction with its Matthean parallel (Matt. 19:1–12), one concludes that verse 18 is added to provide a concrete example of the principle laid out in verse 17. If in the past Moses had accommodated divorce by permitting a writ of divorce (Deut. 24:1–4), now with the coming of the kingdom God's creational intention must have its full place, essentially ruling out divorce – at least as it was understood in Mosaic legislation – as an option.[174] At the same time, if 16:1–13 is principally concerned with

---

174. Matthew (5:32; 19:9) provides an 'exception clause' which is absent in Luke.

stewardship, marriage must be regarded as an instantiation of a different kind of stewardship. In the case of divorce and remarriage, there is some sense in which the law remains in force (namely, in its stipulating against adultery) and another sense in which it is annulled (namely, in its granting accommodations for divorce). From yet another angle, Jesus' admonitions against divorce and remarriage are an appropriate complement to his earlier warnings on the worship of mammon (v. 13). If the parable of the shrewd manager points to the dangers of spiritual adultery presented by mammon, an analogous and more literal kind of adultery is warned against here.

ii. Parable of Lazarus (16:19–31)

19. Like the parable of the shrewd manager (16:1–13), the present parable concerns a rich man (*tis ēn plousios*) and is introduced with the identical Greek construction (cf. 16:1), inviting some comparisons between the two narratives. This otherwise anonymous rich man is *dressed in purple and fine linen*; he is also known to have *feasted sumptuously* – all in contrast to the hungry Lazarus (v. 21). Luke's ascription of these activities marks the rich man out with two standard tokens of wealth (fine clothing and an ample diet), even as it aligns him with those unrighteous vacillators who, like Herod, 'put on fine clothing and live in luxury' (7:25). While Jesus' disciples are called to pray in the community's daily bread (*ton epiousion . . . kath' hēmeran*, 11:3), the rich man of this parable has no obvious need for such prayers, as he has daily access to magnificent meals *every day* (*kath' hēmeran*),

20–21. Luke's decision to identify the poor man by name (while the rich man remains anonymous) is notable. Most likely, the parable attempts to connect its hero with the Gentile Lazarus (aka Eliezar) of Damascus who stood to inherit Abraham's estate but was eventually supplanted by the child of promise, Isaac (Gen. 15:2).[175] Such a linkage naturally presents itself, at any rate, on the rich man's subsequent invocation of 'Father Abraham' (v. 24),

---

175. As argued by Cave, 'Lazarus'; contra Lehtipuu, *Afterlife Imagery*,
    pp. 30–31.

together with some consideration of Luke's theme of reversal, whereby the children of promise (biological descendants of Isaac) risk being dispossessed, while the disenfranchised Gentiles (biological descendants of Lazarus) stand to be enfolded. Suffering from some kind of medical condition, this Lazarus is *covered with sores*. The depth of his suffering first comes to surface in Jesus' detail that the poor man, like the prodigal son (15:16), *longed to satisfy his hunger* (*epithymōn chortasthēnai*) but was largely frustrated. To the extent that Luke conjures a mental picture of Lazarus crouching beneath the rich man's table, it is fitting that only dogs (a term which in itself is interchangeable with Gentiles) are willing to consort with him, as they *come and lick his sores*.

22. The two parallel lives described in verses 19–21 now come to a parallel close, with first mention going to Lazarus: *The poor man died and was carried away by the angels to be with Abraham*. In Jewish tradition, Abraham was regarded as one of God's worthies who stood ready to receive the righteous into the afterlife (4 Macc. 13:17; T. Levi 18:4; cf. Luke 13:28–29); he was also seen as the possessor of eschatological secrets (4 Ezra 3:14; Apoc. Ab.). Though the angels (as transporters of the righteous dead) have no clear-cut precedent in the Jewish literature, the apocalyptic motif of angels serving as guides for the righteous was already established by the first century.[176] In striking contrast to the passing of Lazarus, the rich man's death is described with matter-of-fact brevity and no fanfare; his transition to the afterlife includes no mention of either Abraham or angels.

23–24. The rich man is in *Hades*, a realm of the afterlife which for many Jews, particularly those who subscribed to a doctrine of resurrection, amounted to an intermediate state preceding the final judgment.[177] There he endures various torments, including the *agony* of *flames*, insatiable thirst and a tantalizing vision of Lazarus in Abraham's 'bosom' (KJV). Seeing Lazarus so situated, the rich man calls out to *Father Abraham* in the hope of enlisting his familiar companion's services in getting some small relief of moisture to *cool my tongue*.

---

176. Lehtipuu, *Afterlife Imagery*, pp. 198–205.
177. See Bauckham, 'Hades, Hell', *ABD* 3, pp. 14–15.

It is unclear exactly which elements, if any, of this parable are intended to be realistic depictions of eschatological realities. Although almost all pre-modern commentators have understood the parable as offering a true-to-life depiction of the post-mortem state, the majority of modern commentators have maintained that Luke is merely drawing on stock images that would have been most familiar to first-century readers and accordingly should not be taken seriously as an accurate account of the hereafter. In considering these alternatives, it bears stating that interpretative extremes at either end should be avoided. On the one side, Jesus clearly presents the parable as a *story* and therefore the reader should exercise caution before assuming that every element in this tale needs to be integrated into a biblically informed eschatology. On the other side, however, because Luke's description of Hades bears some resemblance to the intermediate state envisioned in other Ancient Jewish texts of the day (e.g. 1 En. 22), and because the accuracy of the topographies of these same texts seems to be taken at face value in other early Christian writers (1 Pet. 3:19; 2 Pet. 2:4; Jude 6), attempts to demythologize the parable wholesale are likely misguided. Careful case-by-case judgments on each detail are required.

25. Abraham answers the rich man by addressing him as *child* (*teknon*), appropriately so not only because the rich man claimed the patriarch as his father but also because the term *teknon* has up to this point in Luke largely been applied to those who have resisted God's grace.[178] In responding to the rich man's specific request, Abraham begins to justify his forthcoming refusal of the request by appealing to a logic of justice. Whereas the rich man received *your good things* (*ta agatha sou*) in the course of his life, Lazarus by contrast met with *evil things* (*kaka*). As a result, Abraham continues, *he is comforted here, and you are in agony*. The verse is difficult because on the face of it Luke seems to be espousing a kind of *reverse* 'health and wealth gospel', implying that there was some sort of inherent virtue in Lazarus's difficulties, even as there was some inherent wickedness in the rich man's enjoyment of fine food and clothing.

---

178. See commentary above on 15:31.

Whatever other theological difficulties such an interpretation might entail, it immediately founders on the fact that Lazarus goes to be with Abraham who in his time was unequivocally wealthy (Gen. 13:2; 14:13–24; 23:13–15; etc.). The key element seems to be the insertion of the possessive pronoun *your* before *good things*. By establishing the rich man's earthly enjoyments as *his* good things, as opposed to good things from God and ultimately for God, Abraham is characterizing the rich man's life as an inhospitable life lived apart from God.[179] That the post-mortem Lazarus receives comfort in the afterlife is a function not of his poverty or his poor health, but rather of a divine principle that requires affording comfort to those whose vexations have been compounded by the inattention of the wealthy.

26. That Abraham should describe a *great chasm* separating *us* from (plural) *you* (*hymōn*) suggests that the rich man representatively speaks for a broader company of the damned who share his grim lot. The description also reflects a geography of the afterlife that is not uncommon in the ancient sources.[180] Those on the rich man's side of the chasm can see the state of the blessed and even converse with at least one individual on the right side of eschatology, but frustratingly they cannot *cross from there*, though they are wanting to do so. Whatever aspects of this account Luke hopes his readers to take more literally than figuratively, it seems an inescapable inference of this parable that the deceased reprobate will be granted some insight into the felicity that could have otherwise been theirs. This is also consistent with similar sentiments in the Gospel, not least where Jesus says that 'There will be weeping and gnashing of teeth when you see Abraham and Isaac and Jacob and all the prophets in the kingdom of God, and you yourselves thrown out' (13:28).

---

179. Abraham was also noted for his hospitality (cf. Josephus, *Ant.* 1.196–200; Philo, *Abraham* 109, 114, 132).

180. Both pagan and Jewish texts imagine a chasm in the afterworld. A chthonic 'great chasm' like the one in this parable is described in 1 En. 18:9–12.

27–28. Abandoning all hope of ameliorating his own situation, the rich man now turns his thoughts to his surviving *five brothers* who are still attached to their *father's house*. His hope is that Lazarus might be sent to *warn* (*diamartyrētai*) them, so that they might repent of their present course, presumably not very different from that of the rich man. The warning is not simply advice: the verb of warning (*diamartyromai*) denotes the granting of a solemn charge, often with legal intimations.[181] At the risk of overreading the parable, the request may imply that when the dead disobedient come to terms with the consequences of their poor choices while alive, their regret centres around not only their own foolishness but also the foolishness of their loved ones. This in turn implies that concern for one's kin is no saving virtue but will in fact characterize many of those who will meet with condemnation.

29. Again, Abraham resists the rich man's request, pointing out that *Moses and the prophets* should provide the five brothers sufficient warning of their need to turn. For that reason, the patriarch suggests, *they should listen to them*. The Greek verb behind *listen* is an aorist imperative active form, *akouō*, lexically and grammatically close to *akouetō* in Jesus' charge rounding off the parable of the sower: 'Let anyone with ears to hear listen!' (8:8). In effect, then, Abraham's directive for the five brothers to listen to the Law and the Prophets is of a piece with Jesus' call for his hearers to listen to his parables. Abraham's proposal further suggests that whatever moral lessons are to be learned from the dead rich man's fate, as well as, on another level, from the parable itself, these truths have already been fully recorded in the Hebrew Scriptures. This is consistent with the portraiture of Luke, who sees Jesus' teaching not as a departure from Torah but as its fullest elaboration (24:44).

30–31. Undeterred by Abraham's resistance to this point, the rich man perseveres, insisting that if someone like Lazarus were to rise from the dead, then surely the brothers would respond favourably. His argument is essentially this: if Moses and the prophets have failed to sway his brothers, it is only because something more stunning needs to occur in order to seize their attention

---

181. Cf. Acts 2:40; 8:25; 10:42; 18:5; 20:21; etc.

and shake them loose from their disobedience – something like a resurrection from the dead. Yet Abraham, as the final authority, puts an end to the dialogue while refuting the point: *If they do not listen to Moses and the prophets, neither will they be convinced even if someone rises from the dead.* What are we to make of Abraham's final rejoinder? First, on a narrative level, the patriarch's words foreshadow the unbelieving opposition which the apostolic church will soon meet in Acts, despite its proclamation of Jesus' resurrection in continuity with the Law and the Prophets. Second, the statement clarifies that as potent a sign as the resurrection may be, it cannot and will not persuade those who have already failed to heed the Scriptures. Third, conversely, Abraham implies that those who would be won to repentance through a resurrection event are also those who would be willing to listen to the Hebrew Scriptures. Therefore, in Luke's theology, resurrection is not so much a catalyst for faith and repentance as a new focal point on which faith and repentance must be trained.

Theology

The first of two pivotal characters in Luke 16 is the shrewd manager, who finally demonstrates his ability to leverage wealth to win friends for himself in the kingdom (16:8–9). By contrast, Lazarus's wealthy acquaintance stewards his resources poorly and pays the price accordingly (16:19–31). Kingdom stewardship means being faithful not just with respect to wealth but also with respect to one's relationships, including the relationship of marriage (16:18). No follower of Jesus actually *owns* anything – all that we do have is simply on loan. On the day of judgment, those who have been found faithful will be those who have properly managed the intersection between their entrusted resources (material and social) and people. As Jesus' disciples increasingly adopt God's kingdom values, they will also have a better grasp of how to steward on behalf of the Lord.

N. Sin and repentance (17:1–19)

Context

On the heels of the story of the rich man and Lazarus (16:19–31), Jesus' ruminations on 'occasions for stumbling' (17:1) reflect on sin's power to trigger further sin in others. Yet 17:1–4 is equally concerned with horizontal forgiveness following the commission of sin – a theme already repeatedly touched upon (6:27–36; 11:4). And because a principled commitment to forgive one's enemies carries the risk that goes with being vulnerable to those same enemies, faith must accompany forgiveness (17:5–6). Already highlighted in the narrative (7:1–10, 50; 8:25, 50; 11:5–13), faith can bring about great feats (17:6). But neither exertion of faith, nor forgiveness, nor acts of service can *merit* commendation. The life of discipleship is a life of continuous service, without the expectation of gratitude or reprieve (17:9). The key idea here is humble service. Jesus' seemingly disparate teachings in 17:1–10 find their common centre in the interrelated themes of forgiveness, faith and service.

The same three themes re-emerge in storied form in Jesus' cleansing of the ten men of leprosy (17:11–19), where the service of the singular returning cleansed man translates itself into praise and thanksgiving (17:15–16). It is faith that prompts all ten men to go to the priest in line with Jesus' instructions (17:14), but it is an even greater and indeed saving faith that leads this one worshipper back to his healer (17:19). That which Jesus prescribes in 17:1–10 now finds embodiment in an unlikely Samaritan with leprosy.

Comment

i. Faith and duty (17:1–10)

1–2. Luke 17:1–10 comprises four sections treating seemingly disparate topics: 'scandalizing' behaviour (vv. 1–2), forgiveness (vv. 3–4), faith (vv. 5–6) and humble service (vv. 7–10).[182] In the first of

---

182. Fitzmyer (p. 1136), erroneously in my judgment, sees the four topoi as 'completely unrelated'.

these sections, Jesus pronounces *woe* (*ouai*) on those who cause stumbling, especially for *one of these little ones*. Similar woes, which amount to a declared curse, have already been pronounced on the religious leaders (11:42–52) and disobedient cities (10:13), as well as on those who somehow exclude themselves from the blessings promised by the Beatitudes (6:24–26). In this instance, however, the pronouncement is made more severe by a consideration of preferred alternatives: *it would be better for you*, Jesus continues, *if a millstone were hung around your neck and you were thrown into the sea*.[183] That Jesus should regard a sentence of death by drowning as preferable to divine judgment suggests, once again in Luke, that eschatological judgment of the wicked will be measured out according to the measure of their sin.[184] In its secular usage, *scandalon* denotes a trap, a snare or an impediment that causes stumbling; in the Jewish and early Christian literature it refers to that which incites another person to sin.[185] The latter is surely in view here. And so Luke urges his readers not just to avoid personal sin but also to avoid activities that provoke other community members to sin. Furthermore, given that the envisaged victims of such scandals are *little ones* (v. 2), with the same noun referring to children in 9:48, one suspects, with support from the parallel Matthew 18:5, that one or more forms of child abuse are in view.

3–4. It is not entirely clear whether the phrase *be on your guard* (*proschete heautois*) logically attaches itself to verses 1–2 or verses 3b–4. But since Jesus elsewhere gives the very same command while warning against especially subtle temptations (12:1; 20:46; 21:34), and since an unforgiving attitude (vv. 3b–4) would seem to be less overt than the behaviour roundly condemned in verses 1–2,

---

183. There's no doubting an upper millstone's effectiveness as a weight: millstones from Jesus' day were generally 1 to 2 feet in diameter and up to a foot wide.

184. It is worth noting: that Jesus can imagine a fate of judgment worse than death poses no small challenge to the doctrine of annihilationism (the belief that the wicked will simply cease to exist following divine judgment).

185. See Bock, p. 1384; BDAG, p. 753.

a connection with verses 3b–4 seems more likely. Notably, the plural *proschete* prepares for a directive pertaining to an individual's interactions with another 'brother' (*adelphos*); the imperative asks the community, in instances of conflict between two individuals, to follow the process outlined in verses 3b–4.

Jesus lays out a linear progression of four stages: the commission of the sin, the offended individual's obligation to *rebuke the offender*, the action of *repentance* and the necessity of forgiveness pending in view of such repentance. Several remarks are in order. First, although verse 4 primarily relates to an offence perpetrated against another believer, the absence of a personal object following the clause *if another disciple sins* would seem to suggest – contrary to what much of Western society would claim – that all sin, public and private, vertical and horizontal, is potentially subject to the church's scrutiny. Second, the act of rebuke is enjoined not as a take-it-or-leave-it option but as a mandatory response to identified sin. Third, in contradistinction to many contemporaneous Jewish texts (e.g. CD IX, 2–8; T. Gad 6:1–7), the requirement of forgiveness is made to depend not on the confessor's perceived sincerity but simply on the act of repentance itself. Jesus' teaching naturally raises the question as to whether his disciples would be free to impose limits on the frequency with which forgiveness might be granted. Anticipating such a question, he imagines an exaggerated scenario in which the offending disciple *sins against you seven times a day* only to seek forgiveness seven times (the number of fullness). The basic idea is clear: no matter the rate at which this prescribed cycle of sin and forgiveness plays out, the repenting offender who seeks forgiveness cannot be denied.[186]

5. Well aware of the persecution that Jesus and his apostolic followers have already faced, the Twelve quickly recognize how the life of radical forgiveness which Jesus has outlined in verses 3–4 potentially puts them at especial risk. For if down through history the prospect of retaliation has dissuaded a lot of malefactors from mischief, what protections would the apostles have left in carrying

---

186. As Nolland (p. 838) aptly puts it, the 'benefit of the doubt lies entirely with the one being forgiven'.

out their much opposed mission? Accordingly, they ask their *Lord* that their faith might be increased.

6. If the apostles' request for increased faith is ignored, it is only because they have misidentified the issue. As Jesus sees it, it is not he who must increase their faith but they who must begin using the faith they already have. And how powerful is that faith, even in its smallest measures! Recalling that the kingdom is like a mustard seed (13:19) that is poised to grow into a much more expansive tree, Luke's reader infers, on the basis of the mustard seed's new term of comparison, that faith has a similar potential for growth. According to Jesus, even such slight faith has power to command *this mulberry tree*, even with its notoriously tenacious roots, to be *uprooted and planted in the sea.* As the final resting place for Pharoah's horsemen and chariots, the bottom of the sea is a symbol of divine judgment. And though Luke appears to be recounting a moment in time when Jesus had drawn his disciples' attention to a nearby tree that just happened to be a mulberry, the choice of a mulberry tree is in fact highly intentional. As the mulberry, as well as the related willow, was a standard symbol for Babylon (Ps. 137:2; Rev. 18:12), and Babylon was a comprehensive metaphor for all that perpetuated exile, Jesus' promise regarding the mulberry amounts to a carefully veiled invitation for the apostles to pray down judgment on the 'Babylonians' of their own day.

7-8. As verses 3-4 have made clear, Jesus is calling his followers to a life of radical forgiveness, and this vocation is rendered all the more daunting by the reality of hostile forces. Therefore, it would not be unreasonable to expect that those who accepted Jesus' terms might subsequently take a self-satisfied pride in their calling – with this in turn giving way to a sense of self-entitlement with respect to God. In order to stem any such attitude, Jesus now offers an analogy (vv. 7-10). *Who among you,* Jesus asks, *would say to your slave who has just come in from ploughing or tending sheep in the field, 'Come here at once and take your place at the table'?* Though in the first-century world ploughing and shepherding were tasks not untypically assumed by servants, it is no accident that both activities are also metaphorized in the scriptural narrative of restoration (shepherding: Jer. 23:1-4; Ezek. 34; ploughing: Isa. 28:24; Jer. 4:3; Hos. 10:12). In the same way, both activities function as symbols for the work of ministry.[187] Neither in the first-century world nor in the coming kingdom, Jesus observes, would servants expect their master to wait on them in this manner (even though, paradoxically, Jesus has promised service like this in 12:37). In the kingdom, as in the realm of workaday life, only after working in the field *and* providing the master with food and drink could servants expect to sit down for dinner.

On a basic level, Jesus' exhortation (vv. 7–8) comes to Luke's readers as a warning against those who might otherwise be tempted either to retire early from a life of service or to pamper themselves in the misguided conviction that they have earned – perhaps by dint of their personal sacrifice – a place of repose at the messianic table. On a more specific level, that Jesus' imagined scenario should include the master being served food and drink surely relates to his recurring role as guest in the Gospel and therefore to a more specific application as well. The point is this: having insisted on the rightful place of the marginalized at the kingdom table (14:21), and having also identified himself with the same marginalized (10:29–36), Luke's Jesus now calls on his followers to wait on his table – as they would later do in Acts (2:46; 4:32; 6:1–7) – even as he soon comes in the guise of the community's poor.[188] The principle bears not so much on self-denial as prioritization: Jesus' injunction does not rule out the prospect of the servants enjoying themselves; rather, they are free to do so *later* or 'after these things' (*meta tauta*).[189]

9. If verses 7–8 ask two questions (the first expecting the answer 'No' and the second expecting the answer 'Yes'), in verse 9 Jesus asks a third and final question (once again expecting a negative response): *Do you thank the slave for doing what was commanded [ta*

---

187. So too Minear ('Luke 17:7–10', pp. 84–85), followed by Tannehill (p. 256).

188. Luke's point is similar to the one made by Matthew's parable of the sheep and the goats (Matt. 25:31–46).

189. It would have been difficult for Luke to have recounted this teaching without also recalling Paul's rebuking the Corinthians for having the poor eat last at their celebration of the Lord's Supper (1 Cor. 11:17–22).

diatachthenta]? The Greek phrase *ta diatachthenta* is a substantive
participial form of *diatassō*, a verb which has a range of meetings
including 'to arrange' and 'to give order'. The semantic range of the
verb yields additional insight. While Jesus is certainly pointing out
the absurdity of his followers chasing after gratitude for keeping
the master's command, *ta diatachthenta* further implies that the disciples' behaviour is beholden not simply to a command but to a new
order introduced by the kingdom. To serve in the light of *what was
commanded* is to live in congruence with this in-breaking reality.

10. Should any of Jesus' servants be tempted to regard their
kingdom service as some kind of special achievement, this would
be immediately undercut not only by what is true of reality (as
defined by Jesus in v. 9), but also by what *is not* true of the servants.
Even at their best, Jesus' servants are *worthless slaves (douloi achreioi)*
or 'good-for-nothing servants'.[190] The presence of the adjective
achreios means that even the most effective of Jesus' servants are in
fact ineffectual; the same Greek descriptor connotes baseness of
character (cf. LXX of 2 Sam. 6:22, where the translator renders the
Hebrew *shophal* with Greek *achreios*). In sum, though Jesus' servants
may be inclined to congratulate themselves on their service,
pointing perhaps to their exceptional character or noticeable effectiveness, or both, such attitudes are belied by their status as *douloi
achreioi*.

ii. Jesus heals ten men of leprosy (17:11–19)

11. Reminding his readers that Jesus was *on the way to Jerusalem*, a
journey which began at 9:51, Luke now plots his location
somewhere *between Samaria and Galilee*. This is curious because as
early as 9:51–56 Jesus had already entered Samaria – presumably
moving southbound from Galilee to Jerusalem.[191] Now he seems

---

190. Following a few others, Green (p. 614 n. 368) and Nolland (p. 842) seek
    to soften the normal force of *achreios*, preferring to render *douloi achreioi*
    as 'servants to whom nothing is owed'. I demur: the NRSV (*worthless
    slaves*) has it right.

191. According to Edwards (p. 482), the 'particular space here traversed
    would be the region of the Decapolis, which protrudes like an

to have turned back north. In any event, Jesus has entered a cultur-ally mixed area populated by both Samaritans and Jews.[192]

12. Approaching the *village*, Jesus is met by *ten lepers* who, as a precaution against defiling Jesus with their uncleanness, keep *their distance*.[193] Though their ethnic composition is never stated, we later learn that at least one within the group is a Samaritan (v. 16). One suspects that for whatever reason the age-old hostility between Jews and Samaritans did not apply to this group; in this regard, the ten men are a kind of prototype for the ethnically comingled church of Acts (Samaritans and Jews, cf. Acts 8:14–17). That there are as many as ten men with leprosy banding together raises the possibility that Jesus is encountering a wandering leper colony or perhaps a village comprising solely those so afflicted. On the latter possibility, his encounter with the ten men is likely intentional if not premeditated.

13. In calling Jesus *Master* (*epistata*), the men employ a term of address that up to this point has been used only by the disciples – and that consistently as part of the lead-up to a miracle. In identifying him by his name *Jesus* (the first time the name is applied by fellow humans in Luke's Gospel), the men convey a level of familiarity or personal knowledge. Their plea is identical to that of Lazarus's rich friend who calls out to Abraham (16:24): *have mercy* (*eleēson*). While the request of Lazarus's wealthy acquaintance was 'too little, too late', the distressed call of the men with leprosy will imminently be honoured.

14. In commanding the men to go *and show yourselves to the priests*, Jesus is requesting compliance with Torah's prescriptions for cleansing people who have serious skin disease (Lev. 14:1–32). In Torah-observant Judaism, those suffering from such a skin condition would need to appear before priests following evidence

---

(note 191 *cont.*) arrowhead into Jewish territory west of the Jordan between Samaria and Galilee'.

192. So too Nolland, p. 846.

193. Leprosy was a condition which rendered one ritually unclean; see Lev. 13:45–46. The term does not necessarily refer to Hansen's disease but may refer to a less serious skin condition.

that their condition had been healed (Lev. 14:1–4). Therefore, in carrying out Jesus' directive (*as they went*), all ten men believe that by the time they find the priests, they will have been visibly healed. In the very act of going, then, all ten exercise faith and are accordingly *made clean.*

In comparing this episode with the earlier cleansing of a man with leprosy in Luke 5:12–16, one notices some instructive differences. In the earlier cleansing, Jesus declares the afflicted man clean (5:13). As has been argued above, in making this pronouncement, Jesus assumed a role reserved for priests; his declaration essentially functioned as the first required declaration of cleansing (Lev. 14:9). If so, this would in turn be followed by the priest's performance of an atoning sacrifice (Lev. 14:10–20a), exactly as commanded in Luke 5:14, preparing for a second declaration of cleanness (Lev. 14:20b).[194] By contrast, the present episode has Jesus issuing neither a declaration of cleanness (as was the case in 5:13) nor instructions regarding an atoning sacrifice (as was the case in 5:14). From this, one infers that the cleansing experienced by the ten men in 17:14 is, as it were, one step short of the cleansing of Luke 5, that is, simply a physical restoration allowing them to initiate the eight-day cleansing ritual outlined in Leviticus 14.

15–16. Though all ten men experience healing en route to the priest, only one *turned back* (*hypestrepsen*) – a verb indicating not only the healed man's outward motion but also his inward repentance.[195] Just a short time earlier, this man, along with the other nine, had been raising his voice (*phōnēn*) in beseeching Jesus (v. 13), but now he alone is *praising God with a loud voice* (*phōnēs megalēs*). Luke's description of the healed man's voice as *loud*, together with his mentioning that he *was a Samaritan*, recalls Scripture's anticipation of universal worship when the nations would worship Yahweh with a 'loud voice' (Pss 47:1; 60:8; 66:8; 98:4). And fluidly moving from praising God (v. 15) to thanking

---

194. See commentary above on 5:12–16.

195. Contra Green (p. 630), who overlooks hints of restoration in v. 18, with its leading marker: repentant returnees.

Jesus (v. 16), the man has effectively blurred the distinction between God and Jesus.[196]

17–18. Jesus is struck not so much by the healed man's response of worship as by the nine's abject failure: *But the other nine, where are they?* As it turns out, only one was *found to return*, that is to say, only one was 'found' in the salvific sense by evincing that salvation in worship. Ironically, though it is unclear how many of the nine were non-Jews, the only one who responded rightly was *this foreigner.* The statement not only reinforces Luke's thematic interest in showing that foreigners rather than Jews were responding to Jesus, but also alludes to Isaiah's prediction that only a tenth would return from exile (Isa. 6:13). The observation that a foreigner should be 'found to return', together with the fact that this foreigner was a tenth of a larger set of recipients of God's grace (the tenth coin of the woman's ten coins), reframes the entire episode as an emblem of the long-awaited return from exile soon to unfold in Luke–Acts.

19. Jesus' parting words to the healed man (*Get up and go on your way; your faith has made you well* [*sesōken se*]) betoken the importance of faith in his salvation. To be sure, though the other nine men had a faith of sorts, verse 19 suggests that only a faith that gives way to worship and thanks is demonstrably a saving faith. And only those with such faith belong to the emergent return from exile now taking shape in Jesus. More than that, because Jesus at this point omits any instruction to go to the priests, as had been earlier issued to him and the other nine men in 17:14, this may hint that the man was now free to entirely forgo the protocols prescribed in Leviticus 14:1–20, including the mandate for offering an atoning sacrifice (vv. 10–20a). On this inference, it can only be either that Jesus would provide the atonement in his impending death or, more likely, that the necessary sacrifice has already been accomplished through the man's praise (Pss 50:23; 141:2; cf. Heb. 13:15; 1 Pet. 2:9).

---

196. Whereas the man of 5:12–16 had fallen on his face (*pesōn epi prosōpon*, 5:12) *before* the act of healing, this man falls on his face (*epesen epi prosōpon*; NRSV *prostrated himself*) *after* it. Across the span of the Gospel, two acts of worship enclose two acts of healing.

Theology

Though the truth is often missed, a biblically informed doctrine of sin requires believers to avoid not only sins of omission and commission, but also seemingly innocent choices that might increase the likelihood of sin in the lives of others. The New Testament term for the effect of such choices is *scandalon* (stumbling block); the act of creating such stumbling blocks, *scandalizomai* (scandalizing). A parade example of such scandalization occurs in Romans 14, when Paul urges 'the strong' to self-restrict their menu options so as not to entice 'the weak' into sinning by openly eating meat sacrificed to idols and so defiling their consciences. The transition from the story of the rich man and Lazarus (at the end of the previous section) to Jesus' teaching on scandalizing (in this section) implies a second level of moral failure on the rich man's part. Not only had the well-clad and well-fed man ignored the plight of the beggar Lazarus; it also seems the case (in the light of 17:1) that his conspicuous consumption had created moral hazards for the beggar – tempting him perhaps towards resentment, envy or any other range of sins that might follow a violated sense of justice. Luke's theology of scandal requires balancing freedom in Christ with sensitivity to the fact that others' perceptions might become a source of stumbling.

Fortunately, whatever the nature of horizontal sin, whether direct or indirect (*scandalizomai*), the community of Jesus-followers must operate by a principle of limitless forgiveness. Such forgiveness is possible because Christ has transformed all believers, like the remnant man with leprosy, from a state of exile and moral uncleanness to a state of restoration, moral cleanness, worship and thanksgiving. The faith of the man with leprosy is also the faith that is necessary for forgiving others. The same faith is also the engine of worship.

O. The coming of the kingdom (17:20–37)

Context

In this passage, Jesus emphasizes both the abruptness and the mystery of the kingdom's arrival. For many of those who witness the Son of Man's eschatological coming, their experience will be like that of the parabolic characters who are met with a rude awakening (12:16–21; 16:19–31). For this reason, Jesus' disciples would be well served to be alert – an exhortation picked up again in 21:5–38. But as to who is finally saved, there is little knowing ahead of time. For here, as in the parable of the sower (8:4–15), the inscrutable nature of God's purposes, worked out at the convergence of divine election and human responsibility, will cut across all stations of life and conventional human categories.

Comment

20–21. Once Jesus' interviewers are identified as *the Pharisees*, one may be forgiven for suspecting some malicious intent. After all, if Jesus could be caught stating on record that the kingdom was about to arrive in his own movement, such an admission just might provide his enemies with some useful political ammunition down the road. But if the Pharisees *were* hoping for self-incriminating statements, they are quickly disappointed: Jesus (anticipating 21:8–9) emphasizes not the predictability of the kingdom's timing but rather the inscrutability of such matters. The coming kingdom is neither susceptible to human observation (*meta paratērēseōs*) nor neatly locatable in time and space.[197]

Quite the contrary, the *kingdom of God is among you*. As to what *exactly* this means, four options obtain. First, it has been widely argued that the prepositional phrase *entos hymōn* is to be taken as not 'among you' but 'within you', rendering the kingdom a spiritual reality already palpable in the Pharisees' inner experience. A second approach, made famous by Bultmann, is to translate the present-tense verb *estin* as a future: 'the kingdom will be among you'. Third, it has been maintained that *hē basielia tou theou entos hymōn estin* essentially means 'the kingdom of God is within your reach'. A fourth option: when Jesus says *the kingdom of God is among you*, he means that the kingdom is present to his hearers through his own person and ministry.

What are we to make of these four options? While the first proposal's sense of 'the kingdom of God is within you' would

---

197. On *paratērēsis*, see Riesenfeld, *TDNT* 8, pp. 148–149.

admittedly be most in keeping with the normal sense of *entos*, this reading falters on two grounds. First, it makes nonsense of the larger Gospel narrative, for if the kingdom is already present within the Pharisees (among others), this squares poorly with their opposition to the kingdom up to this point (cf. e.g. 7:29–30).[198] Second, the concept of a purely interior kingdom forces the acute question as to how a kingdom so defined would relate to Luke's overall vision of a public and objective kingdom, evinced not least in the immediate context. Among the remaining three interpretative options, the fourth option, which Nolland designates 'the most common modern view', is the strongest: the kingdom is among Jesus' hearers insofar as the kingdom is embodied in Jesus himself.[199] At the same time, this reading might also arguably include the third option. For if the kingdom is present in and through Jesus, and this presence once announced becomes a kind of de facto invitation to embrace the kingdom (i.e. by embracing Jesus), then Jesus is also saying in so many words, 'the kingdom of God is well within your reach!'

22. Jesus' turning his attention strictly towards his disciples sets aside verses 22–37 as a private instruction. The first exegetical question to be solved in verse 22 is the meaning of *the days of the Son of Man*. Taking the construction as a genitive of description, one may identify such days with the reign of the Son of Man, inaugurated in Daniel 7:13 and fulfilled in Daniel 12:1–3. In this vein, the partitive '*one* of *these days* [*mian tōn hēmerōn*] of the Son of Man' might be more accurately rendered, according to the style of the Septuagint (see BDAG, pp. 231–232), as 'on the *first* of these days' (as in Acts 20:7 and more significantly Luke 24:1). This would also seem to be the day of coronation on which the Son of Man was expected to judge the unclean pagan rulers (Dan. 7:9–12). It is at any rate a day that the disciples would *long to see* but *will not*. Such eager longing suggests that Jesus has in mind the persecutions, upheavals and apostasy described more fully in 21:12–19.

---

198. Marshall (p. 655), unsuccessfully in my view, argues that the 'you' is indefinite.

199. Nolland, p. 853.

23. In the midst of such distress, some might be tempted to pinpoint the precise arrival of the kingdom with empty promises of *'Look there!' or 'Look here!'* But it is just this speculative urge that the disciples are called to suppress. Jesus' instructions are clear: *Do not go, do not set off in pursuit*, since such reports will prove to be misleading (cf. 21:8).

24. On the face of it, the comparison between the arrival of the Son of Man and *lightning* lighting up *(lampei) the sky* speaks of the unexpected, sudden, glorious and highly public manner of his coming.[200] But in the Hebrew Bible lightning also accompanies Yahweh's assertion of kingship at Sinai (Exod. 19:16; cf. Exod. 19:3–6), implicit in his covenant-making role, just as it was expected to accompany the future coming of the eschatological kingdom.[201] Painted with a scriptural brush, the coming of the Son of Man in his day *is* the coming of the kingdom.[202]

25. No sooner does Jesus affirm the Son of Man's glorious appearing than he confirms his also being subject to *much suffering (polla pathein)*, in keeping with an earlier prediction that 'The Son of Man must undergo *great suffering [polla pathein]*' in connection with his betrayal, crucifixion and resurrection (9:22, emphasis added). But this time, rather than being rejected by 'elders, chief priests, and scribes' (as 9:22 would have it), Jesus is scorned by *this generation*, suggesting a certain fluidity between Israel's leaders and its people. The position of this commentary is that *this generation* is a specialized negative term bearing spiritual, temporal and genealogical freight.[203]

---

200. The Matthean parallel (24:27) has 'shines' (*phainetai*). Luke 17:24 and
    Matt. 24:27 employ two different Greek verbs to convey the sense of
    the Hebrew *zāhār*; these translations are patently drawn from the two
    versions of Dan. 12:3 (Theodotion and LXX, respectively), a verse
    which describes the shining of the resurrected wise.

201. See e.g. Zech. 9:14a ('Then the LORD will appear over them, / and his
    arrow go forth like lightning) and Ps. 97:1, 4 ('The LORD is king! . . .
    His lightnings light up the world; / the earth sees and trembles').

202. Though most translations include the words 'in his day', the phrase is
    text-critically suspect, missing in the important P75 B D.

203. See commentary on 11:29; see also Rieske, 'Two Families'.

26. The fate of the wayward generation of Jesus' day finds anticipation in the 'generation' of Noah's time (Gen. 6:9). And by virtue of their shared resistance to the wicked generation, the comparison (*Just as . . . so too*) between the *days of Noah* and the *days of the Son of Man* creates an analogy between not just the two eras but the two figures themselves. Verse 26 also invites an implicit correlation between Noah and the Son of Man in their respective saving functions, while verse 27 will go on to tease out this analogy in terms of judgment.

27–30. If the destruction of the world in Noah's day (Gen. 6 – 9) supplies one point of comparison with the Son of Man's imminent judgment, the destruction of Sodom and Gomorrah (Gen. 19) in Lot's day provides another (vv. 28–29).[204] Together the two divine interventions anticipate the judgment of the coming Son of Man (v. 30). The shared feature of all three judgments is their unexpected suddenness together with the blind indifference of those being judged.

Whereas four activities are imagined in Noah's day (v. 27), six are catalogued for Lot's day (v. 28), forming a total list of ten activities. Between the two sub-lists there are overlaps and distinctives. In describing the Noachic era, Jesus highlights *marrying and being given in marriage*, institutions invoking a sense of celebration and forward-looking hope (v. 27). Similarly, in recalling the days of Lot, Jesus mentions such future-oriented endeavours as *planting and building*, as well as *buying and selling* (v. 28). Some of these actions 'appear elsewhere in the Lucan story as distractions from what human existence should be about: buying (14:18, 19); eating, drinking and building (12:18–19); selling (19:45)'.[205] The juxtaposition of judgment with *eating and drinking* across verses 27 and 28 is striking not only because the latter activities are predicated of Jesus and his followers (7:34), but also because they are normally evidence of divine blessing (Deut. 12:7; Eccl. 5:18). Yet whatever sense of security these familiar institutions, cultural activities and

---

204. The two judgments were often correlated in Second Temple Jewish
    literature, not least 2 Pet. 2:5–8; see Lewis, *Noah, passim*.
205. Fitzmyer, p. 1171.

blessings might have conveyed in the pre-patriarchal era, once the moment had reached its crisis, all such impressions were quickly shown up as false assurances. So it would be with the coming of the Son of Man.

31a. The phrase *that day* not only continues the description of the coming of the kingdom but also frames this chain of events as the fulfilment of 'that day' promised in the prophets (e.g. Isa. 2:11, 17, 20; Jer. 30:8; Zeph. 3:11). On that day, the one on the rooftop should avoid descending into the *house* in order to retrieve his or her *belongings*. Since first-century rooftops were accessed by either a staircase or a ladder outside the house, Jesus is essentially discouraging any attempt to re-enter the house (after descending from the roof) in the hope of salvaging one's personal belongings. Apparently, the coming crisis would neither allow time for retrieving household possessions nor grant advantage to those who did so. Quite apart from this commentary's interpretation of 21:25–28, which correlates the coming of the Son of Man (21:27) with the Roman siege of Jerusalem (see below), Jesus' warning to those on the rooftop (not to mention 'anyone in the field', v. 31b) suggests that the coming of the Son of Man refers in the first instance not to the parousia (second coming) but to the imminent destruction of Jerusalem in AD 70. That said, it would be inappropriate to overstate the distinction between the two events: 21:25–38 frames the pillaging of the temple as a prelude to the parousia, rendering the two historical events as two different aspects of the same singular moment of divine intervention.[206] The sack of Jerusalem cannot finally be separated from the parousia – and vice versa.

31b–32. When individuals *in the field* (*en tō agrō*), or for that matter anyone in the countryside surrounding Jerusalem, see the foreign armies bearing down, they must resist the temptation to flee towards Jerusalem for safety. Such was the tragic error of *Lot's wife*, who looked back, despite the warning of Genesis 19:17, seeking comfort and security in those things which had been divinely

---

206. Similarly Nolland (p. 861), who writes that 'Luke sees the first-century judgment in Judea at the hands of the Romans . . . as the first installment of a universal judgment'.

targeted for destruction. Lot's wife sets a negative example for those who might look to the Holy City as some kind of divinely protected refuge.

33. Jesus' specific warnings in verses 31–32 are now set out in a maxim: *Those who try to make their life secure will lose it, but those who lose their life will keep it.* The saying's thrust is very close to that of 9:24 ('For those who want to save their life will lose it, and those who lose their life for my sake will save it'), a maxim situated within a larger context spelling out the costs of discipleship. Given the convergence between the prescribed path of discipleship (9:24) and the true path of safety (17:33), it stands to reason that Jesus' faithful hearers would be especially well positioned for surviving the coming disaster. By contrast, those who succumbed to the temptation of securing their life by pitching in to defend Jerusalem would be at gravest risk.

34. While *one will be taken* (whether in judgment or salvation is not clear), *the other* will be *left* (again perhaps in judgment or perhaps in salvation, depending on the meaning assigned to *taken*). Given the gender of the substantives ('the one … the other'), the *two in one bed* are not husband and wife, as one might gather from the English translations, but two males. That this selective snatching occurs at *night* leads us to imagine two related males, such as two brothers, sleeping side by side. All things considered, we are finally led to think of the tenth plague inflicted during the course of the first Passover night against all the firstborn males within Egypt (Exod. 11 – 12). On that night, countless unredeemed Egyptian males were taken in death while still in their beds; meanwhile, those 'covered' by the blood on their doorpost suffered no injury. On this logic, Luke presents the coming of the Son of Man as the trigger for a new exodus from the thrall of Jerusalem. The winnowing of humanity promised by John the Baptizer (3:17) would – in Jesus' vision – find its fulfilment in the Roman attack on Jerusalem, in which one male would be gathered up and the other left, recapitulating the tenth plague.

35. Corresponding to the two males in a bed are two females *grinding meal together* (not necessarily *women* as the NRSV and other translations would have it). On the surface, the simultaneity of the Son of Man's coming and two females grinding meal underscores the suddenness of the former. On a more significant level, however, one recalls that when Yahweh announced the tenth plague, it was promised that death would strike the firstborn of the Pharaoh, as well as the firstborn of the 'female slave who is behind the handmill' (Exod. 11:5). The allusion to Exodus 11:5 only reinforces the exodus story as the template by which his followers were to understand the destruction of Jerusalem. But whereas in the exodus narrative, the female mill-grinders were affected indirectly through the deaths of their male firstborn, Jesus now predicts a judgment that would directly affect women and men alike. By preserving one male and one female from a larger group of four, a pair of males and a pair of females (vv. 34–35), the forthcoming judgment against Israel promises to leave in place that which is necessary for a new creation: a new Adam and a new Eve, constituting the surviving remnant.[207]

37. In asking *Where, Lord?*, the disciples are not enquiring where this great sorting of humanity will take place but rather where the surviving elect will finally land on the far end of such winnowing. Where, in other words, will the surviving remnant be 'left' (or 'taken' as the case may be) in this new post-temple existence?

Jesus' answer to this question has proved to be deeply puzzling, providing scholarly fodder for some two dozen different interpretations.[208] Much of the mystery stems from the wide range of lexical possibilities. Along with the NIV and ESV, the NRSV advances the following rendering for 17:37: *Where the corpse [sōma] is, there the vultures [aetoi] will gather.* Though this translation is common enough, it is vulnerable to two strong objections. In the first place, if Luke had meant 'corpse', why did he not use the word readily available to convey that meaning, namely, *nekros*? In the second place, though *aetos* can mean 'vulture', it more commonly denotes 'eagle'; Ancient Greek more commonly preferred the term *gyps* to signify

---

207. A number of significant manuscripts lack v. 36. Absent a warrant for its inclusion in the canonical text, we omit comment.

208. At the time of his published dissertation, Bridge (*Eagles*, p. 3) counted no fewer than twenty interpretations. More have been added to the literature since. My argument below is largely based on Bridge's thesis.

the carrion-eating vulture. Sensitive to the force of the first objection, other translations (e.g. NAB, NASB) have something like 'Where the *body is*, there also the vultures will be gathered.' But still better is the translation of the KJV (seconded by the ASV and the Douay-Rheims, Wycliffe, Tyndale, Geneva and Bishops Bibles), which does justice to both objections: 'Wheresoever the body is, thither will the eagles be gathered together.'

In answering the disciples' question regarding the future whereabouts of the surviving remnant, Jesus points to his own body (*sōma*). Though Jesus' meaning was likely impenetrable in the original historical situation, the point will receive further elaboration on his subsequent equation of the Passover bread with his *sōma* (22:19), which in turn instantly, at least in Luke's mind, becomes a metaphor for the church. In any event, just as the early church identified itself with the body of the Risen Lord (1 Cor. 10:16; Eph. 3:6; Col. 3:15), verse 37 parabolically identifies the local 'body' of believers as the appointed refuge for gathering 'eagles' (*aetoi*). These 'eagles' are the ones who have renewed their youth 'like the eagle's' (Ps. 103:5) and who, on return from exile, will find new strength as they 'mount up with wings like eagles' (Isa. 40:31): they are the elect.

Theology

Jesus' entrance into the world marked the first glimpse of the dawning of the kingdom of God. By the time of his baptism and first sermon, that kingdom began to take fuller and more conspicuous form. Now in this passage, Luke's readers hear rumblings that this same kingdom would continue to unfold well into the future, first with the destruction of the temple and then, finally and climactically, with the parousia. Anticipated by the prophets, the kingdom of God unfolds progressively and organically through divine self-revelation in Jesus.

True as this may be, it is equally true that when Jesus now enters into the company of the Pharisees, the kingdom of God is fully and completely in their midst. This is because Jesus embodies the kingdom in his person. Jesus is not just the king: he is the *kingdom*. Likewise, in the book of Acts, where the Spirit is, there too is the kingdom.

This has implications for understanding the kingdom's relation to human players. Unlike those who co-identify the kingdom of God with the present-day church, with some group within the church or with some moralizing movement in society, Luke asserts that the kingdom of God is bound up in God's very self. When a community of believers sees itself as a platform for kingdom activity or as a group engaged with the kingdom, this is one thing. Yet it is quite another for the same community to nullify the distinction between their well-intentioned but fallen cause and the kingdom. When the kingdom of God is merely an immanent reality, the inevitable result is a tale of arrogant triumphalism, full of sound and fury but signifying nothing.

P. Two parables about prayer (18:1–14)

Context

Following closely on Luke 17:20–37, an episode which highlighted the importance of alert obedience in the light of the coming kingdom, the present passage concerns a central plank of that obedience: prayer. Together the two parables composing 18:1–14 teach two complementary lessons. In the first place, as the parable of the persistent widow (18:1–8) shows, prayer must be stubbornly tenacious. Yet in the second place, as the parable of the two praying men (18:9–14) indicates, even the most disciplined among God's praying people will fail to gain heavenly audience if their prayers are borne on the wings of spiritual pride. Those who aspire to pray for the coming of the kingdom in every area of life must possess not only a persevering spirit but also a self-effacing humility that admits to the depth of their own sin.

Comment
i. Parable of the persistent widow (18:1–8)

1. Luke prefaces this parable by remarking on its purpose, as it speaks of the disciples' *need [dei] to pray always*. In exhorting believers to continual prayer, Luke 18:1 takes its place alongside other Lukan texts (Luke 11:5–10; Acts 1:14; 2:42), not to mention other verses in the broader New Testament canon (Rom. 12:12; Eph. 6:18; Phil. 4:6; 1 Thess. 5:17; Jas 5:17–18). The topical shift from eschatology (Luke

17:20–37) to prayer is not as stark as it may at first appear, for as far as the disciples are concerned, Jesus' teachings on persistent prayer are simply setting out for them the practical implications of the coming Son of Man. Luke's choice of the infinitive form of *dei* ('it is necessary'), rather than, say, the imperative mood of *proseuchomai*, is noteworthy. As has already been pointed out above, in the Gospel *dei* almost always expresses divine necessity.[209] Thus the presence of the same verb here hints that persevering prayer is crucial to the fulfilment of God's purposes. Because God uses the frailty of human prayer to achieve redemption, the disciples are to pray *and not to lose heart*, even when the parousia delays.[210]

2. The language of the parable's setting (*in a certain city there was a judge . . .*) raises the question as to whether Jesus actually had a certain city (*polis*) or even a certain judge (*krit\u0113s tis*) in mind. Even though Jesus' description of the less-than-ideal judge (one who *neither feared God nor had respect for people*) is a stock description (cf. e.g. Josephus, *Ant.* 1.72 [10.83]), he endorses the point: piety without respect for others is at bottom just another form of ungodliness.

3. Having introduced the second character (*in that city there was a widow*), Jesus has now put on stage two characters diametrically opposed in terms of their respective social standing. Any judge who was aloof to the law of God and the favour of people was likely a powerful and corrupt figure; widows were among the least powerful of all adults in Jewish patriarchal society. And yet, remarkably, this powerless widow will ultimately prevail upon the judge simply by *coming* and speaking, two actions seeming to parallel the two basic components of prayer: coming into God's presence and making one's requests known. The facts of her case are never revealed; nor is there any doubt regarding the justice of her cause. All we know is that she seeks relief from her *opponent* (*antidikon*), a legal term typically applied to a prosecutor or one

---

209. See note on 2:49.

210. Snodgrass (*Intent*, p. 457) appropriately comments: 'Luke's concern in 18:1 is not prayer in general, but praying and not becoming weary . . . *with respect to the eschaton*, the time when deliverance comes' (emphasis original).

bringing a suit, or to Satan (1 Pet. 5:8). That she *kept* coming (the imperfect *ērcheto* is durative) is testimony to her persistence.

4–5. Despite Scripture's insistence on justice for widows (Exod. 22:22; Isa. 1:17; Jer. 22:3; Zech. 7:10), and despite this widow's tireless entreaties, the judge, almost certainly motivated by shady financial incentives, matches her persistence with his own stubbornness; he remains unwilling (*ouk ēthelen*). After an unspecified period of time, however, he relents: *but later he said to himself.*[211] In a moment of refreshingly honest reflection, the judge owns up to his disregard for God and human beings, yet out of exhaustion declares, *I will grant her justice.* He does so fearing that she will *wear me out* (*hypōpiazē me*) – or, more literally, 'beat me down', or even more literally, 'blacken my eye' – with her coming.

6. The concluding Greek of verse 6 sets up a masterful double meaning. In one sense, Jesus the master or *Lord* (*kyrios*) asks his disciples to *listen to what the unjust judge says* (*ho kritēs tēs adikias legei*). In another sense, if we translate *kritēs tēs adikias* not as a genitive of description but as an objective genitive, then the words can be understood – with intimations of the Shema of Deuteronomy 6:4 – quite differently: 'And the Lord says, "Hear what the Judge of all unrighteousness says."' In the first sense, Jesus points to the widow's determination as a fitting illustration of the believer's prayer life. In the second sense, Jesus' exhortation to 'hear' frames persevering prayer as the appropriate outworking of a monotheistic confession that calls believers to obey the judge of all the earth.

7. Drawing out the implications of the parable, Jesus poses a rhetorical question that compares the cause of the widow to the interests of *his chosen ones* (*tōn eklektōn autou*). The term 'chosen one' (*eklektos*) relates to God's elective purposes in the Mosaic covenant (Exod. 19:6) as well as to the Abrahamic promises (Ps. 105:6); the latter in turn provides the backdrop to Isaiah's promises to the 'elect ones' returning from exile (Isa. 43:20; 65:9, 15, 22).[212] Since injustice against widows (as we have here) normally involved the

---

211. This is yet one more example of a soliloquizing Lukan character; see Sellew, 'Interior Monologue'.

212. See Schrenk, *TDNT* 4, pp. 181–182.

misappropriation of their land, and since receiving the inheritance
of the kingdom is the disciples' overriding concern (Luke 11:1–2),
Jesus' promise that God will *grant justice* (*ekdikēsin*) to his praying
elect seems less about divine retribution (though the noun could
denote as much) than about the inheritance associated with the
coming of the kingdom. The parable suggests that such justice is
not granted automatically but is dependent on persevering prayer.
Given the parallel between his 'chosen ones' and 'those who cry
out', it follows that *the* characteristic trait of the elect is that they,
like Anna (2:37), *cry to him day and night.*

The second part of this verse (*will he delay long in helping them?*) is
made difficult by ambiguities in the Greek.[213] Towards making
sense of all this, we must take Jesus' words to be both an echo and
a refutation of Sirach 35:22.[214] Against Sirach, Jesus insists, in
virtually the exact same phrasing, that God *will be* not slow to help
the elect (as a number of interpreters have understood it) but
patient with them (*ep'autois*), that is, the wicked. And it is precisely
this patience with the wicked that explains why God seems so slow
in securing justice for the elect's oppressors. Following others who
take the Greek conjunction *kai* concessively, we can translate the
entire Greek sentence as follows: 'And will not God grant justice
to his elect ones who cry to him day and night, even though he
remains patient with those (wicked) people?'

8. The analogy between the parable's judge and God goes only
so far, for it is not just that God (like the unjust judge) will *grant
justice* but that he (unlike the unjust judge) will do so suddenly (as
suggested by Jeremias) or *quickly.*[215] Divine eagerness to execute
justice does not guarantee that the elect will *perceive* God's
promptness: it does guarantee, however, that the judge of the earth
will move as quickly as divine purposes allow. Notwithstanding the
certainty of these claims, Jesus' encounter with human unbelief

213. The Greek reads: *kai makrothymei ep'autois.* Marshall (pp. 674–675)
    identifies nine different options for translating this text.
214. Sir. 35:22 informs us that God 'will not be patient with them [*mē
    makrothymēsei ep'autois*] [the wicked]' (my translation).
215. Jeremias, *Parables*, p. 155.

leads him to conclude with a haunting question: *when the Son of Man comes, will he find faith on earth?* The final utterance of the parable, Jesus' question invites Luke's hearers to take stock of their faith and reflect on whether they themselves engage God 'day and night' on the pattern of the persistent widow.

ii. Parable of the two praying men (18:9–14)

9–10. The parable of the two praying men connects with the preceding parable in several respects.[216] First, like the previous parable, this parable front-loads the moral of the story while also providing a full-circle wrap-up (vv. 1, 8//vv. 9, 14). Second, the previous parable featured a villain who did not respect people (vv. 2, 4), and this parable addresses those who, like the unjust judge, have *regarded others with contempt*. Third, the two complementary parables focus on complementary individuals at opposite ends of the social spectrum: one empowered (the unjust judge) and the other marginalized (the tax collector). Fourth, both parables feature one religious figure and one non-religious figure, though with different roles. If the irreligious judge is the antagonist in the first story, in this parable the non-religious tax collector serves as the role model. Once again, religious social identity is a poor predictor of kingdom standing.

The parable is specifically meant for *some who trusted in themselves* (*pepoithotas eph'autois*), believing *that they were righteous* (*dikaioi*). The language is reminiscent of Jeremiah 7:4 (LXX), where the prophet lambasts the people of Judah for trusting in themselves (*pepoithate eph'autois*) and their deceptively pious words while engaging in worship.[217] Jesus will quote the very same passage in his temple action (19:46; cf. Jer. 7:11), auguring God's judgment on the temple. Against this background, Jesus' story of two praying men is not just a warning against isolated religious folk but a thinly veiled word of judgment against the temple elite's self-deceptive piety.

Like the legal experts who did not need a physician (5:31–32), the intended audience of this parable had seen themselves as having

---

216. In addition to these points, see Snodgrass, *Intent*, p. 453.
217. So also Edwards, p. 502.

arrived with respect to the demands of the law. While it is true that self-congratulatory prayers like these were not atypical in first-century Judaism, this does not mean, as several Lukan commentators have opined, that such 'normal practices' were also Jesus' norm.[218] On the contrary, as elsewhere in the tradition (Matt. 6:5–8), Jesus is critical of such public, self-serving displays.

The action begins with *two men* going up *to the temple to pray*: a *Pharisee* and a *tax-collector*. The language of *one* [*ho heis*] . . . *the other* [*ho heteros*] picks up on the same construction in 17:34b, where 'one' is taken up from his bed and 'the other' is left behind. By introducing the pair of men with the same syntax, Luke may be hinting that these two individuals, despite their shared activity in a shared space, stand on opposite sides of a great elective divide. If Pharisees were regarded as the epitome of moral rectitude and tax collectors were the parade examples of immorality, the resolution of this story (v. 14) will subvert the first-century reader's expectations.[219]

11. Striking a typical posture of prayer, the Pharisee is *standing by himself* (*statheis pros heauton*). He begins his prayer, as many Ancient Jewish prayers were begun, with a statement of thanksgiving, a *berakah*. But unlike so many scriptural recitations of gratitude, his prayer is not theocentric but self-referential.[220] The Pharisee thanks God that he is *not like other people* or, closer to the sense of the Greek, 'not like the rest of mankind' (NJB), comprising as it does – along with the likes of *this tax-collector* – three categories of sinners (*thieves, rogues, adulterers*). If we take *rogues* (*adikoi*) to refer to individuals who engage in fraudulent and therefore defiling behaviour (cf. CD VI, 11–17), then the three types of sinners roughly correspond to what was a familiar taxonomy known as the 'three nets of Belial': wealth, cultic profanation and adultery (CD IV, 17–18).

Within the Lukan context, *rogues* and *thieves* may be recalling one or more of the bad actors in the parable of the persistent widow,

---

218. See e.g. Edwards, p. 504; Green, p. 648.

219. On tax collectors (or toll collectors), see commentary on 3:12 and 5:27–32.

220. The Greek phrase *pros heauton* may in fact modify not 'standing' but 'praying': 'The Pharisee . . . prayed in regard to himself'.

the rogue judge (*ho kritēs tēs adikias*) and perhaps, on an implicit level, the behind-the-scenes third party hoping to swindle the widow of her land. Thinking himself to be morally superior to such unseemly characters, the Pharisee presents himself as one who is above the fray depicted in 18:1–8. Yet all such posturing is in vain, for Jesus has already condemned the Pharisees for all three named behaviours (11:39, 42; 16:15, 18).[221]

12. Having cleared himself of his peers' moral failings, the Pharisee congratulates himself on his righteous actions, including fasting *twice a week* and giving a *tenth of all my income*. There is no hint that Jesus is critical of the Pharisaical practice of the biweekly (Monday/Thursday) fasting.[222] Much less is there any indication that tithing is problematic (cf. 11:42). Rather, the problem lies with the Pharisee's haughty attitude.

13. The tax collector's spatial position in relation to the other worshippers, his physical posture and his actions all conspire to support his prayer: *God, be merciful [hilasthēti] to me, a sinner!* The contrast between the two characters is now striking. Whereas the Pharisee socially distances himself because he regards himself as superior to his fellow human beings, the tax collector by contrast is *standing far off* (*makrothen hestōs*) out of a deep sense of his own unworthiness. So overwhelming is this conviction, in fact, that he cannot *even look up to heaven* (*oude tous ophthalmous eparai eis ton ouranon*), the locus of God's presence. This makes him humbler than the much humbled rich man in Hades who in fact *did* raise his eyes (*eparas tous ophthalmous*) to Abraham in his bliss (16:23).[223] In *beating his breast*, the outward sign of inward self-humiliation and repentance (Josephus, *Ant.* 10.15), he declares himself not just 'a sinner' but in superlative terms as '*the* sinner' (*tō hamartōlō*). He needs not simply mercy, as most translations attempt to gloss *hilasthēti* ('*be merciful* to me'), but expiation.[224]

---

221. Green, pp. 648–649.

222. The practice's earliest attestation is in Did. 8.1; b. Taʿan. 12a.

223. In 1 En. 13:5, condemned sinners cannot raise their eyes to heaven.

224. See Hermann and Büchsel, '*Hilaskomai* etc.', *TDNT* 3, pp. 300–323.

14. Jesus' summary (circling back to v. 9) makes clear that the Pharisee's self-directed prayer is but a vain attempt to justify himself – effectively aligning him with the Gospel's other self-justifiers (10:29; 16:25). By contrast, the tax collector returns home from the temple justified, fulfilling earlier predictions that the exalted would be brought down and the humble would be exalted (1:52; cf. 14:7–11). That the tax collector's atonement (v. 13) and justification occur without recourse to the temple apparatus hints at an emerging economy where atonement is found no longer in the sacrificial cultus but in faith and repentance.[225] It is precisely this element that forbids Luke's reader from understanding this parable as merely providing an example of personal humility. On the contrary, the parable underscores the revolutionary impact of the kingdom where familiar, existing and deeply ingrained categories of justified and unjustified give way to a whole new configuration rendering the temple all but obsolete.

Theology

Though suffering injustice is part and parcel of life in a fallen world, the Gospel's many predictions of persecution suggest that Christians have been called to be special partakers of this experience. And when Jesus' disciples are confronted with injustice, their first and last response must be prayer. And what are oppressed disciples to pray but that God would secure justice against the adversary. Realistically, those who pray do so with varying levels of faith. Some will see no change to their straitened circumstances and give up praying altogether; others will persevere, continuously calling out to God day and night. Those who choose the latter path promise to have the kind of faith the Son of Man will be looking for on his return.

Yet even the one who prays persistently is not necessarily clear of another set of dangers: the danger of self-righteousness. When Jesus' disciples pray believing that they are more righteous than other people, that other members of humanity are 'bad' while they themselves are 'good', they too have missed the mark. The sheer

225. So too Fitzmyer, p. 1185.

act of prayer is never an end in itself, since even the most pious-sounding prayers can be driven by the engine of a superiority complex and the fuel of spiritual narcissism. If followers of Jesus are to expect their prayers to avail, they must pray perseveringly and with an inward sense that they are, as any human being living or dead, in desperate need of God's mercy.

Q. Upside-down kingdom (18:15–34)

Context
An inward humility that sustains a self-aware and consistent life of prayer must be accompanied by an appropriate perspective on the socially marginalized as well as on one's own social status. Against the surrounding first-century culture, which looked down on children as inferior beings, Jesus extols even the smallest of children (18:15–17). Meanwhile, the idolatrous trappings of wealth must be eschewed, as these values too have no place in the kingdom economy (18:18–30). Such counter-cultural teachings come into focus only against the backdrop of Jesus' impending betrayal and crucifixion (18:31–34). Jesus' third and final prediction of his death not only builds on earlier predictions (cf. 9:22, 28, 43b–44), but also prepares for the passion awaiting him on entering Jerusalem.

Comment
i. Jesus blesses the children (18:15–17)
15. Recognizing that Jesus' life-giving power can be accessed through physical contact (5:40; 8:44–46), people now begin *bringing even infants* (*prosepheron . . . kai ta brephē*) in the hope that he would lay on hands and impart a blessing.[226] The verb *prospherein* sometimes

---

226. Luke's Markan source (10:13–16) retains *paidia* ('children'). By making a change to *brephē*, he makes these the youngest of *paidia*. Though *brephos* normally denotes an infant, as Bock (p. 1469) notes, the use of the same term 'in 2 Tim. 3:15 shows that the term can include early childhood beyond the toddler stage'. In this light, *brephē* here are not entirely helpless infants but sentient toddlers, as seems to be required by v. 17.

denotes cultic offering (e.g. 1 Kgs 18:36; 2 Chr. 29:7; Jer. 14:12; cf. Luke 23:36; Acts 7:42), potentially putting Jesus' reception of the children in the same category as his own presentation at the temple (2:22–40). That Luke records this exchange as Jesus approaches his own atoning death may be related to the Ancient Jewish practice whereby parents brought their children to be blessed by the priest on the eve of the Day of Atonement.[227] The imperfect *prosepheron* ('bringing') indicates repetitive action, showing that Jesus is happy to oblige. But the disciples are persuaded that their master's time and energy would be better devoted to more important matters. And so they begin to rebuke (imperfect *epitimōn*) these suppliants.

16. Though the disciples' instincts are consistent with first-century Hellenistic norms, which regarded children as not yet fully and truly human, Jesus seeks to correct their actions and underlying values. His twofold instruction is stated in positive (*let the little children come to me*) and negative (*do not stop them*) terms. The imperative *do not stop* (*mē kōlyete*) is noteworthy for two reasons. First, it mirrors other occurrences of the same construction (9:50; Acts 8:36; 10:47), where in each case it relates to a context of community self-definition. If Luke's reader gives this parallelism full weight, it may be inferred that children are to be granted bona fide membership within the Jesus community. Second, insofar as Jesus' rebuke lines up with his earlier injunction against causing little ones to stumble (17:2), Luke may also be hinting that the disciples' marginalization of children puts the same children at increased risk of stumbling.

17. In issuing his climactic pronouncement, Jesus shifts attention from the disciples' exclusion of children to the root of such attitudes. He warns that unless the disciples receive *the kingdom of God as a little child*, they cannot ever hope to *enter it*.[228] Whether

---

227. Marshall, p. 682.

228. Tannehill (p. 268) points out that there are two other possibilities for understanding the Greek: (1) 'Whoever does not receive the kingdom as one might receive a child', and (2) 'Whoever does not receive the kingdom of God as if it were a child'. Notwithstanding these possibilities, the consensus translation represented by the NRSV need not be seriously questioned.

receiving the kingdom is temporally prior (so Marshall, p. 683) or logically prior to *entering* the kingdom (highlighting the paradox that the kingdom is both a gift to be received and a space to be entered) is unclear. In any case, the manner of receiving is paramount. Whatever Jesus means by embracing the kingdom as a child, it can mean nothing less than embracing God's reign with a humble simplicity that is innocent of social hierarchies. Jesus' warning inverts the standard pecking order. In the kingdom, it is not the adult but the child who is the most sublime expression of humanity.

ii. The rich ruler (18:18–30)

18. All three Synoptic Gospels tell the story of a certain earnest enquirer. From all three, we learn that he is wealthy; from Matthew (Matt. 19:20), that he is young; and from Luke, that he is a *ruler* (*archōn*) – a term which in the third Gospel often refers to religious leadership.[229] For all we know, he may have even been a member of the very Sanhedrin responsible for declaring Jesus guilty and deserving of death. In any case, he is a socio-economically powerful figure, and this identity – as we shall discover – puts him at a disadvantage in relation to the kingdom. Addressing Jesus as *Good Teacher* (a flattering phase, especially given Judaism's reticence to apply the adjective 'good' to human beings), he is eager to hear Jesus' answer to a standard theological question of the day: *what must I do to inherit eternal life?* Since the phrase *eternal life* was synonymous with the future general resurrection (Dan. 12:2), we suspect that the ruler is less concerned with the fact of his post-mortem existence than with the scope of his future lot.[230] Though this admittedly surfaces more clearly in Matthew (Matt. 19:16–30) and Mark's (Mark 10:17–31) versions of the story, he is likely curious to know whether his current possessions, including real estate property, will carry over into the age to come.[231]

---

229. Edwards, p. 511.

230. For background on this term, see Perrin, 'Eternal Life'.

231. Matthew (19:22) and Mark (10:22) agree that the ruler had 'many *ktēmata*', i.e. many landholdings.

19. Scrutinizing the ruler's term of address, 'Good Teacher' (v. 18), Jesus responds with a question of his own: *Why do you call me good?* On a surface level, the question is rhetorical, as if Jesus were preparing to correct the erroneous assumption that goodness could be ascribed to anyone but God. But on a deeper level, the counter-question prods the ruler into reflecting further on Jesus' goodness, inviting him to consider whether indeed this attribute might have something to do with the fact that God alone is good. Whether or not it is reasonable to expect anyone in the historical situation to have inferred Jesus' divinity from his goodness, Luke invites his post-Easter readers to do nothing less. The question also operates on a third level, for in referring his interviewer back to *God alone* (*heis ho theos*), Jesus reminds him of Israel's monotheistic creed as expressed in the Shema: 'Hear, O Israel: The LORD is our God, the LORD alone' (*ho theos . . . heis*; Deut. 6:4, emphasis added). Whereas Judaism recognized the Shema as *the* rallying cry for Israel's rejection of idolatry, Jesus' nod to this very familiar text poses a subtle but effective challenge to the ruler's idolatrous attachments, predicated on the faulty assumption that goodness *can* be had apart from God.

20. In responding to the ruler, Jesus initially offers a word of commendation (*You know the commandments*), only then to mark the importance of keeping the commandments, more specifically, the seventh, sixth, eighth, ninth and fifth commandments on the order of Deuteronomy 5:17–19 (LXX). Strikingly absent from the makeshift list are the LXX version's first four commandments (against idolatry, graven images, blasphemy and Sabbath-breaking), as well as the tenth commandment (against coveting). Jesus' selective naming of the commandments may well be intended to reflect his interlocutor's selective adherence to the Decalogue.

21–22. Unfazed by the high bar set before him, at least for the moment, the ruler insists that he has *kept all these since my youth*.[232] But now the conversation takes a sudden turn as Jesus issues an

---

232. Though the historical evidence for bar/bat mitzvah is murky, the rabbinic material suggests that age thirteen was considered an age of accountability even in Jesus' day.

observation (*There is still one thing lacking*), a dual command (*Sell all that you own and distribute the money to the poor*), a promise contingent on the fulfilment of this command (*and you will have treasure in heaven*) and finally one last command (*then come, follow me*). Luke's reader is struck first of all by the fact that Jesus' challenge is very concrete and *practical*. Having earlier instructed his followers to 'sell your possessions, and give alms' and 'make purses for yourselves that do not wear out, an unfailing treasure in heaven' (12:33), Jesus turns the wealthy ruler into a specific test case, demonstrating that these demands were meant neither as sheer hyperbole nor as unattainable ideals. Second, Jesus' requirements are *radical*. The ruler is being asked not only to forgo his material possessions but also to experience – in the very act of transferring his wealth to the poor – an inevitable social demotion from vaunted 'ruler' to one of the faceless poor. Third, the gauntlet Jesus throws down is *paradoxical*, in keeping with the nature of the kingdom. Whereas the ruler had probably approached Jesus with the hope of confirming the continuity between his current life trajectory and post-mortem prospects, he is rudely surprised by a 'to do list' that not only is unexpectedly stringent but also cuts to the core of the ruler's deepest commitments.

23. The erstwhile self-satisfied ruler has a decision to make: either he must give up his considerable wealth as per Jesus' instructions or forgo the possibility of following him altogether. Unable to 'have his cake and eat it too', he becomes visibly *sad* and eventually leaves the scene. What becomes of this unnamed ruler we do not know, although it is not impossible, as strands of early church tradition maintained, that Luke expected his first readers to recognize in this story a real-life episode from the otherwise exemplary Joseph of Arimathea (23:50).

24–25. When *Jesus looked at him* and notices that the ruler's countenance had changed, he remarks on the difficulties facing *those who have wealth to enter the kingdom of God*.[233] How great are those

---

233. Impressed by the presence of *perilypon genomenon* in some manuscripts, the ESV translators prefer a different reading: 'seeing that he had become sad'.

difficulties? To drive the point home, Jesus warns that it is *easier for a camel to go through the eye of a needle than for someone who is rich to enter the kingdom of God*. Despite countless sermons stating otherwise, there is absolutely no evidence either of a Jerusalem gate named 'eye of the needle' or of an ancient practice of making camels kneel before it. Jesus' language is merely hyperbolic, stressing the human impossibility of attaining wealth and salvation.

26–27. Scandalized by the implications of Jesus' pronouncement, those *who heard it* ask aloud, as if with one voice, *Then who can be saved?* The confusion of Jesus' audience can be at least partially explained by a pattern within the familiar stories of Scripture, whereby the conspicuously righteous (Abraham, Job and David, to name a few) are also blessed – as evidence of their righteousness – with conspicuous wealth. While this storied pattern must have led the culture to assume a correlation between worldly wealth and divine blessing, now Jesus flatly overturns that assumption by identifying wealth not as the evidence of eschatological blessedness but rather as a *virtually* insurmountable obstacle to it. Were it not for divine intervention in the lives of such wealthy individuals, salvation would be all but impossible.

28–30. Taking all this in, Peter points out – whether in a self-congratulatory or a searching tone – that he and the other disciples have *left our homes* in order to follow Jesus. In turn, Jesus reassures that all those who have surrendered kith and kin (*house or wife or brothers or parents or children*) out of their personal dedication to the kingdom will be duly recompensed. The timing, degree and nature of the divine compensation is notable. First, the onset of kingdom rewards *in this age* is not entirely startling, since Jesus' followers have already in some sense acquired new family members (8:19–21) and new houses (*oikia*) (9:4; 10:8–12), creating a social reality that anticipates the communal lifestyle taken up in Acts (Acts 2:42–47; 4:32–37). With a view to this sharing of social and material resources, Jesus can rightfully declare that kingdom adherents will receive *very much more* (*pollaplasiona*) or 'many times as much' (NASB, NIV) *in this age*. Finally, if new relatives and new homes are promised in this life, the reward for kingdom devotees in the age to come is precisely what the ruler had been seeking: eternal life.

iii. The third passion prediction (18:31–34)

31. As Jesus' long journey to Jerusalem draws to a close, he *took . . . aside* (*paralabōn*) the disciples in a quasi-revelatory exchange (cf. 9:28 with a similar use of the same verb) and issues his third and final passion prediction (cf. 9:22, 43b–44). As in 9:22, the present verses speak of his being killed and raised on the third day. As in 9:43b–44, Jesus predicts a betrayal, but this time specifying Luke 9's 'human hands' as the grasp of 'Gentiles'. Just as the two men in the parable of the two praying men had 'gone up to the temple' (18:9–14), so, too, Jesus announces to the disciples, *we are going up to Jerusalem* – as if forcing the question of whether their actions there will be more like those of the self-righteous Pharisee or the tax collector. That Jesus is taking *the twelve* (as opposed to, say, 'the disciples') into the Holy City frames this event, once again, as the climactic ingathering of the exiled tribes into eschatological Jerusalem.[234] And when they arrive, Jesus forewarns, *everything that is written about the Son of Man . . . will be accomplished* (*telesthēsetai*), just as he had been anticipating all along (12:50). Jesus' expectation of his fulfilling *the prophets* (plural) as the Son of Man is puzzling not only because the Son of Man figures prominently only in the book of Daniel, but also because in that day Daniel was not even categorized among the prophets.[235] This makes it likely that Luke, not to mention Jesus before him, found traces of the Danielic Son of Man throughout the scriptural corpus, at least in texts which combined themes of suffering and vindication. As Nolland summarizes the issue, 'We cannot be sure what texts Luke would have thought of, but Dan 7:13 would surely be in the list.'[236]

32–33. Jesus predicts seven different events. True to his prediction, Jesus will indeed be *handed over to the Gentiles* (22:47–53). Accordingly, it is not just the Jewish leaders who are responsible for Jesus' death but also the Romans. From there, also in keeping with this prediction, he will be *mocked and insulted* (22:63–64; 23:8–12, 35). Luke's passion narrative never mentions either spitting or flogging

234. 'The Twelve' is seldom used in Luke; its last occurrence is in 9:12.
235. See Fitzmyer, p. 1209.
236. Nolland, p. 896.

but the former is reported in Mark (14:65; 15:19) and the latter would be assumed in any crucifixion (Josephus, *J.W.* 2.306–308; 5.449). Certainly, the Evangelist will narrate in detail how Jesus is killed and raised *on the third day.* With the exception of 'insulting' (cf. Luke 11:45; Acts 14:5), the six injuries said to occur prior to the resurrection are drawn right from Luke's source in Mark's Gospel (Mark 10:33–34).

34. The disciples' failure to understand is of a piece with a recurring Lukan theme (cf. 2:50; 9:45). In explicating that failure, the Gospel writer blends factors of divine sovereignty and human responsibility: on the one hand, *they did not grasp what was said*; on the other, *what he said was hidden from them.* This dullness anticipates the moment of clarity after the resurrection (24:32, 45–48), when all these mysterious predictions of sufferings will make sense within the scope of the divine plan.

Theology

The kingdom Jesus preaches is in every sense an upside-down kingdom. This is demonstrated not least in Jesus' insistence that in this new community children embody the ideal – an ironic fact given that children had always been marginalized in the Hellenistic world. Similarly, because the pernicious pull towards evaluating human worth by conventional metrics of social power can exert itself even in the very possession of wealth, kingdom aspirants must be prepared to forsake their property entirely. Though such self-divestiture may appear foolish to the watching world, trans-actions like these remain the better part of wisdom. How so? Because all earthly attachments and advantages relinquished for the sake of the kingdom will be permanently retrieved at the eschatological inheritance (18:29–30). In adhering to this new and strange set of values, Jesus' followers are not following some abstract principle but simply walking in the path of the crucified one. As far as Luke is concerned, the only God-pleasing life is the cruciform life.

R. Approach to Jerusalem (18:35 – 19:27)

Context

The Gospel now comes full circle. In his healing of the blind man, Jesus performs his last miracle of release, closing out the ministry of release first announced at the synagogue in Nazareth (4:18–19). Now, too, in his calling of Zacchaeus, the last of his one-to-one encounters, he brings salvation, delivering on the same Isaianic promise made in that home-town sermon. Both the roadside beggar and the tax collector were saved from out of a crowd that in one way or another impeded their access to Jesus. This is a poignant symbol: if the Son of Man and Son of David (18:39) would become king against the wishes of his adversaries (19:27), those who wish to participate in his reign must be prepared to stand apart from the crowd as they seek to follow him.

Comment

i. Jesus heals the blind man from Jericho (18:35–43)

35. Jericho was principally significant in connection with Joshua's first victory at the beginning of his campaign of conquest. The scriptural account recorded in Joshua 2 and 6, detailing the spies' reconnaissance mission to Jericho and the city's overthrow, respectively, typifies this episode together with the story of Zacchaeus (19:1–10) in two respects. First, if Jesus *is* the king preparing to go to war (14:31), then his initial victory in the approach to Jerusalem comes, just as it did for Joshua, at Jericho. Second, whereas this passage makes a hero out of an anonymous roadside beggar (Mark 10:46 identifies him as Bartimaeus) and the following story celebrates a tax collector who occupies an equally low-status role (19:9–10), the social status of both these Lukan converts mirrors that of the prostitute Rahab.[237] When one considers that all three figures each had a dishonourable vocation, that all three defected to Yahweh's cause and that all three did so against the tide of social pressure, one wonders whether there is more to the geographical setting of 18:35–43 and 19:1–10 than meets the eye.

---

237. On the social shame of begging, see Johnson, p. 283.

The pinpointing of Jericho brings other resonances into play. Eighteen miles due east of the Holy City, Jericho sat on the singular international highway leading to and from Babylon. By leading his retinue on *this* road, the road back from the land of exile (Isa. 40:3; cf. Luke 3:4), Jesus may have been staging his Jerusalem-bound convoy as the long-awaited return from exile.[238] Yet if gestures towards the redemptive story are in play, so too are connections to another part of Luke's narrative. Recalling that the first category of seed in the parable of the sower (8:5) was sown 'along the path' (NIV; *para tēn hodon*), one may be forgiven for wondering whether this blind man's position *by the roadside* (*para tēn hodon*) speaks of his initially precarious situation as a hearer of God's word. More to the point, insofar as the blind man beside the path symbolizes the disciples' initial failure to understand Jesus' passion (18:34) (a failure which will eventually be reversed by sudden insight at Emmaus, 24:31), the blind beggar's starting position beside the road hints that their initial incomprehension was at bottom a failure to hear. Happily, by the end of this encounter, the beggar will soon be following Jesus *on* the road (v. 43), the road *from* exile.[239]

---

238. This is more than plausible, simply because first-century culture seems to have been much more attuned to the symbolic significance of space. Josephus notes, for example, that within little more than a decade after Jesus' death, the messianic pretender Theudas 'convinced most of the crowd to bring along their possessions and to follow him to the Jordan River, since he had said to them that he was a prophet and that on command he would part the river and grant them easy passage through it' (*Ant.* 20.97; my translation). In hoping to part the Jordan, Theudas was not simply trying to perform a random trick. Undoubtedly, as the first step in this messianic uprising, Theudas was hoping to re-enact exactly what Joshua did (where Joshua did it) before conquering the land.

239. This is made explicit in the Markan parable where blind Bartimaeus moves from following Jesus 'by the road' (10:46) to 'on the road' (10:52) (my translations). Curiously, Mark locates the healing of blind Bartimaeus not on Jesus' approach but on his way out of Jericho (10:46), while Matthew (20:29–34) reports two blind men being healed. The apparent discrepancies are hardly irreconcilable; see Bock, pp. 1501–1504.

36. Jericho was a city of no mean size and commerce.[240] And so the blind beggar's ability to detect the *crowd going by* in the midst of the city's hustle and bustle is some indication of the size of Jesus' entourage. With piqued curiosity, he enquires into *what was happening*. Not coincidentally, acts of 'hearing' and 'enquiring' also characterize the parable of the sower's ideal hearer (8:8–9), reminding readers that spiritual interest is not far removed from curiosity.

37–38. The crowd responds to the blind man's question by indicating the approach of one *Jesus of Nazareth*. It is an epithet which, though virtually unparalleled in the Gospel (cf. 4:34), will soon become standard in the church's proclamation of their Risen Lord (Acts 2:22; 3:6; 4:10; 6:14; 22:8; 24:5; 26:9). Along the same lines, Luke's choice of verb for this identification (*they told him*) is *apēngeilan*, denoting – as elsewhere in the narrative – not simply the transfer of information but proclamation.[241] On hearing this response to his enquiry, the beggar cries out to Jesus by a term different from the one used by the crowd: *Son of David*. The phrase not only speaks of Jesus' capacity as healer (Solomon son of David was renowned for his healing abilities; cf. Josephus, *Ant.* 8.42–49), but also more fundamentally underscores Jesus' messianic status.[242] On one level, then, the blind man calls out to Jesus as healer; on another level, his cry 'reminds the reader just who is approaching Jerusalem . . . the Davidic Messiah, the one promised an eternal reign on the throne of his father David (Lk. 1.32–33)'.[243] The blind man's confession reveals that in his understanding he is well ahead of the physically sighted but spiritually blind disciples; it also anticipates the judgment of the crowd when Jesus enters Jerusalem

---

240. This is to be inferred not least from the fact that in 37 BC Mark Antony had granted the city to Cleopatra as a special gift.

241. BDAG, p. 79.

242. The title *Son of David* is not necessarily altogether different from *Jesus of Nazareth*. If the beggar interpreted *Nazōraios* in relation to the Davidic 'shoot [*nēṣer*] of Jesse' (Isa. 11:1), he may have derived Jesus' messianic status, at least in part, from his identity as a Nazarene. See Nolland, p. 900.

243. Strauss, *Davidic Messiah*, p. 307.

(19:38). The man's plea to Jesus is simple and succinct: *have mercy on me!* It is the third and final time Jesus will hear a plea for mercy (cf. 16:24; 17:13).

39. Irritated by the blind beggar's shouting, those *in front* of him sternly *ordered [epetimōn]* him to be silent. This is a striking reversal, since the same verb (*epitimaō*, to rebuke) that is here predicated of the crowd identifying Jesus 'of Nazareth' was earlier predicated of Jesus when he silenced a demon (4:35) who likewise attempted to reveal him as being 'of Nazareth'. Given this observation, Luke's more careful readers will discern that the period of messianic secrecy is drawing to a close: Jesus is now about to be revealed as the Davidic Messiah. Despite the bystanders' attempt to quiet the beggar, he persists all the more, refusing to be silenced on account of his confession.

40–42. Unexpectedly halting in his tracks, Jesus commands *the man to be brought to him* and asks him to articulate his wishes. The elliptical Greek behind the beggar's request (*Lord, let me see again; hina anablepsō*) occasions a response with the same verb: *Receive your sight* (*anablepson*). Recovery of sight (*anablepsis*) is of course exactly what Jesus has promised to bring (4:18; 7:22) as part and parcel of his mission, just as it is the fulfilment of Isaiah's vision of return from exile (Isa. 61:1–2).[244] In granting his request, Jesus credits his suppliant with not just a faith for healing but a saving faith, evinced by the beggar's confession of Jesus as Messiah, his persistence (cf. 18:1–8) and his refusal to be cowed into silence (cf. Acts 4:17–22).

43. At Jesus' word, the blind man's sight is *immediately* restored, yielding a spontaneous corporate act of worship among the *people* (*laos*).[245] Meanwhile, the now-healed man becomes both worshipper and disciple, as he follows Jesus while *glorifying God.* The restored blind man is presented as an ideal disciple. Those whose sight has been restored by Jesus will confess him as Messiah, follow him and glorify God – all the while moving observers to praise (cf. Matt. 5:16). Jesus the king's first victory at Jericho involves not the

---

244. Fitzmyer, p. 1214.
245. See Kodell, 'Use of *Laos*'.

vanquishing of the city's inhabitants but the restoration of a roadside beggar who would not be held back by the crowd.

ii. Zacchaeus (19:1–10)

1–2. Whereas Luke 18:35 had Jesus approaching Jericho, now he is finally entering the city with the intention of only passing through. Zacchaeus's identity as a 'sinner' (19:7) would have been implied by his profession as a tax collector. Within the Roman tax collection system, Zacchaeus's role as something like a regional manager of tax collectors was the obvious source of his wealth. In this respect, the introduced character is doubly notorious: not only has he been willing to exploit his fellow Judeans on behalf of Rome, he has organized others to the same end.

3. Zacchaeus's seeking (*ezētei*) to see Jesus (more exactly, to see *who Jesus was* [*Iēsoun tis estin*]) will mirror the Son of Man's seeking (*zētēsai*) the lost (v. 10). That the tax collector should wish to *see* Jesus is not incidental: seeing Jesus is tantamount to seeing salvation (2:30; 3:6), because Jesus *is* salvation (1:69). Unfortunately, Zacchaeus's efforts are frustrated by two obstacles: the crowd and his own diminutive stature. Yet in Luke's economy of faith, obstacles have a way of quickly becoming opportunities.

4. Responding creatively to his challenges, Zacchaeus in a moment mentally maps out the trajectory of Jesus' entourage and runs *ahead* (*eis to emprosthen*, 'into his presence') in order to climb a sycamore fig tree for a better view. Zacchaeus's behaviour is undignified, if not socially unacceptable: in antiquity running and tree-climbing were the domains of children, not adult males, much less well-established adult males. Yet this is part of Luke's point: Zacchaeus has cast aside all decorum if only to accomplish his objective of seeing Jesus. Some situations, the Evangelist seems to say, demand our jettisoning social convention for the sake of achieving God's purposes.

5. On arriving 'at the place' (*epi ton topon*), Jesus looks up and instructs the tax collector to *hurry* and descend. The reason for such urgency? Jesus clarifies: 'for today it is necessary for me to remain in your house' (my own translation). The adverb *today* (*sēmeron*), here positioned with emphasis at the beginning of the clause, is a Lukan favourite; it is regularly associated – as in this case – with salvation breaking into the present moment in an extraordinary manner (2:11; 4:21; 23:43).[246] Zacchaeus must hurry down the tree because salvation has come *today*! Yet the same salvation is also a matter of divine necessity (*dei*). Though Luke's Jesus was only passing through Jericho (v. 1), his sudden change of plans follows an incorrigible divine will bent on saving. The means and token of that salvation are nothing less than Jesus' remaining (*menei*) in the house of the sinner.

6–7. Described with the same words used in Jesus' invitation (*so he hurried down*; *speusas katabē*), Zacchaeus's compliance is complete. Reaching the ground, he joyfully receives Jesus. Meanwhile, the watching crowd mutters its disapproval, much as the disobedient Sinai generation murmured against God (Exod. 15:24, LXX). The source of their displeasure lies in Jesus' willingness to visit a sinner – and a highly conspicuous one at that. The crowd's disparaging attitude is but an extension of the prejudices earlier expressed by the religious leaders (Luke 5:27–32). Like leader, like follower.

8. That Zacchaeus is described as having *stood there* is curious. Perhaps we are nudged to surmise that when the tax collector first came down, he either knelt or prostrated himself prior to standing back up. At any rate, Zacchaeus next speaks *to the Lord* (*pros ton kyrion*), carrying a twofold meaning pertinent to Jesus as 'sir' and Lord of the universe.

Zacchaeus makes a double promise. First, in immediate response to Jesus' request to stay at his house, he transfers a substantial portion of his own resources to the less-well-to-do, thereby assisting in the very release Jesus announces (cf. 4:18–19). Second, Zacchaeus offers to restore fourfold damages to anyone whom he has defrauded. While Old Testament law normally calls for double restitution in cases of theft (Exod. 22:7), Zacchaeus generously doubles the amount of restitution mandated by law.

9. In response to Zacchaeus's announcement, Jesus now offers his own assurance of salvation. This salvation comes to the tax collector not at some indefinite future moment and in some faraway space but *today* and in Zacchaeus's *house*. The coupling of *today* and

---

246. See Troftgruben, 'Today'.

house in verse 9 mirrors the same word pairing in verse 5, as if to underscore their importance. For the Evangelist, salvation is not merely a matter of individual decision but devolves to the whole *household* (Acts 16:31), not at some indeterminate time in the future but *today*. The basis for and outworking of this salvation is Zacchaeus's filial relationship to Abraham, evinced through the tax collector's open-handedness to the poor and oppressed. It is through Jesus-encounters like these, Luke seems to say, that God is even now raising up children of Abraham, just as John had promised he would (3:8).

10. The explanatory *gar* (*for*) in Jesus' continued summation of the incident clarifies the principal reason for Zacchaeus's new standing: the Son of Man's coming to search for and *save the lost*. Concerning this pronouncement, we are reminded of Luke 15, where in response to the grumbling of the religious leaders (v. 2), Luke's Jesus tells three parables of searching and saving. For the Son of Man, as for Luke's readers, such search-and-rescue operations usually occur through 'chance encounters', the seeming randomness of which belies God's sovereign saving purposes.

iii. Parable of the ten pounds (19:11–27)

11. Jesus' recent declaration that Zacchaeus's house had inherited salvation 'today' (19:9) would have convinced many onlookers *that the kingdom of God was to appear immediately*. And because Zion was to be centre stage for Israel's redemption, Jesus' position *near to Jerusalem*, anticipating his going up to Jerusalem (19:28) and his drawing near to it (19:41), would have only further fuelled such speculations. Now, as many commentators see it, *he went on to tell a parable* in order to squelch any inferences regarding the kingdom's immediacy. In my judgment, however, Jesus is seeking to rectify the people's misunderstanding as it relates not to the timing of the kingdom but to their gratuitous assumption that the arrival of the kingdom would be good news for one and all. In the face of such presumption, Jesus' parable means to say, 'Don't be so sure.'

12. Though the NRSV presents the central figure of Jesus' parable as a *nobleman*, the Greek phrase *anthrōpos tis eugenēs* is better translated 'a man of noble birth' (NIV). The point is worth making, if only because the phrase *anthrōpos tis* puts this figure in the same category as identically named characters headlining Luke's parables (cf. 10:30; 14:16; 15:11; 16:1, 19; 20:9). While in rabbinic parables, the journeying master is typically an allegorical stand-in for God, in Luke's Gospel *anthrōpos tis* typically marks out the Adamic Son of Man, that is, Jesus.

Like the prodigal son (15:13), the nobleman goes off *to a distant country* (*eis chōran makran*). In my interpretation of 15:13, I argued that 'distant country' symbolically represents the land of exile. In the interests of consistency, I provisionally apply the same meaning here. In this case, the period of the master's absence is not the span of time leading up to the parousia (as the parable is traditionally interpreted) but instead the remaining period of Israel's exile, which finally draws to a close with the destruction of the temple in AD 70.[247] The purpose of the nobleman's journey, leading up to his return, is not so much to obtain *royal power* (NRSV) or to 'have himself appointed king' (NIV) as to 'receive for himself a kingdom' (rightly ESV, similarly NASB). Though there is obviously a time lapse between the nobleman's reception of the kingdom and his return, there is 'no hint of a long passage of time to make the reader think . . . of the "delay of the parousia"'.[248]

13. Prior to his departure, the man *summoned ten of his slaves* and allots to them *ten pounds* (*deka mnas*), each pound being equivalent to roughly three and a half months' wages.[249] The allocation of ten coins to ten individuals builds both on the woman's ten silver coins (15:8) and the ten variously responsive men with leprosy (17:12, 17). In the present passage, as in Luke 15 and 17, ten is the number of completion: 'ten slaves/servants' represents the sum of the man's servants; ten pounds, the full accounting of his entrusted wealth. He expects each servant to *do business* [*pragmateusasthe*] *with these until*

---

247. On the destruction of the temple as the end of exile, see commentary below on 21:5–38. On this general line of interpretation, albeit with some variance from my own reading, see Johnson, pp. 288–295; Wright, *Victory of God*, pp. 632–639.

248. Johnson, pp. 293–294.

249. In the Matthean parallel (Matt. 25:14–15), the master confers varying amounts on his servants.

I come back [*en hō erchomai*]. As a qualification of the NRSV's rendering, there is no reason to limit the grammatically awkward *en hō erchomai* to the notion of return, as the verb means 'to come' and 'to go' as well.[250] The verb *pragmateuomai* pertains to the realm of banking and commerce, and so the nobleman is concerned that his servants execute wise management with a view to making a profit.[251] In keeping with his earlier thematizing of wealth, Luke once again asserts that God-given resources are not an end in themselves but tools for investment.

14. The introduction of *the citizens of his country*, hostile to the nobleman, establishes a secondary plot line that would have been completely unrelated to the main plot, were it not for the fact that the fates of his servants and disloyal citizens are decided at the same climactic moment (v. 27). The citizens seem to represent Jews who resist Jesus' assertion of kingship; the servants, Jesus' sympathizers, who have been entrusted with the kingdom charge.

The narrative recounted in verses 12 and 14 bears a striking resemblance to recent political events of the day, when, following the death of Herod the Great (4 BC), his son Archelaus went to Rome in order to convince Caesar Augustus that he – and not his brothers – should be the deceased Herod's successor.[252] Unfortunately for Archelaus, his overture was partially stymied by an envoy of Jews who, having caught wind of the young ruler's aspirations, made their own trip to Rome in order to make a case *against* the would-be king's rule. The delegation was at least partially successful (reducing Archelaus to becoming ethnarch rather than king); a subsequent delegation in AD 6 would have him removed altogether. Though history records no direct reprisals as we find in 19:27, the events of 4 BC, predictably, did

---

250. Guy, 'Interplay', pp. 121–122.

251. Thayer, p. 534.

252. While some commentators see Herod the Great in the background (as he made a similar overture), the case for Archelaus is strengthened by the presence of his palace at Jericho (see Snodgrass, *Intent*, p. 537). Jesus' allusion, in other words, is geographically specific. See Josephus, *Ant.* 17.299–314.

not bode well for Archelaus's later treatment of the citizens (Josephus, *J. W.* 2.111).

The similarities between Archelaus and Jesus' nobleman are not intended to ascribe the historical figure's flaws to the parabolic character but rather to juxtapose the motivations and outcomes of the two envoys, historical and fictive. If the Jewish delegation, hoping to nip Archelaus's kingship in the bud, was motivated by envious hatred (as Josephus tells us), the same dark motivation animates the parable's concerned citizens (and by extension the Sanhedrin soon to face Jesus). In contrast to Archelaus, the nobleman of Luke 19 not only firmly secures his kingdom (v. 15) but also executes judgment against his opposers (v. 27).

15. Having charged his ten servants to invest what had been entrusted to them (v. 13), the nobleman, on securing his kingdom, selectively follows up with three of them (vv. 16–26) *when he returned.* Again, while most commentators link this keeping of accounts with the parousia, the stubborn fact remains that verse 15 leaves no suggestion of a large temporal gap between the nobleman's reception of the kingdom and his return. In Luke's larger narrative, Jesus is declared king in the very next passage (19:38), despite being hated by his opposers (23:2, 37, 38). Soon after that, Jesus' rightful possession of the kingdom is presupposed (e.g. Luke 23:42; Acts 1:6). In other words, he secures the kingdom well before the parousia. On these observations, I suggest that if Luke invites us to look for a coming (*erchomai*) on the part of this kingdom-acquiring *anthrōpos*, we need go no further than the confines of his Gospel, more precisely, the coming (*erchomenon*) of the Son of Man (*huios tou anthrōpou*) to close out the period of exile (21:27). This 'coming' (alluded to in 19:13) has to do not principally with the parousia (though a *sensus plenior* cannot be ruled out) but first and foremost with the destruction of the temple (AD 70).

16–17. The parable's movement from most-effective to least-effective investors puts the emphasis on the climactic failure of the third and final servant rather than on the success of the first. Nevertheless, the success of the first servant is stunning: *Lord, your pound has made ten more pounds.* The master's commendations include a characterological assessment. Because the first servant has *been trustworthy in a very small thing*, he is declared to be *good*, falling into the same category as the good person with a good heart (6:45) and the good soil (8:8, 15). Accordingly, he is granted authority over *ten cities* (cf. Rev. 2:26–27; Wis. 3:8). One cannot ignore the thought-provoking connection with Luke's exorcised demoniac, who proclaimed Jesus' powers throughout the Decapolis (ten cities) (8:26–39; cf. Mark 5:20).

18–19. Like the first servant, the *second* servant refers to the coin left in his possession as *your pound*, reinforcing that there was never any sense in which the servant *owned* that which had been entrusted to him, for everything belongs to God. Though this servant does not realize as great a profit as the first, he still reaps a reward commensurate with his performance: *And you, rule over five cities.*

20. The third and final member of the representative sample, curiously designated as *the other* (*ho heteros*), appears with a report: *Lord, here is your pound. I wrapped it up in a piece of cloth.* Like the first two servants, this 'other' shows appropriate deference (all three servants call the nobleman *Lord*) and presents him with his original coin. But unlike his predecessors, this servant returns no yield. Among the range of options for financial management in the day, the strategy of laying aside the coin in a handkerchief would not have been unprecedented or even inherently suspect (3Q15). Nevertheless, his handling of the coin amounts to a flat rejection of the nobleman's explicit instructions to 'do business' (*pragmateusasthe*; v. 13).

21. Having recounted his course of action, the third servant now explains his anxieties over the nobleman's reputation as a *harsh* (*austēros*) or 'exacting' (JB) *man* (Matt. 25:24 describes the master as *sclēros*, hard). Perhaps, arguably like the ruler Archelaus, the nobleman was renowned for taking (*aireis*) *what you did not deposit* and reaping *what you did not sow*. The characterization is appropriate to Luke's Jesus, as we recall that his disciples picked up (*ērthē*) scraps of bread they did not supply (9:17) and that he himself sought to harvest a yield he did not sow (8:4–8).

22–23. The enraged nobleman does not dispute the third servant's characterization. On the contrary, he confirms it, only to turn the servant's own assessment into a warrant for judgment: '*I will judge you* from your own mouth, *you* evil *slave!*' The words of condemnation combine two words that invoke Jesus' earlier observation that 'the evil person [*ho ponēros*] out of evil treasure produces evil; for it is out of the abundance of the heart that the mouth [*stoma*] speaks' (6:45b). The interplay of 19:22 and 6:45 makes clear that the third servant's malfeasance is not merely a matter of poor judgment: his inaction is a grave moral failure to which his own mouth gives witness. At the very least, the servant could have *put my money into the bank* in order to earn interest.[253]

24–26. As a result of the third servant's maladministration, the nobleman issues the following instructions to *the bystanders*: *Take the pound from him and give it to the one who has ten pounds*. The command is surprising, as common sense might dictate that the one with the most pounds would be the last to need another one (v. 25).[254] But once again, the kingdom operates according to a counter-intuitive principle. In the kingdom, those who steward their possessions faithfully and wisely will see the scope of their management increase, while those who fail to do so will eventually lose whatever they have. In fact, the concluding judgment, together with the nobleman's characterization of the delinquent slave as *ponēros*, puts this character in perilously close company with the nobleman's opposers (vv. 14, 27). Though the text is not especially keen to spell out the final fate of the cautious servant, the main point remains the same: followers of Jesus who invest appropriately in the kingdom will receive greater degrees of 'wealth' and authority. Meanwhile, however, those followers who allow that which has been entrusted to them to sit idle will lose any and all advantage such divine conferrals might have otherwise brought. For Luke, the proof of discipleship consists in one's willingness to invest.

27. Finally circling back to the citizens introduced at verse 14, the nobleman takes the opportunity to deal decisively with his enemies. For most modern readers, the nobleman's words (*But as*

---

253. Though Torah forbade charging interest within the covenantal community (Exod. 22:25; Lev. 25:35–37; Deut. 23:19–20), interest-bearing loans to Gentiles fell well within the scope of permissible behaviour (Deut. 23:20).
254. Verse 25 is text-critically suspect, missing in some important manuscripts (D, W).

for these enemies of mine who did not want me to be king over them – bring them here and slaughter them in my presence) are shocking insofar as they come from a character clearly representative of Jesus. Yet if contemporary sensibilities are offended, it is in part because most of us are unfamiliar with the brutal winner-takes-all political realities of the first-century world. In my judgment, the character's final command primarily looks ahead not to the eschatological judgment (contra most commentators) but to the destruction of the temple.

Theology

On the cusp of becoming king, Jesus offers the parable of the ten pounds in order to illuminate the various responses to his emerging kingship. According to the parable, three different strategies present themselves: the path of bullish kingdom investment (kingdom submission plus investment), the path of risk avoidance (kingdom submission with no investment) and the path of outright kingdom resistance (no submission, no investment). In the parable, the first two servants belong to the first of these categories; the third servant, the second category; and the king's unruly subjects match the third profile. While there is certainly a binary quality to kingdom participation (after all, one is either *in* the kingdom or *outside* it), it is nonetheless true that the kingdom elicits varying shades of response.

The parable will begin to play itself out soon enough in Acts, for whatever early traces of human faithfulness, negligence and opposition appear in that story, these responses to the kingdom will take a crisper and more definite form as the narrative trajectory of Luke's second volume unwinds. Soon enough, lost opportunities (like that of Ananias and Sapphira) will translate into lost authority, while Paul, for example, will capitalize on his God-given opportunity, acquiring geographical 'authority' one city at a time as he undertakes his missionary journeys. Meanwhile, those who oppose the apostolic proclamation mark themselves out as those royal subjects who were never supportive of the nobleman's royal claims.

As much as the parable plays itself out in Luke–Acts, it also provides a template for all human responsiveness to the kingdom. In this vein, the question the Gospel writer poses to his audience is not just 'Are you for or against Jesus?' There is a second and perhaps even more germane question for Luke's readers and it is this: 'If you are for Jesus, how will you leverage the resources with which you have been entrusted?'

Such investment primarily takes two forms: social and financial capital. Many in Jericho praised God for Jesus' healing of the blind man, but it was only the blind man who actually followed Jesus despite the peer pressure of the crowds. Many had lined the streets to see Jesus, but it was only Zacchaeus who, having made a fool of himself in order to see Jesus, was declared a son of Abraham. In response to this declaration, he gives back out of his financial resources. Ten servants had been entrusted with a coin, but only two (a blind man and a tax collector?) are singled out as having properly invested theirs. Christological confession is empty unless accompanied by actions that put one at social or material risk.

Once again, the proper point of departure for obedience is Christology. Those subjects who fail to understand the mystery of the suffering Davidic Son of Man will naturally reject Jesus' kingship. Meanwhile, those servants who mishandle their trust do so not because they fail to take their master's kingship seriously, but because they fail to grasp the king's character and expectations – his determination to reap what he has not sown and to produce something out of nothing. One's personal destiny rises and falls on one's lived-out Christology.

6. MINISTRY IN JERUSALEM (19:28 – 21:38)

A. Entry into Jerusalem (19:28–48)

Context

As Jesus enters Jerusalem, his long journey that began at 9:51 is now drawing to a close. More than that, the whole of Luke's Gospel is drawing to a close. In reviewing the beginning of our story, we recall that the twelve-year-old Jesus was at the temple, listening to the teachers and asking questions (2:46). At this point, at the culmination of his life and ministry, Jesus is *teaching* at the same temple (19:47), just as Israel's returning Messiah was expected to do. In Luke 3, John had promised a messianic 'coming one', while also affirming that God had power to raise up children for Abraham from the very stones (3:7–17). Prior to that, the angels had announced that the birth of Jesus, the 'blessed one' (1:42), signalled peace for the elect (2:14). Now in Jesus' triumphal entry these insights converge, as the crowds declare him the coming one, the blessed one and the one who makes peace available (19:38). That which had been said about

Jesus at the beginning of his life is now finally proving true towards the end of his life.

On his way to Jerusalem, Jesus had both sent out delegations (10:1) and talked about royal delegations (14:31–33). This present section includes yet another delegation (19:28–36), with two disciples tasked with finding Jesus' transportation. In the process of doing so, they declare him Lord (vv. 31, 34). It is a declaration that the crowds will embrace, but one which the Pharisees reject (v. 39). In rejecting Jesus, they demonstrate that the parable of the pounds (19:11–27) is already proving true. The parting of the ways, between those who embrace Jesus as king and those who reject him as such, is now unfolding.

Comment

i. Preparations for the entry (19:28–36)

28–29a. The phrase *after he had said this* links the ensuing action with the previous passage (19:11–27), a parable of a hard-fought kingship and judgment.[1] Jesus is said to be *going up* because the road from Jericho *to Jerusalem* steadily increases in elevation. Just due east of the Holy City were the two villages of Bethphage and Bethany, occupying the eastern elevation of the *Mount of Olives*. The Mount of Olives is symbolically laden not only because this was the route by which King David fled Absalom's rebellion (2 Sam. 15:30) but also because it was written that on the day the Lord would execute judgment against the nations, he would stand with 'his feet . . . on the Mount of Olives, which lies before Jerusalem on the east' (Zech. 14:4).

29b–30. Sending a delegation of *two of the disciples* (the minimum number of persons necessary to establish a legal witness; cf. Deut. 19:15), Jesus commands them to enter *the village ahead of you*. There, so he predicts, the disciples will find a tethered *colt* (*pōlon*), a term typically referring to the offspring of a horse but sometimes used to denote a young donkey. Their task is to untie and – not unlike the way in which Roman authorities would commandeer personal transportation ultimately in Caesar's name – retrieve it for his

---

1. So also Liefeld, p. 1011.

personal use. That Jesus should mount a colt that has *never been ridden* is important in two respects. In the first place, in antiquity if a colt or horse was intentionally unridden, it was normally because it was being set aside for a special ceremonial purpose (e.g. m. Sanh. 25:1). Second, Jesus' remarkable ability to mount an unbroken colt and ride it steadily into the city speaks of his lordship over creation. In appropriating the animal, Jesus prepares to fulfil Zechariah 9:9:

> Rejoice greatly, O daughter Zion!
>   Shout aloud, O daughter Jerusalem!
> Lo, your king comes to you;
>   triumphant and victorious is he,
> humble and riding on a donkey,
>   on a colt, the foal of a donkey.[2]

31. There is no reason to expect that random townsfolk in Jesus' day would allow a pair of strangers simply to help themselves to their horse – no questions asked. There *would* likely be questions, and for one question in particular (*Why are you untying it?*) Jesus pre-supplies an answer: *The Lord needs it* (*ho kyrios autou chreian echei*). Though all the major translations fall in line with this rendering (NRSV), the Greek may be alternatively translated as 'its Lord has need'. The ambiguity, little clarified by a consideration of the basic exegetical data, is almost certainly intentional.[3] By contrasting Jesus' lordship (*kyrios autou*) over the colt (v. 31) with its owners' (*kyrioi autou*) lordship by legal possession (v. 33), with yet another oblique affirmation of their master's ultimate lordship over the animal in verse 34 ('The Lord needs it' [NRSV]/'Its Lord has need'),

---

2. Concerned to tighten the connection with Zech. 9:9, Matthew (Matt. 21:1–9) has Jesus riding (alternately?) both a young horse and a young donkey.

3. In 19:33, Luke changes Mark's 'some of the bystanders' (Mark 11:5) enquiring into the disciples' actions to 'its owners' (*hoi kyrioi autou*). This phrase would favour the alternative translation for v. 31. On the other hand, in support of the standard translation, Luke's 'general use of *chreian echei* has the genitive of the thing required' (Johnson, p. 296).

it is almost as if Luke's triple use of *kyrios* suggests Jesus' lordship encases and overrides all previously existing claims of ownership. Thus, *ho kyrios* means that Jesus is not just 'the master' of the disciples but 'the Lord' in the cosmic sense.[4]

32-34. The two anonymous disciples are identified merely as *those who were sent* (*hoi apestalmenoi*). Connoting a sense of mission, the same verb (*apostellō*) has already been used in connection with the sending out of the paired disciples – also 'ahead of him' – during the missionary campaign of the seventy-two (10:1). Later in the story, in the parable of the king going to war (14:31–33), the king sends ahead (*aposteilas*) a delegation suing for peace (14:32). In retrospect, both 'sendings' seem to prepare for the present delegation. If in Luke 10 the thirty-six pairs of disciples are to proclaim the nearness of the kingdom ahead of the king (10:9), now a single pair comes to Jerusalem on Jesus' behalf in preparation for his arrival. And if 14:31–33 provides any clue, this pair of disciples *is* the fulfilment of that parabolic embassy suing for peace. After all, when word gets out – as it certainly would – that the disciples are appropriating a colt because '*its* Lord has need', the mere circulated report of this event will come to function as a last-ditch appeal for repentance. When the two disciples arrive, they find events unfold exactly as Jesus predicted (confirming his trustworthiness as a prophet): the unridden and tethered colt is on hand, the question is presented and they answer just as they had been told.

35. On bringing the colt back to Jesus, the disciples begin spreading out *their cloaks on the colt*. The makeshift drapery corresponds to what one might have expected to see on the horse of a victorious Roman ruler. That *they set Jesus on it* means that the disciples are physically seating Jesus on the colt: Jesus is not just unilaterally claiming his kingship, for the disciples are participating in making him king.

36. The disciples' spreading out their cloaks on the back of the colt is now matched by the crowd's *spreading their cloaks on the road*. Worn by men and women alike, the cloak or *himation* was a

---

4. As argued more fully by Rowe, *Narrative Christology*, pp. 159–163.

rectangularly shaped mantle made of heavy cloth, usually wool or linen. And because, like other items of personal clothing, the cloak was an extension of personal identity, the very act of laying one's cloak at the feet of another was an expression of submission and honour.[5] Still more, the practice of laying one's clothing on the path of a processing king is historically well established and signified the ascription of royal or military-leadership status.[6] That the crowds create a path out of their own garments 'on the way' (*en tē hodō*) shows that they are responding to John the Baptizer's ministry of preparing the way of the Lord (3:4–5; cf. Isa. 40:3–5).

ii. Triumphal entry (19:37–44)

37. In his final approach to Jerusalem, Jesus descends westwards from the *Mount of Olives*. Whereas up to this point roadside supporters have been busy lining his trajectory with their cloaks (v. 36), now the energy mounts as *the whole multitude of the disciples* spontaneously breaks into vocal worship. They express themselves *joyfully*, signalling that the promised day of rejoicing (6:23) is now beginning to dawn. The public designation of Jesus as Messiah is a shift from earlier episodes. Earlier Jesus had silenced a demonic spirit who declared Jesus the priestly Messiah with a loud voice (*phōnē megalē*; 4:33), but now he unreservedly receives the disciples' messianic adulation – uttered with the same *loud voice* (*phōnē megalē*; cf. 17:15).

38. The disciples' cheers combine strains of Psalm 118:26 with a variation of the angels' chorus at Jesus' birth (2:14). It is not surprising that the crowds are singing lines from Psalm 118: it is Passover time and Psalm 118 belonged to the annual liturgy of psalms rehearsed every Passover in anticipation of Israel's return from exile. Yet there is a Christological significance to all this. On the story level, the crowd's chant from Psalm 118:26 (*Blessed is the king / who comes in the name of the Lord!*) puts Elizabeth's declaration of Jesus as the 'blessed one' (1:42) right alongside John's prediction of a messianic 'coming one' (3:16; 7:19). Wittingly or unwittingly,

---

5. For fuller discussion, see Rothe, *Roman Identity*.

6. Josephus, *Ant.* 11.325–339; 12.312, 348–349; 16.12–15; 1 Macc. 4:19–25; 5:45–54; 10:86; 13:43–51; 2 Macc. 4:21–22.

Elizabeth and John once darkly expressed what is now coming clearly into view: Jesus is the messianic fulfilment of Psalm 118, the Davidic restorer destined to bring Israel back from exile.

39. The Pharisees are not necessarily *in the crowd* (*apo tou ochlou*) but perhaps 'part of the crowd' or even, most likely, 'apart from the crowd'. Keenly watching Jesus' every move, they demand that the *Teacher* rebuke his *disciples*. Such a rebuke is justified in their view because the disciples are implying not only that their master is the catalyst of return from exile but also that he is the messianic 'coming one'. Their resistance shows that they are the king's enemies in the parable of the pounds (19:27).

40. In introducing Jesus' ministry, John the Baptizer had punningly remarked on God's ability to raise up sons (Hebrew *bānîm*) of Abraham from stones (Hebrew *'ăbānîm*) (3:8). Jesus' disciples, now receiving him, are also sons of Abraham in just this sense (1:55; 13:16; 19:9). Should these disciples/sons remain *silent*, Jesus intones, building on John's pun and drawing on Habakkuk 2:11, the very *stones would shout out*, thereby discharging the vocation which would otherwise fall to children of Abraham. Though patently hyperbolic, it should not go unremarked that inanimate objects can and do give voice to God's glory (e.g. Pss 19:1–4; 148:1–10). If the stones are poised to shout out, as Jesus claims, it only means that the creation is ready to respond to the revelation of the Messiah, even if that response is humanly imperceptible.

41. Jesus has already declared the blessedness of those 'who weep now' (6:21b). Now one reason for such sorrow comes into view: as he draws *near* Jerusalem, Jesus weeps over the grim judgment awaiting the city (vv. 42–44). True, others before Jesus (Jeremiah, for example) had wept over the city. But Jesus' lament is climactic and summative.

42. Despite his disciples' celebration of peace 'in heaven' above (19:38b), the city below, Jesus warns, will tragically remain ignorant of those things conducive to peace (*ta pros eirēnēn*). Understood against 14:32, Luke's Jesus presents himself as the parabolic king suing for peace. That this same peace is *hidden from your eyes* suggests that Jesus' offer of divine shalom is a mystery veiled every bit as much as the mystery of the kingdom itself (8:10).

43. As in previous sieges of Jerusalem, Jesus predicts that the city's enemies will *set up ramparts around you*, only then to enclose the city walls. With the same roles but a different set of actors, this was the all-too-familiar script of exile.[7] At the same time, Jesus' prediction would turn out to be factually accurate, retrospectively confirming his prophetic status as far as Luke's post-AD 70 readers were concerned.[8]

44. So thorough will Jerusalem's devastation be that Jesus is compelled to cast visions of the city – its inhabitants as well as its architecture – being crushed *to the ground (edaphiousin)*. To reinforce the point, he further predicts that *they will not leave within you one stone upon another (ouk aphēsousin lithon epi lithon en soi)*. The Greek phrasing is grammatically awkward, likely owing to a strained allusion to Haggai 2:15, a verse which speaks of the days before the construction of the temple, that is, a time before there was *one stone upon another*. The point is that the promised demolition of the sacred space will mean a reversal of the temple construction project undertaken centuries earlier in Haggai's time.[9] At the same time, Josephus's record of the Romans' razing of the temple and surrounding city (*J.W.* 7.1–4) means that, once again in retrospect, Jesus' words are meant to be taken quite literally. At bottom, the city's tragic failure was a failure to recognize *the time of your visitation (ton kairon tēs episkopēs)*.

iii. Temple action (19:45–48)

45. Given that many Jews expected the coming Messiah to purge the temple of evildoers, Jesus' temple action fits hand-in-glove with contemporary messianic hopes.[10] His focus on *those who were selling*

---

7. Isa. 29:1–4; Jer. 6:6–21; 8:18–22.

8. Fitzmyer (p. 1254) sees in Luke for 'instance, allusion to the earthworks thrown up by the Romans . . . the circumvallation of Jerusalem, a wall of thirty-nine furlongs (*stadia*) encircling the whole city . . . the firing of the temple gates . . . [and] the battering of the fortress Antonia'. See Josephus, *J.W.* 5.466, 508; 6.24–28, 93, 228.

9. Derrett, 'No Stone'.

10. The parade example of such expectation surfaces in Pss Sol. 7:21–30.

things there (*tous pōlountas*) is less a demonstration against the
monetization of religion (as is commonly believed) than a protest
against various financial abuses as these were perpetrated by the
front-facing offices of the temple priesthood and by the priesthood
itself.[11] Among such abuses (seemingly alluded to in v. 46) was the
practice of dramatically inflating exchange rates on the temple
coinage necessary for purchasing on-site animals.[12] Within the
purview of redemptive history, as the fulfilment of Zechariah
14:21b ('And there shall no longer be traders in the house of the
LORD of hosts on that day'), the temple action also signals the
arrival of the day of the Lord. In this light, Jesus' effort *to drive out*
(*ekballein*) the merchants aims not to reform the temple but to judge
it, sealing this event as a watershed moment in the eschatological
scenario. Just as Yahweh's response to disobedient Israel culminated in his driving (*ekballein*) the nation out from the land (e.g. Jer.
29:14; Ezek. 11:9), Jesus' driving out (*ekballein*) frames the temple
action as a symbolic prelude to exile.

46. Following Mark 11:15–17, Luke condenses what was
originally a fulsome sermon at the temple into a crisp conflation of
supporting Scriptures: Isaiah 56:7 (v. 46a) and Jeremiah 7:11 (v. 46b).
In quoting the latter Hebrew scripture, Jesus invokes a larger
passage that not only castigates the Judahites for their deceptive
religiosity (Jer. 7:4) and shabby treatment of widows (Jer. 7:6), but
also promises imminent destruction for such offences (Jer. 7:14–15,
20, 30–34). And so, in a breathtaking stroke, the citation of Jeremiah
7:11 thematically builds on the parable of the two praying men
(including a self-deceived Pharisee) in 18:9–14, the parable of the
persistent (and oppressed) widow in 18:1–8 and the immediately
preceding lament over Jerusalem's destruction (19:41–44). Meanwhile, Isaiah 56:7, once duly appreciated in its fuller context, signals
that the eschatological hour had arrived, when Israel's false
shepherds would be judged and the sacred space would be opened

---

11. Neither Jesus nor the Gospel writers were alone in this critique; see T.
    Mos. 5:1–6; b. Yebam. 8a–b; Josephus, *Ant.* 20.180–181; 20.204–207. See
    Perrin, *Jesus the Temple*, pp. 93–99.
12. Perrin, *Jesus the Temple*, p. 98.

up to the Gentiles. Together Jeremiah 7:11 and Isaiah 56:7 imply
the removal of the current temple and the emergence of a new
salvific economy order that coincided with Israel's return from
exile and the consequent inclusion of Gentiles.

47–48. To the vexation of *the chief priests, the scribes, and the leaders of
the people,* he is teaching frequently, *every day* (*to kath'hēmeran*), in fact.
Though such confrontational instruction would eventually prove to
seal his fate, Jesus teaches *kath'hēmeran,* exemplifying what it means
for his disciples to carry their cross *kath'hēmeran* (9:23). And insofar
as Jesus' daily instruction was a means of spiritual nourishment, his
teaching *kath'hēmeran* constitutes – in the terms of Luke 4:4 and Deuteronomy 8:3 – a response to the disciples' prescribed petition for
daily (*kath'hēmeran*) bread (11:3). Meanwhile, as a result of the temple
action, which was understood as a frontal assault on the high priest's
authority, the whole register of Israel's religious leadership now
becomes severely oppositional: from here on out they *kept looking*
(*ezētoun*) or began to look *for a way to kill him.* Yet in contrast to Jesus'
disciples who were told that their seeking would lead to finding
(*zēteite kai heurēsete,* 11:9), the temple leadership's efforts prove fruitless.
Frustrated by the high esteem in which Jesus is held by *all the people,*
they *kept looking* (*ezētoun*) for their opportunity, but *they did not find* [*ouch
euriskon*] *anything they could do.* As the crowds hear him, they are
spellbound (*exekremato*); they 'hung on his words' (NIV, JB, NEB).

Theology

Twice in this section, Luke writes that Jesus the Lord 'has need'
(19:31, 34), even as the Evangelist records Paul saying just the opposite, to wit, that God has no need (Acts 17:25). Of course, both
statements are true in their own way. On the one hand, the Bible
maintains that God is absolutely sovereign, free and self-sufficient;
and it is these attributes that allow the Baptizer to say that God can
single-handedly transform stones into worshipping children of
Abraham (3:8; 19:40). On the other hand, it is equally true that Jesus
– if he is indeed fully human – must rely on earthly resources and
human support. In this section, for instance, he needs a colt and a
cheering crowd to declare his kingship. From this as well as Luke's
fuller story, we learn that when the Lord has need, that need, real yet
qualified, is always an invitation to human co-participation in the

kingdom. To be sure, strictly speaking, God does not *need* us. But so long as Jesus is on his mission, 'the Lord has need' and this sets the groundwork for vocation.

Such vocation ought to engage our human passions at their best. Once Jesus enters Jerusalem, the reaction is polarized, evincing a range of responses across the successive scenes. But no-one experiences greater breadth of feeling than Jesus himself. The joy of the triumphal entry gives way to a profound sorrow over Jerusalem, yielding again to his righteous anger in his temple act. In conveying Jesus' wide-ranging affect, Luke steers his readers away from the trap of an aloof and unfeeling Stoicism. As the Evangelist's readers undertake their own mission, they need to know that the world's mixed reaction to the gospel should be met with a Christ-like mix of joy, sorrow and righteous indignation. If Jesus' followers happen to experience such emotions in the course of their own vocations, it only means that they are experiencing true humanity.

B. Conflict with Jerusalem authorities (20:1–26)

Context

Jesus' controversial temple action (19:45–47) was a direct assault on the authority of the high priest. So it is unsurprising that the temple authorities now seek to neutralize Jesus' demonstration by publicly interrogating him regarding the source of his authority (20:1–8) – all in the hope of discrediting him. This is no standalone exchange but the first in a series of six talks (20:1–8; 20:9–19; 20:20–26; 20:27–40; 20:41–44; 20:45 – 21:4), a combination of dialogues and monologues. Together these six polemic encounters compose a reprise of an earlier series of debates with the religious leaders (5:17 – 6:11), consisting of five passages. As Jesus' death lurked just below the surface in the first extended debate, the same ominous undertone emerges here with the three episodes of this section centring on the parable of the wicked tenants (20:9–19).

On his journey to Jerusalem, when Jesus' detractors had requested a sign as evidence of his authority, in return he promised only the sign of Jonah, a sign of resurrection (11:29–30). In the central hinge of the present section, the parable of the wicked tenants (20:9–19), he once again gestures towards the resurrection.

But this time he also implicitly condemns the regnant priesthood. This condemnation is grounded in his authority as the Christ. The episodes on either side of the parable are like buttresses supporting the same point. On the one side, when Jesus is asked about the source of his authority (20:1–8), he points back to his own baptism under John (3:21–22). On the other side, he points to himself as the one who has greater authority than Caesar (20:20–26).

Comment
i. Jesus' authority questioned (20:1–8)

1. The conventional translation of *one day* (*en mia tōn hemerōn*) has no stronger claim than the alternative 'on the first of the days', that is, the first of Jesus' last days in Jerusalem. On this day, at any rate, Jesus is not simply *teaching the people* but also *telling the good news* (*euangelizomenou*), closing out his ministry just as he began it (4:18). The synonymous parallelism between teaching and telling good news forbids a sharp distinction between the two concepts (cf. Acts 5:42; 15:35): preaching the good news and teaching are two sides of the same coin. All the while, multiple ranks of temple dignitaries, beginning with *the chief priests*, followed by *the scribes* and *the elders*, have come out to meet Jesus head-on – the first within a string of conflictual encounters. As representatives from the same groupings that have been prophetically implicated in Jesus' death (9:22), their presence strikes an ominous tone; their intent is to initiate a kind of informal pre-trial before the official trial.[13] Having made its way up to the upper echelons of the religious hierarchy, the 'problem of Jesus' has reached a critical tipping point.

2. When the temple leadership asks *by what authority are you doing these things*, the *things* (*tauta*) in view are Jesus' actions in the temple (19:45–48).[14] Their focus on this issue, rather than on a slew of

---

13. Entrapment was legally permissible when it came to building a case against a deceiver (i.e. a *mesit*) who induced others towards idolatry (Deut. 13:7); see Schnabel, *Jesus in Jerusalem*, p. 247.

14. Contra Fitzmyer (p. 1273), who argues that it was merely Jesus' willingness to teach in the temple that occasioned the leaders' question.

other potentially offending matters, is understandable, if only because the temple action constituted the most explicit condemnation of the temple hierarchy up to this point. But rather than complain about Jesus' actions in general terms, the Jewish leadership have come to realize that their forthcoming legal case against him would have more teeth if they could corner him on the issue of authority. According to the Jewish world view, authority was embedded in a cosmic, hierarchical chain that culminated in the person of Yahweh, and any rightful earthly authority was derived either directly from God or through one or more intermediary designates duly authorized by God.[15] In this light, the leaders' challenge would have forced him on to the horns of a dilemma. On the one hand, if he admitted to *not having* authority to cleanse the temple, he would have instantly and publicly discredited himself. On the other hand, if he claimed in fact to *have* the authority to perform the temple action, and that apart from official approval, this could be seen as a blasphemous usurpation of the high priestly office, an act punishable by death.[16] It seemed that any way that Jesus dared to answer the question, the consequences would be devastating.

3–4. Rather than oblige the Jewish leaders, however, Jesus counters their question with a question of his own (not an uncommon move in rabbinic debate), relating to their assessment of John the Baptizer: was the baptism of John *from heaven, or was it of human origin?* The counter-question is a brilliant rejoinder on several levels. On the first level, Jesus' comeback deflects the leaders' entrapment by forcing their transparency on an issue that would – if the truth were to get out – lead to an intolerable loss of political support from among the people. On another level, by drawing the watching public's attention to John's baptism, Jesus is calling everyone's attention to hearsay reports of his own baptism under the Baptizer (3:21–22). For those willing to connect the dots,

---

15. See Edwards, 'Authority of Jesus'.

16. In this respect, the temple authorities' query is simply the same question that had inwardly nagged at the religious leaders who were present at Jesus' healing of the paralysed man (5:21).

this reminder made for a convincing syllogism. If John really was a prophet sent from God, as the people held (20:6), then the Baptizer's corroboration of Jesus' baptism, which had identified him as the beloved Son of God (3:22), could only mean that Jesus *was* in fact the Son of God. In short, whereas the temple leaders question Jesus' qualifications for performing the temple action, Jesus refocuses the issue by indirectly pointing to John's uncontested credibility and his crucial role as witness to the heavenly voice. The counter-question is not merely a clever diversionary tactic but, as per the principle enunciated in 8:18, a request that the religious leaders come to terms with the knowledge they already (should) have before requesting more information.[17]

5–7. Huddling together the leaders quickly agree that Jesus' counter to their heads-you-lose-tails-I-win question has now put *them* in a catch-22. If they grant John's divinely granted authority, they would then have to explain why they conspicuously failed to embrace his message (v. 5). Alternatively, if they publicly state that John spoke without divine backing, being *of human origin*, they might even suffer stoning (v. 6), the punishment due to those who failed to acknowledge true prophets (Deut. 13:1–11). The only way out of the dilemma was to plead ignorance: *So they answered that they did not know where it came from* (v. 7). Not that this is a particularly attractive option, for here they 'must shamefully admit that they, the religious leaders, do not know'.[18]

8. Since, in the presence of the watching crowds, the temple leaders are unable to frame a definite answer to Jesus' question, he is – so to speak – 'off the hook' in answering the leaders' question (v. 2). Bystanders in the crowd would have interpreted Jesus' deft rhetorical move, turning the tables in such a way as to confound his questioners, as a clear victory. On the other side of the ledger, the temple leaders, left confused and flummoxed by the encounter they had initiated, are made to bear the mantle of public shame.

---

17. As Edwards (p. 561) puts it, 'The counterquestion of Jesus contains the seeds of truth the Sanhedrin pretends to desire'.

18. Tannehill, p. 288.

ii. Parable of the wicked tenants (20:9–19)

9. In this the very last of his parables, once more beginning with the familiar *anthrōpos tis* (*a man*; cf. 10:30; 14:16; 15:11; 16:1, 19; 20:9), Jesus issues an ominous warning to his opponents, even though his message is directed to *the people*. As in many rabbinic parables, the man who goes off to a faraway country stands for God. The vineyard would have been easily recognized as a symbol for Israel (Isa. 5:1–10); the tenants, as priests tasked with ensuring Israel's fruitfulness.

10–12. At the appointed hour, the landowner sends a servant to collect the produce that has come due. In a disturbing twist, the messenger is beaten.[19] Because Israel's prophets are designated as 'servants of God' (e.g. 1 Kgs 18:36; 2 Kgs 14:25; Dan. 6:20), the hapless figure likely represents any and all 'first-wave prophets' who were persecuted for their message. After all, in the first-century agricultural world, slaves often managed fields on behalf of their owners and thus were authorized to speak for those who sent them, much as the prophets were authorized to speak for God.[20] The parable's second servant, who receives treatment even more shameful than the first, likewise refers to God's rejected prophets, perhaps even those who are sent to follow up on Yahweh's initial plea for repentance. A third servant attempts the same mission, but to no avail. With hostilities escalating, this one is wounded and cast out.

13. In a last-ditch effort to secure the tenants' respect, the owner astonishingly sends his *beloved son* (*huios . . . ho agapētos*). The epithet is an obvious reference to Jesus, who at his baptism was declared to be *ho huios . . . ho agapētos* (3:22). By extension, the same phrase also refers to Isaac, who is designated *huion . . . ton agapēton* (Gen. 22:2, LXX). Since Isaac's sacrifice was thought to provide the basis for cultic atonement, the death of the beloved son is likewise marked out as atoning.

14–15a. The tenants immediately recognize the final messenger as the vineyard-owner's appointed heir, reminiscent of another

---

19. Significantly, Luke uses the same verb, *dērō*, to describe the beating of Jesus and the apostles. See Luke 22:63; Acts 5:40; 16:37.

20. Green, pp. 706–707.

heir, the Suffering Servant (Isa. 53:12). Mired in their wickedness, the tenants' deliberations mimic those of Joseph's murderous brothers: *let us kill him (apokteinōmen auton*; cf. Gen. 37:20). Their plotting reveals not only their growing viciousness but also their motivations of envy and greed. Even so, in a re-enactment of Ahab's shocking expropriation of Naboth's vineyard (1 Kgs 21:1–16), the tenants throw the son out of the vineyard and kill him. This amalgam of intertextual resonances pertains less to Jesus' enemies than to Jesus himself. For just as Joseph suffered grave injustice for the ultimate good of a nation (Gen. 50:20), so it will be with Jesus. Likewise, just as Naboth was deprived of his inheritance on the basis of trumped-up charges, Jesus too will know what it means to play victim to an envious and power-hungry elite. As the antitype of both Joseph and Naboth, Jesus not only stands in the gap for his people as perpetrators of injustice but also identifies with his people as those who have suffered injustice.

15b–16. Following the parable's tragic close, Jesus asks what the landowner might do to the tenants, only to answer his own rhetorical query: he will *destroy those tenants and give the vineyard to others.* On hearing the violent ending of the parable, transparently about the temple leadership, Jesus' hearers are appalled by his prediction and protest indignantly (*Heaven forbid!*).

17. Now challenging his audience's incredulity, Jesus calls on his hearers to interpret Psalm 118:22 (Luke's third Christological use of the psalm; cf. 13:35; 19:38): *The stone that the builders rejected / has become the cornerstone.* At least several layers of meaning are in play. First, building on a Hebrew pun between 'stone' (*'eben*) and 'son' (*bēn*), already well established in Daniel 2 (in reference to the crushing, stone-like temple) and Daniel 7 (in reference to the Son of Man), Jesus implicitly identifies himself as both the parable's beloved son and as the cornerstone of the long-awaited eschatological temple, precisely as anticipated – as far as first-century Jewish readers were concerned – by Psalm 118. Second, whereas Psalm 118 tells the story of royal humiliation leading to exaltation, Jesus invites the people to make sense of the parable and by extension the imminently unfolding chain of events along the same lines. The thinly veiled point seems clear enough: as the climactic prophet who is more than a prophet, Jesus offers himself as the afflicted and exalted one par excellence, simultaneously (as the cornerstone) the basis for atonement and (as the new Isaac-style son) the priestly figure offering himself for the atonement. It is an atonement to be secured, ironically enough, through his rejection. That which the priestly 'tenants' failed to do – this is fully undertaken by Jesus himself.

18–19. Like the stone of Daniel 2:34–35 and 44–45, the cornerstone will have a crushing effect on those pagan forces who feel its weight. As for those who fall on top of the stone (because they have stumbled on who the stone is and what he represents; cf. Isa. 8:14–15), they too will be broken to pieces. In either case, so Jesus warns those who link arms with the now-condemned temple leadership, the result is judgment. None of this is lost on the scribes and chief priests, who are now more than ever convinced that Jesus must be removed. The only factor restraining them now is their fear of losing the public's goodwill.

iii. Taxes to Caesar (20:20–26)

20. Tightening their grip, Jesus' opponents watch him closely for the third time (cf. 6:7; 14:1). In order to trap him, they send spies who pass themselves off as *honest* with respect to their support for Jesus. Earlier it was his opponents' hypocrisy that prevented them from interpreting 'the present time' (12:56). Now the same duplicity drives them to active entrapment. Their goal is to force Jesus into a verbal misstep that will give them sufficient cause to hand him to the *jurisdiction* of Pilate.

21. The delegation speaks flatteringly to Jesus, emphasizing his reputation as one who does not *show deference* or, more woodenly, 'receive the face' (*lambaneis prosōpon*). The Semitic expression 'you do not receive the face' is ironic since Jesus will momentarily show that indeed he does not receive the face of Caesar on the coin, ultimately because it is an idolatrous image widely regarded as an extension of the emperor's divine image.[21]

22–23. Jesus sees right through their trick question. On the one hand, if Jesus goes on record advocating not paying taxes to Caesar,

---

21. On emperor worship in the NT era, see Perrin, 'Imperial Cult'.

this would make Jesus liable for sedition, a very serious offence in Roman eyes. On the other hand, if he agrees that all Jews should cheerfully pay Caesar's tax, he would instantly lose credibility with the masses who expected the Messiah to release Israel from Rome. Jesus has been cast on to the horns of a dilemma.

24. In response, Jesus asks his questioners to produce a denarius, a coin which in Jesus' day would have carried Tiberius's face on one side and the words 'Pontifex Maximus' ('Most High Priest') on the reverse. This background is important for understanding the thrust of Jesus' words. For by asking specifically about the coin's *head* or 'image' (*eikon*, the Greek equivalent of the Hebrew *ṣelem*), a word which in Jewish parlance first and foremost denoted an idol, Jesus indirectly highlights its idolatrous function. Similarly, by enquiring into its inscription, he draws attention to a set of engraved words that blasphemously asserted the emperor as chief high priest and sole mediator between humanity and the gods. Obliged to respond to Jesus' very simple question, his opponents acknowledge that both the image and the inscription refer to Caesar (Tiberius).

25. Having intimated the coin's idolatrous properties, Jesus goes on to draw an inference from the very answers supplied by his entrappers: *Then give to the emperor the things that are the emperor's, and to God the things that are God's.* Jesus' response is enigmatic, giving rise to various interpretations. Is Jesus asking his hearers, as some have suggested, to ignore their obligation to the Roman state in the light of the imminent eschaton? Or is he coming out publicly against the anti-Roman Zealots without necessarily pardoning Rome's ways? Or is he suggesting that the question is moot, since there are essentially two realms, Caesar's and God's, and that the first of these falls well outside his spiritual interests? In my view, each of these approaches has insuperable weaknesses.

The best option begins by supposing, as I have argued elsewhere, that Jesus is framing Caesar's story within another familiar story of pagan pretence: that in Daniel.[22] The backdrop of Daniel makes sense not least because the very contrast between 'the things of God' and 'the things of human beings' seems to finds its roots

---

22. See Perrin, *Jesus the Priest*, pp. 239–260.

in Daniel 2:22, where 'the things of God' refers to the revelation of eschatological mystery (cf. 1 Cor. 2:14). We recall that in Daniel's day, the pagan rulers used imperial decrees and inscriptions to force Yahweh's faithful to pay homage to the idolatrous 'image' (Dan. 3:1–7; 6:1–12). In an ironic twist, and in response to the pagan inscriptions and images, the God of Israel leaves his own 'inscription' (Dan. 5:5–28) and sends his own 'son' (Dan. 3:25; 7:14) precisely as the image of God. Understood against this scriptural backdrop, the 'things of Caesar' refer to the token assertions of Roman authority that will eventually prove to be just as futile as the images and inscriptions asserted in Daniel's day. Meanwhile, the things of God are the very image and inscription of God, that is, the Son of Man and his message of judgment against idolaters. On this logic, then, Jesus' command to 'give to Caesar the things of Caesar' invites his hearers to render freely back to the emperor the idolatrous coin that is his due, whether in the form of taxes or other legitimate demands. Meanwhile, to 'give to God the things of God' is to attribute the mysteries spoken by Jesus back to their divine origins.

26. Flummoxed by Jesus' response, the opponents are not only *amazed* but rendered *silent*. Their hope had been to trap Jesus *in the presence of the people*, but now it is they who seemingly have fallen into his trap. They have stumbled on the cornerstone (20:17).

Theology

It is impossible to follow Jesus without a firm grasp of his all-encompassing authority. For this very reason, Jesus' authority remains a central concern in the Gospel. The question as to who (or what) has the authority to set standards of belief and behaviour was not a moot issue in Luke's world. On the contrary, as the gospel made its way across the Roman Empire, the Christians' declaration of Jesus' lordship quickly came into direct conflict with various local and more global authorities. Chief among the global authorities were the temple system and devotion to Rome.

Every fallen-human society has norms of authority that are intrinsically opposed to the authority of Christ. In some cultures, ancestral custom holds final authority. In other societies, the pursuit of money is the end that justifies all possible means. Still, in some highly individualized societies, the ultimate bar of appeal is not reason or the Scriptures but what one subjectively *feels* to be true. In all such instances, the Son of God's authority is relativized. But as Luke makes clear in this passage, things do not end well for those who toy with Jesus' authority. At any rate, we know this: those who reject the Son's authority will be crushed by the cornerstone.

C. Further conflict (20:27 – 21:4)

Context

As Jesus closes out his refutation of his opponents in these four scenes, a chiastic (ABBA) structure emerges. On the outer edges are a question about resurrection (20:27–40) and Jesus' commendation of an impoverished widow (21:1–4). These two episodes in turn straddle a pair of monologues. The first of these concerns the glorious exaltation of the Davidic Messiah (20:41–44); the second, the inglorious self-exaltation of the teachers of the law, as well as their condemnation (20:45–47). The widow is to be commended for giving away her livelihood because, so it seems, she has grasped that her true life awaits her beyond the grave. The teachers of the law will be – to use Mary's words – 'brought down . . . from their thrones' (1:52), ultimately because they will have failed to adopt the eschatological long view, a perspective which the widow has grasped so well. Again and again in the Gospel, Jesus has gestured to his own resurrection. Now in anticipation of the event itself, he enters into an exposition of the topic.

Comment

i. Marriage at the resurrection (20:27–40)

27. Unlike the Pharisees, who espoused the doctrine of resurrection, the politico-religious party of the *Sadducees* denied bodily resurrection (as Luke points out), the existence of angels and demons, and final judgment. (Jesus' argument in this passage refutes all three denials.) Also unlike the Pharisees, who held to the authority of the oral law, the Sadducees relied solely on what the historian Josephus calls the 'law of Moses' (Josephus, *Ant.* 13.297–298; 18.16) – whether the phrase refers to the Pentateuch or the fuller canon is not clear by itself.[23] Hoping to make a compelling *ad absurdum* argument, the Sadducees pose a hypothetical situation (reminiscent of a subplot in Tob. 3:7–15) involving a line of seven brothers who have been successively married to and then each outlived by the same woman. That they *came to him* demonstrates that they, like the scribes and Pharisees, are taking the offensive with the goal of checkmating Jesus in public debate. The convergence of two otherwise antipathic sects in common cause against Jesus shows the far-ranging breadth of antagonism.

28. Jesus' interrogators cite Mosaic legislation (Deut. 25:5–10; cf. Gen. 38:8) regarding prescriptions for levirate marriage (a practice whereby an adult male marries the widow of his childless brother or kinsman with a view to preserving the seed line of the deceased brother/relative). Torah's teaching is clear enough: in the case where a *man's brother dies*, that man is bound to *marry the widow and raise up children for his brother.*

29–33. The gathered Sadducees ask Jesus to imagine an unlikely but still theoretically possible situation in which seven brothers in turn marry and then predecease the same woman, in accordance with levirate law. Each of these seven marriages proves childless, until eventually the woman herself finally dies, prompting the question in verse 33.

34–36. Jesus responds to the Sadducees not so much by answering their question as by challenging its basic premise. By his account, those *who are considered worthy of a place in that age* will in the post-mortem realm exist as celibate beings. In other words, in contrast to the folk in Noah's day who were 'marrying and being given in marriage' (17:27), the resurrected elect will *neither marry nor be given in marriage.* Why? Because marriage will be outmoded by

---

23. A longstanding assumption, not uncommonly repeated in the commentaries (e.g. Bock, p. 1617), is that Jesus builds his argument on Exodus (of all unlikely places) because the Sadducees accept only the Pentateuch as authoritative. But this inference depends on the late testimony of Origen and Jerome writing centuries after the Sadducean party ceased to exist. Evidence closer to the first century indicates that their canon was similar to that of the Pharisees.

the sheer fact that the righteous *cannot die any more*. The implication
here, signalled in the Greek by the explanatory *gar*, is that the
elimination of death somehow obviates the need for or even the
possibility of human procreation. The resurrected righteous
cannot die, furthermore, because *they are like angels and are children
of God*, who are likewise *children of the resurrection*. The future status
of the righteous as *children of God* or 'sons of God' (*huioi . . . theou*;
cf. 6:35) helps to explain why neither marriage nor procreation is
suitable for the next life: 'the basic relationship is one of divine
sonship, perhaps with the implication that men and women are
related to one another as brothers and sisters', whereby 'divine
Fatherhood replaces human parentage'.[24] The status of the
resurrected as sons of God also explains their future angel-like
(*isangeloi*) character (cf. 2 Bar. 51:10; 1 En. 15:4–6), since angels
were regularly called 'sons of God' (e.g. Job 1:6; Ps. 29:1). Luke's
phrase *like angels*, comparable to the parallels at Matthew 22:30 and
Mark 12:25 which claim that the resurrected will be 'as angels' (*hōs
angeloi*), does not mean that the just will *become* angels, but rather
that they will come to share certain angelic attributes appropriate
to the resurrection.

What attributes might these be? First and foremost, by stating
that the resurrected elect are *like angels*, Jesus is aligning himself
with the Jewish conviction that the new creation would be
populated by a functionally androgynous and perfected humanity.[25]
On a secondary level, the future angelic quality of the righteous
cannot be unrelated to the fact that in Luke–Acts the angelic
responsibilities of proclamation (Luke 1:11–19, 26–38; 2:9–21; 24:4;
Acts 1:10), worship (Luke 9:26; 15:10) and comfort (Luke 22:43; Acts
5:19) also fall to believers in this life. In this respect, the believers'
prospect of becoming *like angels* is not a radical break from but a
culmination of their obedient missional life.

37. In asking the Sadducees to revisit their assumptions
regarding the post-mortem state, Jesus is of course presupposing

---

24. Marshall, pp. 737–738, 742.

25. This has already been hinted at multiple times through Luke's
    thematization of gender.

the doctrine of resurrection. But since the belief of resurrection is exactly what is at stake, he must also speak of the matter directly. He does so by adducing evidence *that the dead are raised* from the account of the burning bush (Exod. 3). The clause *where he speaks of the Lord as the God of Abraham, the God of Isaac, and the God of Jacob* is ambiguous, as it is uncertain whether the *he* who *speaks (legei)* is Moses standing in front of the bush, Moses as the author of Exodus recounting the episode, or the bush itself. Though the grammar allows the theoretical possibility of the first option, this remains unlikely in the canonical context, since it is not Moses but the burning bush who identifies Israel's saving God as the God of the three patriarchs. This still makes plausible the second (and commonly accepted) option, whereby Moses' text *speaks* of Israel's God as the God of the three patriarchs. But it may be equally if not more persuasively argued that the bush is the subject of *legei* and is therefore also the originator of the epithet. True, on grammatical grounds, the antecedent term *Moses* (v. 37a) may initially incline the reader to assume Moses (or the Mosaic text) as the subject of *legei*. By the same token, given that the unconsumed burning bush of Exodus 3 lends itself splendidly to the Evangelist as a type of Jesus' exodus-style ministry, death and resurrection, and given, too, that Luke's Jesus himself has already spoken of the three patriarchs in connection with resurrection (13:28), we must agree with the standard patristic interpretation that not only frames the burning bush event as a Christophany but also identifies the pre-existent Jesus as the revealer of the divine moniker. In Luke's theological perspective, the certainty of resurrection does not follow from any inherent immortality of the soul, but from the covenantal promise issued on the cusp of Moses' calling.

38. The Scriptures variously attest that the dead cannot honour God (e.g. Pss 30:9; 115:17; Isa. 38:18). And it is likely on the basis of this logic that Jesus maintains that *he is God not of the dead, but of the living.* The logic might be restated as follows: by revealing the God of Israel as the God of the physically deceased Abraham, Isaac and Jacob, the burning bush implies that the covenantal relationship established with those patriarchs remains vital, involving vital parties, and that *therefore to him all of them are alive.* God's covenantal

commitment to the patriarchs means that death will by no means
have the last word – either over them or over those who belong to
the people of God.

39. As Jesus closes out his argument, some of the Pharisaical
scribes sympathetic to Jesus' position on resurrection, and therefore
also sharing Jesus' opposition to the Sadducees, applaud his efforts.
They come full circle from verse 28 by addressing him as *Teacher*.[26]
Little do such sympathizers understand that this same teacher is
also Lord! Jesus has successfully driven a wedge between the two
allying forces, much as Paul would do with the same two parties
on this same issue in Acts 23:8.

40. The evidence that Jesus had spoken well consists not just in
the substance of his words but also in their effect. As a result of his
refutation of the Sadducees, *they no longer dared to ask him another
question*. Though one might surmise from this statement that the
they refers only to the Sadducees, that this episode proves to be the
last of the debates initiated by Jesus' opponents shows that his
answer here has put an end to all discussion.

ii. Son of David (20:41–44)

41. The long line of questioning directed against Jesus has run
its course. Now it is Jesus' turn to take the offensive and pose a few
questions of his own. The questions centre around his interlocutors'
interpretation of Scripture and of the Christ. The passage begins
he said to them, but who are the *them*? Moreover, who are the ones
saying that *the Messiah is David's Son*? Most likely, Jesus is now
speaking to the people about their religious leaders' faulty messianic understanding (cf. Mark 12:35). Up to this point, the crowds
have only watched from a distance Jesus' bout with the temple elite
(20:1); now they are brought into the conversation. The issue is not
so much whether the Christ could be the Son of David, which in
Luke is taken for granted (1:27, 32–35), but 'in what way' (*pōs*) this
could be so.

---

26. Significantly, the disciples call Jesus 'master' and 'Lord' but never
    'teacher' (Edwards, pp. 577–578).

42–43. As Jesus makes clear, identifying the Messiah as the Son of David is potentially problematized by Psalm 110, where David addresses the enthroned Messiah as a superior, that is, as *Lord*. This is not merely a matter of the title, for to be at Yahweh's right hand is to share his rule.

44. Jesus' question (*David thus calls him Lord; so how can he be his son?*) is not meant to cast doubt either on the Messiah's identity as Son of David or on the validity of Psalm 110. Instead, Jesus highlights the tension in order to push his hearers to think more deeply about just what they were expecting in the Davidic Messiah. Challenging his opponents who expected nothing more than a David redivivus, Jesus prods his hearers to look for – in keeping with the narrative of Psalm 110 – an exalted Melchizedek-like priest who confronts the hostile nations. Yes, the Messiah will be a son of David, but paradoxically, Jesus so much as promises, he will surpass David at the moment of his enthronement. Just how the enthronement of Psalm 110 is fulfilled in reality becomes clear only later on, in Acts 2:34–36.

iii. Hypocrisy of leaders (20:45 – 21:4)

45. Turning away from his opponents (20:41–44), Jesus now addresses his *disciples* directly *in the hearing of all the people*, thereby engaging two sets of listeners: a primary audience of the Twelve and a secondary audience made up of sympathizers and other onlookers. In staging the scene in this way, Luke presents the condemnations (20:45–47) and commendations (21:1–4) issued by Jesus as a kind of charge to the disciples, with the people functioning as witnesses. Viewed in this light, 20:45 – 21:4 serves not only to elucidate some of the sinful behaviours responsible for the destruction of the temple but also to enjoin, through negative and positive examples, certain values on the soon-to-emerge temple community.

46. Having already reproached the scribes once in the Gospel (11:44–52), Jesus now circles back to his critique. But this time his pronouncement of woes is less a rebuke to the bad actors themselves than a warning to his disciples, lest they find themselves ensnared by the same attitudes and behaviours: *Beware of the scribes*. Two condemnable activities are attributed to the temple leaders.

First, they *like to walk around in long robes (en stolais)*, obviously for show.[27] Second, they *love*, not God (as Judaism's chief command requires), but tokens of honour in life's civic, religious and social spheres: greetings *in the market-places*, the *best seats in the synagogues* and the *places of honour at banquets*. All this takes Luke's reader back to Jesus' earlier admonishments directed against the religious elite (11:37–52; 14:7–11), and that he must reissue the warning is ample evidence that those earlier admonishments have fallen on deaf ears.

47. Though Jesus may possibly be referring to a practice whereby scribes took advantage of widows' hospitality (As. Mos. 7:7), a preferable explanation presents itself with the scenario that the lawyers engaged in spiritual grandstanding in order to be entrusted with legal guardianship over the estates of widows – all with a view to embezzling their assets.[28] To make matters worse, *for the sake of appearance* they *say long prayers* – in contrast to the short and compact prayer Jesus had commended to his disciples (11:1–4). In charging the scribes with this 'devouring' (*katesthiousin*), Jesus hopes to expose both the scammers in his midst as well as their motivations of greed. (In Judaism, greed was a form of idolatry which in turn was profaning to the temple – in anticipation of 21:5–36.) Of course, verse 47a is not merely a historical note on the scribes' malfeasance. By including Jesus' warning in his Gospel, Luke signals that Christian leaders would be vulnerable to similar temptations of engaging in religious posturing for the sake of financial gain (1 Thess. 2:5).

As far as such individuals are concerned, Jesus promises, *they will receive the greater condemnation* (cf. 12:47–48). Such a prediction raises at least two questions. First, why would the scribes' behaviour merit *greater* condemnation than other kinds of wrongdoing? Second, what baseline point of comparison is being presumed here? In other words, if the scribes can expect to receive greater judgment, 'greater' with respect to whom and under what circumstances?

---

27. Though the precise social significance of the robes (*stolai*) is unclear, we should probably 'think . . . of ostentatious garments denoting the high office that scribes considered themselves to have' (Nolland, p. 976).

28. As argued by Derrett, 'Houses of Widows'.

Towards answering the first of these two questions, one infers that the scribes' judgment will be more severe simply because the higher the level of spiritual leadership, the greater the responsibility for which one must give account. In taking up the second question, we first observe that the present passage situates itself between, on the one side, the parable of the wicked tenants (20:9–19), which presages the dissolution of the temple cultus, and, on the other side, Jesus' prediction concerning the destruction of the temple (21:5–36). Given this context, I would maintain that the 'greater judgment' in view is both eschatological *and* historical. On a basic level, because this admonishment takes its place alongside other passages in Luke that warn of judgment at the parousia (6:23–25; 12:1–10; 12:35–48), Jesus must be promising that fraudulent religious leaders will absorb the greater punishment at the eschaton. At the same time, because the warning is so closely linked to the impending destruction of the temple, he is also predicting that whatever deleterious impact will be dealt out to Israel's populace in a short time, it would be the temple leaders who would naturally bear the greater brunt of that judgment.

21:1. Among the hallmarks of Jewish piety, few if any were more important than the act of giving. Worshippers offered their freewill *gifts* publicly in the court of the women at the *treasury* or 'hall of the treasury' (Josephus, *Ant.* 19.292–296), situated on an elevated platform some 10 feet or so above ground level. So it was that Jesus *looked up* to see *rich people* mounting the stairs, preparing to deposit their coins into any one of more than a dozen funnel-shaped receptacles dedicated to this purpose (m. Šeqal. 2:1; 6:1, 5).

2–3. But worthier of mention than these rich people is a *poor widow* who offers *two small copper coins (lepta duo)*. The Roman *lepton* was a tiny coin (the diameter of which is equivalent to the width of an adult human pinky) and was of extremely negligible value (0.8% of a day's wage; cf. 12:59). Despite the low value of the widow's offering, Jesus declares that she has *put in more than all of them*, that is, the wealthy. Luke's reference to a widow who has spent her last out of obedience is likely intended to invoke the widow of Zarephath (1 Kgs 17:8–16). To the extent that Luke's Jesus has presented himself as a new Elijah at various points in the Gospel, one might reasonably gather that the nameless widow retains some kind of unique elective status, as well as a unique relationship to Jesus himself.

4. In asserting the relative superiority of the widow's gift, Jesus shifts the emphasis away from the amount of the donation in comparison with other donations to the size of the gift as a proportion of the donor's assets. In contrast to the wealthy who contributed *out of their abundance*, the widow gave *out of her poverty*, for she *put in all she had to live on* (*ton bion hon eichen*), alternatively translated 'the life which she had'. According to Jesus, then, the truly impressive gift is one which entails a depletion of one's own personal resources.[29] Such self-giving would hardly be possible without some trace of faith (9:3), resurrection hope (18:19–30) and love for God (7:41–50). In this respect, the anonymous widow functions as a paragon of kingdom virtues. Moreover, as one who gives her life (*bion*) through financial giving, she anticipates Jesus' giving of his own life through his death. In Luke's kingdom economy, sacrificial financial giving is a means of imitating Christ (cf. 2 Cor. 8:9).

Theology

The last three of the four scenes in this section share a common thread: exaltation. First, Jesus cites Psalm 110, a text which focuses on the exaltation of the Messiah. Then he describes the Pharisees exalting themselves. Finally, Jesus exalts the lowly widow. To summarize all this in theological terms, the Father will exalt the messianic Son, who in turn will exalt his self-giving followers, while the self-serving will be swiftly demoted. All such exaltation (and condemnation) is made possible only by the resurrection, a reality confirmed by the first of the four scenes.

A person's outlook on life, as well as that person's actions and attitudes, will largely depend on the firmness of his or her

---

29. Wright ('Widow's Mites'), followed by Fitzmyer (p. 1320), argues that Jesus is not praising the widow but bemoaning the fact that she has been duped by religious pretenders. Though ingenious, this interpretation does not fit the obvious attempt to contrast the widow with the religious leaders.

resurrection faith. Those who set themselves to garnering human praise or ill-got wealth do so because, though they (like the Jewish leaders Jesus criticizes) believe in the fact of the resurrection, they believe at a deeper level still that their only real fullness is to be found in this life. They live their lives, in other words, as if the resurrection did not matter. But because God is faithful to his covenantal promises, and has proven that faithfulness by having drawn the dead-but-living patriarchs into the divine presence, Jesus' followers can take a long view beyond the horizon of death. Living life in the light of the resurrection means saying 'No!' to the quest for human approbation and ill-got wealth. It also means saying 'Yes!' to giving out of the poverty of all one has. In undertaking the quest for the Risen Jesus' praise, the Gospel suggests, there is no better way to start than with a robustly consistent resurrection faith.

D. Eschatological Discourse (21:5–38)

Context

The present passage is of a piece with the narrative dedicated to Jesus' final visit to Jerusalem. To say that Jesus' entrance into the Holy City had got off to a rocky start would be an understatement. Though he entered as the messianic king (19:28–46), the temple authorities are unwilling to receive him as such. The strained situation is further aggravated by a string of controversies (20:1 – 21:4), the second of which contained a thinly veiled condemnation of the temple leadership. And so when the narrative lens swings from these high-pressure debates to the disciples' appreciation of the temple in 21:5, readers may initially think that they are about to get a break from the emotional intensity. If so, they could not be more wrong, for Luke's so-called Eschatological Discourse (or Olivet Discourse) foretells a series of uncanny and dreadful events culminating in the dissolution of the temple and then, finally, of the cosmos. Steeped in scriptural images, often with oblique meanings, the passage has been subject to a wide variety of interpretations. To anticipate my own reading, I will argue that Jesus connects the coming of the Son of Man with the imminent destruction of the temple, which in turn is the signature lead-up to the great parousia (second coming), referred to in verses 29–36. While this reading of the Eschatological Discourse is a minority interpretation (with most commentators preferring to identify the coming of the Son of Man in vv. 25–28 with the parousia), I believe it is not only justified based on the details of the present text but also an appropriately nuanced understanding of the coming of the Son of Man.[30] In any event, by the end of the Eschatological Discourse, the reader will have discovered that the opposition which Jesus faces in Luke 20 is actually symptomatic of a larger spiritual resistance which will soon be judged—in Jerusalem and throughout the world.

Comment
i. Fall of the temple (21:5–28)

5. Although the *some* speaking about the temple are formally unidentified in Luke, the context, not to mention the parallels in Matthew 24:1 and Mark 13:1, puts the disciples in view. Their focus is on the splendour of the temple, which was legendary.[31] The adjective *kalos* (*beautiful*) speaks not only of the temple stones' aesthetic appeal but also of their impressive size, with many of the surviving retaining wall stones weighing more than a jumbo jet. Since the disciples must have certainly visited the temple numerous times in their lives already, their remarks are not likely to be those of bedazzled tourists. Rather, even as the disciples aspire to gain control of the temple, they are revelling in what they presume to be their future base of operations.[32]

6. Yet Jesus immediately nips any such self-congratulatory musings in the bud by announcing that the temple is on borrowed time. Using phrases regularly connected with the 'Day of the Lord' in particular and judgment in general (Isa. 39:6; Hos. 9:7; Amos 4:2; etc.), Jesus solemnly declares that *the days will come* when the temple

---

30. Space prevents a full exposition of the point here; see Perrin, *Kingdom of God*, ch. 10.
31. Josephus, *Ant.* 15.391–402; *J.W.* 5.184–226.
32. Visions of Messiah and control of the temple seemed to go hand in hand in Ancient Judaism; cf. Pss Sol. 17.

will be destroyed. The predicted destruction is so far reaching that
– as mentioned in 19:44 – not even a stone will be left on another.
When first heard, this statement would have seemed incredible,
given the immensity of the stones. The very possibility of such
heavy building blocks being toppled from lower supporting stones
would demand an extraordinary human feat of engineering. But as
it so happens, Jesus' prediction would prove essentially true
following the destruction of the temple in August AD 70: after
capturing and gutting the temple itself, the Romans did in fact
methodically unstack the stone blocks constituting the temple
walls.

7. The modern reader can hardly imagine the emotive impact of
Jesus' prediction. After all, the temple was the nerve centre of
Judaism – its political, judicial, economic and religious hub. Even
if some sense of this event had already been intimated at various
points in Luke's narrative, still to contemplate Judaism without its
temple was to imagine the unimaginable. Stunned by Jesus'
prediction, the disciples now seek clarification on two issues: the
timing of the temple's destruction and the visible sign that such an
event is imminent. Obliging his followers, Jesus answers precisely
these two questions in verses 10–28, only to go on to speak – as a
kind of bonus – of the so-called second coming in verses 29–36.

8–11. But first by way of preface Jesus issues a few caveats. He
not only warns them against false prophets, destined to come out
of the woodwork, but also warns against their being perturbed by
unsettling events which might otherwise be interpreted as
premonitions of *the end*. All the while, the first order of business for
Jesus' disciples is that they stand guard against the coming
deceivers, who will make spurious messianic claims (declaring *I am*,
ēgo eimi), even as these same religious frauds will persuade many by
connecting contemporary political upheavals with their self-
assigned role in ushering in the end. That such messianic pretenders
did arise after Jesus' time but before Luke's writing of his Gospel
confirms the truth of his prediction. While commentators often
assume that *the end* means the end of the space–time continuum,
this is unlikely. The more pressing concern for the apostolic community and Luke's readership, as Acts 1:6 amply demonstrates, is
not the end of the world but the end of exile, that is, the restoration

of Israel. Insisting on a window of indefinite time between these dire events and the restoration of the tribes, Jesus hopes to pre-empt any apocalyptic hysteria that might be fuelled by such signs and tribulations.

Elaborating on the previous point, Jesus describes the *wars and insurrections* of nations and kingdoms rising up against one another, perhaps with some allusion to the unholy kingdoms of Daniel 7 rising up against one another. Yet along with these political developments there will also be geophysical (*earthquakes*), agri-cultural (*famines*) and celestial (*dreadful portents and great signs*) pointers. Strikingly, each of these signs finds specific instantiation in Acts.[33] In deploying all these images, Jesus is clearly operating within the thought-world of Jewish apocalypticism; the horrific events to which he refers constitute the long-expected 'tribulation', refining the faith of the faithful and thereby bringing added prom-inence to their witness.[34] Sharing with the disciples the widely held belief that a period of intense sufferings would precede the messi-anic era, Jesus is concerned (1) that his followers remain steadfast in the face of impending tribulation, and (2) that they do *not* assume that such tribulation will immediately precede the full coming of the kingdom (restoration). In depicting certain occasions in Acts as the outplaying of events predicted in Luke 21:8–12, the Evangelist not only confirms Jesus' prophetic credentials but also frames the travails of the early church in terms of the messianic tribulation.

12–13. Moving backwards in the timetable of events, Jesus now avers in verses 12–19 that a period of intense persecution will precede the tumultuous signs described in verses 10–11. The focus is on the actions of the persecutors. In the first place, they will 'lay on their hands' (*epibalousin . . . tas cheiras*) or *arrest* Jesus' followers, even as they *persecute* them. The scribes and chief priests come close to perpetrating the former activity against Jesus following his per-formance of the parable of the wicked tenants (20:19), and in Acts

---

33. Earthquakes (4:31; 16:26); famine (11:28); celestial signs (2:1–4, 19–20).

34. On tribulation in Jewish expectation, see Allison, *End of Ages*, pp. 5–25; Pitre, *Jesus*, pp. 41–127.

an aggressive laying on of hands becomes the power brokers' standard response to Christian mission (Acts 4:3; 5:18; 12:4; 21:27). Meanwhile, persecution in a more general sense remains the lot of the prophets and apostles (Luke 11:49; Acts 7:52), even as the church would experience the same at the hands of the pre-Christian Saul (Acts 9:4, 5; 22:4, 7; etc.). In the second place, Jesus promises that there will be many who will betray and/or remand the disciples to the Jewish and Roman seats of executive power: the local synagogues (which served as a local court for non-capital offences) and magistrates, respectively. This follows the pattern established by Jesus (Luke 9:44; 18:32; 20:20; 22:4, 21, 22, 48; 24:7, 20; Acts 3:13) and anticipates what would soon befall the early Christians, especially Paul (Acts 8:3; 12:4; 21:11; 22:4; 28:17). Finally, Jesus foretells that his followers will be led before kings and governors, again in accordance with his own example (Luke 22:66; 23:26) and in alignment with the experience of Paul who is brought before local governors, such as Felix and Festus (Acts 24:1 – 25:22), as well as kings, such as Agrippa (25:23 – 26:32) and even Caesar (28:17–20). The upshot of all such difficult encounters will be *to testify* (*eis martyrion*).[35] As Jesus sees it, the difficulties which will soon befall his disciples are no occasion for self-pity or handwringing, for such persecutions are precisely that which gives the gospel message its platform and its volume.

14–15. While other texts in the New Testament canon enjoin mental preparation for defending the faith (1 Pet. 3:15), here Jesus discourages such forethought. The command should not be over-interpreted. It is unlikely that Jesus is asking his disciples to stop using their brains altogether when put on the spot. Rather, he is reiterating an earlier point, namely, that self-reliant pre-rehearsal of one's defence is bound to fail insofar as it risks defaulting to human wisdom rather than spiritual wisdom, which comes only through the indwelling Spirit (Luke 12:11–12; cf. Mark 13:11). Jesus promises that he himself will provide *words* (NRSV) or 'a mouth' (*stoma*), just as Yahweh granted Moses 'a mouth' in his heated exchanges with

---

35. While it is possible that the sense of the Greek phrase here is 'proof for' the disciples themselves, the context makes this unlikely.

Pharaoh (Exod. 4:11, 15), together with *a wisdom* (*sophian*). Adversaries of the gospel will not be able to resist either. The provision of such Spirit-led eloquence and wisdom comes on display at many points in Acts.[36]

16–17. In the Ancient Near East, the bond of family was the strongest of all bonds. So when Jesus promises that even his followers' closest relatives and friends will turn against them, this indicates not only the extraordinarily high cost of identifying with Jesus' movement but also the degree of animosity which the movement would provoke. One's allegiance to the name of Jesus was to take priority over all other human allegiances and even one's own life. Nor would there be any human refuge outside one's immediate circles, for the disciples could expect only to be hated by all.

18–19. At first glance, Jesus' assurance that *not a hair of your head will perish* stands in formal contradiction to the promise of verse 16, which implies a martyr's fate for at least some. But verse 18 also asks to be understood alongside verse 19, which relates to the disciples' securing of their *souls* (*psychas*). Earlier in the narrative, Luke's Jesus had promised that 'those who want to save their life [*psychēn*] will lose it, and those who lose their life [*psychēn*] for my sake will save it' (9:24). In that context, as well as in the present context, we assume, the saving of one's *psychē* finally occurs through resurrection. This means that Jesus' guarantee for the safety of the disciples' very hairs is not a blanket promise for physical safety (which would in any case be patently disproven in Acts), nor an oblique assurance of spiritual safety (which has no discernible connection to one's hair), nor even a note of assurance that no harm will befall the disciples without divine permission (which is quite different from what the text plainly states) – as various commentators suggest. The point here is that whatever happens, the bodies of the faithful will be restored at the resurrection – hair and all. This does not rule out the possibility of God's providential protection; after all, Paul guarantees the proverbial hair of the sailors' heads in Acts 27:34. But Jesus' saying encourages readers to

---

36. Acts 2:14–41; 3:11–26; 4:5–20; 7:1–53; 13:13–43; 17:16–31; 21:37 – 22:21; 22:30 – 23:10; 24:10–21; 25:8–12; 26:1–29; 28:17–28.

take the long view afforded by God's resurrection power. In the meantime, the disciples' participation in the future resurrection was not to be taken for granted, for it depended on their persisting in *endurance* (*en tē hypomonē*). For Luke, as for the New Testament writers as a whole, assurance of salvation followed not just from faith in the present but also perseverance in the future.

20. Homing in on the signs which would immediately precede the destruction of the temple, Jesus first mentions the presence of besieging armies positioned around Jerusalem. Such is the first indication that the *desolation* of the temple is close at hand. In retrospect, Jesus' words find their fulfilment in the advance of Titus's armies, which, as the historical record shows, did indeed encircle Jerusalem in the spring of AD 70.

21. Having intimated the first sign of the impending desolation, Jesus now expounds on the proper response to this ominous event with three sets of instructions, the first two of which have proven to be a source of scholarly puzzlement. The initial set of instructions (*Then those in Judea must flee to the mountains*) poses difficulties because the historical record, passed down through Eusebius (*Hist. eccl.* 3.5.3), suggests that those who did flee Judea ahead of the Roman army did *not* go into the foothills but, following the suggestion of an oracle, to the plains of Pella in the east. Certainly, it is conceivable that Jesus' directive, handed down orally or through the written Gospel tradition, simply went unheeded by the Christians who chose instead to obey the Pella oracle. Alternatively, perhaps the fleeing Christians went through the foothills on the way to the plain. Again, this is conceivable but hardly satisfying. In my view, the difficulty resolves itself on understanding Jesus' words not as literal advice but as a reference to the mountains precisely as the proverbial refuge of the faithful on the spiritual abdication of Israel's leadership (Ezek. 7:16; Nah. 3:18) in general, and to the actions of the second-century BC hero Mattathias in particular.[37] When the noble Mattathias called out a faithful community following Antiochus IV's sacrilegious offerings on the altar, he 'and

---

37. As far as I am aware, this interpretation was first developed by Wright (*Victory of God*, p. 352).

his sons *fled to the hills*' (1 Macc. 2:28, emphasis added). If Jesus is indeed recalling the example of this Maccabean resistance leader, then the exhortation towards higher ground is not meant to identify a literal escape destination where his followers could safely hide from the Romans. Instead this must be a highly allusive way of saying that the desolation of the cultic space, which had first occurred in Mattathias's time in December 167 BC, was about to replay itself. Jesus' followers would need to respond accordingly with their own version of 'fleeing to the hills'.

Interpretative difficulties also accrue to a literal interpretation of Jesus' second directive (translated in the NRSV as *those inside the city must leave it*). The problem is this: once the Romans had drawn up battle lines in a perimeter outside Jerusalem, eventually supported by a surrounding security wall, it seems unlikely that anyone fleeing from the city could possibly make it past the enemy forces without being apprehended. And if the Romans did catch such a person, we can assume that said person's prospects were not highly favourable. When taken literally, this set of instructions simply makes for bad advice.[38]

Towards remediating this difficulty, I suggest that the language is more allusive than literal, and that most standard English translations (ESV, NET, NIV, NRSV) of verse 21b do us a disservice by translating *kai hoi en mesō autēs ekchōreitōsan* along the lines of 'and let those in the city flee'. A closer word-for-word, and in my view more helpful, rendering of the Greek is actually provided by the KJV: 'and let them which are in the midst of it depart out'.[39] In Septuagintal usage, the prepositional phrase *en mesō* means not just 'in the middle' of some physical space, but also in the middle of social space, that is, cultural, moral or spiritual space occupied by a community. Usage of this kind occurs, for example, in the LXX account of the exodus, when the Israelites are told to depart from

---

38. Schnabel (*Mark*, p. 326) disagrees on this point, maintaining that when the Zealots took over the Temple Mount in the winter of AD 67/68, there was ample time to leave Jerusalem and Judea.

39. As Marshall (p. 772) rightly notes, the pronoun *autēs* ('its') 'must refer back grammatically to *Ioudaia* ("Judea")'.

'the midst of them' (*ek mesou autōn*), that is, from within the mix of Egyptians (Exod. 7:5). Thus it is not implausible that Luke's 'in the midst of it' shows a similar usage, where the 'it' is not so much a defined physical space as a system. Meanwhile, Luke's use of *ekchōreō* (*depart*) is conspicuous since the term is very rare in the biblical canon, occurring only here in the New Testament and three times in the Greek translation of the Hebrew Scriptures. Of these three Old Testament usages (LXX Num. 17:10; Judg. 7:3; Amos 7:12), the first instance occurs in Yahweh's instruction to Moses in the aftermath of Korah's rebellion prior to a moment of horrific divine judgment: 'Get away from this congregation [*ekchōrēsate ek mesou tēs sunagōgēs tautēs*], so that I may consume them in a moment' (Num. 17:10, LXX; 16:45, ET). This occurrence of *mesos* ('midst') in conjunction with *ekchōreō* here is significant, since we have precisely the same word pairing as in Luke 21:21. Therefore, based on the principle of *gezera shawa* (whereby paired words in one scriptural passage illuminate the same paired words in another), I propose that when Luke's Jesus said 'and let them which are in the midst of it depart out', he had Numbers 17:10 (LXX; 16:45, ET) in mind. If so, the inference is clear enough. In declaring that 'those in the midst of it should flee' (*hoi en mesō autēs ekchōreitōsan*) at the sight of the encircling troops, Jesus is not so much giving escape instructions as stating that the wrath of God is, once again, about to be unleashed against a disobedient people. At that point, those who connect the dots of Jesus' words learn that they must eventually make a clean break with the entire socio-religious system that was the temple. Likewise, those in the 'regions' (*chōrais*), the areas which constituted the landholdings of Palestinian Judaism, must also sever their temple ties (v. 21c). If Acts depicts the early Christians maintaining their ties with the Jerusalem temple, Jesus here announces that a time would come when such ties were neither appropriate nor even possible. In retrospect, the period between Pentecost and the destruction of the temple proved for the early Christians to be a period of transitioning out of the Mosaic theocracy – what Paul elsewhere calls 'under the law' (Gal. 4:21, NIV).

22. Jesus' followers are told to break from the temple not only because of the current generation's resistance to Jesus' pro-

clamation (19:43–44), but also on account of Israel's historic disobedience over the course of redemptive history (11:50–51). The
days of vengeance (NRSV) or 'days of punishment' (*hēmerai ekdikēseōs*; cf.
NIV) are presented as a fulfilment of the Scriptures, not least Deuteronomy 32:35, where the 'day of vengeance' (*en hēmera ekdikēseōs*)
marks the day of Israel's exile. Thus, for the disobedient, the fall of
the temple would signal an intensification of exile. Meanwhile, for
Jesus' followers, it would prove that release and return from exile
were underway.

23–24a. In Israel, as in many cultures across the ages, pregnant
women and nursing mothers received special deference. That this
demographic will not be spared the awfulness of the period attests
to the severity of the divine punishment (cf. 23:29). This is all part
of the great distress *on the earth*, the wrath to be directed to this
people. The same women will also incur the sword of Israel's
enemies; the rest will be hauled away into exile.

24b. In the Ancient Near East, as in the Middle East today, as
well as many other parts of the world, the act of trampling confers
shame. The temple grounds had not been entirely immune to this.
In Isaiah 1:12, Yahweh charges Israel with trampling his temple
courts; in Daniel 8:10, 13, it is predicted that both the righteous and
the sanctuary would be trampled as part of the tribulation. Now,
in fulfilment of Daniel 8, the temple courts will again be trampled,
this time by Gentiles. All this will be necessary, Jesus suggests, *until
the times of the Gentiles are fulfilled*, a period which is best understood
along the lines of Paul's insistence that a divinely ordained window
for Gentile conversion would remain operative for a time, even
while Israel continued to be hardened (Rom. 11:1–32). In other
words, the *times of the Gentiles* marks the period of Gentile political
control over Israel and Gentile mission.[40] At the close of this *time*,
so Luke seems to hint, Yahweh would turn his face to Israel again
for its salvation.

25–26. Whereas, as I have mentioned, the majority of commentators understand 21:25–28 as referring to the future return of Jesus,
in my view the celestial signs and political upheavals described in

---

40. So also Green, p. 739; more tentatively, Marshall, p. 774.

these verses correspond better to the events as they were later to transpire in the several years before the temple's downfall, AD 67–69.[41] In this period, the Roman Empire experienced unprecedented levels of instability. In the year AD 69 alone, the so-called 'Year of the Four Emperors', political power was passed through a series of coups from Galba to Otho, from Otho to Vitellius, and from Vitellius to Vespasian. And as each succeeding emperor took power, he appealed to certain astrological signs in the heavens as confirmation of legitimacy, which would then be widely circulated as useful propaganda. So, when Jesus refers to the nations being thrown into anguish by celestial signs, he is predicting such astrological interpretations as propounded by the successive Roman emperors.[42] More than that, and perhaps more fundamentally, Luke sees these events as a fulfilment of Isaiah 13, a passage which predicts the fall of Babylon and underwrites Jesus' discourse at numerous points. So then, Luke's celestial signs, together with the roaring and tossing of the sea, should be understood not as physical phenomena but as the pieces of a scriptural collage, rooted in well-known texts of judgment. That Jesus should equate the temple with Babylon itself (the epitome of wickedness in the Scriptures) not only speaks of the intensity of Jesus' polemic against his detractors, but also sheds light on just what the young church saw itself escaping *from*.

27. At this point, so Jesus promises, the Son of Man will appear – not in the visible person of Jesus but as he is revealed in the destruction of the temple. The backdrop in Daniel 7 remains key. In this passage, we recall, the fundamental problem posed by the four unclean beasts from the sea is the desecrated temple space left in the wake of the four empires, which are represented by the four strange and fierce creatures. When Daniel's Son of Man comes

---

41. The position supported here is essentially identical to that outlined in the commentaries of France on Matthew and Mark. See France, *Mark*, pp. 500–501.

42. In the Greek literature, *synochē* ('anguish') is the visceral negative response to unfavourable omens, including celestial omens; cf. Koester, *TDNT* 7, p. 886–887.

with the cloud and in his glory, he comes to perform an atoning act, which would serve both to consign the unclean beasts to judgment and renew the temple space. On this background, the coming of *the Son of Man . . . in a cloud* is not a picture of Jesus being carried by a vaporous formation or something of the sort; it is rather an image which assures Luke's readers that the fall of the temple is an act of divine judgment *for the very purpose of creating a new sacred space* – sacred space that would begin to form with Pentecost (Acts 2).[43]

28. Having effectively answered the disciples' query posed in verse 7, Jesus now rounds off his discourse by summarizing what he deems to be the most fitting response. Once *these things (toutōn)* start to become visible, Jesus forewarns, that is the cue to remain alert. But what are *these things*? Just this: the immediately preceding list of events which Jesus promised in verses 20–27. Such readiness is necessary because the long-awaited redemption from the current and finally accursed theocracy is at hand.

ii. Parable of the fig tree (21:29–33)

29–31. The break introduced by *then he told them (kai eipen)* marks a shift in subject matter, although not completely discontinuous with verses 5–28. There is also a swing in genre: the text moves from an image-rich discourse to a simple parabolic comparison between blooming foliage and the arrival of the kingdom. Jesus begins by inviting his hearers to observe *the fig tree and all the trees*, pointing out that the sprouting of leaves typically occurs right before summer. Similarly, when *you see these things taking place*, this is evidence that the kingdom is near.

Two exegetical questions immediately arise. First, does the force of Jesus' analogy strictly relate to the arboreal life cycle or is there some added significance in the fact that he employs a *fig* tree in the comparison? Second, what is the referent of *these things*

---

43. Wright (*Victory of God*, p. 345) is on the mark when he writes that the disciples 'had not yet even thought of his being taken from them, let alone that he might come back . . . down to earth riding on a literal cloud. Had Jesus wished to introduce so strange and unJewish an idea to them he would have had a very difficult task.'

(*tauta*)? In answer to the first question, while the majority of commentators would suggest that Jesus specifies the fig tree only on account of the conspicuous difference between the fig's appearance in winter and in early bloom,[44] this commonplace explanation is weakened by the fact that countless deciduous trees exhibit the same seasonal contrast, begging the question as to whether Jesus' choice of *fig* tree was entirely gratuitous. Moreover, we note that Luke adds *and all the trees*, where his source (Mark 13:28) lacked the phrase. If Luke really intended to single out the fig tree due to its having this particular characteristic, then his addition of *and all the trees* is self-defeating. In my judgment, given the scriptural connection between the fig tree and Israel (1 Kgs 4:25; Isa. 28:4; Jer. 8:13; 24:5; Hos. 9:10; Mic. 7:1), a connection already patently exploited in Luke (13:6-9), we must conclude that the fig tree here indeed refers to ethnic Israel, while *all the trees* refers to the Gentile nations.

This judgment provides helpful support in approaching the second problem: the meaning of *these things*. Here again a careful reading of the text invites us to buck the trend of contemporary interpretation. Interpreters who correlate the coming of the kingdom with the sack of Jerusalem (vv. 20-24) are forced into the awkward position of making *these things* (v. 31) point all the way back to the much earlier predictions contained in verses 10-19. But the simpler approach is to assume that *these things* refers to the very last items under discussion, namely, the devastation of Jerusalem (vv. 25-28). In this case, the arrival of the kingdom (v. 31b) is not the destruction of the Holy City but the second coming of Christ (as in 22:18). This coheres well with the interpretation of the trees (fig tree = Israel; 'all trees' = Gentiles) proposed here, since precisely these two people groups are locked in combat in verses 20-28. The sprouting of leaves on both sets of trees, then, is equivalent to *these things* (v. 31a) and the fall of the city (vv. 20-24). For Luke's Jesus, the judgment against Jerusalem is a kind of down payment on the judgment to come with the arrival of the kingdom (v. 31b), the parousia.

---

44. So, e.g., Bock, p. 1687; Green, p. 741.

The implications of the parable are manifold, but at least two points should be noted. First, the comparison suggests that ethnic Israel (*the fig tree*), despite its severe judgment detailed in the discourse, will indeed finally participate in the eschatological blessing along with the nations (*all the trees*). On this note, Jesus holds out a sure salvific hope for Israel. Second, we are reminded that all the nations (Israel and the Gentiles) will realize their full, fruit-bearing potential only at the eschaton, ushering in an indefinite, glorious period symbolized by summer time, the season of agricultural flourishing. In the meanwhile, until the moment of the second coming, Luke's readers must expect that even those nations which are most responsive to the gospel will have yet to reach their fruit-bearing potential. Situating the parable as the capstone to the Eschatological Discourse, the Evangelist hopes to show that just as the persecutions and upheavals in the apostolic era will lead in due course to the fall of Jerusalem, so too even this horrific event will prove to be situated within a larger narrative which culminates with the full advent of the kingdom. The significance of such signs is not the immediacy of restoration but rather its nearness, a nearness which though indeterminate in timing is nonetheless certain.

32. Interpretation of verse 32 depends crucially on the much disputed meaning of *this generation* (*hē genea hautē*). Some commentators take the phrase to signify humanity in general, thus something like: 'Human beings will not cease to exist until all things take place.' While this sense is not impossible, it is inherently unsatisfying since it is difficult to see how such a statement could contribute to Jesus' meaning.[45] Another possibility is that *this generation* refers to the Jewish race, thus reinforcing the hope of salvation for the Jews. But the problem here is that such a meaning would require a highly unusual usage of *genea*. In my view, *this generation* here refers – as it normally does – to a set of people living at a given time, that is, Jesus' contemporaries.[46] In

---

45. As Bock (p. 1690) puts it, this merely 'states the obvious'.
46. So, e.g., Edwards, p. 610; Fitzmyer, p. 1353; Maddox, *Purpose*, pp. 111–115.

other words, Jesus' point is simply that 'all these things' (*panta*), everything from the persecutions to the sack of the temple, will occur within the space of a generation (three or four decades), that is, roughly by AD 70. That the temple actually fell by this date only confirms Jesus' words. This sense of *genea* certainly does not exclude the negative import of 'generation' in the Hebrew Scriptures (Gen. 7:1; Deut. 32:5; Pss 78:8; 95:10) and in Luke elsewhere (cf. Luke 17:25), but the focus is first and foremost on chronology. Luke's interest in preserving this promise is clear enough: assurance of such a swift timetable would certainly benefit Christians who might otherwise be unnerved by charlatan messiahs pressing for more immediate (and usually more violent) solutions to activate the kingdom.

33. On the face of it, the contrast Jesus makes between his words and *heaven and earth* is intended to assert the absolute authority of the former. In claiming that his words will outlast *heaven and earth*, Jesus is more or less saying that his words are divine.[47] However, because *heaven and earth* was also used as a circumlocution for Jerusalem, it is possible that through the phrase Jesus is reaching back to his earlier statements regarding the destruction of the temple.[48] In this case, verse 33 would essentially be Jesus' assurance that though the Holy City may fall, his words will prove true beyond this point and into eternity. It is an intriguing possibility that cannot be ruled out, but hardly changes the essential force of the statement.

iii. Admonition to watchfulness (21:34–36)

34a. The future coming of the kingdom has radical implications for everyday life. Accordingly, Jesus warns his followers – with some help from Isaiah 24:17–20 – that they must take special care of their souls. Left to its own devices, the human heart will be *weighed down* by three elements: *dissipation and drunkenness and the*

---

47. Similarly, Edwards (p. 610): 'The only being who could reasonably make such a claim is God (Isa 52:6).'

48. On 'heaven and earth' as a cipher for Jerusalem in the context of Rev. 21, see Beale, *Revelation*, pp. 1039–1121.

worries of this life.[49] The first two are closely related: *dissipation* (*kraipalē*) often has the sense of a hangover, while *drunkenness* (*methē*) means just that – a state of intoxication. The third element (*worries of this life*) in this short list seems less socially scandalous but its inclusion alongside dissipation and drunkenness suggests that such seemingly innocent concerns are neither as innocent as they appear nor any less insidious with respect to the soul.

34b–35. Those who fail to exercise caution will face certain judgment, come *that day*. Such judgment will come unexpectedly (*apiphnidios*), inescapably (*like a trap*) and universally (against all those 'sitting' on the face of the earth). Those who fail to conform their present-day lives to the impending future reality will one day experience that future reality in all its terrible force.

36. The key is to remain alert (*agrypneite*) and to pray (*deomenoi*), precisely – ironically enough – the same activities which the disciples will *fail* to perform at Gethsemane (22:39–46). While the NRSV and ESV may be right in suggesting that Jesus' followers are to pray for strength (in which case *hina* almost functions as an infinitive), the translation 'pray in order that you might have strength' may be more on target. In other words, Jesus does not call his disciples to pray specifically for strength but to pray with the intended result that they, through the very act of praying, might have the spiritual fortitude to escape such judgment. In either case, while the condemned will be found sitting (perhaps with some allusion to the peevish children sitting in the marketplace, 7:32), the righteous will stand.

iv. Summary (21:37–38)

37. The present verse creates a wrap-around with 19:47, enfolding the substance of Luke 20 – 21. This bracketing serves to show that the verbal attacks directed against Jesus in Luke 20 are not unconnected with the promised tribulations of the following chapter. By spending each evening on the Mount of Olives, Jesus not only hopes to keep his whereabouts concealed from the

---

49. The weighed-down heart is like the stubborn heart of Moses' Pharaoh (cf. Exod. 7:14; 8:15, 32; 9:7, 34).

Jerusalem authorities (thereby avoiding a premature arrest), but also, certainly from Luke's point of view, positions himself as 'the LORD' poised to fight eschatological battle from the Mount of Olives (Zech. 14:3–4).

38. Meanwhile, rising early day by day, *all the people* are eager to hear his teaching. In Lukan usage, *all the people* (perhaps referring to the totality of the elect people of God) are those who respond well to God's revelation in Jesus (7:29; 18:43).

Theology

The implications of the destruction of the temple are manifold. In the first place, whereas under the law Israel had been storing up judgment against itself over the centuries, now with the destruction of the temple that judgment was about to reach its climax. This moment signals the end of life under law and temple, as well as the full emergence of a new salvific economy centred around Jesus Christ. Second, the predicted destruction of the temple gives special urgency to the apostolic mission recorded in Acts. Convinced of Jerusalem's impending doom, the early church's mission to the synagogues in Palestine and throughout the diaspora would have been all the more motivated by the conviction of what God was about to do with the current system. In this respect, as the apostles call out the elect remnant from within the diasporic synagogues, they are essentially continuing the very same new exodus initiated by Jesus. Third and finally, Luke's readers would have understood the destruction of the temple and the emergence of a new Christ-obeying community together as a harbinger of the future transformation of the cosmos into a new creation. This follows from the fact that in Judaism the temple was thought of as a microcosm of the cosmos. When Jesus intimates the temple's devastation, not long after his announcement regarding a new 'cornerstone' (20:17–18), it is no accident that he also speaks of that moment when the physical heavens and earth would give way to a new reality.

In conveying Jesus' words, the Evangelist wants his readers to remain alert and prayerful, with minds and hearts ultimately fixed on the end of history. For Luke along with the rest of the New Testament writers, if there is any event that matches the significance of Easter weekend, it is the parousia. From here on out, all reality is to be interpreted between these two seismic signposts: Jesus' death and resurrection on the one side of history and his future coming on the other. The destruction of the temple is a confirming sign of the latter.

7. PASSION NARRATIVE (22:1 – 23:56)

A. Last Supper (22:1–23)

Context

Luke 22:1–23 centres around the Last Supper, also known as the Lord's Supper. Jesus' farewell paschal meal marks the close of his life, even as it draws together various threads of Luke's story. Taking its place alongside the earthly Jesus' other meals in the Gospel (5:30–32; 7:34; 14:16–24; 15:2, 23–32; 16:21; 19:7), this meal gives definition to all the meals that have gone before and even some that will come after. However clear the intimations of Jesus' messianic status up to this point, his identification with the bread now seals that role. Themes of new exodus now also come to a head, as Jesus' cup saying recalls the formation of the Mosaic covenant in Exodus 24. For Moses and Jesus alike, kingdom and meal converge.

Other subplots also begin to converge. Here the long-brewing animosity of the Jewish leaders comes to a rolling boil, as they engage Judas in betraying his master (22:1–6). More immediately, the emissary which Jesus sends on ahead in 22:7–13 finds earlier parallel in the lead-up to the triumphal entry (19:28–34), suggesting that this king's unusual terms of peace (14:31–32) have both a glorious and a shameful aspect. The glory of the triumphal entry gives way to the shame of the cross.

Comment

i. Judas's betrayal (22:1–6)

1. First commanded on the night of the first Passover (Exod. 12:15–20; 13:3–10; cf. 23:15; 34:18), the *festival of Unleavened Bread* is a seven-day feast held from the fifteenth to the twenty-first day of the month of Abib (March–April). As Luke notes, it is also *called the Passover* – a cause of no little confusion for modern readers. That Luke is compelled to explain the former term with the more familiar latter term indicates that the Evangelist expected his Gospel to be read by Gentiles unfamiliar with the Jewish festivals. The notation serves as the gateway into Luke's passion narrative, where Jesus himself will play the role of the sacrificial animal offering.

2. The *chief priests and the scribes* have been seeking to get rid of Jesus ever since the temple action (19:47). The intervening engagements, including the public debates (20:1 – 21:4) and his prediction of the temple's destruction (21:5–38), have only exacerbated tensions. It is no surprise, then, that the same groups *were looking* [*ezētoun*] *for a way to put Jesus to death* [*anelōsin*], that is, 'to get rid of' (NIV) him. Though it is not immediately clear whether the subordinate clause (*for they were afraid of the people*) reflects on the failure of the temple leaders' attempts on Jesus' life (as the imperfect *ezētoun* might suggest) or on their motives for killing him, the former is more likely. In other words, the leaders' fear of the people is not the incentive for killing Jesus but rather a disincentive for killing him in a hasty and impolitic manner.[1]

---

1. The number of pilgrims visiting Jerusalem during Passover may have exceeded the native population as much as sevenfold. 'Josephus tells us further that the crowd on such feasts were particularly volatile and given to violence (*Jewish War* 1:88–89), an observation he supports with

3. In his struggle with *Satan* since the temptation (4:1–13), Jesus has clearly been getting the upper hand (10:18; 11:18; 13:16). But now the tables *appear* to turn when the evil one physically enters *into Judas*. In canonical perspective, Luke's narratival remark is curious because according to John 13:27, this satanic 'entering' occurred during the Last Supper, not before it. For this reason, unless we contemplate the possibility that Satan entered Judas twice, it would be wise to resist attaching too technical a meaning to this entering. Judas does not exhibit the marks of demonic possession, at least not as we find them in 8:26–39, nor does Luke's wording force the inference. By the same token, Luke could certainly not mean anything less than this: that though Judas remained a culpable and therefore free agent, Satan here begins exerting a controlling influence on his decisions.

Whereas the betrayer has already been introduced as 'Judas Iscariot' (6:16), here he is identified as *Judas called Iscariot*.[2] Iscariot is not a patrilineal name (*nomen*) but a nickname of uncertain derivation. The most common explanation holds it to be a transliteration of Ish Kerioth (man from Kerioth; cf. Josh. 15:25). Alternatively, it may be a variant of the Aramaic *skaryota*, the equivalent of the Latin *sicarius* or 'dagger man'. On this theory, Judas would have had some kind of prior association with the Jewish terrorist group known as the Sicarii. It is, however, questionable that the Sicarii existed as early as Jesus' day. Perhaps the most intriguing if not somewhat speculative etymology is that Iscariot reflects the Aramaic *iskarioutha* meaning 'choking' or 'constriction'.[3] In this case, Judas was called this by fellow Jesus-followers, either posthumously (reflecting Judas's death by hanging; cf. Acts 1:18) or during his lifetime. One can easily imagine him being so named by Jesus himself for reasons we know not. This would at least perfect a certain symmetry, whereby he becomes the evil counterpart to the nicknamed Simon.

---

the description of riots at Passover (2:18–13; 2:223–227) and Pentecost (2:43)' (Johnson, p. 332).

2. This might be to distinguish him from another Judas (son of James), also known as Thaddeus; cf. Acts 1:13.

3. Taylor, 'Iscariot', pp. 379–383.

4. Now the *chief priests* appear not with the scribes (22:2) but with the *officers of the temple police*.[4] Judas goes out to them in order to make a proposition as to how they might *betray* Jesus. First signalled at Judas's introduction (6:16), this betrayal has also been predicted in Jesus' second (9:44) and third (18:32) passion predictions. No evil takes either Jesus or Luke's readers by surprise.

5–6. Unlike Zacchaeus and the crowds who receive Jesus with rejoicing (19:6, 37), the temple leaders rejoice (*echarēsan*) at Judas's willingness to come forward. To incentivize the would-be betrayer to make good on his proposal, they also *agreed* [*synethento*] *to give him* silver. The corresponding verb *syntithēmi* has overtones of contractual obligations. By contrast, the verb indicating Judas's consenting response (*exōmologēsen*) has a religious or confessional aspect, especially in Jewish and Christian literature (e.g. Ps. 29:5, LXX; 105:47, LXX; Rom. 14:11; 15:9; Rev. 3:5). Perhaps the point of the word choice is to emphasize that Judas's decision to betray Jesus amounts to a public profession of political and religious allegiance, implying – as far as Luke's readers are concerned – that any decision to apostatize from Christ is partially born out of perverse human attachments. Once the die is cast, it is no longer the chief priests and scribes (22:2) who are seeking (*ezētei*) for an *opportunity* to inflict harm on Jesus, but Judas. The evil forces outside the Twelve have now penetrated the community, ensuring that Jesus' destruction will be delegated to a member from within – a sobering warning to the church.

ii. Preparations for Passover (22:7–13)

7–8. The *day of Unleavened Bread* closed out the week-long feast of Unleavened Bread. It was also the day on which the Passover lambs had to be slaughtered. This traditionally occurred several hours before sunset, in time for the Passover meal that night (technically the next day, since Jewish reckoning considered

---

4. The combination recurs at Luke 22:52 and continues into Acts (4:1; 5:24, 26). The officers of the temple police were second only to the chief priests in authority, having responsibility for the security of the temple.

evening the start of a new day). Accordingly, Jesus once again sends an envoy of two disciples (cf. 19:28–34), who are this time named: *Peter and John*. As in 19:29, the verb of sending (*apesteilen*) has connotations of a solemn errand. The same pair will take on a distinctive leadership role in the post-Pentecost church (Acts 3:1–11; 4:1–31); the two apostles also experience, along with James, the transfiguration (Luke 9:28; cf. Luke 8:51).

9–10. The 'What?' and the 'When?' of the Passover meal were already stipulated in the relevant legislation. As for the venue of the Passover, the only stipulation was that it had to be in Jerusalem (Deut. 16:5–8). Though one suspects that between Jesus and the Twelve there likely would have been at least one connection in the city who could host them for the Passover, Jesus takes a different tack. For upon entering the city, Peter and John are told that a certain *man carrying a jar* (*keramion*) will meet them. Though the *keramion* was a ceramic pitcher typically used for carrying wine (e.g. Seneca, *Polyb.* 4.26), this jar is predicted to be filled with *water*. This is probably not unrelated to one of Israel's founding stories, specifically, of Abraham's servant determining Isaac's future spouse by means of a providentially administered water jug (Gen. 24:12–54). If, in the patriarchal narrative, the continuation of the promised seed occurs after a divinely orchestrated event involving a water jar leading to a meal, now Jesus prepares for his own meal with a divinely appointed host who is never finally identified. As for the bearer of the water jar, the two disciples are told to *follow him into the house he enters*.

11. Peter and John are duly led to the owner of the house (*tō oikodespotē tēs oikias*), that is, the household manager. In previous exhortations to watchfulness, Jesus admonishes the disciples to imitate the 'owner of the house' who is ready to serve the returning master at a moment's notice (12:35–48). In Luke 12 the owner of the house must ready himself for the master *returning* from a wedding banquet (12:36). But if we identify the soon-to-come Last Supper (22:14–23) as a covenantal meal not unlike a wedding banquet (5:33–35), then Jesus seems to be on his way to the wedding banquet. Strikingly, whereas the first envoy to secure the colt emphasized Jesus as Lord and true owner of the colt (19:31, 33, 34, 38), here the master instructs his disciples to identify him merely as *the teacher*.

Their quest is to secure a *guest room* (*katalyma*) for the evening's meal. Whereas Jesus' parents were unable to secure a *katalyma* for bringing their child into the world (2:7), divine providence – whether the room was prearranged or not – would reserve Jesus a *katalyma* as he prepared to exit the world.

12–13. As in Mark 14:15, the venue for the Last Supper is described as *a large room upstairs, already furnished* (*anagaion mega estrōmenon*). That the room is *large* would have been a matter of practical necessity, since no fewer than thirteen men were to dine, more if others in addition to the Twelve were also in attendance. At the same time, that the room is *large, already furnished* (meaning that the rug and pillows have been arranged) and *upstairs* may hint that Jesus seeks in this space some kind of crude spatial analogy to the future and expansive kingdom above where he longs to have a meal (22:18). This cannot be overpressed since *anagaion* (upstairs room) may refer to a makeshift rooftop space, precisely the architectural location associated with Jesus' first act of forgiveness (5:17–26). As in 19:28–34, the two disciples discover that everything is just as Jesus said it would be. Accordingly, *they prepared the Passover meal*.

iii. The paschal meal (22:14–23)

14. Drawing on Daniel, Luke consistently employs *the hour* (*hē hōra*) to designate a milestone within the timetable of God's redemptive actions (Luke 1:10; 2:38; 7:21). This is a fortiori the case in his introduction to this pericope: *When the hour* [*hōra*] *came . . .* In stipulating this specific time span, moreover, the Evangelist closes out a trajectory of increasingly compressed time periods, moving from the week-long 'feast' (22:1), to the 'day' (v. 7) and now at last 'the hour' (v. 14). Jesus had earlier reclined to eat (*anepesen*) with the unbelieving Pharisees (11:37), but now *he took his place at the table* (*anepesen*) with more sympathetic company, *the apostles*. In Luke 22 the term sits alongside other designations for Jesus' closest followers: 'In the account of the Last Supper all three words occur for those at the meal: *dōdeka* in 22:3, *mathētai* in 22:11, and *apostoloi* in 22:14.'[5] In identifying the twelve disciples as *apostles* in this

---

5. Just, *Ongoing Feast*, p. 228.

passage, Luke is underscoring their joint role in the ecclesial foundation, together with their shared responsibility for reiterating the Lord's Supper in remembrance of Jesus (v. 19).

15. Jesus' institution of the Lord's Supper rests on a solid footing as a fact of history, having been variously attested not only in the Gospels, but also in one of Paul's earliest writings (Matt. 26:26–29//Mark 14:22–25//1 Cor. 11:23–26; cf. Did. 9.1–5). Still, given the divergences between Mark and Matthew, on the one hand, and Luke and Paul, on the other, specifics relating to putative sources and precise wording remain less clear. Luke's account is the longest among these reports and may in fact depend on a Hebraic or Aramaic source. This theory would at any rate be supported by the Hebraism *I have eagerly desired* (*epithymia epethymēsa*).[6] Jesus' intense desire *to eat this Passover*, more likely referring to the lamb than to the meal as a whole (so, e.g., Marshall, p. 796), implies that this moment retains a singular significance. In fact, given earlier intimations of his death precisely as an *exodos* (9:31), Jesus' transposition of Passover symbols (22:14–23) as a way of interpreting his own death suggests that the journey to Jerusalem (9:51 – 19:44), the bulk of the Gospel, has now reached its climax in this defining moment. Furthermore, that Jesus regards this meal as his final act *before I suffer* implies that his earlier predictions of suffering (9:22; 17:25) are now about to be fulfilled. If in Acts all roads lead to the ends of the earth, then in Luke all roads come together at this juncture, of which the passion and resurrection are arguably but a denouement.

16. Jesus expects not just to suffer soon but also to die. That is, he *will not eat* the Passover *until it is fulfilled in the kingdom of God*. But when exactly is the Passover fulfilled? Or when does Jesus eat it again? Though good arguments can be made for locating this fulfilment at Emmaus or in the bread-breakings of the early church, a stronger case can be made for linking this envisioned Passover to the eschatological meal, corresponding to the parousia and the general resurrection. This judgment is supported in the first instance by the fact that Luke's Jesus has been consistently pointing

---

6. So, e.g., Edwards, p. 624.

to the eschatological meal (12:35–37; 13:28–29; 14:15), *not* to its harbingers post-resurrection or post-Pentecost. Second, the eucharistic oral tradition upon which Luke draws very clearly focuses the Lord's Supper on the second coming (1 Cor. 11:26). On the Evangelist's sacramentology, therefore, the church's performance of the Lord's Supper looks back to the Mosaic exodus and ahead to the final exodus achieved on the attainment of the new creation.

17. By reporting that Jesus *took a cup*, the first of the four cups of the Passover rite, Luke implies that Jesus himself participates in the meal, a supposition confirmed by verse 18 (*'from now on* I will not drink'; emphasis added). Yet he also instructs the Twelve to *divide* the cup's contents *among yourselves*. In typical Passover ritual, only the officiant would partake of the cup. Jesus' instruction that the apostles share the cup is unique and may suggest that he is transferring his leadership role to them, even as he invites his followers to participate in his suffering.

18. As the entitled heir of the vineyard (20:9–19), Jesus promises not to drink of *the fruit of the vine*, a circumlocution for wine (Deut. 22:9; Isa. 32:12; m. Ber. 6:1). His assertion is less a vow of abstinence than, again, a vision of the eschatological feast (note the parallels with v. 16), when *the kingdom of God comes*. As the coming of the kingdom is also one of the leading focal points of the Lord's Prayer (Luke 11:2), one surmises that neither his promised feast (22:8) nor his prescribed prayer (11:2) looks to a gradual coming of the kingdom but rather to a climactic event capping off all of cosmic history.

19–20. Next, attention is drawn to *a loaf of bread* (*arton*) and *the cup* (*to potērion*). Both components, the unleavened Passover bread (Exod. 29:2; Lev. 2:4; Num. 6:19, LXX) and one of the four Passover cups, Jesus now reinterprets wholesale.[7] Whereas Luke 22:14–18 seems to reflect a conventional paschal meal with isolated moments of striking variation, now the whole meal is transformed so as to point entirely

---

7. Though the leading witnesses of the western manuscript tradition omit vv. 19b–20, most commentators (including this one) regard the words as authentically Lukan.

to Jesus. Within Luke's story, the event functions as the centre panel flanked by two other meal scenes: the feeding of the five thousand (9:10−17) and the Emmaus road meal (24:28−35). Like Mark, Luke hopes his readers will connect the dots between Jesus' actions at the Lord's Supper (*took . . . given thanks . . . broke . . . gave*) and the same actions at the feeding miracle (9:16) and at Emmaus (24:30). The three messianic meals are mutually interpretative.

In identifying his body with a broken piece of bread, Jesus foretells his fate on the cross. At the same time, I believe a credible case can be made that Jesus is here identifying himself with the *aphikomen*, that is, the morsel of bread which was placed on the table in expectation of the coming Messiah and eventually metonymically identified with the Messiah.[8] In the light of these considerations, Jesus' implicit invitation to partake of the bread serves as a dual invitation extended to the Twelve to (1) participate in his vocation of brokenness and (2) confess him as Messiah. For Luke's readers, their own participation in the Lord's Supper might signify nothing less.

Meanwhile, the cup saying invokes no fewer than four different Scriptures (Exod. 24:8; Isa. 53:11−12; Jer. 31:31−34; Zech. 9:11). Pointing back to the poured-out blood of the Mosaic covenant (Exod. 24), Jesus' cup, with its own *poured out . . . blood*, represents the establishment of the kingdom, catalysed by Jesus' death, resurrection, ascension and parousia − all encapsulated in the concept of new exodus.[9] The pouring out of this blood *for you* (*hyper hymōn*) indicates that Jesus' death is atoning much as the Suffering Servant atoned on behalf of many, as in Isaiah 53:11−12. Finally, Jesus' identification of the cup as *the new covenant in my blood* gestures to the new covenant of Jeremiah 31:31−34 and the covenant of blood in Zechariah 9:1. Not insignificantly, Jeremiah's anticipated new covenant is a predicted epoch of forgiveness and life in the Spirit.

21−22. Notwithstanding the remarkable, though largely implicit, claims of Jesus' bread and cup sayings, one of the apostles stands

---

8. Some scholars would object to this point, claiming that the evidence of this practice is too late to be relevant to Jesus' setting.

9. See Pao, *New Exodus*, pp. 95−96.

ready to betray Jesus, even as he *is with me*. Indeed, *his hand is on the table*. Yet this comes as no surprise either to God or to Jesus. Whereas Matthew (Matt. 26:24) and Mark (Mark 14:21) ultimately ascribe the betrayer's actions and the Son of Man's resultant *going* to holy writ ('as it is written'), Luke by contrast owes this course of events to what *has been determined*. Notwithstanding the hand of divine providence, the betrayer remains fully culpable for his actions: *woe to that one by whom he is betrayed!*

23. On hearing Jesus' dire warning, the Twelve start *to ask one another* (*syzētein pros heautous*) about this matter. Given the argumentative connotations of the same verb in other Lukan contexts (Acts 6:9; 9:29), however, we find the NET translation appealing: 'So they began to question one another as to which of them it could possibly be who would do this.'[10] Two comments are in order. First, Luke seems to be intentionally drawing attention to the sobering fact that participation in the Lord's Supper is no guarantee against either apostasy or treachery. Second, there is some irony in the fact that once the disciples are informed of a traitor in their ranks, their first inclination is to interrogate one another rather than to countenance the possibility that they themselves might have some role in abandoning Jesus, if not betraying him altogether.

Theology

Up to this point in the story, everyone who has come to Jesus' table has come on an equal footing. The same is certainly true of the Last Supper. Here a motley crew of twelve men, from various backgrounds and persuasions, now take a meal together with Jesus. Around the shared messianic bread and the cup, all embrace their identity as co-heirs of the kingdom and co-participants in a common mission. In taking the bread and cup, all are made equal. Whereas those outside the kingdom look to Graeco-Roman-style meals as one more opportunity to reassert status, Jesus' disciples instead are to locate themselves, with respect to the community and to the world, through the Lord's Supper. The Lord's Supper is

---

10. References pointed out in Green, p. 764 n. 77.

a meal that flattens out worldly hierarchies even as it galvanizes those who follow the Messiah – a Messiah who summarizes his life story by breaking a piece of bread.

The reason that the kingdom poor converge around *meals* is because meals are celebratory at heart. The reason for celebration is Jesus' death and resurrection, and the forgiveness that results from both. Luke retains Jeremiah's phrase '*new* covenant' (22:20; cf. Jer. 31:31–34), a divinely inaugurated economy that promised to include both the spiritual inscribing of the human heart (Jer. 31:33) and forgiveness (Jer. 31:34). As the visible fulfilment of the new covenant itself, the Lord's Supper drives home the fact that God in Christ has not only cancelled past and present sin but also provided power for obedience going into the future. When Jesus' followers re-enact this meal, they are not just remembering Jesus but opening the door to personal and communal transformation.

B. The hour of trial (22:24–46)

Context

The section marked out by Luke 22:24–46 finds its background in at least three earlier portions of the Gospel. First, when Jesus points to himself as 'one who serves' (22:27) and to the disciples as those who sleep (22:46), he is retrospectively explicating the parable of the servants waiting for their master (12:35–40). Second, Jesus' observation that the disciples have stood their ground in the midst of his trials or *peirasmoi* (22:28), together with Luke's demonstration of their failure in the face of more immediate temptation or *peirasmos* (22:40), shows that they are experiencing uneven success in averting the trial or temptation (*peirasmos*) – and this perhaps because they have not sufficiently prayed (11:4). Third and finally, the missionary policies of an earlier day (9:1–6) are now reversed (22:35–38), suggesting that a new era is breaking forth, demanding a new protocol designed for intensified conflict. If there is a theme that runs through Luke 22:24–46, that theme is trial.

Comment

i. True greatness (22:24–30)

24–26. The disciples' accusations and interrogations, all issued in the hope of identifying Jesus' betrayer (v. 23), now lead to self-justifying boasts. On the mistaken assumption that the as-yet unidentified betrayer sat towards the bottom of the group's pecking order, each disciple seeks to prove his innocence in a roundabout way by proving his relative importance (which, so it was thought, would make him a less likely suspect). Of course, as far as Jesus is concerned, this is pure nonsense. While Gentile rulers may have authority over whole nations and therefore *lord it over them*, such bids for power and status were inappropriate for his disciples.[11] In a world where seniority trumps youth and leaders outrank followers, Jesus calls his disciples to become *the youngest* and the *one who serves*, much like the youthful Suffering Servant of Isaiah 53.

27. Jesus reinforces his point by posing a rhetorical question. It is a question that is designed to draw out the hierarchical social roles of the first-century banquet table, where the one who reclines at the dinner table is assumed to be socially superior to the *one who serves*. But after getting his disciples to agree to this hierarchy in theory, Jesus now asserts himself as one 'in the middle of you' (*en mesō hymōn*) and as one who serves, an assertion soon to be made palpable through his death. The call to humble service is no mere suggestion but a command based on Jesus' modelled behaviour. Because the Graeco-Roman social world was completely structured by these hierarchies, any first-century reader would have understood such teaching to be extremely destabilizing.

28–29. Jesus does not merely belittle the disciples' ambitions for greatness; he calls them to a higher and more lasting greatness.

---

11. Though the phrase 'lord it over' someone is almost always pejorative, it would be a mistake to assume the same intrinsically negative overtones here in the shared translation of the NRSV, ESV and NIV. Jesus is simply alluding to the reality of political hierarchies without implying that such structures are inherently abusive or self-serving. See Lull, 'Servant-Benefactor', pp. 290–294; Nelson, *Leadership*, pp. 149–150.

Placing the *you* (*hymeis*) at the beginning of the sentence (followed by a post-positive particle *de*), Luke's Jesus emphasizes the disciples' unique privilege: 'But as for *you*!' Having stuck with Jesus through his *trials* (*peirasmoi*), not least the temptations accompanying the social marginalization that followed Jesus' commitment to the truth (cf. 11:4), the Twelve stand at the brink of inheritance. Indeed, now that the new covenant has been inaugurated through the Last Supper (22:20), it is fitting that Jesus formalize the new leadership role of the Twelve by 'conferring' (*diatithemai*; the verb *diatithēmi* is connotative of covenantal arrangements; cf. Gen. 9:17; 15:18; Exod. 24:8; etc.) on them the very kingdom which the Father had conferred on Jesus.

30. Participation in this kingdom inheritance entails a twofold promise: to eat with Jesus at his messianic banquet table (thus sharing an intimate *relationship* with the Messiah) and to sit as judge over the twelve tribes of Israel (thus sharing in one of the Messiah's central *functions*). The first prospect has already been intimated in the many meal scenes of Luke's narrative (6:21; 9:10–17; 14:12–24; etc.). Meanwhile, the expectation of participating in Israel's judgment has also already been anticipated by earlier hints of the disciples' priestly calling. Since judging was not a royal but a priestly prerogative (Deut. 17:9; 2 Chr. 19:8–11), not to mention the task of the eschatological priests (Ezek. 44:23), Jesus must be alluding to the Twelve's role as those who would oversee the eschatological temple.

ii. Predicted testing (22:31–34)

31. In the light of the Baptizer's early warning that the coming one had a 'winnowing fork . . . in his hand, to clear his threshing-floor and to gather the wheat into his granary' (3:17), one infers that the 'sifting' Jesus envisions here is the very same divinely initiated activity (cf. Amos 9:9). Yet it is also, strangely enough, an activity in which Satan comes to play a voluntary role (cf. Job 1 – 2). Guided by the Gospel's own logic, Luke's readers must conclude that if the devil's temptation had demonstrated Jesus' Messiahship (4:1–13), then Satan's warrant to sift the apostles in the ensuing passion narrative will ultimately serve to show their fragility. The lead apostle is singled out as *Simon*, rather than Peter, likely because his

forthcoming failure is better reflected by his name prior to his
encounter with Jesus.[12]

32. Though Satan is determined to sift the apostles collectively, Jesus mentions only having *prayed for you* (*edeēthēn peri sou*),
that is, Simon alone. The thrust of that prayer is that his *faith may
not fail* (*eklipē*) or quit (v. 32a).[13] Though verse 32b goes on to
presume that Simon will lapse in some fashion, it is not immediately clear whether, despite Jesus' prayer, the disciple's faith
actually does fail in the sense intended by *eklipē*. In any case,
having foreseen his protégé's apostasy, the master also sees his
restoration (*when once you have turned back*). At the point of repentance, so Jesus commands, the disciple must *strengthen your brothers*.
As Luke's sequel will go on to show, Peter will eventually oblige
Jesus by strengthening the church in the first twelve chapters of
Acts. In the light of these words, though Peter's own betrayal of
Jesus is certainly tragic, one is left wondering whether his sin and
restoration actually leave him better equipped to strengthen his
fellow believers.

33–34. Simon is dismayed by Jesus' prediction and objects to it.
Recalling dire warnings of persecution from the Olivet Discourse
(21:12–16), he professes his readiness to accompany Jesus *to prison
and to death* – outcomes with which some of Luke's own readers
would have been directly or indirectly familiar. In response, Jesus
only doubles down on his prediction. Driving home the nearness
and thoroughness of Simon's denial while also filling out specific
details, he promises that *the cock will not crow this day* until the apostle
has *denied* him *three times*. Soon enough the dark prophecy will prove
true (22:54–62).

---

12. The repetition *Simon, Simon* expresses the pathos of the situation. This
     is one of a number of instances of the double vocative in Luke; see
     Edwards, p. 637 n. 87.

13. The verb *ekleipō* tends to express not so much binary success or failure
     as relative lack or failing supply; see BDAG, p. 242.

iii. New instructions (22:35–38)

35–37. At least three problems present themselves in verses 35–36.[14] The first issue pertains to an ambiguity in the Greek syntax, as the precise objects of the two participles *echōn* (having) and *mē echōn* (not having) are indeterminate. Second, why does Jesus forbid reliance on purse and bag in 9:1–3 and 10:1–4, only to rescind the same directives here? Third, how does Jesus' injunction to purchase a sword comport with his earlier stated commitment to non-violence? In an attempt to treat these problems, the following remarks are in order. First, in adjudicating the meaning of the Greek, the majority of commentators are likely correct in supporting the NRSV rendering: *But now, the one who has a purse must take it, and likewise a bag. And the one who has no sword must sell his cloak and buy one.* The second and third issues can be lightly touched on together: Jesus' policy reversal is meant not to discourage trust in God's provision but to alert the Twelve to the fact that a period of intense tribulation, introduced by *but now*, is underway. Jesus' continuing commitment to non-violence, not to mention his self-understanding as Israel's agent of atonement, is evidenced by his claim that Isaiah 53:12 *must be fulfilled in me.* This is further corroborated by his being *counted among the lawless,* a prophecy which turns to reality when he is crucified alongside two *lēstai* (traditionally if not somewhat misleadingly understood as robbers) in 23:32–43. Yet in all this, Jesus' advice to buy a sword is not meant as a literal instruction for the disciples but as a general indication of the conflict to come. In short, the call to purchase a sword 'is a call to be ready for hardship and self-sacrifice'.[15]

38. Over-literalizing Jesus' words, the disciples inform Jesus that there are *two swords* in their possession. In saying as much, they demonstrate that they have failed to grasp what it means for their master to emulate the Suffering Servant. Jesus' retort, *It is enough* (*hikanon estin*), does not intend to say that two swords will suffice as

---

14. In the words of Liefeld (p. 1029), 'this short passage is difficult to interpret'.

15. Marshall, p. 825.

the disciples' weaponry: it is to say that an exasperated Jesus wants the Twelve to drop the whole discussion.

iv. Gethsemane (22:39–46)

39. Whereas Matthew and Mark identify the place of Jesus' last prayer as Gethsemane (Matt. 26:36//Mark 14:32), and John calls it a 'garden' east of the Kidron (John 18:1), Luke's contribution is to locate the so-called 'Garden of Gethsemane' on the *Mount of Olives*. The place name is appropriate for what is about to unfold on the cross, for the Mount of Olives is associated with both judgment and redemption (Zech. 14:4). Given that this was a location where Jesus *went, as was his custom*, one might reasonably suppose that the space was a privately owned area, tucked away within a copse of olive trees and regularly used as home camp for Jesus and his disciples. When Luke reports that *the disciples followed him*, the sentence likely intends something more than the apostles' spatial relationship to their master: for the moment they are engaged as following disciples.

40. In coming to *the place* (*tou topou*), Jesus commands the disciples to pray in connection with the trial (*peirasmon*). Perhaps not coincidentally, 'coming to the place' (*ēlthon epi ton topon*, Gen. 22:9, LXX) is exactly what Abraham did in his hour of trial (*peirasmos*) when tasked with sacrificing his son Isaac. In this case, Jesus is the new Isaac, the promised seed of Abraham and the basis for Israel's atonement going forward. The same prayer that Jesus had enjoined on his disciples as a standard prayer for life in the kingdom (11:4) he now re-enjoins for the purposes of the present crisis: *Pray that you may not come into the time of trial* (*peirasmon*). By itself, the term *peirasmos* can be translated here as trial (NRSV) or test (NJB) or temptation (ESV, KJV, NIV, NASB).[16] Though sharp distinctions cannot be drawn between the three meanings, I prefer the first of these options as the primary sense. In this context, the term *trial* is a semi-technical term relating to a redemptive threshold event, for here Jesus and his disciples are entering into the same kind of testing moment that Abraham (Gen. 22:1) and the exodus-bound

---

16. BDAG, pp. 640–641.

Israelites (Deut. 4:34; 7:19; 29:3) faced – confirming the covenant and launching the new exodus.

41. Though the disciples are called to follow Jesus in his sorrows, he must – so to speak – tread the winepress alone (Isa. 63:3): *he withdrew from them about a stone's throw*, a short distance.[17] In the same way Jesus initiated his ministry (3:21), so now he closes it out – with prayer. This time, however, Jesus is praying on his knees, an untypical posture since Jews generally prayed standing up. Though Jesus' position may indicate his utter submission, more to the point is his recapitulation of Daniel's kneeling posture when he prayed in exile (Dan. 6:10). Daniel's kneeling prayers marked out the days of exile: Jesus now demonstrates the climax of exile by praying on his knees as well.[18]

42. Having already instructed his disciples to call on God as 'Father' (11:2) in their regular prayers, now Jesus uses the term for the first time. Luke's recording of Jesus' term of address is partially motivated by his interest in drawing a parallel with that putatively atoning Isaac, who likewise at his point of crisis called out 'Father!' (Gen. 22:7). It is a common but nevertheless mistaken notion that Jesus was the first in Ancient Judaism to call God 'Father'. More to the point is to assert that whereas pre-Christian Judaism occasionally used this epithet for God when seeking to recall Yahweh's faithfulness in the midst of crisis, the historical Jesus, as evidenced both here and in the Lord's Prayer (11:2), is ultimately responsible for standardizing such prayer language among his followers.[19] The delicate balance of the present verse

---

17. The colloquial English phrase was inspired by translations of this verse.

18. Larkin ('Old Testament Background', pp. 252–253) notes further comparisons: Daniel and Jesus are 'both alone and in communion with God (Dan. x. 2 ff.); both are strengthened (ὅτι ἐνίσχυέ με, Dan. x. 18 Θ) by a heavenly messenger; both are concerned with the will of God as it will be played out in future events; and both having received knowledge of God's will find themselves in need of strength, physical restoration'.

19. Perrin, *Jesus the Priest*, pp. 20–38.

expresses Jesus' psychological wrestling match within. Deferring to the divine will, Jesus pleads with the Father to *remove this cup*, which is the cup of divine wrath (Isa. 51:17–22; Ezek. 23:32–24). At the same time, Jesus affirms that the chief criterion for his future path is not his own desire but the desire of God. The Evangelist intends this prayer as a model for all Christian prayer, in order that the believer's personal interest might take a back seat to the divine will.

43–44. These verses are text-critically disputed. If the external manuscript evidence ever so slightly favours their omission, the internal evidence provides compensatory reasons for their inclusion.[20] Whether or not the words are authentic to Luke, they certainly speak of the extraordinary depths of Jesus' prayer. So weakened is he, both physically and in terms of sheer will, that *an angel from heaven appeared to him and gave him strength.* Entering into a state of anguish, Jesus now prays with increased intensity, with the result that his physiological processes begin to operate in an unusual way, leading to the sweating out of blood.[21]

45–46. Unlike Mark (14:32–42) and Matthew (26:36–46), which recount multiple bouts of prayer with intermediate check-ins with the disciples, Luke recounts only one session of prayer and one conversation between Jesus and his followers. The apostles seem to be emotionally exhausted, as he *found them sleeping because of grief.* Accordingly, he chides them. The disciples must rise up and *pray*, precisely along the lines that Jesus had already commanded: *that you may not come into the time of trial* (11:4). In early Christianity, falling asleep and rising up are metaphors for spiritual lethargy and spiritual alertness, respectively (Eph. 5:14). The same certainly obtains here. The disciples fail Jesus and themselves because they have failed to pray.

---

20. Metzger, *TCGNT*, p. 151.

21. Medically speaking, it may be that Jesus is experiencing hematidrosis, a condition in which the body undergoes so much stress that it begins to sweat blood.

Theology

Whereas the vast majority of first-century Jews expected the tribulation (i.e. the divinely ordained set of trials encapsulated in the word *peirasmos*) to occur *prior* to the messianic reign, this passage clarifies that Jesus' messianic movement would take shape *through* the tribulation. The master indicates, if only indirectly, that his community of followers would face trials both from within and from without. As Luke well knew, Judas's betrayal (22:22) of the Twelve would be only the first of many instances in which a seemingly well-established believer would unexpectedly reject the believing community and then turn on it in an effort to destroy it. On another front, Luke foresees certain external forces (like those in 22:37–38) that would conspire in fierce opposition, seeking among other things to label both Jesus and/or his followers as transgressive. When such trials come, believers have the choice to succumb or to withstand. In other words, they may succumb by responding, for example, with self-righteous finger-pointing (22:24), violent intentions (22:38a) or slothful resignation (22:45). Or they may withstand the *peirasmos* by relying on divine assistance (22:40). The key to such divinely empowered resistance, as Jesus has already implied elsewhere (11:4), is nothing less than watchful prayer (22:41–43). If trials succeed in breaking down a community, it is more often than not because the community has failed to pray.

C. Jesus arrested (22:47–62)

Context

Building on the Last Supper (22:7–38), the so-called 'passion narrative' translates into action that which had been solemnly dramatized at Jesus' last meal. Throughout this section of the story, allegiances to Jesus are revealed for what they are, even as Messiah – in the very crucible of suffering – is revealed for who he is. The arrest scene (22:47–53) throws into sharp relief two approaches to kingdom life: the way of the misguided disciples (the path of armed resistance) or the way of Jesus (the path of blessing and healing). Soon the frailty of the disciples will be on full display with the threefold denial of Peter (22:54–62), proving that Jesus – and only Jesus – is the true Son of Man.

Comment

i. Jesus is apprehended (22:47–53)

47–48. As the crowd (*ochlos*) follows Jesus over the course of his ministry, its allegiance to Jesus has been ambivalent at best (cf. e.g. Luke 3:7–10). In this instance, *a crowd* comes to arrest Jesus. Two steps ahead of them is *one called Judas*, Jesus' predicted betrayer (22:21–22). The depth of his imminent betrayal is brought home in two ways. First, Judas is designated here as *one of the twelve*. The Gospel writer mentions this not to introduce new information but to accentuate the irony and the pathos of his treachery: Israel's Messiah was about to be turned in by a member of his own core group, who otherwise would have been enthroned as one of twelve tasked with judging the twelve tribes of Israel (22:30). Second, he draws near *to kiss him*. Whether or not Judas succeeds in delivering his affectionate greeting (v. 48 seems to imply as much), such a sign of tenderness and devotion will soon be belied by the posse's intentions, as the predicted fate of the Son of Man is now being fulfilled (9:22–24, 43–45; 18:31–34).

49. As if to indicate that they have temporarily lost their exalted titles, the erstwhile 'apostles' of 22:14 are now less grandly identified as *those who were around him*. They ask an honest question: *should we strike with the sword?* The query shows, again, that they have taken literally Jesus' command to buy a sword (22:36) and therefore have misunderstood him altogether. Like the waylaid seed in the parable of the sower, they have become like those who listen but do not understand Jesus' words (8:10).

50. No sooner do the disciples pose their question than one of them (identified as Peter in John 18:10), without waiting for an answer, cuts off the *right ear* of the *slave of the high priest* (identified as one Malchus in John 18:10).[22] The event is preserved in all four Gospels (cf. Matt. 26:51; Mark 14:47; John 18:10–11) and therefore must have been regarded as an important datum. It is curious that Luke should specify the severed appendage as the servant's *right* ear. And the note is made all the more curious by the fact that it

---

22. Like Mark, Luke likely identifies the victim with such specificity in order to establish him as a corroborating witness to Luke's account of the arrest. See Bauckham, *Eyewitnesses*, p. 195.

would be more natural for a right-handed swordsman to take off his opponent's left ear in a swordfight. This perhaps invites the suggestion that the disciple had furtively attempted to strike the high priest's servant from behind.

51. Jesus rebukes the disciples' violent instincts.[23] And if the first half of verse 51 shows what is *not* the kingdom way, the second half indicates what is: *And he touched his ear and healed him.* Among the Gospel writers, only Luke mentions Jesus' healing of the severed ear. Perhaps he does so in order that the first and last healings within his story would revolve around Peter: the inaugural healing performed to relieve Simon's mother-in-law of her fever (4:38–39); and the one wrought here, to 'clean up' after his lead disciple's rash behaviour. Nor is it of little relevance that Jesus' climactic healing was performed on behalf of not a friend's family member but rather a murderous enemy – all in keeping with Jesus' earlier teachings (cf. 6:27–36). In this showdown between official high priest's chief representative (Malchus) and the de facto high priest's chief representative (Peter), Jesus insists that his priestly order play by a different set of rules.

Luke would not have his reader brush too quickly past the fact that Jesus' healing touch has essentially recreated a human ear! There is both Christological and redemptive-historical import in this. According to the Scriptures, it is God who makes the ear (Prov. 20:12). More than that, if exile is the result of God's failing to give ears to hear (Deut. 29:4), the granting of a new ear to the servant of the high priest may be Luke's symbolic way of holding out hope that God would finally return Israel (epitomized in the servant of Israel's leading figure) from exile (cf. Rom. 11:26–27).

52. The composition of the crowd now becomes clearer, being populated by the *chief priests, the officers of the temple police, and the elders.* The convergence of representatives of all the key stakeholders (religious authorities, executive authorities and civil authorities) on the person of Jesus reinforces both the significance of this arrest (in the eyes of Jesus' enemies) and the climactic nature of the

---

23. Even better than NRSV's *No more of this!* is NASB's more emphatic *Stop! No more of this.* Nolland (p. 1088) translates the Greek as 'Allow even this!', meaning that the disciples are to allow the arresting party to have its way.

moment. They are armed *with swords and clubs*, as if prepared for a violent encounter. The posse's self-arming would only be necessary, Jesus observes, if he were a terrorist, robber or *bandit* (*lēstēs*), a *lēstēs* of the kind who – according to his own words in the temple action – gather together in the temple (19:46). Ironically, the crowd of temple-associated personnel approach Jesus as if he were a dangerous rebel, when in fact it is they themselves who play the violent usurpers and show that precisely in the act of arresting Jesus under the cloak of darkness.

53. Luke has already informed his readers that the Jewish leaders resisted the idea of arresting Jesus for fear of the people (22:2). Jesus exposes their cowardly stealth by observing that the same posse that was taking him into custody now had ample opportunity to undertake the same actions publicly while Jesus taught in the temple grounds. An even more fundamental explanation for the arresting authorities' earlier inaction, however, lies in the fact that only now has the Danielic hour of tribulation (Dan. 12:1) arrived. This is *your hour*, just as it is the hour that belongs to the authority of darkness, the principality of Satan.

ii. *Peter renounces Jesus (22:54–62)*

54. The co-regency of the high priests Annas and Caiaphas (3:2) makes it an open question as to whether the *high priest's house* refers to the dwelling of the former or of the latter. The issue does not seem to matter greatly to Luke, for in contrast to his chief source Mark, who frames Jesus' confrontation with Caiaphas as a climactic showdown, Luke downplays the high priest's role. A second layer of meaning seems to obtain in the Greek phrase *eisēgagon eis tēn oikian tou archiereōs* ('they brought him into the house of the high priest'). To his credit, Peter is *following*. But, ominously, he follows *at a distance*. In the light of verse 61, it appears that Peter can watch the proceedings with a comfortable space between himself and those now interrogating Jesus.

55. Exactly who *kindled a fire* is left unsaid.[24] We are left to assume it was the temple support staff. This matters simply

---

24. Fitzmyer (p. 1426) notes the awkwardness of the Greek sentence.

because Jesus was supposed to have kindled his own fire (3:16–17; 12:49), a fire of judgment, but now his opposers kindle their own 'fire of judgment'. Their fire is set *in the middle of the courtyard* (*aulēs*), enclosed on one side by the high priest's house. It is to be recalled that Jesus had earlier spoken a parable about a strong man guarding his own house (*aulēn*) who would be overcome by a stronger man (11:21–22). In some sense, of course, the high priest's administration seeks to do away with Jesus in an attempt to retain control over the possessions of the house. Yet in retrospect, it is the bringing of Jesus into the house/courtyard, en route to his atoning crucifixion and resurrection, that advances the plundering of this strong man's house. In this case, the strong man is not Satan but one of his pawns in the person of Caiaphas. Meanwhile, presumably glancing at Jesus and his interrogators every now and then out of the corner of his eye, Peter sits down with those who had taken a seat at the fire. This posture does not bode well, for, in the Gospel of Luke, those who sit are spiritually and morally vulnerable (e.g. 5:17; 7:32). More than that, like the wicked of Psalm 1:1, Peter sits down in the very middle (*mesos*) of those who oppose Jesus.

56–57. Back in the day, a *servant-girl* would have occupied one of the lowest rungs on the ladder of social power. And yet as she fixes her gaze on Peter in the light (*phōs*) of the fire, she challenges him, quickly causing him to cave in to the pressure of her accusations. Peter's denial is no small thing, for Jesus had previously promised that whatever had been whispered in the dark was destined to be heard in the light (*phōs*, 12:3), and that 'whoever denies me before others' with respect to this whispered message 'will be denied before the angels of God' (12:9). To make matters worse, in denying *any* knowledge of Jesus whatsoever, Peter was going well beyond the scope of the accusation. The fixed gaze of the interrogating young woman would eventually be matched by the disappointed gaze of Jesus (v. 61).

58. Whereas the servant-girl had claimed that Peter was '*with* him', now another person charges him with being '*of* them' (*ex autōn*). The first accusation bears on Peter's willingness to be associated with the person of Jesus, while the second has to do with his commitment to his movement. For Luke's audience hearing this story well after the historical incident, both kinds of commitments would be tested by the church's persecutors. Again Peter fails, this time issuing a curt response: *Man, I am not!* (*anthrōpe ouk eimi*).

59–62. A third interrogator now joins the discussion and *kept insisting* (*diischyrizeto*), repetitively and forcefully, that Peter was *with him* (returning to the servant-girl's point). The give-away evidence for this claim is Simon's identity as a *Galilean*, likely discernible by his accent (cf. Matt. 26:73).[25] Again, for a third time, Peter denies the point. In the light of the later-attested Roman practice of allowing detained Christians three opportunities to recant their faith (or face capital charges), Luke's story certainly would have resonated deeply with any in his audience who knew of other believers who had been forced by the Roman magistrates to choose between apostasy or death. And yet at the very moment of Peter's denial, the cock crows (showing that Jesus was being interrogated throughout the night, since the first cock crow falls between 3 am and 4 am). Still within the scope of Peter's vision, the *Lord turned and looked at Peter.* Now reminded of *the word of the Lord* (22:34), the lapsed disciple departs and breaks down in tears. If the 'word of the Lord' was the original catalyst for Peter's calling (5:5), the same word foresees his temporary apostasy.

Theology

If faith in Christ has both a confessional and a behavioural aspect, then the same must also be true for apostasy from Christ. In Jesus' arrest and Simon Peter's fireside interaction, we see the lead disciple experiencing two kinds of falling away: in the former scene, his disloyalty expresses itself through how he acts; in the latter scene, by what he says. Contemplating the two scenes together, the reader discovers not just the depths to which Peter has sunk but also the ways in which apostasy often takes hold.

---

25. By the fourth century, Julian the Apostate wrote a tractate critical of Christians entitled *Against the Galileans*. How early the term 'Galilean' was used as a moniker for Jesus-followers is hard to tell. It is not unreasonable to suppose that at the time of Luke's writing the term was used opprobriously.

On hearing Luke 22:47–53 for the first time, most members of the Evangelist's audience probably would have inwardly applauded Peter for his bravery in taking on Jesus' arresting party. After all, they would have reasoned right along with Peter, if Jesus were indeed Israel's hoped-for Messiah, then it would only make sense to defend him at all costs, even if that meant using the sword. But as it transpires, this way of thinking turns out to be entirely wrong. Jesus makes this clear with his rebuke: 'No more of this!' What seems brave in the kingdom of this world is actually cowardice in the kingdom of God.

The problem was that though Peter may have had the right goal in mind (establishing Jesus as king), he sought to achieve that goal in his own way, in his strength and by his own devices. The history of the church is littered with stories of believers, some well meaning and others ill motivated, attempting to achieve divine ends by sinful means. God requires not just an all-consuming commitment to the coming of the kingdom but also an equally uncompromising commitment to see that goal through by God's appointed means. Those who adopt Jesus' kingdom goal in theory but swap out his strategy for ushering in that kingdom are already at high risk of becoming apostate.

Believing that Jesus' messianic programme has come to an abrupt end, Peter is no longer willing to endure the social shame of identifying with his master – not even while interacting with the most powerless members of society. As a result, he denies ever having been associated with him and in fact disavows any knowledge of him altogether. Triggered by inward desires and outward pressures, Peter's apostasy, like the apostasy of countless erstwhile believers since, manifests itself in an unwillingness to embrace the person of Jesus, along with his extraordinary claims, *and* a refusal to associate with those who do.

As Luke shares this story, he is aware that many of his readers across the Roman Empire would face social and political pressures to recant their faith. Those who succumb to such pressures would in effect be capitulating to the forces of darkness (22:53). And just as Peter went outside to weep bitterly, so too will those who – whether through word or deed – have rejected Christ after him. Yet happily, those who, like Peter, repudiate Christ only to return can hope to be used for kingdom purposes once again (22:32).

D. Jesus detained (22:63 – 23:25)

Context

In Jesus' encounters with the Jerusalem power base (22:63–71) and the Roman authorities (23:1–25), the cruelty of his punishment comes into full view, as does the treachery which brought such punishment. Having been handed over by a member of his own band, the Son of Man is now betrayed by his people, not to mention the Roman justice system in general. Precisely as the quintessential victim of such injustices, Jesus prepares to atone for injustices of just this kind. Charged with being a false messiah and a false king, Jesus now demonstrates through his suffering what true Messiahship and true kingship is. Having been announced (1:32) and confirmed as the new Davidic ruler (3:22), Jesus demonstrates the surprising nature of that office.

Comment

i. Before the Sanhedrin (22:63–71)

63. In fulfilment of his third passion prediction, where Jesus foretold that the Son of Man would be mocked (*empaichthēsetai*; 18:32), the mocking (*enepaizon*) begins, the first of three rounds of ridicule (23:11, 36). The same men who taunt Jesus now also beat (*derontes*) him. Thus, as the last and greatest of the prophets, Jesus incurs the same fate as the two envoys in the parable of the wicked tenants (20:10–11). Clearly, Luke construes the passion not only as a recapitulation of all righteous suffering that has gone before but also as its climax in the Son of Man.

64. The retainers abusing Jesus must have been aware of his prophetic claims, most conspicuously in connection with his prediction of the temple's demise (21:5–28). For this reason, they now taunt him by blindfolding him and quizzing him on his supernatural insight: *Who is it that struck you?* [26] This dark game may also have to do with a contemporary interpretation of Isaiah 11:3 ('he

---

26. In 23:14, Jesus will be charged with leading others astray. This cannot be unconnected with his claim to the prophetic mantle. In instances where the Scriptures envision people being led astray,

shall not judge by what his eyes see'), which was understood as a messianic *testimonium*. If Jesus really was the Messiah, so the soldiers may have gathered, he would be able to answer their questions blindfolded, since − so it was thought − the Messiah would not require physical sight to make his judgments.

65. The main verb of the verse is the imperfect *elegon*: 'they kept speaking to him' or possibly 'they kept speaking about him'. As they spoke, they reviled (*blasphēmountes*) him with respect to many other things − what 'other things' the Evangelist leaves to our imagination. In this context, the verb *blasphēmeō* seemingly performs multiple duties. In their relation to Jesus as a man, the men 'blaspheme' their prisoner insofar as they subject him to shameful reproach. In relation to Jesus as the emerging high priest, they blaspheme him insofar as they directly challenge his authority (Exod. 22:28). In relation to Jesus as God, they blaspheme him insofar as they insult the divine name. Whether Luke intended only one or two of these meanings, all three blasphemies can legitimately be derived from the text.

66. Though Mark gives the impression that Jesus is interrogated entirely at night, Luke takes pains to report that the proceedings begin only *when day came*. This would not have been an incidental point for Luke's Jewish readers, for according to rabbinic tradition it was required that capital cases be tried during the day (m. Sanh. 4:1).[27] The authorities escort Jesus to the assembly (*presbyterion*), another term for the *council* or Sanhedrin.[28] The Sanhedrin was the supreme council, normally constituted by representatives who may have hailed from different political and geographical constituencies. Though the point is sometimes disputed when applied as a rule of thumb, in this instance (as in Acts 5:21) the council would have likely been convened at the high priest's pleasure.

---

false prophets are the principal bad actors (Exod. 5:4; Num. 15:39; Ezek. 13:18, 22).

27. This of course raises the question whether 'Jesus' trial' was in fact a trial in the formal sense. In my view, the historical evidence points to the legal proceedings being informal in nature.

28. Twelftree, *DJG*, p. 837.

67–68. Up to this point, Jesus' teachings and actions had only been gesturing to his messianic status: he had never in fact claimed to be the Messiah outright, at least not publicly so. Though the interrogations recorded by the other three Evangelists are more far-ranging and dilatory, in Luke's account the temple dignitaries cut right to the chase by asking Jesus, in the terms of Psalm 2, if indeed he is *the Messiah*.[29] The term is synonymous with 'Son of God'. Curiously, he refuses to answer the question, either positively or negatively. Instead he complains about his interlocutors' unbelief as well as their unwillingness to answer his own questions.

69. Despite this apparent evasiveness, Jesus does not leave his interrogators utterly disappointed, for now he makes a claim that at least comes close to answering the question. Whereas Mark (14:62) combines language from Daniel 7 ('Son of Man . . . coming with the clouds'), Psalm 110 ('seated at the right hand') and Zechariah 12:10 ('you will see'), Luke amends the Markan parallel so as to admit only the first two subtexts (while also dropping the Danielic clouds), two texts which were already exegetically coordinated in Jewish interpretation.[30] Drawing on these two passages, Jesus intimates that God will ultimately ensure the submission of the Gentiles, divine rule and eschatological judgment.

70. Jesus' assertion is far more tantalizing than clarifying. What role, if any, Jesus' interrogators wanted to know, did he claim in this eschatological scenario? A follow-up question was necessary: *Are you, then, the Son of God?* Jesus responds: *You say that I am (hymeis legete hoti egō eimi)*. What does Jesus mean by this assertion? On the one hand, it is an overstatement to call this an outright if halting 'admission'.[31] Nor is it the case, on the other hand, that Jesus is refusing to answer by simply 'throwing the

---

29. The phrasing of the question combines 'Messiah' (*christos*) (Ps. 2:2) with the predicate 'you are' from Ps. 2:7. From the first-century Jews' vantage point, this Messiah is one and the same as the promised Davidic ruler.

30. Evans, 'Jesus before Caiaphas'.

31. So Marshall, p. 851.

question back to the temple authorities'.[32] The truth is somewhere in between: it is an answer but it is far from a clear-cut answer. Just as the divine voice had twice affirmed his divine sonship (3:22; 9:35), now the third and final, climactic revelation of the truth comes from Jesus himself, although obliquely. Jesus claims that the Jewish leaders have been saying *that I am* (*hoti egō eimi*). Ironically, they have spent their lives verbally confessing Israel's God as the 'I AM' (*egō eimi*) of the exodus (Exod. 3:14), yet they fail to embrace the 'I AM' of both the first and the new exodus (Isa. 42:6, 8; 43:3, 5, 10, 11; etc.). The subsequent action is explained well by Bock: 'Whatever the exact force [of Jesus' answer], the absence of a denial means that the council has enough from Jesus. In their view he convicts himself.'[33]

71. After Jesus' climactic declaration, no more testimony was necessary. Jesus had indicted himself simply by refusing to reject divine or quasi-divine status. In doing so, in the judgment of the council, he also assigned himself the messianic role. Because it was assumed that the Messiah would arise within the ranks of institutional Judaism, Jesus was clearly a false prophet and a blasphemer of the true high priest. For all these reasons put together, he deserved to die.

ii. Before Pilate (23:1–25)

1. Barely a week prior, 'the whole crowd' (*hapan to plēthos*) of the disciples were praising Jesus as he entered Jerusalem presenting himself as Israel's Messiah: at this juncture 'the whole crowd' (*hapan to plēthos*) of the Sanhedrin rises up in order to bring their alleged Messiah to justice. Except in the case of unusual exceptions, the Romans reserved the right to try and administer cases involving capital charges.[34] For its part, the Sanhedrin knew that it could only go so far. And so they go to Pontius Pilate, Judea's fifth prefect, an office in place ever since the *ethnarche* Archelaus was deposed in AD

---

32. Skinner, *Trial Narratives*, p. 76.

33. Bock, p. 1802.

34. See Chapman and Schnabel, *Trial*, pp. 31–82; Sherwin-White, *Roman Law*, p. 36.

6 and Rome began to exert its control directly over the region (along with Idumea and Samaria). Pilate had a reputation for being a firm (if not inflexible) and ruthless ruler.[35]

2–3. Part of Pilate's daily role involved hearing cases, usually first thing in the morning. The first order of business in each case involved the plaintiffs setting forth a formal statement of the charges. The Jewish leadership makes a twofold claim: first, that Jesus was seditiously preventing Jews otherwise loyal to the emperor from paying their taxes; second, that he was claiming to be the Messiah, a king. Almost certainly struck by the fact that Jewish leaders were willing to turn over one of their own to Rome, Pilate could ill afford to treat this matter lightly. At the same time, he recognizes that the crowd is attempting to manipulate him by alluding to 'hot button' offences that no governor would wish to commit (playing accomplice to a seditious rabble-rouser, for example). Likely convinced of Jesus' innocence early on and reluctant to allow such manipulations to have their intended effect, Pilate will do everything he can to shuffle off responsibility for the case. But not before he asks at least one question: *Are you the king of the Jews?* In response, Jesus answers Pilate precisely the same way he answered the Sanhedrin: *You say . . .*

4–5. Though other Evangelists are more fulsome in their report of Pilate's interchange with Jesus, Luke presents a relatively pared-down account. Whatever his line of interrogation, Pilate returns to the crowd with an initial verdict which complains of lack of evidence. The crowd retorts that Jesus had been busily fomenting dissent *by teaching throughout all Judea, from Galilee where he began even to this place.*

6–7. On discovering that Jesus is a Galilean and therefore under the jurisdiction of Herod Antipas, Pilate sloughs Jesus off to the ruler who had been not only John the Baptizer's executioner but also a menace to Jesus himself. In this respect, whatever Jesus' prospects had been for a favourable outcome, these now become suddenly dim. Since it was Passover, it was not surprising that Herod was in Jerusalem to participate in the festivities.

---

35. See Bond, *DJG*, pp. 679–680.

8. Like the crowds in response to Jesus' miracles (13:17) and Zacchaeus in response to Jesus' impending visit (19:6), Herod rejoices over Jesus. Indeed, he is *very glad* (*echarē lian*). The reason for such joy is that now at least his curiosity might be satisfied. Because Jesus had largely kept among the people, Herod had had no opportunity to see Jesus for himself. He had only heard about him, on account of his words and deeds. Herod's interest in the famed miracle-worker lay in the latter's promise for giving a good circus side act. Like the rest of the 'evil generation' (11:29a), Herod wished to see a sign.

9. Assuming, on the basis of verse 8, that Herod asked Jesus for such a sign, his request goes unfulfilled. This is not surprising. After all, Jesus did promise that those asking for a sign would be disappointed to learn that no sign would be issued except the sign of Jonah (11:29). Filling out a pattern, Luke notes that Herod *questioned him at some length*. In retrospect, when Jesus came into Jerusalem he was met with two rounds of questions (20:21, 27) before his interrogators gave up (20:40). In this second set of questions, issuing from the Roman power and beginning with the mocking questions of the soldiers (22:64), Herod's line of questioning exhausts this stage of Jesus' makeshift trial. Herod will prove to be disappointed not just by Jesus' disinclination to perform a sign but also by his refusal to answer at all. The Gospel writer surely construes this as a fulfilment of Isaiah 53:7:

> He was oppressed, and he was afflicted,
>> yet he did not open his mouth . . .
>> . . . like a sheep that before its shearers is silent,
>> so he did not open his mouth.

10. No doubt the *chief priests and the scribes* standing nearby were especially vexed by Jesus' silence, as it would have seemed like an act of disrespect. Accordingly, they set about accusing him *vehemently* (*eutonōs*), that is, powerfully and vigorously.[36] The initial accusations made in 23:2 are now being delivered with ever increasing intensity.

---

36. BDAG, p. 327.

11. Before remanding Jesus to Pilate, Herod and his retainers use the time to deliver whatever bodily and emotional harm they can. Jesus' abuse was perpetrated not just by a few isolated scoundrels who happened to surround him: *even Herod*, together with *his soldiers*, gets involved. So eager is Herod to join in the ridicule and the manhandling, Luke's grammar suggests, that he is even willing to set aside the dignity of his office. Perhaps in a satirical attempt to imitate a royal enrobing, Herod and his henchmen put an *elegant robe* (*esthēta lampran*) on Jesus. However, the adjectives 'brilliant' or 'shining' might be preferred over the NRSV's *elegant* for *lampros*.[37] In this connection, it is worth noting that Jesus' clothes have earlier been made radiant at the transfiguration (9:29) in anticipation of his high priestly role, and now Herod, even as he puts the robe on his victim's shoulders, is unwittingly participating in Jesus' securing that role. By the time Luke's readers come to Acts 12, they will see that the gesture proves ironic, for just as Herod clothed Jesus with mock royal garb in order to prepare him for his death, Herod himself would don his own royal apparel (*esthēta basilikēn*) which would have no small role in his own death, dealt out by a divine act of judgment (Acts 12:20–23).

12. Whatever the details regarding the relationship between Herod and Pilate before their collaborative efforts to deal with Jesus, it may easily be imagined why Herod disliked Pilate and vice versa. After all, the scope of powers assigned to Pilate must have seemed a heavy indignity, when Herod's father, Herod I, had ruled the whole of Judea single-handedly. Pilate in turn would have been forced to negotiate with the Herodian dynasty at countless turns in his administration. Luke includes this aside to show Jesus' power not just to forge strong relationships in his own camp but also to galvanize opposition from without. Just as the church would make strange bedfellows of those who opposed its mission, the same principle applies to Jesus.

13–17. Now the prefect gives a speech.[38] Summoning Jesus' accusers, Pilate rehearses the initial charges brought against him,

---

37. BDAG, p. 465.

38. The best manuscripts do not include v. 17. It should therefore be excluded from comment.

or at least one of them: *perverting the people* (*apostrephonta ton laon*). Now with the backing of the half-Jew Herod, Pilate is able to declare that, following their own independent cross-examination, Jesus is not guilty. But in order to meet the crowd halfway, as it were, he consents to have him flogged and then ultimately released. This was no small punishment, for Roman flogging was a vicious practice on any showing. The *flagellum* (i.e. the whip) was normally made of leather cords attached at one end to metal balls, porcelain or animal bone. A few strikes were enough to cause excruciating pain and no little loss of blood.

18–19. Yet this was not good enough: as far as the crowd was concerned, nothing short of crucifixion would do. And so the people shout out in unison. Unable even to utter Jesus' name in their collective contempt, they call on Pilate to eliminate his detainee: *Away with this fellow* (*aipe touton*). In exchange for Jesus, they would have one Barabbas released. Whereas Matthew and Mark both note that it was customary to release a prisoner during Passover (Matt. 27:15; Mark 15:6), Luke omits any remarks on this tradition.[39] Clearly it is this tradition to which the crowds are appealing. Following Mark (Mark 15:7), the Evangelist notes that Barabbas was being held for insurrection and murder; Matthew tells us that his first name was Jesus and that he was well known (27:16). There is almost certainly an intended irony in the fact that Jesus Barabbas (Aramaic for 'son of the father') was about to be released for murder and insurrection, while Jesus the true 'Son of the Father' was about to be murdered for the crime of insurrection. If one searched for any evidence that Luke held to a theory of substitutionary atonement, one need not look any further than 23:18.

20–21. Exactly why Pilate was reluctant to oblige the crowds and be done with it is not entirely clear. At some level, the governor is convinced of Jesus' innocence. Still other traditions fill in the picture, ascribing his hesitancy to his convictions that the charges were purely politically motived (Matt. 27:18), warnings from his wife (Matt. 27:19) and intimations of the possibility that Jesus was

---

39. On the *privilegium paschale*, see Schnabel, *Jesus in Jerusalem*, pp. 288–291.

LUKE

in fact a divine messenger (John 19:8). From a political standpoint, Pilate has little choice but to make some attempt to pacify the crowds. He had hoped that the flogging would have satisfied them but reality proved otherwise. Eventually, he calls (*prosephōnēsen*) to the crowds, only to be shouted down by those who repeatedly (iterative imperfect) *kept shouting* (*epephōnoun*). With the repetition of the imperative *crucify* (*staurou*), the crowds now break into an iterative chant.

22–25. This marks the third time that Pilate declares Jesus' innocence (cf. 23:4, 14). Luke construes this not just as compelling evidence of Jesus' actual innocence (since Pilate approaches the case as a largely disinterested party), but also as an anticipation of the threefold verdict of innocence with respect to Paul's case (Acts 23:9; 25:25; 26:31). Both Jesus and Paul are declared innocent; yet their guilt remains in the eyes of their detractors. As for the crowds in Luke 23, they now call out, again exactly as the demons (4:33; 8:28), with *loud shouts* (*phōnais megalais*). Overcome by the opposition of the crowds, Pilate grants the terms of their request. Meanwhile, in further compliance with their demands, he releases Barabbas.

Theology
There is an unmistakeable irony in the way Jesus becomes king. Having fiercely opposed his messianic claims, his enemies now conduct a mock coronation. Jesus is charged with pretending to be king, and his guards therefore pretend to make him king by forcing him to wear a robe. All the while, through the mockery and the beatings, Jesus is in fact becoming the king of the Jews. Not only the king of the Jews but the Lord of the universe.

This helps to put into perspective every expression of anti-Christian sentiment or behaviour. To be sure, anti-Christian persecution – whatever its form or severity – is an injustice that the world could do without. That said, it should also be pointed out that God has a way of taking the fiercest and cruellest persecution, and converting it into something redemptive. If Jesus becomes king through the opposition of sinful people, this means that Jesus' co-heirs will likewise be glorified through the persecutions they endure.

E. Jesus crucified (23:26–56)

Context

Once the legal proceedings had run their course, it now fell to the Romans to crucify Jesus. This turn of events comes as no surprise. Jesus had predicted his execution three times (9:18–22, 44; 18:31–33), even as he predicted that the actions around his death would include abuse of various kinds. As Luke now recounts both this abuse and the crucifixion itself, he once again confirms Jesus' predictive powers and thus his prophetic status. Yet in this section, Jesus is presented as far more than a prophet, for here he is repeatedly declared to be, even if ironically, the king of the Jews, that is, the Messiah. This declaration, formalized in the inscription on the cross, sets the stage for the resurrection (Luke 24): precisely because Jesus was crucified for claiming to be the Messiah, his forthcoming resurrection by the power of God will in the end vindicate that claim. This section focuses not just on Jesus' abusers but also on various individuals from different social backgrounds and geographies who attempt to support or honour Jesus. This of course is a microcosm of what would soon play out on the world's stage. From the very first, Jesus' death unleashes a polarizing controversy over whether the crucified Messiah is to be mercilessly mocked or honoured with all one's being.

Comment

i. Crucifixion (23:26–43)

26. With Roman executions, it was not uncommon for passers-by to be pressed into service, especially if the soon-to-be-executed victims were too weak to carry the *patibulum* (the cross's horizontal beam) by themselves.[40] Weakened by the beatings (22:63), Jesus himself falls into this category of victim, forcing the Romans to enlist a certain (*tina*) Simon of Cyrene. Cyrene, a metropolis on the coast of North Africa, near the modern city of Shahhat in Libya, was no small distance from Jerusalem. Simon's presence is likely to be explained by his having made a pilgrimage to Jerusalem for the

---

40. For historical examples, see Chapman and Schnabel, *Trial*, pp. 282–292.

Passover. That Cyrenians should later be converted at Pentecost (Acts 2:10) and then also join the Cyprians in preaching to the Greeks (Acts 11:20) shows a steadily blossoming work of God. That his son is the same Rufus (cf. Mark 15:21) mentioned in Paul's greetings to the Romans (Rom. 16:13) is an intriguing if not finally provable theory. Yet it is also a probable theory, given that he likely belonged to the early Christian community and that his name would have been instantly recognized by Mark's and Luke's readers alike (why else would he be named?).[41] Simon is said to be coming in *from the country* (*ap'agrou*) or the field, a detail which – perhaps coincidentally, perhaps not – puts him in company with the ideal disciple 'in the field' who does not look wistfully back to his or her past (Luke 17:7, 31). He is forced to carry the cross behind Jesus, a task necessitated by the victim's weakened state. Yet it is also a task which metaphorically lines up with the duties of the disciple (9:23).

27. Whereas Luke began his Gospel recounting how 'the whole assembly of the people' (*pan to plēthos . . . tou laou*) was praying in the temple court (1:10) shortly before Jesus' birth, now *a great number of the people* (*polu plēthos tou laou*) follow him to his death.[42] Whether they were more motivated to gawk cruelly at Jesus or support him in his final hours is unclear. It is clear, however, that the women in this number are already mourning their champion's death, following along much as they did during his itinerancy (8:2–4).

28. According to Deuteronomy 29:11, God's covenant with Israel was not just with the nation's men, but also with its women and children. Therefore, as Jerusalem now decisively cuts itself off from the covenant by putting Jesus to death, its women and children will not be spared from the coming doom. Accordingly, he calls out to his mourners as *daughters of Jerusalem*. If nothing else, the phrase underscores the profound change that had occurred in the space of just a few days. By riding into Jerusalem on a donkey, Jesus had invited – in fulfilment of Zechariah 9:9 – the 'daughter [of]

---

41. On Simon's possible connection with Rufus, see Bauckham, *Eyewitnesses*, p. 52.

42. For the ancient phenomenon of crowds accompanying the condemned to their deaths, see Nolland, pp. 1136–1137.

Jerusalem' to rejoice. Now that invitation had been refused by the city's leaders, the same epithet is repurposed to signal that a judgment like the one described in Jeremiah 4:31 is just over the horizon:

> For I heard a cry as of a woman in labour,
>   anguish as of one bringing forth her first child,
> the cry of daughter Zion gasping for breath.

Jeremiah's 'daughter Zion' gasps, the same verse goes on to tell us, because she is fainting before her killers. The killers in this context would of course be the Roman legions. On the same pattern, when Jeremiah predicts – failing Judah's repentance – the desolation of the temple (Jer. 22:1–5), he goes on to give a similar twofold set of instructions:

> Do not weep for him who is dead,
>   nor bemoan him;
> weep rather for him who goes away,
>   for he shall return no more
>   to see his native land.
> (Jer. 22:10)

Now Jesus gives the same two-tier instructions: those who die now (like Jesus himself) will endure a fate preferable to that of those who shall be expelled from the land. Against the background of these prophetic texts, Jesus' admonition not only points ahead to the grim outcome awaiting the mourning women and their families; it also serves to interpret the Jerusalem leadership's actions as the trigger for deepening exile.

29. At a previous point in the narrative, a blessing was declared on the womb that bore Jesus and the breasts that nourished him (11:27). Now Jesus revises that blessing by stating that Israel's mothers would be better off if they had not had children at all. The *days are surely coming when* that is exactly what they will say.[43] Within

---

43. The phrase *the days are surely coming* is most reminiscent of Jer. 31:31 and the promise of the new covenant (cf. Jer. 7:32; 16:14; 38:31, LXX). If an

Luke's story, we recall, too, that Elizabeth (1:7), the bleeding woman and the dead young girl (8:40–56) are all singled out as women with unfruitful wombs. Though such women have been – in the normal course of things – regarded as cursed, in the future many will look back to declare such women blessed.

30. From Jesus' day down to the present day, Jerusalem has stood encircled by hills and mountains. Now because these same elevations had protected Jerusalem against marauding enemies for centuries, Jesus' vision of Jerusalem's citizens pleading that these peaks collapse inwards towards the city has a sense of utter doom and finality about it. The coming national catastrophe, Jesus predicts, will be the fulfilment of Hosea 10:8: *they will begin to say to the mountains, 'Fall on us'; and to the hills, 'Cover us.'* The prophetic line is part of a larger passage focused on Israel's disobedience and exile, when the altar will be overrun with weeds. Not incidentally, in the Scriptures, mountains and hills are those things which normally cannot be moved (Ps. 46:2; Isa. 54:10, Nah. 1:5), except by cataclysmic events and/or a visitation of God himself.

31. Jesus' last statement to the mourning women may be drawing on a traditional proverb now lost to history. Unfortunately, the proverb's meaning here is not any more recoverable than the context of its origins. Two interpretative issues present themselves. First, who is the subject (the *they*) in the sentence *if they do this . . . ?* Is it the Romans, the Jews, or someone else? Second, whereas the NRSV translates *en tō hygrō xylō* as *when the wood is green*, the Greek may also be translated along the lines of the JB: 'For if men use the green wood like this, what will happen when it is dry?' The former approach understands Jesus to be contrasting two different eras or time periods; the latter distinguishes between two different cases (the case of the green wood versus the case of the dry wood).

In making sense of the statement and allowing Luke's text to be its own best interpreter, we can do worse than refer back to the closing line of John the Baptizer's exhortation: 'Even now the axe

(note 43 *cont.*) allusion is meant here, it means that the issuance of the new covenant is not without judgment on those who fail to participate in it.

is lying at the root of the trees; every tree therefore that does not bear good fruit is cut down and thrown into the fire' (3:9). Green trees at least hold out the hope of fruitfulness, but dry wood is useful only for burning. John's preaching implied that there was still time for Israel to produce fruit and thus gives merit to the possibility that Jesus here is comparing Israel to a green tree. Yet according to Jesus a time is also coming when the green tree will become dry. This must correspond to the same time, referenced by John, when the axe of judgment will be applied and the tree is burned. On this analogy, those who apply the axe – those who 'do these things' – would be the Romans. If their cruelty is on full show in the crucifixion of Jesus, how much more will their viciousness be unleashed when God turns the nation over to judgment.

32. Now Luke returns to reproducing the narrative as told by other Gospels (par. Matt. 27:38//Mark 15:27). I find it remarkable that the NRSV's rendering of verse 32 (*Two others also, who were criminals, were led away to be put to death with him*) is along the lines of every other English translation I have consulted. It is a remarkable thing because it is almost as if the translations conspire to avoid interpreting Luke's Greek – no less accurately – as follows: 'two other criminals [*kakourgoi*] were led away to be executed along with him'.[44] Presumably, the collective avoidance is at least partially motivated by a concern not to scandalize the reader by implying that Jesus is one of three criminals. But in my view, this is exactly Luke's point: in reputation he was among the criminals; he 'was numbered with the transgressors' (Isa. 53:12). At last, Jesus is led for the third and final time (22:54; 23:1), driving home, too, that he, the Suffering Servant, is 'like a lamb that is *led* to the slaughter' (Isa. 53:7, emphasis added).

33. The crowd now comes to *the place that is called The Skull*, a place name which John spells out in its Aramaic equivalency: Golgotha (John 19:17). Our best hypothesis is that the spot of Jesus' crucifixion

---

44. Matthew (Matt. 27:38) and Mark (15:27) specify them as *lēstai*, meaning highway robbers (as in Luke 10) or terrorists. Luke leaves the nature of their wrongdoing less clear.

coincides with the location of the Church of the Holy Sepulchre.[45] Without going into all the details, Luke matter-of-factly reports: *they crucified Jesus*. A longstanding practice among the ancient civilizations but 'perfected' by the Romans, crucifixion was a grim business.[46] Though all crucifixions involved the victim's being transfixed to a cross, there was considerable variation. Though Christian art traditionally shows Jesus crucified on a t-shaped cross, it more likely was shaped like an upper-case 'T', with the horizontal cross-beam sitting on top of the vertical beam. The victim, suspended a few feet off the ground, was nailed through the feet and arms, with the buttocks sometimes made to rest on a wooden stub in order to partially support the body, which in turn would enhance airflow to the lungs and thereby prolong the victim's agony. Jesus is crucified alongside the two criminals: *one on his right and one on his left.*

34. No sooner is Jesus crucified than he prays for forgiveness for his malefactors (6:27–36), just as he had instructed his disciples to pray (11:4). These words anticipate very similar words coming from Stephen during his martyrdom ('Lord, do not hold this sin against them', Acts 7:60).[47] To the bitter end of his life, Jesus executes the office of the praying priest. To the bitter end of the story, he sets the standard for how Luke's readers ought to respond to persecution and even martyrdom. All the while, the soldiers are not the least bit fazed. In fulfilment of Psalm 22:18, *they cast lots to divide his clothing.*

35. Roman crucifixions were spectator events and so it is no surprise that the people assemble themselves simply to watch it all slowly play out. Meanwhile, the leaders continue to revile Jesus (fulfilling Ps. 69:7, 9, 12, 19–20), pointing out that though he was able to save others, he is not willing or able to *save himself.* This is the first of three jibes (cf. vv. 37, 39) ridiculing the seemingly patent fact that Jesus is not finally able to save either others or himself. But

---

45. Parrot, *Golgotha*, pp. 59–65; Schnabel, *Jesus in Jerusalem*, pp. 132–135.

46. See Josephus, *J.W.* 7.203.

47. Luke 23:34a is textually suspect. In my judgment, the coherence with the Lord's Prayer and the theologically rich parallel with Acts 7:60 together make for fairly compelling evidence for counting this text as authentically Lukan. See Marshall, pp. 867–888.

the informed reader of Luke–Acts who is aware of Jesus' saving acts past (Luke 2:11; 7:50; 8:48; 17:19; 18:42) and future (Acts 2:36; 13:23) knows that this is not the case, despite appearances to the contrary. D. A. Carson succinctly summarizes the moment:

> The deeper irony is that, in a way they did not understand, they were speaking the truth. If he had saved himself, he could not have saved others; the only way he could save others was precisely by not saving himself.[48]

36. When Luke records that the *soldiers . . . mocked [enepaixan] him*, this counts as the third and final 'mocking', a triple fulfilment of that which Jesus had predicted (cf. 22:63; 23:11) when he said that the Son of Man would be 'mocked [*empaixthēsetai*] and insulted' (18:32). Yet the soldiers also approach Jesus bearing *sour wine*, that is, a wine vinegar that was common drink among the troops (cf. Ps. 69:21). Since the verb used to describe the soldiers' approach (*proserchomenoi*) is often used in cultic contexts, the reader may be forgiven for seeing this moment as an ironic dramatization of a typical daily temple sacrifice, involving the offering of a lamb along with wine (Num. 28:1–8).[49]

37–39. Mimicking the leaders, the soldiers now call out in a language reminiscent of the devil's (4:3): *If you are the King of the Jews, save yourself!* Parenthetically, Luke inserts a comment confirming the presence of an appended *inscription* or titulus (*epigraphē*), a sign not uncommonly posted on the cross, explaining the reasons for a criminal's punishment (Suetonius, *Cal.* 32.2). Pilate's motivation for designating Jesus King of the Jews, despite his doubts over his guilt, leaves room for speculation. Though Pilate may have possibly done this in an effort to cover himself legally, or to join in with the mockery directed against Jesus, or to disincentivize other would-be messianic pretenders, the solution that makes the best psychological

---

48. Carson, *Scandalous*, p. 29.

49. Luke does not specify whether or not Jesus actually received the wine; Matthew (27:34) and Mark (15:23) report that Jesus declined the wine on tasting it.

sense of the situation is this: Pilate, well aware that he had been
pushed into a corner by the temple leaders, sought to satirize the
Jewish nation.⁵⁰ As time passes, the refrain of *Save yourself!* now falls
from the lips of one of the criminals, though in a modified form.
Whether it was the one on the right or the left is unstated. According
to the Gospel writer, this criminal *kept deriding* (*eblasphēmei*) Jesus,
though we might also take this to mean 'kept blaspheming'.

40–41. Now Luke includes a story omitted by the other Evangelists, traditionally known as the story of the 'Penitent Thief' or the
'Thief on the Cross'. The one thief is now rebuked by the other,
appealing to the fear of God, *since you are under the same sentence of
condemnation.* According to the second malefactor, both he and his
partner in crime are being punished justly. By contrast, Jesus *has
done nothing wrong* (*atopon*).⁵¹ As far as Jesus is concerned, the double
assertion amounts to a personal confession of sin as well as a
Christological confession.⁵²

42. Turning to Jesus, the criminal now gives wings to his faith by
issuing an astonishing request: *remember me when you come into your
kingdom.*⁵³ The request is 'astonishing' because it remarkably takes
three points for granted. First, it assumes that Jesus is in fact a king
(just as the titulus had mockingly suggested). Second, the sentence
also depends on the assumption that this same kingdom transcends
the confinements of normal space and time (a point lost even on the
apostles at this juncture). Third and finally, the criminal's words
imply that Jesus has the wherewithal to enter into that kingdom,
notwithstanding their shared straitened circumstances.

43. In response, as if to underscore the certainty of what he is
about to say, Jesus issues an asseveration of *truly, amēn.* An inter-

---

50. Johnson (p. 378) names the first three reasons without adjudicating
between them.
51. The adjective *atopos* has the meaning of 'out of place' or 'inappropriate';
see BDAG, p. 120. Festus suspends judgment on Paul being *atopos*,
against the charges of the Jewish leaders (Acts 25:5).
52. So too Edwards, p. 696.
53. Some manuscripts have: 'Remember me when you come *in* your
kingdom.'

pretative difficulty lies in determining whether the word *today* (*sēmeron*) modifies Jesus' speaking ('Truly today I tell you ... ') or the rendezvous in paradise ('Truly I tell you, today you will be with me ... '). Because of the natural word order of the Greek and Luke's thematic insistence that salvation is a matter of *today* (2:11; 4:21; 19:9), we conclude that Jesus expects to enter into some kind of intermediate state along with the now-forgiven malefactor – and to do so *today*. Jesus' name for that state is *paradeisos*, derived from a Persian term meaning an enclosed garden. Generations before Jesus, the notion of paradise had already had broad currency in Jewish eschatological thought (1 En. 60:8; 61:12; Pss Sol. 14:2). In promising the 'thief' this paradise, Luke's Jesus is essentially promising to reopen a form of Eden while he assumes an Adamic role (3:38).

ii. Jesus breathes his last (23:44-49)

44. Throughout Luke's Gospel, Jesus has been anticipating the instigation of the new exodus under his authority. The recent Passover meal (22:7-38) confirmed as much. Now a further sign presents itself with the unfolding of the darkness *over the whole land* (*eph' holēn tēn gēn*). In the story of the exodus, darkness came 'over the land' (LXX: *epi gēn*) of Egypt (Exod. 10:21) as part of the penultimate plague, the plague of darkness, immediately preceding the final plague on the firstborn males. As Jesus hung dying, three hours of darkness, lasting from about noon to 3 pm, shrouded the scene, or perhaps the land of Israel, or perhaps again the whole earth (*gēs* could refer to any one of these things). In the Scriptures in general and in Luke in particular (not least in 22:53), darkness is associated with judgment. Here the Gospel writer seemingly interprets the phenomenon as a typological fulfilment of the palpable darkness once felt by the Egyptians prior to the exodus.

45. The eclipsing (*ekliponotos*) of the sunlight by the darkness leads to an even more uncanny event: the rending of the *curtain of the temple* – right down the middle (*meson*).[54] The Greek term

---

54. The textual tradition attests to various verbs in describing the sun. Some important manuscripts have that the sun 'failed' (*ekleipō*); others say that the sun 'darkened' (*eskotisthē*).

katapetasma (curtain) could refer to one of two or even several veils
in the temple grounds, including the curtain spanning the entrance
into the Holy Place from the outside (Exod. 26:36–37). However, if
only on the basis of comparison with Hebrews 10:19–22, one
suspects that Luke has in view here the veil separating the Holy
Place from the Most Holy Place (Exod. 26:31–33), which might
actually have been two veils (m. Mid. 4:7).[55] If God's throne room
was in the Most Holy Place, then the threshold to that most sacred
space was the curtain. And now, through the death of Jesus, it was
rent in two. But what would this event have symbolized for Luke
and his first readers? In part, the tearing of the temple veil pointed
ahead to the coming destruction of the temple. At the same time,
the destruction of the curtain signified that Jesus-followers now
had new and unprecedented access into the presence of God (cf.
Heb. 10:19). Finally, the rending of the veil means that God's
presence was also bursting out to reach beyond the confines of the
temple space. This last implication is certainly confirmed by the
Risen Jesus' instruction to take the gospel to the region and even
to the ends of the earth (cf. Acts 1:8).

46. Moments before dying, Jesus cries out *with a loud voice (phōnē
megalē)*, mirroring at the very beginning of our story Elizabeth's
blessing Mary 'in a loud voice' on discerning Jesus' conception. Yet
in retrospect, Jesus' parting shout is not just the closing bookend
to the story of his life but also a climactic and summative cry. In
relation to the exorcised (or soon-to-be exorcised) demons who
emerge from their human strongholds with a loud voice (4:33; 8:28),
Jesus' cry seemingly absorbs the demonic only to purge it (cf. Zech.
13:2). With respect to those who praise God with a loud voice (17:15;
19:37), Jesus offers the ultimate shout of human praise. In a
definitive response to those who had sought his crucifixion with a
loud voice (23:23), Jesus' loud voice has the last word.

Now calling on his heavenly *Father* for the last time, matching
this time the declaration of the Father at his baptism (3:22), Jesus
prays in the language of Psalm 31:5: *into your hands I commend my spirit.*
In the context of Psalm 31, the prayer is that of one who has been

---

55. Liefeld, p. 1045.

assured of redemption, much as the martyr Stephen would use the same prayer moments before his death (Acts 7:59). With that assurance of God's deliverance, Jesus breathes his last.

47. Earlier in the narrative, the readers met a Roman centurion of extraordinary faith (7:1–10). Now, as if to provide a symmetrical frame which ensconces the story of Jesus within a larger context of imperial power already giving way to the power of the gospel, Luke narrates an episode involving another righteous centurion. (Both of these anticipate the centurion Cornelius in Acts 10.) Observing *what had taken place*, the Roman commander concludes with no uncertainty that Jesus was indeed *innocent* (*diakaios*) or, equally fair, 'righteous' (NIV). On one level, the Evangelist has been keen throughout the trial narrative to establish Jesus' innocence, and the Gentile centurion provides a further witness to that innocence. At the same time, Luke almost certainly repurposes the centurion's declaration as a messianic confession, just as we seem to have in the Synoptic parallels with the messianic epithet 'Son of God', since the 'the righteous one' (*ho dikaios*) was a circumlocution for Messiah (e.g. 1 En. 92; Rom. 1:17). Exactly what is included within the scope of *what had taken place* is partially illuminated by the term *genomenon*, since the singular participle suggests an event or complex of events rather than a series of discrete events. Whereas Matthew (27:54) and Mark (15:39) connect their centurion's confession to the rending of the temple veil, Luke's arrangement suggests that the pervading darkness, the torn curtain and Jesus' expiring prayer conspired to lead him to faith. Finally, in glorifying (*edoxazen*) God, the centurion demonstrates the fulfilment of the eschatological hope: the day when the nations would come to glorify God's name (Ps. 86:9).

48. The convergence of the crowds interested in viewing Jesus' execution has already been noted (23:35). Yet now they observe *what had taken place* (plural neuter: *ta genomena*), meaning not just the events leading up to the centurion's confession, but also – in addition to those things – the confession itself. On taking in this astounding turn of events, they return (NRSV supplies *home* as their destination, while the NIV and KJV do not). As they go, they follow the lead of the praying tax collector (18:13) by beating their breasts as a sign of mourning and self-humiliation. Clearly, such events are meant to invoke Zechariah's vision in which the inhabitants of Jerusalem will 'look on the one whom they have pierced' and 'mourn for him' (Zech. 12:10). Not insignificantly, Zechariah 12:10's mention of a 'pierced one' in turn alludes to the death of King Josiah (2 Chr. 35:20–25; cf. 2 Kgs 23:29–30) occurring at the battle of Megiddo. Well before Jesus' day, that death was interpreted as an atoning death.[56]

49. The inclusion of the Greek particle *de* (*but*) implies a contrast between Jesus' *acquaintances* (*pantes hoi gnōstoi autō*) and the breast-beating crowds who were now leaving the scene. These individuals, who included the women who had followed him from Galilee (8:1–3), had all the while stood (pluperfect: *heistēkesan*) nearby. They too were watching these things, but if the centurion has one angle, and the crowds have a wider angle, the lens of those known to Jesus (*hoi gnōstoi autō*) is wider still. Their presence sets the stage for what is about to follow.

iii. Burial (23:50–56)

50–51. If, in the opening chapters of Luke, a certain Joseph is tasked with a set of responsibilities surrounding Jesus' entrance into the world, in the Gospel's closing chapters another Joseph has another set of responsibilities. That the Evangelist should connect this Joseph with Arimathea was in part to distinguish him from other known individuals of the same name. Yet there may be an added significance. For if, as the evidence suggests, Arimathea is one and the same as Elkanah and Hannah's home town of Ramathaim-Zophim (1 Samuel), this brings us back full circle to the beginning of the story, where a virgin yet pregnant teenager draws on the language of Hannah to praise God for what he would do (Luke 1:46–55). According to Matthew (Matt. 27:57), Joseph of Arimathea was wealthy and a disciple of Jesus. It was in his tomb that Jesus was to be buried (Matt. 27:60). Like Simeon (Luke 2:25), Luke's Joseph was *righteous* and was *waiting expectantly for the kingdom of God*. As a member of the Sanhedrin that had just condemned Jesus to death, he had also resisted the body's decision.

52. Joseph's approaching Pilate for the body of Jesus was a social and political risk. After all, Jesus had been publicly crucified as a

---

56. Laato, *Josiah*, pp. 290–294.

criminal and to request such a favour raised the possibility of being
shamed or surveilled. Ordinarily, in the aftermath of a crucifixion,
the victim's body would be left on the cross, only to be slowly
picked at by vultures and dogs. This was almost a rule in cases of
treason (Tacitus, *Ann.* 6.29), the very charge lodged against Jesus.[57]
For the Ancient Jews, however, unburied bodies were an
abomination; they preferred to bury executed offenders in a
common grave allocated to the criminal dead (m. Sanh. 6:5; t. Sanh.
9:8; Josephus, *Ant.* 5.44).

53–55. Joseph seems to have received permission without
incident, for now he is taking down Jesus' body and wrapping it in
linen, typical of Jewish burial practice. He would have been forced
to move quickly. It was already well after 3 pm and there were pro-
scriptions against carrying the dead on the Sabbath (m. Šabb. 23:5),
which began at sunset. After wrapping the body, Joseph lays it in *a
rock-hewn tomb*. In Jewish antiquity, tombs were reused as they were
handed down family lines. That makes it all the more unusual that
Jesus should be put in a *tomb where no one had ever been laid*. As unusual
as this is, it is also symbolic: the honour of being buried in a completely new tomb fell only to royalty. One last time the Galilean
women follow, if only to observe where and *how his body was laid*.

56. As a precursor to burial, the application of scented powders
such as myrrh and aloe was standard in Jewish burial rites. This was
in an effort not so much to embalm the corpse as to delay
putrefaction. In order to stay one step ahead of the Sabbath, the
women also return home to prepare the mixture with a view to
returning on Sunday morning. After all, Friday night was upon
them, and that meant the onset of Sabbath, which they had every
intention of obeying.

Theology
Salvation has proven to be a major theme in the Gospel. Now, as
Jesus hangs dying on a Roman cross, it has also become a major
preoccupation of his mockers. 'Save yourself – and us!' they call out
– three times, in fact. If Jesus really is the saviour, then why is he

57. See Brown, *Death*, p. 1208.

not saving now? Of course, Luke's point is that Jesus *is* in fact saving. Just as he saves the crucified man next to him by offering him a place in paradise, so too he promises to save all those who, like the criminal, ask to be remembered when the kingdom comes. Salvation comes through Jesus; salvation comes through the cross.

In Luke's story there are some who accept this proposition and others who resist it. Those who resist do so largely because they have fixed notions as to what salvation should look like. For Pilate and the religious authorities, salvation meant the consolidation of political authority. For the cursing malefactor on the cross, salvation meant deliverance without repentance. All of these wanted salvation *on their terms* – not on the terms offered by Jesus. Yet right alongside these figures stand out certain unlikely individuals who respond positively. The criminal on the cross looked to Jesus as the king who would one day usher in his kingdom. Joseph of Arimathea staked his claim in the kingdom by bearing the shame that went with requesting a crucified criminal's body. In the story as well as down through history, Jesus' crucifixion has proven to be a winnowing fork, effectively separating out those who insist on salvation on their own terms from those who accept God's salvation just as it is offered through a crucified king.

8. RESURRECTION NARRATIVE (24:1–53)

A. Resurrection (24:1–35)

Context

Through a heartbreaking turn of events, the long-brewing opposition to Jesus had culminated in his arrest and death (22:1 – 23:56). And with his burial, the Jesus story *seems* to come to an abrupt end – and with it the hopes of a restored Israel. Had the Gospel writer intended his story only as a tragic tale of disappointment and injustice, Luke 23 would have been the perfect place to end.

But as it turns out there is a 'postscript'. And that postscript begins to unfold in two scenes constituting 24:1–35. In the first scene, a critical mass of Luke's lead protagonists gathers around an empty tomb as witnesses. Some, like the two angelic figures (24:4), are witnesses *to* the resurrection; others, namely, the Eleven (24:9) and the women (24:3), are witnesses *of* the resurrection. The second scene centres around a journey leading up to a meal, the last full-blown repast in a series of Lukan meals (5:27–39; 14:1–24; 22:14–38; 24:13–35) and a point of departure for meals in Acts

(Acts 1:4; 10:1 – 11:18; 27:33–38). Revelations of resurrection occur in both scenes – revelations that meet with mixed levels of understanding. Through it all we discover that the Evangelist's story proves not to be a tragedy but a tale of triumph.

Comment

i. Women at the tomb (24:1–12)

1. The action of this passage flows effortlessly from the previous scene. On Friday evening, the women had returned from the tomb to prepare spices for Jesus' burial (23:54–56); on Saturday, they rested in accordance with Sabbath regulations. Now *on the first day of the week . . . they came to the tomb*; eager to attend to Jesus' corpse, they come *at early dawn*. The day and time of the women's arrival invites comparison to the very first dawn of the very first day of the very first week (Gen. 1:3).[1] This would not be inconsistent with Luke's vision of resurrection as a kind of new creation.

2–3. In first-century Jewish burial practices, the deceased were typically buried in two stages.[2] For those who could afford it, deceased bodies were first laid out horizontally in a walk-in loculi tomb. Then, after the body had decomposed over the course of a year, the family would gather the remaining bones for a second burial involving a separate vault and an ossuary or bone box. The tomb described here is likely a loculi tomb, the entrance of which would have been sealed with a large rectangular stone. Since considerable effort would have to go into moving such stones, the women are naturally surprised by the sight of the *stone rolled away*. Even more surprising would have been their failure, on entering the tomb, to 'find the body of the Lord Jesus' (NIV).[3] Nor is the name used insignificant: 'In naming it the body of the *Lord Jesus* Luke is already using the language of Christian faith (cf. I Cor.

---

1. See commentary on Luke 8:22; 20:1.
2. On these details, see Hachlili, 'Burials', *ABD* 1, pp. 789–791. See also Chapman, *DJG*, pp. 97–100 (97–98).
3. The NRSV omits the phrase 'of the Lord Jesus' for text-critical reasons. In my judgment, the full expression is original.

11.23, II Cor. 4.14).'⁴ If for Luke the pre-Easter Jesus is simply 'Jesus', the post-Easter Jesus is frequently deemed the 'Lord Jesus'. He is Lord, because he is risen.

4. The unexplained absence of Jesus' body is not just surprising but also deeply troubling: *they were perplexed [aporeisthai] about this.*⁵ As if this discovery were not overwhelming enough, the women must suddenly come to terms with yet another twist: the presence of *two men in dazzling clothes* standing beside them. Reminiscent of the two patriarchal witnesses at the transfiguration (9:28–36), and anticipating another pair of figures at the ascension (Acts 1:10), the two men are clearly angels; their double verification meets the minimum standard for legally valid testimony (Deut. 19:15).

5. Understandably, the *women were terrified (emphobōn de genomenōn)* and in their stunned state they fall down and *bowed their faces to the ground*, intuiting the need to avert their gaze out of respect for these transcendent beings.⁶ Meanwhile, the two angels put to them a chiding question: *Why do you look for the living among the dead?* The question is of course rhetorical and so does not require an answer. But to make matters perfectly clear, the angels then go on to affirm Jesus' absence from the tomb and the fact of his resurrection.

6–8. Next the angels call to mind Jesus' passion predictions, which included three points: (1) the handing over of the Son of Man, (2) his crucifixion and (3) his resurrection. Even though these predictions were primarily directed to the Twelve, the women were probably also present on at least one of these occasions. If this were not the case, it would be virtually impossible to make sense of verse 8: *they remembered his words.* This is not necessarily to say that the women had utterly forgotten Jesus' predictions regarding the Son

---

4. Lieu, p. 201.

5. Whereas 'perplexity' typically refers to the inability to understand, the verb *aporeō* more narrowly denotes the sense of being at a loss to know what to do next (BDAG, p. 119).

6. Interestingly, Daniel must also bow his face to the ground before the interpreting angel of Daniel 10 (vv. 9, 15), right before the angel's announcement of wars (Dan. 10) leading up to the resurrection of the righteous (Dan. 12).

of Man's strange fate; more likely, they had some recollection along these lines but, without a context in which one might make sense of all this, such words would have been virtually meaningless.

9. In Jewish antiquity, a woman's testimony was regarded with deep suspicion.[7] For this reason there is no small historical and theological significance in the fact that women (and not men), in alerting *the eleven and . . . all the rest*, were the first to relay news of the resurrection. If the honoured office occupied by the Eleven fell only to males, the honour of being the first to witness the resurrection goes to females.

10–11. In order to secure the women's role as witnesses, the Gospel writer identifies the leading figures by name. Mary Magdalene and Joanna have already been mentioned by name as supporters of Jesus (8:2–3); Mary the mother of James has not been previously mentioned.[8] There is also an undetermined number of other women in the party. Together, they take it upon themselves to get the word to the apostles. But their efforts are mostly in vain. Ironically, though the apostles had been tasked with co-leading the fledgling movement, and though they had also been the primary recipients of Jesus' assurances regarding his own resurrection, *they did not believe them*. From their point of view, such a report was an idle tale (*lēros*), pure nonsense.[9]

---

7. In this vein, Josephus (*Ant.* 4.219) declares: 'Let no evidence be accepted from women' (my translation). Yet as Ilan (*Jewish Women*, pp. 163–166) shows, this does not mean that women were altogether barred from bearing witness; merely that their witness was regarded as inferior to that of men.

8. The Greek construction *Maria hē Iakōbou* (literally: Mary of James) may mean 'Mary the wife of James' or 'Mary the daughter of James'. However, in the light of Mark 16:1, it is likely that Mary is James's mother.

9. As the term (used only here in the NT) is sometimes associated with philosophical sophistry, one wonders whether Luke means to compare the Eleven's dismissal of the women's report to the Athenian philosophers' scoffing at Paul's announcement of resurrection (Acts 17:16–34).

12. Although the apostles fail to believe, it is a qualified disbelief.[10] After all, when Peter *ran to the tomb*, this is evidence that he himself did not entirely write off the women's words. On arriving, he finds the strips of *linen* which had been wound around Jesus' lifeless body just a few days before. Understandably, he is amazed, and not knowing what to do next simply returns home.

ii. On the road to Emmaus (24:13–35)

13–14. In this the second of three resurrection scenes, the action breaks down into four parts: (1) the initial meeting (vv. 13–16), (2) the dialogue concerning recent events (vv. 17–27), (3) the meal (vv. 28–32) and (4) the excursion back to Jerusalem (vv. 33–35).[11] Given the events of Easter morning, the disciples are astir with agitation and puzzlement. Two of them, an unidentified disciple and another named Cleopas (both of them outside the surviving Eleven; cf. v. 33), depart from Jerusalem the same day – perhaps indicating an already disintegrating community – and spend the afternoon travelling to Emmaus.[12] Emmaus has been variously located: candidates include modern-day El-Moza (Colonia, 4 miles [4.5 km] west of Jerusalem), Qubeibeh (7 miles [11 km] north-west) and Emmaus Nicopolis (19 miles [30.5 km] west). Our geographical uncertainty is hardly helped by the divergences in the manuscript tradition, with some witnesses showing 60 stadia (= over 7 miles [11 km]) and others 160 (= 20 miles [32 km]). The latter possibility would admirably fit Emmaus Nicopolis but this presumes a lengthy walking distance for one day. In any case, the focus of the travelling companions is not on *where* they are going but *whence* they have

---

10. Whereas there is an outside possibility that the present verse is not original to Luke's Gospel (the RSV relegates it to a footnote), text critics and commentators broadly concur that the notice of Peter's trip to the tomb is authentically Lukan.

11. So Fitzmyer, p. 1559.

12. That the community was already beginning to erode is suggested by Smith, *Easter Gospels*, p. 113. That there are *two* travellers is significant, given the necessity of multiple witnesses in vouching for this resurrection event (Deut. 19:15).

come, and the events that had just transpired that morning. Just as Jesus had revealed himself to the Twelve 'on the way' to Jerusalem in 9:51 – 19:48, so now once again Jesus is on the road, this time with two disciples heading *away* from Jerusalem.

15–16. Coming up from behind, the Risen Jesus joins the two men as they walk and talk. There is no sense of either surprise or strangeness at his doing so. Jesus appears as an anonymous ordinary man who happens to be travelling the same road. The travellers' shared failure to recognize him is a matter not of providential intervention but spiritual blindness; their faith-weak eyes were held back from recognizing him (cf. 9:45; 18:34).[13] While the Evangelist has little interest in explaining the precise mechanics of the disciples' imperception, non-recognition is obviously an important component of the scene, just as it is in several of the fourth Gospel's resurrection accounts (John 20:14–15; 21:4). In Luke, sight has to do with faith and salvation (2:30; 6:39; 10:23; etc.); failure to see has to do with unbelief and spiritual estrangement.

17–18. Saddened by recent events, the two disciples continue their discussion in the presence of their new-found travelling companion, who asks about their topic. The two men are apparently so surprised by the question – more exactly, by the ignorance which prompted it – that they stop in their tracks (*estathēsan*). Then, with some incredulity, Cleopas enquires how it is possible even for a stranger to remain oblivious to that which has happened *in these days* (*hēmērais tautais*) – the same *hēmērais tautais* Jesus predicted much earlier in his ministry (cf. 5:35).

19. While Jesus feigns ignorance, the two travellers clarify that they had been talking about *Jesus of Nazareth, a prophet*. The epithet is fitting. Jesus had already been identified as a prophet (4:24; 7:16; 9:19) and challenged as a prophet (7:39); it had also already been intimated that he would share the same dire fate as the prophets (6:23, 26; 11:47–50; 13:33). Further declaring Jesus to be *mighty in deed and word*, the two men strengthen the tie-back (already hinted at in *Jesus of Nazareth*) to the inaugural sermon at Nazareth where he claimed the backing of divine power (4:14–19). The phrase *mighty*

---

13. Contra, e.g., Fitzmyer, p. 1563.

in deed and word also likens Jesus to Moses, whom Stephen elsewhere describes with exactly the same words (Acts 7:22). Luke's Jesus, again like Moses, is also mighty *before God and all the people* (cf. Deut. 34:10–12). The point is that Moses' mantle as prophetic redeemer has now passed a fortiori on to Jesus.

20. Ironically, again in keeping with Jesus' earlier observations regarding the fate of prophets, it was – according to his two companions – the chief priests and leaders of Israel who had handed him over to be crucified. The travellers' remark advances Luke's purposes in two ways. First, it serves an apologetic purpose, explaining how Jesus could simultaneously be the prophetic Messiah and the *rejected* Messiah.[14] Second, it carries a polemic purpose, lumping the temple leadership with the ungodly who had persecuted the prophets in the past. For Luke, Jesus' status as crucified Messiah was no source of embarrassment but rather a vindication of his prophetic claim and an indictment of those who opposed him.

21. The two travellers now reveal their own once-cherished expectations, no doubt representative of the Jesus movement as a whole: on this Jesus they had pinned their hopes for the redemption of Israel. But now, so far as Cleopas and his friend were concerned, these hopes had been all but dashed. Given Jesus' predictions about rising on the third day (9:22; 18:33), the fact that Jesus' execution had taken place three days prior with no further happenings seems to have been the crowning disappointment – *besides all this.*[15] The irony of unwittingly telling this tale of woe to the triumphant Risen Jesus would not have been lost on Luke's readers. Whereas the discovery of the empty tomb *should* have provided initial grounds for faith, the disciples' sadness and disappointment betray their unbelief.

22–24. Wrapping up their strange story, the two travellers recount the women's remarkable encounter at the tomb, which had

14. See Strauss, *Davidic Messiah*, pp. 255–256.

15. Marshall (p. 893) thinks the *besides all this* refers to the Jewish notion that the soul would depart the body only on the third day, but this is doubtful.

been followed by the male disciples' own investigation (24:1–12).[16] On the one hand, the empty tomb afforded evidence that Jesus' predicted resurrection had in fact come to pass; on the other hand, the absence of a Risen Jesus seemed to have scuttled lingering hopes – despite the vision of the angels announcing Jesus' resurrection. True, the male disciples were astonished by the women's report, but it was an astonishment born of unbelief rather than faith (24:11).

25. With his identity still disguised, Jesus then rebukes his conversation partners. They are *foolish*, more precisely, 'without understanding'. The charge implicates not so much the pair's cognitive abilities as their spiritual–moral shortcomings, for they are also *slow of heart to believe* the Scriptures. According to Luke and just about any Jew, the heart, as the seat of one's personal attitudes and commitments, was integral to obeying the highest command (10:27); indeed, it was the key to all obedience (6:45; 8:15). The disciples' failure to correlate recent events with Scripture was at bottom not a hermeneutical failure, but a spiritual failure – a dullness of the heart.

26–27. At the same time, the two travellers also misunderstood the Scriptures: they had failed to appreciate the necessity (*dei*) of Christ's suffering as a precondition of his entering into *his glory* (cf. 9:26) (perhaps implying pre-existence). Jesus' rebuke is striking, especially considering that Second Temple Judaism did not as a general rule anticipate a suffering – much less a resurrected – Messiah. Towards remedying their insufficient grasp of the Scriptures, which had led them to misinterpret recent events, Jesus then proceeds to elucidate the biblical text in reference to himself. He does so, as Luke puts it, *beginning with Moses and all the prophets*. We recall that Jesus had at an earlier point mentioned that unbelief in regard to 'Moses and the prophets' would engender unbelief in regard to resurrection (16:31). Now Luke provides an instance of such disbelief. From the phrase *Moses and all the prophets*, we might

---

16. Interestingly, 24:12 records that only Peter followed up on the women's report, but the gist of 24:24 implies that the apostle was not alone – all consistent with the account in John 20:3–9.

gather that Jesus here offers a systematic exposition through the Pentateuch and the Twelve (Minor Prophets), as representative of *all the scriptures*. But it is more likely that Jesus is not focusing on isolated texts within Torah and the prophetical books, but on persons, patterns and sweeping storylines within the texts.[17] If the pre-Easter community, together with first-century Judaism, had imagined that suffering was an incidental element in the prophetic profile, Jesus now sets the record straight by revealing a *theologia crucis* in the Hebrew Scriptures, written long before the cross.

28–29. Jesus' exposition is presumably still incomplete by the time the travelling party reaches Emmaus. While Cleopas and his friend have arrived at their intended destination, Jesus pretends to have an interest in continuing his journey. In his risen state, no less than in his earthly existence, Jesus does not force himself on his hearers, but instead waits to be invited in for the evening – all in keeping with ideal practices of hospitality.[18] The two men oblige, pointing out that it was already the cusp of evening and that the day had been spent.

30. Not much time would have passed between the men's invitation and their meal together with Jesus, since first-century Jews typically ate dinner before sundown. Here Jesus is found reclining with his hosts, a familiar posture from earlier meal scenes (7:36; 9:14–15). Then, in what would have been an unusual move for any guest, Jesus usurps the role of the host by blessing the evening bread. The series of verbs (*blessed . . . broke . . . gave*) invokes the earlier feeding miracle (9:16), and to a lesser extent the Last Supper (22:19). Just as the feeding of the five thousand signalled the revelatory in-breaking of the kingdom through the ministry of Jesus, and the Last Supper anticipated the final arrival of the kingdom (cf. 22:18), the Emmaus meal reveals Jesus' Messiahship. It also marks one step closer to the eschatological state that Jesus longed for at 22:18.

31. At the very moment of the blessing, the men (as well as any others in the household) instantly recognize Jesus for who he is.

---

17. See Bock, p. 918.
18. See Koenig, *Hospitality*, p. 116.

Again the Evangelist is reluctant to go into much detail on this point, except to say that their eyes are opened, much as the healed blind had their eyes opened (7:21; 18:35–43), and much as, too, Saul would later have his eyes opened (Acts 9:8–18). But in this case the opening of the eyes involves not a restoration of physical sight but an enlivening of the spiritual and mental apparatus. Here recognition comes not by human effort but through the words of blessing over the meal. Luke leaves no doubt about the sacramental implications of the moment: in the corporate sharing of this quasi-Lord's Supper, Christians have the opportunity to recognize the person of Jesus in fresh, powerful ways.[19] No sooner does such recognition occur, however, than Jesus vanishes. His sudden appearance at the beginning of the passage is matched by his equally sudden disappearance: in between this entrance and exit, we now find two transformed lives.

32. Even as the climactic resolution of a clever mystery novel drives the reader back to consider various clues scattered throughout the narrative, the revelatory experience of the Risen Lord forces the disciples to reflect on their experience of Jesus on the road to Emmaus – in particular his scriptural exposition. Apparently, it was not just the persuasiveness of Jesus' explanation en route to Emmaus that clarified matters but *our hearts burning within us*. Theirs was a spiritual experience wrought, simply enough, through the exposition of Scripture. He had 'opened' their eyes through the supper (v. 31), even as he had 'opened' the Scriptures through his exposition (v. 32) – the same Greek verb *dianoigō* governs both actions. On Luke's theology, so it seems, even though human dullness and unbelief may obscure a proper vision of Christ, God is able to penetrate our incomprehension through the Word and the sacrament. In this respect, the Emmaus incident prepares for the central role of preaching and the breaking of bread in Acts.

---

19. Just (*Ongoing Feast*, p. 239) asks, 'Though most commentaries classify the Emmaus meal either as the Eucharist or as an ordinary meal, could it not be a unique meal within the table fellowship matrix that is Eucharistic even if it is not the first Christian Eucharist?'

33. With barely a moment to spare, the two men then rise from the table to make another long journey, this time *back* to Jerusalem, and by this time too in the darkness of night. While the ancients tended to avoid night-time travel, the travellers are willing to bear the risk for theirs is now the urgent goal of informing the community of their experience. At last, they arrive at the house at which the Eleven and the rest have *gathered* (*ēthroismenous*).[20]

34–35. The Jesus community at Jerusalem has convened itself, even at this late hour, because its members too have seen the Risen Lord. While earlier in Luke's narrative Peter had found only isolated linen burial strips and had puzzled over their meaning (v. 12), now Jesus' followers are celebrating the fact that Peter and others had also – at some point during that day after his initial visit to the tomb – witnessed the Risen *Lord*. (While we have no note of this event in Luke or even in the broader Gospel tradition, evidence of this sighting does come by way of 1 Cor. 15:5.) On hearing this news, the two travellers in turn report in detail their own experience with the resurrected Jesus, both on the road and at the dinner table. As the *Lord* in this capacity, Jesus reveals himself to the disciples not simply as their messianic master but as their God.

Theology

Jesus' rising from the dead in Luke 24:1–35 has manifold implications. We might highlight three. First, whereas Jesus had been mockingly crucified as the 'King of the Jews' (23:38), his rising from the dead now vindicates his messianic claim. He *is* in fact, as so many had hoped, 'the one to redeem Israel' (24:21) from exile. Through his resurrection, therefore, Jesus is now the climax and the fulfilment of the Hebrew Scriptures. All prior history has been

---

20. The verb *athroizō* is rare in Scripture but may allude to the prophetic vision of a restored Israel in Ezek. 36:24 ('I will take you from the nations, and gather you from all the countries, and *bring you* [*athroisō*] into your own land'; emphasis added). If so, the Ezekialian subtext hints that the post-Easter community is already experiencing the long-awaited return from exile.

leading up to this moment of resurrection; all subsequent history has been unfolding in the light of it.

Second, through his resurrection Jesus is marked out as God – a point confirmed by his being twice named 'Lord' in this passage. As God, Jesus transcends the natural laws of time, space and human perception. As God, too, he has the power to illuminate dull eyes and open up hardened hearts, granting salvation to whom he will. Since in Judaism the granting of election to salvation was considered a strictly divine prerogative, Jesus' actions at Emmaus reinforce that which can be gathered elsewhere: he is Lord of the universe.

Third and finally, Jesus' resurrection serves as a model and guarantee of the eschatological resurrection for all of God's people. In re-enacting the meal scenes that his disciples remembered so well, the Risen Jesus signals that they too will join him in the celebratory resurrection meal not entirely unlike their earthly meals together. Thus at the resurrection the blessed will enjoy certain continuities with their earthly existence. At the same time, because Jesus' resurrected physical body moves beyond the typical limits of human bodiliness, believers can also expect to inherit a kind of 'physical body plus'. The Emmaus meal brings home the certainty of this hope.

B. Commissioning (24:36–53)

Context

As the Gospel draws to a close, it may be asked how the final two scenes provide closure to Luke's 'orderly account of the events that have been fulfilled among us' (1:1) and what they have to do with the sequel of Acts. On the one hand, the final two scenes may be compared to a flame applied to the frayed end of a nylon rope, cauterizing loose ends into a crisply sealed unity; on the other hand, Luke 24:36–53 also functions like a fine-tooth comb drawn firmly against the same narrative cord, teasing out important threads that will be finally tied together only in the next book.

Looking back, the reader discerns that the promise of peace (2:14) has finally been cashed out (24:36); the promise of joy and laughter (6:21) has come to fruition (24:41). What is more, the Law and the Prophets have come full circle and the Eleven are witnesses to that fact (24:44–48). Yet looking forward, we see that the same Eleven must await the power of the Spirit (24:49) as they prepare to take up their mantle as priests of the new temple order (24:50–53).

Comment

i. Sending with a promise (24:36–49)

36–37. Even as Jesus' closest followers discuss his alleged appearance among themselves, the Risen Lord himself now appears *among them* (*en mesō autōn*), speaking no more than a mere two words in the Greek: *eirēnē hymin* (*Peace be with you*). Far more than an expression of greeting or comfort, Jesus' conveyance of peace carries overtones of salvation. This much follows from Luke's previous usage of *eirēnē*, where divinely imparted peace is the promised lot of the elect (2:14) as well as – like the Hebrew equivalent *šālôm* – the bundle of blessings associated with salvation (7:50; 8:48; 10:5). Notwithstanding the objective reality of this conferred peace, Luke's readers might also expect Jesus' words to have an impact on the disciples' emotional state. If so, then such expectations are rudely disappointed. The glaring contrast between Jesus' declaration of peace and the agitation of the *startled and terrified* disciples may in part, I think, be explained with reference to the parable of the sower (8:1–15).[21] In this programmatic parable, we recall, the word/seed of God fell 'among [*en mesō*] thorns' (8:7) only to be choked out by thorn-like cares growing up with the word (8:14). In this scene, Jesus 'stood among [*en mesō*] them' (24:36) and is unable to communicate due to the *doubts* that *arise in their hearts* (24:38). If this is the case, then the Eleven's difficulty in recognizing the Risen Lord is finally a function of a distracted worldliness. It at least seems partially on account of the disciples' spiritual resistance that they come to believe *that they were seeing* a spirit or *a ghost* (*pneuma*).[22] There is a certain irony here, since from Luke's

---

21. Within Luke's storied world, we should not excuse the disciples' terrified reaction (*ptoēthentes*) as merely human or natural, since Jesus has earlier instructed them not to be terrified (*mē ptoēthēte*) (21:9).

22. The KJV and RSV prefer to translate *pneuma* as 'spirit'.

vantage point the disciples *are* in a sense seeing a spirit – more exactly, the first intimations of the Holy Spirit who would soon overshadow the believing community in Acts 2.

38. At the empty tomb, the women had been asked a rhetorical 'Why?' question (24:5); now the disciples are being asked a similarly probing 'Why?' question. In the opening action of Luke's story, the priest Zechariah is said to be 'terrified' (*etarachthē*) and overwhelmed by fear (*phobos epepesen ep'auton*) on meeting Gabriel (1:12). Now the disciples are being described with similarly unusual language as 'terrified' (*tetaragmenoi*) and gripped by fear (*emphoboi*) (v. 37). For both Zechariah and the apostles, perched on the threshold of a redemptive-historical turning point, such fears are not unrelated to their respective struggles to believe (1:20; 24:41).[23] Once again, in Luke's theology, fear is the unholy manifestation of unbelief.

39–40. Accommodating himself to the state of the disciples, Jesus invites them to examine his hands and feet, pierced as they must have been by the nails of cross (cf. John 20:27). In doing so, he wants to make clear to his bewildered followers that the figure standing before them is not a *ghost* but a physical body of *flesh and bones* existing in substantial continuity with the crucified Jesus.[24] That is, he wants them to *see that it is I myself* (*hoti egō eimi autos*). Yet in applying the phrase *egō eimi* to himself, Luke's Jesus also means to identify himself with the divine epithet: the 'I AM', first mentioned in Exodus 3:14 and spoken of repeatedly in Isaiah 40 – 66 (e.g. Isa. 42:6, 8; 43:3, 5, 25; 44:6, 24; 45:5; 46:4, 9; 48:12, 17; 49:23, 26; 51:15; 60:22). This self-identification in turn possibly attaches a second layer of signification to Jesus' display of his hands and feet.

---

23. See above commentary on Luke 1:12 for possible intertextual connections between Gabriel and Daniel. Such connections, together with the similar descriptions of Zechariah's and the disciples' experience of fear, render it likely that the women's bowing their faces before the angels at the tomb (24:5) is connected with a similar response in Dan 10:9, 15, even as Jesus' words 'Peace be with you' (24:36) are informed by Dan. 10:19 where the angel declares 'peace be with you' (ESV; *shālōm lāk*).

24. On this point, see Talbert, 'Resurrection'.

The astute reader of Luke's Gospel will have noticed that Jesus' feet (*pous*) (7:38, 44, 45, 46; 8:35, 41; 10:39; 17:16) and arms/hands (*cheir*) (3:17; 4:40; 5:13; 13:13) are motifs of especial interest. Now at last, with Jesus' announcement of peace and his self-disclosure as the 'I AM', these seemingly stray pieces come together within the framework of Isaiah 52:6–7, 10 (emphasis added):

> Therefore my people shall know my name; therefore on that day they shall know *that it is I* [LXX: *hoti egō eimi autos*] who speak; here am I.

> How beautiful upon the mountains
>> are the *feet* [LXX: *podes*] of the messenger who announces *peace* [*eirēnēs*],
> who brings good news,
>> who announces salvation,
>> who says to Zion, 'Your God reigns' . . .
> The LORD has bared his holy *arm* [*brachiona*]
>> before the eyes of all the nations;
> and all the ends of the earth shall see
>> the salvation of our God.

As the third Gospel draws to an end, the beauty of Jesus' feet and the strength of his hands take their proper place. Both of these elements are related to Jesus' saving declaration of peace which seals Jesus as the fulfilment of the Isaianic Servant and his agenda as Israel's regathering from among the nations.

41. The phrase *in their joy they were disbelieving* may strike the reader as an oxymoron (a term or phrase with mutually contradictory terms), but we have already sighted the curious convergence of joy and disbelief, again in the parable of the sower, specifically in relation to the shallow soil (8:13). Similarly, the post-Easter disciples are joyful, to be sure, but they still lack the necessary foundation for their faith. Not much better off than the unbelieving but wondering crowds (4:22; 9:43; 11:14; 20:26), they are left *wondering* (*thaumazontōn*). Nor, in their stupor, are they much further along than the wondering (*thaumazōn*) Peter as he surveyed the empty tomb on Easter morning (24:12). Whereas, in Luke's account, the only lasting remedy for such a spiritual condition would be nothing less than the impartation of the Spirit (Acts 2), for now Jesus merely wants to drive home a point as he requests something to eat.

42–43. Obliging Jesus' request, the disciples give him *a piece of broiled fish*, and then watch him take it and eat it. This brief and slightly odd interaction involving some leftover grilled fish seems to carry out several functions. In the first place, Jesus' ingestion of food proves beyond all doubt that he is not a disembodied spirit, for if anything was obvious about spirits, it was that they were unable to eat. Within the story, Jesus' taking of the fish partially mimics the moment in the feeding of the five thousand when Jesus took fish (along with bread) before distributing it (9:16). Only this time the fish has been cooked over a charcoal fire (be it 'broiled' or 'grilled'), perhaps as if to suggest that Jesus' miraculous provisions of fish (5:1–11; 9:12–17) and indeed all his subsequent miraculous provisions would be tinged with the same forgiveness that followed Peter's charcoal-fire denial (22:54–57). Along these lines, it is interesting that whereas Jesus 'gave' (*edidou*) the fish to the disciples at the feeding miracle, it is now the disciples who 'give' (*epedōkan*) the fish to Jesus, shifting the role of host from Jesus to the disciples. Whereas the earthly Jesus had a track record of providing fish *ex nihilo*, it now falls to the disciples to share their store of fish with the same Jesus, whenever that 'Jesus' should suddenly present himself in the guise of human need.

44. The referent of *these* in the clause *these are my words that I spoke* is not Jesus' wording in verses 36–41 but the substance of his passion predictions (9:18–22, 44; 18:31–33). In these passages, as well as at other times in the course of his ministry, Jesus had promised his own resurrection. And now before the disciples' very eyes that promise has been tangibly realized. Jesus' resurrection was not a random trick or an attention-grabbing stunt but the fulfilment of *everything written about me in the law of Moses, the prophets, and the psalms*, that is, the climax of human history.[25] According to Luke, the

---

25. The phrase refers to the whole of the Hebrew Scriptures; as Anderson (*God Raised Him*, p. 183) notes, the 'Scriptures are unambiguously designated as the threefold Hebrew canon: Law of Moses, Prophets, and Psalms (24:44)'.

scriptural canon finds its fulfilment not simply in Jesus but, more exactly, in the *resurrected* Jesus.

45. Yet prior to the disciples' attempt *to understand the scriptures*, it was necessary for Jesus to open *their minds*. Apparently, apart from such illumination, proper understanding would be impossible. This mirrors another post-Easter event, for just as divine insight into Jesus' person came only through the breaking of the bread (24:31), a similar divine intervention proves crucial for illuminating Scripture's meaning. For Luke, then, neither Scripture nor the one to whom Scripture points can be fully grasped apart from the special illuminating work of God.

46–47. Exactly which Scriptures speak of the Messiah's suffering and rising (*on the third day*) is not entirely clear. Equally uncertain is what texts Jesus has in mind when he talks of the scriptural promise that *repentance and forgiveness of sins* would *be proclaimed in his name to all nations*. This is not to say that Jesus' scriptural reasoning is obscure, only that such scriptural points are lucid in varying degrees: the resurrection of the Messiah *on the third day* is perhaps the least clearly expressed; the repentance of the nations is more transparent.[26] In any event, Jesus identifies his own resurrection, precisely as *the Messiah*, not only as the climax of Scripture but also as the necessary and sufficient condition for the preaching of repentance to the nations *beginning from Jerusalem*. The Holy City's status as the hub of the Christian mission is consistent with its exalted role in the prophetic literature; it is also consistent with the structure of Acts, alluded to in Acts 1:8, moving centrifugally from Jerusalem (Acts 1:1 – 8:4) to Judea and Samaria (8:5 – 9:31), and then on to the ends of the earth (9:32 – 28:31).

48. No sooner does Jesus declare the gist of the gospel message than he also emphasizes the disciples' role as *witnesses*.[27] The word 'witness' (*martys*) is a legal term, likely reflecting the disciples'

---

26. With regard to the nations, texts such as Pss 2; 16; 22; 110; Isa. 53; Hos. 6; Zech. 12 – 13 may have emerged at the forefront. For a fuller investigation, see Gronigen, *Messianic Revelation*.

27. The leading position of the personal pronoun *hymeis* ('you') reinforces the emphasis: '*You* are witnesses of these things!'

vocation of testifying to God and his elect Servant – all within the context of the covenantal lawsuit envisioned by Isaiah (Isa. 43:10). As witnesses in this 'Isaianic sense', the disciples are being charged not only with attesting to the sheer fact of Jesus' bodily resurrection but also with publicly interpreting it as the means and the manner by which return from exile would take effect. In this redemptive-historical framework, the resurrection becomes the decisive demonstration of Yahweh's superiority over the gods as well as the grounds on which the nations' idolatry stands condemned. Witness in the New Testament sense ineluctably leads to either redemption or judgment on the part of the hearers.

49. In order to discharge their calling, Jesus knew, the disciples would require sufficient empowerment. For this reason, he declares, *I am sending upon you what my Father promised*, or more literally, 'the promise of my Father' (*epangelian tou patros mou*), the Holy Spirit. With this promise, realized soon enough in Acts 1 – 2, comes a set of instructions: *stay here in the city until you have been clothed with power from on high*.

ii. Ascension (24:50–53)

50. In anticipation of that moment of empowerment, where a missionary charge also precedes ascension (Acts 1:7–9), Jesus leads his followers *out as far as Bethany*, the spot from which he only days before made his final entrance into Jerusalem.[28] It is there that Jesus – now *lifting up his hands* – blesses them. In part, Jesus' blessing is designed to be a departure blessing, not unlike those bestowed by the patriarchs (e.g. Gen. 27:27–29; 48 – 49; Deut. 33 – 34) on their heirs as means of conferring personal presence and even power from beyond the grave (but in Jesus' case, beyond 'beyond the grave'!).[29]

---

28. Atkins ('Ascension', p. 205) appropriately remarks: 'By showing that the departure and blessing of the disciples was at the same place as the entry into Jerusalem, Luke crowns the triumphal entry with the triumphal exit of Christ.'

29. On this aspect, see discussion in Mekkattukunnel, *Priestly Blessing*, pp. 161–170.

More than this, it is also a priestly blessing.[30] As priest representing both God and human beings, Jesus blesses as both God and a human being – at least the *inclusio* with earlier blessing scenes seems to suggest as much. For just as Elizabeth (1:42) and then Simeon had blessed Mary and Joseph (2:34) at the front end of the Gospel, now at its back end the human son of Mary and Joseph returns the horizontal blessing. And whereas in Luke's opening chapters the likes of Zechariah and Simeon had blessed God from below (1:68; 2:28), now God in Christ is returning the blessing from above. Through the resurrection God, human and divine blessing comes full circle.

51. Even as Jesus blesses his disciples, he physically distances himself from them right before being *carried up into heaven*. The seamless transition between Jesus' blessing and heavenward movement points to his continuing intercessory role in the ascension. The theological point is obvious enough: though the resurrected Jesus may be physically withdrawn from his people, symbolized by his withdrawal from his disciples before the ascension, Luke promises that Jesus' presence and power are bound up in his high priestly blessing which he will continue to impart to the faithful.

52–53. The spectacle of an ascending Jesus makes no small impression on the astonished disciples. In response, unlike the different characters kneeling before Jesus in honorific homage (e.g. 5:12), the disciples kneel (*proskynēsantes*) in worship. More than a messiah (vv. 45–47), and more than a priest (v. 50), Luke also wants us to know, Jesus is also very God of very God and worthy of worship – a fitting and climactic point with which to close the Gospel. At the same time, the disciples' worship is but a segue to their return to Jerusalem (*hypestrespan eis Ierousalēm*). This contrasts with a much earlier 'return to Jerusalem', when Jesus' parents returned to the Holy City in search of their son, only finally to find him at the temple (2:43–46). Whereas Mary and Joseph had frantically combed the streets of Jerusalem in search of Jesus, the

---

30. As persuasively argued by Mekkattukunnel, *Priestly Blessing*, pp. 171–219. Contra, e.g., Marshall, p. 909; Nolland, pp. 1227–1228. For the priestly Christological theme in the Gospels overall, see Perrin, 'Jesus as Priest'.

disciples return to Jerusalem *with great joy*, for – *unlike* Mary and Joseph – they are not ignorant of Jesus' whereabouts and are confident that he is once again about the Father's business, this time in the heavenly temple. So, too, the same *great joy* that the angels had promised at Jesus' birth (2:10) is now at last bursting forth through the resurrection and ascension. Finally, like the prophetess Anna who worshipped God continually at the temple (2:36–37), the disciples remain *continually in the temple blessing God*: unlike Anna they *have* received the consolation of Israel (2:38) on the far side of resurrection.

And so the Gospel comes full circle. The Son of the Most High, the Lord God, the Son of David (to name a handful of Jesus' titles), have converged in the person of the risen and ascended Jesus. That which had been glimpsed only dimly in the opening pages of Luke's Gospel has now come into the full light of day – all culminating in a scene of continuing worship centred on Jesus. Meanwhile, Jesus' act of blessing outside Jerusalem hints that the gravitational centre for God's activity is poised to move well beyond the confines of Zion, anticipating the expanding mission in Luke's second volume, the book of Acts.

Theology

In some sense, Jesus' resurrection from the dead is the final word, the end of the story. In another sense, it is only the beginning – the beginning of a new story, the story of the church. That second story awaits to be told in the pages of Acts. Not content to write 'about all that Jesus began to do and to teach' in the Gospel (Acts 1:1, NIV), Luke will go on to tell of the Risen Jesus' deeds as revealed through the Spirit and the church.

Towards setting the stage for the sequel, Jesus in this final pair of episodes confers two roles on the disciples: they are to be both witnesses and priests. As witnesses, their task is to attest to the Risen Christ, preaching repentance for the forgiveness of sins by the power of the Spirit. As priests, duly ordained by the chief high priest Jesus himself, their primary vocation is one of worship. The focal space of this worship is the new holy place occupied by the Risen Lord in his ascended state; the focal object of that worship: Jesus himself. Though there might arguably be some overlap between the responsibilities of witness and priest, together the two roles summarize well all that the apostles will set out to do in Acts.

By implication, what is true of the Eleven is also to be true of the church. Built on the foundation of the apostolate, the church is called to witness and called to serve as a royal priesthood. Individually and corporately, Christians are called to mission and to worship. Though both are exceedingly important, between these two priorities the final emphasis falls on worship. Just as the Gospel of Luke began with worship, so too there it ends. It is as if the very Gospel text is saying that the story of Jesus *must* be wrapped in worship. For, as intimated elsewhere, it is above all those who sit at the Lord's feet who will receive the inheritance – and it will not be taken away from them.